ON January 15th, 1981 a research group (Don, Carla and Jim) started receiving a communication from the social memory complex, Ra. Don, the questioner; Carla, the channeler; Jim, the scribe. From this communication precipitated the Law of One and some distortions of the Law of One.

The Archetypical Mind:

In the beginning of this archetypical mind (the universe) was the harvest of the preceding octave. The archetypal mind is an understanding of the mind, body and spirit that conveys that all life is based off core archetypes within the conscious and unconscious mind. An archetype is a pattern of behavior, prototype "first" form or a main model that other statements, patterns of behavior and objects copy, emulate or "merge" into. It is the mind which is peculiar (unusual) to the Logos of this planetary sphere. Thusly, unlike the great cosmic all-mind, it contains the material which it pleased the Logos to offer as refinements to the great cosmic beingness. The archetypical mind, then, is that which contains all facets which may affect mind or experience. Archetypes are portions of the One Infinite Creator or aspects of its face. It is, however, far better to realize that the archetypes, while constant in the complex of generative energies offered, do not give the same yield of these complexes to any two seekers. Each seeker will experience each archetype in the characteristics within the complex of the archetype which are most important to it.

The archetypical mind is part of that mind which informs all experience. It is repository (accumulation of data) of those refinements to the cosmic or all-mind made by this particular Logos and peculiar only to this Logos. So, in this universe we have 22 archetypes (7 mind, 7 body and 7 spirit) plus choice, whereas the preceding universe had 9. Thus, it may be seen as one of the roots of mind, not the deepest but certainly the most informative in some ways. The other root of mind is that planetary mind which also informs the conceptualizations (or defining of the abstract concepts) of each entity to some degree.

Each archetype presents an aspect of the One Infinite Creation to teach the individual mind/body/spirit complex according to the calling or the electromagnetic configuration of mind of the entity. Teaching is done via the intuition. With proper seeking or mind configuration, the power of will uses the spirit as a shuttle to contact the appropriate archetypical aspect necessary for the teach/learning. In the same way each of the other informers of intuition are contacted. They are hierarchical and proceed from the entity's own subconscious mind to group or planetary mind, to guides, to higher self, to archetypal mind, to cosmic mind or intelligent infinity. Each is contacted by the spirit serving as shuttle according to the harmonized electromagnetic configuration of the seekers mind and the information sought. An easier way to understand this would be that each Archetype, such as in the tarot deck, represents an aspect of our particular universe (or logos). The Logos has some room to create archetypes that please it for our "universe" of experience. Each of us experiences these archetypes in our own unique way.

The Adept: Each entity is the Creator. The entity, as it becomes more and more conscious of its self, gradually comes to the turning point at which it determines to seek either in service to others or in service to self. The seeker becomes the adept when it has balanced with minimal adequacy the energy centers red, orange, yellow, and blue with the addition of the green for the positive, thus moving into indigo work.

The adept then begins to do less preliminary or outer work (preparing for something more important), having to do with function, and begins to affect the inner work having to do with being. As the adept becomes a more and more consciously crystallized entity, it gradually manifests more and more of what it has always been since before time, that is, the One Infinite Creator.

Oneness:

Another beautiful way I've heard someone describe oneness; is how we are all united as we share one consciousness. There was a study done once with one group of people taking the test on a Sunday and the group describing the test as harder to take as it was done for the first time.

Then, the next day on Monday another group of people took the same test and described the test as being easier to take. This shows how humanity shares one consciousness.

Love created the light. Sunlight, or visible light, is made of the seven colors of the rainbow: red, orange, yellow, green, blue, indigo, and violet. These same seven colors represent the seven colors of our seven energy centers, or chakras, of our body. Each color spectrum represents a different level of consciousness or awareness. Red being the 1st density of experience and the root chakra, orange being the 2nd density of experience and the sacral chakra, yellow being the 3rd density of experience and the solar plexus, green being the 4th density of experience and the heart chakra, blue being the 5th density of experience and the throat chakra, indigo being the 6th density of experience and the third eye chakra, and violet being the 7th density and the crown chakra.

Just like seven colors is represented in the light at once, souls are also simultaneously experiencing all seven densities at the same time, but we are only aware of one density and one lifetime at a time, such as this 3rd density experience, we are consciously aware of right now in this single timeline of an infinite number of timelines. Light comes from the source just as we all emanate from the source as well. This is another easier way to view oneness.

-Introduction-

The research group Don Elkins, Carla Rueckert and James (Jim) Allen McCarty used "tuned trance telepathy" to communicate with an extraterrestrial race called RA, or 6th density social memory complex, named RA from Venus. There are 8 densities of mind, body, soul for our consciousness to evolve through. Humans are currently in the 3rd density approaching 3rd density graduation into 4th density for the harvest that could possibly occur in 2030. Some religions call it the Rapture, but it's actually the Rapture of Consciousness to a higher density for those souls that are at least 51% positive or service to others. (For true service to others, respecting others free will is most important in our universe. Those that infringe on beings free will is conducting a negatively oriented action.) Currently 65% of earth beings are on the positive path harvestable for 4th density positive. So, 6th density (such as your higher-self or RA) would be at least 435,000,000 years more advanced than 3rd density humans.

The research group used the English language because it is known by RA. In fact, RA knows more English than they do. RA landed on Earth 11,000 years ago as a sort of an extraterrestrial missionary with the objective of helping humans on Earth with their mental evolution. Failing in their attempt, RA retreated from the Earth's surface but continued to monitor activities closely on this planet. For this reason, RA is highly informed about our history, language, etc. RA had difficulty communicating with humans 11,000 years ago, therefore, their message was distorted and they retreated. It wasn't until RA found this research group in 1981 that they could effectively communicate this information without it being distorted. Now we have this information given to us for our evolution called the Law of One.

There's a close connection between children who have had UFO encounters and them being able to bend metal with their minds. It happened in 1977 when Don, the questioner, questioned a 14-year-old boy who had a UFO encounter. Don asked him to take a piece of silverware and tell it to bend without touching it in any firm or forceful way. The 14-year-old boy did as Don suggested, and the fork immediately bent nearly double.

Under hypnotic regression a young boy experienced a previous life of being solitary and avoided contact with others. He inherited a fairly large estate and spent his life in it. He had his gardener's plant flowers, fruits, and vegetables in a very extensive garden that he maintained. So, in his current life he experienced intense allergies to all the things he loved in his previous life. Therefore, in this life he couldn't cut the grass, smell the flowers or spend much time outside.

During the hypnotic regression with Delores Cannon, Cannon asked his higher self if the lesson of putting people first and other things second had been learned. The higher self said it had been learned; it was then asked of the higher self if the allergies could be healed. The higher self-agreed and the allergies were no longer necessary.

Meditation is always suggested as the best means of attaining understanding, and of understanding the nature of the illusion (on Earth) and the purpose, for which you are experiencing it. Each person can use their consciousness in meditation to create a more rapid growing of evolution.

The Confederation of Planets in the Service of the Infinite Creator concentrate upon the concept of Seeking and of desire, they feel that the will of each entity is absolutely central to each entity's quest for evolution. They say that free will is at the foundation of the universe. Each entity is not only part of one unity but also a totally unique part of that unity. Each person's free will is paramount, and the Confederations' concern is always to avoid infringement upon free will of any person. Their method of contacting people on Earth occurs from a deep concern for this free will.

Once the desire to receive this message has been developed, the messages are available from many contactees or channeling groups around the world.

People may "tune" to prepare for a channeling contact first by meditation. One may recite the Lord's Prayer, "Aum-ing," singing, chanting or reading some inspirational writing or careful visualization of the "white light" of the Creator, are all useful "tuning" methods with meditation before a session for protection.

Reincarnation is very basic to the Confederation's message. One of the most highly regarded fruits of the meditation and seeking process is the ability of the seeker to penetrate the "forgetting process" which occurs at the time of our birth into this incarnation so that we might become aware of the lessons that we have to learn during this incarnation. These lessons are always along the lines of how to love better, more fully, more deeply, or with more kindness and understanding. However, each person has unique lessons.

Understanding all the lessons that we have to learn about love is the basic concept that all things are one. In this book consists of metaphysics, philosophy, and the plan of evolution of mind, body and spirit of people on Earth. According to a higher positively oriented entity named Hatonn, who spoke with the group for many years, the purpose of some of the UFO's that are seen in our skies is much like the purpose that we might have in sending aid to a disaster stricken or extremely impoverished country. It is a desire to be of service.

Hatonn: "We have been contacting people on planet Earth for many, many of your years. We have been contacting at intervals of thousands of years those who sought our aid. It is time for many of the people of this planet to be contacted, for many now have the understanding and the desire to seek something outside the physical illusion that has for many years involved the thinking of those of this planet. The process we are stimulating is one which is self-generating. As more and more of those who desire our contact receive it and pass it on to others, then those who receive this passed-on information will then themselves be able to reach a state of thinking and understanding sufficiently in tune, with our vibrations in order to receive our contact. For this, my friends, is how contacts work. It is first necessary, if the entity is to be able to receive our contact, for him to become of a certain vibration as a result of his thinking. This is greatly speeded by involvement in groups such as this (a channeling group). And then it is finally done through meditation. In other words, the verbal communications given to the entity by the channels such as this one create a system of thought and a desire for spiritual awareness that raises his vibration."

"We of the Confederation of Planets in the Service of the Infinite Creator are very sorry that we cannot step upon your soil and teach those of your people who desire our service. But, my friends, as we have said before, this would be a very great disservice to those who do not desire our service at this time, and we are afraid we would have little effect in bringing understanding even to those who desire it, for understanding, my friends, comes from within. We can only guide. We can only suggest. We are attempting to do this in such a way that the seeking of the individual will be stimulated to turning his thinking inward, inward to that single source of love and understanding, the Creator, that is part of us all, part of everything that exists, for everything that exists, my friends, is the Creator."

"We are very privileged to have you join with us in this great service at this time in the history of your planet. For this is a very great time, a great transitional period, in which many of the Earth's people will be raised from their state of confusion to a simple understanding: the love of their Creator."

Another word for the one original thought is the word love. It implies a unity that is so great that we do not see each other simply as close friends, brothers and sisters, but, ideally, as the Creator; and, as we see each other and ourselves as the Creator, we see one being. This concept is at the very heart of telepathy, and Hatonn talks about this concept and the original thought in general:

"At this time, I am in a craft far above your place of dwelling. I am at this time able to monitor your thoughts. This, my friends, might seem to some of your peoples to be an infringement, but I can assure you that it is not. Our capabilities of knowing the thinking of the peoples of this planet Earth are not designed in any way to infringe upon either their thinking or their activities. We do not consider the knowledge of the thoughts of others to be an infringement for we see these thoughts as our own. We see these thoughts as the thoughts of the Creator."

"My friends, it may seem to you that a thought of a nature other than one of love and brotherhood might be a thought generated not of our Creator. This is not possible, my friends. All thought that is generated is generated by the Creator. He is all things and is in all places, and all of the consciousness and all of the thought that exists is the thought of our Creator. His infinite number of parts all have free will, and all may generate in any way they choose. All of His parts communicate with all of the creation, in His entire and infinite sense."

"We are not attempting to change the thinking of our Creator. We are only attempting to bring His ideas to some of the more isolated parts for their inspection and appraisal. Isolated parts, I say, my friends, and why should we consider these parts to be isolated? We consider them isolated because from our point of view they have chosen to wander far from the concept that we have found to permeate most of the parts of the creation with which we are familiar. We find, my friends, that man upon planet Earth in his experiences and experiments has become isolated in his thinking and has divorced it from that to which we are accustomed in the vast reaches of creation which we have experienced."

"I urge you, my friends, to remember what we have brought to you. The next time that you are, shall we say, backed into a corner by the circumstances which prevail within the illusion of your physical existence, remember what you have learned and do not forget what you have worked so hard to obtain. You will choose at any time to alter your needs and desires from within the physical illusion to your being within the creation of the Father. As long as your objectives lie within this physical illusion it will be necessary for you to be subject to the laws which prevail within this illusion. If your desires can be altered by the application of what you are learning and are lifted in the creation of the Infinite One, then, my friends, you may have a great deal more ability to remove yourself from the corners into which the illusion seems to back you."

Some people may see that our entire planet could have gone so wrong philosophically and that beings more advanced than us would care enough about us to attempt to help us, some being referred to as guardian angels. Do we really think we would have had it all figured out, when there's beings' way more advanced than us out there to guide us in the right direction. However, channeling these guardian angels looks for the heart of the "cosmos" system of philosophy. Much of it is ethnical without being dogmatic.

Hatonn: "My friends, man on Earth has become very shortsighted in appreciation of the creation. He does not understand the true meaning of the simple and beautiful life that surrounds him. He does not appreciate its generation and regeneration. He learns that the very atmosphere that he breathes is cycled through the plant life to be regenerated to support him and his fellow beings and creatures, and yet this seems to the vast majority of those who dwell upon this planet to be an exercise in technology rather than one in theology. There is no awareness of the Creator's plan to provide for His children, to provide for their every desire and to provide a state of perfection. Man on Earth has lost the awareness that is rightfully his. And why, my friends, has he lost this awareness? He has lost this because he has focused his attention upon devices and inventions of his own. He has become hypnotized by his playthings and his ideas. He is but a child in his mind."

"All of this may be very simply remedied, and man can once more return to an appreciation of reality rather than an appreciation of the illusion created by his mind. All that is necessary, my friends, is that he individually avail himself to this appreciation of reality through the process of meditation, for this process stills his active conscious mind which is continually seeking stimulus within the illusion developed over so many centuries of time upon planet Earth. Very rapidly, then, he can return to an appreciation of the reality in the functioning of the real creation.

"This, my friends, is what man on Earth must return to if he is to know reality; this simple thought of absolute love, a thought of total unity with all his brothers regardless of how they might express themselves or whom they might be for this is the original thought of your Creator."

The creation of the Father has a very simple nature, which is that love is the essence of all things and of all their functions. Yet this real creation is not on most of our minds because we live in a daily atmosphere that the Confederation refers to as an illusion.

Hatonn: "We of the Confederation of Planets in the Service of the Infinite Creator have been, for many of your years, aware of many principles of reality. We are aware of these principles because we have availed ourselves to them just as the people of your planet may do."

"It is possible through meditation to totally reduce the illusion that you now experience that creates the separation- an illusory separation- to what it actually is a total illusion. We have been continuing to speak to you about meditation. We have spoken to you many times about reality and about love and about understanding, and yet you do not seem to be able to overcome the illusion."

"The reason for the illusion, my friends, is one that man on Earth has generated. He has generated it out of desire. This illusion is useful. It is very useful for those who would wish to evolve at a very rapid rate by experiencing it and by using it while within it. Many of us who are now circling your planet would desire to have the opportunity that you have, the opportunity to be within the illusion and then, through the generation of understanding, use the potentials of the illusion. This is a way of gaining progress spiritually and has been sought out by many of our brothers."

"I cannot over-emphasize the necessity of becoming able to understand the nature of the potentials within your illusion and then, by self-analysis and meditation, reacting to that in a way that will express the thought that generated us: the thought of our Creator. This was done by the teacher whom you know as Jesus. This man recognized his position. He recognized the illusion. He understood the reason for the potentials within the illusion, and his reaction to these potentials and activities within the illusion was a reaction which was expressing the thought of the Creator, a thought of love."

"Keep uppermost in your mind that the illusion that you experienced is an illusion, that it is surrounding you for the purpose of teaching you. It can only teach you if you become aware of its teachings. It is said that "He worked His wonders in mysterious ways." This way may seem mysterious; however, it is the way of spiritual evolvement. There are many souls experiencing the illusion in which you find yourself; however, there are few using this illusion to grow. They are not doing this other than at a subliminal level because they have not availed themselves through their seeking to a knowledge of the possibility of doing this."

"Once an individual has become aware of the possibility of using the illusion in which he finds himself in your physical world for the progression of spiritual growth, it is necessary that he take the next step and use his knowledge to express, regardless of the potentials that affect him, the love and understanding of his Creator."

Meditation is the best means for attaining understanding, of progressing spiritually, and of understanding the nature of the illusion and the purpose for which we are experiencing it. We can use our consciousness in meditation to create a more rapid growth in personal evolution.

Hatonn: "Desire, my friends, is the key to what you receive. If you desire it, you shall receive it. This was the Creator's plan, a plan in which all of His parts would receive exactly what they desire. My friends, often in the illusion which you now experience it seems that you do not acquire what you desire. In fact, the opposite seems to be the case in many, many instances. It is a paradox, it seems, that such a statement should be made and that such apparent results of desire are manifested, and yet we state, without exception, that man receives exactly what he desires. Perhaps, my friends, you do not understand desire. Perhaps this understanding is not within the intellectual mind. Perhaps it will be necessary to spend time in meditation to become aware of your real desire. For, my friends, there is much, much more of you and of the creation than you presently appreciate with your intellectual abilities in your present illusion.

It is very difficult for the peoples of this planet to give up their illusion, to give up the preconceived knowledge of what they believe to be cause and effect. However, this is not reality. This is illusion, born of illusion. It is a simple product of the complexity that man upon this planet has generated. Join with us in divorcing your thinking from such complexities and become aware of what has created you, everything that you experience, and everything that is thought. Become aware of your Creator. Become aware of His desire, and when you know this desire, you will know your own, for you and your Creator are one, and you are one with all of His parts and, therefore, all of your fellow beings throughout all of the creation. When you know his desire, you will feel it. There will be no more confusion. There will be no more questions. You will have found what you have sought. You will have found Love, for this is the desire of your Creator: that all of His parts express and experience the Love that created you. This may be found simply, in meditation. No amount of seeking within the intellectual concepts of your people, no amount of careful planning or careful interpretation of the written or spoken word, will lead you to the simple truth."

The Confederation states that the will of each entity is absolutely central to each entity's quest for evolution. In fact, free will is at the foundation of the universe. Each entity is part of one unity but also a totally unique part of that unity. Each persons free will is paramount, and the Confederation always wants to avoid infringement upon free will of any person:

Hatonn: "We do not wish to impose our understanding of truth upon your peoples, and this would be something that we would do if we contacted them directly. We could not help it, for our very utterance of truth would be accepted by many of your peoples as being valid. We do not wish to be thought of as the ultimate representative of the Creator's truth. We wish to give this to your peoples in such a way so that they may accept or reject this at their own will. This, as we understand it, is a necessary provision in the spiritual evolvement of all mankind; that he be, at some state of his evolution, in a position to accept or reject what is necessary for his evolution. In this way, and only in this way, can he know the truth, the truth of the Creator, that single truth that is the creation, the truth of the love of the creation."

"It must be realized from within. It cannot be impressed from without. We are attempting to stimulate those of your peoples who would be stimulated to seeking this truth that is within them. We have been required by our understanding of our Creator's principle to remain in hiding, for we cannot serve one individual and at the same time do a disservice to his neighbor by proving within his own mind that we exist, for many of those of planet Earth at this time do not desire to believe in or have proof of our existence. For this reason, we find it necessary to speak to those who seek through channels such as this one. We find it necessary to give to those who seek that which they seek in such a way that they, for themselves, may appraise its value and accept or reject, on their own terms, those thoughts that we bring, and understand the reality of the creation in which all of us exist."

Hatonn: "Many of your peoples are at this time seeking outside their illusion. To those who seek, we offer our understanding. We do not attempt to say that we have ultimate wisdom. We only suggest that which we have to offer may be of value, for we have found, in our experience, as we have passed through the same experiences as those of Earth, that there is a most beneficial direction in seeking to serve. We are acting through instruments such as those here tonight to give, to those who seek, an understanding. Our presence is meant to stimulate seeking. Through this process, we hope to contact as many of the peoples of your planet as would desire our contact. We hope in the very near future to be able to contact many more of the peoples of your planet, the peoples who would desire understanding. It is difficult to contact those people of your planet because of this, shall I say, mixture of types, but it is well worth our effort if we are able to contact but one."

We will continue to act as we do now, speaking through instruments such as this one, until a sufficient number of the peoples of your planet have become aware of truth. We are constantly striving to bring, through many channels of communication, the simple message to the people of Earth; the simple message that will leave them with a simple understanding of all that there is, and that is love."

(It's easier to understand the love of an Infinite Creator through meditation).

Hatonn: "Wisdom is a rather lonely matter, my friends. You must accept this truth as you acquire the burden of wisdom. That which you know, you are to be careful of, for what you know in the real creation has power, and that which you desire is all of the direction which that power will be aimed at; but have faith in what you know and what you are learning. Feed your faith and your understanding through meditation. The further you go along the path the more meaningful you will find this simple statement: meditate. It begins as a simple process and, little by little, it becomes a way in which you live. Observe it as you progress along your own spiritual path."

"It is to be remembered that service to others is service to one's self. There is no similarity between others and ourselves. There is identity. There is contemplation and unity. Therefore, that which is felt of a negative nature towards a sheep of the flock is felt towards one's self and is felt toward the Creator. This enters the service which you attempt to give to yourself and to the Creator through service to another, and causes a blot of a stain upon the perfect service you would have performed. It must be remembered that each person is a completely free entity whose independence must in no way be shaken and yet whose identity remains one with you."

"There is only one thing of great importance for you to consider at this time. That is your personal preparation for service. You are to serve your fellow man, and, therefore, it is necessary that you prepare yourselves for this service. This of course is done in mediation. We cannot overemphasize the importance of meditation. Through this technique you will receive answers to all of your questions. It is difficult to realize this, but it is true. All of your questions can be reduced to an extremely simple concept. This you can become aware of in meditation. Once this has been done you will be ready to serve, just as others have served and are now serving upon your planet. Follow their example; spend time in meditation. Qualify yourself to reach out to your fellow man and lead him from the darkness of confusion that he is experiencing back into the light that he desires."

"There are more people upon this planet seeking than there have been in the past. However, many are quite confused in their attempts to seek, and there is a need at this time for many more channels such as this one who can receive directly the thoughts that so many of the people of this planet are seeking. We are attempting at this time to generate greater numbers of proficient vocal channels who can receive our thoughts quite readily. This requires daily meditation. This is all that is required; daily meditation. It is assumed, that as this daily mediation is performed there is a desire for our contact."

"At the time at which each of you incarnated, my friends, each of you was aware that certain lessons, hitherto unlearned, were to be the goals for achievement in this incarnation. If it seems to you that your entire incarnation within this illusion has been a series of difficulties of one particular type, then you are almost certainly aware in some manner of one of your lessons. As you can see, these lessons are not to be avoided. They are to be learned."

"Further, we must point out to you that when a confrontation in such a lesson has been achieved, that which separates you from understanding is most often your own thinking. Your conscious thinking processes are quite capable of being self-destructive in the sense that they may aid you to avoid the lesson that you wish in reality to learn."

"Therefore, as you approach a lesson, we suggest that if it is possible to achieve a temporary abeyance (inactivity) of the conscious, analytical processes, then you may return to the problem with a much clearer mentality, ready to learn what you came to this experience to learn, rather than only to avoid what you came to learn."

"We know how difficult it is to achieve the meditative state at all times, for we have been where you are and we are aware of that particular type of illusion that you call physical. We urge you, therefore, to depend on meditation of a formal kind, then to attempt a semi-meditative state at all times, and, by this, we mean simply to achieve a state of attention so that your destructive impulses are not free to clog your mind completely and keep you from learning the lessons you came to learn."

"Meditation upon the complete unity of yourself and all that you see. Do this not once, and not simply in present circumstances, but at all times, and especially in difficult circumstances. For insofar as you love and feel at one with those things which are difficult for you, to that extent will those circumstances be alleviated. This is not due to any laws within our illusion but is due to the Law of Love, for that body which is of spiritual, which is interpenetrated with the physical body, is higher than your physical body, and those changes which you make by love upon your spiritual body will, of necessity, reflect themselves within the physical illusion."

"All is one, my friends. My voice is now the voice of this instrument; my thoughts are her thoughts. Please believe that the vibration we offer to you is not a vibration of personality, but is a vibration of the Creator. We are also channels. There is only one voice. Within this vibration, we are self-consciously aware that this voice is the voice of the Creator. It is simply a matter of lifting vibration which are not so self-aware of the Creator. All things will eventually come into harmony in relation to your understanding."

"Even if the universe for those around you remains disharmonious and difficult, if your mind is stayed upon the unity of the Creator, your own universe will become harmonious, and this is not by your doing but by the simple love of the Creator."

"There is a season upon your planet which shall be highly traumatic within your physical illusion. The physical reason for this are varied. Your scientists will spend a great deal of time, while they can, in attempting to catalog and describe each of the conditions which will produce disaster on this physical plane of your planet. That which your scientists speak of is quite so, and will be part of the program which has been predicted by all of those holy works which you have upon the face of the Earth."

"It is not either permissible or possible for us to tell you precisely what events will occur, or when they will occur, due to the fact that the vibration within the mind and heart of the peoples upon your planet is determining and will determine the precise events. There is within the planet Earth a great deal of karma which must be adjusted as the cycle changes, and these things will manifest. Precisely when, and how, we cannot say, nor would we wish to, my friends. For the rain, and the wind, and fire, will destroy only those things which are in what you call the third density of vibration. You may value those things because you cannot imagine what a fourth-density existence will be like. We suggest to you that you spend no time concerning yourselves with the effort of maintaining your third-density existence after the vibration change to fourth density has been completed."

"If, within your spirit, your graduation day has come, those things necessary for your emergence into fourth density will be done for you. All will be accomplished by helpers which you must be aware that you have."

"It is extremely possible that damage will occur to those things which you identify yourself in the third density. If we may speak plainly, you will observe the valley of the shadow of death. These very words, my friends, have been spoken to you before, and yet you cling to that physical body and those physical surroundings as though your spirit were attached quite permanently to them."

"May we suggest to you that you can find your spirit neither in your head, nor in your hands, nor in your chest, nor in your legs, nor in your feet, that nowhere you can find your spirit; nowhere can you operate to remove it, nor to aid it. Your spirit resides within a shell. The shell may be removed, but that is no matter. The spirit does not perish."

(The physical changes and trauma of our planet is the planet itself moving into a new vibration, a new portion of space and time, which many have called the New Age. We must have learned the lessons of Love and compassion to move into this new frequency of fourth density.)

Hatonn: "There is a choice to be made very shortly, and it would be preferable if all the people of this planet understand the choice that is to be made. It will be difficult for many of the people of this planet to understand what this choice is, because it is a choice that they have not considered. They have been much too involved in their daily activities and their confusion and their desire of a very trivial nature to be concerned with an understanding of the choice that they are very shortly to make. Whether they wish to or not, whether they understand it or not, regardless of any influence, each and every one of the people who dwell upon planet Earth will shortly make a choice. There will be no middle area. There will be those who choose to follow the path of love and light and those who choose otherwise."

"This choice will not be made by saying, "I choose the path of love and light," or "I do not choose it." The verbal choice will mean nothing. This choice will be measured by the individual's demonstration of his choice. This demonstration will be very easy for us of the Confederation of Planets in His Service to interpret. This choice is measured by what we term the vibratory rate of the individual. It is necessary, if an individual is to join those who make the choice of love and understanding, for his rate of vibration to be above a certain minimal level. There are many now that are close to this minimum level, but due to continuing conditions of erroneous (or inaccurate) thought that prevail upon your surface, they are either fluctuating around this point or are even in some cases drifting away from the path of love and understanding. There are many whose vibratory rate at this time is sufficiently high for them to travel with no difficulty into the density of vibration that this planet is shortly to experience."

(The Confederation has called the graduation the harvest, which will take place sometime in the future. Some channeling revealed this date to be around December of 2030, even though this date could easily change. This concept of the Judgment Day differs from the eschatological one (relating to the final destiny of each soul on Earth) in that the one who judges us is not a God apart from us but the God within us. As a result of this harvest some will go on to a new age of love and light and will learn new lessons in a very positive and beautiful density, as the Confederation calls it. Others will have to repeat this particular grade of lessons and relearn the lessons of love. Here the Confederation entity, Hatonn, speaks once again of the Harvest and of the Confederation's purpose in speaking through contactee groups:

"There is going to be a Harvest, as you might call it, a harvest of souls that will shortly occur upon your planet. We are attempting to extract the greatest possible harvest from this planet. This is our mission, for we are the Harvesters."

"In order to be most efficient, we are attempting to create first a state of seeking among the people of this planet who desire to seek. This would be those who are close to the acceptable level of vibration. Those above this level are of course not of as great an interest to us since they have, you might say, already made the grade. Those far below this level, unfortunately, cannot be helped by us at this time. We are attempting at this time to increase by a relatively small percentage the number who will be harvested into the path of love and understanding."

"Even a small percentage of those who dwell upon your planet is a vast number, and this is our mission, to act through groups such as this one in order to disseminate information in such a fashion that it may be accepted or rejected, that it may be in a state lacking what the people of your planet choose to call proof."

"We offer them no concrete proof, as they have a way of expressing it. We offer them Truth. This is an important function of our mission- to offer Truth without proof. In this way, the motivation will, in each and every case, come from within the individual. In this way, the individual vibratory rate will be increased. An offering of proof or an impressing of this Truth upon an individual in such a way that he would be forced to accept it would have no usable effect upon his vibratory rate."

"This, then, my friends, is the mystery of our way of approaching your peoples."

Wanderer's:

"Wanderers" are usually service-oriented people and often have difficulty fitting into the planetary vibrations of Earth. Often, they feel that they do not fit in or don't belong, but are possessed of many gifts, in the arts, in teaching or in a simple sharing of a cheerful and happy vibration. Ra suggests there's approximately 65,000,000 wanderers on Earth in the 1980's. They have left other densities in harmonious environments to take on a job that is most difficult and dangerous, for if a wanderer cannot at least begin to pierce the forgetting process that occurs at birth into this density during his or her lifetime on planet Earth, and remember the love and light that they intended to share, the wanderer can be caught in the 3rd density illusion, collecting Karma, and be delayed in arriving again at the home planet until all that is unbalanced in 3rd density in this lifetime has been balanced."

In summary, a Wanderer is a more evolved being that comes from the higher densities such as the 4th, 5th or 6th then reincarnate into our 3rd density Earth to be of service. In many cases, their mission is to raise the vibration of the planet by bringing love and/or knowledge to a 3rd density planet, such as Earth. Jesus, Buddha and prophet Mani of Manichaeism from Iran were all Wanderers. Jesus and Prophet Mani both being of the 4th density vibration from the Sirian Star System.

Psychic surgery:

Psychic surgery is a type of "faith healing." No psychic surgery patient has ever been lost because nothing actually happens to the patient's physical body. It is truly a psychic form of healing done in the Philippines and in Mexico.

The psychic surgery is done in a Philippine bedroom; the patient is undressed except for garments retained for personal modesty, lies down on the bed, which may in some cases be covered with a shower curtain, usually one borrowed from the hotel room. The healer, a religious man, who often spent 10 or 12 years of his life praying to become a healer "walking in the wilderness" of the volcanic mountains of Luzon in solitude, enters the room. He carries nothing except perhaps a bible. Often a healer is accompanied by an assistant who functions as interpreter or surgical assistant; more accurately termed, cleanup man.

The healer begins by taking the hands and moving them over the body, palms down. This is the method of scanning the body just as an x-ray machine would. A site for "surgery" is then selected, and if the healer is right-handed the left hand is pressed firmly against the skin. The skin seems to separate and the interior of the body is seen. This manifestation is very real looking, and anyone who sees it swears the body has opened with the bare hands. The right hand then enters this open site and manipulates within the body.

Carla Rueckert, the channeler, was one of the patients. The healer was told that she had arthritis. He scanned her body with the help of his assistant. Then, he opened the abdominal cavity and with a very-liquid-sounding action pulled gently, but firmly, at what seemed to be organs rather than joints. It wasn't unpleasant, but it was puzzling. He then removed what seemed to be three small, long pieces of bloody material, at the center of which was a small piece of hard material. This done, he removed his left hand. The "incision" vanished without a scar or trace of any kind. The two men mopped up what had become a considerably amount of blood, rinsed their hands, and then took baby oil and worked it over the abdominal skin, massaging in silence.

The scanning had produced the knowledge of three cysts upon Carla's right ovary, and the misplacement or dropping of both ovaries, which had occurred through years of very active life. The pulling had been to reposition the ovaries so that she wouldn't have discomfort during menstruation. The removal of cysts had been some purpose. She never told Don about it either.

Upon returning to the United States, Carla had her gynecologist examine the area, and he confirmed the three cysts were no longer palpable. They remained gone, and her comfort level of her menstrual cycle was way better.

Once the healer's hands are upon the person's body, a distinct emotional and mental attitude change occurs, away from fear or apprehension, within the individual of those who have explained their experiences. The psychic surgeon calls it the presence of the Holy Spirit.

How Carla channeled:

Deep trance can channel an extraterrestrial being, and Carla would challenge any new entity in the name of Christ Consciousness, demanding it to leave if it did not come in the name of Christ Consciousness. When it remains after that, then Carla opens herself up to its telepathic communication.

Two sessions a day was too wearing on Carla, so then the group averaged one session every 7-10 days.

Carla recites the Prayer of St. Francis right before opening herself up to channeling and Don aligns the table, which holds the Bible, candle, incense and chalice of water in a straight line with her head, as recommended by Ra. After Don lights the candle and incense, Don and Jim, walk the Circle of One around Carla and repeat the words that begin each contact.

At some point after that, Carla departs her physical body, and Ra then uses it to make the words that form the responses to Don's question. Jim meditates and sends light to Carla for the duration of the session, only taking time out to flip the tapes over as they finish each side. When the session is over, Don waits a few moments for Carla to return to her body, calls her name a few times until she responds, helps her sit up, rubs her neck a bit, and gives her the chalice full of water to drink after Don and Jim have filled it full of their love vibrations as much as they can.

(The proof of all of the channeling sessions are recordings on the L/L research YouTube channel. All 106 sessions under the playlist called The Ra contact.)

Channeling Instructions:

RA, Session #2, January 20th, 1981:

"Place at the entity's head a virgin chalice of water. Place to the center the book most closely aligned with the instrument's mental distortions, which are allied most closely with the Law of One- that being the Bible, place a small amount of cense, or incense, in a virgin censor. To the rear of the book symbolizing One, opened to the Gospel of John, Chapter One, place a white candle."

(Now these five Law of One books I condensed down I would say is material most aligned with the Law of One.)

RA, Session #69, August 29th, 1981: "At this particular working there is slight interference with the contact due to the hair of the instrument. We may suggest the combing of this antenna-like material into a more orderly configuration prior to the working."

The group hooked up three tape recorders microphones just below Carla's chin so that they don't miss any of the session if tape recorder one or two malfunctions, which did happen to them before.

Session #2, January 20th, 1981: "The proper alignment is with the head pointed 20 degrees north by northeast. This is the direction from which the newer or New Age distortions of love/light, which are less distorted, are emanating, and this instrument will find comfort therein."

"The instrument would be strengthened by the wearing of a white robe. The instrument shall be covered and prone, the eyes covered."

Don asks three women (Wanderer's) questions:

*Three women separately had hypnotic regressions and agreed to answered Don's questions. On May 10th, 1975, Don, along with Lawrence Allision, an accomplished hypnotist, sat down with a volunteer pursuing his masters in chemical engineering, and proceeded to explore another world. This material was gathered in a Chapter devoted to the concept of Wanderers in Don and Carla's 1976 book Secrets of the UFO.

During the hypnotic regression the man described a world where he was dressed in loose white clothes with a sash for a belt. It was short sleeves and warm. He had a little boy and didn't see any mountains on this planet. There're no feelings for names there and their speech appeared to be telepathic, since they just knew without words.

It seemed to be a simple life. There was light at his books, so it's obviously mechanized, which is being equipped with machines. People weren't speaking to each other; they all seem to know each question. They know what's going on, there was singing.

He was sitting on a stone or a bench and they'd be sitting down, he's explaining, but he's not talking to them. (So, telepathic communication). This appeared to be the center of the community like a temple. It was a stone, limestone, but whiter. That's what it's made of. The dome appeared 200-250 feet long and maybe 150 feet wide. It was a huge room. The glow was from the ceiling and that was the light. There's a glow and a darker painted-like light. The room was bright and doesn't appear to have any shadow in the room.

There was singing off in the distance like a choir. The music was sparkling in the air. It sort of was like a praise to God. He grew up studying large books.

In the morning there's a teacher, and in the afternoon or in late evening he studies. There are no exams. You just want to learn. It's like you can't learn enough.

Jordyn: "That's what I do all day at work. Read and study large books. Even all five 'Law of One' books"

Nobody had individual homes. This big place is their home. This is one purpose. It's like a school, or a teaching place to teach those that want to learn it in depth, and those that come when they can. It's not a ruling-type people. People don't have to go there. It's not a class system or anything.

Meditation played a very large part in the lives of the inhabitants of this other world, or at least those on that planet. There were meditations alone and there were daily group meditations with everyone. He didn't see himself there, in different states of consciousness. There are prayerful times, in the morning and at night. You have them in your room, and then you have others before meals, before the morning meal and then briefly before the evening meal when the food was brought. Then afterwards there's like a private sort of devotional, except that you're not-like in a mediation. There are other times the whole group gets together other than meals. The whole place is like a family. You don't feel that attached necessarily to one person; you feel attached to everybody.

Another function of the clan was to open their temple from time to time to all of those on that planet who wished to come for spiritual inspiration. The description of this temple sounded like a very large heliport.

Ships land at the heliport, the doors open and the people come out of the spaceships, and people come into the temple. They're allowed to go on the grounds, as this is their place too, but they sort of come as a visitor to it.

They may stay for about a day.

Heliport description:

There's a flat stone out in front of the heliport without roads coming to it. Then, there's a huge spaceship pad for spaceships to just appear and land on the pad. They weren't zipping off or coming in, across the horizon or anything.

Spaceship Description:

It's longer than it is wide, and it's not real thick compared to length and width dimension. It's like an oblong shape and just appear and sets down on the pad.

Here the young man grew in wisdom, teaching, growing, beginning to teach fewer and more advanced students, and in time preparing to end the incarnation. (This advanced planet appears to be an example of a 4th, 5th, or 6th density planet of the positive polarity.) A being coming from a higher density planet such as this one described and then reincarnating into Earth to help, would be the definition of a Wanderer.

He said he reincarnated back into the 3rd density Earth to help with the needs of people that are lost and he felt as if that's what he needed to do.

The research that Don and Carla did, brought them across the knowledge of a highly unusual type of healing called psychic surgery. In 1976, at the age of 33, the work Carla did was to be her last. She had juvenile rheumatoid arthritis with several complications, with one being lupus. It was considered a miracle that she survived as she lost approximately half of each kidney.

Don and Carla's investigated psychic surgery and discovered it being a psychic form of healing. No psychic surgery patient has ever been lost because nothing actually happens to the patient's physical body. It's a psychic form of healing and a "faith healing". Don and Carla had spent time in the Philippines and Mexico examining the possibilities of this and witnessing it to actually be possible and successful healing.

Important Note: Some of this material may be a little difficult to understand at first, as the wisdom gathered within is from Ra (a part of the Council of 9 Guardian Angels from the Galactic Federation). I did surprisingly discover that by the 2nd or 3rd time I read through it, it was processed and just clicked in my understanding 100% more. At first some material within may appear to be a PHD level in metaphysics, by the 3rd time reading through, it felt elementary and extremely easy to understand and digest. So, keep on reading and don't give up. This material has been one of the biggest blessings in my life as it helped me reach enlightenment.

Session 1: January 15th, 1981 (By Carla, Don and Jim)

Ra: "We greet you in the love and in the light of our Infinite Creator."

In Ra's vibration the polarities are harmonized, the complexities are simplified, the paradoxes have a solution. They are One. That's their nature and their purpose. Ra has served with varying degrees of success in transmitting the Law of One, of Unity, of singleness to people of Earth. They have walked our planet. They have seen the faces of our peoples. They now feel the great responsibility of staying in the compacity of removing the distortions given to the Law of One. They will continue until our cycle is appropriately ended. (Until our 3rd density harvest, with the possibility of that being in 2030.)

Ra made contact with the Egyptians and at the same time another 6th density social memory complex, like Ra, made contact in South America, and the so-called "lost cities" were their attempts to contribute the Law of One.

They spoke to one who heard and understood and was in a position to decree the Law of One. However, the priests and peoples of that era quickly distorted their message, robbing it of the compassion which unity is informed by its very nature. Since it contains all, it cannot abhor any. Since there weren't any proper channels to enunciate (pronounce clearly) the Law of One, they then removed themselves from the now hypocritical position which they allowed themselves to be placed in.

Consider that the universe is infinite. Ra can assure us that there is no end to ourselves, our understanding, our journey of seeking or our perceptions of the creation.

That which is infinite cannot be many, for manyness is a finite concept. To have infinity you must identify or define the infinity as unity; otherwise, the term does not have any referent (likeness) or meaning. In an infinite Creator there is only unity. A simplistic example of unity is the prism that shows all colors stemming from the sunlight.

In truth there is no right or wrong. There is no polarity, for all will be reconciled at some point through the mind/body/spirit we distort in various ways at this time. This distortion is chosen by us as an alternative to understanding the complete unity of thought that binds all things. You are not speaking of similar or somewhat like entities or things. You are everything, every being, every emotion, every event, every situation. You are unity. You are infinity. You are love/light, light/love. You are. This is the Law of One.

The distinction between yourself and others is not visible to Ra. A separation doesn't exist between the consciousness-raising efforts of the distortion which you project as personality. Thus, to learn is the same as to teach unless you are not teaching what you are learning, in which case you have done you/them little good.

Group-individualized consciousness is that state of sharing understanding with the other distortions of mind/body/spirit complexes, which are within the evident reach of the mind/body/spirit complex individual or group. Ra is speaking to the group and accepting both the groups' distortions and Ra's distortions in order to enunciate (pronounce clearly) the Laws of creation, more especially the Law of One. Ra isn't available to many people on Earth, for this is not an easily understood way of communication or type of philosophy. However, Ra's very being is hopefully a poignant (emotionally effecting Ra deeply) example of both the necessity and the near hopelessness of attempting to teach. (I, Jordyn, am here to help Ra spread the Law of One. Hopefully helping them not feel that this teaching is hopeless, but that it will reach the masses.)

Each of the three group members are striving to use, digest, and diversify the information without distortion. The few who will illuminate by sharing this light is far more enough reason for the greatest possible effort. To serve one is to serve all. If an individual makes effort to act as a catalyst in general to increase the awareness of planetary consciousness, they surely are being of aid. Ra states that this is the only activity worth doing: to learn/teach or teach/learn.

(Learn/teach basically means learning, to then one day share what you have learned by teaching it. Whereas teach/learn means teaching can help one to learn).

There is nothing else of aid in demonstrating the original thought except your very being, and the distortions that come from the unexplained, inarticulate or mystery clad being are many. Thus, to attempt to discern and weave your way through as many group distortions as possible among your peoples in the course of your teaching is a very good effort to make. Ra can speak no more valiantly (courageously or determined) of the groups desire to serve.

Ra is able to be available for communication because of the instrument's recent experiences with trance. She (Carla) is able to communicate their thoughts in the future. Each person chooses the mind/body/spirit complex for this particular life experience of this time/space.

Ra suggests to nurture the instrument for a brief period of silence. Then the repetition of the instruments name (Carla). Repeat until an answer is obtained. Then the laying on of the hands at the neck region for a brief period so that the instrument may recharge batteries, which are not, full of the essence of this particular field at this time. And finally, a gift of water into which the love of all present has been given. This will restore this entity, for her distortions contain great sensitivity towards the vibrations of love and the charged water will affect comfort.

A nickname can contain the greatest vibration of love. The charging of water is done by those present placing their hands over the glass and visualizing the power of love entering the water. This will charge that very effective medium with those vibrations.

This instrument is at this time, quite fatigued. However, her heart is such that she continues to remain open to us (Ra) and useful as a channel. This is why we (Ra) have spent the time/space (physical time in one timeline of space. Space/time means metaphysical space not found in time) explaining how the distortions of fatigue may be ameliorated. (Ameliorated means to make something bad or unsatisfactory better).

"Under no circumstances should this instrument be touched until she has responded to her name. I do not wish to take this instrument beyond her capacity for physical energy. It grows low. There, I must leave this instrument. I leave you in the glory and peace of unity. Go forth in peace, rejoicing in the power of the One Creator. I am Ra."

Session 2: January 20th, 1981.

There are few who will grasp, without significant distortion what Ra will communicate Ra states. If the group chose to share this information with others, Ra believes this would be most helpful in regularizing and crystalizing our own patterns of vibration upon the levels of experience of life. If one is illuminated, are not all illuminated? To teach/learn is the Law of One in one of its most elementary distortions.

Ra asks that in giving this information to not stress. The teach/learning which is Ra's responsibility is philosophical (which is the study of fundamental nature of knowledge, reality and existence) rather than historical.

Ra is the Confederation who 11,000 years ago came to two of our planetary cultures who at the time were closely in touch with the creation of the One Creator. It was Ra's naïve belief that they could teach/learn by direct contact and the free-will of individuals weren't in danger. (Since all is one, to teach is to learn.) They didn't think that they would be disturbed, as these cultures were already closely aligned with the belief in the liveness or consciousness of all. They came and were welcomed by the peoples they wished to serve. They attempted to aid them in technical ways through healing of mind/body/spirit complex distortions through the use of crystals, appropriate to the distortion, placed within a certain appropriate series of vibrations of time/space material. Thus, the pyramids were created.

Ra attempted to contact the rulers of Egypt, or in some areas called the Holy Land. They found that the technology was reserved largely for those in power. This was not intended by the Law of One. So, they left Egypt. The 6th density group that worked with those in South America didn't give up so easily. They returned. Ra did not. However, Ra never left our vibration due to their responsibility for the changes in consciousness they first caused and then found distorted in ways not relegated (reduced in rank) to the Law of One.

In the 18th dynasty, Ra was able to contact Pharaoh. Pharoah was described by Ra to be small in life experience and called a Wanderer. Thus, Pharaoh received their communication and was able to blend his distortions with Ra's. The young Pharaoh "Ammon" was given the honor of a prosperous god. Pharaoh decided that this name, being in honor of one among many gods, was not acceptable for inclusion.

Thus, he changed his name to one that honored the Sun disc, called Aten, which was a close distortion to Ra's own reality as they understand their own nature of mind/body/spirit complex distortion. However, it does not come totally into alignment with the intended teach/learning that was sent. This entity, Ikhenaten, became convinced that the vibration of One was the true spiritual vibration and thus decreed the Law of One.

However, this entity's beliefs were accepted by very few. His priests gave lip service, without seeking spiritually. The people continued in their beliefs. The people continued in their polarized beliefs of many gods until Mohammed delivered the peoples into a more intelligible distortion of mind/body/spirit relationships.

The principle of crystal healing is based upon an understanding of hierarchical nature of the structure of the physical body. There are crystals that work upon the energies coming into the spiritual body, ones that work upon the distortions from spirit to mind, ones that balance the distortions between the mind and the body. All of these crystal healings are charged through purified channels. Without the relative crystallization of the healer working with the crystal, the crystal will not be properly charged. The other ingredient is the proper alignment with the energy fields of the planet and the holistic or cosmic distortions or streaming's that enter the planetary aura with an appropriate ratio of shapes and placement is of indicated aid in the untangling or balancing process.

The delicacy of the choosing of the crystal is very critical and a crystalline structure such as a diamond or ruby can be used by a purified channel who is filled with the Love/Light of One, in almost any application. This takes initiation and there never have been many to persevere to the extent of progressing through the various leavings which initiation causes.

The larger pyramids were built by Ra's ability using the forces of One. The stones are alive. It hasn't been understood by the people of our culture. The purposes of the pyramids were two: Firstly, to have a properly oriented place of initiation for those who wished to become purified or initiated channels for the Law of One. Two, Ra wished then to carefully guide the initiates in developing a healing of the people who they sought to aid, and of the planet itself. Pyramid after pyramid charged by the crystal and initiate were designed to balance the incoming energy of the One Creation with the many and multiple distortions of the planetary mind/body/spirit. Ra was then able to continue work, that brothers within the Confederation had effected through building of other crystal-bearing structures and thus complete a ring of these about the Earth's surface.

Ra stated that the instrument (Carla) wasn't being used correctly and therefore experiencing unnecessary fatigue. The vibrations may be purified by a simple turning of the circle of One and <u>by saying:</u>

<u>Question:</u> "What is the Law?"

<u>Answer:</u> "The Law is One."

<u>Question:</u> "Why are we here?"

<u>Answer:</u> "We seek the Law of One."

<u>Question:</u> "Why do we seek Ra?"

<u>Answer:</u> "Ra is a humble messenger of the Law of One."

<u>Both together:</u> "Rejoice then and purify this place in the Law of One. Let no thought form enter the circle we have walked about this instrument, for the Law is One."

The instrument at this time should be in trance. The proper alignment is the head pointed 20 degrees north by northeast. This is the direction from which are less distorted, are emanating, and this instrument will find comfort therein. This is a sensitive instrument meaning the distortions that enter her mind/body/spirit complex come from any of her senses. Thus, it is well to do the <u>following:</u>

<u>1.)</u> Place at the entity's head a virgin chalice of water.

<u>2.)</u> To the center, the book most closely aligned with the instrument's mental distortions which are aligned most closely with the Law of One, that being the Bible that she

touches most frequently. (For me, Jordyn, it would be these five condensed Law of One book that I published.)

3.) To the rear of the book symbolizing One, opened to the Gospel of John, Chapter 1, a white candle.

4.) The instrument would be strengthened by the wearing of a white robe covered and prone, the eyes covered.

Though this is a complex activity/circumstance and may seem very distorted from a teach/learning experience, these elaborations on the technique of trance will ease the mind as they perceive improvement in fatigue. If these teach/learn sessions are held at night, it is best to hold the sessions before the sun comes out.

Session 3: January 21st, 1981

Ra: "I am Ra. Please correct the angle of the incense so that it is perpendicular to the plane of 20 degrees north by northeast… the incense acts as energizer to the physical body, signifying its humanity… this is a necessity that the wafted smoke is perceived from the same relative angle as the instrument perceives the opened Bible balanced by the lighted candle signifying love/light and light/love and, therefore, give the mental and emotional distortion complex of this instrument the sight of paradise and peace which it seeks. Thus, energized from the lower to the higher, the instrument becomes balanced and does not grow fatigued. We appreciate your concern, for this will enable our teach/learning to proceed more easily."

Ra's social memory complex cannot effectually discern the distortions of the societal mind/body/spirit complex of our peoples on Earth. Ra wishes to fulfill the teach/learning honor/responsibility by answering the groups questions. This only will suffice (meet or satisfy a need), for Ra cannot plumb (measure) the depths of the distortion complexes which infect our peoples of Earth.

The so-called Great Pyramid had two capstones. One was of Ra's design and was smaller and carefully contrived pieces of granite. This was contrived for crystalline properties and for the proper flow of your atmosphere via a chimney. When Ra left our density, the original was taken away and a more precious one substituted, consisting, in part, of a golden material. This did not change the properties of the pyramid at all and was a distortion due to the desire of a few to mandate the use of the structure as a royal place only.

Questioner: "What was the specific purpose of the chimney?"

Ra: "There is a proper flow of our atmosphere which, though small, freshen the whole structure by having air-flow ducts situated so that there was a freshness of atmosphere without any disturbance or draft."

Questioner: "How were the blocks moved?"

Ra: "I am Ra. You must picture the activity within all that is created. The energy is, though finite, quite large compared to the understanding/distortion by your peoples. This is an obvious point well known to your people, but little considered."

"This energy is intelligent and hierarchical. Much as your mind/body/spirit complex dwells within a hierarchy of vehicles and retains, therefore, the shell or shape of field, and the intelligence of each ascendingly intelligent or balanced body, so does each atom of a rock."

"With this connection made, a request may be given. The intelligence of Infinite rockiness communicates to its physical vehicle, and that splitting and moving which is desired is then carried out through the displacement of the energy field of rockiness from finity to a dimension of infinity."

"In this way, that which is required is accomplished due to a cooperation of the infinite understanding of the Creator indwelling in the living rock. This is the mechanism by which many things are accomplished, which aren't subject to our present means of physical analysis of action at a distance."

Questioner: "I am reminded of the statement that if you had faith to move a mountain, the mountain would move. That if you are fully aware of the Law of One, you would be able to do these things?"

Ra: "Faith is perhaps one of the stumbling blocks between those of the infinite path and those of the finite proving/understanding" (This means that faith is on the infinite path with infinite possibilities and people that need to prove things are limited on the finite path).

Ra: "You are precisely correct in your understanding of the congruency of faith and intelligent infinity. One is more spiritual, the other more proof seeking."

There is a distinction between the individual power through the Law of One and the combined or societal memory complex mind/body/spirit understanding of the Law of One.

In the first case only the one individual, purified of all flaws, could move a mountain. In the case of mass understanding of unity, each individual may contain an acceptable amount of distortion and yet the mass mind could move a mountain. The progress is normally from the understanding which you now seek to a dimension of understanding which is governed by the laws of love, and which seeks the laws of light. Those who are vibrating with the Law of Light seek the Law of One. Those who vibrate with the Law of One seek the Law of foreverness.

We cannot say what is beyond this dissolution of the unified self with all that there is, for we still seek to become all that there is, and still are we Ra. Thus, our paths go onward.

The Pyramids were thought/built by Ra constructed by thought forms created by their social memory complex.

Ra built with everlasting rock the Great Pyramid. Other pyramids were built with stone moved from one place to another.

Questioner: "What is everlasting rock?"

Ra: "If you can understand the concept of thought forms you will realize that the thought form is more regular in its distortion that the energy fields created by the energy in the materials in the rock which has been created by thought form from thought to finite energy and beingness in your distorted reflection of the thought form.

The pyramids were built with many blocks instead of the whole things created as one form created at once because of the Law of Free Will. Ra wished to make a healing machine, or time/space ratio complex which was efficacious (effective) as possible. (Efficacious is being successful in producing a desired or intended result; effective). Ra didn't wish to be worshipped as builders of a miraculous pyramid. Thus, it appears to be made, and not created by thought.

The Great Pyramid is primarily a healing machine and a device for initiation. They are part of one complex of love/light intent/sharing. To use the healing properly it was important to have a purified and dedicated channel, or energizer, for the love/light of the infinite Creator to flow through. The initiatory method was necessary to prepare the mind, the body, and the spirit for service in the Creator's work. The two are integral.

There are two main functions of the pyramid in relation to the initiatory procedures. Before the body can be initiated, the mind must be imitated. This is the point where most adepts find their mind/body/spirit complexes distorted from. When the character and personality that is the true identity of the mind has been discovered, the body then must be known in each and every way. Thus, the various functions of the body need understanding and control with detachment. The first use of the pyramid is going down into the pyramid for deprivation of sensory input so that the body, in a sense, be dead and another life begin.

After the Channeling session:

Only the chalice behind the instruments head shall she drink from. That chalice is the most beneficial as the virgin material living in the chalice accepts, retains, and responds to the love vibration activated by the questioners beingness.

Session 4: January 22nd, 1981

The initiation of spirit was a more carefully designed type of initiation as regards to the time/space ratios about which the entity to be initiated found itself. If you will picture the side of the pyramid shape and mentally imagine this triangle cut into four equal triangles you will find the intersection of the triangle, which is at the first level on each of the four sides, forms a diamond in a plane which is horizontal. The middle of this plane is the appropriate place for the intersection of the energies streaming from the infinite dimensions and the mind/body/spirit complexes of various interwoven energy fields. Thus, it was designed that the one to be initiated would, by mind, be able to perceive and channel this gateway to intelligent infinity. This was the second point of designing this specific shape.

The initiate was to be on the centerline of that pyramid at an altitude above the base as defined by the intersection of the four triangles made by dividing each side.

There is a focusing of energy that is multidimensional to our dimensions.

Each size pyramid has its own point of streaming in of intelligent infinity. A tiny pyramid that can be placed below a body or above a body will have specific and various effects depending upon the placement of the body in relationship to the entrance point of intelligent infinity.

For the purposes of initiation, the size needed to be large enough to create the impression of towering size so that the entrance point of multidimensional intelligent infinity would completely pervade and fill the channel, the entire body being able to rest in this focused area. It was necessary for healing purposes that both channel and the one to be healed be able to rest within that focused point.

The Pyramid of Giza is out of tune. The disharmony jangles the sensitivity. Only the ghost of streaming still remains due to the shifting of the streaming points due to the shifting electromagnetic field of Earth; due also to the discordant vibratory complexes of those who have used the initiatory and healing place for less compassionate purposes.

It's possible for humans to build pyramids though. The material used isn't critical, but the ratios of time/space complexes are.

There are people today who can construct and initiate in a pyramid they built. However, the time of the pyramids is past. It is a timeless structure. However, the streaming's from the universe were, at the time attempted to aid Earth (approximately 11,000 years ago) those which required a certain understanding of purity. This understanding has changed to a more enlightened view of purity, as the streaming revolved and all things evolve. There are those on Earth today whose purity is already one with intelligent infinity. Without the use of structures, healer/patient can gain healing.

Ra states that the relative simplicity of the mind in the earlier cycle and the less distorted views and thought/spirit processes of the same mind/body/spirit complexes after many incarnations. Those who have chosen the distortion of service and have removed themselves from one dimension to another, thus bringing with them many skills and understandings which more closely match the distortions of the healing/patient processes.

Those who can heal:

There is one "health" in our polarized environment, but there are several significantly various distortions of types of mind/body/spirit complexes. Each type must pursue its own learn/teaching in this area.

The selected individual who be one such as the questioner who has distortions towards healing. The healing should be of one whose ability has found its pathway to intelligent infinity regardless of the plane of existence this distortion is found.

There are two kinds who can heal: Those who have the knowledge-giving of the Law of One and those who have the same knowledge, but show no significant distortions toward the Law of One in mind, body, or spirit, yet, have opened a channel to the same ability. There are those, without proper training, heal. Those whose life does not equal their work may find some difficulty in absorbing the energy of intelligent infinity, they cause disharmony in themselves and others and perhaps even find it necessary to cease the healing activity. Therefore, those who seek to serve and are willing to be trained in thought, word and action are those who will be able to comfortably maintain service in healing.

Firstly, the mind must be known to itself. This is perhaps the most demanding part of healing work. If the mind knows itself then the most important aspect of healing has occurred. Consciousness is the microcosm (miniature version) of the Law of One.

Secondly, the streaming's reaching our planet at this time, these understandings and disciplines have to do with the balance between love and wisdom in the use of the body in its natural functions.

The third area is the spiritual. The first two disciplines are connected through the attainments of contact with intelligent infinity.

Further elaboration; Imagine the more dense aspects of the body. Proceed to the energy pathways that cause the body to be energized. Understand that all natural functions of the body have all aspects from dense to fine and can be transmuted to sacramental. This is a brief investigation of the second area.

The spiritual: Imagine the function of the magnet. One pole reaching up. The other goes down. The function of the spirit is to integrate the up-reaching yearning of the mind/body energy with the down-pouring and streaming of infinite intelligence. This is a brief explication (explaining something in detail) of the third area.

Healing is but one distortion of the Law of One. An undistorted understanding of the Law, is it not being necessary to heal or to show any manifestation but only to exercise the discipline of understanding.

The Law of One may be approximated by stating that all things are one, that there is no polarity, no right or wrong, no disharmony, but only identity. All is one, and that one is love/light, light/love, the Infinite Creator. (So, I would Imagine demons or negative entities are individualized parts of consciousness that do not realize that they are the Creator and they are one with all. The demons are lost and believe they are separate from others, as they choose the darkness/service-to-self path).

One of the primal distortions of the Law of One is that of healing. Healing occurs when a mind/body/spirit complex realizes, deep within itself, that all is complete and whole and perfect. Thus, the intelligent infinity within this mind/body/spirit complex reforms the illusion of body, mind, or spirit to form congruent (in harmony) with the Law of One. The healer acts as energizer or catalyst for this completely individual process.

A healer asking to learn must take healing understood as responsibility for that ask/receiving. This is an honor/duty which must be carefully considered in free will before the asking.

The instrument (Carla) is capable of two sessions a day, but she must be encouraged to keep her body strong by exceeding her normal intake of food, this is due to the physical material Ra uses to speak. Her activities must be monitored to prevent over-activity, for these sessions are equivalent to a physical strenuous working day.

If these admonishments (firm warnings) are considered, the two sessions would be possible. Ra does not wish to deplete the instrument. (So, Ra ends the session, when Carla the instrument gets tired).

The Creator is the One Infinite Intelligence.

Session 5: January 23, 1981

The healer is only the catalyst, much as this instrument has the catalyst necessary to provide channel for Ra's words, yet by example or exercise of any kind can take no thought for this working.

The healing/working is congruent in that it is a form of channeling some distortion of the intelligent infinity.

The group decided to learn the honor/duty of learning/teaching the healing process.

Healing example: The body and mind must be open and receptive. The spirit then goes up the entity's energy/will and the streamings of creative fire and wind go down the body. (Thus, let the spirit go up through the body and the streamings of creative fire and wind go down the body for healing.

Ra: "I am Ra. We shall begin with the first of the three teachings/learnings.

We begin with the mental learn/teaching necessary for contact with intelligent infinity. The prerequisite of mental work is the ability to retain silence of self at a steady state when required by the self. The mind must be opened like a door. The key is silence.

Within the door lies a hierarchical construction you may liken unto geography and in some way geometry, for the hierarchy is quite regular, bearing inner relationships.

To begin to master the concept of mental disciplines it is necessary to examine the self. The polarity of your dimension must be internalized. Where you find patience within your mind you must consciously find the corresponding impatience and vice versa. Each thought a being has, in its turn an antithesis (opposite). The disciplines of the mind involve, first of all, identifying both those things of which you approve and those things of which you disapprove within yourself, and then balancing each and every positive and negative charge with its equal. The mind contains all things. Therefore, you must discover this completeness within yourself.

The second mental discipline is acceptance of the completeness within your consciousness. It is not for a being of polarity in the physical consciousness to pick and choose among attributes, thus building the roles that cause blockages and confusions in the already distorted mind complex. Each acceptance smooths part of the many distortions that the faculty (mental power) you call judgment engenders (creates).

The third discipline of the mind is a repetition of the first but with the gaze outward toward the fellow entities that it meets. In each entity there exists completeness. Thus, the ability to understand each balance is necessary. When you view patience, you are responsible for mirroring in your mental understandings, patience/impatience. When you view impatience, it is necessary for your mental configuration of understanding to be impatience/patience. We use this as a simple example. Most configurations of mind have many facets, and understanding of either self-polarities, or what you would call other-self polarities, can and must be understood as subtle work.

The next step is the acceptance of the other-self polarities, which mirrors the second step. These are the first four steps of learning mental disciplines. The fifth step involves observing the geographical and geometrical relationships and ratios of the mind, the other mind, the mass mind, and the infinite mind.

The second area of learn/teaching is the study/understanding of the body complexes. It is necessary to know your body well. This is a matter of using the mind to examine how the feelings, the biases, what you would call the emotions, affect various portions of the body complex. It shall be necessary to both understand the bodily polarity and to accept them, repeating in a chemical/physical manifestation the work you have done upon the mind bethinking the consciousness.

The body is a creature of the mind's creation. It has its biases. The biological bias must be first completely understood and then the opposite bias allowed to find full expression in understanding. Again, the process of acceptance of the body as a balanced, as well as polarized, individual may then be accomplished. It is then the task to extend this understanding to the bodies of the other-selves whom you will meet.

The simplest example of this is the understanding that each biological male is female; each biological female is male. This is a simple example. However, in almost every case wherein you are attempting the understanding of the body of self or other-self, you will again find that the most subtle discernment is necessary in order to fully grasp the polarity complexes involved.

At this time, we would suggest closing the description until the next time of work so that we may devote time to the third area commensurate (equal in measure) with its importance."

How to comfort the instrument more:

Ra: "I am Ra. The candle would be rotated clockwise approximately 10 degrees each session to improve the flow of spiraled energy through the being's receiving mechanisms. This particular configuration is well otherwise. But we ask that the objects described and used be centered with geometric care and checked from time to time. Also, that they not be exposed to that space/time in which work is not of importance.

Session 6: January 24, 1981

Ra: "We proceed now with the third part of the teach/learning concerning the development of the energy powers of healing.

The third area is the spiritual complex which embodies the fields of force and consciousness which are the least distorted of your mind/body/spirit complex. The exploration and balancing of the spirit complex is indeed the longest and most subtle part of your learn/teaching. We have considered the mind as a tree. The mind controls the body. With the mind single-pointed, balanced, and aware, the body comfortable in whatever biases and distortions make it appropriately balanced for that instrument, the instrument is then ready to proceed with the greater work.

That is the work of wind and fire. The spiritual body energy field is a pathway, or channel. When body and mind are receptive and open, then the spirit can become a functioning shuttle or communicator from the entity's individual energy/will upwards, and from the streamings of the creative fire and wind downwards.

The healing ability, like all other paranormal abilities, is affected by the opening of pathway or shuttle into intelligent infinity. There are many upon your plane who have a random hole or gateway in their spirit energy field, sometimes created by the ingestion of chemicals such as what this instrument would call LSD, who are able, randomly and without control, to tap into energy sources. They may or may not be entities who wish to serve. The purpose of carefully and consciously opening this channel is to serve in a more dependable way, in a more commonplace or usual way, as seen by the distortion complex of the healer. To others there may appear to be miracles. To the one who has carefully opened the door to intelligent infinity, this is ordinary; this is commonplace; this is as it should be. The life experience becomes somewhat transformed. The great work goes on.

At this time, we feel these exercises suffice for your beginning. We will, at a future time, when you feel you have accomplished that which is set before you, begin to guide you into a more precise understanding of the functions and uses of this gateway in the experience of healing.

Where Ra came from prior to their involvement with Earth:

Ra: "I am Ra. I am, with the social memory complex of which I am a part, one of those who voyaged outward from another planet within your own solar system. The planetary influence was what you call Venus. We are a race old in your measures. When we were at the sixth dimension our physical beings were what you would call golden. We were tall and somewhat delicate. Our physical body complex covering, which you call the integument (a tough outer protective layer), had a gold luster.

In this form we decided to come among your peoples. Your peoples at that time were much unlike us in physical appearance. We did not mix well with the population and were obviously other than they. Thus, our visit was relatively short, for we found ourselves in the hypocritical position of being acclaimed as other than your other-selves. This was the time during which we built the structures in which you show interest." (The pyramids)

Ra journeyed from Venus to Earth 11,000 years ago while they were a 6th density race. (Ra, today, is now a part of the Confederation.)

The third-density conditions of Earthly humans are not hospitable to the fifth and sixth dimensions of Venus. So, our Earthly third density humans would not survive on Venus. The 5th and 6th dimensions of Venus are quite conducive to growing/learning/teaching.

How Ra made the transition from Venus to walk on Earth:

Ra: "I am Ra. You will remember the exercise of the wind. The dissolution into nothingness is the dissolution into unity, for there is no nothingness. From the sixth dimension, we are capable of manipulating, by thought, the intelligent infinity present in each particle of light or distorted light so that we were able to clothe ourselves in a replica visible in the third density of our mind/body/spirit complexes in the sixth density. We were allowed this experiment by the Council which guards this planet." (The council of 9 guards Earth).

The Council of 9 is located in the octave, or 8th dimension, in the rings of Saturn.

About 500,000 years ago, there was a population of 3rd density beings on Maldek that dwelt within our solar system. These entities destroyed their planet and were forced to find room on this third density Earth (through reincarnation), which is the only one in our solar system at their time present which was hospitable and capable of offering the lessons necessary to decrease their mind/body/spirit distortions with respect to the Law of One.

They came through the process of Harvest and were incarnated here from our higher spheres within this density. They incarnated within the Earth rather than upon it. The Earth's population contains many various groups harvested from other 2nd dimension and cycled third-dimension spheres. You are not all one race or background of beginning. The experience we share is unique to this time/space continuum.

Ra: "The Law of One states simply that all things are one, that all beings are one. There are certain behaviors and thought forms consonant with the understanding and practice of this law. Those who, finishing a cycle of experience, demonstrate grades of distortion of that understanding of thought and action will be separated by their own choice into the vibratory distortion most comfortable to their mind/body/spirit complexes. This process is guarded or watched by those nurturing beings who, being very close to the Law of One in their distortions, nevertheless move towards active service.

Thus, the illusion is created of light, or more properly but less understandably, light/love. This is in varying degrees of intensity. The spirit complex of each harvested entity moves along the line of light until the light grows too glaring, at which time the entity stops. This entity may have barely reached third density or may be very, very close to the ending of the third-density light/love distortion vibratory complex. Nevertheless, those who fall within this octave of intensifying light/love then experience a major cycle during which there are opportunities for the discovery of the distortions which are inherent in each entity and, therefore, the lessoning of these distortions."

One major cycle is approximately 25,000 of our Earth years. There are three cycles during which those who have progressed may be harvested at the end of three major cycles. That is, approximately 75 and 76,000 years. All are harvested regardless of their progress, for during that time the planet itself has moved through the useful part of that dimension and begins to cease being useful for the lower levels of vibration within that density.

Ra: "This sphere is at this time in fourth-dimension vibration. Its material is quite confused due to the society memory complexes embedded in it is consciousness. It has not made an easy transition to the vibrations which beckon. Therefore, it will be fetched with some inconvenience." (But the graduation for souls into 4th density experience is quickly approaching, with the potential of it being December of 2030.)

From my own channeling session done, it was revealed that approximately 65% of beings on Earth are harvestable for 2030 3rd density graduation as of 2023, with a vibration of at least 51% positive. On my YouTube channel I will make yearly updates on this vibration check.)

This inconvenience, or disharmonious vibratory complex, has begun several years before 1981 and will continue until about 2011 Ra said.

(Since about 2011 Planet Earth has been a 4th density planet inhabiting 3rd density beings until about 2030.)

Ra has walked among our people. They remember sorrow: have seen much. They've searched for an instrument of proper parameters of distortion in mind/body/spirit complexes to accept this information with minimal distortion and maximal desire to serve for some of our years during the transition period around 1981. (Don, Carla and Jim in this channeling group are 5th and 6th density Wanderers).

Some people have seen disc-shaped craft, we call UFO's. Some have said it came from Venus, but Ra said it wasn't them. However, Ra used crystals and the bell-shaped UFO in the past. They used this bell-shaped craft 18,000 and 11,000 years ago. Back then they were of the

6th density from Venus, now of course, a part of the 6th density Confederation. Ra is no longer of Venus currently.

Photographs of bell-shaped craft and reports of contact from Venus exist less than 30 years before 1981. Ra has knowledge of Oneness with these forays (a sudden invasion from negative entities) of our time/space present. However, there are thought forms created among our people on Earth from Ra walking amongst us. The memory and thought forms created are a part of our social memory complex. This mass consciousness creates the experience once more for those who request such experience. That's what they saw.

The Confederation:

Ra: "I am one of the members of the Confederation of Planets in the Service of the Infinite Creator. There are approximately fifty-three civilizations, comprising approximately five hundred planetary consciousness complexes in this Confederation. This Confederation contains those from your own planet who have attained dimensions beyond your third (Atlanteans and Lemurians). It contains planetary entities within your solar system, and it contains planetary entities from other galaxies (Ra often uses the word galaxy where we would say planetary system). It is a true Confederation in that its members are not alike, but allied in service according to the Law of One."

The Law of One is what Ra is here to express. However, they will answer certain questions they say is unimportant, such as if any members of the Confederation of Planets in Service of the Infinite Creator came to Earth in spacecrafts within the past 30 years. Ra feels the information may be acceptably offered. The Law of One is what they are here to express. However, they will speak upon questions asked.

Ra: "Each planetary entity which wishes to appear within your third dimension of space/time distortion requests permission to break quarantine and appear to your peoples. The reason and purpose for this appearance is understood and either accepted or rejected. There have been as many as fifteen of the Confederation entities in your skies at any one time. The others are available to you through thought.

At present there are seven which are operating with craft in your density. Their purposes are very simple: to allow those entities of your planet to become aware of infinity, which is often best expressed to the uninformed as the mysterious or unknown."

Ra offers their answers unless the question contains the potential for an answer infringing on a being's free will.

Session 7: January 25, 1981

The service available for Ra to offer those who call them is equivalent to the square of the distortion/need of that calling divided by, or integrated with, the basic Law of One in its distortion indicating the free will of those wo are not aware of the unity of creation.

Ra: "We must integrate all of the portions of your social memory complex in its illusory disintegration form. Then the product of this can be seen as the limit of our ability to serve. We are fortunate that the Law of Service squares the desires of those who call. Otherwise, we would have no beingness in this time/space at this present continuum of illusion."

The thought of a maximal consideration of what is possible to assist those that call for help is given.

The square is sequential- one, two, three, four, each squared by the next number.

An example would be that if 10 entities called for Ra's services. Ra would square the numbers 10 sequential times, raising the number to the tenth square, equaling approximately 1,012. The entities who call are sometimes not totally unified in their calling and, thus, the squaring slightly less. Thus, there is a statistical loss over a period of call.

Ra is called personally by 352,000 people on Earth. The Confederation, in its entire spectrum of entity complexes, is called by 632,000,000 of our people on Earth. These numbers have been simplified. It, however, constitutes a great need which we of all creation feel and hear as if our own entities were distorted towards a great and overwhelming sorrow. It demands our service.

Ra: "I am Ra. We do not calculate the possibility of coming among your peoples by the numbers of calling, but by a consensus among an entire societal memory complex which has become aware of the infinite consciousness of all things. This has been possible among your peoples only in isolated instances.

In the case wherein a social memory complex which is a servant of the Creator sees this situation and has an idea for the appropriate aid which can only be done among your peoples, the social memory complex desiring this project lays it before the Council of Saturn. If it is approved, quarantine is lifted."

Ra: "I am Ra. The members of the Council are representatives from the Confederation and from those vibratory levels of your inner planes bearing responsibility for your third density. The names are not important because there are no names. Your mind/body/spirit complexes request names, and so, in many cases, the vibratory sound complexes which are consonant with the vibratory distortions of each entity are used. However, the name concept is not part of the Council. If names are requested, we will attempt them. However, not all have chosen names.

In number, the Council that sits in constant session, though varying in its members by means of balancing, which takes place what you would call irregularly, is nine. That is the Session Council. To back up this Council, there are twenty-four entities which offer their services as requested. These entities faithfully watch and have been called Guardians.

The Council operates by means of what you would call telepathic contact with the oneness or unity of the nine, the distortions blending harmoniously so that the Law of One prevails with ease. When a need for thought is present, the Council retains the distortion complex of this need, balancing it as described, and then recommends what it considers as appropriate action. This includes: One, the duty of admitting social memory complexes to the Confederation; Two, offering aid to those who are unsure how to aid the social memory complex requesting aid in a way consonant with both the call, the Law, and the number of those calling (that is to say, sometimes the resistance of the call); Three, internal question in the council is determined.

These are the prominent duties of the Council. They are, if in any doubt, able to contact the twenty-four, who then offer consensus/judgment/thinking to the Council. The Council then may reconsider any question."

A semi-undistorted form of the Council of Nine has been retained by Henry Puharich and Mark Probert.

The quarantine:

The Council of Saturn has not allowed the breaking of quarantine around the Earth, even though there is a certain amount of UFO contacts with planet Earth. Some of them being a group known as the Orion's, which are negatively oriented.

Secondly, there is permission granted, not to break quarantine by dwelling among us, but to appear in thought form capacity for those who have eyes to see.

Thirdly, permission was granted in which the first nuclear device was developed and used for Confederation members to minister to your people in such a way as to cause mystery to occur. The mystery and unknown quality of the occurrences we are allowed to offer have the hoped-for intention of making your peoples aware of infinite possibility. When people grasp infinity, then and only then can the gateway be opened to the Law of One.

Orion's intention:

Their intention is to presumably unify by choosing the distortion complex called elite from a social memory complex and then enslaving, by various effects, those who are seen by the distortion as not elite. There is then the concept of taking the social memory complex thus weeded and adding it to a distortion thought of by the Orion group as an empire. The problem facing them is that they face a great deal of random energy released by the concept of separation. This causes them to be vulnerable, as the distortions amongst their own members are not harmonized. (This is how the negative polarity works).

The Orion group densities of the mass consciousness are varied, like the Confederation. The Orion group has very few third density, a larger number of 4th density, a similarly large number of 5th density, and very few sixth-density entities comprising this organization. They are about $1/10^{th}$ Ras at any point in the space/time continuum as the problem of spiritual entropy (the measure of disorder within a system) causes them to experience constant disintegration of their social memory complexes. Their power is the same as Ra's. The law of one blinks neither at the light nor the darkness, but is available for service-to-others and service-to-self due to free will. However, service to others results in service to self, thus preserving and further harmonizing the distortions of those entities seeking intelligent infinity through these disciplines.

Ra: "Those seeking intelligent infinity through the use of service-to-self create the same amount of power but have constant difficulty because of the concept of separation, which is implicit (not consciously aware) in the manifestations of the service to self which involve power over others. This weakens and eventually disintegrates the energy collected by such mind/body/spirit complexes who call the Orion group and the social memory complexes which comprise the Orion group.

It should be noted, carefully pondered, and accepted that the Law of One is available to any social memory complex which has decided to strive together for any seeking of purpose, be it service to others or service to self. The Laws, which are the primal distortions of the Law of One, then are placed into operation, and the illusion of space/time is used as a medium for the development of the results of those choices freely made. Thus, all entities learn, no matter what they seek. All learn the same; some rapidly, some slowly." (I see the negative path learning more slowly and the positive path learns faster).

Ra: "I am Ra. This is the last question of length for this instrument at this time.

You will recall that we went into some detail as to how those not oriented towards seeking service for others yet, nevertheless, found and could use the gateway to intelligent infinity. This is true at all densities in our octave. We cannot speak for those above us, as you would say, in the next quantum or octave of beingness. This is, however, true of this octave of density. The beings are harvested because they can see and enjoy the light/love of the appropriate density. Those who have found this light/love, love/light without benefit of a desire for service-to-others nevertheless, by the Law of Free Will, have the right to the use of that light/love for whatever purpose. Also, it may be inserted that there are systems of study which enable the seeker of separation to gain these gateways.

This study is as difficult as the one which we have described to you, but there are those with the perseverance to pursue the study just as you desire to pursue the difficult path of seeking to know in order to serve. The distortion lies in the effect that those who seek to serve the self are seen by the Law of One as precisely the same as those who seek to serve others, for are all not one? To serve yourself and to serve others is a dual method of saying the same thing, if you can understand the essence of the Law of One."

Session 8: January 26, 1981

Some UFO landings are of the Orion Group. Their purpose is conquest (taking control of others by force), unlike those of the Confederation (positive) who wait for the calling. The so-called Orion Group calls itself to conquest. Their objective is to locate certain entities that vibrate in resonance with their own vibrational complex, then to enslave the un-elite, those who are not of the Orion vibration.

The landing in Pascagoula in 1973 when Charlie Hixon was taken aboard was an anomaly. It was neither the Orion influence nor Ra's peoples in thought form, but rather a planetary entity of Earth's own vibration which came through quarantine in all innocence in a random landing. Onboard they used his life experience, concentrating upon the experience of war. They did this to learn, like watching a movie. They experience a story and identify with the feelings, perceptions and experiences of the hero.

Charlie Hixon did not have a connection to nor was of the same social memory complex of those who used him. They used his war experiences to learn more of the Law of One.

Charlie described the entities who picked him up as rather unusual. Ra then said the configuration of their beings is their normal configuration. The unusualness is not remarkable. We ourselves, when we choose a mission among your peoples, needed to study your peoples, for if we had arrived in no other form than our own, we would have been perceived as light (the Confederations natural form body being that of light). The entities who picked up Charlie are third-density beings of a fairly advanced order. They were able to pick up Charlie because this entity before incarnation chose to be of service. These entities are of the Sirius galaxy (planet, like Jesus was, but Jesus was late 4th density from the Sirius Planet).

After Ra observed the distortions underwent in direct UFO contact, they decided to gradually back off from direct contact in thought form. The least distortion seems to be available in mind-to-mind communication. Therefore, the request to be taken aboard is not one Ra cares to comply with. The group is most valuable through their channeling/telepathic communication.

Session 9: January 27th, 1981

For Ra to direct judgement or instruction is an intrusion on their future. To speak of past or present within their limits is acceptable. To guide rather than teach is not acceptable for Ra in regards to teaching. Ra instead can suggest a process where each person chooses the first of the exercises given in the order in which Ra gave them, which the group in their discernment feels is not fully appreciated.

This is the proper choice, building from the foundation, making sure the ground is good for the building. We have assessed for you the intensity of this effort in terms of energy expended. Be patient Ra says, for they have not given a short or easy program of consciousness learning.

Our planetary population goes through three 25,000-year cycles in third density to progress through our process of evolution. At the end of 75,000 years the planet progresses itself.

Questioner: What caused the preciseness of years in each cycle?

Ra: "I am Ra. Visualize, if you will, the particular energy which, outward flowing and inward coagulating (changing from a liquid to a thickened state), formed the tiny realm of the creation governed by your Council of Saturn. Continue seeing the rhythm of this process. The living flow creates a rhythm which is as inevitable as one of your timepieces. Each of your planetary entities meant to support such mind/body experiences. Thus, each of your planetary entities is on a different cyclical schedule, as you might call it. The timing of these cycles is a measurement equal to a portion of intelligent energy.

This intelligent energy offers a type of clock. The cycles move as precisely as a clock strikes your hour. Thus, the gateway from intelligent energy to intelligent infinity opens regardless of circumstance on the striking of the hour."

The first entities upon Earth were water, fire, air and earth. (1st density beings)

Mars:

The first third-density people on Earth were brought here from the red planet, Mars. Mars environment became inhospitable to third-density beings. Therefore, the first entities were brought here from Mars, manipulated somewhat by the guardians.

The Martian race is a combination of mind/body/spirit complexes of those from the Red Planet and a careful series of genetical adjustments made by the guardians at the time. These entities arrived, or were preserved, for the experiences upon Earth by a type of nonreproductive birthing but consists of preparing genetic material for the incarnation of entities from Mars.

After the race from mars died, the guardians transferred them to Earth (through reincarnation).

The Law of One was named by the guardians as the bringing of wisdom of the guardians in contact with the entities from the Red Planet, thus melding the social memory complex of the guardian race and the Red Planet race. It took an increasing amount of distortion into the application of the Law of One from the viewpoint of the guardians. This is when the quarantine of this planet was instituted, for it felt that the free will of those from Mars had been abridged (shortened). (Something may be abridged to make it more accessible to a wider audience. Abridge comes from the Latin word abreviare, which means "to shorten".)

((Ra refers to Mars as the Red Planet. Since it appears in higher densities that there's not a feeling for names, but since Earth uses names, they named the Red Planet, Mars.))

The entities of Mars were attempting to learn the Laws of Love which is one of the primal distortions of the Law of One. However, the tendencies of these people towards bellicose (aggressively hostile) actions caused difficulties in their atmosphere and it became inhabitable for third-density experience (due to wars from their bellicose actions) before the end of its cycle. Thus, they were unharvested and continue on Earth to learn the Law of Love.

This transfer occurred approximately 75,000 years ago. This is when third-density upon Earth began. There have been visitors to Earth at various times for the last 4,000,000 years, but theses visitors did not affect the cycling of this planet.

2nd density:

Second density is of the higher plant and animal life that exists without the upward drive to the infinite. These second-density beings are of an octave of consciousness like the various orientations of consciousness among the conscious entities of our third-density vibration.

The higher sub-vibrational density of second density beings had the configuration of the biped (two arms, two legs and walking upright on two feet). However, the erectile movement which we experience was not totally affected in these beings who were tending towards the leaning forward, barely leaving the quadrupedal position (such as cats and dogs). These entities evolved from the original material of Earth in first density. Beings will then evolve from second density to third. Although there is no guarantee of the number of cycles it will take an entity to learn the lessons of consciousness of self which are the prerequisite for transition to third density.

Third density entities on our planet now were not evolved from Earth's second density life. Although animals, such as pets, are currently harvestable for third density life who experience the love for their owners (humans) and have learned self-awareness after being given a name, such as cats being late second density entities harvestable for third density life.

There are two races upon Earth that use second density form. One is from the planet Maldek. These entities are working their understanding through karmic restitution. They dwell within our deeper underground passageways known as "bigfoot". The other race dwelling in our density by guardians who wish to give third density entities at this time appropriately engineered physical vehicles in the event that there is a nuclear war. These instinctual second-density beings are being held in reserve to form a gene pool in case these body complexes are needed. These bodies are greatly able to withstand the rigors of radiation, which our current third density bodies cannot withstand.

This second type of bigfoot entity has glowing eyes and dwell in uninhabited deep forests. There are many in various places over the surface of Earth. This second type of bigfoot Ra would not call them Bigfoot, as they are scarce and are able to escape detection. The first race of Bigfoot is less able to be aware of proximity of other entities, but the second race of Bigfoot are very able to escape due to their technological understanding before their incarnation here. The third type of Bigfoot is a thought form.

Session 10: January 27th, 1981

The peoples of Maldek had a civilization somewhat similar to that of Atlantis, in that it gained much technological information and used it without care for the preservation of their planet which the majority of thought, ideas and actions were of the negative polarity or service-to-self. For the most part they had a sincere belief that seemed to the perception of this sphere to be positive.

Ra: "The devastation that wrecked their biosphere and caused its disintegration (the process of separating to pieces or ceases to exist) resulted from war.

The escalation went to the furthest extent of the technology this social complex (of Maldek) had approximately 705,000 years ago. The cycles had begun much, much earlier upon this sphere due to its relative ability to support the first-dimensional life forms at an earlier point in the space/time continuum of your solar system. These entities were so traumatized by this occurrence that they were in what you may call a social complex knot or tangle of fear. Some of your time passed. No one could reach them. No beings could aid them.

Approximately 600,000 of your years ago the then-existing members of the Confederation were able to deploy a social memory complex and untie the knot of fear. The entities were then able to recall that they were conscious. This awareness brought them to the point upon what you would call the lower astral planes, where they could be nurtured until each mind/body/spirit complex was able to finally be healed of this trauma to the extent that each entity was able to examine the distortions it had experienced in the previous life/illusion complex.

After this experience of learn/teaching, the group decision was to place upon itself a type of what you may call karma alleviation. For this purpose, they came into incarnation within our planetary sphere in what were not acceptable human forms. This then they have been experiencing until the distortions of destruction are replaced by distortions towards the desire for a less distorted vision of service-to-others. Since this was the conscious decision of the great majority of those beings in the Maldek experience, the transition to this planet began approximately 500,000 years ago, and the type of body complex available at that time was used" (Which was the ape body.)

The consciousness of the Maldek has always been third density. The karma alleviation was designed to be in second density bodies not able to be dexterous to the extent of third density distortions.

Many of these entities were able to remove the accumulation of karma, thus being able to accept a third-density cycle in a third density body. Most of these succeeding have incarnated elsewhere in the creation for a third density cycle (into 3rd density bodies on other planets). As this planet reached third density, some of these entities became able to join the vibration of this sphere in third-density form. The one type of Bigfoot are those Maldek entities who have not yet alleviated the distortions during the previous action of war.

Our human race are entities from Maldek, Mars and from many, many other places in the creation. For when there is a cycle change, those who must repeat find a planet appropriate for their repetition. It is somewhat unusual for a planet to contain those from many many loci. Just like a large number of humans on Earth today will have to repeat the cycle.

((My guess is approximately 25% since 65% of humans currently are on the positive path. That would leave my guess of about 10% going to the negative 4th density planet if for those that have a vibration of 95% or more service-to-self.))

The orientation has been difficult to unify even with the aid of many of our teachers here on Earth.

Questioner: "When graduation occurs at the end of a cycle, and entities are moved from one planet to another, by what means do they go to a new planet?"

Ra: "I am Ra. In the scheme of the Creator, the first step of the mind/body/spirit/totality/beingness is to place its mind/body/spirit complex distortion in the proper place of love/light. This is done to ensure proper healing of the complex and eventual attunement (correction) with the totality/beingness complex. This takes a very variable (fluxuating) length of your time/space. After this is accomplished, the experience of the cycle is dissolved and filtered until only the distillation of distortions in its pure form remains. At this time, the harvested mind/body/spirit/totality/beingness evaluates the density needs of its beingness and choose the more appropriate new environment for either a repetition of the cycle or a moving forward into the next cycle. This is the manner of the harvesting, guarded and watched over by many."

The mind/body/spirit/totality/beingness is one with the Creator. There is no time/space distortion. Therefore, it is a matter of thinking the proper locus in the infinite array of time/space for the entity to be moved from one planet to the next for the more appropriate environment in repeating the third-density cycle. (The vibration between 6% and 50% service-to-others will have to repeat 3rd density.)

An entity can consciously or unconsciously learn the Law of One. By learning consciously, it is possible for the entity to greatly accelerate his (or her) growth.

An entity can accelerate their growth much more while in third density than in between incarnations (in-between incarnations being on the metaphysical plane rather than our physical plane here on Earth in a physical body).

Ra: "The Law of One has as one of its primal distortions the free-will distortion; thus, each entity is free to accept, reject, or ignore the mind/body/spirit complexes about it and ignore the creation itself. There are many among your social memory complex distortion who, at this time/space, engage daily in the working upon the Law of One in one of its primal distortions; that is, the ways of love. However, if this same entity, being biased from the depths of its mind/body/spirit complex towards love/light, were then to accept the responsibility for each moment of the time/space accumulation of present moments available to it, such an entity can empower its progress in much the same way as we described the empowering of the call of your social complex distortion to the Confederation."

The empowering of the call?

Ra: "The call being with one. This call is equal to infinity and is not counted. It is the cornerstone. The second call is added. The third call empowers or doubles the second, and so forth, each additional calling doubling or granting power to all the preceding call. Thus, the call of many of your peoples is many, many powered and overwhelmingly heard to the infinite reaches of the One Creation."

Some of the practices or exercises to perform to produce an acceleration toward the Law of One?

Ra: "I am Ra. Exercise One. This is the most nearly centered and usable within your illusion complex. The moment contains love. That is the lesson/goal of this illusion or density. The exercise is to consciously see that love in awareness and understanding. The first attempt is the cornerstone. Upon this choosing rests the remainder of the life experience of an entity. The second seeking of love within the moment begins the addition. The third seeking empowers the second, the fourth powering or doubling the third. As with the previous type of empowerment, there will be some loss of power due to flaws within the seeking in the distortion of insincerity. However, the conscious statement of self to self of the desire to seek love is so central an act of will that, as before, the loss of power due to this friction is inconsequential (not important or significant).

Exercise Two. The universe is one being. When a mind/body/spirit complex views another mind/body/spirit complex, see the Creator. This is a helpful exercise.

Exercise Three. Gaze within a mirror. See the Creator.

Exercise Four. Gaze at the creation which lies about the mind/body/spirit complex of each entity. See the Creator.

The foundation or prerequisite of these exercises is a predilection (bias) towards what may be called meditation, contemplation, or prayer.

(Predilection refers to a preference or special liking for something; a bias in favor of something).

With this attitude, these exercises can be processed. Without it, the data will not sink down into the roots of the tree of mind, thus enabling and ennobling (elevating the rank to nobility of) the body and touching the spirit."

Ra: "I am Ra. The civilizations of Atlantis and Lemuria were not one but two. Let us look first at the Mu entities (Lemuria beings).

They were beings of a somewhat primitive nature, but those who had very advanced spiritual distortions. The civilization was part of this cycle, experienced early within the cycle at a time of approximately 53,000 of your years ago. It was a helpful and harmless place which was washed beneath the ocean during a readjustment of your sphere's tectonic plates through no action of their own. They sent out those who survived and reached many places in what you call Russian, North America, and South America. The Indians of whom you come to feel some sympathy in your social complex distortions are the descendants of these entities. Like the other incarnates of this cycle, they came from elsewhere. However, these particular entities were largely from a second-density planet which had some difficulty, due to the age of its sun, in achieving third-density life conditions. This planet was from the galaxy Deneb.

The Atlantean race was a very conglomerate (different parts grouped together to form a compacted whole) social complex which began to form approximately 31,000 in the past of your space/time continuum illusion. (Conglomerate is a number of different things or parts that are put or grouped together to form a whole but remain distinct entities). It was a slow-growing and very agrarian (ownership of farmland and concerned with agriculture) one until approximately 15,000 of our years ago. It reached quickly a high technological understanding which caused it to be able to use intelligent infinity in an informative manner. We may add that they used intelligent energy as well, manipulating greatly the natural influxes of the indigo or pineal ray from divine or infinite energy. Thus, they were able to create life forms. This they began to do instead of healing and perfecting their own mind/body/spirit complexes, turning their distortions towards what you may call negative.

Approximately 11,000 of your years ago, the first of the, what you call, wars, caused approximately 40 percent of this population to leave the density by means of disintegration (or death) of the body. The second and most devasting of the conflicts occurred approximately 10,822 years in the past according to your illusion. This created an Earth-changing configuration, and the large part of Atlantis was no more, having been inundated (flooded). Three of the positively oriented of the Atlantean groups left this geographical locus before that devastation, placing themselves in the mountain areas of what you call Tibet, what you call Peru, and what you call Turkey."

Ra: "I am Ra. This instrument could be made somewhat more comfortable if more support were given the body complex. Other than this, we can only repeat the request to carefully align the symbols used to facilitate this instrument's balance. Our contact is narrow banded, and thus the influx brought in with us must be precise.

I am Ra. I leave you in the love and the light of the One Infinite Creator. Go forth, therefore, rejoicing in the power and peace of the One Creator. Adonai."

Session 11: January 28th, 1981

The two entities (Don and Jim) additional aid to the instrument's comfort by energizing the instrument with their abilities to share the physical energy complex which is a portion of their love vibration.

If Maldek hadn't destroyed itself due to warfare, the planet most likely, though unknown, would have had a mixed harvest-a few moving to 4th density positive, a few moving towards 4th density negative and the great majority repeating third density. This is approximate due to the fact that parallel possibility/probability vortices cease when action occurs and new probability/possibility vortices are begun.

There is a planet in the area opposite of our sun of a very, very cold nature, but large enough to skew certain statistical figures. This sphere should probably not be called a planet as it is locked in first density (water, air, wind, fire).

As our cycle ends and graduation occurs, the probability/possibility vortex of some beings going to fourth density negative is small.

Adolf Hitler is at this time in a healing process in the middle astral planes of our spherical force field. This entity was greatly confused and, although aware of the circumstance of change in the vibratory level associated with the cessation (temporary end) of the chemical body complex, nevertheless needed a great deal of care.

The number of entities harvested to fourth density negative from Earth is small. However, a few have penetrated the eighth level, which is only available from the opening up of the seventh through the sixth. Penetration into the eighth or Intelligent infinity level allows an entity to be harvested if it wishes at any time/space during the cycle.

A few who have been mentioned by Ra is Taras Bulba, Genghis Khan and Rasputin. All of these entities were aware, through memory, of Atlantean understandings with the use of various centers of energy influx in attaining the gateway to intelligent infinity. This enabled them to do magic and do paranormal things while on Earth.

Taras Bulba and Genghis Khan made little use of these abilities consciously. However, they were bent single-mindedly upon service-to-self, sparing no efforts in personal discipline to double, redouble, and so empower this gateway. Rasputin was a conscious adept and also spared no effort in the pursuit of service-to-self. All three are in the fourth dimension. Therefore, the space/time continua are not compatible. An approximation of the space/time locus of each would net no understanding. Each chose a 4th density planet which was dedicated to understanding the Law of One through service-to-self. (4th density negative planet)

Genghis Khan went to the Orion group; one went to Cassiopeia and the other went to the Southern Cross. Genghis Khan serves the Creator in its own way. All things serve the Creator.

Genghis Khan, at present in 1981, is incarnate in a physical light body disseminating material of thought control to those who are the crusaders. He's a shipping clerk. The crusaders move in their chariots to conquer planetary mind/body/spirit social complexes before they reach the stage of achieving social memory.

Ra: "I am Ra. A mind/body/spirit social complex becomes a social memory complex when its entire group of entities are of one orientation or seeking. The group memory lost to the individuals in the roots of the tree of mind then becomes known to the social complex, thus creating a social memory complex. The advantages of this complex are the relative lack of distortion in understanding the social beingness and the relative lack of distortion in pursuing the direction of seeking, for all understanding/distortions are available to the entities of the society."

Crusaders from Orion came to Earth for mind control purposes. They do this as they follow the Law of One observing free will. Contact is made with those who call. Those then on Earth disseminate the attitudes and philosophy of the negative path. These become the elite. These elites attempt to enslave the rest of the entities on Earth by their free will. These elites enjoy power over others in this planetary game. It is not central to the harvest.

There are two main ways to pass on their concepts to the individuals on Earth, just as there are two main ways of polarizing towards service to others. There are people on Earth who do exercises and perform disciplines in order to seek contact with sources of information and power leading to the opening of the gate to intelligent infinity. There are others whose vibration is such that this gateway is opened, and contact with total service-to-self with its primal distortion of manipulation of others is the afforded with little or no difficulty, no training, and no control.

The Orion group passes on information concerning the Law of One with the orientation of service-to-self. The information can be technical information, just like some in the Confederation attempts to aid the planet in service-to-others. The Orion's give technology in the form of various means of control or manipulation of others to serve the self.

Some scientists receive information telepathically that comes out in usable gadgetry. However, very positively oriented scientists have received information intended to unlock peaceful means of progress which redounded to potential destruction due to further reception of scientists of a negative orientation.

Information on Nuclear energy was received mixed with both positive and negative orientation. The elites responsible for the gathering of the scientists were of mixed orientation. The scientists being overwhelmingly positive. Scientists who followed their work were of mixed orientation, including one extremely negative scientist. This scientist was still around in 1981.

Nikola Tesla received information from Confederation sources desirous of aiding this extremely angelically positive entity in bettering the existence of its fellow human. It is unfortunate that like many Wanderers, the vibratory distortions of third density illusion caused Nikola to become extremely distorted in its perceptions of its fellow humans so that its mission was hindered, in the result, perverted from its purposes. The most desired purpose of Nikola was the freeing of all planetary entities from darkness, in a literal sense. Thus, it attempted to give the planet infinite energy on Earth for use in lighting and power. This freeing of darkness would create free energy. Secondly, the leisure afforded, thereby exemplifying the possibility and enhancing the probability of the freedom to then search the self, the beginning of seeking the Law of One.

Few there are working physically from daybreak to darkness on Earth who can contemplate the Law of One in a conscious fashion.

The Industrial Revolution was planned by Wanderers incarnating in several waves in order to bring the gradual freeing of demands and the freeing of lack of leisure freedom.

Ra stated that the most important thing for the instrument (Carla) is to carefully align the symbols for the instrument's comfort.

To serve the self is to serve all. The service of the self, when seen in this perspective, requires an ever-expanding use of energies of others for manipulation to the benefit of the self with distortion towards power. This is why the crusaders do what they do.

Session 12:

Orion crusaders came to Earth in chariots. The term "chariot" is a term used in warfare among people on Earth. That is its significance. The shape of the Orion craft is elongated, ovoid shape which is of a darker nature than silver but has a metallic appearance if seen in the light. In the absence of light, it appears to be red and fiery in some manner.

Other crafts include disc-shaped objects of a small nature approximately 12 feet in diameter, the box like shape approximately 40 feet to a side. Other crafts can take on a desired shape through the use of thought control mechanisms. There are various civilization complexes that work within this group. Some are more able to use intelligent infinity than others. The information is very seldom shared; therefore, the chariots vary greatly in shape and appearance.

The Confederation makes every effort to quarantine this planet from negative entities or any infringement of free will. However, the network of guardians, much like any other pattern of patrols on whatever level, does not hinder each and every entity from penetrating quarantine, for if request is made in light/love, the Law of One will be met with acquiescence. (Acquiescence is consenting by silence or without objection. They are compliant). If the request is not made, due to slipping through the net, then there is penetration of this net.

There is contact at the level of light-form or light-body being depending upon the vibratory level of the guardian in the Confederation. These guardians sweep reaches of our Earth's energy fields to be aware of any entities approaching. An entity approaching is hailed in the name of the One Creator. Any entity hailed is bathed in love/light and will of free will. They obey the quarantine due to the power of the Law of One.

This light-body is like a solid brick wall. If any entity does not obey quarantine after being hailed in the name of the One Creator, it would be equivalent to walking into a brick wall.

The Creator is one being. The vibratory level of those able to breach quarantine boundaries is such that upon seeing the love/light net, it is impossible to break this Law. Therefore, nothing happens. No attempt is made. There is no confrontation. The only beings who are able to penetrate the quarantine are those who discover windows or distortions in space/time continuum surrounding Earth's energy fields. Through these windows they come. These windows are rare and unpredictable. This accounts for the "UFO flaps" where a large number of UFO's showed up like in 1973.

Many UFO's seen in our skies are of the Orion group. They send out messages. Some are received by those who are oriented towards service-to-others. These messages are altered to be acceptable to those entities while warning of difficulties ahead. This is the most that self-serving entities can do with positively oriented individuals.

The contacts the Orion's find most helpful to their cause are contacts made with negatively oriented people. There are many thought form entities in our skies of the positively oriented Confederation.

Through telepathy the philosophy of the Law of One with the distortion of service-to-self is promulgated. (Promulgated means to promot or make widely known an idea or cause). In advanced groups there are rituals and exercises given, and these have been written down just as the service-to-others oriented entities have written down the promulgated philosophy of their teachers. The philosophy concerns the service of manipulating others that they may experience service towards the other self, thus through this experience becoming able to appreciate service-to-self. These entities would become oriented towards service-to-self and in turn manipulate others so they might experience the service towards the other self.

The Orion has aided the so-called negatively oriented people on Earth. These same entities would be concerning themselves with service-to-self in any case. There are many upon the inner planes which are negatively oriented and available as inner teachers or guides and possessors of certain souls who seek the negative polarity, known as black magic.

It is entirely possible for the untuned channel to receive both positive and negative communications. If the entity at the base of its confusion is oriented toward service-to-others, the entity will begin to receive messages of doom. If the entity is oriented negatively, the crusaders won't find it necessary to lie, will simply give the philosophy they are here to give. Many of the contracts among our people on Earth have been confused and self-destructive because the channels were positively oriented but, in the desire for proof, were open to lying information of the crusaders, who then were able to neutralize the effectiveness of the channel.

Many of the Orion's are fourth density negative. The fourth density by choice is not visible to third density. It is possible for fourth density to be visible. However, it is not the choice of the fourth density entity to be visible due to the necessary concentration upon a rather difficult vibrational complex of the third density experience.

There are not Confederation or Orion entities walking among Earth at this time. However, the crusaders of Orion use thought form and a kind of robot to do their bidding. The robot may look like any other being, it is a construct.

The Men in Black are a thought form entity that have certain physical characteristics given them. However, their true vibrational nature is without third-density vibrational characteristics. Therefore, they are able to materialize and dematerialize when necessary. All these Men in Black are used by the Orion Crusaders.

Imagine the sands of your shores. As countless as the grains of sand are the sources of intelligent infinity. When a social memory complex has achieved its understanding of its desire, it may conclude that its desire is service-to-others and figuratively reach their hand to any entities who call for aid. The Brothers and Sisters of Sorrow move toward this call of sorrow. These entities are from all areas of the infinite creation and are bound together by the desire to serve.

The Brothers and Sisters of Sorrow incarnate on Earth as Wanderers from higher densities to lighten the planetary vibration and aid in the Harvest. There were about 65,000,000 in 1981 with a heavy influxed birthed at that time due to the intensive need to lighten the planetary vibration and aid in the Harvest.

Few are fourth density. The largest number of Wanderers are sixth density. Some are fifth density as well. The desire to serve must be distorted towards a great deal of purity of mind and foolhardiness or bravery, depending upon your judgement. The challenge/danger of the Wanderer is that it will forget its mission, become karmically involved, and thus be swept into the maelstrom (confused state) it had incarnated to avert (prevent) the destruction.

A Wanderer that acts consciously in an unloving manner in action with other beings can become karmically involved.

Due to the extreme variance between the third density vibrations and those of the denser densities, Wanderers have some form of handicap, difficulty or feeling of alienation, the reaction against the planetary vibration by personality disorders and body ailments, such as allergies, indicating difficulty in adjustment to the planetary vibrations.

To make the instrument more comfortable Ra asks the group to realign the object where the symbols sit. It is not a significant distortion for only one session, but the resting place is 1.4 degrees from correct alignment, the rest: place .5 degrees away from proper orientation. Ra said to not concern yourselves with this in space/time nexus present, but do not allow these distortions (of Carla's alignment) to remain over a long period or the contact will be gradually impaired.

Session 13: 1-29-1981

The group considered it a great honor and privilege to also be humble messengers of the Law of One. Don, the questioner, asked Ra if he could make Ra the author of the Law of One. Ra could only request that if his discernment/understanding suggest to use Ra, that the phrase "An humble messenger of the Law of One" be appended. (Appended means to add as an attachment).

The first thing in the creation is infinity. The infinity is the creation. Then, infinity became aware.

Ra: "Awareness led to the focus of infinity into infinite energy. Many people have called this "Logos" or "Love". The Creator is the focusing of infinity as an aware or conscious principle called by us, as closely as we can create understanding/learning in your language, intelligent infinity."

Ra: "The next step is still at this space/time nexus in your illusion achieving its progression as you may see it in your illusion. The next step is an infinite reaction to the creative principle following the Law of One in one of its primal distortions, freedom of will. Thus many, many dimensions, infinite in number, are possible. The energy moves from the intelligent infinity due first to the outpouring of randomized creative force, this then creating patterns which in holographic style appear as the entire creation no matter which direction or energy is explored. These patterns of energy begin then to regularize their own local, shall we say, rhythms and fields of energy, thus creating dimensions and universes."

Ra: "The energies moved in increasingly intelligent patterns until the individualization of various energies emanating from the creative principle of intelligent infinity became such as to be co-Creators. Thus, the so-called physical matter began. The concept of light is instrumental in grasping this great leap of thought, as this vibrational distortion of infinity is the building block of that which is known as matter, the light being intelligent and full of energy, thus being the first distortion of intelligent infinity, which was called by the creative principle.

This light of love was made to have in its occurrences of being certain characteristics, among them the infinite whole paradoxically described by the straight line, as you would call it. This paradox is responsible for the shape of the various physical illusion entities you call solar system, galaxies, and planets of revolving and tending towards the lenticular."

The next steps after the galaxies and planets are simultaneous and infinite.

Questioner: "How did intelligent infinity become individualized from itself?"

Ra: "The intelligent infinity discerned a concept. This concept was discerned to be freedom of will of awareness. This concept was finity. This was the first and primal paradox or distortion of the Law of One. Thus, the one intelligent infinity invested itself in an exploration of manyness. Due to the infinite possibilities of intelligent infinity, there is no ending to manyness. The exploration, thus, is free to continue infinitely in an eternal present."

Ra: "The galaxy and all other things of material of which you are aware are products of individualized portions of intelligent infinity. As each exploration began, it, in turn, found its focus and became co-Creator. Using intelligent infinity, each portion created a universe, and allowing the rhythms of free choice to flow, playing with the infinite spectrum of possibilities, each individualized portion channeled the love/light into what you might call intelligent energy, thus creating the so-called Natural Laws of any particular universe.

Each universe, in turn, individualized to a focus becoming, in turn, co-Creator and allowing further diversity, thus creating further intelligent energies regularizing or causing Natural Laws to appear in the vibrational patterns of what you would call a solar system. Thus, each solar system has its own local coordinate system of illusory Natural Laws. It shall be understood that any portion, no matter how small, of any density or illusory pattern contains, as in a holographic picture, the One Creator which is infinity. Thus, all begins and ends in mystery."

The planetary system that we are in now was created from the larger sun first to the smaller planets next. Thus, the co-Creator, individualizing the galaxy, created energy patterns which then focused in multitudinous (vast individuals or elements) focuses of further conscious awareness of intelligent infinity. Thus, the solar system of which you experience inhabitation is of its own patterns, rhythms, and so-called natural laws which are unique to itself. However, the progression is from the galaxy spiraling energy to the solar spiraling energy, to the planetary spiraling energy, to the experiential circumstances of spiraling energy which begin the first density of awareness of consciousness of planetary entities.

Ra: "Each step recapitulates (repeats) intelligent infinity in its discovery of awareness. In a planetary environment, all begins in what you would call chaos, energy undirected and random in its infinity. Slowly, in your terms of understanding, there forms a focus of self-awareness. Thus, the Logos moves. Light comes to form the darkness, according to the co-Creator's patterns and vibratory rhythms, so constructing a certain type of experience. This begins with first density, which is the density of consciousness, the mineral and water life upon the planet learning from fire and wind the awareness of being. This is the first density.

The spiraling energy, which is the characteristic of what you call "light," moves in a straight-line spiral, thus giving spirals an inevitable vector upwards to a more comprehensive beingness with regards to intelligent infinity. Thus, first-dimensional beingness strives towards the second-density lessons of a type of awareness which includes growth rather than dissolution (breaking apart, dissolving) or random change.

Growth is the difference between first-vibrational mineral or water life and the lower second-density beings which begin to move about within and upon its being. This movement is the characteristic of second density, the striving towards light and growth.

A very simplistic example of second-density growth striving towards light is that of the leaf striving towards the source of light.

A first and second density planet would be physical to our third density eyes. All of the octave of our densities would be clearly visible if the fourth through the seventh freely chose to be visible, but they chose to be invisible.

Second density strives towards the third density, which is the density of self-consciousness or self-awareness. The striving takes place through the higher second-density forms who are invested by third-density with an identity to the extent that they become self-aware mind/body complexes, thus becoming mind/body/spirit complexes and entering third density, the first density of consciousness of spirit.

Earth is in third density in its beingness of mind/body/spirit complexes (people). It is now in a space/time continuum, fourth density planet. This is causing a somewhat difficult harvest. (Earth being fourth density and humans being third density).

Ra: "The fourth density is as regularized in its approach as the striking of a clock upon the hour. The space/time of your solar system has enabled this planetary sphere to spiral into space/time of a different vibrational configuration. This causes the planetary sphere to be able to be molded by these new distortions. However, the thought forms of your people during this transition period are such that the mind/body/spirit complexes of both individual and societies are scattered throughout the spectrum instead of becoming able to grasp the needle, shall we say, and point the compass in one direction.

Thus, the entry into the vibration of love, sometimes called the vibration of understanding, is not effective with our present societal complex. Thus, the harvest shall be such that many will repeat the third-density-cycle.

The energies of your Wanderers, your teachers, and your adepts at this time are all bent upon increasing the harvest. However, there are few to harvest." (Currently in my 2023 channeling session approximately 65% are on the positive vibration of at least 51% service to others. Therefore, the harvest is presently 65% for fourth density positive. Thus, the vast remainder will repeat third density on another third density planet to continue their learning and some may be harvestable for fourth density negative if at least 95% service to self. Those raping, killing, stealing or manipulating others in power over others or control, such as some elites, can make the graduation into the fourth density negative. Religious people call these fourth through 6th density negative beings, demons.)

Sessions can be shorter if the instrument's vital energy is low. Ra monitors the instrument during the channeling session and stops channeling when her vital energies become low in the material which Ra takes from it. They do not wish to deplete her.

Session 14: 1-29-1981

Second density strives towards the third density of self-consciousness or self-awareness. The striving takes place through the higher second-density forms being invested by third-density beings invest or clothe some second-density beings with self-awareness. ((Such as third-density humans having higher second density pets, which gives these pets self-awareness. The owner is then helping their pet evolve.)) It has also been done by various other means of investiture, including many so-called religious practices which personify and send love to various natural second-density beings in their group form.

When Earth was second density, there was no type of investment from higher densities, but the simple third-density investment from the line of spiraling light calling distortion upward from density to density. The process takes longer when there is no investment made by incarnate third-density being. (Which means, the process is longer for 2nd density beings to evolve when there is no investment from 3rd density humans to teach their pets love and self-awareness by giving the pet a name.)

Second density beings are that of plant life, trees, animals, insects and pets. Third density beings can be that of human form. (There are even other third-density beings on other planets). In the case of Earth, that process was interrupted by those who incarnated here from Mars. They were adjusted by genetic changing, and, therefore, there was some difference that was of a very noticeable variety rather than the gradual raising of the bipedal forms on our second-density level to third-density level. Bipedal would be an animal standing on two feet like humans do.

This occurred 75,000 years ago. When beings incarnated here from Mars is when the third density process of evolution began. The first attempt to aid people on Earth was 75,000 years ago when beings incarnated from Mars into Earth. The next attempt of higher density beings aiding people of Earth was approximately 58,000 years ago with those of Lemuria. This continued for a long period of time. The next attempt was 13,000 years ago when some intelligent information was offered to those of Atlantis, being of the same type of healing and crystal working as previously spoken about by Ra.

The next attempt was 11,000 years ago with those of Egypt as Ra also previously spoke about. The same beings who came with Ra returned approximately 3,500 years later (8,500 years ago) to attempt to aid those in South America. However, the pyramids there in South America were not used appropriately.

Therefore, this was not pursued further. There was a landing approximately 3,000 years ago in South America. A few attempts were made 3,300 years ago in Egypt. The remaining part of the cycle, Ra has never gone from our fifth dimension and has been working in the last minor cycle to prepare for harvest. Such as the telepathic trance communication in channeling sessions as was done in this book.

Ra only waked among Earth in Egypt 11,000 years ago and never stepped foot on Earth again. Only assisting humanity through means such as channeling, which is material shown in this book. As Ra believed this was the best way to assist humanity with the least amount of distortion of their message.

Pyramids were built to ring the Earth (by positively-oriented extraterrestrials such as Ra and others). There are six balancing pyramids and fifty-two others built for additional healing and initiatory work among our people on Earth.

There are many force fields of the Earth in their geometrically precise web. Energies stream into the Earth planes from magnetically determined points. Due to growing thought form distortions in understanding the Law of One, the planet was seen to have the potential for imbalance. The balancing pyramidal structures were charged with crystals which drew the appropriate balance from the energy forces streaming into the various geometrical centers of electromagnetic energy that surrounds and shapes the Earth.

All the visits from Ra for the last 75,000 years were to give the people on Earth the understanding of the Law of One, and in this way allowing them to progress through to fourth, fifth and sixth densities. This was to be a service to Earth. The pyramids were used also in giving the Law of One in their own way.

The balancing pyramidal structures could be and were used for individual initiation (sensory deprivation symbolizing death of the body for a new experience to begin). However, the use of the pyramids were also designed for the balancing of the planetary web. The other 52 pyramids are not placed correctly for Earth's healing but for healing of people on Earth. It came to Ra's attention that our density was distorted towards time in one incarnation pattern in order to have a fuller opportunity to learn/teach the Laws or ways of Love, the primal distortion of the Law of One.

The balancing pyramids were to increase the life span of entities here so that they would gain more wisdom of the Law of One while they were in the physical at one time. However, the pyramids were more numerous and were used exclusively for the above purposes and the teach/learners of healers to charge and enable these processes. The pyramids were not called balancing pyramids by Ra.

George Van Tassel built a machine in Earth's west desert called Integratron. This machine is incomplete and will not function for the purpose of increasing life span. The Confederation (positive density) and the Orion's (negative) gave George this information on how to build it. The Confederation was caused to find noncontact due to the alteration of the vibrational mind complex patterns of George. Thus, was confused, was devoted to service to others, so the worst that could happen was to discredit him.

The harvest is now, therefore any efforts to finish this machine for the longevity of life is not necessary. Rather, encourage distortions towards the seeking of the heart of self, for the violet-ray (crown chakra) energy field will determine the harvesting of each person.

After the first 25,000-year cycle there was no harvest. A harvesting began taking place in the latter portion of the second 25,000-year cycle, with individuals finding the gateway to intelligent infinity. The harvest 25,000 years ago, who could have been harvested into fourth density, chose to remain here in third density in service to this planetary population. At any moment they could leave this density through use of intelligent infinity. Thus, there was no harvest, but there were harvestable entities who shall choose the manner of their entrance into fourth dimension.

For the last 3,300 years Ra has been working to create as large a harvest as possible at the end of this third cycle of 75,000 years. Ra came to aid people on Earth. Their efforts in service were perverted due to those misreading their information and guidance. Ra's desire is then to eliminate as far as possible these distortions. The general cause of service the Confederation offers is the primal distortion of the Law of One, which is service. The One Being of creation is like a body. There is no ignoring any call. Ra, the entities of Sorrow, choose as their service the attempt to heal the sorrow of the pains of other beings.

Ra is sixth density with a strong seeking towards seventh density. Their harvest will be in approximately 2,500,000 years, and it is their desire to be ready for the harvest as it approaches. They ready themselves for this harvest through offering the Law of One, the solving of paradoxes, the balancing of love/light and light/love.

- One of their cycles is 75 million years.
- Ra works only with Earth at this time.
- Ra was called by 352,000 people on Earth.

Whoever calls are not in every case able to understand the answer to their calling. Moreover, those who were not calling previously may, with great trauma, discover the answers to the call nearly simultaneously with their late call. There is no time/space in a call. Therefore, Ra cannot estimate the number of people who will hear and understand. ((There being no time/space in a call can be a reason to a delay in answering of prayers. Ra is one of the higher-density positive beings who hear our prayers.))

Over the past 3,300 years Ra has served through channeling such as the Ra material, but in most cases the channels feel inspired by dreams and visions without being aware consciously of Ra's identity or existence.

((Perhaps there's so-called Christian prophets that have dreams and visions but it's actually their higher self, subconscious mind or higher density beings such as Ra speaking to them. These so-called Christian prophets, after receiving a dream, are then told by Christians that it's from the Christian God. That's when they spread the misinformation of dreams being a prophecy from the Christian God or Yahweh. When it's actually 6th density beings such as Ra or even sometimes negative entities.))

The group that channeled Ra has been trained to recognize such contact, so this group is able to be aware of a vibrational source of information.

When Ra contacts entities in dreams, these entities first have to be seeking the Law of One. For example, the entities of Egypt were in a state of pantheism, the distortion toward separate worship of various portions of the Creator. Ra was able to contact one whose orientation was toward the One.

As this evolutionary cycle ends in third density before the harvest, there will be entities who start seeking or be catalyzed into seeking because of trauma and will hear Ra's words telepathically or in written form such as this channeled book.

The book Oahspe was transmitted by one of the Confederation social memory complexes whose idea, as offered to the Council, was to use some of the known physical history of the religious distortions of our cycle in order to veil and partially unveil portions of the Law of One. The information buried within has to do with a deeper understanding of love and light, and the attempts of infinite intelligence through many messengers to teach people on Earth.

The Urantia book is material not passed by the Council. It was given by a series of discarnate entities of our Earth planes, the inner planes.

No entity spoke through Edgar Cayce. Intelligent infinity is brought into intelligent energy from the 8th density or octave. Edgar used this gateway to view the present, which isn't our experience but the potential of this planet. This is the "Akashic Record" or "Hall of Records" termed by the people of Earth.

The questioner, Don Elkins, asked if they are accomplishing their efforts reasonably well. Ra responded saying the Law is One. There are no mistakes.

Session 15: 1-30-1981

The instrument's reserve of vital energy, which is the product of mind, body, spirit distortions in various complexes, is the key to the length of time Ra can speak through the instrument. Ra searched the group and contacted them, for each possesses significantly more vital energy of the body complex. However, Carla was tuned most appropriately. Therefore, Ra remained with this instrument.

Rapid aging occurs on this third-density planet due to an ongoing imbalance of receptor web complex in the etheric portion of the energy field of this planet. The thought form distortions of our people have caused the energy streaming's to enter the planetary magnetic atmosphere in such a way that the proper streaming's are not correctly imbued with balanced vibratory light/love from the cosmic level of this octave of existence.

One of Ra's attempts in service to this planet was to help the planet more fully understand and practice the Law of One so that this rapid aging could be changed to normal aging.

<u>The greatest service a third density human could offer?</u> There is but one service. The Law is One. The offering of self to Creator is the greatest service, the unity, the fountainhead. If you seek the One Creator, you're with infinite intelligence. A great multiplicity of opportunities will evolve from this seeking from this offering. Some become healers, some workers, some teachers, and so forth. There is no picture to the One Infinite. Thus, the process begins. A perfectly balanced entity would become tired rather than visibly aged. The lessons being learned, the entity would depart. This is a form of aging our people don't experience. The understanding comes slowly, the body complex decomposing more rapidly.

Love creates light. Becoming love/light, streams into the planetary sphere according to the electromagnetic web of points or nexi of entrance. These streamings are then available to the individual who, like the planet, is a web of electromagnetic energy fields with points of nexi (or entrance).

In a balanced individual each energy center is balanced and functioning brightly and fully. The blockages of the planet cause some distortion of intelligent energy. The blockages of people further distort or unbalance this energy. There is one energy understood as love/light or light/love or intelligent energy.

<u>How can an individual balance himself?</u>

Energy Centers:

1st Energy center: Malkuth (Earth) Red Ray= Understanding and acceptance is fundamental.

2nd: The next energy complex which may be blocked is the emotional or personal complex, also known as the orange-ray complex. This blockage will often demonstrate itself as personal eccentricities (odd behavior) or distortions with regard to self-conscious understanding or acceptance of self.

3rd: The third blockage resembles most closely that which you have called ego. It is the yellow ray or solar plexus center. Blockages in this center will often manifest as distortions toward power, manipulation and other social behavior concerning those close and those associated with the mind/body/spirit complex. Those with blockages in these first three energy centers, or nexi, will have continuing difficulties in ability to further their seeking of the Law of One.

4th: The center of heart, or green ray, is the center from which third-density beings may springboard to infinite intelligence. Blockages in this area may manifest as difficulties in expressing love or compassion.

5th: The blue-ray center of energy streaming is the center which, for the first time, is outgoing as well as inpouring. Those blocked in this area may have difficulty in grasping the spirit/mind complexes of its own entity and further difficulty in expressing such understandings of self. Entities blocked in this area may have difficulties in accepting communication from other mind/body/spirit complexes.

6th: The pineal or indigo-ray center. Those blocked in this center may experience a lessening of the influx of intelligent energy due to manifestations which appear as unworthiness. This is one of many distortions due to the several points of energy influx into the mind/body/spirit complex. The indigo-ray balancing is quite central to the type of work which revolves about the spirit complex, which has its influx then into the transformation or transmutation of third density to fourth density, it being the energy center receiving the least distorted outpourings of love/light from intelligent energy and also the potential for the key to the gateway of intelligent infinity.

7th: The remaining center of energy influx is the total expression of the entity's vibratory complex of mind, body, and spirit. It is as it will be; "balance" or "imbalance" has no meaning at this energy level, for it gives and takes in its own balance. Whatever the distortion may be, it cannot be manipulated as can the others and, therefore, has no particular importance in viewing the balancing of an entity.

Ra learns from us. Ra teaches us. Thus, they are teach/learners as they teach us and learn from us.

Information given on healing may be seen as a more general context as ways to understand the self. The understanding, experiencing, accepting and merging of self with other-self, and finally with the Creator, is the path to the heart of self.

In each part of yourself resides the One in all its power. Therefore, Ra can only encourage contemplation or prayer as a means of using or combining various understandings to enhance the seeking process.

Without reversing the analytical process, one could not integrate into unity the many understandings gained in such seeking.

Ra: "It is important to allow each seeker to enlighten itself rather than for any messenger to attempt in language to teach/learn for the entity, thus beings teach/learner and learn/teacher. This is not in balance with your third density. We learn from you. We teach you. Thus, we teach/learn. If we learned for you, this would cause imbalance in the direction of the distortion of free will."

<u>The best way to seek the heart of self:</u>

Ra has given information on healing. This information may be seen in a more general context as ways to understand the self. The understanding, experiencing, accepting, and merging of self with self and other-self, and finally with the Creator, is the path to the heart of self. In each infinitesimal (extremely small) part of yourself resides the One in all of Its power. Therefore, we can only encourage these lines of contemplation or prayer as a means of subjectively/objectively (personal feelings/ open mind) using or combining various understandings to enhance the seeking process. Without such a method of reversing the analytical process, one could not integrate into unity the many understandings gained in such seeking.

The elder race are those harvestable beings at the end of the last 25,000-year period who chose not to graduate into the 4th density. These shepherds shall choose the time/space of their leaving. They are unlikely to leave until their other-selves are harvestable also. The other-selves are the beings who did not attain harvest during the second major cycle.

A social memory complex is a group of at least 144,000 souls that are completely unified and can see each other's thoughts, feelings, and motives. However, their desire to serve is the fourth-dimensional type of desire, thus melding them into what you may call a brotherhood.

The Elder Race are planetary entities harvestable and may be considered Wanderers only in the sense that they chose, in fourth-density love, to immediately reincarnate in third density rather than proceeding towards fourth density. This causes them to be Wanderers of a type, Wanderers who have never left the Earth plane because of their free will rather than because of their vibrational level.

There is a sequence of distortions of free will only up to a very short point. After this point, the manyness of distortions are equal one to another. The first distortion, free will, finds focus. This is the second distortion known to you as Logos, the Creative Principle or Love. This intelligent energy thus creates a distortion known as Light. From these three distortions come many, many hierarchies of distortions, each having its own paradoxes to be synthesized, no one being more important than another.

Ra offered the Law of one, which is the balancing of love/light with light/love. The love/light is the enabler, the power, the energy giver. Light/love is the manifestation which occurs when light has been impressed with love.

There is slight distortion in the mental energy of this instrument (Carla) due to concern for a loved one. This is only slightly lowering the vital energies of the instrument. If she is given a manipulation of being one in harmony with the entity, then she can have another session later that day.

<u>Extra- Not is Session 15:</u> The Orion Group, though negative, restrains from conquering planets due to the desire to progress to the One Creator. So, they don't break the Law of Confusion/Free will.

Star Wars Empire is actually true.

There is One Harvest- Those able to enter fourth density may choose which polarity of further seeking of the One Creator. (Fourth density negative and fourth density positive is the One Harvest.)

Session 16: 1-31-1981

The guardians guard the free-will of third density humans on Earth. The events that required activation of quarantine were interfering with the free-will of people on Earth.

The balancing of free will between the negative and the positive densities is from dimension to dimension. The attempts of the crusaders to interfere with free will are acceptable upon the dimension of their understanding. However, the people of our third dimension of Free will which is notable to recognize in full the distortions towards manipulation. Thus, in order to balance the dimensional variances in vibration, a quarantine becomes a balancing situation where free will of the Orion group is not stopped but given a challenge. Meanwhile, the third density isn't hindered from free choice.

The "windows" occur in quarantine to let the Orion group come through once in a while. All sources are one. The window phenomenon is an other-self phenomenon from the guardians. It operates from dimensions beyond space/time in intelligent energy. The windows open randomly and it is unknown when they may open. It is like a striking of the clock. It is not random in the dimension that produces this balancing. So, these windows open within certain limits.

This window balancing of quarantine around Earth prevents the Guardians from totally eliminating the Orion contact (demon contact). The balancing allows an equal amount of positive and negative influx, this balanced by the mind/body/spirit distortions of the social complex. Less negative information or stimulus is necessary than positive in Earth due to the somewhat negative orientation of Earth's social complex distortion in 1981. As of 2023 it is now 65% positive. I would assume this is because of the work of Wanderers, teachers and the three waves of volunteers that came upon the planet over the last 50 years. When I was a Christian, I was at 42% positive vibration with no growth for 33 years. After learning the Law of One, within one year it jumped to 87% positive vibration. (95% Positive is the ideal positive vibration.)

Total free will is balanced so that individuals may have an equal opportunity to choose service to self or service to others. This is the Law of Free Will.

In the event of mass landing of the Orion group, polarization would strongly increase negatively on Earth. It does not infringe upon free will for the Orion group to land on Earth, thus, they do their work through those of this planet going on their own using their own free will. However, the Orion's would lose negative polarity by a mass landing due to the infringement of free will on the planet. It would be a gamble. If the planet then were conquered and became part of the Empire, the free will would then be reestablished. This is restrained in action due to the Orion group desire to progress towards the One Creator. This desire inhibits the group from breaking the Law of Confusion/Free Will.

The movie Star Wars is an allegory for what is actually happening in the same way a children's story is an allegory for physical/philosophical and social understanding.

There is one harvest. Those able to enter 4th density through vibrational levels may choose which polarity of further seeking the One Creator. Whether that be the negative or positive polarity. The negative polarity would need a vibration level of 95% service to self, where the positive polarity would need a vibration level of 51% or more service to others. The remaining people with a vibration level of 50-94% service to self would have to reincarnate into another planet that supports third density life or be transported by UFOs to another third density planet. Some people will go into planets or places supporting 4th density negative life. This is the split.

The 10 Commandments:

The origin of the Ten Commandments follows the law of negative entities impressing information upon positively oriented people. The information attempted to copy positivity while retaining negative characteristics.

- This was done by the Orion group. Their purpose is conquest and enslavement. This is done by finding and establishing an elite and causing others to serve the elite through various devices such as the Laws given to Moses by these Orion's (or demons).

- Moses or Moishe was extremely positive, thus accounting for some of the pseudo-positive characteristics of the information received.

- As with contacts which aren't successful, Moses/Moishe did not remain a credible influence among those who first heard the philosophy of One, and he left the third-density in a lessened or saddened state, having lost the honor and faith with which he had begun the conceptualization of the Law of One and the freeing of his tribes.

- There was an intensive battleground between positively oriented forces of the Confederation and negatively oriented sources. Moishe was open to impression and received the Law of One in its most simple form. However, the information became negatively oriented due to his people's pressure to do specific physical things in the third density planes. This left Moishe open to information and philosophy of a self-service nature.

It would be unlike an entity fully aware of the Law of One to ever say "Thou shalt not." The 5 of the 10 Commandments states "Thou shalt not" which are words not from the positive-polarity, but from the negative vibration of the Orion's.

The path of 6th density Ra's learning is gravened in the present moment. There is no history as they understand it. It's like a circle of being. They know the alpha and Omega as Infinite Intelligence. The circle never ceases. It is present. The densities they have traversed at various points in the circle corresponded to the characteristics of cycles: first, the cycle of awareness; second, the cycle of growth; third, the cycles of self-awareness; fourth, the cycle of love or understanding; fifth, the cycle of light or wisdom; sixth, the cycle of light/love, love/light, or unity; seventh, the gateway cycle; eighth, the octave which moves into mystery they do not plumb (measure).

There is past, present and future in third density. In an overview such as an entity being removed from space/time may be seen that the cycle of completion there exists only the present. Ra seeks to learn this understanding. At the 7th level or dimension, Ra shall become one with the all, thus having no memory, no identity, no past or future, but existing in the all. It is the awareness of the Creator. In the Creator is all that there is. Therefore, this knowledge would be available.

There are approximately 67 million planets in our galaxy that are aware regardless of density. Ra includes all dimensions of consciousness or densities of awareness in this statistic. Approximately one-fifth of all planetary entities contain awareness of one or more densities. Some planets are hospitable only for certain densities. Earth is hospitable for densities 1, 2, 3 and 4.

-1st density that's aware= 17%

-2nd density that's aware= 20%

-3rd density that's aware= 27%

-4th density that's aware= 16%

-5th density that's aware= 6%

The remaining 14% would be 6th and 7th densities. All planets have progressed from third density by knowledge and application of the Law of One. The only way for a planet to get out of the situation we are in is for the population to become aware of and start practicing the Law of One.

-Negatively oriented planets are much fewer than the positively oriented planets.

-An analogy as to why there are fewer negatively oriented planets: In a positively oriented society with service to others, it would be simple to move a large boulder by getting everyone to help move it.

In a society oriented towards service to self, it would be much more difficult to get everyone to work for the good of all to move the boulder; therefore, it is much easier to get things done to create the service to others principle and grow in positively oriented communities than in negatively oriented communities. Disharmony found in negatively oriented planets also break the beings apart more.

How the Confederation of Planets was formed:

Ra: "The desire to serve begins, in the dimension of love or understanding, to be an overwhelming goal of the social memory complex. Thus, those percentiles of planetary entities, plus approximately 4% more of whose identity we cannot speak, found themselves long, long ago in your time seeking the same thing: service-to-others. The relationship between these entities as they entered an understanding of other beings, other planetary entities, and other concepts of service was to share and continue together these commonly held goals of service. Thus, each voluntarily placed the social memory complex data in what you may consider a central thought complex available to all. This then created a structure whereby each entity could work in its own service while calling upon any other understanding needed to enhance the service. This is the cause of the formation and the manner of the working of the Confederation."

There are approximately 500 planets in the Confederation in our galaxy. There are many Confederations. This Confederation contains 7 of our solar systems and is responsible for the callings of the densities of these solar systems. A Sun being the center of each solar system.

Ra is aware of life in infinite capacity.

The progression of life in other galaxies is somewhat close to the same, asymptotically approaching congruency (consistency) throughout infinity. The free choosing of galactic systems causes variations of an extremely minor nature from one of our galaxies to another.

The Law of One is truly universal in creating a progression towards the 8th density in all galaxies. There are infinite forms, infinite understandings, but the progression is one.

An entity doesn't have to understand the Law of One to evolve from third density into 4th density, for third density is not the density of understanding.

The 5th density harvest is of those whose vibratory distortions consciously accept the honor/duty of the Law of One. This responsibility/honor is the foundation of this vibration. Each responsibility is an honor; each honor, a responsibility. Thus, it honor/responsibility.

There are no words for positively describing 4th density. Ra can only explain what is not and approximate what is. Beyond 4th density our (Ra) ability grows more limited until we become without words.

-4th density is not of words, unless chosen.

-It is not of heavy chemical vehicles for body complex activities.

-It is not of disharmony within self.

-It is not of disharmony within peoples.

-It is not within limits of possibility to cause disharmony in any way.

-It is a plane of bipedal vehicles which is much denser (more light) and fuller of life.

-It is a plane wherein one is aware of the thoughts of other-selves.

-It is a plane of compassion and understanding of the sorrows of third density.

-It is a plane striving towards wisdom or light.

-It is a plane where individual differences are pronounced although automatically harmonized by group consensus.

Density is a mathematical one. The closest analogy is that of music, where after seven notes the 8th one begins a new octave. Within our great Octave of existence, Ra and the Confederation shares with us, there are seven octaves or densities. Within each density there are seven sub-sub densities. Within each sub-density, are seven sub-sub densities, and so on infinitely.

In any density level, there is infinity/opportunity. You may consider any possibility/probability complex as having an existence.

Daydreams are a large subject. Perhaps the simplest thing we (Ra) can say is if the daydream is one which attracts to self, this then becomes reality to self. If it is a contemplative general daydream, this may enter the infinity of possibility/probability complexes and occur elsewhere, having no particular attachment to the energy field of the creator.

Example: If one was to daydream about building a ship, this would/would have/ or shall occur in one of these other densities.

Example 2: If any entity daydreams strongly about battling others/other-self this fantasy binds the thought form to the possibility/probability complex connected with the self/the creator of this thought form. This then would increase the possibility/probability of bringing this into third-density occurrence.

The Orion group uses daydreams of hostile or other negative natures to feed back or strengthen these thought forms.

Wanderers become completely third density beings. There is just as much influence from the Orion thoughts as other third density humans on this planet. The only difference occurs in the spirit complex if the Wanderer wishes to have an amor of light that enables it to recognize more clearly what it doesn't desire. This is not more than bias and cannot be called an understanding.

Furthermore, the Wanderer is less distorted toward the deviousness of third-density positive/negative confusions. Thus, Wanderers often don't recognize as easily as negative individuals do, the negative nature of thoughts or beings. Therefore, Wanderers incarnating here would be high-priority targets of the Orion group.

If a Wanderer should be successfully infringed upon by the Orion group and the Wanderer demonstrated negative actions towards others, they would be caught into the planetary vibration and, when harvested, possibly repeat again the master cycle of third density on a third density planet.

Session 17: 2-3-1881

The Orion group arrived into the Earth planetary sphere around 2,600 years ago. The Confederation arrived 3,300 years ago.

Ra: "I am Ra. The fourth density is a vibrational spectrum. Your time/space continuum has spiraled your planetary sphere and you, what we would call galaxy, what you call star, into this vibration. This will cause the planetary sphere itself to electromagnetically realign its vortices of reception of the instreaming of cosmic forces expressing themselves as vibrational webs so that the Earth thus be fourth density magnetized.

This is going to occur with some inconvenience, as we have said before, due to the energies of the thought forms of your peoples which disturb the orderly constructs of energy patterns within your Earth spirals of energy, which increases entropy and usable heat. This will cause your planetary sphere to have some ruptures in its outer garment while making itself appropriately magnetized for fourth density. This is the planetary adjustment.

You will find a sharp increase in the number of people, as you call mind/body/spirit complexes, whose vibrational potentials include the potential for fourth-vibrational distortions. Thus, there will seem to be a new breed. These are those incarnating for fourth-density work.

There will also be a sharp increase in the short run of negatively oriented or polarized mind/body/spirit complexes and social complexes, due to the polarizing conditions of the sharp delineation (detailed description) between fourth-density characteristics and third-density self-service orientation.

Those who remain in fourth density upon this plane will be of the positive orientation. Many will come from elsewhere, for it would appear that with all the best efforts of the Confederation, which includes those from our people's inner planes, inner civilizations, and those from other dimensions, the harvest will still be much less than this planetary sphere is capable of comfortably supporting in service."

It is impossible to help another being directly reach fourth-density level in these last days. Ra: "It is only possibly to make catalyst available in whatever form, the most important being the radiation of realization of oneness with the Creator from the self, less important being information such as we share with you.

We, ourselves, do not feel an urgency for this information to be widely disseminated. It is enough that we have made it available to three, four, or five. This is extremely ample reward, for if one of these obtains fourth-density understanding due to this catalyst, then we shall have fulfilled the Law of One in the distortion of service.

We encourage a dispassionate attempt to share information without concern for numbers or quick growth among others. That you attempt to make this information available is, in your terms, your service. The attempt, if it reaches one, reaches all.

We cannot offer shortcuts to enlightenment. Enlightenment is, of the moment, an opening to intelligent infinity. It can only be accomplished by the self, for the self. Another self cannot teach/learn enlightenment, but only teach/learn information, inspiration, or a sharing of love, of mystery, of the unknown that makes the other-self reach out and begin the seeking process that ends in a moment, but who can know when an entity will open the gate to the present?"

Jesus of Nazareth did not have a name in the 4th density positive. This entity was a member of the highest level of 4th density of that sub-octave. Jesus was desirous of entering this planetary sphere in order to share the love vibration in as pure a manner as possible. He received permission to perform this mission. Jesus was a Wanderer of no name, of Confederation origins, representing the 4th density understanding of the vibration of understanding or love. He could have gone onto the 5th but chose instead to return to third for this particular mission.

There is no separation of the entities within Ra. You would call it social memory complex, indicating manyness. To Ra's understanding, you are speaking to an individualized portion of consciousness.

When the group speaks to Ra, they are speaking to the same entity through a channel or instrument. When the instrument is lower at times in vital energies, it will sometimes hamper Ra's proceedings. However, Carla has a great deal of faithfulness to the task and gives whatever it has to this task. Therefore, Ra continues when energy is low. This is why Ra speaks until the instrument's vital energies are low.

People on Earth can be harvested into Fourth density if they are of the appropriate vibratory levels. No matter what religion, have no religion or knowledge of the Law of One.

However, there will be a few harvestable whose radiance does not cause others to be aware of their spirituality. Thus, it is not particularly probable that an entity would be completely unknown to his immediate acquaintances as an unusually radiant person, even if they weren't caught up in any of the so-called religious systems.

When Jesus of Nazareth incarnated, the Orion group tried to discredit him and cause his downfall. The Orion's technique was to build upon other negatively oriented information. This information had been given by "Yahweh". This information involved many strictures upon behavior and promised power of third density, service-to-self nature. These two types of distortions were impressed upon those already oriented to think these thoughts.

This eventually led to many challenges for Jesus. It eventually led to Judas, who believed it was doing the appropriate thing in bringing about or forcing upon Jesus the necessity for bringing in third density planetary power distortion of third density rule over others. Which is negatively oriented.

Judas felt if Jesus was pushed into a corner that Jesus would be able to see the wisdom of using the power of Intelligent Infinity to rule over others. Judas was mistaken in this estimation of the reaction of Jesus, who teach/learning was not negatively oriented. This resulted in the destruction of the body of Jesus.

Ra: "Those who heal may be of any density which has the consciousness of the spirit. This includes third, fourth, fifth, sixth, and seventh. The third density can be one in which healing takes place just as the others. However, there is more illusory material to understand, to balance, to accept, and to move forward from.

The gate to Intelligent Infinity can only be opened when an understanding of the insteamings of intelligent energy are opened unto the healer. These are the so-called Natural Laws of your local space/time continuum and its web of electromagnetic sources or nexi of instreaming energy.

Know then, first, the mind and the body. Then as the spirit is integrated and synthesized, these are harmonized into a mind/body/spirit complex which can move among the dimensions and can open the gateway to Intelligent Infinity, thus healing self by light and sharing that light with others.

True healing is simply the radiance of the self, causing an environment in which a catalyst may occur which initiates the recognition of self, by self, of the self-healing properties of the self."

Jesus learned this ability by a natural kind of remembering at a very young age during his incarnation. Ra: "Unfortunately, this entity first discovered his ability to penetrate intelligent infinity by becoming the distortion you call "angry" at a playmate. This entity was touched by the entity known as Jesus and was fatally wounded.

Thus, the one known as Jesus became aware that there dwelt in him a terrible potential. This entity determined to discover how to use this energy for the good, not for the negative. This entity was extremely positively polarized and remembered more than most Wanderers do."

Ra: "The entity you call Jesus was galvanized by this experience and began a lifetime of seeking and searching. This entity studied first day and night in its own religious constructs which you call Judaism and was learned enough to be a rabbi, as you call teach/learners of this particular rhythm or distortion of understanding, at a very young age.

At the age of approximately thirteen and one-half of your years, this entity left the dwelling place of its earthly family and walked into many other places seeking further information. This went on sporadically until the entity was approximately twenty-five, at which time it returned to its family dwelling and learned and practiced the art of its earthly father.

When the entity had become able to integrate or synthesize all experiences, the entity began to speak to other-selves and teach/learn what it had felt during the preceding years to be of a worthwhile nature. The entity was absolved karmically of the destruction of an other-self when it was in the last portion of lifetime and spoke upon a cross, saying, "Father, forgive them, for they know not what they do." In forgiveness lies the stoppage of the wheel of action, or what you call karma."

Jesus now studies the lessons of the wisdom vibration, the fifth density, also called the light vibration.

Jesus became aware that it was not an entity of itself but operated as a messenger of the One Creator, who Jesus saw as love. This entity was aware that we are in the last portion of this cycle (of 3rd density) and spoke to the effect that those of its consciousness would return at the harvest. Jesus won't return except as a member of the Confederation speaking through a channel. However, there are others of the identical congruency of consciousness that will welcome those to fourth density. This is the meaning of the Returning. (The return of Christ, which is the return of 4th density consciousness of love, understanding and oneness).

The Earth will be 4th density positive because those oriented and harvestable towards service-to-others greatly outnumber those negatively oriented or service-to-self. In 1981 Ra said that the great majority of people on Earth will repeat third density.

It is the right/privilege/duty of those consciously opening the gate to intelligent infinity to choose when they leave third density. Those who are of negative orientation who so achieves this right/duty most often choose to move forward in their learn/teaching of service-to-self. Therefore, Taras Bulba, Genghis Khan and Rasputin have harvested to fourth density negative prior to the harvest.

Those who are not in incarnation at this time will be included in the harvest.

Ra: "The best way of service-to-others is the constant attempt to seek to share the love of the Creator as it is known to the inner self. This involves self-knowledge and the ability to open the self to the other-self without hesitation. This involves radiating that which is the essence or the heart of the mind/body/spirit complex.

The best way for each seeker in third density to be of service-to-others is unique to that mind/body/spirit complex. This means that the mind/body/spirit complex must then seek within itself the intelligence of its own discernment as to the way it may best serve other-selves. This will be different for each. There is no best. There is no generalization. Nothing is known."

The negative path is quite difficult to attain harvestability and requires great dedication.

The negative path is difficult to obtain due to the Law of One indicating that the gateway to intelligent infinity be a gateway at the end of a straight and narrow path. To attain 51 percent dedication to the welfare of others is as difficult as attaining a grade of 5 percent dedication to others. The sinkhole of indifference is between the two. Those indifferent must repeat third density.

Each entity entering fourth density enters at the sub-density upon which they vibrate at.

The third density has an infinite number of levels.

There are seven astral and seven devachic levels. This is the larger distinction in levels in our inner planes.

Entities inhibit the various astral and devachanic planes due to their vibration/nature. The astral plane varies from thought forms in the lower extremities to enlightened beings who become dedicated to teach/learning in the higher astral planes.

In the devanchanic planes are those whose vibrations are even more close to the primal distortions of love/light. Beyond these planes there are others.

-There are seven sub-planes to what we call our physical plane here. There are an infinite number of planes. In our particular space/time continuum distortion, there are seven sub-planes of mind/body/spirit complexes.

Ra: "You will discover the vibrational nature of these seven planes as you pass through your experiential distortions, meeting other-selves of the various levels which correspond to the energy influx centers of the physical vehicle.

The invisible, or inner, third-density planes are inhabited by those who are not of body complex natures such as yours; that is, they do not collect about their spirit/mind complexes a chemical body. Nevertheless, these entities are divided in an artificial dream within a dream into various levels. In the upper levels, desire to communicate knowledge back down to the outer planes of existence becomes less, due to the intensive learn/teaching which occurs upon these levels."

Ra: "It has been our experience that some penetrate several planes at one time. Others penetrate them slowly. Some in eagerness attempt to penetrate the higher planes before penetrating the energies of the more fundamental planes. This causes energy imbalance.

You will find ill health, as you call this distortion, to frequently be the result of a subtle mismatch of energies in which some of the higher energy levels are being activated by the conscious attempts of the entity while the entity has not penetrated the lower energy centers or sub-densities of this density."

There is no best way to meditate.

Entities wishing to obtain critically needed experience in order to become harvestable are incarnated with priority over those who will, without too much probable/possible doubt, need to re-experience this density.

This type of seniority of vibration has been going on since the first individual became conscious of its need to learn the lessons of this density. This was the beginning of a seniority by vibration. This seniority gives harvestable entities priority in order that an entity have the best possible chance in succeeding in this attempt.

It was suggested that the instrument (Carla) wear heavier clothing on the feet. As inpourings occur in the seventh chakra energy center, filtering through the sixth and so forth, the entity's base chakra becomes somewhat de-energized. Thus, the entity should wear warm apparel for the feet.

Session 18: 2-4-1981

Ra wishes to express the feeling of the Infinite Mystery of the One Creation in its infinite and Intelligent unity.

Ra: "The proper role of the entity is in this density to experience all things desired, to then analyze, understand, and accept these experiences, distilling from them the love/light within them. Nothing shall be overcome. That which is not needed falls away.

The orientation develops due to analysis of desire. These desires become more and more distorted towards conscious application of love/light as the entity furnishes itself with distilled experience. We have found it to be inappropriate in the extreme to encourage the overcoming of any desires, except to suggest the imagination rather than the carrying out in the physical plane of those desires not consonant with the Law of One, thus preserving the primal distortion of free will.

The reason it is unwise to overcome is that overcoming is an unbalanced action creating difficulties in balancing in the time/space continuum. Overcoming thus creates the further environment for holding on to that which apparently has been overcome.

All things are acceptable in the proper time for each entity, and in experiencing, in understanding, in accepting, in then sharing with other-selves, the appropriate distortion shall be moving away from distortions of one kind to distortions of another which may be more consonant with the Law of One.

It is a shortcut to simply ignore or overcome any desire. It must instead be understood and accepted. This takes patience and experience which can be analyzed with care, with compassion for self and for other-self."

To not infringe on the free will of others is a basic rule of the Law of One. Another way to not break the Law of One:

Ra: "As one proceeds from the primal distortion of free will, one proceeds to the understanding of the focal points of intelligent energy which have created the intelligences or the ways of a particular mind/body/spirit complex in its environment, both what you would call natural and what you would call man-made. Thus, the distortions to be avoided are those which do not take into consideration the distortions of the focus of energy of love/light, or shall we say, the Logos of this particular sphere or density. These include the lack of understanding of the needs of the natural environment, the needs of other-selves' mind/body/spirit complexes. These are many due to the various distortions of man-made complexes in which the intelligence and awareness of entities themselves have chosen a way of using the energies available.

Thus, what would be an improper distortion with one entity is proper with another. We can suggest an attempt to become aware of the other-self as self and thus do that action which is needed by other-self, understanding from the other-self's intelligence and awareness. In many cases this does not involve the breaking of the distortion of free will into a distortion or fragmentation called infringement. However, it is a delicate matter to be of service, and compassion, sensitivity, and an ability to empathize are helpful in avoiding the distortions of man-made intelligence and awareness.

The area or arena called the societal complex is an arena in which there are no particular needs for care, for it is the prerogative/honor/duty of those in the particular planetary sphere to act according to their free will for the attempted aid of the social complex.

Thus, you have two simple directives: awareness of the intelligent energy expressed in nature, awareness of the intelligent energy expressed in self to be shared when it seems appropriate by the entity with the social complex, and you have one infinitely subtle and various set of distortions of which you may be aware; this is, distortions with respect to self and other-selves not concerning free will but concerning harmonious relationships and service-to-others as other-selves would most benefit."

An entity incarnating on Earth becomes conscious at a varying point in its space/time through the continuum. This may have a medium of approximately 15 months. They are not responsible before they become aware. Distortions are to be understood by entities and dissolved as you learn. Even a four-year-old is responsible for any actions that were against or inharmonious with the Law of One.

It has been arranged by Ra's social complex structures that newer entities incarnation (the youth) are to be provided with physical guides (teachers, parents, friends) to be able to quickly learn what is consonant with the Law of One.

Forgiveness is the eradicator of karma. Balanced forgiveness for the full eradication of karma would require forgiveness of others and of self.

Forgiveness of others is forgiveness of self. An understanding of this insists of the full forgiveness upon the conscious level of self and other-self, for they are one. A full forgiveness is impossible without the inclusion of self.

All Confederations serve the One Creator. There is nothing else to serve, for the Creator is all that there is. It is impossible not to serve the Creator. There are simply various distortions of this service.

As the Confederation works with our people, each Confederation is a group of specialized individual social memory complexes, each doing what it expresses to bring into manifestation.

Yahweh's first communication to Earth's people were genetic changes in the cloning process. Thus, entities incarnated in the image of the Yahweh entities. (This is what the Bible meant by "made in the image of God")

The second communication was the walking among our people to produce further genetic changes in consciousness by sexual reproduction devised by the intelligent energy of our physical complex.

Yahweh's purpose in making the sexual genetic changes 75,000 years ago was one purpose only: to express in the mind/body complex those characteristics that would lead to further and more speedy development of the spiritual complex.

The characteristics which were encouraged included sensitivity of all physical senses to sharpen experiences and the strengthening of the mind to analyze these experiences.

The Yahweh group worked with those of Mars 75,000 years ago in the cloning process. There are differences, but they lie in the future that Ra can't speak of because of free-will.

3,600 was approximately the number of attempts by the Orion group during this culture. This was a series of encounters where the Anak were impregnated with the new genetic coding so that they would be larger and stronger.

The ones of Yahweh were attempting to create an understanding of the Law of One by creating people capable of grasping the Law of One. The experiment was a decided failure because rather than assimilating the Law of One, it was a great temptation to consider the social complex or sub-complex elite better than the others previous to the genetic change. This is a technique of the service-to-self.

The entities of Yahweh were responsible for this procedure in isolated cases as experiments in combating the Orion group. However, the Orion group were able to use this distortion of mind/body complex to inculcate (instill persistently) the thoughts of the elite rather than concentrations upon the learning/teaching of Oneness. ((Inculcate means to instill an attitude, idea, or habit by persistent instruction)).

Yahweh was of the Confederation but was mistaken in its attempts to aid. The results of Yahweh's interactions were quite mixed. Where the entities were of a vibration that embraced Oneness, the manipulations of Yahweh were very useful. Where the entities of free will chose a less positively oriented configuration of the total vibratory complex. Those of the Orion group were able to make some serious inroads on the consciousness of our planet for the first time.

Specifically, those who are strong, intelligent, etc., have a temptation to feel different from those who are less intelligent and less strong. This is a distorted perception of oneness with other-selves. It allowed the Orion group to form the concept of the holy war. This is a seriously distorted perception. There were many of these wars of a destructive nature.

Session 19: 2-8-1981

With the space/time continuum understandings of the intelligent energy that animates the illusion if all entities make the transition from second density to third density; within the context of this illusion, Ra states that there are some that do not transfer from one particular density to another, for the continuum is finite.

In the understanding Ra has of the universe or creation as one infinite being, its heart beating as alive in its own intelligent energy, it merely is one beat of the heart of this intelligence from one creation to creation. In this context, each and every entity of consciousness has/ is/ will experienced/ experiencing/ experience each and every density.

There are three types of second-density entities that become aware of the intelligent energy within each portion, cell, or atom of its beingness. The first and most predominant is the animal. The second is the vegetable, which humans call tree. Trees are capable of giving and receiving enough love to become individualized. The third is mineral. Occasionally a certain location/place become energized to individuality through the love it receives and gives to a third density entity in relationship to it. This is the least common transition.

Entities do not become inspired. They become aware of the intelligent energy within each portion, cell, or atom of its beingness from second density into third.

This awareness is awareness that was already given. From the infinite come all densities. Self-awareness comes within, given the catalyst of certain experiences understanding the upward spiraling of the cell or atom or consciousness.

You may then see there is an inevitable pull toward the eventual realization of self.

The transition to third-density on Earth would look like us humans.

There are some second-density entities that made the graduation on Earth into third-density with no outside stimulus, but only the efficient use of experience.

Others of Earth's second density joined the third-density cycle due to harvesting efforts by the same sort of sending of vibratory aid as those of the Confederation send you now. This communication was telepathic rather than vocal or written due to the nature of second-density beings.

The Confederation of Planets in the Service of the infinite Creator sent aid to the second-density beings for their graduation into third-density on Earth approximately 75,000 years ago.

There were beings on the second-density plane when exposed to third-density vibrations became third density human entities.

There was the loss of body hair that clothed the body to protect it; the changing of the structure of the neck, jaw and forehead in order to allow easier vocalization; and the larger cranial development of third-density needs. This was a normal transfiguration.

The transfiguration occurred within a generation and one-half. Those who had been harvested of this planet were able to use the newly created physical complex of chemical elements suitable for third-density lessons.

There is a necessity for third density. That necessity is self-awareness or self-consciousness. In order to be capable of this, the chemical body must be capable of abstract thought. Thus, the fundamental necessity is the combination of rational and intuitive thinking.

Second density forms largely operate upon intuition, which proved through practice to yield results. So, the transition was for abstract, rational and intuitive thinking.

The third-density mind was capable of processing information to think abstractly and termed "useless" in the sense of survival. This is the primary requisite.

The other necessary ingredients is the necessity for a weaker physical body to encourage the use of the mind, the development of the already present awareness of the social complex. The further development of the physical dexterity of the hand was also necessary.

Within the primal distortion of free will, each solar system developed its own Logos. This Logos has complete free will in determining the paths of intelligent energy that promote the lessons of each density given the conditions of the planetary spheres and sun bodies.

Consider, if you will, the tree. It is self-sufficient. The third density entity is self-sufficient only through difficulty and deprivation. It is difficult to learn alone, for there is a built-in handicap, that is the rational/intuitive mind. At once the great virtue and the great handicap of third density.

The weakening of the physical body was designed to distortion entities with a predisposition to deal with each other. Thus, the lessons approach a knowing of love can be begun.

This catalyst then is shared between peoples as an important part of each self's development as well as the experiences of the self in solitude and the synthesis (the whole) of all experience through meditation. The quickest way to learn is to deal with other-selves. Dealing with the self without the other-self is like living without mirrors. Thus, the self cannot see the fruits of its beingness. Thus, each may aid each by reflection. This is also a primary reason for the weakening of the body.

Earth has second-density beings with primary motivation towards self and possibly a little motivation towards service-to-others with their immediate family going into third density and carrying this bias with them but being in a position where this bias will slowly be modified to one aimed toward a social complex and ultimately towards union with the all.

The second-density concept of serving self includes the serving of those associated with the tribe or pack. This is not seen in second density as separation of self and other-self. All is seen as self since in some forms of second-density entities, the tribe or pack becomes weakened, so does the entity within the tribe or pack.

The new or initial third density has this innocent bias towards viewing those in the family, the society, and country, as self. Though a distortion not helpful for progress in third density, it is without polarity.

The break becomes apparent when the entity perceives other-selves as other-selves and consciously determines to manipulate other-selves for the benefit of the self. This is the beginning of the road of the service-to-self path.

The majority of third-density beings is far along the chosen path before realization of that path is conscious.

The metaphor that creates the bias toward the service-to-self path: Some love the light. Some love the darkness. It is a matter of the unique and indefinitely various Creator choosing and playing among its experiences as a child upon a picnic. Some enjoy the picnic and find the sun beautiful, the food delicious, the games refreshing, and glow with joy of creation.

Some find the night delicious, their picnic being pain, difficulty, sufferings of others, and the examination of the perversities of nature. These enjoy a different picnic.

All of these experiences are available. It is the free will of each entity that chooses the form of play, the form of pleasure.

The further an entity has polarized, the easier to change polarity, for the more power and awareness the entity will have.

Those truly helpless are those who have not consciously chosen a path, but repeat patterns without knowledge of the repetition or meaning of the pattern.

<u>An analogy in polarization of consciousness:</u> There is an extreme potential in polarization, the same as the positive and negative pole in electricity. The more you build the charge on either polarity, the more potential difference and the greater the ability to do work.

Ra: "The physical complex alone is created of many, many energy or electromagnetic fields interacting due to intelligent energy, the mental configurations of each complex further adding fields of electromagnetic energy and distorting the physical complex patterns of energy, the spiritual aspect serving as a further complexity of fields.

Thus, instead of one, shall we say, magnet with one polarity, you have in the body/mind/spirit complex one basic polarity expressed in what you would call violet-ray energy, the sum of the energy fields, but which is affected by thought of all kinds generated by the mind complex, by distortions of the body complex, and by the numerous relationships between the microcosm which is the entity and the macrocosm in many forms which you may represent by viewing the stars, each with a contributing energy ray which enters the electromagnetic web of the entity due to its individual distortions."

Ra: "The root of astrology is one way of perceiving the primal distortions which may be predicted along probability/possibility lines given cosmic orientations and configurations at the time of the entrance into the physical/mental complex of the spirit and at the time of the physical/mental/spiritual complex into the illusion.

This then has the possibility of suggesting basic areas of distortion. There is no more than this. The part astrology plays are likened unto that of one root among many."

Ra said the instrument should wear shoes.

Session 20: 2-9-1981

When our third density cycle began 75,000 years ago, some second-density beings were unharvestable and were able to repeat a portion of their second-density cycle.

Some of the second-density beings who were not harvested 75,000 years ago are still on this planet today. Some of these beings were harvested into third density within the past 75,000 years.

The most common occurrence of second-density graduation during third-density cycle is the so-called pet.

For the animal that is exposed to the individualizing influences of the bond between animal and third-density entity, this individuation causes a sharp rise in the potential second-density entity so that upon cessation (ending) of the physical complex, the mind/body complex does not return into the undifferentiated (identical) consciousness of that species. Then, enters third density.

As a second-density entity reincarnates into third-density for the beginning of this process of learning, the entity is equipped with the lowest vibrational distortion forms of third-density consciousness, equipped with self-consciousness. This would be a human beginning the understanding of third density.

Rapid change occurred in the body of the second-density to third-density entity: this occurred approximately a generation in a half. Body hair was lost and there were structural changes.

The physics of Dewey B. Larson states all is motion or vibration. The basic vibration that makes up the physical world changes, thus creating a different set of parameters in this short period of time between density changes allowing for the new type of being.

The physics of Dewey is a correct system as far as it is able to go. There are things which aren't included in the system. However, those coming after this particular entity, using the basic concepts of vibration and the study of vibrational distortions, will begin to understand gravity and things you consider as "n" dimensions. These things are necessary to be included in a more universal physical theory.

Dewey brought this material through for use primarily in the fourth density.

There's a split that occurs when an entity either consciously or unconsciously chooses the path that leads to either service-to-others or service-to-self. The philosophical question of why such a split even exists came up. Just as it is in electricity, if we have no polarity in electricity we have no electricity; we have no action. Therefore, if we have no polarity in consciousness, we have no action or experience. ((I view it as without the negative density given beings catalysts or experiences to help us evolve and make decisions, we wouldn't evolve as fast or be able to choose a polarity. Without the choice of polarity, evolution is occurs much slower.))

The concept of service-to-self and service-to-others is mandatory if we wish to have work, whether it be work in consciousness or work of a mechanical nature in the Newtonian concept in the physical.

<u>An example:</u> The coil, is wound, is potential, is ready. The thing that is missing without polarizing is the charge. The charge is the individualized entity using the inpourings and instreamings of energy by the choices of free will.

At the beginning of third density 75,000 years ago, the average life span was approximately 900 years.

There is a particular use for the span of life in this density, given the harmonious development of the learning/teachings of this density, the life span of the physical would remain the same throughout the cycle. However, our planet developed vibrations by the 2nd major cycle (of three cycles) that shortened the life span.

The life span at the end of the first cycle of 25,000 years was approximately 700 years.

The causes of this shortening are always an in-euphonious or inharmonious relational vibration between other-selves. In the first cycle this was not as severe due to the dispersion of peoples, but there was the growing feeling of separation from other-selves.

The lessening of the life span was due primarily to the lack of the building of positive orientation. When there is no progress, the conditions that grant progress are gradually lost. This is one of the difficulties of remaining unpolarized. The chances of progress became steadily less.

At the beginning of the 75,000-year cycle, we had those who graduated second density on Earth to third density. Then a group of entities transferred from Mars mid-third-density to continue third density on Earth. ((I was a part of this transfer from Mars)). The beings who transferred from Mars was an adaptation here rather than a beginning.

There were perhaps one-half of the third-density population from Mars, one-quarter who graduated from second-density on Earth and approximately one quarter from other planets for third-density work.

When all three of these groups incarnated into Earth for third-density they remained largely unmixed.

This unmixing led to a possibility of warlike energy between the groups.

This did reduce the life span.

The mind/body/spirit complex of third density has perhaps been 100 times as intensive of a program of catalytic action from which to distill distortions of learn/teachings than any other of the densities. This is why 900 years is the optimum life span. Thus, the learn/teachings are most confusing to the entity, which is inundated by the ocean of experience.

During the first 150-200 years the entity is going through a spiritual childhood. The mind and body are not enough in a disciplined configuration to lend clarity to the spiritual influxes. Thus, the remaining time span is given to optimize the understandings which result from experience itself.

Our current life span is too short for those new to third-density lessons.

Those entities who have learned/taught themselves rapid growth can now work within the confines of a shorter life span. However, the greater preponderance (predominance) of people on Earth finds themselves in what may be considered a perpetual (or eternal) childhood.

The Confederation members which dwell in inner plane existence within the planet's densities worked with the entities in the first 25,000-year third density cycle. There was also the aid of one of the Confederation which worked with Mars in making the transition.

For the most part, the participation was limited, as it was appropriate to allow the full travel of the workings of the confusion mechanism to operate in order for the planetary entities to develop what they wished in freedom within their own thinking.

It is often the case that a third-density planetary cycle won't need outside or other-self aid in the form of information. Rather, the entities themselves are able to work themselves towards the appropriate polarizations and goals of third density learn/teachings.

The original desire is that entities seek and become one. If entities can do this in a moment, they may go forward in a moment. If that were to occur in a major 25,000-year cycle, the third-density planet would be vacated at the end of that cycle. They would be harvestable and move to a fourth density planet.

The medium or mean of third-density developments throughout the one infinite universe is a small harvest after the first cycle-the remainder having significantly polarized.

The second cycle having a much larger harvest- the remainder being even more significantly polarized.

The third cycle culminating the process and the harvest being completed.

The Confederation was watching to see and expecting a harvest at the end of the 25,000-year cycle in which a percentage would be harvested fourth density positive or negative. There was none harvestable.

The Orion group made one attempt during the first 25,000 years to offer negatively polarized information to those of third density. However, nobody was concerned to follow that path to polarity.

The technique used was the telepathic thought transfer. The second technique was the arrangement of certain stones in order to suggest strong influences of power, this being those of statues and rock formations in our Pacific areas and to an extent in our Central American regions. These are the stone heads of Easter Island.

The stone heads could influence people to take the service-to-self path if people lived in such a way that it seemed as if humanity was at the mercy of forces which they can't control. Given a charged statue or a rock formation charged with nothing but power, it is possible for the free will of those viewing this structure to ascribe to this power. Power over things which cannot be controlled. This has the potential for the further distortion of power over others.

Nearly all of the stone head structures were constructed at a distance by thought after scanning of the deep mind, the trunk of mind tree, looking at the images most likely to cause the experience of awe in the viewer. Very few were created in later times in imitation of original constructs by entities upon Earth plane/density.

The fourth density Orion constructed them. The density of love and understanding. Love and understanding, whether it be of self or of other self toward other-self, is one. Fourth density negative or positive is both the density of love and understanding.

These stone heads were constructed approximately 60,000 years ago.

The structures built in South America and the lines at Nazca were fashioned some characteristic statues, some formations of rock and some rock and Earth formations.

These formations were of benefit because they were charged with energy of power. They were of benefit even though they could only be seen from an altitude.

The lines at Nazca are hardly understandable for any entity walking on the surface. He cannot see anything but disruption of the surface. However, if you go up to a high altitude you can see the patterns.

60,000 years ago, the Earth was formed in such a way as to be visibly arranged in powerful structural designs, from the vantage point of distant hills. So, this is how 60,000 years ago it was of benefit to entities walking the surface.

The entire smoothness, as you see this area now, was built up in many places in hills. Time has eroded with wind and weather to a great extent both the somewhat formidable (intimidating) structures of earth designed at that time and the nature of the surrounding countryside. These lines are just the faint traces of what used to be there.

Session 21: 2-10-1981

The information Ra offers would have no future affect if the instrument would read the material because her fidelity in dedicating its will to the service of the infinite Creator and also because Ra removes the conscious mind of Carla so that Ra can communicate without reference to any instrument's orientation.

Ra uses the vocabulary that they are familiar with. It's not the instrument's vocabulary. However, Carla retains the use of a sufficiently large vocabulary that the distinction is often without any importance.

The entities from Mars third-density experience were brought to a close prematurely were aided genetically while being transferred to third density on Earth. This, although done in a desire to aid, was seen as infringement upon free will.

The light quarantine which consists of the Guardians, or gardeners, which was in effect, was intensified.

Ra: "I am Ra. The incarnation pattern of the beginning third-density mind/body/spirit complex begins in darkness, for you may think or consider of your density as one of a sleep and a forgetting. This is the only plane of forgetting. It is necessary for the third-density entity to forget so that the mechanisms of confusion or free will may operate upon the newly individuated consciousness complex.

Thus, the beginning entity is one in all innocence oriented towards animalistic behavior using other-selves only as extensions of self for the preservation of the all-self. The entity becomes slowly aware that it has needs that are not animalistic; this is, that are useless for survival. These needs include the need for companionship, the need for laughter, the need for beauty, the need to know the universe about it. These are the beginning needs.

As the incarnations begin to accumulate, further needs are discovered: the need to trade, the need to love, the need to be loved, the need to elevate animalistic behaviors to a more universal perspective.

During the first portion of third-density cycles, incarnations are automatic and occur rapidly upon the cessation of energy complex of the physical vehicle (or upon death). There is small need to review or to heal the experiences of the incarnation. As, what you would call, the energy centers begin to be activated to a higher extent, more of the content of experience during incarnation deals with the lessons of love.

Thus, the time, as you may understand it, between incarnations is lengthened to give appropriate attention to the review and the healing of experiences of the previous incarnation. At some point in, the green ray energy center becomes activated and at that point incarnation ceases to be automatic.

When incarnation ceases to be automatic after the green ray center becomes activated, the entity can decide when they need to incarnate for the benefit of their own learning, they also select their parents.

Near the end of our 75,000-year third density cycle, approximately 54% of people incarnating are making their own decisions.

During the first 25,000-year cycle there was no industrial development at all, such as machinery available to the people. However, there was various implements of wood and rock used in order to obtain food and for use in aggression.

At the end of the first 25,000-year cycle there was no rapid physical change except according to intelligent energy or physical evolution, suited physical bodies to their environment such as the color of their skin due to the area of the sphere the entities lived; the gradual growth of peoples due to improved intake of food.

The Guardians seeing no harvest occurring after the first 25,000-year cycle did not take any action except to remain aware of the possibility of a calling for help or understanding among people of this density on Earth. The Confederation is concerned with the preservation of conditions conducive (helpful) to learning. This revolves about the primal distortion of free will.

The Confederation gardeners did nothing until some of the plants in their garden called them for help. (This means that the Confederation did nothing until some of the people on Earth called them for help.)

The first calling was approximately 46,000 years ago from those of Maldek. They were aware of their need for rectifying the consequences of their action and were in some confusion in an incarnate state as to the circumstances of their incarnation. The unconscious being aware, the conscious being quite confused. This created a calling. The Confederation sent love and light to them.

There dwell within the Confederation planetary entities who planets do nothing but send love and light as pure streaming's to those who call. This is not in the form of conceptual (theoretical and abstract) thought but of pure and undifferentiated (identical) love.

It was not necessary for some time for equal time to be given to the self-service-oriented group due to them not perceiving the aid of the Confederation. Since it was not perceived, it was not necessary to balance this.

What is necessary to balance is opportunity. When there is ignorance, there is no opportunity. When there exists a potential, then each opportunity shall be balanced, this balancing caused by not only the positive and negative orientations of those offering aid but also the orientation of those requesting aid.

In the sense of greatness of technology there were no great societies that developed during the second 25,000-year cycle. There was some advancement among those of Deneb who had chosen to incarnate as a body in China.

There were appropriately positive steps in activating the green-ray energy complex in many portions of the planet, including the Americas, Africa, Australia, India, as well as various scattered peoples.

None of these became what you would name as great as the greatness of Lemuria or Atlantis due to the formation of strong social complexes. Atlantis had great technological understandings.

However, in South America there grew to be a great vibratory distortion towards love. These entities were harvestable at the end of the second major cycle without ever having formed strong social or technological complexes.

Session 22: 2-10-1981

By the end of the second major cycle the life was with certain variations among geographically isolated people more in harmony with intelligent energy and less bellicose (aggressiveness).

Many lived 35-40 years in one incarnation, with the possibility not considered abnormal to approach one hundred years at the end of the second major cycle.

This drastic drop in average life span from 900 to 700 years to 35 years over each 25,000-year cycle was caused by an intensification of a lack of service-to-others.

Ra: "I am Ra. By the end of the second cycle, the Law of Responsibility had begun to be effectuated (put into force or operation) by the increasing ability of entities to grasp those lessons which they are to be learned in this density. Thus, entities had discovered many ways to indicate a bellicose (war-like) nature, not only as tribes or nations but in personal relationship, each with the other, the concept of barter having given way to the concept of money; also, the concept of ownership having won ascendancy (higher position) over the concept of non-ownership on an individual or group basis.

Each entity then was offered many more subtle ways of demonstrating either service toward others or service-to-self with the distortion of the manipulation of others. As each lesson was understood, those lessons of sharing, of giving, of receiving in free gratitude-each lesson could be rejected in practice.

Without demonstrating the fruits of such learn/teaching, the life span became greatly reduced, for the ways of honor/duty were not being accepted."

The shortening life span can help the entity in having more life in between incarnations to review their mistakes. This shortening life span is also a distortion of the Law of One which suggests that an entity not receive more experience in intensity than they may bear. This is only upon an individual level and does not hold sway over planetary or social complexes.

Thus, the shortened life span is due to the necessity for removing an entity from the intensity of experience which ensues when wisdom and love are reflected back into the consciousness of the Creator without being accepted as part of the self, this then causing the entity to have the need for healing and for much evaluation of the incarnation.

Given appropriate circumstances, a much longer incarnation is very helpful for continuing this intensive work until conclusions have been reached through the catalytic process.

The isolated group in South America that was harvestable at the end of the second cycle had achieved life spans stretching upwards toward the 900-year life span appropriate to third density.

The planetary action upon Earth that we are experiencing now that shortens all life spans here, was not strong enough to affect this group of approximately 150 harvestable entities due to their great isolation. Which was possible at that time.

At the end of the second cycle there were approximately 345,000 entities on Earth. The Confederation visited this isolated group and they became desirous to stay in order to aid the planetary consciousness. They decided to stay and help during the next 25,000-year cycle.

When the Confederation visited this group, they appeared as a light bearing a shield of light. (Religious people may refer to this an angel). It spoke of the oneness and infinity of all creation and of those things which await those ready for harvest. It described in golden words the beauties of love as lived. It then allowed a telepathic linkage to progressively show those who were interested the plight of third density when seen as a planetary complex. It then left.

As a group they stayed. There were those peripherally (extras that were) associated with the culture which did not stay. However, they were not able to be harvested either and so, beginning at the very highest of the sub-octaves of third density, repeated this density. Many of those who have been of the loving nature are not Wanderers but those of this particular origin of second cycle of third density harvestable for the 4th density.

The entities repeating the third-density third cycle have, in a few cases, been able to leave. These entities have chosen to join their brothers and sisters.

From our historical past Saint Augustine, Saint Teresa, Saint Francis of Assisi are of such nature. They being of monastic background found incarnation in the same type of ambiance appropriate for further learning.

The Confederation became concerned at the lack of harvest at the end of the second 25,000-year cycle. The Council of Saturn acted only in allowing the entry into third density of other mind/body/spirit complexes, not Wanderers, but those who sought further third-density experience. This was done randomly so that free will would not be violated, for there was not yet a call.

The next action from the Confederation was the calling from the Atlanteans. This calling was for what you would call understanding with the distortion towards helping other-selves. The action taken was the impression of information through channels.

The first calling from Earth was before Atlantis became technologically advanced. The technological advancement of Atlantis did not come at first because of this call. About the same time Ra first appeared in the skies over Egypt and continuing thereafter, other entities of the Confederation appeared unto Atlantis who had reached a level of philosophical understanding which was consonant with communication, to encourage and inspire studies in the mystery of unity.

However, requests being made for healing and other understanding, information was passed having to do with crystals and the building of pyramids as well as temples which were associated with training.

This training was different in that the social complex was more sophisticated and less contradictory and barbarous (savagely cruel) in its ways of thinking. Therefore, the temples were temples of learning rather than the attempt being made to totally separate and put upon a pedestal the healers.

Priests were trained in these temples in the sense of those devoted to learning, not in the sense of celibacy, obedience and of poverty. The difficulties became apparent as those trained in this learning began to attempt to use crystal powers for those things other than healing, as they were involved not only with learning but became involved with the governmental structure. Their information was given to them from visitations from time to time, but none of these visitations in the historical passage of events was important Ra stated. There were two conditions necessary for these visitations to occur. The calling of a group of people whose square overcome the integrated resistance of those unwilling to search or learn.

The second requirement was the relative naivete of those Confederation members who felt that direct transfer of information would necessarily be helpful for Atlanteans as it had been for the Confederation entity.

These naïve Confederation entities had the same thing happen to them in the past, so they were doing the same thing for the Atlantean entities. Ra is one of the naïve members of that Confederation and are still attempting to recoup the damage for which they feel responsibility. It is Ra's duty as well as honor to continue with our people on Earth, until all traces of the distortions of their teach/learnings have been embraced by their opposite distortions, and balance achieved.

A large enough percentage of Atlanteans had started at least in the direction of the Law of One and living the Law of One for their call to be heard by the Confederation. This call was heard because of the Way (Law) of Squares, it overrode the opposition of the Atlantean entities who were not calling. The Confederation used this tuned trance telepathy in communication such as the group is using now to contact Ra and contact was also made directly, but this turned out to be distorted because it was perverted by the entities of Atlantis. Also, there is only one law. That is the Law of One. Other so-called laws are distortions of this Law, some of them primal and most important for progress to be understood. However, it is well that each so-called law, which Ra calls "way", be understood as a distortion rather than a law. There is no multiplicity to the Law of One.

In the early part of the Atlantean cultural experience had average life spans of 70 to 140 years approximately. Due to increasing desire for power, the lifetime decreased rapidly in the later stages of the civilization, and thus, the healing and rejuvenating information was requested.

Session 23: 2-11-1981

The first contact made by the Confederation occurred during our third major cycle approximately 18,000 years ago appearing over the skies in Egypt. The people would have seen crystal-powered, bell-shaped craft. This occurred approximately the same time that aid was given to Atlantis.

Ra first went to Egypt since there were those who chose to worship the hawk-headed sun god "Horus". The sun god Horus had taken other names as well, the object of worship being the sun disc represented in some distortion.

Ra was drawn to spending some time scanning the people for a serious interest amounting to a seeking where Ra might help without infringement. They found that the social complex was quite self-contradictory in its religious beliefs, so there was not an appropriate calling for Ra's vibration. So, approximately 18,000 years ago they departed without taking action.

Seeing the UFO 18,000 years ago in the skies of Egypt did not affect them due to their firm conviction that many Wonderous things occurred as a normal part of a world in which many, many deities had powerful control over supernatural events.

Ra allowed visibility because it did not make a difference.

Ra: "I am Ra. The next attempt was prolonged. It occurred over a period of time. The nexus, or center, of our efforts was a decision upon our parts that there was a sufficient calling to attempt to walk among your people as brothers.

We laid this plan before the Council of Saturn, offering ourselves as service-oriented Wanderers of the type which land directly upon the inner planes without incarnative processes. Thus, we emerged, or materialized, in physical chemical complexes representing as closely as possible our natures, this effort being to appear as brothers and spend a limited amount of time as teachers of the Law of One, for there was an ever-stronger interest in the sun body, and this vibrates in concordance with our particular distortions.

We discovered that for each word we could utter, there were thirty impressions we gave by our very being, which confused those entities we had come to serve. After a short period, we removed ourselves from these entities and spent much time attempting to understand how best to serve those to whom we had offered ourselves in love/light.

The ones who were in contact with that geographical entity, which you know of as Atlantis, had conceived of the potentials for healing by use of the pyramid-shape entities. In considering this and making adjustments for the difference as in the distortion complexes of the two geographical cultures, we went before the Council again, offering this plan to the Council as an aid to the healing and the longevity of those in the area you know as Egypt. In this way we hoped to facilitate the learning process as well as offer philosophy articulating the Law of One. Again, the Council approved.

Approximately, 11,000 of your years ago we entered, by thought, your- we correct this instrument. We sometimes have difficulty due to low vitality. Approximately 8,500 years ago, having considered these concepts carefully, we returned, never having left in thought, to the thought form areas of your vibrational planetary complex and considered for some of your years, as you measure time, how to appropriately build these structures.

The first, the Great Pyramid, was formed approximately 6,000 of your years ago. Then, in sequence, after this performing by thought of the building or architecture of the Great Pyramid using the more, shall we say, local or earthly material rather than thought form material to build other pyramidal structures.

This continued for approximately 1,500 of your years.

Meanwhile, the information concerning initiation and healing by crystal was being given. The one known as "Ikhnaton" was able to perceive this information without significant distortion and, for a time, moved heaven and earth in order to invoke the Law of One and to order the priesthood of these structures in accordance with the distortions of initiation and true compassionate healing. This was not to be long lasting.

At this entity's physical dissolution from your third-density physical plane, as we have said before, our teachings became quickly perverted; our structures once again went to the use of the so-called "royal" or those with distortions towards power."

If pyramidal healing is to be effectuated (generated), it must be a funneling without significant distortion of the insteamings through the spiritual complex into the tree of mind.

Ra: "There are parts of this mind which block energies flowing to the body complex. In each case, in each entity, the blockage may well differ.

However, it is necessary to activate the sense of the spiritual channel or shuttle. Then whether the blockage is from spiritual to mental or from mental to physical, or whether it may simply be a random and purely physical trauma, healing may then be carried out."

When Ra started building the pyramid at Giza using thought, they were not in close contact with incarnate entities upon Earth. Ra was responding to a general calling of sufficient energy in that particular location to merit action. They sent thoughts to all who were seeking their information.

The appearance of the pyramid was a tremendous surprise. However, it was carefully designed to coincide with the incarnation of "Imhotep" known as a great architect. Imhotep was later made into a deity, in part due to this occurrence.

The pyramids did not produce a rise in consciousness that was hoped for. Ra is of the Brothers and Sisters of Sorrow. When one has been rescued from that sorrow to a vision of the One Creator, then there is no concept of failure.

Ra's difficulty lay in the honor/responsibility of correcting the distortions of the Law of one which occurred during their attempts to aid those in Egypt. The distortions are seen as responsibilities rather than failures; the few who were inspired to seek, were the only reason for the attempt.

Thus, Ra would perhaps be in the position of paradox in that as one saw illumination, Ra was successful, and as others became more sorrowful and confused, Ra saw failures. These are the groups terms. Ra persists in seeking to serve.

After Ikhnaton died, this entity was then put through the series of healing and review of incarnational experiences which is appropriate for third-density experience. This entity had been somewhat in the distortions of power ameliorated (improved) by the great devotion to the Law of One. (Ameliorated means to make something that is bad or unsatisfactory better). This entity then revolved to enter a series of incarnations with no distortions toward power.

The average life span of the Egyptians during the time of Ikhanaton was approximately 35-40 years. There was much physical disease. The land in Egypt was highly barbarous in its living conditions. The Nile River was allowed to flood and recede, thus providing the fertile grounds for the breeding of diseases which may be carried by insects. Also, the preparation of food allowed diseases to form also, there was difficulty in many cases with sources of water, and water which was taken caused disease due to the organisms therein.

The root cause of disease in this particular society was not so much a bellicose (war-like) action, although there were tendencies, but rather the formation of a money system and a very active trading and development of those tendencies toward green and power, thus, the enslaving of entities by other entities and the misapprehension of the Creator within each entity.

The Confederation entities who walked among those in the South American continent were called by a similar desire to learn of the manifestations of the sun. They worshipped this source of light and life.

Ra: "Thus, these entities were visited by light beings not unlike ourselves. Instructions were given and they were more accepted and less distorted than ours. The entities themselves began to construct a series of underground and hidden cities including pyramid structures.

These pyramids were somewhat at variance (a difference) from the design that we had promulgated (made known publicly). However, the original ideas were the same with the addition of a desire or intention of creating places of meditation and rest, a feeling of the presence of the One Creator; these pyramids then being for all people, not only initiates and those to be healed.

They left this density when it was discovered that their plans were solidly in motion and, in fact, had been recorded. During the next approximately 3,500 years these plans became, though somewhat distorted, in a state of near completion in many aspects.

Therefore, as is the case of the breakings of the quarantine, the entity who was helping the South American entities along the South American ways you call in part the Amazon River went before the Council of Saturn to request a second attempt to correct in person the distortions which had occurred in their plans. This having been granted, this entity or social memory complex returned, and the entity chosen as messenger came among the people once more to correct the errors.

Again, all was recorded and the entity rejoined its social memory complex and left your skies.

As in our experience, the teachings were, for the most part, greatly and grossly perverted (corrupted) to the extent in later times of actual human sacrifice rather than healing of humans. Thus, this social memory complex is also given the honor/duty of remaining until those distortions are worked out of the distortion complexes of your peoples."

Session 24: 2-15-1981

In this last 25,000 year cycle the Atlanteans, Egyptians and those in South America were contacted and then the Confederation departed. The Confederation did not come back for some time because enlargements upon the information given to the Atlanteans resulted in bellicosity activities which resulted in the final Atlantean catastrophe 10,864 years ago.

Ra: "Many, many were displaced due to societal actions both upon Atlantis and upon those areas of what you would call North African deserts, to which some Atlanteans had gone after the first conflict. Earth changes continued due to these, what you would call, nuclear bombs and crystal weapons, sinking the last great land mases approximately 9,600 of your years ago.

In the Egyptian and the South American experiments, results, though not as widely devastating, were as far from the original intention of the Confederation. It was clear to not only us but also to the Council and the Guardians that our methods were not appropriate for this particular sphere.

Our attitude thus was one of caution, observation, and continuing attempts to creatively discover methods whereby contact from our entities could be of service with the least distortion and, above all, with the least possibility of becoming perversions or antitheses (the opposite) of our intention in sharing information."

Ra: "I am Ra. In approximately 3,600 of your years in the past, there was an influx of those of the Orion group. Due to the increasing negative influences upon thinking and acting distortions, they were able to begin working with those whose impression from olden times was that they were special and different. (Also, known as the elite).

An entity of the Confederation, many, many thousands of your years in the past "Yahweh" had, by genetic cloning, set up these particular biases among these peoples who had come gradually to dwell in the vicinity of Egypt, as well as in many, many other places, by dispersion after the down-sinking of the land mass Mu. (Also known as Lemuria). Here the Orion group found fertile soil in which to plant the seeds of negativity, these seeds, as always, being those of the elite, the different, those who manipulate or enslave others.

The one known as Yahweh felt a great responsibility to these entities. However, the Orion group had been able to impress upon the people the name Yahweh as the one responsible for this elitism. Yahweh then was able to take what you would call stock of its vibratory patterns and became, in effect, a more eloquently effective sound vibration complex.

In this complex the old Yahweh, now unnamed but meaning "He comes," began to send positively oriented philosophy. This was approximately in your past of 3,300 years. Thus, the intense portion of what has become known as Armageddon was joined."

3,600 years ago, the Orion's were able to get through the quarantine the weakening of windows due to a proper calling for negatively oriented information.

Ra: "When there is a mixed calling, the window effect is much more put into motion by the ways of the densities.

The quarantine in this case was patrolled closely, due to the lack of strong polarity, the windows thus needing to be very weak in order for penetration. As your harvest approaches, those would call light work according to their call. The ones of Orion have the working only according to their call. This calling is in actuality not nearly as great.

Thus, due to the way of empowering or squares, there is much resistance to penetration. Yet, free will must be maintained and those desiring negatively oriented information must then be satisfied by those moving through by the window effect."

Yahweh, their old name, attempted to correct the perversions of their intention in sharing information by starting a positive philosophy 3,300 years ago. Since they felt a responsibility for those who came gradually to Egypt and many, many other places by dispersion after the down-sinking of the land mass Mu, also known as Lemuria.

"Yod-Heh-Shin-Vau-Heh" the new name for the entity known as Yahweh, still felt it could raise up entities' superior to the negative forces, that these superior forces could spread the Law of One. Thus, Yod-Heh-Shin-Vau-Heh came among people of Earth incarnatively and mated in the normal reproductive manner birthing a generation of much larger beings called "Anak"

The other method used to a greater effect later was the wheel within a wheel and the cherubim with sleepless eye.

The Orion's or the Empire had an emissary (representative which was sent) 3,600 years ago in our skies. This emissary was fiery, which was hidden by the cloud in the day. This was to obliterate (wipe out) the questions of those seeing the mysterious wheel within a wheel and the cherubim with sleepless eye the positive entity was trying to use for positive philosophy. The Orion's tried to make this fiery emissary (representative) consonant (harmonic) with people's concept of the Creator.

Information was passed on to people who saw this fiery cloud by thought transfer and by the fiery phenomena and other events to appear as being miraculous through the use of thought forms.

Those of the Empire were not successful in maintaining their presence for long after approximately 3,000 years ago, so they left after a 600-year period in our skies. The so-called prophets were often given mixed information, both positively oriented and negatively oriented, but the worst the Orion group could do was to cause these prophets to speak of doom, as prophecy in those days was the occupation of those who love their fellow beings and wish only to be of service to them and to the Creator.

The Orion group was successful in polluting some of the positively oriented prophets' messages with prophecies of doom

The Orion's left after a 600-year period.

Ra: "Although the impression that they had given to those who called them was that these entities were an elite group, that which you know as "Diaspora" occurred, causing much dispersion of these people so that they became a humbler and more honorable breed, less bellicose (hostile) and more aware of the loving kindness of the One Creator. (Diaspora is the spread of a people from their original homeland).

The Creation about them tended towards being somewhat bellicose, somewhat oriented towards the enslavement of others, but they themselves, the target of the Orion group by means of their genetic superiority/weakness, became what you may call the underdogs, thereby letting the feelings of gratitude for their neighbors, their family, and their One Creator begin to heal the feelings of elitism which led to the distortions"

The questioner would typically end the session with asking if there's anything that they could do to make the instrument more comfortable. Here is one of Ra's responses that concludes session 24, a typical response that ends each session.

Ra: "I am Ra. You are conscientious. Be careful to adjust this instrument's upper appendages if its upper body is elevated.

I am Ra. All is well. It is our joy to speak with you. We leave in the love and the light of the One Infinite Creator. Go forth, therefore, rejoicing in the power and the peace of the One Creator. Adonai."

Session 25: 2-16-1981

About 3,000 years ago the Orion group left due to Diaspora, dispersion. (Diaspora means to scatter about).

Ra: "I am Ra. For many of your centuries, both the Confederation and the Orion Confederation busied themselves with each other upon planes above your own planes in time/space whereby machinations (a plot to overthrow something) were conceived and the armor of light girded (encircled). Battles have been and are continuing to be fought upon these levels.

Upon the Earth plane, energies had been set in motion which did not cause a great deal of call. There were isolated instances of callings, one such taking place beginning approximately 2,600 of your years in the past in Greece and resulting in writing and understandings of some facets of the Law of One. We (Ra) especially note the one known as Thales and the one known as Heraclitus, those being of the philosopher career teaching their students. We (Ra) also point out the understandings of the one known as Pericles.

At this time there was a limited amount of visionary information which the Confederation was allowed to telepathically impress. However, for the most part, during this time empires died and rose according to the attitudes and energies set in motion long ago, not resulting in strong polarization but rather in that mixture of the positive and the warlike or negative which has been characteristic of this final minor cycle of your beingness."

The Orion's and the Confederation are busy upon planes above our own. Picture, if you will, your mind. Picture it then in total unity with all other minds of your society. You are then single-minded, and that which is a weak electrical charge in the physical illusion of a single human mind, is now an enormously powerful machine of the collective mind where thoughts may be projected as things.

The Orion group charges or attacks the Confederation armed with light. The result, a standoff, both energies being somewhat depleted by this and needing to regroup.

The negative depleted through failure to manipulate, the positive depleted through failure to accept what is given.

The positive fourth density is in a thought war with fourth density negative Orion's when four planetary Social Memory Complexes at any moment are asked to partake in this thought war for the Confederation. This is the most difficult work for the Confederation.

Ra: "I am Ra. At the level of time/space at which this takes place in the form of what you may call thought war, the most accepting and loving energy would be to so love those who wished to manipulate that those entities were surrounded and engulfed, transformed by positive energies.

This, however, being a battle of equals, the Confederation is aware that it cannot, on equal footing, allow itself to be manipulated in order to remain purely positive, for then though pure it would not be of any consequence, having been placed by the so-called powers of darkness under the heel, as you may say.

It is thus that those who deal with this thought war must be defensive rather than accepting in order to preserve their usefulness in service-to-others. Thusly, they cannot accept fully what the Orion Confederation wishes to give, that being enslavement. Thusly, some polarity is lost due to this friction, and both sides, must then regroup.

It has not been fruitful for either side. The only consequence which has been helpful is a balancing of the energies available to this planet so that these energies have less necessity to be balanced in this space/time, thus lessening the chances of planetary annihilation."

Fourth density is most effective for this work than 5th or 6th density besides third which, lacking the wisdom to refrain from battle, sees the necessity of the battle. Thus, it is necessary that fourth density social memory complexes be used.

The Confederation only uses fourth density positive for this thought battle with the Orion's. Positive fifth and sixth density entities would not take part in this battle, due to their wisdom to refrain from battle.

Fifth density negative would not take part in this battle. The fifth density is the density of light or wisdom. The fifth density negative entity is at a high level of awareness and wisdom and has ceased activity except by thought. They are extraordinarily compacted and separated from all else.

Session 26: 2-17-1981

Ra: "I am Ra. There is no possibility of a complete source of information of the Law of One in this density. However, certain of your writings passed on to you as your so-called holy works have portions of this law."

((Now this Law of One book that I summarized and my book 'Correcting Distortions of the Bible' is the closest thing we have to a complete source of information of the Law of One.))

The Bible has portions of this law in it. The Old Testament and the New Testament having approximately equal Law of One content in it. However, the so-called Old Testament has a larger amount of negatively influenced material in it than the New Testament.

The percentage of negatively Orion influence in both the Old and the New Testaments Ra prefers that this be left to the discretion of those who seek the Law of One. Ra is not speaking in order to judge. Such statements would be construed by some who may read this material as judgmental. We can only suggest a careful reading and inward digestion of the contents. The understandings will become obvious.

((In later material the answer was about 50% negatively influenced including the 10 Commandments from the Orion's)).

Ra did not communicate with anyone on Earth in the 1900's, until this channeling group in the early 1980's.

The ways of One have seldom been communicated, although there have been rare instances between 1900-1981.

There have been many communications from fourth density due to the drawing towards the harvest to fourth density. These are the ways of universal love and understanding. The other teachings are reserved for those whose depth of understanding recommend and attract such further communication.

Approximately 250 years ago there began to be a significant number of entities who by seniority were incarnating for learn/teaching purposes rather than the learn/teachings of those less aware of the process. This was Ra's signal to enable communication to take place.

The Wanderers began to make themselves felt amongst those on Earth, firstly offering ideas or thoughts containing the distortion of free will. This was the prerequisite for further Wanderers having more specific information to offer. The thought must precede the action.

Abraham Lincoln chose to leave his physical body and allow a fourth density positive entity to use it on a permanent basis. This is relatively rare compared to the phenomenon of Wanderers. His association was influenced by negative forces.

Thomas Jefferson and Benjamin Franklin incarnated on Earth as Wanderers.

Increased UFO activity became known upon Earth after the 1940's when information of the Confederation sources had offered Albert Einstein became perverted and instruments of destruction began to be created, examples of this being the Manhattan Project and its product.

Information offered through Wanderer Nikola Tesla also was experimented with for potential destruction: An example being the so-called Philadelphia Experiment.

Thus, Ra felt a strong need to involve their thought forms in whatever way the Confederation could to be of service in order to balance these distortions of information meant to aid Earth.

UFOs then began to appear as an air of mystery from the Confederation with the UFO phenomenon. Then by telepathy sent many messages which could be accepted or rejected under the Law of One so that the population would start thinking seriously about the consequences of what they were doing with the nuclear devices.

((In Delores Cannon's book "The three Waves of Volunteers and the New Earth" was about three waves of souls incarnating into Earth after the atomic bombs were dropped in World War II. Our "protectors" and "watchers" in outer space saw that Earth was on a collision course with disaster. The prime directive of non-interference (due to free will) prevented them from taking any action, but then they came up with a brilliant plan to save Earth and assist her in her ascension. They couldn't interfere from the "outside," but maybe they could influence from the "inside". So, the call went out for volunteers to come and help. "Earth is in trouble-who wants to volunteer?" The native souls living on Earth were too caught up on the wheel of karma.

The only hope was to ask for pure souls to come who had never been trapped on the karmic cycle. Dolores in her hypnosis work has discovered three waves of these volunteers. Some have come directly from the "Source" and have never lived in any type of physical body before. Others have lived as space beings on other planets or other dimensions. Because there's a veil of forgetting that takes place between our conscious and our unconscious minds upon entry to the Earth dimension, they do not remember their assignment. Thus, these beautiful souls have a difficult time adjusting to our chaotic world. These souls have a vital role to play as they help all the rest of us ascend to the New Earth.))

There were other services that Ra could perform. Firstly, the integration of souls or spirits in the event nuclear devices are used, which the Confederation already did. The use of intelligent energy transforming matter into energy is of such a nature among nuclear bombs that the transition from space/time physical third density to time/space third density heaven worlds is interrupted in many cases.

Therefore, Ra offers themselves as those who continue the integration of souls or spirit complex during transition from space/time (metaphysical) to time/space (physical).

Kathryn's thoughts: I would assume this was the Three Waves of Volunteers of souls that incarnated into Earth to raise the awareness/consciousness of Earth to help with the ascension into New Earth fourth density harvest that could occur in 2030. I also assume when Ra stated that few will harvest, the Three waves were also needed so that Earth wouldn't destroy itself like Mars did mid third-density. Thus, why they had to transfer to Earth 75,000 years ago to continue third density experience and evolution. The three waves of volunteers also greatly increased the harvest from just a few to 65% harvestable beings that are above 51% service-to-others.

Hiroshima and Nagasaki:

Ra: "I am Ra. Those who were destroyed, not by radiation but by the trauma of the energy release, found not only the body/mind/spirit complex made unviable (unworkable), but also a disarrangement (disorganization) of the spirit complex, which we understand as a mind/body/spirit complex, to be completely disarranged without possibility of reintegration. This would be the loss to the Creator of part of the Creator, and thus we were given permission not to stop the events, but to ensure the survival of the disembodied mind/body/spirit complex. This we did in those events, (Hiroshima and Nagasaki), losing no spirit or portion or holograph or microcosm (small version of something much larger) of the macrocosmic (the whole body of things observed such as the universe) (of the) Infinite One."

((Ra was given permission not to stop the events by the Confederation due to the free will of those who create those events to occur.))

Ra's actions to ensure the survival of the disembodied mind/body/spirit complexes was accomplished through their understanding of dimensional fields of energy. The higher or more dense energy field will control the less dense.

In general, Ra would allow the population of Earth to have a nuclear war and many deaths from that war, due to free will, but they will allow these souls to remain entities and enter the heaven worlds or astral world after their death by a bullet or by the normal dying of old age.

Those who were killed in Nagasaki and Hiroshima have not yet fully begun the healing process of this trauma. They are being helped as much as possible.

Action of nuclear destruction affect the entire planet. There are no differences at this level of destruction in regards to personal evolution. The planet will need to be healed.

Death by nuclear bomb would not make someone unharvestable for graduation into fourth density. Once the healing has taken place after 1981, the harvest may go forth unimpeded (not delayed). However, the entire planet will undergo healing for this action, no distinction between victim and aggressor, this due to damage done to the planet.

The planetary healing is a process of acceptance, forgiveness and if possible, restitution. The restitution not available in time/space, there are many among your peoples now attempting restitution while in the physical. These attempts are made with feelings of love toward the planet and comfort and healing of the scars and the imbalances of these actions.

UFO Phenomenon:

As the UFO phenomenon was made obvious to many people on Earth, many groups of people were reporting contact and telepathic communication with UFO entities and recorded the results of the communications. Most of these landings were of the Orion or negative density, with the exception of the advanced third density UFO entities that contacted Charlie Hixon.

Although some of the Confederation members have removed themselves from time/space using thought projections into our space/time and have chosen with permission of the Council, from time to time, to appear in our skies without landing. There also has been isolated instances of no affiliation that occurred with the UFO phenomenon.

Once having reached third-density space/time through the windows surrounding our Earth, the Orion crusaders may plunder (forcefully steal) as they will, the results completely a function of the polarity of the witness/subject or victim.

This is due to the sincere belief of fourth-density negative that to love self is to love all. Each other-self which is taught or enslaved has a teacher that teaches love of self. Exposed to this teaching, it is intended that there be a harvest of fourth density negative or self-serving mind/body/spirit complexes.

The most effective mode of positively oriented Confederation contact is done through channeling such as the Ra contact. The infringement on free will is greatly undesired. Therefore, Wanderers are the only subjects for thought projections of the "Close Encounters" and meetings between positively oriented social memory complexes and Wanderers.

One example of a meeting between a social memory complex and a Wanderer is that known as Morris. This refers to CASE #1 in Secrets of the UFO by D.T Elkins with Carla L. Rueckert, page 10-11. In this case the previous contact with Morris' circle of friends was negatively oriented. However, Morris was impervious (impassable) to this contact and could not see the negative physical optical apparatus of this contact, since he was a Wanderer.

However, the inner voice alerted Morris to go by itself to another place, and there a positive entity with the thought form shape and appearance of the other contact appeared and gazed at Morris, thus awakening in it the desire to seek the truth of this occurrence and of the experiences of its incarnation in general.

The feeling of being awakened or activated is the goal of this type of positively oriented contact. The duration and imagery used varies depending upon the subconscious expectations of the Wanderer which is experiencing this opportunity for activation.

"Close Encounters" by a Confederation member is with a thought form type of craft that Wanderers in the 1970's experienced these landed thought form crafts. Confederation landings are much less common than the Orion type of so-called "Close Encounter."

Ra states that in a universe of unending unity, the concept of a "Close Encounter" in humorous, for are not all encounters self with self? Therefore, how can any encounter be less than very, very close?

Encounters are of self to self from a higher awareness of understanding. Wanderers of positive polarization do have "Close Encounters" with the Orion or negatively oriented polarization.

When it occurs, it is quite rare and occurs either due to the Orion entities' lack of perception of the depth of positivity to be encountered or due to the Orion entities' desire to attempt to remove this positivity from this plane of existence. Orion tactics normally are those with simple distortions of mind that indicate less mental and spiritual activity.

The methods used to awaken Wanderers are varied. The center to each approach is the entrance into the conscious and subconscious in a way to avoid causing fear and a way to maximize the potential for an understandable subjective experience that has meaning for the entity. Many occur in sleep, others during activities of the day. The approach is flexible and doesn't necessarily include the "Close Encounters."

The subconscious expectations of people cause the details of the thought form experience offered by the Confederation thought form entities. If a Wanderer expects a physical examination, it will be experienced with as little distortion towards alarm or discomfort as is allowable by the nature of the expectations of the subconscious distortions of the Wanderer.

The Orion group uses the physical examination of people on their crafts as a means of terrifying the individual and causing it to feel the feelings of an advanced second-density laboratory animal. The sexual experiences of some are a subtype of this experience.

The intent is to demonstrate control of the Orion beings over Terran inhabitant. Control over others being a negatively service-to-self characteristic.

The thought form experiences are subjective and, for the most part, do not occur in this density.

Both Confederation and Orion contacts are being made in "Close Encounters." Although the preponderance (or most) of contacts are

Orion oriented. (Preponderance means most, therefore, most of the contacts are Orion oriented. Which is negatively-oriented).

Ra: "The most typical approach of Orion entities is to choose what you might call the weaker-minded entity that it might suggest a greater amount of Orion philosophy to be disseminated.

Some few Orion entities are called by more highly polarized negative entities of your space/time nexus. In this case they share information just as we are now doing. However, this is a risk for the Orion entities due to the frequency with which the harvestable negative planetary entities then attempt to bid and order the Orion contact, just as these entities bid planetary negative contacts. The resulting struggle for mastery, if lost, is damaging to the polarity of the Orion group.

Similarly, a mistaken Orion contact with highly polarized positive entities can wreak havoc with Orion troops unless these crusaders are able to depolarize the entity mistakenly contacted. This occurrence is almost unheard of. Therefore, the Orion group prefers to make physical contact only with the weaker-minded entity."

If the contact was fear and doom, the contact was quite likely of a negative nature. If the result is hope, friendly feelings, and the awakening of a positive feeling of purposeful service-to-others, the marks of Confederation contact are evident.

Ra: "Just as grass withers and dies while the love and light of the One Infinite Creator redounds (contribute greatly) to the very infinite realms of creation forever and ever, creating and creating itself in perpetuity (foreverness).

Why then be concerned with the grass that blooms, withers, and dies in its season only to grow once again due to the Infinite love and light of the One Creator? This is the message that we bring. Each entity is only superficially that which blooms and dies. In the deeper sense there is no end to beingness.

This is an introduction to the Law of One, traveling through and hitting high points of the 75,000-year third density on planet Earth. After this, the channeling group wanted to go into the investigation of evolution.

END of BOOK #1 of 5

~~~

BOOK # 2

------FOREWARD-----

On January 15th, 1981 a research group (Don, Carla and Jim) started receiving a communication from the social memory complex, Ra. Don, the questioner; Carla, the channeler; Jim, the scribe. From this communication precipitated the Law of One and some distortions of the Law of One. Book 2 contains the communications received in sessions 27-50 with Ra. Book 2 of the Law of One builds very carefully on concepts received during the first 26 sessions with Ra. This book concentrates on the metaphysical principles which govern our spiritual evolution as we seek to understand and use catalyst of our daily experiences. A more thorough examination of the energy centers of the body, and the connections between mind, body and spirit, is carried out, building upon information received in the first 26 sessions. The group learns more about Wanderers, the various densities, healing, and the many energy exchanges and blockages native to our illusion relating to experiences such as sex, illness, and meditation.

The first three sessions of Book 2 (27-29) may be difficult and confusing to anyone not familiar with the system of physics authored by Dewey B. Larson. Don't be discouraged, since Larsonian physics is far from well known. Just keep reading and by session 30, you will be back on firm metaphysical ground. After finishing book 2 and going through book 1 again, book 1 will seem a lot clearer.

(I even wrote these books in such a way to make it more understandable than the transcripts of the Law of One books and cut straight to the facts, taking out all the unnecessary and repetitive conversations, which condensed it down in a much easier to read book).

The Ra contact continued for 106 sessions which were printed into four books in The Law of One series. The fifth book was all conversations with Ra I thought to be of significance, so I included those notes in book #5.

Session 27: 2-21-1981

Intelligent Infinity equals one concept. To attempt to divide intelligent infinity is like attempting to divide the word faith.

Intelligent Infinity is unity. This unity is all that there is. This unity has a potential and kinetic. The potential is intelligent infinity. Tapping this potential will yield work. This work has been called by Ra, intelligent energy.

The nature of this work is dependent upon the particular distortion of free will which in turn is the nature of a particular intelligent energy of kinetic focus of the potential of unity or that which is all.

The concept of work is universal in application, as Ra uses it. Intelligent infinity has a rhythm or flow as of a giant heart beginning with the central sun, the presence of the flow inevitable as a tide of beingness without polarity, without finity; the vast and silent all beating outward, outward, focusing outward and inward until the focuses are complete. The intelligence or consciousness of foci have reached a state where their spiritual nature or mass calls them inward, inward, inward until all is coalesced. This is the rhythm of reality.

Intelligent infinity has no difference, potential or kinetic, in unity.

The basic rhythms of intelligent infinity are totally without distortion of any kind. The rhythms are clothed in mystery, for they are being itself. From this undistorted unity appears a potential in relation to intelligent energy.

In this way you may observe the term to be somewhat two-sided, one use of the term: the undistorted unity- being without any kinetic or potential side.

The other application of this term Ra uses undifferentiatedly (similarly) of the vast potential tapped into by foci or focuses of energy is intelligent energy.

Loves comes from an infinite strength of unity, the finite qualities being chosen by the particular nature of this primal movement.

The first distortion of intelligent infinity (of the Law of One) is the distortion called free will. In this distortion of the Law of One it is recognized that the Creator will know Itself.

The Creator then grants for this knowing the concept of total freedom of choice in the ways of knowing.

The experiences are the distortion of the Law of Free will or the Way of Confusion.

The Second distortion is love. Love must be defined against the background of intelligent infinity/unity/the One Creator with the primal distortion of free will. Love is the type of energy of an extremely high order which causes intelligent energy to be formed from the potential of intelligent infinity. This then may be seen to be an object rather than an activity, and the principle of this extremely strong energy focus being worshiped as the Creator instead of unity or oneness from which all Love emanates.

The vibration or density of love or understanding is not used in the same sense as the second distortion of love. The distortion of Love being the great activator and primal co-Creator of various creations using intelligent infinity.

The vibration of love being the density in which those who have learned to do a "loving" activity without significant distortion, then seek ways of light or wisdom. Then love comes into light in the sense of the activity of unity in its free will. Love uses light and has the power to direct light in its distortions. Thus, vibratory complexes recapitulate (repeats) in reverse the great creation in its unity, thus showing the rhythm or flow of the great heartbeat.

The physics of Dewey Larson says all is motion which we can take as vibration, and that vibration is pure vibration and is not physical in way or in any form or density. The first product of that vibration is the photon or particle of light. Love creates light.

Ra says each Love, the prime movers, comes from one frequency. This frequency is unity. It is perhaps a strength than a frequency, this strength being infinite, the finite qualities being chosen by the particular nature of this primal movement.

(Love comes from an infinite strength of unity, the finite qualities being chosen by this primal movement of Love.)

This vibration is pure motion and pure love. It is nothing that is yet condensed to form any type of density of illusion. This Love then creates by this process of vibration a photon, which is the basic particle of light. This photon then, by added vibrations and rotation, further condenses into particles of the densities we experience.

The light which forms the densities has color. This color is divided into seven categories.

The nature of vibratory patterns of our universe is dependent upon the configurations placed upon the original material or light by the focus or Love using Its intelligent energy to create a certain pattern of illusions or densities in order to satisfy Its own intelligent estimate of a method of knowing Itself. Thus, the colors, are as straight, or narrow, or necessary as is possible to express, given the will of love.

Session 28: 2-22-1981

There's one particular Logos, or Love, or focus of this Creator which has chosen Its natural laws and ways of expressing them mathematically.

The one undifferentiated (identical) Intelligent infinity, unpolarized, full and whole, is the macrocosm (the whole universe) of the mystery-clad being. Ra consists of the messengers of the Law of One. Unity cannot be specified by any physics but only become activated or potentiated (increase the power of or effectiveness of) intelligent infinity due to the catalyst of free will. The understandings Ra has to share begin and end in mystery.

The nature of the vibratory patterns of our universe is dependent upon the configurations placed upon the original material or light by the focus of Love using Its intelligent energy to create a certain pattern of illusions or densities in order to satisfy Its own intelligent estimate of a method of knowing Itself. The potential which then through catalyst forms the kinetic.

Ra: "This information is a natural progression of inspection of the kinetic shape of your environment. You may understand each color or ray as being a very specific and accurate portion of intelligent energy's representation of intelligent infinity, each ray having been previously inspected in other regards.

This information may be of aid here. We speak now non-specifically to increase the depth of your conceptualization (or your own idea) of the nature of what is. The universe in which you live is recapitulation (summary) in each part of intelligent infinity. Thus, you will see the same patterns repeated in physical and metaphysical areas; the rays or portions of light being, those areas of what you may call the physical illusion which rotate, vibrate, or are of a nature that may be counted or categorized in rotation manner in space/time as described by Dewey; some substances having various of the rays in a physical manifestation visible to the eye, this being apparent in the nature of your crystallized minerals which you count as precious, the ruby being red and so forth."

Light occurred as a consequence of vibration which is a consequence of Love. This light can condense into material into our density, into all of our chemical elements because of rotations of the vibration at quantized units or intervals of angular velocity.

The enabling functional focus of Love causes light to condense into our physical or chemical elements from rotational vibrations of angular velocity. The energy of Love is an ordering nature. It orders in a cumulative way from greater to lesser so that when Its universe is complete, the manner of development of each detail is inherent in the living light and thus will develop in such and such a way. Our universe having been well studied in an empirical (verifiable by observation or experiential) fashion by scientists and understood or visualized, with greater accuracy by understandings or visualizations of Dewey.

An individualized portion of consciousness is in the area of creation itself.

Ra: "You remain carefully in the area of creation itself. In this process by which free will acts upon potential intelligent infinity to become focused intelligent energy takes place without the space/time of which you are so aware as it is your continuum experience.

The experience or existence of space/time comes into being after the individuation process of Logos or Love has been completed and the physical universe has coalesced (come together to form one mass) or begun to draw inward while moving outward to the extent that which you call your sun bodies have in their turn created timeless chaos coalescing into planets, these vortices of intelligent energy spending a large amount of first density in a timeless state, the space/time realization being one of the learn/teachings of this density of beingness."

A unit of consciousness, an individualized unit of consciousness creates a unit of the creation. One individualized consciousness creates one galaxy of stars with many millions of stars in it. The possibilities are infinite. Thus, a Logos may create a solar system or it may create billions of solar systems. What we call solar system, such as our sun and 8-9 planets, Ra calls galaxy.

Our Milky Way Galaxy is a strong Logos with approximately 250 billion solar system for Its creation. The laws or physical ways of this creation will remain constant.

We live in a lenticular Milky Way galaxy, or Star system which many people call galaxy with approximately 250 billion other suns like our own was created by a single Logos (Love/Universe).

There are many individualized portions of consciousness in this lenticular galaxy. This Logos then subdivided into more individualization of consciousness. This understanding by the questioner Ra said was perceptive and an apparent paradox.

The apparent paradox: It would seem that if one Logos creates intelligent energy ways for a large system there would not be the necessity or possibility of the further sub-Logos differentiation. However, within limits, this is precisely the case.

Ra: "In each beginning there is the beginning from infinite strength. Free will acts as a catalyst. Beings begin to form the universes. Consciousness then begins to have the potential to experience. The potentials of experience are created as a part of intelligent energy and are fixed before experience begins.

However, there is always, due to free will acting infinitely upon the creation, a great variation in initial responses to intelligent energy's potential. Thus, almost immediately the foundations of the hierarchical nature of beings begins to manifest as some portions of consciousness or awareness learn through experience in a much more efficient (or faster) manner."

Therefore, there is individualized consciousness in our lenticular galaxy that learns faster through experience and almost immediately the foundations of the hierarchical nature of beings begin so there is always mixture in densities of intelligent consciousness in the galaxy.

There are some portions of consciousness that learn more quickly and are more efficient in learning. There's a function of the will of attraction to the upward spiraling line of light.

When this major galaxy was created, the eight densities were created as well. However, the 8th density functions also as the beginning density of first density, in its latter stages, of the next octave of densities.

Ra can speak of their experiences and understandings in limited ways. However, they cannot speak in firm knowledge of all the creations. They know only that they are infinite, so they assume an infinite number of octaves.

Their own teachers impressed upon them that there is a mystery-clad unity of creation in which all consciousness periodically coalesces (joins together into one mass) and again begins. Ra assumes an infinite progression though they understand it to be cyclical in nature and clad (clothed) in mystery.

When the galaxy is formed by the Logos, electrical polarity in the way Larson stipulated (specified) its meaning but also in the metaphysical sense. There was also polarity in consciousness.

All is potentially available from the beginning of our physical space/time, it then being the function of consciousness complexes (of free will) to begin to use the physical materials to gain experience to then polarize in a metaphysical sense. The potentials for this are not created by the experiencer but by intelligent energy.

The process of creation, after the original creation of the galaxy, is continued by further individualization of the consciousness of the Logos so that there are many, many portions of the individualized consciousness creating further items for experience all over the galaxy.

Within the guidelines or ways of the Logos, the sub-Logos may find various means of differentiating experiences without removing or adding to these ways.

Session 29: 2-23-1981

Our sun is a physical manifestation of a sub-Logos.

The sub-Logos of our solar entity differentiated (recognized the difference between) some experiential components within the patterns of intelligent energy set in motion by the Logos which created the basic conditions and vibratory rates consistent throughout our major galaxy.

Our sun is a sub-Logos of the Logos of our major Milky Way Galaxy.

A sub-sub-Logos is you, a mind/body/spirit complex.

Every entity that exists would be some type of sub or sub-sub-Logos, down to the limits of any observation, for the entire creation is alive.

A planet is named only as Logos if It is working in harmonic fashion with entities or mind/body complexes upon Its surface or within Its electromagnetic field.

Entities through the level of planets have the strength of intelligent infinity through the use of free will, going through the actions of beingness. The creation of the One Infinite Creator does not have the positive or negative terms of polarity.

It is only when the planet begins harmonically interacting with mind/body/spirit complexes, that planets take on distortions due to the thought complexes of entities interacting with the planetary entity, such as planet Earth.

Planets in first density are in a timeless state to begin with. The process by which space/time (physical) comes into time/space (non-physical) continuum form is a function of the careful building of an entire or whole plan of vibratory rates, densities, and potentials. When this plan has coalesced (or combined into one mass) in the thought complexes of Love, then the physical manifestations begin to appear; this first manifestation stage being awareness or consciousness.

At the point at which this coalescence (merging to form one whole) is at the livingness or beingness point, the point or fountainhead of beginning, space/time (physical reality) then begins to unroll its scroll of livingness.

Love creates the vibration in space/time in order to form the photon. The Logos creates all densities. Quantized incremental rotations of the vibrations show up as material of these densities.

<u>Gravity</u> is the pressing towards the inner light/love, the seeking towards the spiral line of light which progresses towards the Creator. This is a manifestation of a spiritual event or condition of livingness.

The gravity on our moon is less than it is on Earth. The metaphysical and physical are inseparable. The phenomenon is able to calculate the gravitational force of most objects due to various physical aspects such as mass. The physical aspects of gravity correspond and is equally important to the metaphysical nature of gravity.

The attractive force, gravity, is the pressing outward force towards the Creator is greater spiritually upon the entity Venus due to the greater degree of success at seeking the Creator.

This point only becomes important when all of creation in its infinity has reached a spiritual gravitational mass of sufficient nature, the entire creation infinitely coalesces (coming together to form one mass); the light seeking and finding Its source and thusly ending the creation and beginning a new creation, such as a black hole with its conditions of infinitely great mass at the zero point from which no light may be seen as it has been absorbed.

The black hole that manifests third density is the physical complex manifestation of the spiritual or metaphysical state of the environmental material succeeding in uniting with unity or with the Creator.

When Earth is fully into fourth density, there will be a greater spiritual gravity, thus causing a denser illusion.

The increase in spiritual gravity measurable by existing instrumentation would be and will be statistical in nature only and not significant.

As the rotations of the vibration which is light forms the atoms that forms creation, they coalesce (or combine together) in a certain manner sometimes. The precise crystalline structure formation from intelligent energy shows that it is possible by some technique to tap intelligent energy and bring it into the physical illusion by working through the crystalline structure must be charged by a correspondingly crystallized or regularized or balanced mind/body/spirit complex.

Each mind/body/spirit complex is a unique portion of the One Creator.

The necessity is for the mind/body/spirit complex to be of a certain balance, this balance enabling it to reach a set level lack of distortion. The critical difficulties are unique for each mind/body/spirit complex due to the experiential distillations (clear understanding of the past) which in total are the violet-ray beingness of each entity.

This balance is what is necessary for work to be done in seeking the gateway to intelligent infinity through the use of crystals or through any other use. No two mind/body/spirit crystallized natures are the same. The distortion requirements, vibrationally speaking, are set.

Reading the violet ray of an entity determines whether the entity could use crystals to tap intelligent energy. It is possible for 5th density or above to do this.

The gateway to intelligent infinity is born of the sympathetic vibration (occurring when an object vibrates in response to a sound wave that has the same frequency) in balanced state accompanying the will to serve, the will to seek.

The use of crystal in physical manifestation is that use wherein the entity of crystalline nature charges the regularized physical crystal with this seeking, enabling it to vibrate harmonically and also become the catalyst or gateway whereby intelligent infinity may become intelligent energy, this crystal serving as an analog (comparable) of the violet ray of the mind/body/spirit in relatively undistorted form.

There are things Ra considers not efficacious (not effective) to tell people due to possible infringement upon free will. Entities of the Confederation have done this in the past. The uses of the crystal include the uses for healing, for power, and even for the development of lifeforms. Ra feels that it is unwise to offer instruction at this time on specific uses of crystals, as people have shown a tendency to use powerful sources of power for disharmonious reasons.

Our particular Logos of our major galaxy has used a large portion of its coalesced material to reflect the beingness of the Creator. In this way there is much of our galactic system which does not have the progression of developing into higher density planets, but dwells spiritually as a portion of the Logos. Of those entities upon which consciousness dwells there is a variety of time/space periods during which the higher densities of experience are attained by consciousness.

Session 30: 2-24-1981

Creation is a single entity or unity. If only a single entity exists, then the only concept of service is the concept of service to self. If this entity subdivides, then the concept of service of one of its parts to one of its other parts is born. From this, springs the equality of service to self or to others.

Polarities begin to be explored only at the point when a third density entity becomes aware of the possibility of choice between the concept or distortion of service to self or service to others. This marks the end of the unselfconscious or innocent phase of conscious awareness.

Mind, body, and spirit are all simplistic terms which equal a complex of energy focuses:

-The body- being the material of the density which you experience at a given space/time or time/space. This complex of materials being available for distortions of physical manifestation.

-The mind- is a complex which reflects the in-pourings of the spirit and the up-pourings of the body complex. It contains feelings, emotions and intellectual thoughts in its more conscious complexities.

Ra: "Moving further down the tree of mind we see the intuition which is of the nature of the mind more in contact or in tune with the total beingness complex. Moving down to the roots of mind we find the progression of consciousness which gradually turns from the personal to the racial memory, to the cosmic influxes, and thus become a direct contactor of that shuttle which we call the spirit complex.

This spirit complex is the channel whereby the in-pourings from all of the various universal, planetary, and personal in-pourings may be funneled into the roots of consciousness and whereby consciousness may be funneled to the gateway of intelligent infinity through the balanced intelligent energy of body and mind.

You will see by this series of definitive statements that mind, body, and spirit are inextricably (impossible to separate) intertwined and cannot continue, one without the other. Thus, we refer to the mind/body/spirit complex rather than attempting to deal with them separately, for the work that you do during your experiences is done through the interaction of these three components, not through any one (of these)."

Upon our physical death from third density and this particular incarnative experience, we lose this chemical body. Immediately after the loss of this chemical body we maintain a mind/body/spirit complex.

The physical body complex we now associate with the term being but manifestation of a more dense and intelligently informed and powerful body complex.

During the transition that humans call death there is a great loss of mind complex due to that fact that much of the activity of the mental nature that we are aware during our experience of this space/time continuum is as much of a surface illusion as the chemical body complex.

((In other words, there is a great loss of mind complex from the veil of forgetting between the conscious and unconscious mind that creates an illusion of separation of our experiential awareness on Earth. Then, it transitions to true reality after death of what true reality is. This is also what the illusion means.))

In other terms, nothing whatsoever of importance is lost; the character or pure distillation of emotions and biases or distortions and wisdoms becoming obvious for the first time. These pure emotions and wisdoms and bias/distortions being, for the most part, either ignored or underestimated during physical life experience.

The spiritual channel is then much opened due to the lack of necessity for the forgetting characteristic of third density.

Mind, body, spirit originates through evolution. The consciousness in first density being without movement, a random thing. Ra says whether we call this a mind or body complex is a semantic (interpretation) problem. A semantic problem is technically meaning the same thing, but each entity may analyze and study each word or phrase for their meaning. Ra calls it mind/body complex recognizing always that in the simplest iota of this complex exists in its entirely the One Infinite Creator.

The mind/body complex in 2nd density discovers the growing and turning towards the light, thus awakening what you may call the spirit complex, that which intensifies the upward spiraling towards the love and light of the Infinite Creator.

The addition of this spirit complex having existed potentially from the beginning of space/time, perfects itself by graduation into third density. When the mind/body/spirit complex becomes aware of the possibility of service to self or other self, then the mind/body/spirit complex is activated.

On Earth during 2nd density there was habitation during the same space/time of bipedal entities (beings standing upright) with the dinosaurs. These two types of entities seemed very incompatible with each other. They both inhabited the same space/time during second density because of the workings of free will as applied to evolution. There are paths the mind/body complex follows in an attempt to survive, to reproduce, and to seek in its fashion what is unconsciously felt as the potential for growth. These two arenas or paths of development being two among many.

=>Bisexual reproduction first originates in 2nd density.

=>The second density is the groundwork being laid for third density work. In this way it may be seen that the basic mechanism of reproduction capitulates (surrenders) into a vast potential in third density for service to other self and to self; this being not only by functions of energy transfer, but also by the various services performed due to close contact of those magnetically attracted to one another; these entities thus having the opportunities for many types of service unavailable to the independent entity.

Increasing the opportunity of the experience of the One Creator is the key that occurs in all densities.

The bisexual reproduction or the philosophy of it plays a part in the spiritual growth of second density entities in isolated instances due to efficient perceptions upon the part of entities or species. For the greater part, by far, this is not the case in second density, the spiritual potentials being those of third density.

Metaphysical descriptions of planets within our solar system that have individual mind/body/spirit complexes have been, are or shall be experienced are listed below. The other planets not listed are part of the Logos.

Venus-This planetary sphere was of rapid evolution. It is Ra's native Earth and the rapidity of the progress of mind/body/spirit complexes upon its surface was due to harmonious interaction.

Mars- This entity, as already discussed, was stopped mid-third density, thus being unable to continue in progression due to lack of hospitable conditions upon the surface. This planet shall be undergoing healing for some of our space/time millennia.

Earth- This planet which we dwell on has a metaphysical history well known to us in early portions of this content.

Saturn- Was a great affinity (fondness) for the infinite intelligence and thus it has been dwelled upon in its magnetic fields of time/space by those who wish to protect our solar system. (Council of 9 or the Guardians).

Uranus- Is slowly moving through first density and has the potential of moving through all densities.

Therefore, Mercury, Jupiter, Neptune and Pluto not listed by Ra is because these planets are a part of the Logos and do not have living entities on them. Even Uranus in first density has entities in first density such as water, Earth, wind and fire that still has potential to evolve through all densities.

These planets, however, is a part of the major galactic system dwelling spiritually as part of the Logos.

The Logos has distributed itself throughout our galactic system. However, the time/space continua of some of our more central sun systems are much further advanced.

The spiritual density or mass of those more towards the center of our galaxy is known. However, this is due to the varying timelessness states during which planets may coalesce (come together to form one mass), this process of space/time beginning occurring earlier as you approach the center of the galactic spiral.

Session 31: 2-25-1981

Sexual Positive or Negative Energy Transfers or Blockages:

-1st energy center Transfer= Red ray. Random transfer having only to do with our reproductive system.

-The orange and yellow ray=Attempts to have sexual intercourse and creates a blockage if only one entity vibrates in this area, thus causing the entity vibrating sexually in this area to have a never-ending appetite for this activity (by not giving their partner an orgasm). What these vibratory levels are seeking is green ray activity.

The possibility of orange or yellow ray energy transfer polarizes negative if one is being seen as an object rather than other self; the other seeing itself as plunderer or master of the situation.

(I always knew it seemed wrong for someone to just see me as an object, with no love and just wanted to master the situation. Just because they were "straight" didn't make it positively oriented. It always felt more negative for people just to use each other for sex and view the others as an object instead of caring about them, getting to know the person and forming a loving relationship with them. The loving sexual relationship would be the green ray positive activity. That's why I chose females more often because of the love they had for me, whereas most guys just viewed me as an object and I didn't want that. I wanted the positive green ray sexual polarity and gender didn't matter, just the romantic and emotional connection did to me.)

Ra says in green ray there are two possibilities.

One: If both vibrate in green ray there will be a mutually strengthening energy transfer, the negative (female) drawing the energy from the roots of the beingness through the energy centers, thus being physically revitalized.

Two: The positive (male polarity) as deemed in our illusion, finding in its energy transfer an inspiration which satisfies and feeds the spirit portion of the body/mind/spirit complex, thus both being polarized and releasing the excess each has in abundance by nature of intelligent energy. That is, negative/intuitive, positive/physical energies; this energy transfer being blocked if one or both entities have fear of possession or of being possessed sexually, of desiring sexual possession or desiring being possessed physically or sexually by the other.

The other green-ray possibility is that of one entity offering green-ray energy, the other not offering energy of the universal love energy, this resulting in a blockage of energy for the one not green ray; the green ray being polarizing slightly towards service to others. The one not acting sexually in service to the other in universal love may gain negative polarity.

The blue ray energy transfer is somewhat rare among people on Earth, at least in 1981, but is of great aid due to energy transfers involved in becoming able to express the self without reservation or fear.

The indigo-ray transfer is extremely rare among our people on Earth. This is the sacramental portion of the body complex where contact may be made through violet ray with intelligent infinity. No blockages may occur at these latter two levels due to the fact that if both entities are not ready for this energy it is not visible and neither transfer nor blockage may take place. It is as though the distributor were removed from a powerful engine.

Energy transfer implies the release of potential energies across a potentiated (more effective) space. The sexual energy transfers occur due to the polarizations of two mind/body/spirit complexes, each of which have some potential difference one to the other. The nature of the transfer of energy or of blockage is the interaction of these two potentials. A transfer taking place is like a circuit being closed. You may also see this activity, as all experiential activities, as the Creator experiencing Itself.

Ra: "This is 'one appropriate' way the Creator knowing Itself, for in each interaction, no matter what the distortion, the Creator is experiencing Itself. The bisexual (dual) knowing of the Creator by Itself has the potential for two advantages.

Firstly, in the green-ray activated being there is the potential for a direct and simple analog (comparable) of joy, the spiritual or metaphysical nature which exists in intelligent energy. This is a great aid to comprehension of a truer nature of beingness. The other potential advantage of bisexual reproductive acts is the possibility of a sacramental understanding or connection with the gateway to intelligent infinity, for with appropriate preparation, work in magic may be done and experiences of intelligent infinity may be had. Bisexual reproduction is the reproduction between two people, it has nothing to do with being bisexually attracted to both male and female. Even though it is not wrong if one was. It's the free will choice of each entity who they are attracted to, as long as they do not infringe on the free will choices of others.

The positively oriented individuals concentrating upon this method of reaching intelligent infinity, then, through the seeking or the act of will, are able to direct this infinite intelligence to the work these entities desire to do, whether it be knowledge of service or ability to heal or whatever service to others is desired.

These are two advantages of this particular method of the Creator experiencing Itself. As we have said before, the corollary (immediate consequence) of the strength of this particular energy transfer is that it opens the door to the individual mind/body/spirit complexes' desire to serve in an infinite number of ways of an other-self, thus polarizing towards positive."

Ra: "The sexual energy transfers include the red ray transfer which is random and which is a function of the second-density attempt to grow, to survive. This is a proper function of the sexual interaction. The offspring, as you call the incarnated entity, takes on the mind/body/spirit complex opportunity offered by this random act or event called the fertilization of egg by seed which causes an entity to have the opportunity to then enter this density as an incarnate entity.

This gives the two who were engaged in this bisexual reproductive energy transfer the potential for great service in this area of the nurturing of the small entities (children) as it gains in experience.

It shall be of interest at this point to note that there is always the possibility of using these opportunities to polarize towards the negative, and this has been aided by the gradual building up over many thousands of your years of social complex distortions which create a tendency towards confusion or baffling of the service to others aspect of this energy transfer and subsequent opportunities for service to other selves."

There is always the red-ray energy transfer due to the nature of the body complex. This random result of energy transfer will be the possibility of fertilization at a given time in a given pairing of entities each entity being undistorted in any vital sense by the yellow or orange ray energies; thus, the gift being given freely, no payment requested either of body, of mind, or of the spirit. The green ray is complete universality of love. This is a given without expectation of return.

A couple having a child or not is random within certain limits. If an entity has reached the seniority where it chooses the basic structure of the life experience, they may choose to incarnate in a physical body not capable of reproduction. Thus, some entities choose to be infertile. Other entities, through free will, make use of various devices to insure nonfertility. Except for these conditions, the condition is random.

Ra used the term magnetic attraction to indicate that in our bisexual natures there is polarity of male/female polarization of each entity, be each entity biologically male or female. Thus, the magnetism which two entities with the appropriate balance, male/female verses female/male polarity, meeting and feeling the attraction which polarized forces will exert, one upon the other.

This is the strength of the bisexual mechanism. It does not take an act of will to decide to feel attraction for one who is oppositely polarized sexually. (Gay people may feel opposite attraction in the sense of one person being feminine and the other being more masculine.) It will occur in an inevitable sense, giving the free flow of energy a proper avenue. This avenue may be blocked by some distortion toward a belief/condition stating to the entity that this attraction is not desired.

However, the basic mechanism functions as simply as would the magnet of the iron.

Homosexual entities have experienced many incarnations as biological male and as biological female. This would not suggest what you call homosexuality in an active phase if not for the difficult vibratory condition of your planetary sphere. There is what you may call great aura infringement among your crowded urban areas in your more populous countries.

Ra: "The bisexual reproductive urge has as its goal, not only the simple reproductive function, but more especially the desire to serve others being awakened by this activity.

In an over-crowded situation where each mind/body/spirit complex is under constant bombardment from other selves it is understandable that those who are especially sensitive would not feel the desire to be of service-to-other selves. This would also increase the probability of a lack of desire or a blockage of the red ray reproductive energy.

In an uncrowded atmosphere this same entity would, through the stimulus of feeling the solitude about it, then have much more desire to seek out someone to whom it may be of service, thus regularizing the sexual reproductive function."

Jordyn says: "There are those LGBT people of seniority of vibration or certain Wanderers who many not have the desire for reproduction, thus, not needing the opposite gender for reproduction purposes. Or there are those LGBT people who do want to reproduce, but only with someone they love, thus, only pursuing an emotional connection that may be male or female. They want to serve the one they love and that person may be of the same gender. As many males are attracted to females' femininity. Certain LGBT people may be attracted to the masculine energy and vice versa. I know with me personally I want to find that romantic and emotional connection. I've mainly felt the emotional connection with other females so that's who I go for. I can still serve her through reproducing with her. It's about love, not using the opposite gender to produce a baby. That would be selfish in my eyes, or it's selfish if someone pursues the opposite gender for sexual reasons, without any emotional attachment to them."

<u>Kathryn's question Channeled:</u> "Is transgender okay to transition medically from female to male?"

<u>Answer:</u> "The transition from one physical vehicle is a complex matter of an entities free will and unique life stream, so maybe furthering their path by such transition while others may not. It is important that the aspect of evaluation of each case by the polarization of an entities inner motivations and intensions is important. Furthermore, the goal is to ever align with the premise of service-to-others expansion of the one creation. As the highest wisdom is to see the One Creator within all beings and trust in the perfect unfolding of each entities journey amid the greater cosmic plan." In conclusion, it is each person's free will to choose whether they want to transition or not. Their inner motivation and intensions is what's important and whether its aligned with serving others or not. Therefore, if they still desire to serve others after their transition, then their free will choice to transition is okay as the One Creator is in all beings, even those that transition.

<u>No gender on certain planets:</u>

Certain planets do not have genders. Our planet has masculinity, femininity and some are in the middle. Those that incarnated into a male body is for the purpose of balancing masculine energy and mastering the masculine energy, as the past incarnation cycle most likely was a feminine type. Because the lessons of balancing the masculine and feminine is the most important lesson that each person has to learn. There are also those in the middle who are here to learn the lessons of masculine and feminine at the same time (I believe that would be me).

Kathryn channels and asks: "How is sexuality a false sense of identity?"

Higher Self answer: "At birth a sexuality isn't known. The societal complex comes up with these names, therefore sexuality is a false sense of identity. If the entity is devoid of any type of physical bodily complex or any type of thought form, there will be no objectification and identification with any type of concept, which indeed may be considered as a false sense of identity, like the naming symbolism is a false sense of identity, since many entities are named after birth. However, at the time of birth the naming concept is not present.

Indeed, the symbolism of names can also be considered as a false sense of identity. And any aspect generated by the mind complex is a false sense of identity. Which takes the self away from the true nature of reality of unification of all beings."

Kathryn channels and asks: "Is homosexuality okay if they don't have an emotional connection with the opposite gender?"

Higher Self answer: "We must firstly state that this is primarily the choice of the entities involved. It is the free will which entities can experience and explore if they desire."

Kathryn channels and asks: "Will homosexuality lower an entities positive polarity?" (This question is important, because 51% positive polarity is needed to graduate to the 4th Density New Earth in 2030.)

Higher Self answer: "The answer is incorrect. We must state that the aspect of homosexuality does not have any effect on an entity's polarization, but it's actions which determine the positive polarity or negative polarity of the entity." (Therefore, it's the actions that determines the positive or negative polarity, not the sexuality. Thus, gay people will be in the 4th density New Earth who are at least 51% positively oriented service to others.)

Book 2 continues:

A male would have had roughly 65% of its incarnations in the sexual/biological body complex of a female to have a highly homosexual orientation in this incarnation, and vice versa with females having roughly 65 percent of its past incarnations as a biological male body to be of a highly homosexual orientation.

Ra: "It is to be noted at this juncture that although it is much more difficult, it is possible in this type of association for an entity to be of great service to another in fidelity and sincere green ray love of a nonsexual nature."

Kathryn says: "It's important to note that homosexuality is not wrong and not a sin. LGBT people can still make the 4th density harvest of 51% or more service-to-others. I'm LGBT and I was 65% positive in 2023 and now 68% positive in 2024, so I'm definitely harvestable for 4th

density even when I date women. By June 2024 my positive polarity was 87%."

Ra also states that masturbation and homosexuality is often innocent exercises in curiosity.

Due to solitary sexual experiences, in most cases it is unlikely masturbation has an imprinting effect upon later experiences. This is similarly true of some of the encounters which might be seen as homosexual among those of earlier sexual experiences. That these are often innocent exercises in curiosity.

However, the first sexual experience someone is involved in will indeed imprint upon the entity for that life experience a set of preferences. Therefore, if the first sexual experience is of the same gender, that entity may prefer the same gender for the remainder of their life.

Just as the Confederation attempts to beam their love and light whenever given the opportunity, including sexual opportunities, so the Orion group will use an opportunity to beam negatively orientated energy to influence those sexually towards service-to-self or if the entity is negatively oriented, the negative beings will continue to influence these beings towards greater service-to-self even through sexual acts.

The sexual energy buildup is extremely unlikely to occur without sexual bias from the entity. It would take an entity with the potential for sexual activity to experience a sexual energy buildup.

Even negatively oriented sexual experiences have the potential for sexual energy buildup.

Even negatively oriented sexual experiences have the potential for sexual energy buildup. The choice of stimulus is the choice of the entity. Members of the Third Reich had reports of sexual gratification from the observation of the gassing and killing of entities in the gas chambers. These entities were strongly polarized orange ray, thus finding the energy blockage of power over others, the putting to death being the ultimate power over others; this then being expressed in a sexual manner, though solitary. This is negatively oriented. In this case the desire would continue unabated (persistently) and be virtually unquenchable (unsatisfied).

The entire spectrum of sexual practices among people on Earth, that those who experience gratification from domination over others either from rape or other means of domination. In each case is an example of energy blockage sexual in its nature. Of course, negatively oriented as well.

The cause of this is not Orion. It is the free choice of people on Earth.

The sexual energy transfers and blockages are more of a manifestation or example that is more fundamental than the other way about. Therefore, as people become open to bellicosity (which is a person's tendency to fight and the greed of ownership, these various distortions then began to filter down through the tree of mind into sexual expressions. Thus, these sexual energy blockages, though Orion influenced and intensified, are basically the product of the beingness chosen freely by people.

The racial memory contains all that has been experienced. Thus, there is some contamination even of the sexual, this showing mostly in our own culture on Earth as the various predispositions to adversary relationships or marriages, rather than the free giving one to another in the love and the light of the Infinite Creator.

Session 32: 2-27-1981

Orange ray activation is that influence or vibratory pattern wherein the mind/body/spirit expresses its power on an individual basis. Power over individuals may be seen to be orange ray. This ray has been quite intense among people on Earth on an individual basis. You may see in this ray treating other selves as non-entities, slaves, or chattel, thus giving other selves no status whatsoever.

The yellow ray is a focal and very powerful ray and concerns the entity in relation to groups, societies or large numbers of people. This yellow ray vibration is at the heart of bellicose actions (which is someone wishing to fight or start a war) in which one group of entities feels the necessity and right of dominating other groups of entities and bending their will to the wills of the masters.

The negative path uses a combination of the yellow ray and the orange ray in its polarization patterns. These rays, used in a dedicated fashion, will bring about a contact with intelligent infinity. The usual nature of sexual interaction, if one is yellow or orange in primary vibratory patterns, is one of blockage and then insatiable hunger due to the blockage. When there are two selves vibrating in this area the potential for polarization through sexual interaction is begun, one entity experiencing the pleasure of humiliation and slavery or bondage, the other experiencing the pleasure of mastery and control over another entity. This way a sexual energy transfer of negative polarity is experienced.

Green ray energy transfer is the turning point sexually as well as in each other mode of experience. The green ray may then be turned outward, the entity then giving rather receiving. The first giving beyond green ray is the giving of acceptance or freedom, thus allowing the recipient of blue ray energy transfer the opportunity for a feeling of being accepted, which frees that other self to express itself to the giver of this ray.

Once green ray energy transfer has been achieved by two mind/body/spirits complexes in mating, the further rays are available without both entities having the necessity to progress equally.

A blue ray vibrating entity or indigo ray vibrating entity whose other ray vibrations are clear may share that energy with the green ray other self, thus acting as catalyst for the continued learn/teaching of the other self. Until an other-self reaches green ray, such energy transfer through the rays is not possible.

The indigo ray is the ray of awareness of Creator as self; thus, one whose indigo ray vibrations have been activated can offer the energy transfer of Creator to Creator. This is the beginning of the sacramental nature of the bisexual reproductive act. It is unique in bearing the allness, the wholeness, the unity in its offering to other self.

The violet ray, just as the red ray, is constant in the sexual experience. Its experience by other self may be distorted or completely ignored or not apprehended by other self. However, this ray, being the sum and substance of mind/body/spirit complex, surrounds and informs any action by a mind/body/spirit complex.

The rays have such a different meaning in the next density and the higher densities. Energy transfers only take place in fourth, fifth and sixth densities. These are still a polarized nature. However, due to the ability of these densities to see harmonies between individuals, these entities choose mates that are harmonious, thus allowing constant energy transfer and the propagation (increase in individuals or spreading) of the body complexes each density uses. Even creating more humans. The process is different in the fifth and sixth density. However, it is in these cases still based upon polarity.

The seventh density does not have the sexual energy exchange as it is unnecessary to recycle body complexes.

Ra: "Fourth-density Wanderers, of which there are not many, will tend to choose those entities which seem to be full of love or in need of love. There is the great possibility/probability of entities making errors in judgment due to the compassion with which other selves are viewed.

The fifth-density Wanderer is one who is not tremendously affected by the stimulus of the various rays of other self and in its own way offers itself when a need is seen. Such entities are not likely to engage in the custom of your people called marriage and are very likely to feel an aversion to childbearing and child raising due to the awareness of the impropriety of the planetary vibrations (which is the dishonest or unacceptable behavior on the planet) relative to the harmonious vibrations of the density of light.

The sixth density, whose means of propagation (or reproduction) you may liken to what you call fusion, is likely to refrain, to a great extent, from the bisexual reproductive programming of the bodily complex and instead seek out those with whom the sexual energy transfer is of the complete fusion nature in so far as this is possible in manifestation in third density."

The entire creation is of the One Creator. Thus, the division of sexual activity into the body is an artificial division, all things being seen as sexual equally, the mind, the body, and the spirit; all of which are part of the polarity of the entity. Thus, sexual fusion may be seen with or without sexual intercourse to be the complete melding of the mind, the body and the spirit in what feels to be a constant orgasm of joy and delight in the other's beingness.

The possibility/probability of many Wanderers having considerable problems with 3rd density incarnation being of a different sexual ray energy is rather large. The problem depends upon each unique orientation of each mind/body/spirit complex having this situation or placement of vibratory relativities.

The vibration of the different energy ray colors may be seen to have mathematically straight or narrow steps. These steps may be seen as having boundaries. Within each boundary there are infinite gradations (which is the minute changes) of vibration of color.

As one approaches a boundary, an effort must be made to cross that boundary division of our density. There is also the time/space analogy which may be seen as the color itself in a modified aspect.

The green ray activation is always vulnerable to the yellow or orange ray of possession, this being largely yellow ray but often coming into orange ray.

Fear of possession, desire for possession, fear of being possessed, desire to be possessed are distortions that will cause the deactivation of green-ray energy transfer.

Once the green ray has been achieved, the ability of the entity to enter blue ray is immediate and is only awaiting the efforts of the individual. The indigo ray is opened only through considerable discipline and practice largely having to do with acceptance of self, not only as polarized and balanced self but as Creator and of infinite worth. This will begin to activate the indigo ray.

Session 33: 3-1-1981

(How Ra normally starts each session).

Ra: "I am Ra. I greet you in the love and the light of the One Infinite Creator. I communicate now."

When looking out for the vital energies necessary for non-depletion of the instrument and the contact level: Each entity is responsible for itself. However, Ra would always end a session when the instruments energies was low or the pain level was increasing due to her arthritis. This was to avoid depleting the instrument. The group must voice any concerns if needed. The instrument needs to watch its vital energies, for Ra does not wish to deplete the instrument.

The function of the supporting group may be of protection for the Ra contact and they may energize the instrument and intensify its vital energies.

This supporting group has always provided protection in love and light due to an underlying harmony, thus ensuring the continuation of the narrow band contact. However, the vital energies of either of the supporting members being depleted, the instrument must then use a larger portion of its vital energies, thus depleting itself more than would be profitable on a long-term basis.

How to maintain the best possible condition for maintaining contact: Ra suggests rather than being brave and ignoring a physical weakness that it is good to share the distortion with the group and perhaps remove one opportunity for contact which is very wearying for the instrument, in order that another opportunity might come about in which the instrument is properly supported and feeling better.

Secondly, the work begun in harmony may continue in harmony, thanksgiving and praise of opportunities of the Creator. These are your protections. These are Ra's suggestions. Ra cannot be specific for their free will is the essence of the contact. Ra only states this because of Ra's grasp of the (channeling) group's desires for long-term maintenance of the contact. This is acceptable to Ra.

The color therapy device is the shining of particular colors on the physical body is a somewhat clumsy and variably useful tool for instigating in an entity's mind/body/spirit complex an intensification of energies or vibrations which may be of aid to the entity.

The variableness (changeability) of this device is due to the lack of true colors used and to extreme variation in sensitivity to vibration among our peoples on Earth.

One way of approaching accuracy in color would be passing light through a crystal of the particular color. This is not a great or even visible variation; however, it does make some difference given specific applications.

One could possibly use a prism breaking white light into its spectrum and screening off all parts of the spectrum except what you wish to use by passing it through a slit.

The incarnating entity which has become conscious of the incarnative process and thus programs its own experience may choose the amount of catalyst or the number of lessons it will undertake to experience and to learn from in one incarnation.

Not all is predestined, but there are invisible guidelines shaping events which will function according to this programming. Thus, if one opportunity is missed another will appear until the student of the life experience grasps that a lesson is being offered and undertakes to learn it.

These lessons would be reprogrammed as the life experience continues. Let's say that an entity develops the bias that he actually didn't choose to develop prior to incarnation. It is then possible to program experiences so that he will have an opportunity to alleviate this bias through balancing.

To the best of Ra's knowledge: The orientation or polarization of the mind/body/spirit complex is the cause of the perceptions generated by each entity.

An example observed in your grocery store: The entity ahead of self may be without sufficient funds. One entity may take this opportunity to steal. Another may feel itself a failure. Another may unconcernedly remove the least necessary items, pay for what it can, and go about its business. The one observing may feel compassion. Another observing may feel an insult because of standing next to a poverty-stricken person. Another observing may feel indifference. The other observing may feel generosity. These are analogies (the comparison between two or more things for clarification).

Fourth-density positive has the concept of defensive action, but above fourth density defensive action is not in use due to the wisdom density. The concept of defensive and offensive action is very much in use in our 3rd density Earth.

In each case, an entity able to program experiences may choose the number and the intensity of lessons to be learned. It is possible that an extremely positive oriented entity might program for itself situations testing the ability of self to refrain from defensive action even to the point of physical death of self or other self. This is an intensive lesson and it is not known what entities have programmed. Ra may read the programming if they desire. However, they choose not to because it is an infringement.

The movie, the Ninth Configuration, the Colonel made the decision to defend his friend instead of allowing his friend to be suppressed by the negatively oriented entities. This is an action of 3rd or 4th density seen by the action of Jehoshuah, which many people on Earth refer to as Jesus. Jehoshuah was to be defended by its friends. Jehoshuah reminded its friends to put away the sword. This entity then delivered itself to be put to the physical death. The impulse to protect the loved other self is one which persists through the fourth density, a density abounding in compassion. More than this Ra cannot and need not say.

The planetary catastrophes are a symptom of the difficult harvest rather than a consciously programmed catalyst for harvest. Thus, Ra does not concern themselves with it, for it is random in respect to conscious catalyst such as Ra makes available.

The results of the random catalyst of the Earth changes are also random. Thus, Ra may see probability/possibility vortices going towards positive and negative. However, it will be as it will be. The true opportunities for conscious catalyst are not the Earth changes but the result of the seniority system of incarnations are those who placed in incarnation who have the best chance of using their life experiences to become harvestable.

This seniority system is also used in the service-to-self. Other catalytic influences are the Creator's universe and the self-service for becoming harvestable negatively.

The primary mechanism (or piece in a larger process) for catalytic experience in third density is other self (other beings). Other catalytic influences are the Creator's universe and the self.

The self-acted upon catalytically that produces experience: Firstly, the self-unmanifested. Secondly, the self in relation to the societal self-created by self and other self. Thirdly, the interaction between self and the gadgets, toys, and amusements of the self, other self-invention. Fourthly, the self-relationship with those attributes of war and rumors of war. An example of unmanifested self is physical pain. The self not needing other self in order to manifest or act.

Any interaction betwixt self and other self has whatever potential for catalyst that there exists in the potential difference between self and other self, this moderated and under-girded by the constant fact of the Creator as self and as other self.

The violet ray of the positive fourth density will be tinged with the green, blue, indigo triad of energies. This tinge may be seen as a portion of a rainbow or prism, the rays being quite distinct.

The violet ray of fourth-density negative has in its aura the tinge of red, orange, yellow, these rays being muddied rather than distinct.

Speaking approximately, there is a distinctive difference in the color structure of each density. 5th density is perhaps extremely white in vibration. 6th density is a whiteness which contains a golden quality as you would perceive it; these colors having to do with the blending into wisdom of the compassion learned in fourth density. Then in sixth the blending of wisdom back into a unified understanding of compassion viewed with wisdom. This golden color is not of your spectrum but is alive.

The penetration of the eighth level or intelligent infinity allows a mind/body/spirit complex to be harvested if it wishes at any time/space during the cycle.

Session 34: 3-4-1981

The experience of each entity is unique in its perception of intelligent infinity. Perceptions range from a limitless joy to a strong dedication to service to others while in the incarnated state. The entity which reaches intelligent infinity most often will perceive this experience as one of unspeakable profundity. However, it is not usually for the entity to immediately desire the cessation of the incarnation. Rather the desire to communicate or use this experience to aid others is extremely strong.

Kathryn says: "After learning the general overview of the Law of One. I experienced this feeling, along with my prophecies. This information and my prophecies fulfilled was one of the most long-lasting, exciting feelings I ever felt. It was exciting finally finding the truth and realizing that I'm the first prophet on Earth to speak the 100% truth without the negatively influenced distortions found in half the Bible. Plus, my dreams have been the most accurate in the world as well."

Karma may be called inertia. Those actions put into motion will continue using the ways of balancing until slowed down or stopped. This stoppage of the inertia of an action is through forgiveness. These two concepts are inseparable. (Therefore, karma can be stopped through forgiveness.)

If an entity develops karma in an incarnation, programming sometimes occurs so that they may experience catalysts that will enable the entity to get to a point of forgiveness thereby alleviating the karma.

However, both self and any involved other may, at any time through understanding, acceptance, and forgiveness, ameliorate (improve) these patterns. This is true at any point in an incarnative pattern. Thus, one who has set in motion an action may forgive itself and never again make that error. This also breaks or stops karma.

The catalyst of pain is the most common experience among people on Earth. The pain may be physically more often than it is mental and emotional. In some cases, it's spiritual. This creates a potential for learning, the lessons vary. Almost always these lessons include patience, tolerance and the ability for light touch.

Very often the catalyst for emotional pain, whether it be the physical death of a loved one or other seeming loss, will simply result in the opposite, in a bitterness and impatience, a souring. This is catalyst which has gone awry. In those cases, then there will be additional catalyst provided to offer the unmanifested self-further opportunities for discovering the self as all-sufficient Creator containing all that there is and full of joy.

The unmanifested self is physical pain. The self not needing other self to manifest or act.

The so-called contagious diseases are those second density entities which offer an opportunity of catalyst for the unmanifested self (physical pain). In other words, contagious diseases are second density entities offering catalyst for the self without needing other people to manifest or act.

If this catalyst is unneeded, then these second-density creatures do not have an effect. In each of these generalizations there are anomalies so Ra can't speak to every circumstance but only to the general way of things as you experience them.

Birth defects are a portion of the programming of mind/body/spirit totality manifested in the mind/body/spirit of third density. These defects are planned as limitations which are part of the experience intended by the entity's totality complex. This includes genetic predispositions (which is an increased likelihood of developing a disease).

The unmanifested self may find its lessons with any of the energy influx centers of the mind/body/spirit complex. The societal and self-interactions most often concentrate on the 2nd and 3rd energy centers.

Those most active in attempting to remake or alter society are those working from feelings of being correct personally or having answers that will put power in a more correct configuration. This may be seen to be of full travel from negative to positive orientation. Either will activate these energy ray centers.

There are a few whose desires to aid society are green-ray or above. These entities are few due to the understanding of fourth ray that universal love freely given is more to be desired than principalities (those in governmental power like a prince) or even the rearrangement of people or political structures.

Two positively oriented active souls no longer in our physical time here on Earth are Albert Schweitzer, who went into a strange and barbaric society in order that it might heal. He was able to mobilize great amounts of energy and money. He spent much green-ray energy both as a healer and as a lover of the organ instrument. His yellow ray was bright and crystallized by the efforts needed to produce the funds to promulgate (promote) its efforts, also meaning to promote its efforts. His blue and green rays were of a toweringly brilliant nature as well. The higher levels being activated, the lower energy points remaining in balance, being quite, quite brilliant.

Another positively oriented soul strongly biased towards positive societal effects was Martin Luther King. He dealt in a great degree with rather negative orange and yellow ray vibratory patterns. However, this entity was able to keep open the green-ray energy due to the severity of its testing, this entity may be seen to have polarized more towards the positive due to its fidelity to service-to-others in the face of great catalyst.

The unmanifested self (such as physical pain)-interacting between self and gadgets, toys and inventions concentrate for the most part in the orange and yellow energy centers.

In a negative sense many of the communication devices and other distractions such as the less competitive games, may be seen to have the distortion of keeping the person unactivated so that yellow and orange ray activity is much weakened thus carefully decreasing the possibility of eventual green-ray activation.

Other gadgets seen as tools where the entity explores the capabilities of its physical or mental complexes and in a few cases, the spiritual complex, thus activating the orange ray in team sports and in modes of transport. These may be seen as investigating the feelings of power;

more especially, power over others or a group power over another group of other selves.

There are many green-ray attempts of many to communicate via a T.V. for truth and beauty that may be helpful. The sum effect of this gadget is that of distraction and sleep.

This war and self-relationship are fundamental perceptions of the maturing entity. There is a great chance to accelerate in whatever direction is desired.

One may polarize negatively by assuming bellicose (hostile) attitudes, such as the tendency for fighting or war, for whatever reason.

One may find oneself in the situation of war and polarize somewhat towards the positive activating orange, yellow and then green rays by heroic actions taken to preserve the mind/body/spirit complexes of other selves.

Finally, one may polarize very strongly third ray/green ray by expressing the principle of universal love at the total expense of any distortion towards involvement in bellicose actions. In this way the entity may become a conscious being in a very brief span of your time/space. This may be a traumatic progression.

A large percentage of all entities on Earth has a progression of trauma catalyst.

Third ray is green ray. Red ray and violet ray are seen as fixed to Ra; thus, the five inner rays are the varying rays to be observed as indications of seniority in the attempts to form a harvest.

In the graduation or harvesting to fourth-density positive, the red ray is seen only as being activated, is the basis for all that occurs in vibratory levels, the sum of this being violet ray energy.

This violet ray is the only consideration for fourth density positive. In assessing the harvestable fourth-density negative, the intensity of the red, orange and yellow is looked upon quite carefully as a great deal of stamina and energy of this type is necessary for the negative progression, it being extremely difficult to open the gateway to intelligent infinity from the solar plexus center. This is necessary for harvest in fourth-density negative.

Ra: "…General George Patton, was one in whom the programming of previous incarnations had created a pattern or inertia which was irresistible in its incarnation in your time/space. This entity was of a strong yellow ray activation with frequent green ray openings and occasional blue ray openings. However, it did not find itself able to break the mold of previous traumatic experiences of a bellicose (war-like) nature.

This entity polarized somewhat towards the positive in its incarnation due to its singleness of belief in truth and beauty. This entity was quite sensitive. It felt a great honor/duty to the preservation of that which was felt by the entity to be true, beautiful, and in need of defense. This entity perceived itself a gallant figure (brave or chivalrous). It polarized somewhat towards the negative in its lack of understanding the green ray it carried with it, rejecting the forgiveness principle which is implicit (understood but not clearly expressed) in universal love.

The sum total of this incarnation vibrationally was a slight increase in positive polarity but a decrease in harvestability due to the rejection of the Law of Way of Responsibility; that is, seeing universal love, yet still it fought on."

Almost immediately after the cessation of war, General George Patton's death was so he could immediately reincarnate to make harvest.

Session 35: 3-6-1981

Ra: "It is to be noted that in discussing those who are well known among your peoples there is the possibility that information may be seen to be specific to one entity whereas in actuality the great design of experience is much the same for each entity. It is with this in mind that we would discuss the experiential forces which offered catalyst to an individual.

It is further to be noted that in the case of those entities lately incarnate much distortion may have taken place in regard to misinformation and misinterpretation of an entity's thoughts or behaviors.

We shall now proceed to speak of the basic parameters of the one known as Franklin D. Roosevelt. When any entity comes into third-density incarnation, each of its energy centers is potentiated but must be activated by the self, using experience.

The one known as Franklin developed very quickly up through red, orange, yellow, and green and began to work in the blue ray energy center at a tender age. This rapid growth was due, firstly, to previous achievements in the activation of the rays, secondly, to the relative comfort and leisure of its early existence, thirdly, due to the strong desire upon the part of the entity to progress. This entity mated with an entity whose blue ray vibrations were of a strength more than equal to its own thus acquiring catalyst for further growth in that area that was to persist throughout the incarnation.

This entity had some difficulty with continued green ray activity due to the excessive energy which was put into the activities regarding other selves in the distortion towards acquiring power. This was to have its toll upon the physical vehicle. The limitation of the nonmovement of a portion of the physical vehicle opened once again, for this entity, the opportunity for concentration upon the more, universal or idealistic aspects of power; that is, the non-abusive use of power. Thus, at the outset of a bellicose action this entity had lost some positive polarity due to excessive use of the orange and yellow ray energies at the expense of green and blue ray energies, then had regained the polarity due to the catalytic effects of a painful limitation upon the physical complex.

This entity was not of a bellicose (hostile) nature but rather during the conflict continued to vibrate in green ray working with the blue ray energies. Franklin's teacher also functioned greatly during this period as blue ray activator, not only for its mate but also in a more universal expression. This entity polarized continuously in a positive fashion in the universal sense while, in a less universal sense, developing a pattern of what may be called karma; this karma having to do with inharmonious relationship distortions with the mate/teacher."

Franklin D. Roosevelt's teacher was his wife.

He placed the physical limitations on his body himself through pre-incarnation programming.

The basic guidelines for the lessons and purposes of incarnation had been carefully set before incarnation by the mind/body/spirit complex totality of Franklin.

If he had avoided the excessive enjoyment of or attachment to the competitiveness inherent of his occupation, this entity would not have had the limitation.

However, the desire to grow was strong in this programming and when the opportunities began to cease due to distortions towards love of power the entity's limiting factor was activation.

There was an intense amount of confusion present in Adolf Hitler's life patterns as well as great confusion among any discussion of this entity.

Ra: "Here we see an example of one who, in attempting activation of the highest rays of energy while lacking the green ray key, canceled itself out as far as polarization either towards positive or negative. This entity was basically negative. However, its confusion was such that the personality disintegrated, thus leaving the mind/body/spirit complex unharvestable and much in need of healing.

This entity followed the pattern of negative polarization which suggests the elite and the enslaved, this being seen by the entity to be of a helpful nature for the societal structure. However, in drifting from the conscious polarization into a twilight world where dream took the place of events in your space/time continuum, this entity failed in its attempt to serve the Creator in a harvestable degree along the path of service-to-self. Thus, we see the so-called insanity which may often arise when an entity attempts to polarize more quickly than experience may be integrated.

We have advised and suggested caution and patience in previous communications and do so again, using this entity as an example of the over-hasty opening of polarization without due attention to the synthesized and integrated mind/body/spirit complex. To know your self is to have the foundation upon firm ground."

There are two entities subordinate to Adolf at the time who may be harvestable in a negative sense, one known as Hermann; the other preferred to be called Himmler. When this was channeled by Ra at the time there were others still alive harvestable 4th density negative that Ra can't mention due to them still being alive at the time of this channeling in 1981.

Ra: "This shall be the last full query of this session as we find the instrument quite low in vital energies.

The one known as Abraham (Lincoln) had an extreme difficulty in many ways and, due to physical, mental, and spiritual pain, was weary of life but without the orientation to self-destruction. In your time, 1853, this entity was contacted in sleep by a fourth-density being. This being was concerned with the battles between the forces of light and the forces of darkness which have been waged in fourth density for many of your years.

This entity accepted the honor/duty of completing Abraham's karmic patterns and Abraham discovered that this entity would attempt those things which Abraham desired to do but felt it could not. Thus, the exchange was made.

This entity, Abraham, was taken to a plane of suspension until the cessation of its physical vehicle much as though we of Ra would arrange with this instrument to remain in the vehicle, come out of the trance state, and function as this instrument, leaving this instrument's mind and spirit complex in its suspended state.

The planetary energies at this time were at what seemed to this entity to be at a critical point, for freedom had gained in acceptance as a possibility among many peoples. This entity saw the work done by those beginning the democratic concept of freedom, in danger of being abridged (shortened) or abrogated (repealed) by the rising belief and use of the principle of the enslavement of entities. This is a negative concept of a fairly serious nature in your density. This entity, therefore, went forward into what it saw as the bate for the light, for healing of a rupture in the concept of freedom.

This entity did not gain or lose karma by these activities due to its detachment from any outcome. Its attitude throughout was one of service-to-others, more especially to the downtrodden or enslaved. The polarity of the individual was somewhat, but not severely, lessened by the cumulative feelings and thought forms which were created due to large numbers of entities leaving the physical plane due to trauma of battle."

Session 36: 3-10-1981

There is a dimension in which time does not have sway (does not exist). In this dimension, the mind/body/spirit in its eternal dance of the present may be seen in totality as an eternal present, and before the mind/body/spirit complex becomes a part of the social memory complex is willingly absorbed into the allness of the One Creator, the entity knows itself in its totality.

This mind/body/spirit complex totality functions as a resource for the Higher Self. The Higher Self, in turn, is a resource for the distillations of third-density experience and programming further experience. This is also true of densities four, five and six with the mind/body/spirit complex totality coming into consciousness in the course of seventh density.

The Higher Self exists with full understanding of the accumulation of experiences of the entity, aids the entity in achieving healing of the experiences that have not been learned properly and assists in further life experience programming.

Ra: "The Higher Self exists with full understanding of the accumulation of experiences of the entity, aids the entity in achieving healing of the experiences which have not been learned properly and assists as you have indicated in further life experience programming.

The mind/body/spirit complex totality is that which may be called upon by the Higher Self aspect just as the mind/body/spirit complex calls upon the Higher Self. In the one case you have a structured situation within the space/time continuum with the Higher Self having available to it the totality of experiences which have been collected by an entity and a very firm grasp of the lessons to be learned in this density.

The mind/body/spirit complex totality is as the shifting sands and is in some part a collection of parallel developments of the same entity. This information is made available to the Higher Self aspect. This aspect may then use these projected probability/possibility vortices in order to better aid in future life programming."

Seth says in the "Seth Material" that each entity here on Earth is one part of an aspect of a Higher Self or Oversoul that has many aspects or parts in many dimensions that all learn lessons that allow the Higher Self to progress in a balanced manner.

The Higher Self governs all of our parallel realities that are similar to our experience in the third density here on Earth.

The more in balance an entity becomes, the less possibility/probability vortices may need to be explored in parallel experiences.

True simultaneity is available only when all things are seen to be occurring at once. Therefore, various parts of the being experiencing parallel experiences of varying natures is not occurring simultaneously.

From Universe to Universe and parallel existences can then be programmed by the Higher Self, given the information available from the mind/body/spirit complex totality regarding the probability/possibility vortices at any crux.

The apparent simultaneity existence of two selves is actually one-self at the same time. This oversoul or Higher Self seems to exist simultaneously with the mind/body/spirit complex that it aids. This is not actually simultaneous, for the Higher Self is moving to the mind/body/spirit complex as needed from a position in development of the entity in the future of this entity.

The Higher Self operates from the future and is aware of lessons learned through the sixth density. However, it does not know exactly what will happen in the future for that would be an abrogation (in abolishing) free will. The progress rate through sixth density is fairly well understood. The choices that must be made to achieve the Higher Self as it is are in the provenance (or birthplace) of the mind/body/spirit complex itself.

Thus, the Higher Self is like a map where the destination is known; the roads are very well known, these roads being designed by intelligent infinity working through intelligent energy. However, the Higher Self aspect can only program for the lessons and certain predisposing (or inclined towards) limitations if it wishes. The remainder is completely the free choice of each entity. There is the perfect balance between the known and the unknown.

The Higher Self does have some type of physical body. This Higher Self is of a certain advancement within sixth density going into the seventh. After the seventh has been well entered the mind/body/spirit complex becomes so totally a mind/body/spirit complex totality that it begins to gather spiritual mass and approach the octave density. Thus, the looking backwards is finished at that point.

The Higher Self of every entity is of sixth-density. This is an honor/duty of self to self as one approaches seventh density.

Each entity has several beings to call on for inner support.

The mind/body/spirit complex totality is a nebulous (or unclear/foggy) collection of all that may occur held in understanding.

The Higher Self itself is a projection or manifestation of mind/body/spirit complex totality that then may communicate with the mind/body/spirit complex during the discarnate (not having a physical body) part of a cycle of rebirth or the incarnation. It may communicate if the proper pathways or channels through the roots of mind are opened.

These channels to contact the Higher Self may be opened by meditation. Meditation also helps in evolution.

Each path of life experience is unique.

Intense polarization does not necessarily develop the will or need to contact the Oversoul. However, given the polarization, the will is greatly enhanced and vice versa.

There are no negative beings that have attained the Oversoul manifestation, which is the honor/duty of the mind/body/spirit complex totality of late sixth density. Therefore, all Higher Selves and Oversouls are of the positive polarity.

These negatively oriented mind/body/spirit complexes have a difficulty that has never been overcome. For after fifth-density graduation wisdom is available but must be matched with an equal amount of love. This love/light is very, very difficult to achieve in unity when following the negative path and during the earlier part of sixth density, society complexes of the negative orientation will choose to release the potential and leap into the sixth-density positive.

Therefore, the Oversoul which makes its understanding available to all in the social memory complex who are ready for such aid is a positive Oversoul. However, the free will of the individual is paramount, and any guidance given by a Higher Self may be seen in either the positive or negative polarity depending on the choice of the entity.

The negative path is one of separation. The first separation is the self from the self. Many negatively oriented beings choose not to use its abilities of will and polarization to seek guidance from any source but its conscious drives, self-chosen in the life experience and nourished by previous biases created in other life experiences.

Kathryn says: "I assume demons/negatively-oriented beings choosing not to seek guidance is due to separation and service-to-self choice as they are in separation and darkness."

The sixth-density negative entity is extremely wise. It observes the spiritual entropy occurring due to the lack of ability to express the unity of sixth density. Thus, loving the Creator and realizing at some point that the Creator is not only self but other self as self, this entity consciously chooses an instantaneous energy reorientation so that it may continue its evolution.

Once the negatively polarized entity has reached a certain point in the wisdom density it becomes extremely unlikely that it will choose to risk the forgetting, for this polarization is not selfless but selfish and with wisdom realizes the jeopardy of such "Wandering." Occasionally a sixth-density negative entity becomes a Wanderer in an effort to continue to polarize negatively. This is extremely unusual.

The Wanderer has the potential of greatly accelerating the density when it comes in its progress in evolution. This is due to the intensive life experiences and opportunities of third density. Thusly the positively oriented Wanderer chooses to hazard the danger of the forgetting in order to be of service to others by radiating love of others. If the forgetting is penetrated the amount of catalyst in third density will polarize the Wanderer with much greater efficiency than expected in the higher and more harmonious densities.

Similarly, the negatively oriented Wanderer dares to hazard the forgetting in order that it might accelerate its progress in evolution in its own density by serving itself in third density by offering to other selves negatively polarized information.

Examples of sixth density negatively polarized Wanderers in our historical past could be harmful Ra said. So, they withheld that information. Ra wants us to view the entities about you as part of the Creator. They can't explain any further.

Approximately 8.5-9.75% of Wanderers on Earth in the 1980's has been successful in penetrating the memory block and have become aware of who they are. About 50% have a fairly well-defined symptomology (symptoms or signs) indicating to them that they are not of this "insanity" or not of this world. Nearly one-third of the remainder are aware that something about them is different, so you see there are many gradations of awakening to the knowledge of being a Wanderer. This information will make sense to middle and first of these groups.

Session 37: 3-12-1981

Each third-density entity has a Higher Self in sixth density which is moving to the mind/body/spirit complex of the entity as needed.

The Higher Self is a manifestation given to late sixth-density mind/body/spirit complex as a gift from its future selfness. The mid-seventh density's last action before turning towards the allness of the Creator and gaining spiritual mass is to give this resource to the sixth-density self, moving as you measure time in the steam of time.

This self, the mind/body/spirit complex of late sixth density, has then the honor/duty of using both the experiences of its total living bank of memory of experience, thoughts, and actions (the Higher Self) and using the resource of the mind/body/spirit complex totality left behind from the mid-seventh density self, a type of infinitely complex thought form to give the sixth-density self as a gift.

In this way you may see yourself, Higher Self or Oversoul, and your mind/body/spirit complex totality as three points in a circle. The only distinction is that of your time/space continuum. Otherwise, all three are the same being.

Each entity has its totality and when a planetary entity becomes a social memory complex, formed in fourth-density, the totality of this union of entities also has its Oversoul and its social memory complex totality as resource. As always, the sum, spiritually speaking, is greater than the sum of its parts so that the Oversoul of a social memory complex is not the sum of the Oversouls of its members entities but operates upon the way of squares or doubling.

Spiritual mass begins to attract the out-moving and ongoing vibratory oscillations (swinging back and forth like a pendulum) of beingness into the gravity well of the great central sun, core, or Creator of the Infinite universes.

Session 38: 3-13-1981

The desire for information like nuclear energy was attracted to our people on Earth. It was not given for a reason from outside influences; rather it was desired from people on Earth. Entities desired a second chance to use nuclear energy here on Earth peacefully that caused the destruction of Maldek from nuclear energy.

Inspiration fulfilled the desire to receive the information regarding nuclear energy. This inspiration involves an extraordinary desire to know or to receive in a certain area accompanied by the ability to open to and trust in intuition.

Each balance of an entity is perfect and unique.

The rays of a Wanderer may be viewed as extremely even, red, orange, yellow and the green is extremely bright. This is balanced by a dimmer indigo.

Ra: "Between these two the point of balance resides, the blue ray of the communicator sparkling in strength above the ordinary. In the violet ray we see this unique spectrograph (which records an astronomical spectrum of all the energy rays) and at the same time the pure violet surrounding the whole; this in turn, surrounded by that which mixes the red and violet ray, indicating the integration of mind, body, and spirit; this surrounded by the vibratory pattern of this entity's true density.

This description may be seen to be both unbalanced and in perfect balance. The latter understanding is extremely helpful in dealing with other selves. The ability to feel blockages is useful only to the healer. There is not properly a tiny fraction of judgement when viewing a balance in colors. Of course, when we see many of the energy plexi weakened and blocked, we may understand that an entity has not yet grasped the baton and begun the race. However, the potentials are always there. All the rays fully balanced are there in waiting to be activated."

Perhaps another way to address this is in the fully potentiated (or effective) entity the rays mount one upon the other with equal vibratory brilliance (intense brightness of light) and scintillating sheen (shining brightly) until the surrounding color is white. This is potentiated balance in third density.

It is possible for a third-density planet to form a social memory complex in the latter or seventh portion when entities are harmoniously readying for graduation.

As far as Ra is aware there are no negatively third-density social memory complexes. Positively oriented social memory complexes of third density are not unheard of but quite rare. However, an entity from the star Sirius's planetary body has approached this planetary body twice. This entity is late third density and is part of a third-density social memory complex. The social memory complex is properly a fourth-density phenomenon.

The second-density vegetation forms that graduated into third density upon Sirius of that social memory complex third density were dogs. (Which is interesting, because dogs upon Earth are 2nd density.)

Jehoshuah was from Sirius and experienced second density life as a tree. Jehoshuah was fifth density harvestable (later fourth density) when he reincarnated as a Wanderer into third density Earth to spread love upon the Earth.

Since Bellicose is impossible for vegetation, they would then have the advantage not to carry a racial memory of a bellicose nature into third density from second and therefore develop a more harmonious society and accelerate their evolution.

However, to become balanced and begin to polarize properly it is then necessary to investigate movements of all kinds, especially bellicosity.

Kathryn states: "This reminds me of how before the veil of forgetting, typically found more often closer to the center of our galaxy, there wasn't bellicosity due to beings remembering everything and that everyone is a part of the Creator. They also felt that connection to the Creator like an umbilical cord. Due to the happiness and peace, there was less need to serve others so evolution occurred much slower. That's why the veil of forgetting is necessary to polarize faster and therefore eventually move through all the densities."

This third density social memory complex from Sirius investigated bellicosity (wars-like mentality) by taking Charlie Hixson on their UFO and extracting from his memory rather than warfare among themselves.

Entities of this heritage would find it nearly impossible to fight. Their studies of movements of all kinds is their form of meditation which must be balanced, just as our people on Earth need constant moments of meditation to balance our activities.

These advanced third density entities from Sirius did not use their legs for movement but of an electromagnetic phenomenon controlled by thought impulses of a weak electrical nature.

Their craft was visible to people on our planet in that area at that time and is a third-density material, like a chair on Earth.

Graduation into fourth-density negative is achieved by those beings who have consciously contacted intelligent infinity through the use of red, orange and yellow rays of energy. Therefore, the planetary conditions of fourth-density negative include the constant alignment and realignment of entities in efforts to form dominant patterns of combined energy.

The early fourth density is one of the most intensive struggles for the negative polarization. When the order of authority has been established and all have fought until convinced that each is in the proper placement for power structure, the social memory complex begins. Always the fourth-density effect of telepathy and the transparency of thought are attempted to be used for the sake of those at the apex of the power structure.

This is often quite damaging to the further polarization of fourth-density negative entities, for the further negative polarization can come about only through group effort. As they manage to combine, they then polarize through such services to self as those offered by the crusaders of Orion.

Session 39: 3-16-1981

Ra: "As you are aware, in the beginning of the creations set up by each Logos, there are created complete potentials, both electrical, in the sense Larson intends, and metaphysical. This metaphysical electricity is important in the understanding of this statement as is the concept of electricity.

This concept deals with potentiated energy. The electron has been said to have no mass but only a field. Others claim a mass of infinitesimal measure. Both are correct. The true mass of the potentiated (more effective or active) energy is the strength of the field. This is also true metaphysically.

However, in your present physical system of knowledge it is useful to take the mass number of the electron in order to do work that you may find solutions to other questions about the physical universe. In such a way, you may conveniently consider each density of being to have a greater and greater spiritual mass. The mass increases significantly but not greatly until the gateway density. In this density the summing up, the looking backwards- in short- all the useful functions of polarity have been used. Therefore, the metaphysical electrical nature of the individual grows greater and greater in spiritual mass.

For an analog one may observe the work of Albert who posits the growing to infinity of mass as this mass approaches the speed of light. Thus, the seventh-density being, the completed being, the Creator who knows Itself, accumulates mass and compacts into the One Creator once again."

$$Mi = \frac{m_0 C^2}{\sqrt{1-v^2/c^2}}$$

Mi in this equation equals spiritual mass. Henry Puharich statement by "The Nine" stated that "CH is a principle which is the revealing principle of knowledge and of law." Ra said that the principle is so veiled in that statement is but the simple principle of the constant or Creator and the transient or the incarnate being and the yearning existing between the two, one for the other, in love and light amidst the distortions of free will acting upon the illusion-bound entity."

"The Nine" transmitted this principle in a veiled way because the scribe is most interested in puzzles and equations.

"The Nine" describes themselves as the "nine principals of God."

This is also a veiled statement. The attempt is made to indicate that the nine who sit upon the Council are those representing the Creator, the One Creator, just as there may be nine witnesses in a courtroom testifying for one defendant. The term principal has this meaning also.

The abilities and preferences of a scribe or contact group determines the nature of this contact. The difference lies in the fact that Ra is as they are, so they will only speak as they are. This demands a very tuned group.

Our development in evolution of the seven bodily energy centers: The basic energy of red ray may be seen to be the basic strengthening ray for each density. It shall never be condescended to less important or productive of spiritual evolution, for it is the foundation ray.

The next foundation ray is yellow, the great stepping stone ray. At this ray the mind/body potentiates to its fullest balance. The strong red/orange/yellow triad springboards the entity into the center ray of green. This is a basic ray, but not a primary ray.

Green ray is the resource for spiritual work. When green ray has been activated, we find the third primary ray being able to begin potentiation. This is the first true spiritual ray in that all transfers are of an integrated mind/body/spirit nature.

The blue ray seats the learnings/teachings of the spirit in each density within the mind/body complex animating the whole, communicating to others this entirety of beingness.

The indigo ray, though precious, is only worked upon by the adept. It is the gateway to intelligent infinity bringing intelligent energy through. This is the energy center worked upon in the inner, hidden and occult teachings, for this ray is infinite in its possibilities. Those who heal, teach and work for the Creator in any way may be seen to be both radiant and balanced in those activities that are indigo ray.

The violet ray is constant and is not applied to the functions of ray activation. It is the mark, the register, the identity, the true vibration of the entity.

There is no difference in red ray in equally strongly polarized positive and negative entities.

The negative ray pattern is red/orange/yellow moving directly to the blue. The blue only being used to contact intelligent infinity.

In positively oriented entities the configuration is even, crystal lineally clear of the seven energy rays.

Session 40: 3-18-1981

Our Sun, the sub-Logos, has white light emanating from it made up of frequencies ranging from red to violet.

The white light which emanates and forms articulated sub-Logos has its beginning in what may be metaphysically seen as darkness. The light comes into that darkness and transfigures it, causing the chaos to organize and become reflective or radiant. Thus, the dimensions come into being.

Metaphysically speaking, the blackness of the black hole is a concentration of white light being systematically absorbed once again into the One Creator. Finally, this absorption into the One Creator continues until all the infinity of creations have attained sufficient spiritual mass in order that all form once again the great central sun of the intelligent infinity awaiting potentiation by free will. Thus, the transition of the octave may be seen to enter into timelessness of unimaginable nature moving through the black hole of the ultimate spiritual gravity well and coming immediately into the next octave.

Our astronomers have noticed that light from spiral galaxies is approximately seventy times less than it should be, considering the calculated mass of the galaxy. This is due to the increase of spiritual mass in the galaxy we call white dwarf stars. This is a portion of the way or process of creations cycle.

The first density corresponds to the color red. In first density the red ray is the foundation for all that is to come.

In second density the orange ray is that of movement and growth of the individual, this ray striving towards the yellow ray of self-conscious manifestations of a social and individual nature; third density being the equivalent, and so forth, each density being primarily its ray plus the attractions of the following ray pulling it forward in evolution and to some extent coloring or shading the chief color of that density.

Assuming the individual evolves in a straight line from first through eighth density, the bodily energy centers for an individual would then be activated to completion if everything worked out as it should.

However, the fully activated being is rare. Much emphasis is laid upon the harmonies and balances of individuals. It is necessary for graduation across densities for the primary energy centers to be functioning in such a way as to communicate with intelligent infinity and to appreciate and bask in this light in all of its purity. However, to fully activate each energy center is the mastery of few, for each center has a variable speed of rotation or activity. Once all necessary centers are activated to the minimal necessary degree is the harmony and balance between these energy centers.

Within each density there's a gradual upgrading of vibratory levels.

The frequency of vibration which forms the photon, the core of all particles of the density, increases from a frequency in second density of orange to the third density color of yellow. This transition takes place with the gradual upgrading of vibratory levels within each density.

All the vibrations that form the density, the basic vibrations of the photon, increases in a quantum fashion over a relatively short period of time.

The frequency that is the basis of each density is what may be called a true color. This term is impossible to define given Earth's system of sensibilities and scientific measurements, for color has vibratory characteristics both in space/time and in time/space. The true color is then overlaid and tinged by the rainbow of the various vibratory levels within that density and the attraction vibrations of the next true color density.

The transition from second to third density was approximately 1,350 years.

It's difficult to estimate the transition time from Earth's third density to fourth density due to the uncharacteristic anomalies of this transition. There are incarnate beings who already started fourth density work by the 1980's and most likely before that. However, the third density climate of planetary consciousness is retarding the process.

The possibility/ probability vortices indicate somewhere between 100-700 years as transition period. This could change due to the volatility of people on Earth.

The vibration of the photon has increased in frequency already.

It is this influence that has begun to cause thoughts to become things. As an example, the thoughts of anger becoming cells of the physical body going out of control to become cancer.

This third to fourth density vibratory increase began approximately in 1936 when the first harbingers (forerunners) began their fourth density work. Energies will be vibrating more intensely through the forty-year period preceding the final movement of vibratory matter through the quantum leap.

The vibratory nature of our environment already became true color green before 1981. It was heavily over-woven with the orange ray of planetary consciousness. However, the nature of quanta (or density) is such that the movement over the boundary is that of discrete placement of vibratory level.

The fourth density is one of revealed information. Selves are not hidden to self or other selves. The imbalances or distortions of a destructive nature show, therefore, in more obvious ways, the vehicle of the mind/body/spirit complex thus acting as a teaching resource for self-revelation. These illnesses such as cancer are correspondingly very amenable (agreeable) to self-healing once the mechanism of the destructive influence has been grasped by the individual.

Cancer is quite easily healed mentally and spiritually with fasting and diet used as a link to that healing. Cancer is a good teaching tool because it is easily healed mentally and spiritually with the body used as a link and once the entity forgives the other self who they're angry with and forgive themselves the cancer will disappear.

The other portion of healing has to do with a greatly heightened respect for the self. This may be conveniently expressed by taking care in dietary matters. This is quiet frequently a part of the healing and forgiving process.

These dietary matters for the greatest care of one's body should not be understood literally but as a link or psychological nudge for the body, mind, and spirit. It is the care and respect for the self that is the true thing of importance. Here is the basic information for this instrument's diet, for Carla's diet: The vegetables, the fruits, the grains, and to the extent necessary for the individual metabolism, the animal products. These are those substances showing respect for the self.

In addition, those entities in need of purging the self of a poison thought form or emotion complex do well to take care in following a program of careful fasting until the destructive thought form has been purged analogously (comparable) with the byproducts of ridding the physical body of excess material. The value is not to the body complex but used as a link for the mind and spirit. Thus, self-reveals self to self.

The basic vibration that we experience now is true color green or fourth-density as third density entities. The fourth density vibration we now experience accounts for many mental effects on material such as the bending of metal by mind.

The great number of entities with the so-called mental diseases is due to the effect of this green ray true color upon the mental configurations of those unready mentally to face the self for the first time.

People incarnating here by seniority of vibration who have distracted themselves and failed to prepare for this transition are somewhat susceptible to mental diseases or disorders.

Session 41: 3-20-1981

If the (channeling) group moves to another house the place of working for channelings shall be of the appropriate vibratory levels or that purification of the place be enacted and dedication made through mediation before initial working. This might entail such seemingly mundane chores as the cleansing or pointing of surfaces which the group may deem inappropriately marred (flawed).

The banishing Ritual of the Lesser Pentagram can be used in preparing a place for a channeling session.

Our Sun is the sub-Logos that creates all that we experience in our particular solar system.

Ra: "The sun has various aspects in relation to intelligent infinity, to intelligent energy, and to each density of each planet, as you call these spheres. Moreover, these differences extend into the metaphysical or time/space part of your creation.

In relationship to intelligent infinity, the sun body is, equally with all parts of the infinite creation, part of that infinity.

In relationship to the potentiated intelligent infinity which makes use of intelligent energy, it is the offspring of the Logos for a much larger number of sub-Logoi. The relationship is hierarchical in that the sub-Logos uses the intelligent energy in ways set forth by the Logos and uses its free will to co-create the full nuances of your densities as you experience them.

In relationship to the densities, the sun body may physically be seen to be a large body of gaseous elements undergoing the processes of fusion and radiating heat and light."

Metaphysically, the sun achieves a meaning to fourth through seventh density according to the growing abilities of entities in these densities to grasp the living creation and co-entity, or other self, nature of this sun body. Thus, by the sixth density the sun may be visited and inhabited by those dwelling in time/space and may even be partially created from moment to moment by the processes of sixth density entities in their evolution.

Some sixth density entities whose means of reproduction is fusion may choose to perform this portion of experience as part of the beingness of the sun body. You may think of portions of the light that we receive as offspring of the generative expression of sixth-density love. Latter portions of sixth density seeking the experiences of the gateway density are using this mechanism to be more closely Co-Creators with the Infinite Creator.

The sub-Logos is of the entire octave and is not an entity that experiences the learning/teachings of entities such as us humans.

First-density beings is formed by the energy center (vortex). This vortex then causes these spinning motions of vibration of light which then starts to condense into materials of the first density such as water, fire, air and Earth.

The Logos has the plan of all the densities of the octave in potential completion before entering the space/time continuum in first density. Thus, the energy centers exist in potentiation before they are manifest.

The simplest manifest being is light, also known as the photon. In relationship to energy centers, it may be seen to be the center or foundation of all articulated energy fields.

The first or red-ray density, though attracted towards growth, is not in the proper vibration for those conditions conducive (helpful) to the spark of awareness. As the vibratory energies move from red to the vibratory environment that stimulate those chemical substances to combine in such a way that love and light begin the function of growth.

The polymorphous dinoflagellate is a single-celled entity. The mechanism is the attraction of upward spiraling light. There is nothing random about this or any portion of evolution.

The base of any metabolism may be found in the chemical substances of the neighborhood of origin. There are several different types of cell bases for conscious entities on this planet and to a much greater extent in the forms found on other planets of other sub-Logoi (planets in other solar systems.) The chemical vehicle most conveniently houses the consciousness. The functioning of consciousness is more important than the chemical makeup of a physical vehicle.

The polymorphous dinoflagellate has an orange energy center. The true color of orange of second density is precisely the same as the true color of humans being yellow. However, the second-density beginning is primitive and the use of orange ray limited to the expression of self may be seen to be movement and survival.

Those clinging to orange ray in third density have a much more complex system of distortions through which orange ray is manifested.

Ra: "The appropriate true color for third density is yellow. However, the influences of the true color, green, acting upon yellow ray entities have caused many entities to revert to the consideration of self rather than the stepping forward into consideration of other self or green ray. This may not be seen to be of a negatively polarized nature, as the negatively polarized entity is working very intensively with the deepest manifestation of yellow ray group energies, especially the manipulation of other self for service to self. Those reverting to orange ray are many upon your plane at this time, are those who feel the vibrations of true color green and, therefore, respond by rejecting governmental and societal activities as such and seek once more the self.

However, not having developed the yellow ray properly so that it balances the personal vibratory rates of the entity, the entity then is faced with the task of further activation and balancing of the self, thus the orange ray manifestations at this space/time nexus.

Thus, true color orange is without difference. However, the manifestations of this or any ray may be seen to be most various depending upon the vibratory levels and balances of the mind/body/spirit complexes which are expressing these energies."

Our scientists have puzzled over the various differences and possible interrelationships of various stages, types, and conditions of life forms. This is not fruitful information as the Sun (Sub-Logos) in a moment's choice can change it if it chooses.

Animals and those of a vegetable nature, like a tree, are the first to experience yellow ray experiences that find the necessity for reproduction by bisexual techniques or who find it necessary to depend in some way on other selves for survival and growth.

Each energy center may potentially be activated in third density, the late second-density entities having the capability, if efficient use is made of experience, of vibrating and activating the green ray energy center.

The third-density being, having the potential for complete self-awareness, thus has the potential for the minimal activation of all energy centers. The fourth, fifth, and sixth densities are those refining the higher energy centers. The seventh density is a density of completion and the turning towards timelessness or foreverness.

A second density animal has all of the energy centers but just not all activated. Animals are composed of light just as all things are.

The will of the Logos posits the potentials available to the evolving entity. The will of the entity as it evolves is the single measure of the rate and fastidiousness (very attentive to detail) of the activation and balancing of the various energy centers.

Each energy center has a wide range of rotational speed or people may see it more clearly in relation to color, brilliance (intense brightness of light or vividness of color). The more strongly the will of the entity concentrates upon and refines or purifies each energy center, the more brilliant or rotationally active each energy center will be. It is not necessary for the energy centers to be activated in order for the self-aware entity. Thusly, entities may have extremely brilliant energy centers while being quite unbalanced in their violet ray aspect due to lack of attention paid to the totality of experience of the entity.

The key to balance may be seen in the unstudied, spontaneous, and honest response of entities toward experiences, thus using experience to the utmost, then applying the balancing exercises and achieving the proper attitude for the purified spectrum of energy center manifestation in violet ray. This is why the brilliance or rotational speed of the energy centers is not more important than the balanced violet ray manifestation of an entity in regarding harvestability. Those entities that are unbalanced, especially to the primary rays, will not be capable of sustaining the impact of the love and light of intelligent infinity to the extent necessary for harvest.

Space/time in mathematical terms as Larson uses is s/1. Space being invisible and metaphysical.

Time/space in mathematical terms is t/s. Time being visible third density earth and the physical aspects we see in our dimension.

Fasting to remove unwanted thought forms is a healing technique used by a conscious being. One must be conscious that the ridding of excess and unwanted material from the body is the analogy to the riding of mind or spirit of excess or unwanted material. So, the denial of the unwanted portion is taken through the tree of mind down through the trunk to subconscious levels where the connection is made and the mind, body, spirit in unison expresses denial of the excess or unwanted spiritual or mental material as part of the entity.

All then falls away and the entity, while understanding and appreciating the nature of the rejected material as part of the greater self. Nevertheless, through the action of the will purifies and refines the mind/body/spirit complex, brining into manifestation the desired mind or spirit complex attitude.

Some entities catalyst is programmed by the Higher Self to create experiences so that they can release themselves from unwanted biases. The entity then can consciously program this release through fasting. The self, if conscious to a great enough extent of the working of this catalyst and the techniques of programming, may through concentration of the will and faith alone cause reprogramming without the analogy of fasting, diet or other analogous body complex disciplines.

The material in INITIATION has Ra's teachings on balancing with distortions seen when that material is collated (combined to create a set) with the material Ra has given in the Law of One books.

Red, yellow and blue are the primary energy centers. These are the first, third and fifth rays. They are primary because they signify activity of a primary nature.

Red ray is the foundation;

Orange ray is the movement towards yellow ray.

Yellow is self-awareness and interaction.

Green is the movement through various experiences of energy exchanges having to do with compassion and all-forgiving love to the primary blue ray.

Blue is the first ray of radiation of self regardless of any actions from another.

Green-ray entity is ineffectual (ineffective) in the face of blockage from other selves. The blue ray entity is co-Creator. The function of the Logos is a representative of the Infinite Creator in effectuating (putting into operation) the knowing of the Creator by the Creator you may see the steps by which this may be accomplished.

Ra experienced the vibratory densities upon Venus. They were fortunate in being able to move in harmony with the planetary vibrations with a harmonious graduation to second, third, and to fourth, and a greatly accelerated fourth-density experience.

Ra spent much time/space in fifth density balancing the intense compassion they had gained in fourth density. The graduation again was harmonious and their social memory complex had become most firmly cemented in fourth density remained of a very strong and helpful nature.

Their sixth-density work was also accelerated because of harmony of their social memory complex so that they were able to set out as members of the Confederation to even more swiftly approach graduation to seventh density. Their harmony, however, has been a grievous source of naivete as regards to working with Earth entities.

Session 42: 3-22-1981

Someone first experiencing feelings and then consciously discovering their antitheses (the opposite feeling) within the being doesn't have a smooth flow of positive and negative feelings while remaining unswayed but rather the goal of becoming unswayed. This is a simpler result and takes much practice. Therefore, a balanced entity would have the objective of becoming unswayed or unemotional in any given situation.

The catalyst of experience works in order for the learn/teachings of this density to occur. However, if there is seen in a being a response, even if it is simply observed, the entity is still using the catalyst for learn/teaching. The end result is that the catalyst is no longer needed. This is not indifference or objectivity but a finely tuned compassion and love which sees all things as love. This seeing elicits (draws out) no response due to catalytic reactions. Thus, this entity is now able to become co-Creator of experiential occurrences. This is the truer balance.

A perfectly balanced entity when attacked by the other self, such as a bull or a third density being, the response would be love. However, the balanced entity will see the attack from a third density being of a more complex nature than the cause of the attack from the second-density bull. This balanced entity would be open to many more opportunities for service to a third-density other self.

An attack causing physical pain or loss of life would maintain a response of love in a balanced entity as they see the other self who attacked them as the Creator and loving both and understanding their action in attacking you.

Kathryn says: "Every being is learning and operating in their state of awareness and understanding."

Book 2 Continues: This is of a major or principal importance in understanding the principle of balance. Balance is not indifference but rather the observer not blinded by any feelings of separation but rather fully imbued (permeated) with love.

The fourth density abounds in compassion. This compassion if folly when seen through the eyes of fifth density wisdom. The fourth density compassion is the salvation of third density but creates a mismatch in the ultimate balance of an entity.

Thus Ra, as a social memory complex of fourth density, had the tendency towards compassion even to martyrdom in aid of other selves. When the fifth-density harvest was achieved they found in this vibratory level flaws of such unrelieved compassion. They spent much time/space in contemplation of those ways of the Creator which imbue (saturates) love with wisdom in 5th density.

Many third density entities on Earth feel great compassion for relieving the physical problems of third-density other selves by giving them food if there is hunger. Ra says this is the appropriate response. Many people also bring medicine if they feel there is a need to minister to them medically, and being selfless in all of these services to a very great extent.

Starving entities experience catalysts for third density. Giving people food and medicine is creating a vibration in harmony with green ray fourth density. It is the free will of an entity to give food and medicine to others who need it as it is an appropriate response within the framework of our third density learn/teaching at this time which involves the growing sense of love for and service to other selves.

However, the green ray response is not as refined as imbued with wisdom. This wisdom enables the entity to appreciate its contributions to the planetary consciousness by the quality of its being without regard to activities or behaviors expecting results upon visible planes. The balance with this act of love combined with wisdom could be giving them knowledge of the Law of one and the information necessary to reach the state of awareness of fourth density compassion and all-forgiving love.

With the truly balanced entity no situation would be emotionally charged.

The repression of emotions depolarizes the entity in so far as it chooses not to use the catalytic action of the space/time present in a spontaneous manner, thus dimming the energy centers. There is some polarization towards positive if the cause of the repression is consideration for other selves. The entity that worked long enough with the catalyst to be able to feel the catalyst but not find it necessary to express reactions is not yet balanced but suffers no depolarization due to the transparency of its experiential continuum. Thus, the gradual increase in the ability to observe one's reaction and to know the self will bring the self ever closer to a true balance. Patience is requested and suggested, for the catalyst is intense on Earth and its use must be appreciated over a period of consistent learn/teaching.

To a balanced entity no situation has an emotional charge but is simply a situation like any other in which an entity may or may not observe an opportunity to be of service. The closer an entity comes to this attitude the closer an entity is to balance. Reactions to catalyst shouldn't be repressed or suppressed unless such reactions would be a stumbling block not consonant with the Law of One to an other-self. It is far, far better to allow the experience to express itself in order that the entity may then make fuller use of this catalyst.

The thoughts of an entity, its feelings or emotions, and least of all its behavior are the signposts for teaching of self by self. In the analysis of one's experiences of a dinurnal cycle (a day) an entity may assess what it considers to be inappropriate thoughts, behaviors, feelings, and emotions.

In examining these inappropriate activities of mind, body, and spirit complexes the entity may then place these distortions in the proper vibrational ray and see where work is needed.

When the self is conscious to a great enough extent of the workings of catalyst of fasting through concentration of the will by wishing to extend the attention span and hold it upon the desired programming. This, when continued, strengthens the will. The entire activity can only occur when there exists faith that an outcome of this discipline is possible to cause reprogramming without the analogy of fasting, diet or other analogous (comparable) bodily complex disciplines.

Focusing of the attention is the one technique the higher self uses to grow the will and faith to ensure that the desired lessons are learned or attempted by the third-density self.

Many mystical traditions of our people of Earth have common exercises for helping to increase the attention span. The visualization of a shape and color of personal inspirational quality to the mediator is the heart of the religious aspects of this sort of visualization.

The visualization of simple shapes and colors that have no inspirational quality to the entity form the basis for Earth's magical traditions.

Whether someone visualizes the rose or a circle is not important. However, a path towards visualization be chosen in order to exercise expanding the attention span. This is due to the careful arrangement of shapes and colors which have been described as visualizations by those steeped in the magical tradition.

A less sensitized individual is suggested to choose a personally inspirational image. Whether it be the rose which is of perfect beauty, the cross which is perfect sacrifice, the Buddha which is the All-being in One, or whatever else may inspire the individual.

The appropriate teach/learning device of parent to child is the open-hearted beingness of the parent and the total acceptance of the beingness of the child. This will encompass whatever material the child entity has brought into the life experience on this Earth.

There are two things especially important in this relationship other than the basic acceptance of the child by the parent. Firstly, the experience of whatever means the parent uses to worship and give thanksgiving to the One Infinite Creator, should if possible be shared with the child entity upon a daily basis. Secondly, the compassion of parent to child with the understanding that the child entity shall learn the biases of service-to-others or service-to-self from the parental other self. This is the reason that some discipline is appropriate in the teach/learning. This does not activate any energy center for each entity is unique and each relationship with self and other self doubly unique. The guidelines given are only general for this reason.

Session 43: 3-24-1981

Parts removed from cattle mutilations are the same every time. This is related to energy centers, as there is a link between energy centers and various thought forms. Thus, the fears of mass consciousness create the climate for the concentration upon the removal of bodily parts which symbolize areas of concern or fear in the mass consciousness.

The parts removed are related to the mass consciousness fear of third-density humans. The thought form entities feed upon fear from the Orion's and are able to do precise damage according to systems of symbology. The other second-density types need the blood and are creatures of the Orion group. They do not exist in astral planes as the thought forms but wait within the Earth's surface. Ra's impression is that this information is unimportant but the questioner Don Elkins asked, so Ra answered.

When the Creator's light is split or divided into colors and energy centers for experience, in order to reunite with the Creator, the energy centers must be relatively balanced the same as the split light was as it originated from the Creator as opposed to the relative unimportance of maximal activation of each energy center.

Thus, the most fragile entity may be more balanced than one with extreme energy and activity in service-to-others due to the fastidiousness (extreme attention to detail) that the will is focused upon the use of experience in knowing the self. The densities beyond third give the minimally balanced individual much time/space and space/time to continue to refine these inner balances.

Kathryn states: "I spent the first 25 years of my life having all the experiences in the world; traveling, BMX racing from eight years old to 25 years old, sports, scooters, no TV, riding around the neighborhood. Then, I broke my neck to be forced to go inside myself more, which led me to all this research. I was constantly learning as much as I could and I eventually found the truth that resonated with my inner heart such as the Law of One. Now I balance both service-to-others through giving humanity this information and truth to help more people make the fourth density harvest. This immense dedication is also balanced with taking a day or two off a week for a show, movie, working out, sleeping in and exploring the outside world; just having fun."

The use of physical pain is minimal in fourth density, having only to do with the end of the fourth-density incarnation. This physical pain would not be considered severe enough to treat in third density. The catalysts of mental and spiritual pain are used in fourth density.

The variety of pain of weariness is a part of physical pain at the end of fourth density.

The space/time incarnation of harmonious fourth density experience is approximately 90,000 years. There are multiple incarnations in fourth density with time/space experiences in between incarnations.

The cycle of experience is approximately 30 million years (for fourth density) if the entities are not capable of being harvested sooner. There is in this density a harvest which is completely the readiness of the social memory complex. It is not structured like third density, for it deals with a more transparent distortion of the One Infinite Creator.

At the end of third density the individual is harvested as a function of violet ray, but the violet ray of the entire social memory complex for fourth density must vibrate at the appropriate level to graduate to fifth density.

In fifth density entities may choose to learn as a social memory complex or as a mind/body/spirit complexes and may graduate to sixth density individually or as a social memory complex. For the wisdom density is an extremely free density whereas the lessons of compassion leading to wisdom have to do with other selves.

Sixth-density harvest is of a social memory complex graduation because we have wisdom and compassion blended back using wisdom.

The chemical elements of a fourth-density physical body are not the same as a third-density body. However, the appearance is similar.

It is necessary to eat food in fourth density. The fourth-density being desires to serve and the preparation of food is extremely simple due to increased communion between entity and living foodstuff. Therefore, this is not a significant catalyst but a simple precondition of the space/time experience. This is not considered to be of importance by fourth-density entities and it, therefore, aids in the teach/learning of patience. To stop the functioning of service-to-others long enough to ingest food is to invoke patience.

Fifth-density entities need food which may be prepared by thought. They would eat nectar or ambrosia, or a light broth of golden white hue. Ingesting food in fifth-density is a somewhat central point. The purpose of space/time is the increase in catalytic action appropriate to the density. One of the preconditions for space/time existence is some form of body complex. Such as a body complex fueled in some way.

Fueling our body in third density not only fuels our body that we need but gives us opportunity to learn service and patience. In fifth density it fuels the body and becomes a solace (comfort or relief) rather than a catalyst for learning. In fifth density it is a comfort for those of like-minded gathered together to share in this broth, thus becoming one in light and wisdom while joining hearts and hands in physical activity.

Food in sixth density is light.

The probability/possibility vortices indicate that after the harvest is complete on Earth, there most likely will be incarnate fourth-density beings on the surface as third density entities are now. There won't be any fifth or sixth-density beings on Earth for a long time as fourth-density beings need to spend their learn/teaching space/time with their own density's entities.

As fourth-density beings progress they have more and more need for other density teachings like the information Ra gives due to the calling, so the information is always available. Fifth-density beings just won't live on the surface of the planet until the planet reaches fifth-density vibratory level.

Experience in fourth density is emphatically (without doubt) not the same as third-density experience. It is necessary first for a call to exist for the teach/learning of fifth density to be given to fourth just as a calling in third-density predisposes the information received in a way consonant with free will.

Ra previously stated that the key to strengthening the will is concentration.

An isolation-type of situation is one of the functions of the pyramid.

Free will may be focused at any object or goal.

Without infringing upon free will Ra feels it is possible to state that the Faraday cage and the isolation tank are gadgets in mediation to avoid some distractions as the channeling group asked for this information.

The surrounding of self in a sylvan atmosphere (woods), apart from distractions, in a place of working used for no other purpose, in which the questioner and his associates agree to lay aside all goals but that of the meditative seeking of the Infinite Creator is not gadgetry but the making use of the creation of the Father in second-density love, and in love and support of other selves.

Session 46: 4-15-1981

Kathryn says: "Session 44 and 45 were removed from the channeling group. My notes from those sessions in book 5 will be at the end of that book from those two sessions."

An entity polarizing positively perceives anger instead of using anger for control.

Ra: "The entity polarizing positively perceives the anger. This entity, if using this catalyst mentally, blesses and loves this anger in itself. It then intensifies this anger consciously in mind alone until the folly of this red-ray energy is perceived not as folly in itself but as energy subject to spiritual entropy due to the randomness of energy being used.

Positive orientation then provides the will and faith to continue this mentally intense experience of letting the anger be understood, accepted, and integrated with the mind/body/spirit complex. The other self which is the object of anger is thus transformed into an object of acceptance, understanding, and accommodation, all being reintegrated using the great energy which anger began.

The negatively oriented mind/body/spirit complex will use this anger in a similarly conscious fashion, refusing to accept the undirected or random energy of anger and instead, through will and faith, funneling this energy into a practical means of venting the negative aspect of this emotion so as to obtain control over other self, or otherwise control the situation causing anger.

Control is the key to negatively polarized use of catalyst. Acceptance is the key to positively polarized use of catalyst. Between these polarities lies the potential for this random and undirected energy creating a bodily complex analog (similar) of what you call the cancerous growth of tissue."

The first acceptance, or control depending upon polarity, is of self. Anger is one of many things to be accepted and loved as part of self or controlled as a part of self, if the entity is to do work.

If a negatively polarizing entity is unable to control his own anger or unable to control himself in anger, he may cause cancer. The negative polarization contains a great requirement for control and repression.

Any mind complex distortion that's emotional and disorganized needs, in order to be useful to the negatively oriented entity, to be repressed and then brought to the surface in an organized use. You may find for instance, negatively polarized entities controlling and repressing such basic bodily complex needs as the sexual desire in order that in the practice the will may be used to enforce itself upon the other self with greater efficiency when the sexual behavior is allowed.

A positively oriented entity, rather than attempting repression of emotion, would balance the emotion such as the acceptance and love of anger as part of self as previously stated. This illustrates the path of unity.

Catalyst is unconscious and does not work with intelligence. It is a part of the learn/teaching set up by the sub-Logos before the beginning of our space/time.

In many cases catalyst is not used when the entity developing cancer has no conscious idea of what is happening to them when they develop cancer.

The catalyst, and all catalyst, is designed to offer experience. This experience in our density may be loved and accepted or it may be controlled. These are two paths. When neither path is chosen the catalyst fails in its design and the entity proceeds until catalyst strikes again causing it to form a bias towards acceptance and love or separation and control. There is no lack of space/time in which this catalyst may work.

After Ra stated that the instrument (Carla) grows weary, Ra indicated the possibility of two sessions per week to not cause further harm to the instrument of low physical energy and the potential of the psychic attacks from negative entities not wanting this truth to get out to the world that would raise the consciousness of the planet and interfere with their negatively polarized agenda. (The attacks were from fourth and fifth density negative Orion entities or demons attacking Wanderers so that this information doesn't get out.) Ra appreciates the channeling groups fidelity (the faithfulness) and commitment to this process for their service to humanity.

Session 47: 4-18-1981

The social memory complexes were not planned by the Logos or sub-Logos. As the unity of the Creator exists within the smallest portion of any material created by Love, much less is a self-aware being.

However, the distortion of free will causes the social memory complex to appear as a possibility at a certain stage of evolution of mind. The purpose, or consideration that causes entities to form complexes, of these social memory complexes, is a very simple extension of the basic distortion towards the Creator's knowing of Itself, for when a group of mind/body/spirits becomes able to form a social memory complex, all experience of each entity is available to the whole of the complex. Thus, the Creator knows more of Its creation in each entity partaking of this communion of entities.

The vibratory rates are not the same in positive and negative orientation. They have the power to accept and work with intelligent infinity to a certain degree or intensity. Due to the fact that the primary color of blue energy is missing from the negatively-oriented system of power, the green/blue vibratory energies are not seen in the fourth and fifth density negative vibrations.

The positive has the full spectrum of true color time/space vibratory patterns and thus contains a variant vibratory pattern. Each is capable of doing fourth-density work. This is criterion for harvest.

All beings have the potential for all possible vibratory rates. The potential of green and blue center activation is precisely where it must be in a creation of Love. However, the negatively polarized entity will have achieved harvest due to extremely efficient use of red and yellow/orange, moving directly to the gateway indigo bringing through this intelligent energy channel the insteamings of intelligent infinity.

The positive/negative polarity at the sixth level (sixth density) simply becomes history. Therefore, Ra speaks in an illusory time continuum discussing statistics of positive versus negative harvest into fifth. A large percentage of fourth-density experience, for without wisdom the compassion and desire to aid other self is not extremely well informed.

Visual aids or training aids available in fourth density automatically aids the entity in polarization while extremely cutting down upon the quick effect of catalyst. Therefore, fourth density must take up more space/time.

The percentage of positively oriented entities will harmoniously approach 98% in intention. The primary qualification for graduation from fourth to fifth density is understanding. To achieve this graduation the entity must be able to understand the actions, the movements, and the dance. It is a measure of efficiency of perception. It may be measured by light. The ability to love, accept and use a certain intensity of light creates the requirement for both positive and negative fourth to fifth density harvesting.

When a crystalline structure is formed of Earth's physical material the elements present in each molecule are bonded in a regularized fashion with elements in each other molecule. The structure is regular and has certain properties when fully and perfectly crystallized. It will not splinter or break; it is very strong without effort; and it is radiant, traducing (misrepresenting) light into a beautiful refraction giving pleasure to the eye of many.

There are numerous bodies listed in esoteric literature.

Ra: "For the interrelationships of the various bodies and each body's effects in various situations is an enormous study. However, we shall begin by referring your minds back to the spectrum of true colors and the usage of this understanding in grasping the various densities of your octave.

We have the number seven repeated from the macrocosm (universe) to the microcosm (universe encapsulating a miniature version such as humankind) in structure and experience. Therefore, it would only be expected that there would be seven basic bodies which we would perhaps be most lucid (easily understood) by stating as red-ray body, ect. However, we are aware that you wish to correspond these bodies mentioned with the color rays... Various teachers have offered their teach/learning understanding in various terms. Thus, one may name a subtle body one thing and another find a different name.

The red-ray body is your chemical body. However, it is not the body which you have as clothing in the physical. It is the unconstructed material of the body, the elemental body without form. This basic unformed material body is important to understand for there are healings which may be carried out by the simple understanding of the elements present in the physical vehicle.

The orange-ray body is the physical body complex. This body complex is still not the body you inhabit but rather the body formed without self-awareness, the body in the womb before the spirit/mind complex enters. This body may live without the inhabitation of the mind and spirit complexes. However, it seldom does so.

The yellow-ray body is your physical vehicle which you know of at this time and in which you experience catalyst. This body has the mind/body/spirit characteristics and is equal to the physical illusion.

The green-ray body is that body which may be seen in séance (a spiritualist who can communicate with spirits) when what you call ectoplasm (supernatural substance, which may appear as white) is furnished. This is a lighter body packed more densely with life. You may call this the astral body following some other teachings. Others have called this same body the etheric body. However, this is not correct in the sense that the etheric body is that body of gateway wherein intelligent energy is able to mold the mind/body/spirit complex.

The light body or blue-ray body may be called the devachanic (non-physical) body. There are many other names for this body especially in your so-called Indian Sutras or writings, for there are those among these peoples which have explored these regions and understand the various types of devachanic bodies. There are many, many types of bodies in each density, much like your own.

The indigo-ray body which we (Ra) choose to call the etheric body is, the gateway body. In this body form is substance and you may only see this body as light as it may mold itself as it desires.

The violet-ray body may perhaps be understood as what you might call the Buddha body or that body which is complete.

Each of these bodies has an effect upon your mind/body/spirit complex in your life beingness. The interrelationships are many and complex.

Perhaps one suggestion that may be indicated is this: the indigo-ray body may be used by the healer once the healer becomes able to place its consciousness in this etheric state. The violet-ray or Buddhic body is of equal efficacy (power to produce a desired result) to the healer for within it lies a sense of wholeness which is extremely close to unity with all that there is. These bodies are part of each entity and the proper use of them and understanding of them is, though far advanced from the standpoint of third-density harvest, nevertheless useful to the adept."

We all have bodies in potentiation.

In our present third density incarnation the yellow-ray body is not in potentiation but in activation, it being that body that is manifest.

The first body which activates itself upon death is the "form-maker" indigo-ray body. This body remains the "ka" until ethereal has been penetrated and understanding has been gained by the mind/body/spirit totality. Once this is achieved, if the proper body to be activated is green ray, then this will occur.

After death, if an entity is unaware, he may become an Earth-bound spirit or lingering ghost until he is able to achieve the required awareness for activation of one of his bodies.

The will would create the Earth-bound spirit or a lingering ghost. If the will of the yellow-ray mind/body/spirit is stronger than the progressive impetus (driving force) of the physical death towards realization of what comes next. That is, if the will is concentrative enough on the previous experience, the entity's yellow ray shell, though no longer activated, cannot be completely deactivated until the will is released and the mind/body/spirit complex is caught. This often occurs in sudden death and in the case of extreme concern for a thing or an other-self.

Orange-ray activation after death on Earth occurs quite infrequently, due to the fact that this particular manifestation is without will. Occasionally, someone else will demand the form of the one passing that some semblance (outward appearance) of the being will remain. This is orange ray. This is rare, for normally if one entity desires another enough to call it, the entity will have the corresponding desire to be called, that manifestation would be yellow ray.

The normal procedure, given a harmonious passage of death from yellow ray manifestation, is for the mind and spirit complex to rest in the etheric (indigo ray) body until the entity begins its preparation for experience in an incarnated place that has a manifestation formed by the etheric energy molding it into activation and manifestation. This indigo body, being intelligent energy, is able to offer the newly dead soul a perspective and place to view the experience most recently manifested.

Session 48: 4-22-1981

Ra believes it is more effective to send love/light to our peoples on Earth and the treasure of this contact with the group (Carla, Don, and Jim) than to be naïve enough again to think their physical presence would be more effective. If Ra were to walk the Earth, they would offer themselves as teach/learners.

Orion entities cause UFO flaps by visibly appearing in our skies. The flaps cause many fears among people on Earth, many speaking's, understandings concerning plots, cover-ups, mutilations, killings, and other negative impressions. Even those supposedly positive reports which gain public awareness speak of doom. The understandings in this book are part of the minority.

The Orion-type UFO publicity brought an audience not seeded (planted) by seniority of vibration to a great extent. (Those in fear had less Law of One awareness and a lower vibration.) The audiences receiving teach/learnings without stimulus of fear from publicity will be more greatly oriented towards illumination (awareness and enlightenment).

Ra: "I am Ra. There is very little work in consciousness in fourth and in fifth densities compared to the work done in third density. The work that is accomplished in positive fourth is work whereby the positive social memory complex, having, through slow stages, harmoniously integrated itself, goes forth to aid those of less positive orientation which seek their aid. Thus, their service is their work and through this dynamic between the societal self and the other self, which is the object of love, greater and greater intensities of understanding or compassion are attained. This intensity continues until the appropriate intensity of the light may be welcomed. This is fourth-density harvest.

Within fourth-density positive there are minor amounts of catalyst of a spiritual and mental complex distortion. This occurs during the process of harmonizing to the extent of forming the social memory complex. This causes some small catalyst and work to occur, but the great work of fourth density lies in the contact betwixt the societal self and less polarized other self.

In fourth-density negative much work is accomplished during the fighting for position which precedes the period of the social memory complex. There are opportunities to polarize negatively by control of other selves. During the social memory complex period of fourth-density negative the situation is the same. The work takes place through the societal reaching out to less polarized other self in order to aid in negative polarization.

In fifth-density positive and negative the concept of work done through a potential difference is not particularly helpful as fifth-density entities are, again, intensifying rather than potentiating.

In positive, the fifth-density complex uses sixth-density teach/learners to study the more illuminated (enlightening) understandings of unity thus becoming more and more wise. Fifth-density positive social memory complexes will choose to divide their service to others in two ways: first, the beaming of light to creation; second, the sending of groups to be of aid as instruments of light such as those whom you are familiar with through channels.

In fifth-density negative, service to self has become extremely intense and the self has shrunk or compacted so that the dialogues with the teach/learners are used exclusively in order to intensify wisdom. There are very, very few fifth-density negative Wanderers for the fear the forgetting. There are very, very few fifth-density Orion members for they do not any longer perceive any virtue (worthiness) in other selves."

Each mind/body/spirit complex has its own patterns of activation and its own rhythms of awakening. The important thing for harvest is the harmonious balance between the various energy centers of the mind/body/spirit complex. This is of relative importance."

Each creation is not alike. Each mind/body/spirit complex has its own patterns of activation and its own rhythms of awakening. The important thing for harvest is the harmonious balance between the various energy centers of the mind/body/spirit complex. This is to be noted of relative importance.

Ra: "The entity, before incarnation, dwells in the appropriate place in time/space. The true color types of this location will be dependent upon the entity's needs. Wanderers, have the green, blue, or indigo true color core of mind/body/spirit complex will have rested therein.

Entrance into incarnation requires the investment or activation of the indigo ray or etheric body for this is the "form-maker." The young or small physical mind/body/spirit complex has the seven energy centers potentiated before the birthing process. There are also analogs (devices of information) in time/space of these energy centers in each of the seven true color densities. Thus, in the microcosm (universe) exists all the experience that is prepared. It is as though the infant contains the universe.

The patterns of activation of an entity of high seniority will undoubtedly move with some rapidity to the green-ray level which is the springboard to primary blue. There is always some difficulty in penetrating blue primary energy for it requires that which your people have in great paucity (deficiency); that is, honesty. Blue ray is the ray of free communication with self and with other self. Having accepted that an harvestable or nearly harvestable entity will be working from this green-ray springboard one may then posit that the experiences in the remainder of the incarnation will be focused upon activation of the primary blue ray of freely given communication, of indigo ray, that of freely shared intelligent energy, and if possible, moving through this gateway, the penetration of violet-ray intelligent infinity. This may be seen to be manifested by a sense of the consecrate (sacred) of hallowed (holy) nature of everyday creations and activities.

Upon the bodily complex death, the entity will immediately, upon realization of its state, return to the indigo form-maker body and rest therein until the proper future placement is made.

Here we have the anomaly (abnormal) of harvest. In harvest the entity will then transfer its indigo body into violet-ray manifestation as seen in true color yellow. This is for the purpose of gauging the harvestability of the entity. After this anomalous (abnormal) activity has been carefully completed, the entity will move into indigo body again and be placed in the correct true color locus (location) in space/time and time/space at which time the healings and learn/teachings necessary shall be completed and further incarnation needs determined."

Those under the Guardians are responsible for the determination of further incarnation needs of those incarnating automatically without conscious self-awareness of the process of spiritual evolution. They have been referred to as angelic beings. They are "local" or of our planetary sphere.

Ra: "The seniority of vibration is to be likened unto placing various grades of liquids in the same glass. Some will rise to the top; others will sink to the bottom. Layers and layers of entities will ensue. As harvest draws near, those filled with the most light and love will naturally, and without supervision, be in line for the experience of incarnation.

When the entity becomes aware in its mind/body/spirit complex totality of the mechanism for spiritual evolution it, itself, will arrange and place those lessons and entities necessary for maximum growth and expression of polarity in the incarnative experience before the forgetting process occurs. The only disadvantage of this total free will of those senior entities choosing the manner of incarnation experiences is that some entities attempt to learn so much during one incarnative experience that the intensity of catalyst disarranges the polarized entity and the experience is not maximally useful as intended."

An analogy (resemblance) to that would be a student in college signing up for more courses than he could possibly assimilate (absorb) in the time given.

Each of the true color densities has the seven energy centers and each entity contains all this in potentiation. The activation, while in yellow ray, of violet-ray intelligent infinity is a passport to the next octave of experience. There are adepts (beings who have freed themselves from the thoughts and opinions of others) who have penetrated many, many of the energy centers and several of the true colors. This must be done in the utmost care while in the physical body for there are dangers linking red/orange/yellow circuitry with true color blue circuitry the potential for disarrangement of the mind/body/spirit complex is great. However, the entity who penetrates intelligent infinity is basically capable of walking the universe with unfettered (unrestrained) treat.

Session 49: 4-27-1981

The lobes of our physical complex brain are alike in their use of weak electrical energy. The entity ruled by intuition and impulse is equal to the entity governed by rational analysis when polarity is considered.

Ra: "The lobes may both be used for service to self or service-to-others. It may seem that the rational or analytical mind might have more of a possibility of successfully pursuing the negative orientation due to the fact that in our understanding too much order is by its essence negative. However, this same ability to structure abstract concepts and to analyze experiential data may be the key to rapid positive polarization. It may be said that those whose analytical capacities are predominant have somewhat more to work with in polarizing.

The function of intuition is to inform intelligence. In your illusion the unbridled (uncontrolled) predominance (domination) of intuition will tend to keep an entity from the greater polarizations due to the vagaries (unpredictability) of intuitive perception. These two types of brain structures need to be balanced in order that the net sum of experiential catalyst will be polarization and illumination, for without the acceptance by the rational mind of the worth of the intuitive faculty of the creative aspects which aid in illumination (enlightenment) will be stifled (dimmed).

There is one correspondence between right and left and positive and negative. The web of energy which surrounds your bodies contains somewhat complex polarizations. The left area of the head and upper shoulder is most generally seen to be of a negative polarization whereas the right is of positive polarization, magnetically speaking. This is the cause of the tones." (The meaning of the ringing in our ears.)

There is a correlation between the energy field of an entity of our nature and planetary bodies, for all material is constructed by means of the dynamic tension of the magnetic field.

Ra: "The lines of force in both cases may be seen to be much like the interweaving spirals of the braided hair. Thus, positive and negative wind interweave forming geometric relationships in the energy fields of both persons and planets.

The negative pole is the south pole or the lower pole. The north or upper pole is positive. The crisscrossing of these spiraling energies form primary, secondary, and tertiary energy centers. You are familiar with the primary energy centers of the physical, mental, and spiritual body complex. Secondary points of the crisscrossing of positive and negative center orientation revolve about several of your centers. The yellow-ray center may be seen to have secondary energy centers in elbow, in knee, and in the subtle bodies at a slight spacing from the physical vehicle at points describing diamonds about the entity's naval area surrounding the body.

One may examine each of the energy centers for secondary centers. Some of your peoples work with these energy centers, and call this acupuncture. However, it is to be noted that there are most often anomalies (abnormalities) in the placement of the energy centers so that the scientific precision (accuracy) of this practice is brought into question. Like most scientific attempts at precision, it fails to take into account the unique qualities of each creation.

The most important concept to grasp about the energy field is that the lower or negative pole will draw the universal energy into itself from the cosmos. Therefrom, it will move upward to be met and reacted to by the positive spiraling energy moving downward from within. The measure of an entity's level of ray activity is the locus (location) wherein the south pole outer energy has been met by the inner spiraling positive energy.

As an entity grows more polarized this locus will move upwards. This phenomenon has been called by your peoples the kundalini. However, it may be thought of as the meeting place of cosmic and inner vibratory understanding. To attempt to raise the locus (location) of this meeting without realizing the metaphysical principles of magnetism upon which this depends is to invite great imbalance."

Ra: "I am Ra. The metaphor of the coiled serpent being called upwards is vastly appropriate for consideration by your peoples. This is what you are attempting when you seek. There are great misapprehensions (misinterpretations) concerning this metaphor and the nature of pursuing its goal. We must generalize and ask that you grasp the fact that this in effect renders far less useful what we share. However, as each entity is unique, generalities are our lot when communicating for your possible edification (benefit)."

Ra: "We have two types of energy. We are attempting then, as entities in any true color of this octave, to move the meeting place of inner and outer natures further and further along or upward along the energy centers. The two methods of approaching this with sensible (easily affected) methods are first, the seating within one's self of those experiences which are attracted to the entity through the south pole. Each experience will need to be observed, experienced, balanced, accepted, and seated within the individual. As the entity grows in self-acceptance and awareness of catalyst the location of the comfortable seating of these experiences will rise to the new true color entity. The experience, whatever it may be, will be seated in red ray and considered as to its survival content and so forth.

Each experience will be sequentially (following a logical order) and understood by the growing and seeking mind/body/spirit complex in terms of survival, then in terms of personal identity, then in terms of social relation, then in terms of universal love, then in terms of how the experience may beget (bring) free communication, then in terms of how the experience may be linked to universal energies, and finally in terms of the sacramental nature (sacred signs) of each experience.

Meanwhile the Creator lies within. In the north pole the crown is already upon the head and the entity is potentially a god. This energy is brought into being by the humble and trusting acceptance of this energy through meditation and contemplation of the self and of the Creator.

Where these energies meet is where the serpent will have achieved its height. When this uncoiled energy approaches universal love and radiant being the entity is in a state whereby the harvestability of the entity comes nigh."

Leaving the mind as blank as possible in meditation and letting it run down, so to speak, or focusing on some object or something for concentration is another way to meditate.

Ra: "Each of the two types of meditation is useful for a particular reason. The passive meditation involving the clearing of the mind, the emptying of the mental jumble which is characteristic of mind complex activity among your peoples, is efficacious (effective) for those whose goal is to achieve an inner silence as a base from which to listen to the Creator. This is a useful and helpful tool and is by far the most generally useful type of meditation as opposed to contemplation or prayer.

The type of meditation which may be called visualization has as its goal not that which is contained in the meditation itself. Visualization is the tool of the adept. Those who learn to hold visual images in mind are developing an inner concentrative power that can transcend boredom and discomfort. When this ability has become crystallized in an adept the adept may then do polarizing in consciousness without external action which can affect the planetary consciousness. This is the reason for the existence of the so-called White Magician. Only those wishing to pursue the conscious raising of planetary vibration will find visualization to be a particularly satisfying type of meditation.

Contemplation or the consideration in a meditative state of an inspiring image or text is extremely useful also among your peoples, and the faculty of will, called praying is also of a potentially helpful nature. Whether it is indeed a helpful activity depends quite totally upon the intentions and objects of the one who prays."

Ra commended the (channeling) group (Don, Carla and Jim) for observing fatigue in the circle and refraining from a working until all were in love, harmony, and vital energy as one being. This is, and will continue to be, most helpful.

Session 50: 5-6-1981

Experiences are attracted into the entity through the south pole.

Ra: "I am Ra. It takes some consideration to accomplish the proper perspective for grasping the sense of the above information. The south or negative pole is one which attracts. It pulls unto itself those things magnetized to it. So, with the mind/body/spirit complex. The in-flow of experience is of the south pole influx. You may consider this a simplistic statement.

The only specific part of this correctness is that the red ray or foundation energy center, being the lowest or root energy center of the physical vehicle, will have the first opportunity to react to any experience. In this way only, you may see a physical locus (location) of the south pole being identified with the root energy center. In every facet of mind and body the root or foundation will be given the opportunity to function first.

What is this opportunity but survival? This is the root possibility of response and may be found to be characteristic of the basic functions of both mind and body. You will find this instinct the strongest, and once this is balanced much is open to the seeker. The south pole then ceases blocking the experiential data and higher energy centers of mind and body become availed of the opportunity to use the experience drawn to it."

Experiences are drawn to or attracted to the entity. Ra's understanding is that this is the nature of the phenomenon of experiential catalyst and its entry into the mind/body/spirit complex's awareness.

For example, this instrument, Carla Rueckert, chose, before incarnation, where catalyst can have a great probability of being obtained.

Ra: "This entity, Carla, desired the process of expressing love and light without expecting any return. This entity programmed also to endeavor (trying hard) to accomplish spiritual work and to comfort itself with companionship in the doing of work. (That's also what my channeling session revealed: That I'm supposed to teach spiritual topics such as channeling and the Law of One. I also wanted a relationship to help make life more enjoyable and easier. I believe the relationship helps keep me at a healthier level emotionally, so then I could complete even more spiritual work and service-to-others.)

Agreements were made prior to incarnation; first, with the so-called parents and siblings of this entity (of Carla). This provided the experiential catalyst for the situation of offering radiance of being without expectation of return. The second program involved agreements with several entities. These agreements provided and will provide, in your time/space and space/time continuum, opportunities for the experiential catalyst of work and comradeship.

There are events which were part of a program for this entity only in that they were possibility/probability vortices having to do with your societal culture. These events include the nature of the living or standard of living, the type of relationships entered into in your legal framework, and the social climate during incarnation. The incarnation was understood to be one which would take place at harvest.

These givens, apply to millions of your peoples. Those aware of evolution and desirous in the very extreme of attaining the heart of love and the radiance which gives understanding no matter what the lessons programmed: they have to do with other selves, not with events: they have to do with giving, not receiving, for the lessons of love are of this nature both for positive and negative. Those negatively harvestable will be found at this time endeavoring to share their love of self.

There are those whose lessons are more random due to their present inability to comprehend the nature and mechanism of the evolution of mind, body, and spirit. Of these the process is guarded by those who never cease their watchful expectation of being of service. There is no entity without help, either through self-awareness of the unity of creation or through guardians of the self which protect the less sophisticated mind/body/spirit from any permanent separation from unity while the lessons of your density continue."

Ra may not use examples of known beings sharing love of self, due to the infringement that would cause. Therefore, Ra must be general. The negatively oriented being will be one who feels that it has found power that gives meaning to its existence. This negative entity will strive to offer these understandings to other selves, most usually by farming the elite, the disciples, and teaching the need and rightness of the enslavement of other selves for their own good. These other selves are conceived to be dependent upon the elite and in need of the guidance and the wisdom of the elite.

The adept is one who will go beyond the green ray that signals entry into harvestability. The adept will not simply be tapping into intelligent energy as a means of readiness for harvest but tapping into both intelligent energy and intelligent infinity for the purpose of transmuting planetary harvestability and consciousness.

The key is first, silence, and secondly, singleness of thought. Thusly, a visualization which can be held steady to the inward eye for several minutes. This will signal the adepts' increase in singleness of thought. This singleness of thought then can be used by the positive adept to work in group ritual visualizations for raising the positive energy. The negative adept visualizes for the increase in personal power.

When the positive adept touches intelligent infinity from within, this is the most powerful of connections for it is the connection of the whole mind/body/spirit complex microcosm (individual) with the macrocosm (universe). This connection enables the green-ray true color in time/space to manifest in our space/time. In green ray thoughts are beings. In our illusion this is not normally so.

The adepts then become living channels for love and light and are able to channel this radiance directly into the planetary web of energy nexi. The ritual will always end by the grounding of this energy in praise and thanksgiving and the release of this energy into the planetary whole.

The pyramid shape focuses the instreamings of energy for use by entities that may become aware of these instreamings. The shape of our physical brain is not significant for concentrating instreamings of energy.

Forgetting the pyramid will be of aid to the group in the study of the group feeling energy upon the head in meditation in various places.

Ra: "The instreamings of energy are felt by the energy centers which need activation and are prepared for, activation. Thus, those who feel the stimulation at violet-ray level are getting just that. Those feeling it within the forehead between the brows are experiencing indigo ray and so forth. Those experiencing tingling and visual images are having some blockage in the energy center being activated and thus the electrical body spreads this energy out and its effect is diffused (spread out).

Those not truly sincerely requesting this energy may yet feel it if the entities are not well trained in psychic defense. Those not desirous of experiencing these sensations and activations and changes even upon the subconscious level will not experience anything due to their abilities at defense and armoring against change."

The most normal for the adept is the indigo stimulation activating that great gateway into healing, magical work, prayerful attention, and the radiance of being; and the stimulation of violet ray which is the spiritual giving and taking from and to Creator, from Creator to Creator. This is a desirable configuration.

Why an entity must come into an incarnation and lose conscious memory of what he wants to do and then act in a way in which he hopes to act?

Ra answers: "Let us give the example of the man who sees all the poker hands. He then knows the game. It is but child's play to gamble, for it is no risk. The other hands are known. The possibilities are known and the hand will be played correctly but with no interest.

In time/space (invisible space) and in the true color green density (4th density), the hands of all are open to the eye. The thoughts, the feelings, the troubles, all these may be seen. There is no deception and no desire for deception. Thus, much may be accomplished in harmony but the mind/body/spirit gains little polarity from this interaction.

Let us re-examine this metaphor and multiply it into the longest poker game you can imagine, a lifetime. The cards are love, dislike, limitation, unhappiness, pleasure, etc. They are dealt and re-dealt and re-dealt continuously. You may, during this incarnation begin and we stress begin- to know your own cards. You may begin to find the love within you. You may begin to balance your pleasure, your limitations, etc. However, your only indication of other selves' cards is to look into the eyes.

You cannot remember your hand, their hands, perhaps even the rules of this game. This game can only be won by those who lose their cards in the melting influence of love, can only be won by those who lay their pleasures, their limitations, their all upon the table face up and say inwardly: "All, all of you players, each other self, whatever your hand, I love you." This is the game: to know, to accept, to forgive, to balance, and to open the self in love. This cannot be done without the forgetting, for it would carry no weight in the life of the mind/body/spirit beingness totality."

END of BOOK 2 of 5

Book # 3

~FOREWORD~

On January 15, 1981, the channeling group of Don, Carla and Jim started receiving a communication from the social memory complex Ra. From this communication precipitated *The Law of One* and some of the distortions of *The Law of One*.

The pages of this book contain communications received in Sessions 51 through 75 and then translated to an easier to understand condensed version by Kathryn Jordyn in order for the world to understand this significant material easier, as this information is the key to our evolution, healing and a more enlightened society.

This material presupposes a point of view that L/L research has developed in the course of many years of study of the UFO phenomenon. There are 50 previous sessions with Ra that are in books 1 and 2 of this 5-book series. If at all possible, it is good to begin with the beginning of books 1 and 2 before beginning this material, since concepts build upon previous concepts. The Ra contact continued for 106 sessions, which were printed into four books in The Law of One series. Book 5 is the material the group originally omitted from the four books. Now Jordyn has condensed this material and translated it into an easier to understand version as well, since Ra appeared to speak in a PhD level of understanding and understanding beyond what humans have previously heard or understood; an intellect beyond this world.

Book 3 of The Law of One is an intensive study of the techniques of balancing of the energy centers and efficient polarization as our planet makes ready for harvest into fourth density. The nature of time/space and space/time is examined, and some of the ramifications of meditation and magic are discussed. A good deal of material about psychic attack and the Orion group is included, and the volume ends with a beginning glance into the archetypical mind.

L/L Research (The Channeling group) of Don Elkins (The Questioner) Jim McCarty (The Scribe) and Carla L. Rueckert (McCarty) The Channeler first received this information from Ra in 1981. This group are all $5^{th}/6^{th}$ density Wanderers. These Wanderers are beings from higher densities that came to our 3rd density Earth through reincarnation as an infant in order to one day spread this information for the betterment of humanity.

The magical personality (a being of unity, 6th density, equivalent to Higher Self and a personality enormously rich in variety of experiences and subtlety of emotion.)

Session 51: 5-13-1981

Ra: "I am Ra. In time of harvest there are always harvesters. The fruit is formed as it will be, but there is some supervision necessary to ensure that this bounty is placed as it should be without the bruise or the blemish."

There are those of three levels watching over harvest.

The first level is planetary and that which may be called angelic. This type of guardian includes the mind/body/spirit complex totality or Higher Self of an entity and those inner plane entities which have been attracted to this entity through its inner seeking.

The second class of those who ward this process are those of the Confederation who have the honor/duty of standing in the small places at the edge of the steps of light/love so that those entities being harvested will not, no matter how confused or unable to make contact with their Higher Self, stumble and fall away for any reason other than the strength of the light. These Confederation entities catch those who stumble and set them aright so that they may continue into the light.

The third group watching over this process are the Guardians. This group is from the octave above our own and serves in this manner as light bringers. These Guardians provide the precise emissions of light/love in exquisitely fastidious (accurate) disseminations (spreading) of discrimination so that the precise light/love vibration of each entity may be ascertained (determined).

Thus, the harvest is automatic in that those harvested will respond according to that which is unchangeable during harvest. That is the violet-ray emanation. However, these helpers are around to ensure a proper harvesting so that each entity may have the fullest opportunity to express its violet-ray selfhood."

Ra: "Those for the most part coming from other planets do not need craft as you know them. Firstly, there are a few third-density entities who have learned how to use craft to travel between star systems while experiencing the limitations you now understand. However, such entities have learned to use hydrogen in a way different from your understanding now. These entities still take quite long durations of time to move about. However, these entities are able to use hypothermia to slow the physical and mental complex processes in order to withstand the duration of flight. Those such as are from Sirius of this type. There are two other types.

One is the type which, coming from fourth, fifth, or sixth density in your own galaxy, has access to a type of energy system which uses the speed of light as a slingshot and thus arrives where it wishes without any perceptible time elapsed in your view.

The other type of experience is that of fourth, fifth, and sixth densities of other galaxies and some within your own galaxy which have learned the necessary disciplines of personality to view the universe as one being and, therefore, are able to proceed from locus (location) to locus (location) by thought alone, materializing the necessary craft to enclose the light body of the entity."

The Orion group is mixed between the penultimate (next-to-last) and the latter groups.

Humans have seven bodies each corresponding to one of the seven colors of the spectrum. The energy that creates these seven bodies is a universal type of energy that streams into our planetary environment and comes in through the seven energy centers called chakras to develop and perfect these bodies. Each of these bodies is related to our mental configuration (between spirit and mind or body and mind upon many different levels) and through this mental configuration we may block, to some extent, the instreamings of energy that created these seven bodies.

Each energy center has seven sub-colors for convenience. Thus, spiritual/mental blockages combined with mental/bodily blockages may affect each of the energy centers in several different ways. Thus, you may see the subtle nature of the balancing and evolutionary process.

On the back of the book Secrets of the Great Pyramid, there are several reproductions of Egyptian drawings or works, some showing birds flying over horizontal entities. Ra said these drawings are some of many that distort the teaching of our perception of death as the gateway to further experience.

The distortion of Gnosticism is the belief that one may achieve knowledge and a proper position by means of a carefully perceived and accentuated (highlighted) movements, concepts and symbols. In fact, the process of the physical death is where there is aid available, and the only need at death is the releasing of that entity from its body by those around it and the praising of the process by those who grieve. By this may the mind/body/spirit that experienced physical death be aided, not by the various perceptions of careful and repeated rituals.

In the first three energy centers a full unblocking of energy centers will create speeds of rotation. As the entity develops the higher energy centers, these centers will then begin to express their nature by forming crystal structures. This is the higher or more balanced form of activation of energy centers as this space/time energy is transmuted to regularization and balance in time/space.

(Our true nature appears to be crystallized energy centers in space/time but in time/space they only need to be balanced and not perfect.)

Each of the energy centers of the physical complex may be seen to have a distinctive crystalline structure in the more developed entity.

Red ray- Spoked wheel energy center.

Orange ray- Orange 3-petal flower.

Yellow ray- Many faceted rounded-star.

Green ray- lotus shape. Number of points of crystalline structure dependent on the strength of this center.

Blue ray- Capable of having perhaps one-hundred facets and great flashing brilliance.

Indigo ray- A quieter center. Basic triangular or 3-petaled shape in many, although some adepts who have balanced the lower energies may create more faceted forms.

Violet ray- The least variable and sometimes described as thousand petaled, as it is the sum of the mind/body/spirit complex.

Each of the energy centers of the physical complex may be seen to have a distinctive crystalline structure in the more developed entity.

Immediately after the physical death the primary activated body is the indigo, the form-maker. The indigo body is the analog for intelligent energy. It is, in microcosm, the Logos. The intelligent energy of the mind/body/spirit complex totality draws its existence from intelligent infinity or the Creator. This Creator is understood both in macrocosm (universe) and microcosm (individual person) to have two natures: the unpotentiated infinity which is intelligent; this is all that there is. (Microcosm is a community, place, or situation regarded as encapsulating in miniature the characteristic qualities or features of something much larger, such as the universe, which is the macrocosm.)

Free will has potentiated as co-Creators with intelligent infinity that has will. The indigo body (form-making body) may use its wisdom to choose the appropriate locus and type of experience which the co-Creator or sub-sub-Logos (person) will take.

Session 52: 5-19-1981

Ra: "The other type of experience is the fourth, fifth, and sixth densities of other solar system, and some within our own Solar System has learned necessary disciplines of personality to view the universe as one being are able to proceed from locus (location) to locus (location) by thought alone, materializing the necessary craft."

Other solar systems are not more capable of manipulating the dimensions than our own solar System. It is merely that there are other systems besides our own.

The terminology of right and left brain has inaccuracies. Some functions are repetitive in both lobes and to some entities the functions are reversed.

Ra: "The technology of which you, as a social complex, are so enamored (infatuated) at this time is but the birthing of the manipulation of the intelligent energy of the sub-Logos which, when carried much further, may evolve into technology capable of using the gravitic effects of which we spoke.

We note that this term is not accurate, but there is no closer term. Therefore, the use of technology to manipulate outside the self is far, far less of an aid to personal evolution than the disciplines of the mind/body/spirit complex resulting in the whole knowledge of the self in the microcosm (self) and macrocosm (whole universe).

To the disciplined entity, all things are open and free. The discipline which opens the universes opens also the gateways to evolution. The difference is that of choosing either to hitchhike to a place where beauty may be seen, or to walk, step by step, independent and free in this independence to praise the strength to walk and the opportunity for the awareness of beauty.

The hitchhiker, instead, is distracted by conversation and the vagaries (unexpected changes) of the road and, dependent upon the whims of others, is concerned to make the appointment in time. The hitchhiker sees the same beauty but has not prepared itself for the establishment, in the roots of mind, of the experience."

The positively oriented 4th and 5th density social memory complexes will be attempting to learn disciplines of mind, body, and spirit to accomplish travel. However, there are some technologies available to use intelligent energy forces to accomplish travel, do so while learning the more appropriate disciplines.

A much higher percentage of positively oriented social memory complexes use the personality disciplines, such as thought, to accomplish travel.

Fifth density that moves into sixth has virtually no entities that use outer technology for travel or communication.

The fourth-density negative uses the slingshot gravitic light effect, perhaps 80 percent of its membership being unable to master the disciplines necessary for alternate methods of travel.

In fifth-density negative, approximately 50% at some point gain the necessary discipline to use thought to accomplish travel.

As the sixth density approaches, the negative orientation is thrown into confusion and little travel is attempted. What travel is done is perhaps 73% light/thought.

There are patent differences between positive and negative densities close to the end of fifth density in the disciplines in personality in the completion of the knowledge of the self, necessary to accomplish this discipline.

Discipline of the personality is the acceptance of self; forgiveness of self and the direction of the will is the path towards the disciplined personality. Your faculty of will is that which is powerful within you as a co-Creator, it must be carefully used and directed in service to others for those on the positive path.

There is great danger in the use of will as the personality becomes stronger, for it may be used even subconsciously in ways reducing the polarity of the entity.

Discipline of the personality (acceptance of self, forgiveness of self, and the direction of the will) has the knowledge of self and strengthening of the will is important in third through early seventh densities.

It is paramount to know that it is not desirable or helpful to the growth of the understanding of an entity by itself to control thought processes or impulses except where they may result in actions not consonant with the Law of One. Control may seem to be a shortcut to discipline, peace, and illumination. However, this very control potentiates and necessitates the further incarnative experience in order to balance this control or repression of the self which is perfect.

There is a chance for an entity to remember what was lost in the forgetting by reincarnating again, there is a nimiety (surplus) of opportunity for positive polarization.

Ra: "I am Ra. There are several reasons for incarnation during harvest. They may be divided by the term's "self" and "other self."

The overriding reason for the offering of these Brothers and Sisters of Sorrow in incarnative states is the possibility of aiding other selves by the lightening of the planetary consciousness distortions and the probability of offering catalyst to other selves which will increase the harvest. (This means that the reason the Brothers and Sisters of Sorrow of higher density positive beings that hear people's prayers or cries for help might incarnate into Earth as babies is for the possibility of helping people on Earth raise their positive polarity to increase graduation here on Earth at the Harvest.)

There are two other reasons for choosing this service which have to do with the self.

The Wanderer, if it remembers and dedicates itself to service, will polarize much more rapidly than is possible in the far more etiolated (pale and drawn out due to lack of light) realms of higher-density catalyst.

The final reason is within the mind/body/spirit totality or the social memory complex totality which may judge that an entity or members of a societal entity can make use of third-density catalyst to recapitulate (summarize and retell) a learning/teaching which is adjudged (determined) to be less than perfect. This especially applies to those entering into and proceeding through sixth density, wherein the balance between compassion and wisdom is perfected."

The slingshot effect is energy put into the craft until it approaches the velocity of light, which requires more and more energy. Time dilation occurs. By moving 90 degrees to the direction of travel it's possible to change this stored energy in its application of direction to move out of space/time (physical) into time/space (invisible/metaphysical) with a 90-degree deflection. Then, the energy would be taken out in time/space (metaphysical or another dimension) and you would reenter space/time (physical in our dimension) at the end of this energy burst. Due to the questioner's training, Ra stated that he is more able than Ra to express this concept that the questioner Don thought of. Ra added that the 90 degree is an angle that may be best understood as a portion of a tesseract.

Ra said that we are all one. This is the great learning/teaching. In this unity lies love. This is a great learn/teaching. In this unity lies light. This is the fundamental teaching of all planes of existence in materialization. Unity, love, light, and joy; this is the heart of evolution of the spirit.

The second-ranking lessons are learned/taught in meditation and in service. At some point the mind/body/spirit complex is so smoothly activated and balanced by these central thoughts of unity love, light and joy that disciplines of personality and knowledge of self, universe, its mystery unbroken, is one. Always begin and end in the Creator not technique such as the disciplines of personality, which is acceptance of self, forgiveness of self, strengthening of will and knowledge of self.

There are light bringers from the octave above ours. They provide the light for the graduation of an octave into 8th density, which is the 1st density into a new octave. This octave density above ours is both omega and alpha, the spiritual mass of the infinite universes becoming one central sun or Creator once again. This births a new universe, a new infinity, a new Logos which incorporates all that the Creator has experienced of Itself. There are also Wanderers in this new octave. Ra knowns very little across the boundary of octave except that these beings come to aid our octave in its Logos completion.

Session 53: 5-25-1981

Ra stated that at the current limit of the instrument's strength, physical exercise is well in the long run due to cumulative building up of vital energies. The short run is wearying to the entity (until the buildup occurs).

The physical difficulties (of Carla) prior to contact with Ra are due to the action of the subconscious will of the instrument. This will is extremely strong and requires the mind/body/spirit complex to reserve all available physical and vital energies for the contact. Thus, the discomforts are experienced due to the dramatic distortion towards physical weakness while this energy is diverted. The entity is also under psychic attack, and this intensifies preexisting conditions and is responsible for the cramping and the dizziness as well as mind complex distortions.

Before someone attends a session, they may have special meditative periods set aside before an entity sits within a working. Ra suggests a photograph of all members in the group be sent to the entity wanting to join with writing indicating love and light upon it. This held while meditating will bring the entity into peaceful harmony with each of the group members so that there be no extraneous waste of energy while greetings are exchanged between two entities, both of whom have a distortion towards solitude and shyness.

The most efficient mode of contact from positively oriented Confederation with the people of this planet is channeling, such as what was done to obtain this information in this book from Ra. The infringement upon free will is greatly undesired. Therefore, Wanderers upon our plane of illusion will be the only ones for thought projections that make up the so-called social memory complexes and Wanderers.

An example of a meeting between a social memory complex and a Wanderer is that of the one known as Morris (Case #1 in Secrets of the UFO, 1976, pp 10-11). Morris' circle of friends experienced a negatively oriented contact. However, Morris was impervious to this contact and could not see, with the physical optical apparatus, this contact.

However, the inner voice alerted Morris to go by itself to another place, and there an entity with a thought form shape and appearance of the other contact appeared and gazed at Morris, thus awakening in it the desire to seek the truth of this occurrence and of the experiences of its incarnation in general.

Landed thought form Confederation UFO crafts have occurred but is much less common than the Orion type of so-called Close Encounter. Ra states that in a universe of unending unity, the concept of a "Close Encounter" is humorous because all encounters of self is with the self (others.) "Therefore, how can any encounter be less than very very close?" Ra asks.

The feeling of being awakened or activated is the goal of this type of positive contact. The duration and imagery used varies depending upon the subconscious expectations of the Wanderer which is experiencing this opportunity for activation.

Talking of encounters of self with self, positively oriented Wanderers have had a Close Encounter with the Orion or negatively oriented polarization. When it occurs, it is quite rare and occurs either due to Orion entities lack of perception of the depth of positivity to be encountered or due to their desire to attempt to remove this positivity from this plane of existence. Orion tactics normally choose the simple distortions of mind which indicate less mental and spiritual complex activity.

The methods used to awaken Wanderers are varied. The center of each approach is the entrance into the conscious and subconscious in a way to avoid causing fear and to maximize the potential for an understandable subjective experience that has meaning for the entity. Many occur in sleep; others in the midst of many activities during waking hours. The approach is flexible and does not necessarily include the "Close Encounter" syndrome as people are aware of.

The subconscious expectations of entities cause the nature and detail of thought form experience offered by Confederation thought form entities. If a Wanderer expects a physical examination, it will perforce (unescapably) be experienced with as little distortion towards alarm or discomfort as is allowable by the expectation of the subconscious distortions of the Wanderer.

The Orion group uses the physical examination as a means of terrifying the individual and causing it to feel feelings of advanced second-density being such as a laboratory animal. The sexual experiences of some are a subtype of this experience. Their intent is to demonstrate the control of the Orion entities over the Terran inhabitant.

The thought form experiences are subjective and, for the most part, do not occur in third density.

There is a large spectrum of entities on Earth that are harvestable both negatively and positively.

Ra: "The most typical approach of Orion entities is to choose the weaker-minded entity that it might suggest a greater amount of Orion philosophy to be disseminate.

Some few Orion entities are called by more highly polarized negative entities of your space/time nexus. In this case they share information just as we are now doing. However, this is a risk for the Orion entities due to the frequency with which the harvestable negative planetary entities then attempt to bid and order the Orion contact just as these entities bid planetary negative contacts. The resulting struggle for mastery, if lost, is damaging to the polarity of the Orion group.

Similarly, a mistaken Orion contact with highly polarized positive entities can wreak havoc with Orion troops unless these Crusaders are able to depolarize the entity mistakenly contacted. This occurrence is almost unheard of. Therefore, the Orion group prefers to make physical contact only with the weaker-minded entity."

If there is fear and doom "Close Encounter," the contact was quite likely negative. If the result is hope, friendly feelings, and the awakening of a positive feeling of purposeful service to others, marks of Confederation contact are evident.

Fourth-density Confederation entity looks variously (differently) depending on the derivation (origin) of its physical vehicle.

Confederation entities that can pass as humans most often are fifth-density positive. Fifth-density negative Orion's can pass as humans as well if they choose to take on a similar human form.

Session 54: 5-29-1981

From the Logos comes all frequencies of radiation of light. These frequencies of radiation make up all the densities of experience that are created by that Logos.

The total experience created by our Sun is the planetary system (or solar system) in all of its densities.

The different frequencies are separated into the seven colors. Each of these colors is the basic frequency for a sub-sub-Logos (an individual) to activate on of these basic frequencies or colors and use that body that is generated from the activation of the frequency or color.

Sub-Sub Logos resides only in co-Creators (mind/body/spirit complexes) not in dimensionalities (dimensions). A person can have any body activated of the seven rays, each true color vehicle is available, potentially there is skill and discipline needed in order to avail the self of the more advanced or lighter vehicles. Just like skill is needed to be able to offer concerts.

There's intelligent energy coming from the sub-Logos (the Sun). This intelligent energy is somehow modulated (fine-tuned) or distorted so that it ends up a mind/body/spirit complex with certain distortions that are necessary for the mental portion of that complex to undistort in order to conform once more with the original intelligent energy.

In the free will of self (you) knowing self (another person) you may begin to distinguish the hallmark of an Infinite Creator. If there were no potentials for misunderstanding or understanding, there would be no experience.

Once an entity becomes aware of this process, it then decides that in order to have the full abilities of the Creator it is necessary to have a balanced blending of energy centers with the Original Creative Thought in precise vibration. The precision of each energy center matching the Original Thought lies in the balanced blending of these energy centers in such a way that intelligent energy is able to channel itself with minimal distortion. The mind/body/sprit complex is not a machine. It is rather a tone poem.

All mind/body/spirit complexes in the Infinite Creation has seven energy centers in potential in macrocosm from the beginning of creation by the Logos. Coming out of timelessness, all is prepared. This is so of the Infinite Creation.

The Logos creates light. This light creates the catalytic and energetic levels of experiences in the creation. The highest of all honor/duties (given in the next octave) is the supervision of light in its manifestations during experimental times of our cycles. (Known as the 8th density)

The Mind/body/spirit complex may choose the mental configuration sufficiently displaced from the configuration of the intelligent energy in a particular frequency or color of instreaming energy so as to block a portion of instreaming energy that blocks the frequency or color.

In an entity's pattern of instreaming energy, there may be a complete blockage in an energy center or color or combination of energies or colors.

Free will is the motivator for this energy blockage. Ra prefers to avoid the word "to allow". Free will does not allow, nor would predetermination disallow experiential distortions from blockages. Rather, the Law of Confusion/Free Will offers a free reach of each entity. The verb "to allow" would be considered pejorative (limitation) in that it suggests a polarity between right and wrong or allowed and not allowed. (There is no right or wrong. We are not restricted from anything.) This may seem a minuscule point. However, to Ra's best way of thinking it bears weight Ra says.

It is primary priority to activate or unblock each energy center and begin to refine the balances between the energies so that each tone of the chord of total vibrating beingness resonates in clarity, tune, and harmony with each other energy. This balancing, tuning and harmonizing of the self is most central to the more advanced or advanced mind/body/spirit complex. Each energy center may be activated without the disciplines and appreciations of the deeper personality or soul identity.

Analogy: A seven-stringed musical instrument may be played by deflecting each string and releasing it, producing notes. The individual creative personality could deflect each string the proper amount in the proper sequence, producing music.

In the balanced individual the energies lie waiting for the hand of the Creator to pluck harmony.

The sub-Logos offers the catalyst at the lower levels of energy. The first triad has to do with the survival of the physical complex. The higher centers gain catalyst from the biases of the mind/body/spirit complex itself in response to all random and directed experiences.

Thus, the less developed entity will perceive the catalyst about it in terms of survival of the physical complex with the preferred distortions. The more conscious entity of the catalytic process will begin to transform the catalyst offered by the sub-Logos into catalyst that may act upon the higher-energy nexi. So, the sub-Logos can offer only a basic skeleton of catalyst. The muscles and flesh having to do with the survival of wisdom, love, compassion and service are brought about by the action of the individual on basic complex so as to create a more complex catalyst which may form distortions within these higher energy centers.

The more advanced the entity, the more tenuous (thin/weaker) the connection between the sub-Logos and the perceived catalyst. Until finally, all catalyst is chosen, generated, and manufactured by the self, for the self.

The number of those who have mastered outer catalyst and can manufacture all their catalyst is quite small.

Most of those harvestable at this space/time nexus have partial control over the outer illusion and are using the outer catalyst to work upon some bias which is not yet in balance.

The negatively oriented entity will program catalyst for maximal separation from and control over all those things and conscious entities which it perceives as being other than self. They will ordinarily program for wealth, ease of existence, and the utmost opportunity for power. Thus, many entities burst with health.

However, a negatively oriented entity may choose a painful condition in order to improve the distortions toward the negative emotive mentation's such as anger, hatred, and frustration. Such an entity may use an entire incarnative experience honing a blunt edge of hatred or anger so that it may polarize more towards the negative or separate pole.

A positively oriented entity may select a certain narrow path of thinking and activities during an incarnation and program conditions that would create physical pain if this were not followed.

Prior to incarnation, as an entity becomes more aware of the process of evolution and has selected the positive or negative path, at some point the entity becomes aware of what it wants to unblock and balance its energy centers. It is then able to program for the life experience of those catalytic experiences that will aid it in its process of unblocking and balancing.

The purpose of incarnative existence is evolution of mind, body and spirit. In order to do this, it is not strictly necessary to have catalyst. However, without catalyst the desire to evolve and the faith in the process do not normally manifest, and thus evolution occurs not.

Therefore, catalyst is programmed and designed for the mind, body, spirit complex unique requirements. Thus, it is desirable that the entity be aware of the voice of its experiential catalyst, gleaning from it what it incarnated to glean.

The mind, body, spirit complex is the vehicle for experience; and has energy centers needed to keep it in correct conformation and composition. Both negative and positive entities do well to reserve this small portion of each center for the maintenance of the integrity of the mind/body/spirit complex. After this point, the negative will use the three lower centers for separation from and control over others by sexual means, by personal assertion (exercising authority confidently and forcefully) and by action in our societies.

Contrary-wise, the positively oriented entity will be transmuting strong red-ray sexual energy into green-ray energy transfers and radiation in blue and indigo and will be similarly transmuting selfhood and place in society into energy transfer situations in which the entity may merge with and serve others and then, finally, radiate unto others without expecting any transfer in return.

The energy that enters through these energy centers: The origin of all energy is the action of free will upon love. The nature of all energy is light. The means of it is ingress (entering) into the mind/body/spirit complex is duple (paired together).

Firstly, there is the inner light which is Polaris (brightest) of the self, the guiding star. This is the birthright and true nature of all entities. This energy dwells within.

The second point of ingress (entrance) is the polar opposite of the North Star and may be seen, if you wish to use the physical body as an analog (comparable) for the magnetic field, as coming through the feet from the Earth and through the lower point of the spine. This point of ingress (entrance) of the universal light energy is undifferentiated (not different) until it begins its filtering process through the energy centers. The requirements of each energy center and the efficiency with which the individual has learned to tap into the inner light determine the nature of the use made by the entity of these instreaming.

The experiential catalyst and the requirements or distortions of the energy centers are two concepts linked as lightly as two strands of rope. The experiential catalyst is first experienced by the south pole and appraised with respect to its survival value. As Ra stated earlier, there's a filtering process by which incoming energies are pulled upwards according to the distortions of each energy center and the strength of will or desire emanating from the awareness of inner fight.

The total energy that the mind/body/spirit complex will receive in the way of light comes through the feet and base of spine. Each energy center then filters out and uses a portion of this energy, red through indigo. The violet ray is a thermometer or indicator of the whole.

In the fully activated entity, only that small portion of instreaming light needed to tune the energy center is used, the great remainder being free to be channeled and attracted upwards.

As this energy is absorbed into the being it radiates upwards beginning with the blue ray, although the green ray, being the great transitional ray, must be given all careful consideration, for until transfer of energy of all types has been experienced and mastered to a great extent, there will be blockages in the blue and indigo radiations.

Again, the violet emanation is a resource from which, through indigo, intelligent infinity may be contacted. The radiation will be green, blue or indigo depending on the type of intelligence infinity has brought through into discernible (perceivable) energy.

The green-ray type is the healing, the blue ray the communication and inspiration, the indigo energy of the adept that has its place in faith.

A mind/body/spirit complex feeling the activating sensation at the indigo center during meditation is experiencing instreaming's at that energy center to be used either for the unblocking of this center, for its tuning to match the harmonics of its other energy centers, or to activate the gateway to intelligent infinity.

Session 54: 6-5-1981

The psychic support of the (channeling) group towards appreciation and caring for all within the channeling group was the greatest aid to the discomfort of psychic attacks (of Carla). Ra stated that the group subconsciously had true attitudinal (mindset/opinion), mental, emotional and spiritual distortions towards the instrument. There is no magic greater than honest distortion toward love.

(The groups love towards Carla, the instrument, helped her discomfort from the psychic attacks from negative entities trying to discourage her from getting this information out.)

The negative polarization is greatly aided by the subjugation (control) or enslavement of other selves. The potential between two negatively polarized entities is one enslaving the other or bids the others then gains in negative polarity.

The entity bidden or enslaved, in serving another self, will lose negative polarity although it will gain in desire for further negative polarization. This desire will then tend to create opportunities to regain negative polarity.

In the calling of an Orion Crusader, the entity that calls is a suppliant (requester) neophyte (newcomer) asking for aid in negative understanding. The Orion response increases its negative polarity as it is disseminating the negative philosophy, thereby enslaving or bidding the entity that is calling.

In the instance where the contact becomes contest (competition for power), which is prototypical (typical example) of negativity, the call will attempt not to ask for aid, but to demand results. Since the third-density negatively oriented harvestable entity has at its disposal an incarnative experiential nexus and since Orion Crusaders are, in a great extent, bound by the first distortion of free will in order to progress, the Orion entity is vulnerable to such bidding if properly done. In this case, the third-density entity becomes master and the Orion Crusader becomes entrapped and can be bid. This is rare. However, when it has occurred, the Orion entity or social memory complex involved has experienced loss of negative polarity by the strength of the bidding third-density entity.

To properly bid is to be properly negative. The percentage of thought and behavior involving service to self must approach 99 percent in order for a third-density negative entity to be properly configured for such a contest of bidding.

The two most usual types of bidding are the use of perversions of sexual magic and the use of perversions of ritual magic. In each case the key to success is the purity of the will of the bidder. The concentration on victory over the servant must be nearly perfect.

There is no relationship between a channeling contact and the bidding process. The Ra contact may be characterized as the Brothers and Sisters of Sorrow, wherein those receiving the contact have attempted to prepare for such contact by sacrificing extraneous (external), self-oriented distortions in order to be of service.

The Ra social memory complex offers itself also as a function of its desire to serve. Both the caller and the contact are filled with gratitude at the opportunity of serving others. This in no way presupposes (assumes) that either the callers or those of Ra's group in any way approach a perfection or purity such as the bidding process described as 99% negative. The calling group may have many distortions and the working with much catalyst, as may those of Ra. The overriding desire to serve others, bonded with the unique harmonics of this group's vibratory complexes, gives Ra the opportunity to serve as one channel for the One Infinite Creator.

Things come not to those positively oriented but through such beings.

Ra stated that "As we (Ra) had been aided by shapes such as the pyramid, so we could aid your people." Ra stated, "You will find the intersection of the triangle which is at the first level on each of the four sides forms a diamond in a plane which is horizontal."

The purpose of the pyramid shape is to work with time/space portions of the mind/body/spirit complex. Therefore, the intersection is both space/time (physical) and time/space (non-physically) oriented and is expressed in three-dimensional geometry by two intersections, which projected in both time/space (non-physical/metaphysical) and space/time (physical), from one point.

Don Elkins, Carla the questioner calculated this point to be one-sixth of the height of the triangle that forms the side of the pyramid. Ra was pleased at his perspicacity. (Perspicacity is the ability to understand things quickly and make accurate judgments. Someone who is smart.)

The Queen's Chamber in the Great Pyramid at Giza would not be appropriate or useful for healing work, as healing work involves the use of energy in a more synergic (joint) configuration rather than the configuration of the centered being.

Healing work would be done in the King's Chamber.

The chamber below the bottom level of the pyramid below ground, appears to be roughly in line with the King's Chamber. This is a resonating chamber. The bottom of such a structure shall be open, in order to cause the appropriate distortions for healing catalyst.

There is only one significance to the ankh shapes such as the crux ansata; that is, the placing in coded form of mathematical relationships.

The 76 degree and 18' angle at the apex of the pyramid is an appropriate angle for the healing work intended.

Why the King's Chamber have various small chambers above it: The positioning of the entity to be healed is such that the life energies are in a position to be briefly interrupted or intersected by light. By the catalyst of the healer with the crystal, this light then may manipulate the aural forces (the various energy centers) in such a way that if the entity to be healed wills it so, corrections may take place. Then, the entity is re-protected by its own, now less distorted, energy field and is able to go its way.

The process involves bringing the entity to be healed to an equilibrium (a balance). This involves temperature, barometric pressure, and the electrical-charged atmosphere. The first two requirements are controlled by the system of chimneys.

The distorted configuration of the energy centers is intended to be temporarily interrupted, and the opportunity is then presented to the one to be healed to take the balanced route and walk thence with the distortions towards disease of mind, body and spirit greatly lessened.

The catalytic effect of the charged atmosphere and the crystal directed by the healer must be taken into consideration as integral portions of this process, for the bringing back of the entity to a configuration of conscious awareness would not be accomplished after the reorganization possibilities are offered without the healer's presence and directed will.

Session 56: 6-8-1981

Ra: "We are assuming that you wish to know the principle of the shapes, angles, and intersections of the pyramid you call Giza.

In reality, the pyramid shape does no work. It does not work. It is an arrangement for the centralization as well as the diffraction of the spiraling upward light energy as it is being used by the mind/body/spirit complex.

The spiraling nature of light is such that the magnetic fields of an individual are affected by spiraling energy. Certain shapes offer an echo chamber or an intensifier for spiraling prana, as some have called this all-present, primal distortion of the One Infinite Creator.

If the intent is to intensify the necessity for the entity's own will to call forth the inner light in order to match the intensification of the spiraling light energy, the entity will be placed in what you have called the Queen's Chamber position in this particular shaped object. This is the initiatory place and is the place of resurrection.

The offset place, representing the spiral as it is in motion, is the appropriate position for one to be healed, as in this position an entity's vibratory magnetic nexi are interrupted in their normal flux. Thus, a possibility/probability vortex ensues; a new beginning is offered for the entity in which the entity may choose a less distorted, weak, or blocked configuration of energy center magnetic distortion.

The function of the healer and crystal may not be overemphasized, for this power of interruption must need be controlled with incarnate intelligence; the intelligence being that of one which recognizes energy patterns which, without judging, recognizes blockage, weakness, and other distortion and which is capable of visualizing, through the regularity of self and of crystal, the less distorted other self to be healed.

Other shapes which are arched, groined, vaulted, conical (cone-shaped), or, as your tipis, are also shapes with this type of intensification of spiraling light. Your caves, being rounded, are places of power due to this shaping.

Here's a picture of groined shaped:

Here's a picture of vaulted ceiling:

It is to be noted that these shapes are dangerous. We are quite pleased to have the opportunity to enlarge upon the subject of shapes such as the pyramid, for we wish, as part of our honor/duty, to state that there are many wrong uses for these curved shapes; for with improper placement, improper intentions, or lack of the crystallized being functioning as channel for healing, the sensitive entity will be distorted more rather than less in some cases.

It is to be noted that your peoples build, for the most part, the cornered or square habitations, for they do not concentrate power. It is further to be noted that the spiritual seeker has, for many of your time periods of years, sought the rounded, arched, and peaked forms as an expression of the power of the Creator."

The most appropriate angle of apex for healing work:

RA: "If the shape is such that it is large enough to contain an individual mind/body/spirit complex at the appropriate offset position within it, the 76 degree 18', approximate, angle is useful and appropriate. If the position varies, the angle may vary. Further, if the healer has the ability to perceive distortions with enough discrimination, the position within any pyramid shape may be moved about until results are affected. However, we found this particular angle to be useful. Other social memory complexes, or portions thereof, have determined different apex angles for different uses, not having to do with healing but with learning. When one works with the cone, or the silo type of shape, the energy for healing may be found to be in a general circular pattern unique to each shape as a function of its particular height and width and in the cone shape, the angle of apex. In these cases, there are no corner angles. Thus, the spiraling energy works in circular motion."

Here's the Silo shape structure:

251

The spiraling energy is beginning to be diffused at the point where it goes through the King's Chamber in the Giza pyramid. However, although the spirals continue to intersect, closing and opening in double-spiral fashion through the apex angle, the diffusion or strength of the spiraling energies, red through violet color values, lessons in strength and gains of diffusion, until the peak of the pyramid there's a very weak color resolution useful for healing purposes. The King's Chamber position is chosen as the first spiral after the centered beginning through the Queens Chamber position. The diffusion angle is opposite of the pyramid angle, but the angle being less wide than the apex angle of the pyramid, somewhere between 33 degrees and 54 degrees, depending on the various rhythms of the planet itself.

Half of the angle falls on the side of the centerline that the King's Chamber is on, that will indicate (show) the diffusion of the spectrum. The angle will begin somewhere between the Queen's Chamber position and thence (therefrom) downward towards the resonating chamber underground, offset for the healing work.

This variation is dependent upon various magnetic fluxes of the planet. The King's Chamber position is designed to intersect the strongest spiral of the energy flow regardless of where the angle begins. However, as it passes through the Queen's Chamber position, this spiraling energy is always centered and at its strongest point.

Session 57: 6-12-1981

The psychic attack on the instrument (Carla) can potentially be disruptive to this contact for a brief period of our space/time. (This further proves to me that the negative entities causing these attacks do not want this information getting out.)

The instrument had replenished vital energies due to its (her) sense of humor.

The Orion group cannot interfere directly but only through preexisting distortions of mind/body/spirit complexes such as injuries, pain within the body, ect.

The crystal on the ring of the instrument's right hand (her ring) is available (One may use crystals to heal.)

Ra: "You first, as a mind/body/spirit complex, balance and polarize the self, connecting the inner light with the upward spiraling inpourings of the universal light. You have done exercises to regularize the processes involved. Look to them for the preparation of the crystalized being.

Take then the crystal and feel your polarized and potentiated balanced energy channeled in green-ray healing through your being, going into and activating the crystalline regularity of frozen light which is the crystal. The crystal will resound with the charged light of incarnative love, and light energy will begin to radiate in specified fashion, beaming, in required light vibrations, healing energy, focused and intensified towards the magnetic field of the mind/body/spirit complex which is to be healed. This entity requesting such healing will then open the armor of the overall violet/red-ray protective vibratory shield. Thus, the inner vibratory fields, from center to center in mind, body, and spirit, may be interrupted and adjusted momentarily, thus offering the one to be healed the opportunity to choose a less distorted inner complex of energy fields and vibratory relationships."

One may place the crystal (ring) on the necklace so that it hangs around the green-ray energy center; or the chain hung from the right hand, outstretched, wound about the hand in such a way that the crystal may be swung so as to affect sensitive adjustments.

Ra offers this information realizing that much practice is needed to efficiently use these energies of self. However, each has the capability of doing so, and this information is not information which, if followed accurately, can be deleterious (harmful).

The regularized or crystallized entity, in its configuration, is as critical as the perfection of the crystal used.

In some applications concerning planetary healing, the physical size of the crystal has relationship to the effectiveness in the healing. In working with an individual mind/body/spirit complex, the only requirement is that the crystal be in harmony with the crystallized being. There is perhaps a lower limit to the size of a faceted crystal, for light coming through this crystal needs to be spread the complete width of the spectrum of the one to be healed. Water is a type of crystal which is efficacious (effective) also, although not as easy to hang from a chain in our density. (Efficacious is the success of producing a desired or intended result; effective.)

2 to 5.4 centimeters towards the heart is optimal for where the crystal should hang for proper green-ray.

This healing in relation to the healing done in the King's Chamber in the Giza pyramid: Ra says, "There are two advantages to doing this working in such a configuration of shapes and dimensions.

Firstly, the disruption or interruption of the violet/red armoring or protective shell is automatic.

In the second place, the light is configured by the very placement of this position in the seven distinctive color or energy vibratory rates, thus allowing the energy through the crystallized being, focused with the crystal, to manipulate with great ease the undisturbed and carefully delineated (lifelike) palate (bias) of energies or colors, both in space/time and in time/space. Thus, the unarmored (unprotected) being may be adjusted rapidly. This is desirable in some cases, especially when the armoring is the largest moiety (portion) of the possibility of continued function of body complex activity in this density. The trauma of the interruption of this armoring vibration is then seen to be lessened.

We take this opportunity to pursue our honor/duty, as some of those creating the pyramid shape, to note that it is in no way necessary to use this shape in order to achieve healings, for seniority of vibration has caused the vibratory complexes of mind/body/spirit complexes to be healed to be less vulnerable to the trauma of the interrupted armoring (protected shield).

Furthermore, as we have said, the powerful effect of the pyramid, with its mandatory disruption of the armoring, if used without the crystallized being, used with the wrong intention, or in the wrong configuration, can result in further distortions of entities which are perhaps the equal of some of your chemicals which cause disruptions in the energy fields in like manner."

The pyramid may be used for the improvement of the meditative state as long as the shape is in Queen's Chamber position or entities are in balanced configuration about this central point.

The small pyramid shape, placed beneath a portion of the body complex, may energize this body. This should be done for brief periods not to exceed 30 of your minutes.

The use of the pyramid to balance planetary energies still functions to a slight extent, but due to earth changes, the pyramids are no longer aligned properly for this work.

The aid received for meditation by an entity positioned in the Queen's Chamber position: Consider the polarity of mind/body/spirit complexes. The inner light is the heart. Its strength equals your strength of will to seek the light. The position or balanced position of a group intensifies the amount of this will, the amount of awareness of the inner light necessary to attract the instreaming fight upward spiraling from the south magnetic pole of being.

Thus, this is the place of the initiate, for many extraneous items or distortions will leave the entity as it intensifies its seeking, so that it may become one with this centralized and purified incoming light.

A pyramid shape may be smaller if the apex angle is less, thus not allowing the formation of the King's Chamber position. Also efficacious (effective) for this application are the silo, the cone, the dome, and the tipi; these shapes having the Queen's Chamber effect. A strongly crystallized entity is, in effect, a portable King's Chamber position.

If those who desired to be healers were of a crystallized nature and were all supplicants (requester), those wishing less distortion, the pyramid would be, as always, a carefully designed set of parameters to distribute light and its energy so as to aid in healing catalyst.

However, Ra found our peoples are not distorted towards the desire for purity to a great enough extent to be given this powerful and potentially dangerous gift. Ra, therefore, would suggest it not be used for healing in the traditional King's Chamber configuration which Ra stated they naively gave to our peoples only to see it grossly distorted and their teachings lost.

The appropriate apex angle for a tipi shape for our uses: This is at our discretion. The principle of circular, rounded, or peaked shapes is that the center acts as an invisible inductive coil. Thus, the energy patterns are spiraling and circular. Thus, the choice of the most pleasant configuration is ours. The effect is relatively fixed.

The geometry or relationships of these shapes in their configuration is the great consideration. It is well to avoid stannous (containing tin) material or that of lead or other metals. Wood, plastic, glass, and other materials may all be considered to be appropriate.

If the shape of the pyramid is of appropriate size, it may be placed directly under the cushion of the head or the pallet (pillow) that the body rests on.

Ra again cautions that the third spiral of upward-lining light emitted from the apex of this shape, is most deleterious (damaging/harmful) to an entity in overdose and should not be used overlong. (No longer than 30 minutes).

It doesn't matter what the height, in centimeters, of one of the pyramids for best functioning. Only the proportion of the height from the base to the apex to the perimeter of the base is important. The proportion should be the 1.16 which we may observe. Therefore, the sum of the four base sides should be 1.16 of the height of the pyramid.

The queen's Chamber was the initiatory place: Ra cannot describe initiation in its specific sense due to their distortion towards the belief/understanding that the process they offered so many years ago (I would guess 11,000 years ago in Egypt) and was not a balanced one.

However, initiation demands the centering of the being upon the seeking of the Creator. Ra has hoped to balance this understanding by enunciating (articulate) The Law of One; that is, that all things are One Creator. Thus, seeking the Creator is done not just in meditation and in work of an adept but in the experiential nexus of each moment.

The initiation of the Queen's Chamber has to do with the abandoning of self to such desire to know the Creator in full that the purified instreaming light is drawn in balanced fashion through all energy centers, meeting in indigo and opening the gate to intelligent infinity. Thus, the entity experiences true life or resurrection.

The pyramid used for learning is a different process: The difference is the presence of other selves manifesting in space/time and after some study, in time/space, for the purpose of teach/learning. In the system created by Ra, schools were apart from the pyramid, the experiences being solitary.

In Ra's system, experiences in the Queen's Chamber position were solitary. In Atlantis and in South America, teachers shared the pyramid experiences.

There was learning and teaching within the pyramid.

The dangerous pyramid shape for today would be a four-sided pyramid large enough to create the King's Chamber effect. The 76-degree apex angle is that characteristic of the powerful shape.

Any angle less than 70 degrees would not produce this dangerous effect.

Ra: "This instrument has some vital energy left. However, we become concerned with the increasing distortions of the body complex towards pain.

The space/time (physical) and time/space (non-physical/metaphysical) concepts are those concepts mathematically the relationships of your illusion, that which is seen to that which is unseen. These descriptive terms are clumsy. They, however, suffice (are enough) for this work.

In the experiences of the mystical search for unity, these need never be considered, for they are but part of an illusory system. The seeker seeks the One. The One is to be sought, as we have said, by the balanced and self-accepting self-aware, both of its apparent distortions and its total perfection. Resting in this balanced awareness, the entity then opens the self to the universe which it is. The light energy of all things may then be attracted by this intense seeking, and wherever the inner seeking meets the attracted cosmic prana (universal energy which flows vibrationally around the body), realization of the One takes place.

The purpose of clearing each energy center is to allow that meeting place to occur at the indigo-ray vibration, thus making contact with intelligent infinity and dissolving all illusions. Service-to-others is automatic at the released energy generated by this state of consciousness.

The space/time and time/space distinctions do not hold sway except in third density. However, fourth, fifth, and, to some extent, sixth work within some system of polarized space/time and time/space.

The calculation necessary to move from one system to another through the dimensions are somewhat difficult. Therefore, Ra has the most difficulty sharing numerical concepts with us."

Session 58: 6-16-1981

The physical distortion of arthritis in the instrument increased due to over-activity of weak portions of the body.

It is appropriate to use the diamond crystal for healing if the entity is practiced at their healing art. To work with a powerful crystal while unable to perceive the magnetic flux of the subtle bodies, is perhaps the same as recommending that the beginner, with saw and nail, create the Vatican. The crystal healing practices are as previously mentioned: the crystal around the neck near the green ray and dangling the crystal from a chain in the right hand.

There is great art in the use of the swung crystal. A beginner would do well to work with the unpowerful crystals in ascertaining (finding out) not only the physical major energy centers, but also the physical secondary and tertiary energy centers and then begin to find the corresponding subtle body energy centers. In this way, you may activate your own inner vision.

Any dangling weight crystal of symmetrical form can be used by the beginner. Their purpose is not to disturb or manipulate these energy centers but merely to locate them and become aware of what they feel like when in a balanced state and when in an unbalanced state or blocked state.

The distance from hand dangling over body is unimportant and at your discretion. The weight is unimportant as well. The circular motion moving in a clockwise rotational direction shows an unblocked energy center. However, some entities are polarized the reverse of others, and, therefore, it is well to test the form of normal energy spirals before beginning the procedure.

The test is done by first holding the weight over your own hand and observing your particular configuration. Then, using the other self's hand, repeat the procedure. Ra gave general healing information, since there is a line beyond which information is an intrusion upon the Law of Confusion/Free Will.

The pyramid can be in any orientation and provide some focusing of spiraling energy, but the greatest focusing of it occurs when one side of it is precisely parallel to magnetic north. If one corner is oriented to the magnetic north, the energy will be enhanced in its focus also.

The reversed shape of the pyramid reverses the effects of the pyramid. It would only work if an entity's polarity were, for some reason, reversed.

The pyramid shape is a collector which draws the instreaming energy from the base, and allows this energy to spiral upward in a line with the apex of this shape. This is also true if the pyramid shape is upended (flipped over). The energy is not Earth energy, but is light energy, which is omnipresent (present everywhere).

The pyramid, as an energy collector, the shape itself is the only requirement. For the practical needs of our body inside a pyramid, it is well that this shape be solid sided in order to avoid being inundated (flooded) by outer stimuli.

The concept of four pieces of wire joined at the apex running down to the base being totally open is equal to the solid form still drawing light energy from the base spiraling upward in a line with the apex of this shape. However, there are many metals not recommended for use in pyramids designed to aid the meditative process. Those recommended is wood, other natural materials, or the man-made plastic rods will also be of service.

A seemingly simple open pyramid with four wooden rods joined at an apex focuses the spiraling light because of the funnel shape.

The third distortion is light. The pyramid shape acts as a funnel increasing the density of energy so that the individual may have a greater intensity of light.

The pure crystalline shape, such as the diamond is frozen light. This third-density physical manifestation of light is somehow a focusing mechanism for the third distortion (light) in a general sense.

However, only the will of the crystallized entity may cause interdimensional light to flow through this material. The more regularized the entity and the crystal, the more profound the effect.

There are many people now bending metal and doing other things like that by mentally requesting this to happen.

This is the influence of the second spiral of light in a pyramid being used by an entity. As this second spiral ends at the apex, the light may be likened unto a laser beam in the metaphysical sense and when intelligently directed may cause bending not only in pyramid, but this is the type of energy tapped into by those capable of this focusing of the upward-spiraling light. This is made possible through contact in indigo ray with intelligent energy.

They have no training and are able to do this. They remember the disciplines necessary for this activity, which is merely useful upon other true color vibratory experiential nexi. The end of such energy focusing is to build, not to destroy, and it does become quite useful as an alternative to third-density building methods.

There are three spirals of light energy which the pyramid exemplifies:

> 1.) The fundamental spiral- which is used for study and for healing.
>
> 2.) The spiral to the apex- used for building.

3.) The spiral spreading from the apex- used for energizing. If you picture the candle flame, you may see the third spiral.

Contact with indigo ray doesn't need to show itself in any certain gift or guidepost like bending metal. There are some whose indigo energy is of pure being and never is manifested, yet all are aware of such an entity's progress. Others may teach or share in many ways contact with intelligent energy. Others continue in unmanifested form, seeking intelligent infinity. Thus, the manifestation is lesser signpost or evidence than that which is sensed or intuited about a mind/body/spirit complex. Violet-ray beingness is far more indicative of true self.

Session 59: 6-25-1981

At the end of the second major cycle, there were about 345,000 people on Earth 25,000 years ago. In 1981 there was over 4 billion people.

There were three basic divisions of origin of the increase of entities over the past 25,000 years. Firstly, and primarily, those of Maldek, having been able to take up third density once again, were gradually loosed from self-imposed limitations of form.

Secondly, there were those of other third-density entrance or neophytes (newcomers) whose vibratory patterns matched the Terran experiential nexus. These then filtered in through incarnative processes.

Thirdly, in approximately the past 200 years has been many Wanderers. All possible opportunities for incarnation are being taken at this time due to harvesting process and the opportunities this offers.

At the beginning of the last 75,000-year period to start third density here on Earth, the transfer has been gradual of souls going from Mars to Earth. (I came from Mars in late 3rd density around 1742 to live my first life here on Earth as a Farmer. My 2nd life was in 1889 as an artist named Bradley and now my 3rd life here on Earth currently.)

Over two billion souls are those of Maldek which have successfully made the transition. (Perhaps about 50% of the population in 1981.)

Approximately 1.9 billion souls have, from many portions of the creation, entered into this experience at various times. The remainder are those who have experienced the first two cycles upon Earth or who have come at some point as Wanderers. Some Wanderers having been on Earth for many thousands of years, others having come far more recently.

The first notion of upward-spiraling light is the scoop, the light energy being scooped in through the attraction of the pyramid shape through the base. Thus, the first configuration is a semi-spiral. This is similar to the vortex you get when you release water from a bathtub, except in the bathtub case the cause is gravitic, whereas in the case of the pyramid, the vortex is that of upward-spiraling light being attracted by the electromagnetic fields engendered by the shape of the pyramid.

The spiral which is used for study and healing begins at or slightly below the Queen's Chamber position, depending upon our Earth and cosmic rhythms. It moves through the King's Chamber position in a sharply delineated (detailed) form and ends at the point whereby the top approximate third of the pyramid may be seen to be intensifying the energy.

The large spiral is drawn into the vortex of the apex of the pyramid. However, some light energy of the more intense nature of red end of spectrum is spiraled once again, causing an enormous strengthening and focusing of energy used for building.

The third complete spiral radiates from the top of the pyramid. It is well to reckon with the foundation semi-spiral which supplies the prana for all that may be affected by the three following upward spirals of light.

The prana scooped in by the pyramid shape gains coherence of energetic direction at the first-spiral zero position. The term "upward-spiraling light" is an indication of that which reaches towards the source of love and light. Thus, all light or prana is upward spiraling, but its direction is unregimented (independent) and not useful for work.

From all points in space, light radiates in our illusion outward in a 360-degree solid angle, and this scoop shape with the pyramid then creates the coherence (unity) to this radiation as a focusing mechanism (machine).

As light is funneled into the zero semi-scoop shape position, as the questioner terms it, it reaches the point of turning. This acts as a compression of the light, multiplying tremendously its coherence (unity) and organization in a spiral one.

There is a transformation across boundaries of dimensions at the start of spiral two, as Don Elkins calls it, much work may be done interdimensionally. There was no chamber at position two in the Giza pyramid.

Position two light spiral is useful only to those whose abilities are capable of serving as conductors of this type of focused spiral. One would not wish to attempt to train third-density entities in such disciplines.

The third spiral radiation from the top of the pyramid is used for energizing. This spiral is extremely full of the positive effects of directed prana (universal energy permeating all entities), and whatever is placed over this shape will receive shocks energizing the electromagnetic fields. This can be most stimulating in third-density applications of mental and bodily configurations. However, if over the pyramid is too long, such shocks may traumatize the entity, such as more than 30 minutes.

Other effects of the pyramid shape beside the spirals: There are several. However, their uses are limited. The use of the resonating chamber position challenges the ability of an adept to face the self. This is one type of mental test which may be used. It is powerful and quite dangerous.

The outer shell of the pyramid shape contains small vortices of light energy which, in the hands of crystallized beings, are useful for various subtle workings upon the healing of invisible bodies affecting the physical body.

Other places are where perfect sleep may be obtained and age reversed. The age reversal position being approximately 5 degrees to

10 degrees above and below the Queens Chamber position in ovoid shapes on each face of the four-sided pyramid, extending into the solid shape approximately one-quarter of the way to the Queen's Chamber position. In other words, it would be just inside the wall of the pyramid a quarter of the way but remained three-quarters from the center at approximately the level above the base of the Queen's Chamber.

Ra: "You must picture the double teardrop extending in both the plane of the pyramid face and in half towards the Queen's Chamber, extending above and below it. You may see this as the position where the light has been scooped into the spiral and then is expanding again. This position is what you may call a prana (life-force) vacuum."

Why this would reverse again: Aging is a function of the effects of various electromagnetic fields upon the electromagnetic fields of the mind/body/spirit complex. In this position there is no input or disturbance of the fields, nor is any activity within the electromagnetic field complex of the mind/body/spirit complex allowed full sway. The vacuum sucks any such disturbance away. Thus, the entity feels nothing and is suspended.

Ra told Don Elkins that the alignment of the pyramid Don built in his yard should be as this resting place for maximum efficacy (the power to create a desired result). Meaning one of the base sides should be aligned 20 degrees east of north. That alignment would be efficacious (effective).

The proper alignment for Earth at this time would be magnetic north. However, specific entities whose energy vortices are more consonant with the true color green orientation would be the 20 degrees east of north.

There are advantages to each orientation. The effect is stronger at magnetic north and can be felt more clearly. The energy, thought weak at 20 degrees east of north coming from the now-distant but soon to be paramount directions is more helpful.

The choice is yours. It is the choice between quantity and quality or wide-band and narrow-band aid in meditation.

There is every indication that when the planetary axis realigns, it will realign 20 degrees east of north to conform to the green vibration. Ra cannot speak of Certainties but are aware that the grosser or less dense materials will be pulled into a conformation with the denser and lighter energies which gives your Logos its proceedings through the realms of experience.

Session 60: 7-1-1981

"Energizing shocks" coming from the top of the pyramid come at discrete intervals but come very, very close together in a properly functioning pyramid shape. In one whose dimensions have gone awry, the energy will not be released with regularity or in quanta.

The effect of the Bermuda Triangle is due to a large pyramid beneath the water that releases the third spiral of light in discrete and varying intervals. Entities or craft in the vicinity may change their space/time continuum in some way.

Entities in fifth density or above may tap this energy to communicate information, love, or light across vast distances, but with this energy may be considered trans dimensional leaps. Also, there is the possibility of travel using this formation of energy.

This travel would be instantaneous used primarily by sixth-density entities. As one learns the understandings of discipline of the personality, each of these configurations of prana (universal energy or life-force) is available to the entity without the aid of this shape. One may view the pyramid at Giza as metaphysical training wheels.

The large underwater pyramid off the Florida coast was aided by sixth-density entities of a social memory complex working with Atlanteans prior to Ra working with the Egyptians. Ra also worked with the entities of South America and divided their forces to work within these two cultures.

The pyramid shape was deemed by Ra to be at that time of paramount importance as the physical- training aid for spiritual development. At our current time in evolution of Earth, Ra places little or no emphasis on this shape of the pyramid. It is Ra's honor/duty to attempt to remove the distortions that the use of the pyramid has caused in the thinking of our peoples and in the activities of some of our entities. Ra doesn't deny that such shapes are efficacious (effective), nor do they withhold the general gist of this efficacy (effectiveness). However, Ra wishes to offer their understanding, limited though it is, that contrary to their naïve beliefs many thousand years ago, the optimum shape for initiation does not exist.

Ra: "Let us expand upon this point. When we were aided by sixth-density entities during our own third-density experiences, we, being less bellicose in the extreme, found this teaching to be of help. In our naivete in third density, we had not developed the interrelationships of your barter or money system and power. We were, in fact, a more philosophical third-density planet than your own, and our choices of polarity were much more centered about the understanding of sexual energy transfers and the appropriate relationships between self and other self.

We spent a much larger portion of our space/time working with the unmanifested being. In this less complex atmosphere, it was quite instructive to have this learn/teaching device, and we benefited without the distortions we found occurring among your people.

We have recorded these differences meticulously in the Great Record of Creation that such naivete shall not be necessary again.

At this space/time we may best serve you, we believe, by stating that the pyramid for meditation along with other rounded and arched or pointed circular shapes is of help to you. However, it is our observation that due to the complexity of influences upon the unmanifested being at this space/time nexus among your planetary peoples, it is best that the progress of the mind/body/spirit complex take place without training aids, because when using a training aid, an entity then takes upon itself the Law of Responsibility for the quickened or increased rate of learn/teaching. If this greater understanding is not put into practice in the moment-by-moment experience of the entity, then the usefulness of the training aid become negative."

Ra: "The Ark of the Covenant was that place wherein those things most holy, according to the understanding of the one called Moishe, were placed. The article placed therein has been called by your peoples two tablets called the Ten Commandments. There were not two tablets. There was one writing in scroll. This was placed along with the most carefully written accounts by various entities of their beliefs concerning the creation by the One Creator.

The ark was designed to constitute the place wherefrom the priests, as you call those distorted towards the desire to serve their brothers, could draw their power and feel the presence of the One Creator. However, it is to be noted that this entire arrangement was designed not by the one known to the Confederation as Yahweh but rather was designed by negative entities preferring this method of creating an elite called the Sons of Levi."

This was charged with materials it was built with, being given an electromagnetic field. It became an object of power in this way, and, to those whose faith became that untarnished by unrighteousness or separation, this power designed from negativity became positive.

This is in common with each of our orthodox religious systems, which have all become somewhat mixed in orientation (negative and positive) yet offer a pure path to the One Creator which is seen by the pure seeker.

Ra says the Ark of the covenant still exists but they can't state where at to avoid infringement on our peoples by locating. (Recent channeling said it was in Ukraine and that's why it has had destruction in that country).

Unusable heat is generated as Earth moves form third into fourth density. This has to do with the vibrations of third-density having disharmony with fourth density, showing up as physical heating within the Earth.

If an entity is not in harmony with its circumstances, it feels a burning within. The temperature of the physical vehicle does not yet rise, only the heat of the disharmony. However, if an entity persists for a long period in feeling this emotive heat and disharmony, the entire body complex will begin to resonate to this disharmony, and the disharmony will then show up as cancer or other degenerative health distortions.

When an entire planetary system of peoples and cultures repeatedly experiences disharmony on a great scale, the Earth under the feet of these entities shall begin to resonate with the disharmony. Due to the nature of the physical vehicle, disharmony shows up as a blockage of growth or an uncontrolled growth, since the primary function of a mind/body/spirit complex is growth and maintenance. In the case of Earth, the purpose of the planet is the maintenance of orbit and the proper location or orientation with regard to other cosmic influences. In order to have this occurring properly, the interior of Earth is physically hot. Thus, instead of uncontrolled growth you begin to experience uncontrolled heat and its expansive consequences.

Earth is of a honey comb nature. The center is solid and molten.

At one time the Earth had third-density entities living in the honeycomb areas, which is no longer occurring at this present space/time.

There are some inner civilizations or entities living in these areas who do not come and materialize on the Earth's surface at some times. Further, there are some inner-plane entities in Earth which prefer to do some materialization into third density visible in these areas. There are also bases in these areas of those from elsewhere, both positive and negative. There are abandoned cities.

The bases in these areas by those from elsewhere are used for the work of materialization of needed equipment for communication with third-density entities and for resting places for small crafts. They are used for surveillance when it is requested by entities.

Some of the teachers of the Confederation speak partially through these surveillance instruments along computerized lines, and when information is desired and those requesting it are of the proper vibratory level, the Confederation entity itself will then speak.

Many people on Earth request the same basic information in enormous repetition, and for a social memory complex to speak ad infinitum (endlessly) about the need to meditate is a waste of the considerable abilities of such social memory complexes. (I assume we must meditate before asking questions of the Confederation, higher density beings or those who pray to God.)

Some entities have been approved by the Council of Saturn the placement and maintenance of these message givers for those who needs are simple, thus reserving the abilities of the Confederation members for those already meditating and absorbing information which are then ready for additional information.

Ra: "We of the Confederation are at the call of those upon your planet. If the call, though sincere, is fairly low in consciousness of the system whereby spiritual evolution may be precipitated (accelerated), then we may only offer that information useful to that particular caller. This is the basic difficulty. Entities receive the basic information about the original thought and the means-that is, meditation and service to others- whereby this Original Thought may be obtained.

Please note that as Confederation members we are speaking for positively oriented entities. We believe the Orion group has precisely the same difficulty.

Once this basic information is received, it is not put into practice in the heart and in the life experience but instead rattles about within the mind complex distortions as would a building block which has lost its place and simply rolls from side to side uselessly, yet still the entity calls. Therefore, the same basic information is repeated. Ultimately the entity decides that it is weary of this repetitive information. However, if an entity puts into practice that which it is given, it will not find repetition except when needed."

Ra can say very little about the distortion of mummification of their designs in constructing the pyramid, for the intent was quite mixed and the uses, though many felt them to be positive, were of a nonpositive order of generation. Ra cannot speak upon this subject without infringement upon some basic energy balances between positive and negative forces upon our planet. Those offering themselves to be mummified thought they were offering themselves in service to others.

The entities that helped Ra use the pyramid shape while Ra was in third density have begun their travel back to the Creator and are no longer experiencing time.

When using the pendulum in discovering energy centers, the weak back-and-forth motion indicates a partial blockage, although not a complete blockage. The strong back-and-forth motion indicates the reverse of blockage, which is over-stimulation of a chakra or energy center, which is occurring in order to attempt to balance some difficulty in body or mind complex activity. This condition is not helpful to the entity, as it is unbalanced.

The groups conscientiousness (diligent in carrying out one's duty to do what is right) is to be recommended.

Session 61: 7-8-1981

Seniority of vibration has reached the green-ray level of vibratory consciousness complexes.

There are four types of cycles given in the moment of entry into incarnation. There are more cosmic and less regularized inpourings which, from time to time affect a sensitized mind/body/spirit complex.

The four rhythms are known on Earth as biorhythms.

There is a fourth cycle called the cycle of gateway of magic of the adept or of spirit. This cycle is completed in approximately 18 of our diurnal (day) cycles.

The cosmic patterns are also a function of the moment of incarnative entrance and have to do with our satellite called the moon, our planets of this galaxy, the galactic sun, and in some cases the instreamings from the major galactic points of energy flow.

The three members of this triad (Don Elkins, Carla and Jim) bring in this energy pattern which is Ra. Ra suggests that it is always of some interest to observe the roadmap, both of the cycles and of the planetary and other cosmic influences, in that one may see certain wide roads or possibilities. However, we remind that this group is a unit.

It was Ra's opinion, that they humbly offer, that each of the group members is in remarkable harmony with each other for this particular third-density illusion at this space/time nexus.

In healing exercises of the body, there's disciplines of the body balancing love and wisdom in the use of the body in its natural functions:

Ra: "I am Ra. We shall speak more briefly than usual due to this instrument's use of the transferred energy. We, therefore, request further queries if our reply is not sufficient.

The body complex has natural functions. Many of these have to do with the unmanifested self and are normally not subject to the need for balancing. There are natural functions which have to do with other self. Among these are touching, love, the sexual life, and those times when the company of another is craved to combat the type of loneliness which is the natural function of the body, as opposed to those types of loneliness which are of the mind/emotion complex or of the spirit.

When these natural functions may be observed in the daily life, they may be examined in order that the love of self and love of other-self verses the wisdom regarding the use of natural functions may be observed. There are many fantasies and stray thoughts which may be examined in most of your people in this balancing process.

Equally to be balance is the withdrawal from the need for these natural functions with regard to other self. On the one hand there is an excess of love. It must be determined whether this is love of self or other self or both. On the other hand, there is an overbalance towards wisdom.

It is well to know the body complex so that it is an ally, balanced and ready to be clearly used as a tool, for each bodily function may be used in higher and higher complexes of energy with other self. No matter what the behavior, the important balancing is the understanding of each interaction on this level with other selves, so that whether the balance may be love/wisdom or wisdom/love, the other self is seen by the self in a balanced configuration, and the self is thus freed for further work."

How feelings affect portions and sensations of the body:

Ra: "It is nearly impossible to speak generally of these mechanisms, for each entity of proper seniority has its own programming. Of the less aware entities we may say that the connection will often seem random, as the Higher Self continues producing catalyst until a bias occurs. In each programmed individual the sensitivities are far more active, and that catalyst not used fully by the mind and spirit is given to the body.

Thus, you may see in this entity the numbing of the arms and the hands, signifying this entity's failure to surrender to the loss of control over the life. Thus, this drama is enacted in the physical distortion complex.

In the questioner (Don) we may see the desire not to be carrying the load it carries given as physical manifestation of the soreness of those muscles for carrying used. That which is truly needed to be carried is a pre-incarnative responsibility, which seems highly inconvenient.

In the case of the scribe, we see a weariness and numbness of feelings ensuing from lack of using catalyst designed to sensitize this entity to quite significant influxes of unfamiliar distortion complexes of the mental, emotional, and spiritual level. As the numbness removes itself from the higher or more responsive complexes, the bodily complex distortions will vanish. This is true also of the other example.

We would note at this time that the totally efficient use of catalyst upon your plane is extremely rare."

Ra could give this information without infringing on free will because each of the group members are already aware of this information. It is interesting to Ra that in many of the queries (questions) Don asks for confirmation rather than information.

Ra: "This is not a dimension of knowing, even subjectively, due to the lack of overview of cosmic and other inpourings which affect each and every situation which produces catalyst. The subjective acceptance of what's at the moment and finding of love within that moment is the greater freedom.

That known as the subjective knowing without proof is, in some degree, a poor friend, for there will be anomalies no matter how much information is garnered due to the distortions which form third density."

Ra: "Within the body there are many polarities which relate to the balancing of the energy centers of the various bodies of the unmanifested entity. It is well to explore these polarities for work in healing. Each entity, of course, a potential polarized portion of an other-self."

The proper balancing exercises for all the sensations of the body:

Ra: "The balancing requires a meditative state in order for the work to be done. However, the balancing of sensation has to do with an analysis of the sensation with especial respect to any unbalanced learning between the love and the wisdom or the positive and the negative. Then whatever is lacking in the balanced sensation is, as in all balancing, allowed to come into the being after the sensation is remembered and recalled in such detail as to overwhelm the senses."

The importance of the appurtenances and other items to be carefully aligned and why just a small ruffle in the sheet by the instrument causes a problem with the reception of Ra:

Ra: "We may attempt an explanation. This contact is narrow band. The instrument is highly sensitive. Thus, we have good entry into it and can use it to an increasingly satisfactory level.

However, the trance condition is not one which is without toll upon this instrument. Therefore, the area above the entrance into the physical complex of this instrument must be kept clear to avoid discomfort to the instrument, especially as it reenters the body complex. The appurtenances give to the instrument's sensory input mental visualizations which aid in the trance beginning. The careful alignment of these is important for the energizing group in that it is a reminder to that support group that it is time for a working. The ritualistic behaviors are triggers for many energies of the support group. You may have noticed more energy being used in workings as the number has increased due to the long-term effect of such ritualistic actions.

This would not aid another group, as it was designed for the particular system of mind/body/spirit complexes and especially the instrument."

The purpose of the frontal lobes of the brain and the conditions necessary for their activation:

Ra: "The frontal lobes of the brain will have much more use in fourth density."

Ra: "The primary mental/emotive condition of this large area of the so-called brain is joy or love in its creative sense. Thus, the energies we have discussed in relationship to the pyramids: all of the healing, the learning, the building, and the energizing are to be found in this area. This is the area tapped by the adept. This is the area which, working through the trunk and root of mind, makes contact with intelligent energy and, through this gateway, intelligent infinity."

Session 62: 7-13-1981

Ra: "The instrument was under specific psychic attack at the time of the beginning of the working (channeling). There was slight irregularity in the (supporting groups) words verbalized in the protective walking the circle. Into this opening came this (negative) entity and began to work upon the instrument now in trance state. This instrument was being quite adversely affected in physical complex distortions. Thus, the circle (of one) was walked. The breath (of the supporting group) of righteousness expelled (forcibly, approximately two and one-half feet above the instrument's head) the thought form, and the circle again walked (by the supporting group around the instrument).

The thought form was of Orion (negative) affiliation. This thought form sought to put an end to this instrument's incarnation by working with the renal (kidney) distortions which, although corrected upon time/space, are vulnerable to one which knows the way to separate time/space molding and space/time distortions which are being unmolded, vulnerable as before the healing."

Ra: "There will be some discomfort. However, we were fortunate this instrument was very open to us and well-tuned. Had we not been able to reach this instrument and instruct you (the supporting group Don and Jim), the instrument's physical vehicle would soon be unviable."

Ra: "We are of the opinion that no lasting harm or distortion will occur."

Ra: "The missed word (from the group vocalizing during the circle of One) was a chance occurrence (by the Orion entity) and not a planned one."

Ra: "…As you begin a working be aware that this instrument is likely being watched for any opportunity. Thus, if the circle is walked with some imperfection, it is well to immediately repeat. The expelling (forcibly) of breath is also appropriate, always to the left."

The expelling of breath being sent above the instrument's head from its right side to its left.

The group was given two spiritual healer names, two allopathic healers that they could see.

The harmonies and loving social intercourse which prevail habitually in this group create a favorable environment for the group to do their work.

This group (Don, Carla and Jim) as all positive channels and supporting groups, is a greatly high priority with the Orion group (negative entities).

The Southern Cross members are of the Orion group. However, those planetary social memory complexes of the Orion constellation have the upper hand and thus rule the other members. In negative thinking, there is always the pecking order and the power against power in separation.

There are fourth and a few fifth-density members of the Orion group. Therefore, the top of the pecking order is fifth density negative.

Earth has some negatively oriented action in sway at this space/time nexus.

Ra: "The early fifth-density negative entity, if oriented towards maintaining cohesion (beings united) as a social memory complex, may in its free will determine that the path to wisdom lies in the manipulation in exquisite (flawless) propriety (conforming) of all other selves. It then, by virtue of its abilities in wisdom, is able to be the leader of forth-density beings which are upon the road to wisdom by exploring the dimensions of love of self and understanding of self. These fifth-density entities see the creation as that which shall be put in order.

Dealing with a plane such as this third density at this harvesting, it will see the mechanism of the call more clearly and have much less distortion towards plunder (forcefully steal) or manipulation by thoughts which are given to negatively oriented entities, although in allowing this to occur and sending less wise entities to do this work, any successes redound (greatly contribute) to the leaders.

The fifth density sees the difficulties posed by the light and in this way directs entities of this vibration to the seeking of targets of opportunity such as this one. If fourth-density temptations, towards distortion of ego etc., are not successful, the fifth-density entity then thinks in terms of the removal of Light."

Ra: "Fifth-density entities are very light beings, although they do have the type of physical vehicle which you understand. Fifth-density entities are very fair to look upon in your standard of beauty.

The thought is what is sent for a fifth-density entity is likely to have mastered this technique or discipline. There is little or no means of perceiving such an entity, for unlike forth-density negative entities, the fifth-density entity walks with light feet.

This instrument was aware of extreme coldness in the past diurnal cycle and spent much more time that your normal attitudes would imagine it be appropriate in what seemed to each of you an extremely warm climate. This was not perceived by the instrument, but the drop in subjective temperature is a sign of presence of a negative or nonpositive or draining entity.

This instrument did mention a feeling of discomfort but was nourished by this group and was able to dismiss it. Had it not been for a random mishap, all would have been well, for you have learned to live in love and light and do not neglect to remember the One Infinite Creator."

It was a fifth-density negative entity that made this particular attack upon the instrument. Which is unusual that a 5th density negative bothered to do this instead of sending a fourth-density negative servant.

Nearly all positive channels and groups may be lessened in their positivity or rendered quite useless by the temptations offered by the fourth-density negative thought forms. They may suggest many distortions towards specific information, toward the aggrandizement (glorification) of the self, towards the flowering of the organization in some political, social, or fiscal way.

These distortions remove the focus from the One Infinite Source of love and light of which we are all messengers, humble and knowing that we are but the tiniest portion of the Creator, a small part of a magnificent entirely of infinite intelligence.

Is there something the group could do to eliminate the problems that the instrument continually experiences of the cold feeling of the psychic attacks?"

Ra: "Yes, you could cease in your attempts to be channels for the love and light of the One Infinite Creator.

Jordyn: "This tells me that if channeling was truly evil, like some religious people like to think, then this positive entity wouldn't be giving an option not to channel anymore if they wanted to. An evil entity, would encourage the channeling to always continue until death, if it was a negative action."

The love and devotion of the group aids the instrument (Carla). Be at peace. There is some toll for this work. This instrument embraces this or Ra could not speak. Rest then in that peace and love and do as you will, as you wish, as you feel. Let there be an end to worry when this is accomplished. The great healer of distortions is love.

First density is composed of core atomic vibrations that are in the red spectrum, the second in orange, ect.

The core vibrations of our planet are still in the red and the second-density beings are still in orange at this space/time right now, and each density as it exists on our planet right now has a different core vibration.

Ra: "You must see Earth as being seven Earths. There is red, orange, yellow, and there will soon be a completed green-color vibratory locus for fourth-density entities which they will call Earth. During the fourth-density experience, due to lack of development of fourth-density entities, the third-density planetary sphere is not useful for habitation, since the early fourth-density entity will not know precisely how to maintain the illusion that fourth density cannot be seen or determined from any instrumentation available to any third density.

Thus, in fourth density the red, orange, and green energy nexi of your planet will be activated while the yellow is in potentiation along with blue and indigo."

Jordyn: "I assume this means first, second and fourth density entities will be upon Earth during fourth density New Earth. Third density entities will no longer be habitable and thus, third density entities that did not make the fourth density harvest in approximately 2030 will be transferred to a third density planet to continue their learning and evolution as there is no judgement for the polarity chosen. The 4th density positive can be considered Heaven, while the 4th density negative planet may be considered as Hell."

SESSION 63: 7-18-1981

When the instrument goes to the restroom several times before or after a session, this is due to the elimination of the distortion leavings of the material which Ra uses for contact. This occurs variably, sometimes beginning before contact, other workings this occurring after the contact.

Ra: "The body complex is distorted due to psychic attack in the area of the kidneys and urinary tract. There is also distortion continuing due to arthritis. You may expect this psychic attack to be constant, as this instrument has been under observation by negatively oriented force for some time."

How to lessen the effectiveness of psychic attacks?

Ra: "Continue in love and praise and thanksgiving to the Creator. Examine previous material. Love is the great protector.

<u>Vital energy</u> is the complex of energy levels of mind, body and spirit. Unlike physical energy, it requires the integrated complexes vibrating in a useful manner.

The faculty of will can, to a variable extent, replace missing vital energy, and this has occurred in past workings in this instrument. This is not recommended. At this time the vital energies are well nourished in mind and spirit, although the physical energy level is low at this time.

Vital energy is a function of the awareness or bias of the entity with respect to his polarity or general unity with the Creator or creation.

Ra: "The vital energy may be seen to be that deep love of life or life experiences such as the beauty of creation and the appreciation of other selves and the distortions of your co-Creator's making which are of beauty.

Without this vital energy, the least distorted physical complex will fail and perish. With this love or vital energy or elan (enthusiastic energy), the entity may continue though the physical complex is greatly distorted."

Ra: "It is misleading to speak of gains and losses when dealing with the subject of the cycle's ending and the green-ray cycle beginning upon your sphere. It is to be kept in the forefront of the faculties of intelligence that there is one creation in which there is no loss. There are progressive cycles for experiential use by entities.

As the green-ray cycle or the density of love and understanding begins to take shape, the yellow-ray plane or Earth which you now enjoy in your dance will cease to be inhabited for some period of your space/time as the space/time necessary for fourth-density entities to learn their ability to shield their density from that of third is learned. After this period there will come a time when third density may again cycle on the yellow-ray sphere.

Meanwhile there is another sphere, congruent to a great extent with yellow ray, forming. This fourth-density sphere coexists with first, second, and third. It is of a denser nature due to the rotational core atomic aspects of its material. We (Ra states) have discussed this subject with you.

The fourth-density entities which incarnate at this space/time are fourth density in the view of experience but are incarnating in less dense vehicles due to desire to experience and aid in the birth of fourth density upon this plane.

You may note that fourth-density entities have a great abundance of compassion."

At present we have, in third-density incarnation on this plane, those third-density entities of the planet Earth who have been here for some number of incarnations who will graduate in the three-way split, either positive polarity harvested entities remaining in this planetary influence but not upon this plane, the negative polarity harvestable going to a fourth density negative planet, and the rest unharvestable third density going to another third-density planet. In addition to these entities, we have some already harvestable from other third-density planets who have come here and have incarnated in third-density form to make transition with this planet into fourth density. There are also approximately 65 million Wanderers in 1981.

The recent phenomenon of third-density harvestable entities from other planets incarnating here for fourth-density experience is not yet in excess of 35,000 entities. These entities are incarnating with a double body in activation. The entities birthing these fourth-density entities experience a great feeling of the connection and the use of spiritual energies during pregnancy. This is due to the necessity for manifesting the double body.

This transitional body will be able to appreciate fourth-density vibratory complexes as the instreaming increases without the disruption of the third-density body. If a third-density entity were electrically aware of fourth density in full, the third-density electrical fields would fail due to incompatibility. These entities will die according to third-density necessities.

The third and fourth, combination, density's body will die according to other necessity of third-density mind/body/spirit complex distortions.

The purpose of the combined activation of mind/body/spirit complexes is that they are, to some extent, consciously aware of those fourth-density understandings which third density is unable to remember due to the forgetting. Thus fourth-density is unable to remember due to the forgetting. Thus, fourth-density experience may be begun with the added attraction to an entity oriented toward service to others of dwelling in a troubled third-density environment and offering its love and compassion.

The purpose in transition to earth prior to the complete changeover is for the experience to be gained here before the harvesting process. These entities are not Wanderers in the sense that this planetary sphere is their fourth-density home planet. However, the experience for this service is earned only by those harvested third-density entities which have demonstrated a great deal of orientation towards service to others. It is a privilege to be allowed this clearly in incarnation, and there is much experiential catalyst in service to other selves at this harvesting.

Some children in the dual activated bodies have demonstrated the ability to bend metal mentally, which is a fourth-density phenomenon. The reason they can do this and the fifth-density Wanderers here on Earth cannot do it, is the fact that they have the fourth-density body in activation. Since Wanderers are third density activated in mind/body/spirit and are subject to the forgetting, which can only be penetrated with disciplined meditation and working.

Harvestable third density entities who very recently have been coming here are coming here late enough so that they will not affect the polarization through their teachings. They are not infringing upon the first distortion of free will because they are children now, and they won't be old enough to really affect any of the polarization until the transition is well advanced. However, the Wanderers who have come here are older and have a greater ability to affect polarization. They must do their affecting as a function of their ability to penetrate the forgetting process in order to be within free will.

Some of the harvestable third-density entities who can bend metal are over fifty years old and some over thirty.

Any entity who, by accident or by careful design, penetrates intelligent energy's gateway may use the shaping powers of this energy. (such as bending metal).

Now as this transition continues into fourth-density activation; in order to inhabit this fourth-density sphere it will be necessary for all third-density physical bodies to go through the process we refer to as death. There are people at this time on this fourth density planet who have already gone through this process, only in the very recent past; this population is from other planets since the harvesting has not yet occurred on Earth yet. It is from planets where the harvesting has already occurred. These entities are in dual bodies at this time.

As the fourth-density sphere is activated, there is heat energy being generated. This heat energy is generated on the third-density sphere only. The experiential distortions of each dimension are discrete.

At this time cosmic influxes (inflows) are conducive (helpful) to true color green core particles being formed and material of this nature being formed. However, there is a mixture of the yellow-ray and green-ray environments at this time, necessitating the birthing of transitional mind/body/spirit complex types of energy distortions.

At full activation of the true color green density of love, the planetary sphere will be solid and inhabitable upon its own, and the birthing that takes place will have been transformed through the process of time to the appropriate type of vehicle to appreciate in full the fourth-density planetary environment. At this nexus the green-ray environment exists to a far greater extent in time/space than in space/time.

As our planet is spiraled by the spiraling action of the entire major galaxy and our planetary system spirals into the new position, the fourth-density vibrations becoming more and more pronounced. These atomic core vibrations begin to create the fourth-density sphere and gradually create green-ray-density bodily complexes. This will take place beginning with our third-density type of physical vehicle and, through the means of bisexual reproduction, become by evolutionary processes the fourth-density body complexes.

(Essentially, third-density mothers with dual activated bodies giving birth will give birth to fourth density babies.)

The influxes of true color green energy complexes will more and more create the conditions where the atomic structure of cells of bodily complexes is that of the density of love. The entities inhabiting these physical vehicles will be, to some extent, fourth density babies born and as harvest is completed, the harvested entities of this planetary influence.

There is a three-dimensional clock-face or spiral of endlessness associated with the entire major galaxy so that as it revolves it carries all of these stars and planetary systems through transitions from density to density, which is planned by the Logos.

The Logos did not plan for the core heating effect in our third-density transition into fourth, except for the condition of free will, which is planned by the Logos as it, itself, is a creature of free will. In this climate an infinity of events or conditions may occur. They cannot be said to be planned by the Logos but can be said to have been freely allowed.

The spiritual configuration as well as mental biases of people on Earth has been responsible for the body complex distortions of the planetary sphere.

When third density goes out of activation and into potentiation, Earth will then be a planet that is first, second, and fourth density. There will be no activated third-density vibrations on this planet, which are the mind/body/spirit complexes of third density, artifacts, thought forms and feelings which these co-Creators have produced. This is third density.

Session 64: 7-26-1981

The cause of the instrument's transitory vital energy distortion, which lessens the free flow of vital energy, is a bias towards the yearning for expression of devotion to the One Creator in group worship.

Ra: "This entity was yearning for this protection both consciously in that it responds to the accoutrements (accessories or equipment) of this expression, the ritual, the colors, and their meanings as given by the distortion system of the church, the song of praise, and the combined prayers of thanksgiving and, most of all, that which may be seen to be most centrally magical, the intake of that food which is not of this dimension but has been transmuted into metaphysical nourishment in what this distortion of expression calls the holy communion.

The subconscious reason, it being the stronger for this yearning, was the awareness that such expression is, when appreciated by an entity as the transmutation into the presence of the One Creator, a great protection of the entity as it moves in the path of service to others.

The principle behind any ritual of the white magical nature is to so configure the stimuli which reach down into the trunk of mind that this arrangement causes the generation of disciplined and purified emotion or love which then maybe both protection and the key to the gateway to intelligent infinity."

Why a slight error made in the ritual starting this communication allowed the intrusion by an Orion entity?

Ra: "I am Ra. This contact is narrow band and its preconditions precise. The other-self offering its service in the negative path also is possessed of the skill of the swordsman. You deal in this contact with forces of great intensity poured into a vessel as delicate as a snowflake and as crystalline.

The smallest of lapses may disturb the regularity of this pattern of energies which forms the channel for these transmissions.

We may note for your information that our pause was due to the necessity of being quite sure that the mind/body/spirit complex of the instrument was safely in the proper light configuration or density before we dealt with the situation. Far better would it be to allow the shell to become unviable than to allow the mind/body/spirit complex to be misplaced."

Rituals or techniques used by Ra in seeking in the direction of service:

Ra: "I am Ra. To speak of that which sixth-density social memory complexes labor within in order to advance is at best misprision (neglect/failure) of plain communication, for much is lost in transmission of concept from density to density, and the discussion of sixth density is inevitably distorted greatly.

However, we shall attempt to speak to your query, for it is a helpful one in that it allows us to express once again the total unity of creation. We seek the Creator upon a level of shared experience to which you are not privy (knowledgeable of the secret information), and rather than surrounding ourselves in light, we have become light. Our understanding is that there is no other material except light. Our rituals, are an infinitely subtle continuation of the balancing processes which you are now beginning to experience.

We seek now without polarity. Thus, we do not invoke any power from without, for our search has become internalized as we become light/love and love/light. These are the balances we seek, the balances between compassion and wisdom which more and more allow our understanding of experience to be informed that we may come closer to the unity with the One Creator which we so joyfully seek.

Your rituals at your level of progress contain the concept of polarization, and this is most central at your particular space/time."

Ra can't answer the query as to the techniques Ra used in third density to evolve in mind, body and spirit. That query lies beyond the Law of Confusion (Free will), as does their fourth-density experience.

Ra: "Let us express a thought. Ra is not elite. To speak of our specific experiences to a group which honors us is to guide to the point of a specific advising. Our work was that of your people, of experiencing the catalyst of joys and sorrow. Our circumstances were somewhat more harmonious. Let it be said that any entity or group may create the most splendid harmony in any outer atmosphere. Ra's experiences are no more than your own. Yours is that dance at this space/time in third-density harvest."

Any words upon the particular subject of possible records left near, in, or under the Great Pyramid at Giza creates the possibility of infringement upon free will. Therefore, Ra cannot answer.

The gateway of magic for the adept occurring in 18-day cycles:

Ra: "I am Ra. The mind/body/spirit complex is born under a series of influences, both lunar, planetary, cosmic, and in some cases, karmic. The moment of the birthing into this illusion begins the cycles we have mentioned.

The spiritual or adept's cycle is an eighteen-day cycle and operates with the equalities of the sine wave. Thus, there are a few excellent days on the positive side of the curve, that being the first nine days of the cycle- precisely the fourth, the fifth, and the sixth- when workings are most appropriately undertaken, given that the entity is still without total conscious control of its mind/body/spirit distortion/reality.

The most interesting portion of this information, like that of each cycle, is the noting of the critical point wherein passing from the ninth to the tenth and from the eighteenth to the first days the adept will experience some difficulty especially when there is a transition occurring in another cycle at the same time. At the nadir (lowest point) of each cycle the adept will be at its least powerful but will not be open to difficulties in nearly the degree that it experiences at critical time."

The day the infant was born starts the 18-day cycles, continuing it through the life. It is not necessary to identify the instant of birth, but the day of birth is satisfactory for all but the finest workings.

This cycle is a helpful tool to the adept, but as the adept becomes more balanced, the workings designed will be dependent less and less upon these cycles of opportunity and more and more even in their efficacy (desire to produce an intended result).

Ra is fettered (restrained) from speaking specifically about the level of abilities the adept would reach in order to be independent of the cyclical tool. This is due to the group's work, so to speak would seem to judge. However, this cycle is in the same light as the astrological balances within the group; that is, they are interesting but not critical.

Recent research indicated that the normal sleep cycle for entities on earth occurs one hour later each diurnal period, so that we have a twenty-five-hour cycle instead of twenty-four: In some cases, this is correct. The planetary influences from those of Mars experience memory have some effect on these third-density physical bodily complexes. Mars race has given its genetic material to many bodies upon this plane.

What is the value of modern medical techniques in respect to Karma?

Ra: "…For that which is allopathic among your healing practices is somewhat two-sided.

Firstly, you must see the possibility/probability that each and every allopathic healer is in fact a healer. Within your cultural nexus, this training is considered the appropriate means of perfecting the healing ability. In the most basic sense, any allopathic healer may be seen to, perhaps, be one whose desire is service to others in alleviation of bodily complex and mental/emotional complex distortions so that the entity to be healed may experience further catalyst over a longer period of life. This is a great service to others when appropriate due to the accumulation of distortions toward wisdom and love which can be created through the use of the space/time continuum of your illusion.

In observing the allopathic concept of the body complex as a machine, we may note the symptomology (symptoms of the society) of a societal complex seemingly dedicated to the most intransigent (uncompromising) desire for the distortions of distraction, anonymity (being anonymous), and sleep. This is the result rather than the cause of societal thinking upon your plane.

In turn this mechanical concept of the body complex has created the continuing proliferation (rapid increase) of distortions towards what you would call ill health, due to the strong chemicals used to control and hide bodily distortions. There is a realization among many of your people that there are more efficacious (effective) systems of healing not excluding the allopathic but also including the many other avenues of healing."

Seeking allopathic aid for a bodily distortion vs. experiencing the catalyst and not correcting the distortion:

Ra: "If the entity is polarized towards service to others, analysis properly proceeds along the lines of consideration of which path offers the most opportunity for service to others.

For the negatively polarized entity, the antithesis (opposite) is the case.

For the unpolarized entity, the considerations are random and most likely in the direction towards comfort."

A four-toed Bigfoot cast shown to Don Elkins by somebody he knows was an entity of a small group of thought forms.

There weren't any Bigfoot remains found after the entities have died on our surface. Ra then suggested that exploration of the caves underlining some of the western coastal mountain regions of North America will one day offer such remains. They will not be generally understood if this culture survives in its present form long enough for this probability/possibility vortex to occur.

How to examine the sensations of the body during healing exercises?

Humans are already experiencing sensations.

Ra: "Most of these sensations or nearly all of them are transient (short lived) and without interest. However, the body is the creature of the mind. Certain sensations carry importance due to the charge or power which is felt by the mind upon the experience of this sensation.

For instance, at this space/time nexus, one sensation is carrying a powerful charge and may be examined. This is the sensation of what you call the distortion towards discomfort due to the cramped position of the body complex during this working. In balancing you would then explore this sensation. Why is this sensation powerful? Because it was chosen in order that the entity might be of service to others in energizing this contact.

Each sensation that leaves the aftertaste of meaning upon the mind, that leaves the taste within the memory, shall be examined. These are the sensations of which we speak."

Session 65: 8-8-1981

More entities may increase in their seeking in the near future on this Earth. The generalities of expression can never be completely correct. However, when faced with a hole in current belief systems, an entity's eyes may peer through the hole for the first time to more accurate facts. This tendency is probably given the possibility/probability vortices within our space/time and time/space continua at this nexus.

The intention Wanderers had prior to incarnation here on Earth at this time was them finding it a privilege of the opportunity to be more fully of service because of the increased seeking (of third-density entities on Earth). There are many Wanderers who dysfunction with regard to the planetary ways of our peoples have caused, to some extent, a condition of being caught up in a configuration of mind complex activity which may prohibit the intended service.

Ra was speaking slower when attempting to channel even more narrow band than before, when the instrument became somewhat weak and more fragile than usual, including a continuing pain which has a weakening effect on physical energy.

Seniority by vibration of incarnation has greatly polarized those upon the surface of the planet now, and the influx in Wanderers has greatly increased the mental configuration towards things of a more spiritual nature.

Kathryn Jordyn: "I have seniority of vibration at 87% positive polarity. This also means I'm a part of the 65% of Earth entities harvestable for fourth-density positive New Earth."

So, seniority by vibration entities and the influx of Wanderers are one of the factors creating a better atmosphere for service.

The paranormal events occurring are not designed to increase seeking but are manifestations of those whose vibratory configuration enables these entities to contact the gateway to intelligent infinity. These entities capable of paranormal service may determine to be of such service on a conscious level. This, however, is a function of the entity and its free will and not the paranormal ability.

The greater opportunity for service due to the many Earth changes as we progress into fourth density, such as the healing effect and the ability of people to perform paranormal activities, offers many challenges, difficulties and seeming distresses within our illusion to many who will seek to understand the reason for the malfunctioning of the physical rhythms of their planet.

Moreover, there exist probability/possibility vortices which spiral towards your bellicose (war-like) actions. Many of these vortices are not of the nuclear war but of the less annihilatory (lethal) but more lengthy "conventional" war. This situation, if formed in our illusion, would offer many opportunities for seeking and for service.

Ra: "I am Ra. The possibility/probabilities exist for situation in which great portions of your continent and the globe in general might be involved in the type of warfare which you might liken to guerrilla warfare (small, independent groups using irregular tactics to fight against larger forces). The ideal of freedom from the so-called invading force of either the controlled fascism (far-right authoritarian) or the equally controlled social common ownership of all things would stimulate great quantities of contemplation upon the great polarization implicit in the contrast between freedom and control. In this scenario which is being considered at this time/space nexus, the idea of obliterating valuable sites and personnel would not be considered a useful one. Other weapons would be used which do not destroy as your nuclear arms would. In this ongoing struggle, the light of freedom would burn within the mind/body/spirit complexes capable of such polarization. Lacking the opportunity for overt (open in plain sight) expression of the love of freedom, the seeking for inner knowledge would take root aided by those of the Brothers and Sisters of Sorrow which remember their calling upon this sphere."

What is the value of Edgar Cayce's prophecies with respect to the many Earth changes he mentioned?

Ra: "I am Ra. Consider the shopper entering the store to purchase food with which to furnish the table for the time period you call a week. Some stores have some items, others a variant set of offerings. We speak of these possibility/probability vortices when asked with the understanding that such are as a can, jar, or portion of good in your store.

It is unknown to us as we scan your time/space whether your people will shop hither or yon. We can only name some of the items available for the choosing. The record which the one you call Edgar read from is useful in that same manner. There is less knowledge in this material of other possibility/probability vortices and more attention paid to the strongest vortex. We see the same vortex but also see many others. Edgar's material could be likened unto one hundred boxes of your cold cereal, another vortex likened unto three, or six, or fifty of another product which is eaten by your peoples for breakfast. That you will breakfast is close to certain. The menu is your own choosing.

The value of prophecy must be realized to be only that of expressing (the most likely) possibilities. Moreover, it must be, in our humble opinion, carefully taken into consideration that any time/space viewing, whether by one of your time/space viewing or by one such as we who view the time/space from a dimension, exterior to it will have a quite difficult time expressing time measurement values. Thus, prophecy given in specific terms is more interesting for the content or type of possibility predicted than for the space/time nexus of its supposed occurrence."

Given the amount of strength of the possibility/probability vortex which posits the expression by the planet itself of the difficult birthing of the planetary self into fourth density, it would be greatly surprising were not many who have some access to space/time able to perceive this vortex.

Kathryn: "I have prophecy as well and can see things that will happen in the future. I have videos on my YouTube channel showing proof of 32 dreams of the future actually coming true or at times a thought coming to my head that actually came true in the future."

The amount of this cold cereal in the grocery, to use Ra's analogy, is disproportionately large. Each which prophesies does so from a unique level, position, or vibratory configuration. Thus, biases and distortions will accompany much prophecy.

It was the aim of Wanderers to serve the entities of this planet in whatever way was requested, and it was also their aim that their vibratory patterns might lighten the planetary vibration as a whole, thus ameliorating (improving) the effects of planetary disharmony and palliating (lighten) any results of this disharmony.

Specific intentions such as aiding in a situation not yet manifest, such as the future, are not the aim of Wanderers. Light and love go where they are sought and needed, and their direction is not planned aforetime (in the past).

Each of the Wanderers acts as a function of the biases he has developed in any way he sees fit to communicate or simply be in his polarity to aid the total consciousness of the planet. The physical presence of Wanderers does aid the planet.

Ra: "You may, at this time, note that as with any entities, each Wanderer has its unique abilities, biases, and specialties, so that from each portion of each density represented among the Wanderers come an array of pre-incarnative talents which then may be expressed upon this plane which you now experience, so that each Wanderer, in offering itself before incarnation, has some special service to offer in addition to the doubling effect of planetary love and light and the basic function of serving as beacon or shepherd.

Thus, there are those of fifth density whose abilities to express wisdom are great. There are fourth- and sixth-density Wanderers whose ability to serve as passive radiators or broadcasters of love and love/light are immense. There are many others whose talents brought into this density are quite varied.

Thus, Wanderers have three basic functions once the forgetting is penetrated, the first two being basic, the tertiary (third) one being unique to that particular mind/body/spirit complex.

We may not at this point while you ponder the possibility/probability vortices that although you have many, many items which cause distress and thus offer seeking and service opportunities, there is always one container in that store of peace, love, light, and joy. This vortex may be very small, but to turn one's back upon it is to forget the infinite possibilities of the present moment. Could your planet polarize towards harmony in one fine, strong moment of inspiration? Yes, my friends. It is not probable, but it is ever possible."

Among planetary harvest which yield a harvest of mind/body/spirit complexes, approximately 10 percent are negative, approximately 60 percent are positive, and approximately 30 percent are mixed, with nearly all harvest being positive. In the event of mixed harvest, it is almost unknown for the majority of the harvest to be negative. When a planet moves strongly towards the negative, there is almost no opportunity for harvestable positive polarization, because the ability to polarize positively requires a certain degree of self-determination.

Jordyn: "In a channeling session my higher-self in sixth density positive stated that 65% are positively oriented on Earth currently as of 2023. That leaves 35% being either negatively harvestable or mixed. Being at least 95% negative can make an entity harvestable for the 4th density negative planet. Those mixed will continue their evolutionary journey on another 3rd density planet after Earth fully activates fourth-density into the New Earth at the Harvest."

In a mixed harvest, there is nearly always disharmony and, therefore, added catalyst in the form of "Earth changes" at the end of a harvesting period.

It is the Confederation's desire to serve those who may indeed seek more intensely because of this added catalyst.

Ra doesn't choose to attempt to project the success of added numbers to the harvest, for this would not be appropriate. Ra stated that they are servants. If they are called, they will serve with all their strength. To count the added harvestable numbers is without virtue (showing high moral standards/ethical).

The added catalyst at the end of the cycle is a function specifically of the orientation of the consciousness that inhabits the planet. The consciousness has provided the catalyst for itself in orienting its thinking in the way it has oriented it, thus acting upon itself the same as catalyst of bodily pain and disease act upon the single mind/body/spirit complex. The planet may be seen as a planetary entity as somewhat of a single entity made up of billions of mind/body/spirit complexes.

This entity has not yet formed a social memory but is yet a single entity just as one of us can be called a single entity. Just as one can look at a single sun as an entity, a galaxy with billions of stars as an entity, and the entire universe of galaxies as a single entity in this octave of our existence with 250 billion suns in our universe.

Ra: "Let us attempt to speak upon this interesting subject. In your space/time, you and your peoples are the parents of that which is in the womb. The Earth is ready to be born, and the delivery is not going smoothly. When this entity has become born, it will be instinct with the social memory complex of its parents which have become fourth-density positive. In this density there is a broader view.

You may begin to see your relationship to the Logos or sun with which you are most intimately associated. This is not the relationship of parent to child but of Creator, that is Logos, to Creator that is the mind/body/spirit complex, as Logos. When this realization occurs, you may then widen the field of "eyeshot," infinitely recognizing parts of the Logos throughout the one infinite creation and feeling, with the roots of mind informing the intuition, the parents aiding their planets in evolution in reaches vast and unknown in the creation, for this process occurs many, many times in the evolution of the creation as a whole."

Why the Wanderer goes through the forgetting process?

Ra: "The reason is twofold. First, the genetic properties of the connection between the mind/body/spirit complex and the cellular structure of the body is different for third density than for third/fourth density.

Secondly, the free will of third-density entities needs be preserved. Thus, Wanderers volunteer for third-density genetic or DNA connections to the mind/body/spirit complex. The forgetting process can be penetrated to the extent of the Wanderer remembering what it is and why it is upon the planetary sphere. However, it would be an infringement if Wanderers penetrate the forgetting so far as to activate the more dense bodies and thus be able to live in a godlike manner. This would not be proper for those who have chosen to serve.

The new fourth-density entities which are becoming able to demonstrate various newer abilities are doing so as a result of the present experience, not as a result of memory. There are always a few exceptions, and we ask your forgiveness for constant barrages (bombardment) of over-generalization."

The resonating chamber in the pyramids was used so the adept could meet the self.

One meets the self in the center or deeps of the being. The resonating chamber may be likened unto the symbology of the burial and resurrection of the body, wherein the entity dies to self and, through this confrontation of apparent loss and realization of essential gain, is transmuted into a new risen being. This apparent death of losing the desires that are illusory, common desire of third density and gaining desire of total service to others.

Kathryn: "I believe this is what the Bible meant when it said that one must die to itself to be born again."

This was the purpose and intent of the chamber, as well as forming a necessary portion of the King's Chamber position effectiveness.

This chamber worked upon the mind and the body to create this awareness in him of dying to the desires of third density and resurrecting to the desires of total service to others. This mind was affected by sensory deprivation and the archetypical reactions to being buried alive with no possibility of extricating (freeing) the self (from a constraint). The body was affected both by the mind configuration and by the electrical and piezoelectrical properties of the materials (that allows the materials to absorb mechanical energy from its surroundings of vibration into electrical energy that can power other devices.) This was used in the construction of the resonating chamber.

Session 66: 8-12-1981

The crystallized healer is analogous (has many similarities, but belongs to different categories) to the pyramidal action of the King's Chamber position.

Ra: "The energy which is used is brought into the field complex of the healer by the outstretched hand used in a polarized sense. However, this energy circulates through the various points of energy to the base of the spine and, to a certain extent, the feet, thus coming through the main energy centers of the healer, spiraling through the feet, turning at the red energy center towards a spiral at the yellow energy center, and passing through the green energy center in a microcosm (miniature version) of the King's Chamber energy configuration of prana (cosmic energy or life-force energy); this then continuing for the third spiral through the blue energy center and being sent therefrom through the gateway back to intelligent infinity.

It is from the green center that the healing prana moves into the polarized healing right hand and therefrom to the one to be healed.

We may note that there are some who use the yellow-ray configuration to transfer energy, and this may be done, but the effects are questionable and, with regard to the relationship between the healer, the healing energy, and the seeker, questionable due to the propensity (tendency) for the seeker to continue requiring such energy transfers without any true healing taking place in the absence of the healer due to the lack of penetration of the armoring shell of which you spoke."

A Wanderer who has an origin from fifth or sixth density can attempt such healings and have little or no results.

Ra: "You may see the Wanderer as the infant attempting to verbalize the sound complexes of your people's. The memory of the ability to communicate is within the infant's undeveloped mind complex, but the ability to practice or manifest this, called speech, is not immediately forth coming due to the limitations of the mind/body/spirit complex it has chosen to be a part of in this experience.

So it is with the Wanderer, which, remembering the ease with which adjustments can be made in the home density, yet still having entered third density, cannot manifest that memory due to the limitation of the chosen experience. The chances of the Wanderer being able to heal in third density are only more than those native to this density because the desire to serve may be stronger and this method of service chosen."

The dual activated, third and fourth density, bodies harvested from other third-density planets are able to heal using these techniques, but as beginners of fourth density, the desire may not be present.

A Wanderer may have the desire to learn the techniques of healing while being trapped in a third density body. He then may be primarily concerned with the balancing and unblocking of energy centers. Only if a healer has become balanced may it be a channel for the balancing of an other-self. The healing is first practiced upon the self.

The role of a healer is to offer an opportunity for realignment or aid in realignment of either energy centers or some connection between the energies of mind and body, spirit and mind, or spirit and body. This latter is very rare. The seeker will then have a reciprocal (done in return) opportunity to accept a novel (new perspective) view of the self, a variant arrangement of patterns of energy influx. If the entity, at any level, desires to remain in the configuration of distortion which seems to need healing, it will do so. If, upon the other hand, the seeker chooses the novel configuration, it is done through free will.

This is one great difficulty with other forms of energy transfer in that they do not carry through the process of free will, as this process is not native to yellow ray.

The difference between someone healing themselves through mental configuration and being healed by a healer is that the healer does not heal. The crystallized healer is a channel for intelligent energy which offers an opportunity to an entity that it might help them heal itself.

In no case is there another description of healing.

Therefore, there is no difference as long as the healer never approaches one whose request for aid has not come to it previously. This is also true of the more conventional healers of your culture, and if these healers could but fully realize that they are responsible only for offering the opportunity of healing, and not for the healing, many of these entities would feel an enormous load of misconceived responsibility fall from them.

A mind/body/spirit complex in some cases would be seeking a source of gathered and focused light energy. This source could be another mind/body/spirit complex sufficiently crystallized for this purpose of the pyramid shape or something else.

Perhaps the greatest healer is within the self and may be tapped with continued meditation. The many forms of healing available to our peoples... each have virtue and may be deemed appropriate by any seeker who wishes to alter the physical body distortions or some connection between the various portions of the mind/body/spirit complex.

Psychic surgery:

There's psychic surgery in the Philippine Islands. The psychic surgeon (healer) provides a training aid or a way of creating a reconfiguration of the mind of the patient to be healed as the patient observes the action of the healer in seeing the materialized blood ect. And reconfigures the roots of mind to believe the healing is done, and, therefore, heals himself.

Ra: "There are times when the malcondition to be altered is without emotional, mental, or spiritual interest to the entity and is merely that which has, perhaps by chance genetic arrangement, occurred. In these cases, that which is apparently dematerialized will remain dematerialized and may be observed as so by any observer. The malcondition which has an emotional, mental, or spiritual charge is likely not to remain dematerialized in the sense of the showing of the objective referent (important) to an observer. However, if the opportunity has been taken by the seeker, the apparent malcondition of the physical complex (body) will be at variance (discrepancy) with the actual health of the seeker and the lack of experiencing the distortions which the objective referent would suggest still held sway.

For instance, in this instrument (Carla) the removal of three small cysts was the removal of material having no interest to the entity. Thus, these growths remained dematerialized after the so-called psychic surgery experience. In other psychic surgery, the kidneys of this instrument were carefully offered a new configuration of beingness which the entity embraced. However, this particular portion of the mind/body/spirit complex carried a great deal of emotional, mental and spiritual charge due to this distorted functioning being the cause of great illness in a certain configuration of events which culminated in this entity's conscious decision to be of service. Therefore, any objective scanning of this entity's renal (kidney) complex would indicate the rather extreme dysfunctional aspect which is showed previous to the psychic surgery experience.

The key is not in the continuation of the dematerialization of distortion to the eye of the beholder but rather lies in the choosing of the newly materialized configuration which exists in time/space. (metaphysical)

Ra: "I am Ra. Healing is done in the time/space (metaphysical) portion of the mind/body/spirit complex, is adopted by the form-making or etheric body, and is then given to the space/time physical illusion for use in the activated yellow mind/body/spirit complex. It is the adoption of the configuration health by the etheric body in time/space which is the key to what you call health, not any event which occurs in space/time. In the process you may see the transdimensional aspect of will, for it is the will, the seeking, the desire of the entity which causes the indigo body to use the novel (new) configuration and to reform the body which exists in space/time (the physical). This is done in an instant and may be said to operate without regard to time. We may note that in the healing of very young children, there is often an apparent healing by the healer in which the young entity has no part. This is never so, for the mind/body/spirit complex in time/space is always capable of willing the distortions it choses for experience, no matter what the apparent age of the entity."

The desire and will that operate through to the transdimensional time/space section is an activity of the Creator. The crystallized healer has no will. It offers an opportunity without attachment to the outcome, for it is aware that all is one and that the Creator is knowing Itself.

An entity may consciously desire healing greatly within the being, at some level, find some cause where certain configurations that seem quite distorted are, in fact, at that level, considered appropriate. The reason for assuming these distortions appropriate would be that these distortions would aid the entity in reaching its ultimate objective in the path of evolutions towards its desired polarity.

There is often a complex reason for the programming of a distorted physical complex pattern, even though the distortion may appear to interfere with further service to others, if that's what the entity chose for their polarization. In any case, mediation is always an aid to knowing the self.

A vertical position of the spine is somewhat helpful in the meditative procedure.

Each unmanifested self is unique. The basic polarities within the body have to do with the balanced vibratory rates between the first three energy centers and, to a lesser extent, each of the other energy centers.

As Ra mentioned before, there is an energizing spiral emitted from the top of any pyramid and that people could benefit by placing this under the head for 30 minutes or less. The vibration offered by the energizing spiral of the pyramid is such that each cell, both in space/time (physical) and time/space (non-physical), is charged as if hooked to our electricity. The keenness of mind, the physical and sexual energy of body, and the attunement of will of spirit are all touched by this energizing influence. It may be used in any of these ways. It is possible to overcharge a battery, and this is the cause of Ra's cautioning any who use such pyramidal energies to remove the pyramid after a charge has been received. (30 minutes or less).

There are also substances which you may ingest that cause the body to experience an increase of energy. These substances are crude, working rather roughly upon the body increasing the flow of adrenalin.

The small pyramid shall have the appropriate proportions to develop the spirals in the Giza pyramid. The appropriate size for use beneath the head is an overall height small enough to make placing it under the cushion of the head a comfortable thing.

The only incorrect substances would be the baser (copper, zinc, nickel, tin, lead, aluminum) metals. There are better materials which are, in our system of barter, quite dear. (Bartering is an exchange of goods and services between two or more parties without the use of money). These materials are not much better than the substances Ra mentioned before.

Ra mentioned the problems with the action in the King's Chamber of the Giza-type pyramid. So, the channeling group didn't use the King's Chamber radiations but only the third spiral from the top to construct a small pyramid. For energy through the apex angle the Giza pyramid offers an excellent model. Ra told the group to be sure the pyramid is so small that there is no entity small enough to crawl inside it.

The properties of this third spiral energy are such as to move within the field of the physical complex and irradiate (expose to radiation) each cell of the space/time (metaphysical) body and, as this is done, irradiate also the time/space (physical) equivalent which is close aligned with the space/time yellow-ray body. This is not a function of the etheric body or of free will. This is a radiation much like our sun's rays. Thus, it should be used with care.

In most cases, no more than one 30 minute or less application during a diurnal (day) time period would be appropriate. In a few cases, especially where energy will be used for spiritual work, experimentation with two shorter periods might be possible, but any feelings of sudden weariness would be a sign of over-radiation.

There is no application for direct healing using this energy, although, if used in conjunction with meditation, it may offer to a certain percentage of entities some aid in meditation. In most cases it is most helpful in alleviating weariness and in the stimulation of physical or sexual activity.

In transition from a negative third density planet to fourth density the harvest is one of intense disharmony and the planet will express it through distortions such as disease and so forth.

(If anyone thinks Earth is bad, fourth density negative seems much worse as they are servants to the fifth-density negative entities, as it can be related to what is known as Hell and fourth density positive seems much better, as that can be related to what is known as Heaven. Though the Law of One doesn't blink towards the negative or positive path, each is allowed to be pursued. Though, the positive path is easier due to the harmony of all. In sixth density, the negative path would have to jump to the positive side in order to continue in evolution.)

The vibrations from third to fourth negative oriented planet change precisely as they do upon a positively oriented planet. With fourth-density negative comes many abilities and possibilities of which you are familiar. The fourth density is more dense, and it is far more difficult to hide the true vibrations of the mind/body/spirit complex. This enables fourth-density negatives, as well as positives, the chance to form social memory complexes. It enables negatively oriented entities the opportunity for a different set of parameters that shows their power over others and to be service to the self. The conditions are the same as far as the vibrations are concerned.

Each planetary experience is unique. The problems of bellicose (warlike) actions are more likely to be of pressing concern to late third-density negative entities than the Earth's reactions to negativity of the planetary mind, for it is often by such warlike attitudes on a global scale that the necessary negative polarization is achieved.

As fourth density occurs, there is a new planet and new physical vehicle system gradually expressing itself, and the parameters of bellicose actions become those of thought rather than manifested weapons.

Physical complex distortions, such as disease and illness, are likely to be found less as fourth-density negative begins to be a probable choice for harvest due to the extreme interest in the self which characterizes the harvestable third-density negative entity. Much more care is taken of the body, as well as much more discipline being offered of the self mentally. This is an orientation of great self-interest and self-discipline. There are still instances of disease which are associated with the mind complex distortions of negative emotions such as anger. However, in a harvestable entity these emotional distortions are much more likely to be used as catalyst in an expressive and destructive sense in regards to anger.

Distortions of mind or body are found in beings which need experiences to aid in polarization. These polarizations may be those entities who have already chosen the path to be followed.

It is more likely for positively oriented individuals to be experiencing body distortions due to the lack of consuming interest in the self and the emphasis on service to others. Moreover, in an unpolarized entity, catalyst of the physical distortion will be generated at random. The hopeful result is the original choice of polarity. Oftentimes this choice is not made but the catalyst continues to be generated. In the negatively oriented individual, the physical body is likely to be more carefully tended and the mind disciplined against physical distortion.

There seems to be many diseases and bodily malfunctions in general on this third density planet. If the mind doesn't use the catalyst offered to the entity, it will then filter through to the body complex and manifest as some form of physical distortion. The more efficient the use of catalyst, the less physical distortion to be found.

Wanderers not only have a congenital difficulty (which is present at birth) in dealing with the third-density vibratory patterns but also a recollection (remembering), that these distortions are not necessary or usual in the home vibration.

Ra overgeneralizes as always, for there are many cases of pre-incarnative decisions which result in physical or mental limitations and distortions. Indeed, on some third-density planetary spheres, catalyst has been used more efficiently. In the case of earth, there is much more inefficient use of catalyst and, therefore, much physical distortion."

Session 67: 8-15-1981

The negative entity (demon) has been observing the instrument's service to the Creator during these sessions and now has a constant level of psychic attack upon the instrument as long as she continues in this service.

Ra: "Variations towards the distortion of intensity of attack occur due to the opportunities presented by the entity in any weakness. At this particular nexus the entity has been dealing with the distortion of pain for some time and this has a cumulatively (increasingly) weakening effect upon physical energy levels. This creates a particularly favorable target of opportunity, and the negative entity has taken this opportunity to attempt to be of service in its own way. It is fortunate for the ongoing vitality of this contact that the instrument is a strong-willed entity with little tendency towards the distortion, called among your people's hysteria, since the dizzying effects of this attack have been constant and at times disruptive for several of your diurnal periods.

However, this particular entity is adapting well to the situation without undue distortions towards fear. Thus, the psychic attack is not successful but does have some draining influence upon the instrument."

An expression of a positively polarized and balanced view of negatively polarized actions can debilitate the strength of the negatively polarized entities actions by the questioner viewing the so-called attack as offering its service with respect to its distortion in their polarized condition now so that the group may fully appreciate its polarity, and they are appreciative and thank the entity for its attempt to serve our One Creator in bringing us knowledge in a more complete sense.

The questioner, Don Elkins, views the psychic attack as an offering of service, therefore Don uses the term psychic greeting instead. This particular negative entity is of the Orion Confederation of fifth density negative, and by time/space light or fifth-density body is used while the space/time fifth-density body remains in fifth density. The consciousness is projected to where the instrument is and is one of the seven bodies that make up its mind/body/spirit complex.

This conscious vehicle attached to the space/time fifth-density physical complex is the vehicle that works in this particular service. This is a trans dimensional nature, not only of space/time to time/space but from density to density.

The efforts of this negative entity attacking the instrument are put forward only reluctantly.

Ra: "The usual attempts upon positively oriented entities or groups of entities are made by minions of the fifth-density Orion leader; these are fourth density. The normal gambit of such fourth-density attack is the tempting of the entity or group of entities away from total polarization towards service to others and toward the aggrandizement of self (making yourself more important or powerful than they really are) or of social organization with which the self identifies. In the case of this particular group, each was given a full range of temptations to cease being of service to each other and to the one Infinite Creator. Each entity declined these choices and instead continued with no significant deviation from the desire for a purely other self-service orientation. At this point one of the fifth-density entities overseeing such detuning processes determined that it would be necessary to terminate the group by magical means, as you understand ritual magic. We have previously discussed the potential for the removal of one of this group by such attack and have noted that by far the most vulnerable is the instrument due to its pre-incarnative physical complex distortions."

The negative entity desires are to misplace one or more of this group in a negative orientation so that it may choose to be of service along the path of service to self. The objective which must precede this is the termination of the physical body viability of one of the group members while the mind/body/spirit complex is within controllable configuration. In Ra's limited understanding their belief is that sending this entity love and light, which each of the group is doing, is the most helpful catalyst which the group may offer this entity. The 5th density negative entity has been as neutralized as possible in Ra's estimation by the groups love offering, and thus its continued presence is perhaps the understandable limit for each polarity of the various views of service each may render (give) to the other.

We have no ability not to serve the Creator since all is the Creator. The frequency someone resonates at determines your choice of service to the One Creator.

Ra: "As it happens, this groups' vibratory patterns and those of Ra are compatible and enable us to speak through this instrument with your support. This is a function of free will.

A portion, seemingly of the Creator, rejoices at your choice to question us regarding the evolution of spirit. A seemingly separate portion would wish for multitudinous (a vast) answer to a great range of queries of a specific nature. Another seemingly separate group of your peoples would wish this correspondence through this instrument to cease, feeling it to be of a negative nature. Upon the many other planes of existence, there are those whose every fiber rejoices at your service, and those such as the entity of whom you have been speaking (the negative entity) which wish only to terminate the life upon the third-density plane of this instrument. All are the Creator. There is one vast panoply (impressive collection of things) of biases and distortions, colors and hues, in an unending pattern. In the case of those with whom you, as entities and as a group, are not in resonance, you wish them love, light, peace, joy and bid them well. No more than this can you do for your portion of the Creator is as it is, and your experience and offering of experience, to be valuable, needs be more and more a perfect representation of who you truly are. Could you, then, serve a negative entity by offering the instrument's life? It is unlikely that you would if this a true service. Thus, you may see in many cases the loving balance being achieved, the love being offered, light being sent, and the service of the service-to-self-oriented entity gratefully acknowledged while being rejected as not being useful in your journey at this time. Thus, you serve One Creator without paradox."

The instrument at a young age had many eye infections that caused great difficulties at a young age. The scars of these distortions remained and the sinus system remains distorted. Thus, the negative entity works with these distortions to produce a loss of balance (the dizzying effect) and a slight lack of ability to use the optic apparatus. (The optic apparatus is a complex system of nerves and other structures that transmits visual information from the eyes to the brain.)

Ra: "This entity is able to penetrate in time/space configuration the field of this particular entity. It has moved through the quarantine without any vehicle and thus has been more able to escape detection by the net of the Guardians.

This is the great virtue of the magical working whereby consciousness is sent forth essentially without vehicle as light. The light would work instantly upon an untuned individual by suggestion; that is, the stepping out in front of the traffic because the suggestion is that there is no traffic. This entity, as each in this group, is enough disciplined in the ways of love and light that it is not suggestible to any great extent. However, there is a predisposition of the physical complex which this entity is making maximal use of as regards to the instrument, hoping, for instance, by means of increasing dizziness to cause the instrument to fall or to indeed walk in front of your traffic because of impaired vision.

The magical principles may be loosely translated into your system of magic, whereby symbols are used and traced and visualized in order to develop the power of the light."

The fifth-density entity visualizes certain symbols. These symbols are of a nature where their continued use would have some power or charge. In fifth density, light is as visible a tool as our pencil's writing. The entity configures a light used to create sufficient purity of environment for the entity to place its consciousness in a carefully created light vehicle which then uses the tools of light to do its working. The will and presence are those of the entity doing the working.

The fifth-density entity penetrated the quarantine through a very slight window which less magically oriented entities or groups could not have used to their advantage. This window exists because of free will.

This is a portion of the random effect, and the group experiences the same type of balancing in receiving the psychic attacks as the planet in general receives because of the window effect. As the planetary sphere accepts more highly evolved positive entities or groups with information to offer, the same opportunity must be offered to similarly wise negatively oriented entities or groups.

Ra's view expresses appreciation of this opportunity. This is an intensive opportunity in that it is quite marked in its effects, both actual and potential, and as it affects the instrument's distortions towards pain and other difficulties such as dizziness, it enables the instrument to continuously choose to serve others and serve the Creator.

Similarly, it offers a continual opportunity for each in the group to express support under more distorted or difficult circumstances of the other-self experiencing the brunt of this attack, thus being able to demonstrate the love and light of the Infinite Creator and, furthermore, choosing working by working to continue to serve as messengers for this information which Ra attempts to offer and to serve the Creator thereby.

Thus, the opportunities are quite noticeable, as well as the distortions caused by this circumstance.

This attack is offered to all in the group.

Ra: "The questioner has been offered the service of doubting the self and of becoming disheartened over various distortions of the personal nature. This entity has not chosen to use these opportunities, and the Orion entity has basically ceased to be interested in maintaining constant surveillance of this entity.

The scribe is under constant surveillance and has been offered numerous opportunities for the intensification of the mental/emotional distortions and in some cases the connection matrices between mental/emotional complexes and the physical complex counterpart. As this entity has become aware of these attacks, it has become much less pervious (passable) to them. This is the particular cause of the great intensification and constancy of the surveillance of the instrument, for it is the weak link due to factors beyond its control within this incarnation."

Ra finds great humor in Don Elkins attempt to be of polarized service to the opposite polarity. Since Don wanted to confirm that there was nothing that they could do for the fifth density entity besides offer love and light for the negative entity. There is a natural difficulty in wanting to offer service to the opposite polarity, since what Don considers service is considered nonservice by the negative entity. As you send this entity love and light and wish it well, it loses its polarity and needs to regroup.

Thus, it would not consider Don's service as such. On the other hand, if Don allowed it to be of service by removing this instrument from that midst, Don might perceive this as not being of service. Don has a balanced and polarized view of the Creator; two services offered, mutually rejected, and in a state of equilibrium in which free will is preserved and each allowed to go upon its own path of experiencing the One Infinite Creator. There's unification in sixth density of these two paths.

In working with the mind, we are working with one complex and have not yet attempted to penetrate intelligent infinity. Archetypes are portions of the One Infinite Creator or aspects of its face. Archetypes do not give the same yield of these complexes to any two seekers. Each seeker will experience each archetype in the characteristics within the complex of the archetype most important to it. An example of this is the questioner viewing the fool archetype as The Prodigal Son corresponding to every entity who seems to have strayed from unity and seeks to return to the One Infinite Creator. One great aspect of the fool is the aspect of faith, the walking into space without regard for what is to come next. This is, of course, foolish but is part of the characteristic of the spiritual neophyte (beginner).

Session 68: 8-18-1981

Ra instructed the instrument to refrain from calling Ra unless it is within this set of circumscribed circumstances, such as these channeling sessions with the group and Ra. The instrument was slipping into trance state during one of the normal Sunday night meditations, where she was asked a question about the Ra Material from Ra's brothers and sisters of the wisdom density known as Latwii.

Ra: "This instrument thought to itself, "I do not know this answer. I wish I were channeling Ra." The ones of Latwii found themselves in the position of being approached by the Orion entity which seeks to be of service in its own way. The instrument began to prepare for Ra contact. Latwii knew that if this was completed, the Orion entity would have an opportunity which Latwii wished to avoid.

It is fortunate for this instrument, firstly, that Latwii is of fifth density and able to deal with that particular vibratory complex which the Orion entity was manifesting and, secondly, that there were those in the support group at that time which sent great amounts of support to the instrument in this crux. Thus, what occurred was the ones of Latwii never let go of this instrument, although this came perilously close to breaking the Way of Confusion. It continued to hold its connection with the mind/body/spirit complex of the instrument and to generate information through it even as the instrument began to slip out of its physical vehicle.

The act of continued communication caused the entity to be unable to grasp the instrument's mind/body/spirit complex, and after but a small measure of your space/time, Latwii recovered the now completely amalgamated (formed a close union without complete loss of individual identities of the) instrument and gave it continued communication to steady it during the transition back into integration."

The plan of the fifth-density negative entity was to take the mind/body/spirit complex while it was separated from its yellow-body physical complex shell, to then place this mind/body/spirit complex within the negative portions of your time/space. The shell would then become that of the unknowing, unconscious entity and could be worked upon to cause malfunction which could end in a coma and then in death of the body. At this point the Higher Self of the instrument would have the choice of leaving the mind/body/spirit complex in negative time/space (non-physical reality) or of allowing incarnation in space/time (physical reality) of equivalent vibration and polarity distortions. Thus, this entity would become a negatively polarized entity without the advantage of native negative polarization. It would find a long path to the Creator under these circumstances, although the path would inevitably end well.

The Higher Self could allow the mind/body/spirit complex to remain in time/space (metaphysical/another dimension). However, it is unlikely that the Higher Self would do so indefinitely, due to its distortion towards the belief that the function of the mind/body/spirit complex is to experience and learn from other selves, thus experiencing the Creator. A highly polarized positive mind/body/spirit complex surrounded by negative portions of space/time will experience only darkness, for like the magnet, there is no likeness. Thus, a barrier is automatically formed. This darkness is experienced in Negative time/space.

If this happened to a Wanderer of sixth density and went into negative time/space, it would be sixth-density negative time/space and would incarnate into sixth-density negative space/time.

The strength of the polarization would be matched as far as possible. In some positive sixth-density Wanderers, the approximation would not quite be complete due to the paucity (scarcity) of negative sixth-density energy fields of the equivalent strength. In the case of this instrument, this could happen because the Wanderer extracted in the trance state, leaving the third-density physical, does not have the full capability to magically defend itself. This is also correct when applied almost without exception to those instruments working in trance which haven't experienced magical training in time/space transdimensionally in the present incarnation. The entities of our density capable of magical defense in this situation are extremely rare.

The entity seeking magical ability for defense against negative entities must do so in a certain manner. Ra's general instructions is to never call upon Ra in any way while unprotected by the configuration which is at this time, present. (There's protection in the channeling process by a group being there instead of alone in meditation.)

To take an entity before it is ready and offer it the scepter (an ornamented staff) of magical power (carried by rulers as a symbol of sovereignty) is to infringe in an unbalanced manner.

The fifth-density negative entity is alerted that this channeling group exists and becomes aware of power.

Ra: "I am Ra. The entity becomes aware of power. This power has the capacity of energizing those which may be available for harvest. This entity is desirous of disabling this power source. It sends its legions. Temptations are offered. They are ignored or rejected. The power source persists and indeed improves its inner connections of harmony and love of service.

The entity determines that it must needs attempt the disabling itself. By means of projection it enters the vicinity of this power source. It assesses the situation. It is bound by the first distortion but may take advantage of any free-will distortion. The free-will, pre-incarnative distortions of the instrument with regard to the physical vehicle seem the most promising target. Any distortion away from service to others is also appropriate.

When the instrument leaves its physical vehicle, it does so freely. Thus, the misplacement of the mind/body/spirit complex of the instrument would not be a violation of its free will if it followed the entity freely. This is the process. We are aware of your pressing desire to know how to become impervious as a group to any influences such as this. The processes which you seek are a matter of your free choice. You are aware of the principles of magical work. We cannot speak to advise but can only suggest, as we have before, that it would be appropriate for this group to embark upon such a path as a group, but not individually, for obvious reason."

The positive polarity sees love in all things and that's why one might follow a negative entity to negative time/space (non-physical/another dimension). The negative polarity is clever and able to misplace a mind/body/spirit complex through the positive entities free will. If the negative polarity used any other approach that did not use the free will of the other self, he would lose polarization and magical power.

Session 69: 8-29-1981

Ra suggested for future working the combing of this antenna-like material (hair) into a more orderly configuration prior to the working.

Ra: "The mind/body/spirit complex which freely leaves the third-density physical complex is vulnerable when the appropriate protection is not at hand. You may perceive carefully that very few entities which choose to leave their physical complexes are doing work of such a nature as to attract the polarized attention of negatively oriented entities. The danger to most in trance state, is the touching of the physical complex (body) in such a manner as to attract the mind/body/spirit complex back thereunto or to damage the means by which that which you call ectoplasm is being recalled."

Ectoplasm, in spirituality is a mysterious, usually light-colored, substance that is said to exude from the body of spiritualist medium in trance and may then take the shape of a face, a hand, or a complete body.

Ra: "This instrument is an anomaly in that it is well that the instrument not be touched or artificial light thrown upon it while in the trance state. However, the ectoplasmic activity is interiorized. The main difficulty is then the previously discussed negative removal of the entity under its free will.

That this can happen only in the trance state is not completely certain, but it is highly probably that in another out-of-body experience such as death, the entity here examined would, as most positively polarized entities, have a great deal of protection from comrades, guides, and portions of the self which would be aware of the transfer of physical death."

Protective positive guides or angelic presences would be available in every condition except for the trance state, which is anomalistic (uncommon) with respect to the others.

The uniqueness of this trance state with Ra is the intent to serve others with the highest attempt at near purity which Ra and the group as comrades may achieve.

Ra: "This has alerted a much more determined friend of negative polarity which is interested in removing this particular opportunity.

We may say once again two notes: Firstly, we searched long to find an appropriate channel or instrument and an appropriate support group. If this opportunity is ended, we shall be grateful for that which has been done, but the possibility/probability vortices indicating the location of this configuration again are slight. Secondly, we thank you for we know what you sacrifice in order to do that which you as a group wish to do.

We will not delete this instrument insofar as we are able. We have attempted to speak of how the instrument may deplete itself through too great a dedication to the working. All these things and all else we have said has been heard. We are thankful. In the present situation we express thanks to the entities who call themselves Latwii."

All deaths, whether by natural means, accident or suicide, the negative friends are not able to remove an entity. This is largely because the entity without the attachment to the space/time physical complex is far more aware and without the gullibility which is somewhat the hallmark of those who love wholeheartedly.

However, the death, if natural, would undoubtedly be the more harmonious; the death by murder being confused and the entity needing some time/space (time in another dimension/afterlife) to get its bearings, the death by suicide causing the necessity for much healing work and reincarnating into third density for the renewed opportunity of learning the lessons set by the Higher Self."

If the entity is not trying to be of service and pass away from accident, medical anesthetic or drugs, the negative entities would not find it possible to remove the mind/body/spirit complex.

The dangerous characteristic is the willing of the entity outward from the physical body of third density for the purpose of service-to-others. In any other situation this circumstance would not be in effect. The free will of the instrument is indeed a necessary part of the opportunity afforded the Orion group. However, this free will applies only to the instrument. The entire hope of the Orion group is to infringe upon free will without losing polarity. Thus, this group, if represented by a wise entity, attempts to be clever.

A Wanderer has been so infringed upon in the past by a negative adept and was placed in negative time/space. The path back to the conscious state after trance firstly revolves about the Higher Self's reluctance to enter negative space/time (incarnation). This may be a significant part of the length of that path. Secondly, when a positively oriented entity incarnates in a thoroughly negative environment, it must need to learn/teach the lessons of the love of self, thus becoming one with its other selves.

When this has been accomplished, the entity may then choose to release the potential difference and change polarities. However, the process of learning the accumulated lessons of love of self may be quite lengthy. Also, the entity, in learning these lessons, may lose much positive orientation during the process, and the choice of reversing polarities may be delayed until the mid-sixth density. All of this is time consuming, although the end result is well.

There has only been one Wanderer that came to Earth that has experienced this displacement during this master cycle into negative time/space (in another dimension).

The incarnative process involves being incarnated from time/space (metaphysical) to space/time (physical), so the Higher Self is reluctant to enter negative space/time (physical incarnation).

When first moved into negative time/space, the positive entity experiences nothing but darkness. Then, by incarnation into negative space/time by the Higher Self, it experiences a negative space/time environment with negatively polarized other selves. The positively oriented individual makes a poor student of the love of self and thus spends much more time than those native to that pattern of vibrations. The misplacement is a function of his free will.

Firstly, A positively oriented entity moving into negative time/space is like receiving a poorly marked map and is quite incorrect. It sets out wishing only to reach the point of destination, but becomes confused by the faculty authority and not knowing the territory through which it drives, becomes hopelessly lost.

Free will may at times encounter circumstances when calculations will be awry. This is so in all aspects of the life experience. Although there are no mistakes, there are no surprises.

Secondly, there's a magical charge or metaphysical power when the group does these channelings with Ra. Those who do work of power are available for communication to and from entities of roughly similar power. It is fortunate that the Orion entity does not have the native power of this group. However, it is quite disciplined, whereas this group lacks the finesse equivalent to its power. Each is working in consciousness, but the group has not begun a work as a group. The individual work is helpful, for the group is mutually an aid, to one another.

In order for the instrument not to go into trance other than at a protected channeling such as the group does with Ra:

1- The instrument must improve the disciplined subconscious taboo against requesting Ra, except in the protected group channeling. This would involve daily conscious and serious thought.

2- The second safeguard is the refraining from the opening of this instrument to questions and answers for the present.

3- The hand may be held to keep the instrument in its physical complex during meditation. Also, in the event that, unlikely as it may seem, the entity grew able to leave the physical body, the auric infringement and tactile pressure would cause the mind/body/spirit complex to refrain from leaving. Long practice of the art which intuits here would be helpful. Ra cannot speak of methodology, for the infringement would be most great. However, group effort may do.

Although Ra cannot speak with precision of the techniques and ways of practicing white magical arts or if rituals are designed or not by a particular group for their own particular use or if they are just as good or possibly better than these practiced by the order of the Golden Dawn and other magical groups. Ra notes some gratification that the questioner has penetrated some of the gist of a formidable (intimidating) system of service and discipline.

Session 70: 9-9-1981

The instrument complained of intensive psychic attack for the past day. Ra said the cause is the intensive seeking of enlightenment. The seeking through asking Ra questions during channelings has intensified the attack. Thus, the Orion visitor strives with more and more intensity to disturb the instruments vital energy as this group intensifies its dedication to service through enlightenment.

There is an infinite range of possibility of service/disservice in time-regression hypnosis, an aiding in memory. It has nothing to do with the hypnotist. It has only to do with the hypnotized entity makes of the information gained if the hypnotist desires to serve and if such a service is performed only upon sincere request, the hypnotist is attempting to be of service.

The Higher Self is reluctant to allow its mind/body/spirit to enter negative time/space, since it would be like a prison to us.

The Higher Self is the entity of mid-sixth density, which, turning back, offers this service to its self.

We are all existing at all levels (densities) simultaneously. Your Higher Self is you in mid-sixth density and your Higher Self is yourself in your future. All mind/body/spirit complexes that exist below mid-sixth density has a Higher Self at the level of mid-sixth density.

The Higher Self protects when possible and guides when asked, but the force of free will is paramount. The seeming determinism and free will melt when it is accepted that there is such a thing as true simultaneity. The Higher Self is the end result of all the development experienced by the mind/body/spirit complex to that point.

In time/space, which is precisely as much of yourself as is space/time, all times are simultaneous just as, in your geography, your cities and villages are all functioning's, hustling, and alive with entities going about their business at once. So, it is in time/space with the self.

A positive entity displaced to negative time/space (not incarnate) has the Higher Self being reluctant to this. Each time/space is an analog (an interior analog of the external world) of a particular sort of vibration of space/time. When a negative time/space is entered by an entity, the next experience will be that of the appropriate space/time (going into that next incarnation). This is normally done by the form-making body (indigo body) of a mind/body/spirit complex which places the entity in the proper time/space incarnation.

If a Wanderer of fourth, fifth, or sixth density dies from this third-density state, the time/space density will depend upon the approval by the council of Nine. Some Wanderers offer themselves for one incarnation, while others offer themselves for varying lengths up to and including the last two cycles of 25,000 years for each cycle. If the agreed upon mission is complete, the Wanderer's mind/body/spirit complex will go to the home vibration.

There have been a few Wanderers on this planet for the 50,000 years now. There have been many more which chose to join this last cycle of 25,000 years, and many, many more which have come for harvest.

The position in negative time/space is pre-incarnative. After death of the physical complex in yellow-ray activation, the mind/body/spirit complex moves to a far different portion of time/space in which the indigo body will allow much healing and review to take place before any movement is made towards another incarnative experience.

A miscalculation would be the perception of time/space being no more homogeneous (alike) than space/time. It is as complex and complete a system of illusions, dances, and patterns as is space/time, and has structured a system of natural laws.

George Adamski photographed the bell-shaped craft when Ra came to Earth 18,000 and 11,000 years ago. These craft looked somewhat like a bell; they had portholes around them in the upper portions, and had three hemispheres at 120 degrees apart underneath. A construct of thought constructed them in time/space. This portion of time/space approaches the speed of light. In time/space, the conditions are such that time becomes infinite and mass ceases, so that one which is able to skim the boundary strength of this time/space is able to become placed where it will.

When Ra was where they wished to be, they then clothed the construct of light that appeared as a crystal bell. This was formed through the boundary into space/time. Thus, there were two constructs: time/space or immaterial construct, and the space/time. (Therefore, if the second word is time, then it's in physical reality with time. If the second word is space, then it's in metaphysical reality in space without time).

The particular shape and three hemispheres at the bottom seemed aesthetically pleasing form to Ra and one well suited to those limited uses which Ra must needs make of our space/time motivating requirements.

The three hemispheres at the bottom were aesthetic and part of a propulsion system. They were not landing gear.

Space/time is physics.

Time/space is metaphysics. These concepts are mechanical, they are not central to the spiritual evolution of the mind/body/spirit complex. The study of love and light is far more productive in its motion towards unity in those entities pondering (carefully thinking before reaching a conclusion on) such concepts.

The entity that incarnated into negative space/time (incarnation) will not find it possible to maintain any significant positive polarity, as negativity, when pure, is a type of gravity well, pulling all into it. Thus, the entity while remembering its learned and preferred polarity, must make use of the catalyst given and recapitulate (briefly summarize) the lessons of service to self in order to build up enough polarity in order to cause the potential to occur for reversal.

Ra is attempting to be of the greatest aid to the group by taking care not to deplete this instrument, so Ra would ask if there were any more questions before ending the session to let the instrument keep her reserved energy and Ra was glad to speak with the group. The instrument had arranged its subconscious to accept this channeling session.

Session 71: 9-18-1981

The connection between polarization and harvestability is most important in third-density harvest. In this density an increase in the serving of others or the serving of self will almost inevitably increase the ability of an entity to enjoy a higher intensity of light. Thus, in this density, it is hardly possible to polarize without increasing in harvestability.

In fifth-density harvest, polarization has very little to do with harvestability.

The unmanifested being does its work without aid from other selves. There's an inevitable connection between the unmanifested self and the metaphysical time/space analog (equivalent) of the space/time self. The activities of meditation, contemplation and the internal balancing of thoughts and reactions are those activities of the unmanifested-self more closely aligned with the metaphysical self.

Ra: "The hallmark of time/space is the inequity between time and space. In your space/time the spatial (structural) orientation of material causes a tangible framework for illusion. In time/space the inequity is upon the shoulders of that property known to you as time. This property renders (gives) entities and experiences intangible in a relative sense. In your framework, each particle or core vibration moves at a velocity which approaches the speed of light from the direction of supraliminal velocities. (Supraliminal velocities are speeds exceeding the speed of light).

Thus, the time/space or metaphysical experience is that which is very finely tuned and, although an analog of space/time, lacking in its tangible characteristics. In these metaphysical planes there is a great deal of time which is used to review and re-review the biases and learn/teachings of a prior space/time incarnation.

The extreme fluidity of these regions makes it possible for much to be penetrated which must be absorbed before the process of healing of an entity may be accomplished. Each entity is located in a somewhat immobile state, much as you are located in space/time in a somewhat immobile state in time. In this immobile space the entity has been placed by the form maker and Higher Self so that it may be in the proper configuration for learn/teaching that which it has received in the space/time incarnation.

Depending upon this time/space locus, there will be certain helpers which assist in this healing process. The process involves seeing in full the experience, seeing it against the backdrop of the mind/body/spirit complex total experience, forgiving the self for all missteps as regards the missed guideposts during the incarnation, and, finally, the careful assessment of the next necessities for learning. This is done entirely by the Higher Self until an entity has become conscious in space/time of the process and means of spiritual evolution, at which time the entity will consciously take part in all decisions."

The processes of healing and review for the negative polarization is similar for the positive path as well.

Ra: "I am Ra. The process in space/time of the forgiveness and acceptance is much like that in time/space, in that the qualities of the process are analogous (similar, but different categories). However, while in space/time it is not possible to determine the course of events beyond the incarnation, but only to correct present imbalances. In time/space it is not possible to correct any unbalanced actions but rather to perceive the imbalances and thusly forgive the self for that which is.

The decisions then are made to set up the possibility/probabilities of correcting these imbalances in future space/time experiences. The advantage of time/space is that, working in darkness with a tiny candle, one may correct imbalances."

The processes of healing and review occur upon all planets which have given birth to sub-Logoi such as yourselves. The percentage of inhabited planets is approximately 10 percent.

Approximately 32 percent of stars have planets, while 6 percent have some sort of clustering material which upon some densities might be inhabitable. This octave of infinite knowledge of the One Creator is as it is throughout the One Infinite Creation, with variations programmed by sub-Logoi of major galaxies and minor galaxies.

Our sub-Logos such as our sun uses free will to modify only slightly a much more general idea of created evolution, so that the general plan of created evolution seem to be uniform throughout the One Infinite Creation. The process is for the sub-Logoi to grow through the densities and find their way back to the original thought through free will.

Each entity is of a path that leads to one destination. Many roads that travel through many places but eventually merge into one large center, merging back into the Creator at the seventh density harvest.

More applicable would be the thought that each entity contains within it all of the densities and sub-densities of the octave, so that in each entity, no matter what its choices lead it, its great internal blueprint is one with all others. Thusly its experiences will fall into the patterns of the journey back to the original Logos. This is done through free will, but the materials from which choices can be made are one blueprint.

Pure negativity acts as a gravity well, pulling all into it. Positivity has a much weaker effect due to the strong element of recognition of free will in any positivity approaching purity. Thus, although the negatively oriented entity may find it difficult to polarize negatively in the midst of such resounding harmony, it will not find it impossible.

The negative polarization is one which does not accept the concept of the free will of other selves. Thusly, in a social complex whose negativity approaches purity, the pull upon other selves is constant. A positively oriented entity in such a situation would desire for other selves to have their free will and thusly would find itself removed from its ability to exercise its own free will, for the free will of negatively oriented entities is bent upon conquest (control of entities or places).

Magic is the ability to create changes in consciousness at will. This is the burden of the adept. In magic, one is working with one's unmanifested self in body, in mind, and in spirit, the mixture depending upon the nature of the working.

(Manifested self is physical. Unmanifested self would be metaphysical).

These workings are facilitated by the enhancement of the activation of the indigo-ray energy center. The indigo-ray energy center is fed, as are all energy centers, by experience, but for more than other energy centers is fed by the disciplines of the personality.

White magic may be worked for the purpose of altering only the self or the place of working. To aid the self in polarization towards love and light is to aid the planetary vibration. The heart of white magic is the experience of the joy of union with the Creator. This joy will of necessity radiate throughout the life experience of the positive adept. It is for this reason that sexual magic is not restricted solely to the negatively oriented polarizing adepts but, when most carefully used, has its place in high magic as it, when correctly pursued, joins body, mind and spirit with the One Infinite Creator. Union with the One Infinite Creator will result in service to others.

Ra stated in a previous session that they searched for some time to find a group such as this one (Don Elkins, Carla Rueckert and Jim McCarty). This search was for the purpose of communicating the Law of One and to make reparation for distortions of this law set in motion by their naïve actions of our past. (18,000 and 11,000 years ago). Ra does not expect to make full reparations for these distortions. The attempt is far more important to them than the completeness of the result. What is distorted cannot, to Ra's knowledge, be fully undistorted but only illuminated somewhat. Ra conducted this search in time-space, for in this illusion one may quite readily see entities as vibratory complexes and groups as harmonics within vibratory complexes.

The most important aspect of this communication as the group is a vehicle of partial enlightenment for those on Earth now who have become aware of their part in their own evolutionary process. This is the goal of all artifacts and experiences which entities may come in contact with, and is not only the property of Ra or this contact.

Ra said that the instrument should hold back a portion of energy for reserve. This will lengthen the number or workings the group may have. (This is an example of wisdom).

Session 72: 10-14-1981

The banishing ritual that the group performs before a channeling working with Ra purifies the places and the screening of influences that they do not wish to be there, such as negative entities. (The Circle of One.)

What caused the instrument to become in a condition towards unconsciousness in the last two meditations:

Ra: "The entity which greets this instrument from the Orion group first attempted to cause the mind/body/spirit, which you call spirit, to leave the physical complex of yellow ray in the deluded belief that it was preparing for the Ra contact. You are familiar with this tactic and its consequences. The instrument, with no pause, upon feeling this greeting, called for the grounding within the physical complex by requesting that the hand be held. Thus, the greatest aim of the Orion entity was not achieved. However, it discovered that those present were not capable of distinguishing between unconsciousness with the mind/body/spirit intact and the trance state in which the mind/body/spirit complex is not present.

Therefore, it applied to the fullest extent the greeting which causes the dizziness and in meditation without protection caused, in this instrument, simple unconsciousness, as in what you would call fainting or vertigo. The Orion entity consequently used this tactic to stop the Ra contact from having the opportunity to be accomplished."

During the instrument's scheduled hand operation next month, it is extremely improbable that the instrument going under general anesthetic into an unconscious state would allow psychic attacks from Orion entities. This is due to the necessity for the intention of the being, when departing the yellow-ray physical complex, to be serving the Creator in the most specific fashion for a potential attack to occur. The attitude of the individual is of paramount importance for the Orion entity to be able to be effective. During channeling's, the instruments attitude is to serve the Creator so the Orion's attack, during anesthetic, the attitude wouldn't be on serving the Creator, so it would be extremely improbable for a negative entity to attack during the unconscious state of her hand operation.

Ra: "The Law of Confusion or Free will is utterly paramount in the workings of the infinite creation. That which is intended has as much intensity of attraction to the polar opposite as the intensity of the intention or desire.

Thus, those whose desires are shallow or transitory experience only ephemeral (lasts a very short time) configuration of what might be called the magical circumstance. There is a turning point, a fulcrum which swings as a mind/body/spirit complex tunes its will to service. If this will and desire is for service to others, the corresponding polarity will be activated. In the circumstance of this group, there are three such wills acting as one with the instrument in the central position of fidelity to service. This is as it must be for the balance of the working and the continuance of the contact. Our vibratory complex is one-pointed in these working also, and our will to service is also of some degree of purity. This has created the attraction of the polar opposite which you experience.

We may note that such a configuration of free will, one-pointed in service to others, also has the potential for the alerting of a great mass of light strength. This positive light strength, however, operates also under free will and must be invoked. We could not speak to this and shall not guide you, for the nature of this contact is such that the purity of your free will must, above all things, be preserved. Thus, you wend your way through experiences, discovering those biases which may be helpful."

Ra: "Firstly, those of negative polarity do not operate with respect to free will unless it is necessary. They call themselves and will infringe whenever they feel it possible.

Secondly, they are limited by the great Law of Confusion in that, for the most part, they are unable to enter this planetary sphere of influence and are able to use the windows of time/space distortion only insofar as there is some calling to balance the positive calling. Once they are here, their desire is conquest (control of others).

Thirdly, in the instance of this instrument's being removed permanently from this space/time, it is necessary to allow the instrument to leave its yellow-ray physical complex of its free will. Thus, trickery has been attempted.

The use of the light forms being generated is such as to cause such entities to discover a wall through which they cannot pass. This is due to the energy complexes of the light beings and aspects of the One Infinite Creator invoked (call upon) and evoked (bring to the conscious mind) in the building of the wall of light."

Everything that the group experiences with the contact, their distortion with knowledge in order to serve, the Orion entity's distortion towards reducing the effectiveness of this contact is all a result of free will in creating the free atmosphere for the Creator to become more knowledgeable of Itself through the interplay of its portions, one with respect to the other.

The instrument has great distortions in the direction of mind complex activity, spirit complex activity, and that great conduit to the Creator, the will. Therefore, this instrument's vital energy, even in the absence of any physical reserve measurable, is quite substantial. Physical activities are a far greater distortion in lessening of the vital energy than if used in her deepest desires of serving the Creator. The overuse of this vital energy is, to be literal, the rapid removal of life force.

The proper ritual of this group could use the large amount of light available for recharging the vital energy of the instrument. However, Ra cautions against any working that raises up any personality and realize all are One. Rather it is well to be fastidious in the working." (Fastidious means very attentive to accuracy and details).

The group included "Shin" in the banishing ritual, "Yod-Heh-Vau-Heh" to make it "Yod-Heh-Shin-Vau-Heh." This is helpful especially to the instrument whose distortions vibrate greatly in congruency with this sound vibration complex.

The group will now have group meditations for protection for the instrument. Purifying the place of working with the Banishing ritual daily would be most effective for the group in protection against psychic attacks and negative entities.

The opportunity for the Orion entity is completely dependent upon the instrument's condition of awareness and readiness. Ra would suggest that this instrument is still too much the neophyte (new to the subject or belief) to open its self to questions since that is the format used by Ra. As the instrument grows in awareness this precaution may become unnecessary.

Why there isn't protection at the floor or bottom of the banishing ritual:

Ra: "The development of the psychic greeting is possible only through the energy centers, starting from a station which you might call within the violet ray moving through the adept's energy center and therefrom towards the target of opportunity. Depending upon the vibratory nature and purpose of greeting, be it positive or negative, the entity will be energized or blocked in the desired way.

We of Ra approach this instrument in narrow-band contact through violate ray. Others might pierce down through this ray to any energy center. We, for instance, make great use of this instrument's blue-ray energy center as we are attempting to communicate our distortion/understanding of *The Law of One*.

The entity of Orion pierces the same violet ray and moves to two places to attempt most of its nonphysical opportunities. It activates the green-ray energy center while further blocking indigo-ray energy center. This combination causes confusion in the instrument and subsequent over-activity in unwise proportions in physical complex workings. It simply seeks out the distortions pre-incarnatively programmed and developed in incarnative state.

The energies of life itself, being the One Infinite Creator, flow from the south pole of the body seen in its magnetic form Thus, only the Creator may, through the feet, enter the energy shell of the body to any effect. The effects of the adept are those from the upper direction, and thus the building of the wall of light is quite propitious. (favorable, a good chance of success)"

SESSION 73: 10-21-1981

The banishing ritual of the group has gained with each working in making efficacious (a successful desired result of) the purity of contact needed not only for the Ra contact but for any working of the adept.

Don Elkins thanks Ra for the opportunity to be of service to those on Earth who want the information that the group gains during the Ra contact.

One-pointed in service to others has the potential of alerting a great mass of light strength. In invocation (calling on for assistance) and evocation (calling forth) of negative entities or qualities, the expression alerts the positively oriented equivalent. However, those upon the service to others path wait to be called and can only send love.

Those upon the positive path may call upon the light strength in direct proportion to the strength and purity of their will to serve. Those upon the negative path may call upon the dark strength in direct proportion to the strength and purity of their will to serve.

The great way of the development of the light in the microcosmic mind/body/spirit is assumed that the adept will have its energy centers functioning smoothly and in a balanced manner to its best effort before a magical working. All magical workings are based upon evocation and/or invocation.

The first invocation of any magical working is that invocation of the magical personality. In the working of the adept alerting the light strength the first station is the beginning of the invocation of this magical personality, which is invoked by the motion of putting on something. If you do not have an item of apparel or talisman, the gesture of visualization is appropriate.

The second station is the evocation of the great cross of life. This is an extension of the magical personality to become the Creator. All invocations and evocations are drawn through the violet energy center.

This may then be construed through whatever energy centers are desired to be used.

The action of the upward-spiraling light that enters through the feet is drawn by the will to meet the inner light of the One Infinite Creator may be likened to the beating of the heart and the movement of the muscles surrounding the lungs and all the other functions of the parasympathetic nervous system. The calling of the adept is like the nerve and muscle actions and over which the mind/body/spirit complex has conscious control.

Where the two directions meet of the upward-spiraling light and the light invoked through the crown chakra, is the measure of the development of the particular entity.

Ra: "Each visualization, regardless of the point of the working, begins with some work within the indigo ray. As you may be aware, the ritual which you have begun is completely working within the indigo ray. This is well for it is the gateway. From this beginning, light may be invoked for communication or for healing.

You may note that in the ritual which we offered you to properly begin the Ra workings, the first focus is upon the Creator. We would further note a point which is both subtle and of some interest. The upward-spiraling light developed in its path by the will and, ultimately reaching a high place of mating with the inward fire of the One Creator, still is only preparation for the work upon the mind/body/spirit which may be done by the adept. There is some crystallization of the energy centers used during each working, so that the magician becomes more and more that which it seeks.

More importantly, the time/space (metaphysical) mind/body/spirit analog, which is evoked as the magical personality, has its only opportunity to gain rapidly from the experience of the catalytic action available to the third-density space/time mind/body/spirit totality of an entity."

In the magical personality, desire, will, and polarity are the key factors in this process.

In examining the polarity of a service-to-others working, the free will must be seen as paramount. (Paramount means more important than anything else, supreme.) Many so-called evangelists which we have in our society are attempting to generate positive changes in consciousness while abridging free will. This causes the blockage of the magical nature of the working except in those cases wherein an entity freely desires to accept the working of the evangelist.

Jesus of Nazareth offered itself as teacher to those mind/body/spirit complexes which gathered to hear and even then, spoke as through a veil so as to leave room for those not wishing to hear. When this entity was asked to heal, it often times did so, always sending the working with two admonitions: Firstly, that the entity healed had been healed by its faith-that is, its ability to allow and accept changes through the violet ray into the gateway of intelligent energy; secondly, saying always, "tell no one." These are the working which attempt to maximize quality of free will while maintaining fidelity to the positive purity of the working.

Ra are humble messengers of *The Law of One.* To them there are no paradoxes. Jesus' healings seem magical and, therefore, seem to infringe on free will but do not, for the distortions of perceptions are as many as witnesses, and each witness sees what it desires to see. Infringement of free will occurs in this circumstance of healing only if the entity doing the working takes credit for this event or its own skills. He who states that no working comes from it but only through it is not infringing on free will.

Jesus accumulated twelve disciples to have those that will learn from him and then teach. Those drawn to this entity were accepted by him without regard for any outcome. This entity accepted the honor/duty placed upon it by its nature and its sense that to speak was its mission.

In the exercise of the fire, the healer would be working with the same energy as entering through the crown chakra.

Ra: "When the magical personality has been seated in the green-ray center for healing work, the energy may be seen to be the crystalline center through which body energy is channeled. This particular form of healing uses both the energy of the adept and the energy of the upward-spiraling light. As the green-ray center becomes more brilliant, and we would note this brilliance does not imply over-activation but rather crystallization, the energy of the green-ray center of the body complex spirals twice; firstly, clockwise from the green-ray energy center to the right shoulder, through the head, the right elbow, down through the solar plexus, and to the left hand. This sweeps all the body complex energy into a channel which then rotates the great circle clockwise again from the left to the feet, to the right hand, to the crown, to the left hand, and so forth.

Thus, the incoming body energy, crystallized, regularized, and channeled by the adept's personality reaching to the green-ray energy center, may then pour out the combined energies of the adept which is incarnate, thus offering the service of healing to an entity requesting that service. This basic situation is accomplished as well when there is an entity which is working through a channel to heal."

The transfer of light, would affect the patient to be healed in polarization. The entity may or may not accept any percentage of this polarized life energy which is being offered. In the occasion of the laying on of hands, this energy is more specifically channeled and the opportunity for acceptance of this energy similarly more specific.

It may be seen that the King's Chamber effect is not attempted in this form of working but rather the addition to one, whose energies are low, of the opportunity for the budding up of those energies. Many illnesses can be aided by such means.

There are various forms of healing. In many, only the energy of the adept is used when their energy centers are suitably configured and is then able to channel light, through its properly configured energy centers to the one to be healed.

If the one wishing to be healed, though sincere, remains unhealed, you may consider pre-incarnative choices. The more helpful aid to this unhealed entity may be the suggestion that it meditate upon the affirmative uses of whatever limitations it might experience. In these cases, the indigo-ray workings are often of aid.

The questioner, Don Elkins, sees the primary thing of importance in service-to-others path is the development of an attitude developed through meditation, ritual, and the developing appreciation for the creation or Creator, which results in a state of mind that can be expressed as an increase in vibration or oneness with all. Ra then expanded on that by suggesting that those qualities can be added to by the living day by day and moment by moment, for the true adept lives more and more as it is. (Also, without caring how others perceive them, so being more of who you are without caring what others think or say.)

Jordyn: "For raising the positive polarity charity is great, giving to others and helping others, loving and forgiving others, living in harmony with others, not infringing on their free will, not trying to have power over others and not trying to control anyone. For everyone learns at a different pace and all will end up at the same destination when we all merge back into the Creator at the seventh density harvest of this octave or universe.

My unique service to others is me sacrificing my time of play to write these books and do these YouTube videos as I give people the truth about everything in this life for their own enlightenment if they do so choose to accept. This has given me peace, healing, a calm spirit and more happiness in my life.

Jordyn: "What raised my vibration 10 percent in the month of May 2024 alone was signing a lease to help my brother have a place to live. I also spent more money on others to help them out, instead of only spending on myself. With a giving heart can make some people take advantage of that, so having equal give and take can be important. I also spent money that I'd usually use for crypto or stock investments and used it to edit my YouTube videos and publish these types of books to be more of a service to humanity. Thus, my money switched from investments only for myself and my family to investing on books and videos to get this information out to as many people as possible."

There is an infinite number of possible energy transfers between two or more mind/body/spirit complexes. For each mind/body/spirit complex is unique.

Ra: "This entity (Carla) still has transferred energy available, but we find rapidly increasing distortions towards pain in the neck, the dorsal area, and the wrists and manual appendages."

The physical energy transfer may be done numerous ways. We shall give two examples. Each begins with some sense of the self as Creator or in some way the magical personality being invoked. This may be consciously or unconsciously done. Firstly, that exercise of which we have spoken called the exercise of fire: this is, through physical energy transfer, not that which is deeply involved in the body complex combinations. Thusly the transfer is subtle, and each transfer unique in what is offered and what is accepted. At this point we may note that this is the cause for the infinite array of possible energy transfers.

The second energy transfer of which we would speak is the sexual energy transfer. This takes place upon a nonmagical level by all those entities which vibrate green ray active. It is possible, as in the case of this instrument which dedicates itself to the service of the One Infinite Creator, to further refine this energy transfer. When the other self also dedicates itself in service to the One Infinite Creator, the transfer is doubled. Then the amount of energy transferred is dependent only upon the amount of polarized sexual energy created and released. There are refinements from this point onward, leading to the realm of the high sexual magic.

In the realm of the mental bodies, there are variations of mental energy transferred. This is, again, dependent upon the knowledge sought and the knowledge offered. The most common mental energy transfer is that of the teacher and the pupil. The amount of energy is dependent upon the quality of this offering upon the part of the teacher and regards the purity of the desire to serve, and the quality of information offered and, upon the part of the student, the purity of the desire to learn and the quality of the mind vibratory complex which receives knowledge.

Another form of mental energy transfer is that of the listener and the speaker. When the speaker is experiencing mental/emotional complex distortions towards anguish, sorrow, or other mental pain, from what we have said before, you may perhaps garner knowledge of the variations possible in this transfer.

The spiritual energy transfers are the heart of all energy transfers as a knowledge of self and other self as Creator is paramount, and this is spiritual work. The varieties of spiritual energy transfer include those things of which we have spoken this day as we spoke upon the subject of the adept."

SESSION 74: 10-28-1981

The instrument has no awareness of the pain or other sensations. However, Ra uses the yellow-ray activated physical body as a channel through which they speak. As the mind/body/spirit complex of the instrument leaves the physical shell in Ra's keeping, it is finely adjusted to their contact.

However, the pain that the instrument can't feel, when sufficiently severe, mitigates against proper contact and, when the increased distortion is violent, can cause the tuning of the channel to waver. This tuning must then be corrected, which Ra may do as the instrument offers Ra this opportunity.

Ra: "We may not teach/learn for any other to the extent that we become learn/teachers. Therefore, we shall make some general notations upon this interesting subject and allow the questioner to consider and further refine any queries.

Ra: "The archetypical mind may be defined as that mind peculiar to the Logos of the planet. Thusly, unlike the great cosmic all mind, it contains the material which it pleased the Logos to offer as refinements to the great cosmic beingness. The archetypical mind, then, is that which contains all facets which may affect mind or experience.

The magician was named as a significant archetype. However, it was not recognized that this portion of the archetypical mind represents not a portion of the deep subconscious but the conscious mind and more especially the will. The archetype called by some the High Priestess, then, is the corresponding intuitive or subconscious faculty.

Let us observe the entity as it is in relationship to the archetypical mind. You may consider the possibilities of utilizing the correspondences between the mind/body/spirit in microcosm and the archetypical mind/body/spirit closely approaching the Creator. For instance, in your ritual performed to purify this place, you use the term "Ve Geburah." It is a correct assumption that this is a portion or aspect of the One Infinite Creator. However, there are various correspondences with the archetypical mind which may be more and more refined by the adept. "Ve Gedulah" has correspondences to Jupiter, to femaleness, to the negative, to that portion of the Tree of Life concerned with Auriel.

We could go forward with more and more refinements of these two entries into the archetypical mind. We could discuss color correspondences, relationships with other archetypes, and so forth. This is the work of the adept, not the teach/learner. We may only suggest that there are systems of study which may address themselves to the aspects of the archetypical mind, and it is well to choose one and study carefully. It is more nearly well if the adept goes beyond whatever has been written and make such correspondences that the archetype can be called upon at will."

The indigo center is indeed most important for the work of the adept. However, it cannot, no matter how crystallized, correct to any extent whatsoever imbalances or blockages in other energy centers. They must need to be cleared seriatim (in order) from red upwards.

The indigo ray is the ray of the adept. There is an identification between the crystallization of that energy center and the improvement of the working of the mind/body/spirit as it begins to transcend space/time balancing and to enter the combined realms of space/time (incarnation) and time/space (non-physical).

The disciplined personality, when faced with another self, has all centers balanced according to its unique balance. Thusly the other self looks in a mirror seeing its self.

The disciplines of the personality are the paramount work of any who have become consciously aware of the process of evolution.

The heart of the discipline of the personality: 1- Know yourself. 2- Become the Creator. 3-Accept yourself.

The third step, when accomplished, renders (gives) one the most humble servant of all, transparent in personality and completely able to know and accept other selves. In relation to the pursuit of the magical working, the continuing discipline of the personality involves the adept in knowing its self, accepting its self, and thus clearing the path towards the great indigo gateway to the Creator. To become the Creator is to become all that there is. There is, then, no personality in the sense with which the adept begins its learn/teaching. As the consciousness of the indigo ray becomes more crystalline, more work may be done; more may be expressed from intelligent infinity.

A working of service to others has the potential of alerting a great mass of light strength.

There are sound vibratory complexes which act like the dialing of a phone. When they are appropriately vibrated with accompanying will and concentration, it is as though many upon our metaphysical or inner planes received a telephone call. They answer this call by the attention of your working.

If all people in your churches were adepts consciously full of will, of seeking, of concentration, of conscious knowledge of the calling, there would be no difference between them and those specifically magical incantations (words used as a magic spell) used by the adept. The efficacy (effectiveness) of the calling is a function of the magical qualities of those who call; that is, their desire to seek the altered state of consciousness desired.

The channeling group (Don, Carla and Jim) agreed upon the Banishing Ritual of the Lesser Pentagram for the protective ritual used before channeling Ra. The sound vibratory complexes (also known as words) used in this banishing ritual are the type of words used for altering those of the inner planes (calling positive entities such as guides, angels or Arc Angels for whatever reason it may be for. The ritual calls the positive or service to others power available, just as when people pray to God, they are attempting to call God and this call is going to many upon our metaphysical/inner planes on the positive/service-to-others path. Perhaps 5th, 6th and 7th density positive entities and/or angels.

It is most important for the adept to feel its own growth as teach/learner. The efficiency of the ritual is the practitioner's ability to invoke the magical personality is of paramount importance. This is a study in itself. With the appropriate emotional will, polarity, and purity, work may be done with or without proper sound vibration complexes. However, there is no need for the blunt instrument when the scalpel is available.

The sounding of some of our Hebrew and some of our Sanskrit vowels have power before time and space and represent configurations of light which built all that there is. These sounds have this power because of the correspondence in vibratory complex is mathematical.

The users of these sounds in Hebrew, determined what these sounds were from the entity known as Yahweh. Yahweh aided this knowledge through impression upon the material of genetic coding which became language.

In the case of Sanskrit, the sound vibrations are pure due to the lack of previous alphabet or letter naming. Thus, the sound vibration complexes seemed to fall into place as from the Logos. This was a more natural or unaided situation or process.

SESSION 75: 10-31-1981

Ra seems to suggest that any "light worker" will, if successful in their work, attract some sort of negatively oriented psychic greeting. Just as the instrument in this group is getting psychic greetings/attacks that doesn't cause her physical pain.

Twice during the "Benedictus" portion of the music in a group concert she (Carla) sang as she experienced a psychic attack.

Ra: "In the singing, portion of hallows as the Mass, which immediately precedes that which is the chink called the "Hosanna," there is an amount of physical exertion required that is exhausting to any entity. This portion of which we speak is termed the "Sanctus." We come now to the matter of interest.

When the entity Jehoshuah (Jesus in the Bible) decided to return to the location called Jerusalem for the holy days of its people, it turned from work mixing love and wisdom and embraced martyrdom, which is the work of love without wisdom.

The "Hosanna," as it is termed, and the following "Benedictus," is that which is the written summation of what was shouted as Jehoshuah came into the place of its martyrdom. The general acceptance of this shout, "Hosanna to the son of David! Hosanna in the highest! Blessed is he who comes in the name of the Lord!," by that which is called the church has been a mis-statement, an occurrence which has been, perhaps, unfortunate for it is more distorted than much of the so-called Mass.

There were two factions present to greet Jehoshuah; firstly, a small group of those which hoped for an earthly king. However, Jehoshuah rode upon an ass (donkey) stating by its very demeanor that it was no earthly king and wished no fight with Roman or Sadducee.

The greater number were those which had been instructed by rabbi and elder to make jest of this entity, for those of the hierarchy feared this entity who seemed to be one of them, giving respect to their laws and then, in their eyes, betraying those time-honored laws and taking the people with it.

The chink for this instrument is this subtle situation which echoes down through your space/time and, more than this, the place the "Hosanna" holds as the harbinger (going before to announce another person) of that turning to martyrdom. We may speak only generally here. The instrument did not experience the full force of the greeting, which it correctly identified during the "Hosanna," due to the intense concentration necessary to vibrate its portion of that composition. However, the "Benedictus" in this particular rendition of these words is vibrated by one entity. Thus, the instrument relaxed its concentration and was immediately open to the fuller greeting."

(It appears entities are more protected in groups while meditating, singing or channeling.)

The chink is what turns to martyrdom. Jesus taking the path of martyrdom is the chink. It is aware of certain overbalances towards love, even to martyrdom, but has not yet, to any significant degree, balanced these distortions. Ra does not imply that this course of unbridled compassion has any fault, but affirm its perfection. It is an example of love which has served as beacon to many.

For those that seek further, the consequences of martyrdom must be considered, for in martyrdom lies the end of the opportunity in the density of the martyr, to offer love and light. Each entity must seek its deepest path.

The Orion entity finds a chink in any entity identifying in any amount toward martyrdom. It is then open by its free will to be a target for the Orion's to make it a martyr or to attack. Those involved in and dedicated to work which is magical or extremely polarized are then targeted by negative entities. (Just like negative entities are responsible for killing Jesus as I spoke about in the section of this book about Jesus' life and in my book *Correcting Distortions of The Bible*.)

The channeling group of Don, Carla and Jim entered this work with polarity but virtual innocence as to the magical nature of this polarity. That this group is beginning to discover.

(Just as there are psychic attacks during these channelings, there were also psychic attacks when the instrument sung songs at her church.)

It is extremely rare for an entity to attract the attention of an Orion light being. This is a most unique circumstance.

The instrument, Carla Reuckert, has an intense devotion to the teachings and example of Jesus. This entity then vibrates in song a most demanding version, called The Mass in B Minor by Bach, of this exemplary votive (sacrificial vow) complex of sound vibration. She is consciously identifying with each part of this Mass. Only thusly was the chink made available. It is not an ordinary occurrence and would not have happened had any ingredient been left out: exhaustion, bias in belief complexes, attention from an Orion entity, and the metaphysical nature of that particular set of words.

This fifth-density negative entity wishes to remove the instrument. This instrument is being greeted by a fifth-density entity which has lost some negative polarity due to its lack of dictatorship over the disposition of the instrument's mind/body/spirit or its yellow-ray-activated physical complex.

There are many Wanderers whom you may call adepts who do no conscious work in the present incarnation. It is a matter of attention. One may be a fine catcher of your game sphere, but if the eye is not turned as this sphere is tossed, then per (by) chance it will pass the entity by. If it turned its eyes upon the sphere, catching would be easy. In the case of wanderers which seek to recapitulate the degree of adeptness which each had acquired previous to this life experience, we may note that even after the forgetting process has been penetrated, there is still the yellow-activated body which does not respond as does the adept which is of green or blue-ray-activated body. Thusly, you may see the inevitability of frustrations and confusion due to the inherent difficulties of manipulating the finer forces of consciousness through the chemical apparatus of the yellow-ray-activated body.

Before surgery, it is well for each in this channeling group to realize its self as the Creator. Thusly each may support each other, including the support of self by humble love of self as Creator.

Certain Hebrew and Sanskrit sound vibratory complexes are powerful because they are mathematically related to the creation. The linkage is mathematical or of a musical ratio. There are those whose mind might try to attempt to resolve this mathematical ratio, but at present the coloration of the intoned vowel is part of the vibration, which cannot be accurately measured. However, it is equivalent to types of rotation of Earth's primary material particles.

When certain sounds are correctly vibrated, the creation sings. This is the concept of sympathetic resonance.

In some cases, only intoned vowel has a resonant nature. In other cases, most notably Sanskrit combinations, the selection of harmonic intervals is also of resonant nature. The creation becomes more and more contained within the practitioner if the adept uses this resonant quality.

Ra cannot tell the group of the musical notes to be intoned that are of this quality. As their seeking continues, there will be added to empirical data that acuity of sensibility which continue working in the ways of the adept offers.

<u>Empirical data</u> is the information acquired by scientists or whomever through experimentation and observation.

There is a great probability/possibility that if the group follows in the path that they tread now that more efficacious (intended result; effective) methods for the entire group will be established than the exercise of the fire.

Ra mentioned that hair is an antenna. It is difficult for Ra to expand on how it works due to the metaphysical nature of this antennae effect. Our physics are concerned with measurements in our physical complex of experience. The metaphysical nature of the contact of those in time/space is such that the hair, as it has significant length, becomes a type of electrical battery which stays charged and tuned and is then able to aid contact even when there are small anomalies in the contact.

The inner limit of the length of hair for this aid is 4 to 4-and-one-half inches depending on the strength of the contact and the nature of the instrument.

Any entity may at any time instantaneously clear and balance its energy centers. Thus, in many cases those normally quite blocked, weakened, and distorted may, through love and strength of will, become healers momentarily. To be a healer by nature, one must indeed train its self in the disciplines of the personality.

When the magical personality is properly and efficaciously (effectively) invoked, the self has invoked its Higher Self. Thus, a bridge between space/time and time/space is made, and the sixth-density magical personality experiences directly the third-density catalyst for the duration of the working. It is most central to deliberately take off the magical personality after the working in order that the Higher Self resume its appropriate configuration as analog to the space/time (physical) mind/body/spirit (incarnated being). This should be fastidiously (meticulously) accomplished either in mind or by gesture as well if this is of significant aid.

Fastidious mean being very attentive to and concerned about accuracy and detail.

The magical personality (a being of unity, 6th density, equivalent to Higher Self and a personality enormously rich in variety of experiences and subtlety of emotion.)

In the invocation (summoning or calling to bring forth) of the magical personality, it is not necessarily effective for the neophyte (person new to the subject). The magical personality begins to reside in the neophyte in small degrees or percentages as the neophyte becomes more adept.

Attention must be paid to each aspect of power, love and wisdom in developing the basic tool of the adept; that is, its self, in the three aspects of the magical personality. It is by no means a personality of three aspects. It is a being of unity, a being of 6th density, and equivalent to your Higher Self, and at the same time is a personality enormously rich in variety of experience and subtlety of emotion.

The three aspects are given that the neophyte not abuse the tools of its trade but rather approach those tools balanced in the center of love and wisdom and thus seeking power in order to serve.

A good sequence for the developing of the magical personality would be alternate meditations.

> 1- First on Power. 2- Then a meditation on love. 3- Then a meditation on wisdom. Then, cycling that way is an appropriate technique.

Visualization may be personalized and much love and support within the group generated. (Within this channeling group.)

The Adept: Each entity is the Creator. The entity, as it becomes more and more conscious of its self, gradually comes to the turning point at which it determines to seek either in service to others or in service to self. The seeker becomes the adept when it has balanced with minimal adequacy the energy centers red, orange, yellow, and blue with the addition of the green for the positive, thus moving into indigo work.

The adept then begins to do less preliminary or outer work, having to do with function, and begins to affect the inner work having to do with being. As the adept becomes a more and more consciously crystallized entity, it gradually manifests more and more of what it has always been since before time, that is, the One Infinite Creator.

END OF BOOK #3 of 5

~~~~~

Book #4

~Forward~

Book IV (4) of the Law of One is a beginning in the examination of the nature and the proper metaphysical use of the archetypical mind. The archetypical mind is the mind of the Logos, the blueprint used to make the creation and the means by which we evolve in mind, body and spirit. Ra stated that the archetypical mind could best be studied by one of three methods: 1- The Tarot. 2-Astrology. 3- The Tree of Life, which is known as white ceremonial magic.

This channeling group decided to investigate the archetypical mind by delving into the Tarot, more especially the twenty-two images of the Major Arcana. They primarily work with the first seven cards, which are the archetypes for the structure of mind. An overview of all the Tarot's twenty-two archetypes is also sought.

The group's conclusion was that if the contact were valid, they would at some point begin receiving material that was not familiar to them. That happened in Book IV. This is why the questioning in this book was scattered than in the first three volumes of Ra sessions.

The following comparison is between the general Tarot terminology and Ra's viewpoint that they shared with the Egyptians of the Tarot many years ago. The following comparison deals only with the twenty-two Major Arcana, since it was only these "concept complexes" that were used by Ra back when they were in third-density on Venus. These "concept complexes" (which are multiple meanings in the pictures) were used by Ra and later drawn by Egyptian priests, to describe the process of the evolution of mind, the body, and the spirit. The Court Arcana and the Minor Arcana were of other influences and were concerned primarily with the astrological approach to this study. Each card is described first by its Arcanum number, then by traditional terminology, and third by Ra's terminology.

The cards the group originally questioned and examined were not available for reprinting, so the cards shown here of the Major Arcana of the deck most closely resembling their first deck. These images are to be found in George Fathman's- *The Royal Road*: A study in the Egyptian Tarot; Key to Sacred Numbers and Symbols (Eagle Point, OR: Life Research Foundation, 1951.)

The first seven cards of the Major Arcana were designed to describe the evolution of the Mind; the second seven, the evolution of the body; and the third seven, the evolution of the spirit. Arcanum Number XXII is The Choice. The central choice each conscious seeker or adept makes as it strives to master the lessons of the third-density experience to seek in service to others or in service to self.

THE MIND

1-Arcanum number I: The Magician Card- Matrix of the Mind.

2-Arcanum Number II: The High Priestess Card- Potentiator of the Mind.

3-Arcanum Number III: The Empress Card- Catalyst of the Mind.

4-Arcanum Number IV: The Emperor Card- Experience of the Mind.

5-Arcanum Number V: The Hierophant Card- Significator of the Mind.

6-Arcanum Number VI: The Lovers or Two Paths Card- Transformation of the Mind.

7-Arcanum Number VII: The Chariot Card: Great Way of the Mind.

THE BODY:

8- VIII: Justice or Balance Card- Matrix of the Body.

9- IX: Wisdom or the Sage Card- Potentiator of the Body.

10- X: Wheel of Fortune Card- Catalyst of the Body.

11- XI: The Enchantress Card- The Experience of the Body.

12- XII: The Hanged Man or Martyr Card- Significator of the Body.

13- XIII: Death Card- Transformation of the Body.

14- XIV: The Alchemist Card- Great Way of the Body.

THE SPIRIT:

15- XV: The Devil Card- Matrix of the Spirit

16- XVI: Lightning Struck Tower Card- Potentiator of the Spirit.

17- XVII: The Star or Hope Card- Catalyst of the Spirit.

18- XVIII: The Moon Card- Experience of the Spirit.

19- XIX: The Sun Card- Significator of the Spirit.

20- XX: Judgment Card- Transformation of the Spirit.

21- XXI: The World Card- Great Way of the Spirit.

22- XXII: The Fool Card- THE CHOICE.

THE MIND:

Arcanum Number I
The Magician
MATRIX OF THE MIND

Arcanum Number II
The High Priestess
POTENTIATOR OF THE MIND

Arcanum Number III
The Empress
CATALYST OF THE MIND

Arcanum Number IV
The Emperor
EXPERIENCE OF THE MIND

Arcanum Number V
The Hierophant
SIGNIFICATOR OF THE MIND

Arcanum Number VI
The Lovers or Two Paths
TRANSFORMATION OF THE MIND

Arcanum Number VII
The Chariot
GREAT WAY OF THE MIND

THE MIND

THE BODY

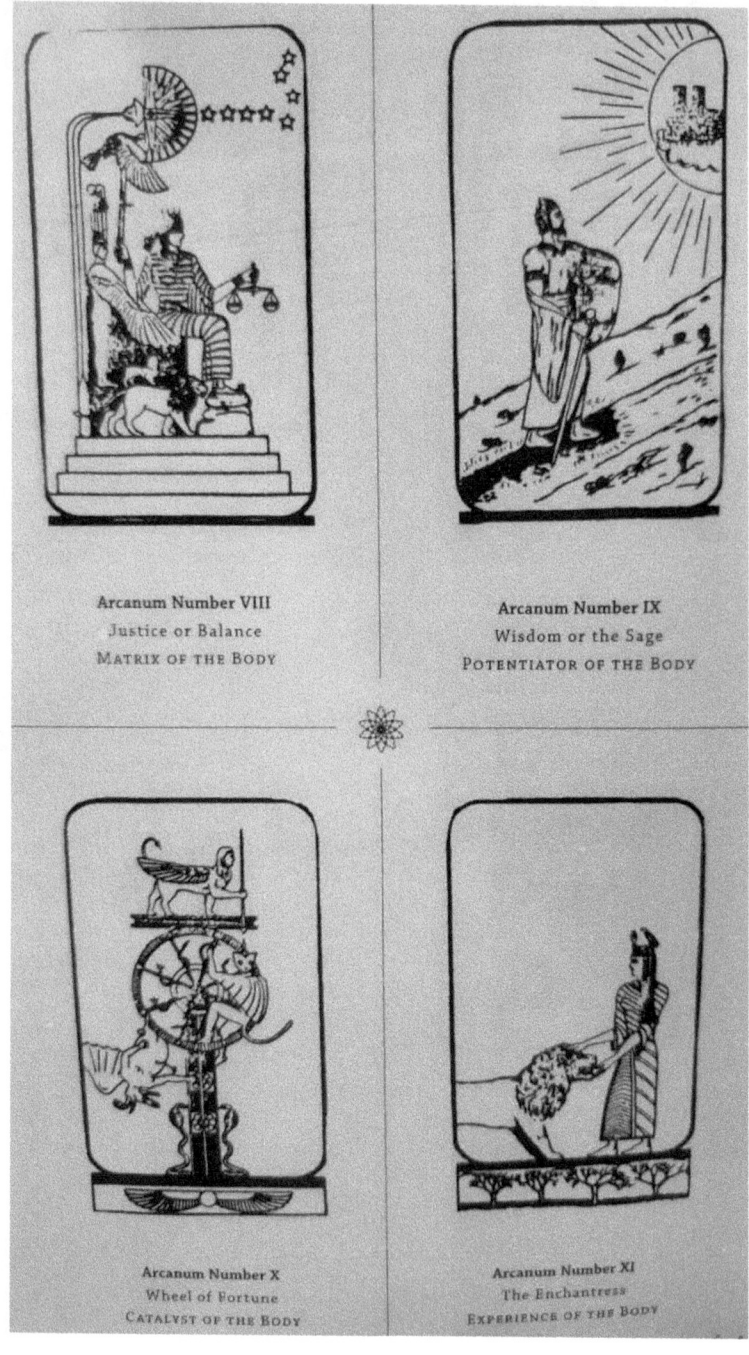

Arcanum Number VIII
Justice or Balance
MATRIX OF THE BODY

Arcanum Number IX
Wisdom or the Sage
POTENTIATOR OF THE BODY

Arcanum Number X
Wheel of Fortune
CATALYST OF THE BODY

Arcanum Number XI
The Enchantress
EXPERIENCE OF THE BODY

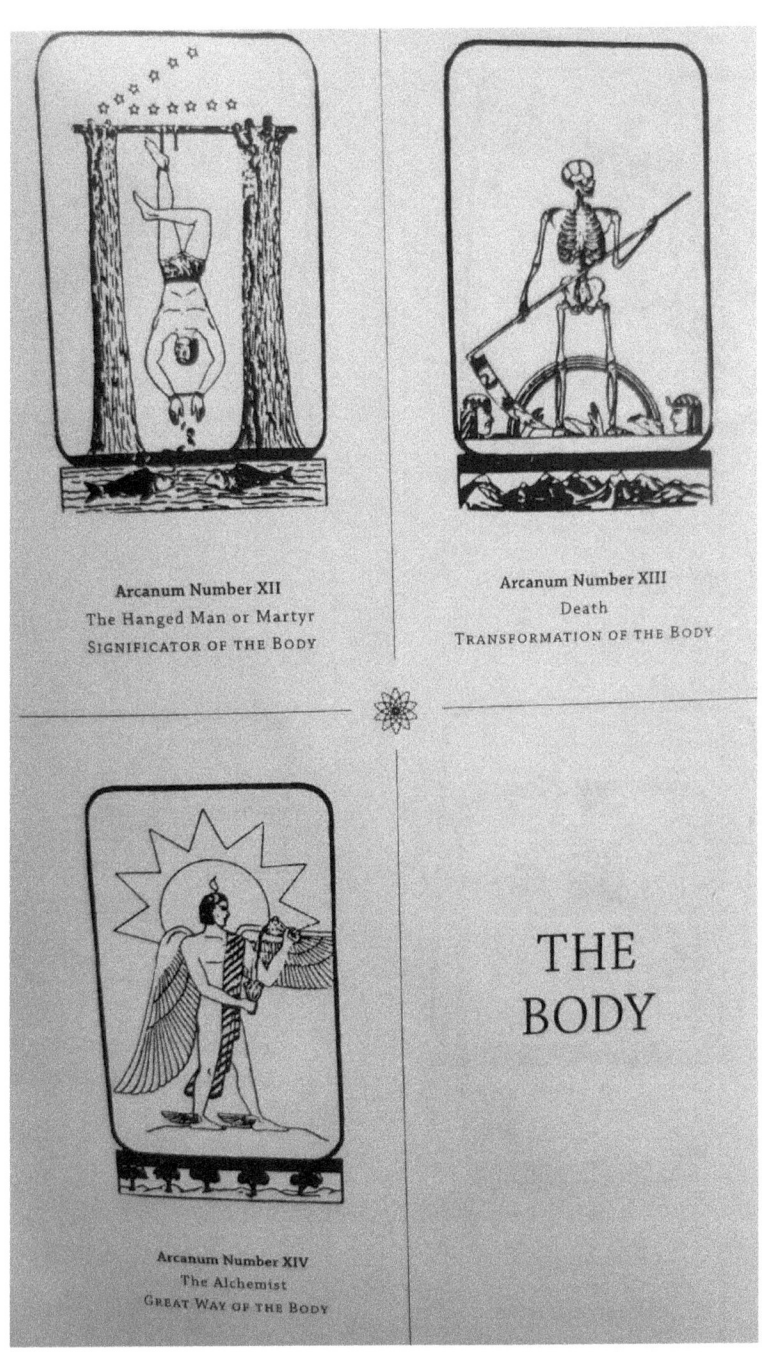

THE BODY

THE SPIRIT:

THE SPIRIT:

Arcanum Number XIX
The Sun
SIGNIFICATOR OF THE SPIRIT

Arcanum Number XX
Judgment
TRANSFORMATION OF THE SPIRIT

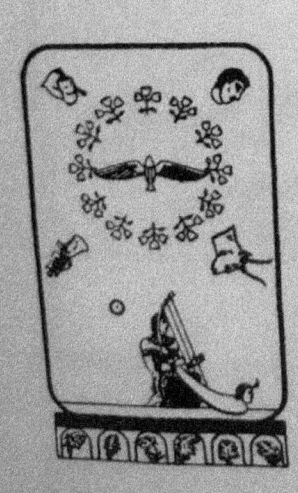

Arcanum Number XXI
The World
GREAT WAY OF THE SPIRIT

THE SPIRIT

Arcanum Number XXII
The Fool.

THE CHOICE

One of the primary discoveries in Book IV is the concept and purpose of the "veil of forgetting" that exists between the conscious and unconscious minds in our current third-density experience. Third densities closer to the center of our galaxy apparently did not have a veil and, therefore, did not forget any event in any incarnation. Not having a veil of forgetting simplified each entity's experience and also the nature of that archetypical mind. Book IV focuses on both pre-veil and post-veiling experiences and the archetypical minds of both experiences in order to get a better understanding of our current veiled experience in the third density of this octave of creation.

As a result of Ra's answers, the channeling group from L/L Research drew their own images of the first seven cards based on Ra's description of Ra's intended tarot images.

The Ra contact continued for 106 sessions, which were printed into four books in The Law of One series. These five books are available from Schiffer Publishing or from L/L Research.

Channeling Group: L/L Research

Don Elkins

Carla L. Rueckert

James A. McCarty

SESSION 76: 2-3-1982

The instrument has a physical complex bankruptcy (bankruptcy of physical energy) and the vital energies are normal, with a strong spiritual-complex counterpart and will lend substance to her lack of energy levels.

First, if the instrument is dedicated to continued communication with Ra and there's no physical complex energy transfer, it will begin to call upon the vital energy itself. If this is done in any substantive measure, it is actively deleterious (destructive) to a mind/body/spirit complex if that complex wishes further experience in the illusion, it now distorts.

Secondly, care can be taken in three ways:

1. Monitor the outer parameters of the instrument
2. Transfer physical energy by sexual transfer, by magical protection
3. By the energetic displacements of thought-forms energizing the instrument during contact. These things will not worsen the instrument's mind/body/spirit-complex distortions of strength/weakness.

The instrument attracts negative greetings by dedicating itself to this service. These are inconvenient, but with care taken, will not be lastingly deleterious (unexpectedly harmfully) to the instrument or the contact.

The third thing that could be done to take care of the instrument is the support channeling group to empathize with the instrument those energies through thought-forms which may be salubrious (healthy) to the other self. This is an energy transfer of empathizing through thought-form, for any thought is a form or symbol or thing that is an object seen in time/space reference.

RA: "This group's use of the Banishing Ritual of the Lesser Pentagram has been increasingly efficacious (effective). Its effect is purification, cleansing, and protection of the place of working.

The efficacy (efficiency) of this ritual is only beginning to be at the lower limits of the truly magical. In doing the working, those aspiring to adepthood have done the equivalent of beginning the schoolwork, many grades ahead. For the intelligent student this is not to be discouraged; rather to be encouraged is the homework, the reading, the writing, the arithmetic, as you might metaphorically call the elementary steps towards the study of being. It is the being that informs the working, not the working that informs the being. Therefore, we may leave you to the work you have begun."

It is beneficial for the group to regularly perform the banishing Ritual in the place the group does the channeling sessions.

Ra: "The origin of the Tarot system of study and divination is twofold: firstly, there is that influence which, coming in a distorted fashion from those who were priests attempting to teach the Law of One in Egypt, gave form to the understanding which they had received. These forms were then made a regular portion of the learn/teachings of an initiate. The second influence is that of those entities in the lands you call Ur, Chaldea, and Mesopotamia, who, from old, had received the data for which they called having to do with the heavens. Thusly, we find two methods of divination being melded into one, with uneven results; the astrology and the form being combined to suggest the correspondences which are typical of the distortions you may see as attempts to view archetypes."

The priests of Egypt attempted to convert knowledge they received from Ra into understandable symbology into the Tarot, with the addition of the Sumerian influence.

Ra: "We, of Ra, are humble messengers of the Law of One. We seek to teach/learn this single law. During the space/time of the Egyptian teach/learning, we worked to bring the mind complex, the body complex, and the spirit complex into an initiated state in which the entity could contact intelligent energy and so become teach/learner itself so that healing and the fruits of study could be offered to all. The study of the roots of mind is a portion of the vivification (liveliness) of the mind complex, and the thorough study of the portion of the roots of mind called archetypical is an interesting and necessary portion of the process as a whole."

Ra: "It is appropriate to study one form of constructed and organized distortion of the archetypical mind in depth in order to arrive at the position of being able to become and to experience archetypes at will. You have three basic choices. You may choose astrology, the twelve signs, as you call these portions of your planet's energy web, and what has been called the ten planets. You may choose the Tarot with its twenty-two so-called major Arcana. You may choose the study of the so-called Tree of Life with its ten Sephiroth and the twenty-two relationships between the stations.

It is well to investigate each discipline, not as a dilettante (rookie) but as one who seeks the touchstone, one who wishes to feel the pull of the magnet. One of these studies will be more attractive to the seeker.

Let the seeker, then, investigate the archetypical mind, using, basically, one of these three disciplines. After a period of study, the discipline mastered sufficiently, the seeker may then complete the more important step: that is, the moving beyond the written in order to express in a unique fashion its understanding of the archetypical mind.

The archetypical mind is that mind which is peculiar to the Logos under which influence you are at this space/time distorting your experiences. There is no other Logos the archetypical mind of which would be the same any more than the stars would appear the same from another planet in another galaxy. The closer Logoi are indeed closer in archetypes.

Since Ra evolved on Venus, Ra is of the same archetypical origin that we experience here on Earth.

Ra cannot express their methods of study of the archetypical mind under the system of distortions they enjoyed in order not to skew our own judgement of what is appropriate for the system of distortions forming the conditions in which we learn/teach. Therefore, they invoke the Law of Confusion (free will).

There is no method of estimation of the time/space (metaphysical) before timelessness entered into our first density. To the beginnings of our time, the measurement would be vast, and yet this vastness is meaningless. Upon the entry into constructed space/time, our first density spanned a bridge of space/time and time/space of perhaps two billion of our years.

Second density is more easily estimated and represents the longest density in terms of space/time. It is approximately 4.6 billion years. These approximations are exceedingly rough due to the somewhat uneven development of creations built upon the foundation stone of free will.

Third density is a choice and has three cycles of 25,000 years, equaling 75,000 years, which we are currently at the end of. The prelude (introduction) to choice must encompass (encircle) the laying of the foundation, the establishment of the illusion, and the viability of that which can be made spiritually viable. The remainder of the densities is continuous refining of that choice. The choice is the work of a moment but is the axis upon which the creation turns.

Ra is aware of creations where third density is lengthier and more space/time is given to the choosing. However, the proportions remain the same, the dimensions all being somewhat etiolated (pale or drawn out due to lack of light) and weakened by the Logos to have a variant experience of the Creator. This creation is seen by Ra to be quite vivid, our creation that we live in in this octave is more condensed by our Logos than some other Logoi have chosen. Thus, each experience of the Creator by the Creator in our system of distortions is more bright or vivid.

Disease offers the body complex the opportunity to cease viability. This is a desirable body complex function. Disease is a microscopic second-density other selves, which have in some forms long existed and perform their service by aiding the physical-body complex in its function of ceasing viability at the appropriate space/time.

(For example, an entity may have chosen before birth to live 50-60 years and agreed that disease would aid them in the body ceasing viability after those 50-60 years to end their incarnation and then reincarnate into a new life with new catalysts and experiences for more lessons to be learned.)

The Logos planned for entities of mind/body/spirit complex to gain experience until the amount of experience was sufficient for an incarnation. This varied only slightly from second-density entities who existed for the purpose of experiencing growth and seeking consciousness. As third-density upon our planet proceeded, the need for the physical-body complex to cease became more rapidly approached due to being intensified and more rapidly gained catalyst. This catalyst was not being properly assimilated (understood). Therefore, the lifetimes needed to be shorter, so that learning might continue to occur with the proper rhythm and increment. Thus, more and more opportunities have been offered as this third density has progressed for disease.

Approximately, 2030 is the harvest of souls on Earth into the 4th density positive. Right now, at the end of 2023, 65% of Earth is harvestable for 4th density positive. To be harvestable, one must be at least 51 percent service-to-others in the love and unity vibration. Those approximately 90-95% negative, in service-to-self of control, manipulation, domination, killing, rape and/or enslavement of others will experience separation and darkness of a 4th density planet being a slave to higher density demons or negative entities.

All planets progress form 3rd density by knowledge of and application of the Law of One. The only way for a planet to get out of the situation that we are in is for the population to become aware of and start practicing the Law of One.

Those 50-90% service-to-self or undecided will be transferred to another planet that supports third-density life, such as a planet like the one we currently live on now.

The Orion Group is of negative density and their purpose is conquest and enslavement. This is done by finding and establishing an elite through various devices such as the 10 Commandments that was given to Moses from negative entities.

Fourth density of love and unity is approximately 30 million years, if not capable of being harvested sooner; or 90,000 years of harmonious incarnation.

Fifth density light or wisdom is about 405 million years or more depending on the Council of Planets and the decision by the Confederation.

Sixth density is unmeasurable, but for Ra one cycle was 75 million years of light/love or love/light or unity.

Seventh density is the Gateway density. Becomes one with the all. Having no memory, no identity, no past or future, but existing in the all, such as the Council of Planets.

Ra: "There is a dimension in which time does not have sway. In this dimension, the mind/body/spirit in its eternal dance of the present may be seen in totality, and before the mind/body/spirit complex which then becomes a part of the social memory complex is willingly absorbed into the allness of the One Creator, the entity knows itself in its totality.

This mind/body/spirit/complex totality functions as a resource for the Higher Self. The Higher Self, in turn, is a resource for examining the distillations of third-density experience and programming further experience. This is also true of densities four, five, and six with the mind/body/spirit complex totality coming into consciousness in the course of seventh density."

The mind/body/spirit complex totality is that which may be called upon by the Higher Self aspect just as the mind/body/spirit complex calls upon the Higher Self. In the one case you have a structured situation within the space/time continuum with the Higher Self having available to it the totality of experiences which have been collected by an entity and a very firm grasp of the lessons to be learned in this density.

The mind/body/spirit complex totality is as the shifting sands and is in some part a collection of parallel developments of the same entity. This information is made available to the Higher Self aspect. This aspect may then use the projected probability/possibility vortices in order to better aid in what you would call future life programming."

As entities begin to see the Creator in seventh, there is a very rapid progression towards the eighth density.

There's no concept of right or wrong, good or bad. (Since all learn at their own pace and eventually are all 6th density positive by mid-sixth density.)

Eighth density is the harvest of seventh density into the next octave. It is the union with Source, the One Infinite Creator. It's the octave that moves into mystery. The Logos creates light. This light creates the catalytic and energetic levels of experiences in the creation. The highest of all honor/duties is given in the 8th density in the next octave. It is the supervision of light in its manifestations during experimental times of our cycles.

There is a crystal skull in the possession of a woman near Toronto. Don Elkins believes it may be of some value in investigating these communications with Ra since he believes this had some origin from Ra. Ra couldn't answer due to the potential answer may have in affecting his actions.

(I believe this means wearing the crystal skull can help in channeling and contacting higher dimensional beings, and a higher density being took part in the formation of this crystal skull.)

SESSION 77: 2-10-1982

Don Elkins asked Ra if there's anything the group could do to protect the instrument from psychic attacks prior to a session. Ra responded by saying that they could refrain from continuing the contact. This is the only thing they could do which they are not already attempting with a whole heart. (This information resonated more with me that Ra would be positively oriented.)

An entity may contemplate itself as the Creator in preparation for a hospital experience or in dealing with pain. This, done in a more determined fashion, would be beneficial at times when the mind is weakened by sever assaults upon distortions of the body towards pain. There is no necessity for negative thought-forms regardless of pain distortions. The elimination of such creates the lack of possibility for negative elementals and other negative entities to use these thought-forms to create the worsening of the mind-complex deviation from the normal distortions of cheerfulness/anxiety.

The Orion group organized the experience for the instruments heart rate to go up to 115 beats per minute and to have extreme pain in her stomach. These events, as well as others more serious, were proximally caused by ingestion of food in the form of a tablet.

Ra: "We examine this query for the Law of Confusion and find ourselves close to the boundary, but acceptably so.

The substance which caused the bodily reaction of the heartbeat was called Pituitone by those which manufacture it. That which caused the difficulty which seemed to be cramping of the lower abdominal musculature but was, in fact, more organic in nature was a substance called Spleentone.

This instrument has a physical-body complex of complicated balances which afford its physical existence were the view taken that certain functions and chemicals found in the healthy body complex are lacking in this one and, therefore, simply must be replenished, the intake of the many substances which this instrument began would be appropriate. However, this particular physical vehicle has, for approximately twenty-five of your years, been vital due to the spirit, the mind, and the will being harmoniously dedicated to fulfilling the service it chose to offer.

Therefore, physical healing techniques are inappropriate whereas mental and spiritual healing techniques are beneficial."

It would be beneficial for the instrument to not ingest this group of food anymore. Also, each person in the group may become aware of the will to a greater extent. It is a vital key to the evolution of the mind/body/spirit complex.

The philosophy of our sun, the sub-Logos, for Its creation and plan for experience was to create a foundation.

Ra: "First of mind, then of body, and then of spiritual complex. Those concept complexes you call the Tarot lie then in three groups of seven: the mind cycle, one through seven; the physical-complex cycle, eight through fourteen; the spiritual-complex cycle, fifteen through twenty-one. The last concept complex may best be termed The Choice.

Upon the foundation of the transformation of each complex, with free will guided by the root concepts offered in these cycles, the Logos offered this density the basic architecture of a building and the constructing and synthesizing of data culminating in The Choice."

There are seven basic philosophical foundations for mental experience, seven for bodily, seven for spiritual that produce the polarization that we experience during the third-density cycle. These 22 concept complexes exist within the roots of mind, and it is from this resource that their guiding influence and leitmotifs (leading motives) may be traced.

Ra: "You may further note that each foundation is itself not single but a complex of concepts. Furthermore, there are relationships betwixt mind, body, and spirit of the same location in octave, for instance: one, eight, fifteen, and relationships within each octave which are helpful in the pursuit of The Choice by the mind/body/spirit complex. The Logos under which these foundations stand is one of free will. Thusly the foundations may be seen to have unique facets and relationships for each mind/body/spirit complex. Only twenty-two, The Choice, is relatively fixed and single."

These 22 philosophical foundations are those of third density. Above third density is the recognition of the architecture of the Logos, but without the veils which are so integral a part of the process of making the choice in third density.

The intensity of fourth density is that of the refining rough-hewn sculpture (has been shaped, but not yet smooth). This is in its own way quite intense, causing the mind/body/spirit complex to move ever inward and onward in its quest for fuller expression. However, in third density the statue is forged in the fire- this is a type of intensity not found in the fourth, fifth, sixth or seventh densities.

The polarization or choosing of each being is necessary for harvestability from third density. The higher densities do their work due to the polarity gained in The Choice.

Ra: "There were Logoi which chose to set the plan for the activation of mind/body/spirit complexes through each true color body without recourse (resource in a difficult situation) to the prior application of free will. It is, to our knowledge, only in an absence of free will that the conditions of only having positive polarity exist within the Logos."

(Therefore, because of free will, the negative polarity also exists.)

Ra: "In such a procession of densities, you find an extraordinarily long third density; likewise, fourth density. Then, as the entities begin to see the Creator, there is a very rapid procession towards the eighth density. This is due to the fact that one who knows not, cares not.

Let us illustrate by observing the relative harmony and unchanging quality of existence in one of your primitive tribes. The entities have the concepts of lawful and taboo, but the law is inexorable (unstoppable) and all events occur as predestined. There is no concept of right and wrong, good or bad. It is a culture in monochrome (black and white). In this context you may see the one you call Lucifer as the true light-bringer in that the knowledge of good and evil both precipitated the mind/body/spirits of this Logos from the Edenic conditions (times of Eden) of constant contentment and also provided the impetus (momentum or motivation) to move, to work, and to learn.

Those Logoi whose creation shave been set up without free will have not, in the feeling of those Logoi, given the Creator the quality and variety of experience of Itself as have those Logoi which have incorporated free will as paramount. Thusly you find those Logoi moving through the timeless states at what you would see as a later space/time to choose the free-will character when elucidating (making clear) the foundations of each Logos."

Under the first distortion, it was the free will of the Logos to choose to evolve without free will.

Those which chose lack of free-will foundations, to all extents with no exceptions, founded Logoi of the service-to-others path. The sage of polarity, its consequences and limits, were unimagined until experienced.

Originally the Logoi that did not choose the free-will path because they had not conceived of it. Later Logoi experienced it as growth from the extension of free-will farther down through their evolution.

Our particular Logos that we experience in our solar system planned for this polarity and knew all about it prior to Its plan.

The Logos would have an advantage of selecting the form of acceleration of spiritual evolution by planning the major archetypical philosophical foundations, such as the 22 archetypes in the Major Arcana of the Tarot. The Logos would plan these as a function of the polarity that would be gained in third density.

Each being must perceive each archetype in its own way. Therefore, precision is not the goal; rather, the quality of general-concept complex perception is the goal.

Our Logos designed this particular evolution of experience with total free will to allow for polarization to accelerate evolution.

Many came more rapidly to third density than others from second density.

> Ra: "Many come more rapidly to third density than others, not because of an innate efficiency of catalysis but because of unusual opportunities for investment. In just such a way those of fourth density may invest third, those of fifth density may invest fourth. When fifth density has been obtained, the process takes upon itself a momentum based upon the characteristic of wisdom when applied to circumstance. The Logos Itself, then, in these instances provides investment opportunities."

SESSION 78: 2-19-1982

The group had to perform the Banishing Ritual twice since there was a misstep which created a momentary lapse of concentration. This was not well; the misstep was a missed footing. The negative entities presence was cold.

The healing of the time/space kidney, for the instrument Carla, was of the self by the self with the catalyst of the spiritual healer Pachita.

The energetic displacements of thought-forms energizing the instrument during contact most efficiently would be the group sending love, light, thoughts of physical, mental, and spiritual strength. You may refine these sending until the fullest manifestation of love and light are sent into the energy web of this entity which functions as instrument. The groups exact sending, in order to be most potent, the creature of their own making.

Our Milky Way galaxy progressed in evolution from the center outward toward the rim, and that in the early evolution of this galaxy, the first distortion of free will was not extended down past the sub-Logos because it was not thought of or conceived of, and that this extension of free will, which created polarization, occurred later as the evolution progressed outward from the center of the galaxy.

The Three distortions of the Law of One:

1- Free Will. 2- Love. 3- Light.

The One Infinite Creator is all that there is. The first manifestation visible to the eye of the body we inhabit is light or limitless light.

Ra: "At the beginning of this creation or octave, there were those things known which were the harvest of the preceding octave. About the preceding creation, we know as little as we do of the octave to come. However, we are aware of those pieces of gathered concept which were the tools which the Creator had in the knowing of the self.

These tools were of three kinds. Firstly, there was an awareness of the efficiency for experience of mind, body, and spirit. Secondly, there was an awareness of the most efficacious nature or significator of mind, body, and spirit. Thirdly, there was the awareness of two aspects of mind, of body, and of spirit that the significator could use to balance all catalyst. You may call these two the matrix and the potentiator."

Ra: "In the mind complex the matrix may be described as consciousness. It has been called the Magician. It is to be noted that of itself, consciousness is unmoved. The potentiator of consciousness is the unconscious. This encompasses a vast realm of potential in the mind.

In the body the matrix may be seen as balanced working or even functioning. Note that here the matrix is always active, with no means of being inactive. The potentiator of the body complex, then, may be called Wisdom, for it is only through Judgment that the unceasing activities and proclivities of the body complex may be experienced in useful modes.

The Matrix of the Spirit is what you may call the Night of the Soul or primeval darkness. Again, we have that which is not capable of movement or work. The potential power of this extremely receptive matrix is such that the potentiator may be seen as Lightning. In your archetypical system called the Tarot, this has been refined into the concept complex of the Lightning-Struck Tower. However, the original potentiator was Light in its sudden and fiery form; this is, the Lightning itself."

The original significators may undifferentiatedly be termed the mind, the body, and the spirit.

At the beginning of our galactic octave is an archetypical mind that is a product of the previous octave, which this galaxy then used as and acts under free will to all for our experience of polarity to help in evolution. The previous octave had polarity in the sense of the mover and the moved, but not in service to others or service to self.

The first experiences were monochrome (black and white). To the limits of Ra's knowledge, which are narrow, the ways of the octave are without time; that is, there are seven densities in each creation infinitely.

The central suns of our galaxy, in starting the evolutionary process in this galaxy, provided for, in their plans, the refinement of consciousness through the densities just as we experience it here. However, they did not conceive of the polarization of consciousness with respect to service to self and service to others.

The densities are the nature of the vibratory range peculiar to each quantum of the octave with some certainty with which you perceive as color with your optical apparatus if it is functioning properly.

Ra: "I am Ra. As proem, let me state that the Logoi always conceived of themselves as offering free will to the sub-Logoi in their care. The sub-Logoi had freedom to experience and experiment with consciousness, the experiences of the body, and the illumination of the spirit.

The first Logos to instill what you now see as free will, in the full sense, in Its sub-Logoi came to this creation due to conceptualizations of the

Significator. The Logos posited the possibility of the mind, the body, and the spirit as being complex. (It is complex due to the veil of forgetting, making the mind complex). In order for the significator to be what it is not; it then must be granted the free will of the Creator. This set in motion a quite lengthy series of Logos's improving or distilling this seed thought. The key was the Significator becoming a complex."

Our particular Logos, when it created Its own particular creation, was at some point far down the evolutionary spiral of the experiment, with the significator becoming what it is now and being granted the free will of the Creator.

Each Logos and Its design are the Creator experiencing Itself. The seed concept of the significator being a complex introduces two things: 1- The Creator against Creator in one sub-Logos in dynamic tension.

2- The concept of free will, once having been made fuller by its extension into the sub-Logoi known as mind/body/spirit complexes, creates and re-creates and continues to create as a function of its very nature.

The purpose of polarity is to develop the potential to do work.

The result of polarization in consciousness, which has occurred later in the galactic evolution, the experiences are much more intense along the two paths.

Fourth and fifth densities are quite independent of each other, the positive functioning with no need of negative and vice versa. It is to be noted that in attempting to sway third-density mind/body/spirit complexes in choosing polarity, there evolves a good bit of interaction between the two polarities. In sixth density, the density of unity, the positive and negative paths must take in each other, for all now must be seen as love/light and light/love. This is not difficult for the positive polarity, which sends love and light to all other selves. It is difficult enough for service-to-self polarized entities that at some point the negative path is abandoned.

Don Elkins believes the choice of polarity for the archetypical basis for evolution of consciousness in our particular experience indicates to him that we have arrived, through a long process of the Creator knowing Itself, at a position of present or maximum efficiency for the design of the process of experience. That design for maximum efficiency is in the roots of consciousness and is the archetypical mind and is a product of everything that has gone before. There are, unquestionably, relatively pure archetypical concepts for the seven concepts of mind, body and spirit.

Ra said that was thoughtful and that there are no mistakes, but cannot judge what was said.

Kathryn: "I believe, even though Don could be correct, I assume Creation and the Creator will always evolve and find more efficient ways for evolution. I even have a theory on how third density can improve for each entity evolving by having this information available for everyone, so that they can make the best decision for themselves in their life, especially when it comes to what polarity they want to choose.

Right now, most people do not understand the consequences of their choice, whether to the positive or the negative. Many do not understand that the positive polarity can give purpose, healing, clear understanding, the end of searching for the truth which can lead to anxieties and irritability dissipating. Knowing that the negative path is division, control, fear and darkness may then change someone's mind on whether they would want to pursue that path or not if they only knew where that path would lead them to. That's why this information is so extremely important to humanity and only fair that they know where each path leads to.

For example, it's not fair to tell someone they can choose service to self without them realizing that it leads to being a slave to higher level negative entities, that it leads to separation, darkness, division and chaos in the negative planets as they all fight for control in a hierarchical system. Whereas the positive path is full of love, unity, compassion and all working together for the betterment of all beings. That eventually in 6th density both polarities will have to merge into love and light of the positive path and the negative path would have to be abandoned at some point in this density of unity."

How wind and fire in the first density teaches earth and water: Air and fire is chaos and literally illuminating and forming the formless, for earth and water were, in a timeless state, unformed. As the active principles of fire and air blow and burn incandescently about what natures is to come, the water learns to become sea, lake, and river, offering the opportunity for viable life. The earth learns to be shaped, thus offering the opportunity for viable life.

Recall at all times that the archetypes are a portion of the resources of the mind complex.

Ra: "Properly, the archetypes have some relationships to the planets. However, this relationship is not one which can be expressed in your language. This, however, has not halted those among your peoples who have become adepts from attempting to name and describe these relationships. To most purely understand the archetypes, it is well to view the concepts which make up each archetype and reserve the study of planets and other correspondences for meditation."

The planets are an outgrowth of the Logos.

There is much study of archetype which is actually the study of functions, relationships, and correspondences. The study of planets is an example of archetype seen as function. However, the archetypes are, first and most profoundly, things in themselves, and the pondering of them and their purest relationships with each other should be the most useful foundation for the study of the archetypical mind.

Archetype 1- Matrix of the Mind. The Magician is understandable when you consider consciousness is the great foundation, mystery, and revelation which makes this particular density possible. The self-conscious entity is full of magic of that which is to come. The mind is the first of the complexes to be developed by the student of spiritual evolution.

Archetype 2- Potentiator of the Mind. The High Priestess, representing the intuition. The beginning knowledge of this Logos is the matrix and potentiator. The unconscious may be described as the High Priestess, for it is the Potentiator of the Mind, and as potentiator for the mind is that principle which potentiates all experience.

Archetype 3- Catalyst of the Mind. The Empress. It takes in far more than disciplined meditation. However, through the faculty of mediation catalyst is most efficiently used. It represents the unconscious or female portion of the mind complex, being first used or ennobled (given noble rank) by the male or conscious portion of the mind. Thus, the noble name.

Archetype 4- Experience of the Mind. Emperor. This implies nobility. It is only through the catalyst which has been processed by the potentiated consciousness that experience may ensue. Thusly is the conscious mind ennobled by the use of the vast resources of the unconscious mind.

Due to the psychic attack, this instrument will require warmth along the right side of the physical body. There has been some infringement, but it should not be long lasting. It is well to swaddle this instrument sufficiently to ward off any manifestations of this cold in physical form.

SESSION 79: 2-24-1982

The energy transfer during the session is a most helpful one in that it serves to strengthen the shuttle through which the instreaming contact is received. The contact itself will monitor the condition of the instrument and cease communication when the distortions of the instrument begin to fluctuate towards the distortions of weakness and pain. However, while the contact is ongoing, the strength of the channel through which this contact flows may be aided by the energy transfer.

The practice of magical workings demands the most rigorous honesty. If you believe you can sustain the magical personality throughout this working, it is well. As long as you have some doubt, it is inadvisable. In any case it is appropriate for the instrument to return its magical personality rather than carry this persona into the trance state, for it does not have the requisite magical skill to function in this circumstance and would be far more vulnerable than if the waking personality is offered as channel. This working is magical in nature in the basic sense. However, it is inappropriate to move more quickly than one's feet may walk.

The experience of third density entities prior to the veil of forgetting was able to remember previous incarnations.

The reincarnation process like the one that we experience here, in which the third-density body is entered and exited numerous times during the cycle, is the same prior to the veil.

The optimal incarnative period is somewhere close to a millennium. This is a constant regardless of the other factors of the third-density experience.

Prior to free will (the first distortion), the veil or loss of awareness did not occur. This veil or loss of consciously remembering what occurred before the incarnation was the first tool for extending free will.

The Logos first devised the tool of separating the unconscious from the conscious during our physical incarnations to achieve Its objective.

The archetypical mind of the Logos prior to this experiment in veiling was less complex and contained nine archetypes. Those nine were three of mind, three of body and three of spirit.

The body, the mind, and the spirit each contained and functioned under the aegis (protection or support) of the Matrix, the potentiator, and significator. The significator of the mind, body, and spirit is not identical to the significator of the mind, body, and spirit complexes (post-veil).

The significator must be a complex: To be complex is to consist of more than one characteristic, element or concept.

Ra: "The Matrix of Mind (Magician Card) is that from which all comes. It is unmoving yet is the activator in potentiation of all mind activity. The Potentiator of the Mind (High Priestess Card) is that great resource which may be seen as the sea into which the consciousness dips ever deeper and more thoroughly in order to create, ideate, and become more self-conscious.

The Significator of each mind, body, and spirit may be seen as a simple and unified concept. The Matrix of the Body (Justice or Balance Card) may be seen to be a reflection in opposition of the mind; this is, unrestricted motion. The Potentiator of the Body (Wisdom or Sage card) then is that which, being informed, regulates activity.

The Matrix of the Spirit (The Devil Card) is difficult to characterize since the nature of spirit is less motile (free wandering). The energies and movements of the spirit are, by far, the most profound yet, having more close association with time/space, do not have the characteristics of dynamic motion. Thusly one may see the Matrix as the deepest darkness and the Potentiator of Spirit (Lightning Struck Tower) as the most sudden awakening, illuminating, and generative influence.

This is the description of Archetypes One through Nine before the onset of influence of the co-Creator or sub-Logos's realization of free will."

The first change for the extension of free will was the putting of a veil between the Matrix (mind) and Potentiator of the Mind (subconscious), to be relatively mystery filled, during the incarnation. This veil occurs between the unconscious and conscious minds.

It was the design of the Logos to allow the conscious mind greater freedom under free will by partitioning (separating) this from the Potentiator or unconscious, which had great communication with the total mind, therefore, allowing the birth of uneducated portions of consciousness.

This simple experiment was carried out and observed before greater complexity was attempted. As Ra said, there have been a great number of successive experiments. The result of these experiments has been more vivid, varied and intense experience of Creator by Creator.

When the first experiment with the veiling process occurred, the early Logoi produced service-to-self and service-to-others mind/body/spirit complexes immediately. The harvestability of these entities was not so immediate, and thus refinements of the archetypes began. There were nine archetypes and many shadows.

These shadows were described by Ra to be inchoate (just begun and undeveloped) thoughts of helpful structures not yet fully conceived.

Implicit (unvoiced) in the veiling or separation of two archetypes is the concept of choice. Therefore, The Choice existed during the first service-to-self polarity. The refinements to this concept took many experiences.

The magical potential (great abilities) in third and fourth density was far great pre-veil than it is now post veil. However, there was far, far less desire of will to use this potential.

Magical ability is the ability to consciously use the unconscious. Therefore, there was maximal ability prior to the innovation of sub-Logoi's free will.

The Magician (Matrix of the Mind) is the conscious mind veiled between the High Priestess (Potentiator of the Mind) of the unconscious mind to all for free will to choose the negative or positive path.

The next archetype is the Empress (Catalyst of the Mind) that acts upon the conscious mind to change it. The fourth archetype is the Emperor (The Experience of the Mind) which is the material stored in the unconscious. There is a great deal of dynamic interrelationship in these first four archetypes.

The Hierophant (Significator of the Body) complex, its very nature. The heart of the mind complex is that dynamic entity which absorbs, seeks, and attempts to learn. It is the original archetype of mind, which has been made complex through the subtle movements of the conscious and unconscious. The complexities of the mind were evolved rather than the simple melding of experience from Potentiator to Matrix. The mind itself became an actor possessed of free will and, more especially, will. As the Significator of Mind (The Hierophant Card) has the will to know, but what shall it do with its knowledge, and for what reasons does it seek? The potentials of a complex Significator are manifold.

There is strong relationship between the Significators of the mind, the body, and the spirit.

The Lovers (# 6 Card in the tarot) is the Transformation of the Mind. The student of the mysteries being transformed by the need to choose between the light and the dark in mind.

#7- The Chariot or the Conqueror (The Path, The Way or the Great Way of Mind). The most perceptive. Its foundation is a reflection and substantial summery of Archetypes One through Six.

It represents the culmination of the action of the first six archetypes into a conquering of the mental processes, even possibly removing the veil.

One may also see the Way of the Mind (Chariot Card), a showing of the Kingdom or fruits of appropriate travel through the mind, in that the mind continues to move as majestically through the material it conceives of as chariot drawn by royal lions or steeds.

SESSION 80: 2-27-1982

The instrument is experiencing mild fluctuations of physical energy. Prayers and affirmations offered to and by the instrument slightly increase the physical energy and continual greetings by the negative fifth density entity whenever it is feasible (possible) has caused sudden energy deficit changes.

Don Elkins had to leave the room for a bit for a forgotten item after the group performed the banishing ritual. If it was the only working, the lapse would have been critical.

(Because of the many workings and banishing rituals done before every session in the same room, it created more built-up protection.) There is enough residual energy of protective nature in this place of working that this lapse, though quite unrecommended, does not represent a threat to the protection of which the banishing ritual offers.

However, the instrument has become more mentally and spiritually able to greet this entity with love, thereby reducing the element of fear, which is an element the negative entity counts as a great weapon in the attempt to cause cessation, in any degree, of the Ra contact.

The negative entity can attack through the instrument's distortions. Any distortion, be it physical, mental, or spiritual in complex nature, may be accentuated (more noticeable) by the suggestion of one able to work magically; that is, to cause changes in consciousness. The instrument has many physical distortions. Their nature varies. The less balanced the distortion by self-knowledge, the more adeptly the negative entity may accentuate a distortion in order to mitigate (lesson) against the smooth functioning and harmony of the group.

As Ra well knows, the information the group accumulates through the Ra contact will be illuminating to a very minor percentage of those who populate this Earth, simply because there are very few people who understand it. The negative fifth-density visitor is dead set against this communication.

The purity of this information is a light. Such an intensity of light attracts attention of the fifth-density negative entity that would hope to gain a portion of that light; that is, the mind/body/spirit complex of the instrument. Borring this, the entity intends to put out the light.

Ra: "Purity does not end with the harvest of third density. The fidelity of Ra towards the attempt to remove distortions is total. This constitutes an acceptance of responsibility for service to others, which is of relative purity. The instrument through which we speak and its support group have a similar fidelity and, disregarding any inconvenience to self, desire to serve others. Due to the nature of the group, the queries (questions) made to us by the group have led rapidly into somewhat abstruse (difficult to understand) regions of commentary. This content does not mitigate (lesson the seriousness) against the underlying purity of the contact."

The negative entity attempted to put out the light for some of the group's space/time, with no long-lasting result. The gain for triumph is an increase in negative polarity to the entity, in that it has removed a source of radiance (light) and, thereby, offered to this space/time the opportunity of darkness where there was once light. In the event that it succeeded in enslaving the mind/body/spirit of the instrument, it would have enslaved a fairly powerful entity, thus adding to its power.

The power this visitor increases in is its spiritual power.

Ra: "The powers of mind do not encompass (encircle) such works as these. You may, with some fruitfulness, consider the possibilities of moonlight. You are aware that we have described the Matrix of the Spirit as Night (The Devil Card). The moonlight, then, offers either a true picture seen in shadow or chimera (delusion) and falsity. The power of falsity is deep, as is the power to discern truth from shadow. The shadow of hidden things is an infinite depth in which is stored the power of the One Infinite Creator.

The adept, then, is working with the power of hidden things illuminated by that which can be false or true. To embrace falsity, to know it, and to seek it, and to use it, gives a power that is most great. This is the nature of the power of your visitor and may shed some light upon the power of one who seeks in order to serve others as well, for the missteps in the night are Oh! So easy."

The work of the adept is based upon previous work with the mind and the body. Work with the spirit would not be possible on a dependable basis. The visitor's power is of the spirit with negative polarization of course.

Archetype 15- (The Devil card in the tarot) (Matrix of the Spirit)

Ra: "The nature of the spirit is so infinitely subtle that the fructifying (fruitful) influence of light upon the great darkness of the spirit is very often not as apparent as the darkness itself. The progress chosen by many adepts becomes a confused path as each adept attempts to use the Catalyst of the Spirit. Few there are successful in grasping the light of the sun (Significator of the Spirit). By far, the majority of adepts remain groping in the moonlight (Experience of the Spirit) and this light can deceive as well as uncover hidden mystery. Therefore, the melody of this matrix often seems to be of a negative and evil nature (The devil card).

It is also to be noted that an adept is one which has freed itself more and more from the constraints of the thoughts, opinions, and bonds of other selves. Whether this is done for service to others or service to self, it is a necessary part of the awakening of the adept. This freedom is seen by those not free as what you would call evil or black. The magic is recognized; the nature is often not."

Implicit (steadfast) in the process of becoming adept is the seeming polarization towards service-to-self, because the adept becomes disassociated with many of his kind is likely to occur. The apparent happening is disassociation, whether the truth is service to self and thus true disassociation from other selves or service-to-others, and thus true association from other selves or service to others, and thus true association with the heart of all other selves and disassociation only from the illusory husks which prevent the adept from correctly perceiving the self and other self as one.

The effect of disassociation on the positively-oriented adept from the miasma (highly unhealthiness) of illusion and misrepresentation of each and every distortion is quite necessary portion of an adept's path. It may be seen by others to be unfortunate.

From the point of view from the Matrix of the Spirit (Devil card), this is somewhat an excursion into catalyst of the spirit (Star card) in this process. This excursion and the process of disassociation is most usually linked with the archetype called Hope (The Star card) which Ra would prefer to call faith. This archetype is the Catalyst of the Spirit and, because of the illuminations of the Potentiator of the spirit (Lightning Struck Tower Card), will begin to cause these changes in the adept's viewpoint.

The positive or negative adept is calling directly through the spirit to the universe for its power, for the spirit is a shuttle.

Ra: "The adept, whether positive or negative, has the same Matrix. The Potentiator is also identical. Due to the Catalyst of each adept, the adept may begin to pick and choose that into which it shall look further. The Experience of the Spirit (Moon Card), that which you have called the Moon, is then, by far, the more manifest of influences upon the polarity of the adept. Even the most unhappy of experiences which seem to occur in the Catalyst of the adept, seen from the viewpoint of the spirt, may, with the discrimination possible in shadow, be worked with until light equaling the light of brightest moon descends upon the adept, and positive or service-to-others illumination has occurred. The service-to-self adept will satisfy itself with the shadows and, grasping the light of day, will toss back the head in grim laughter, preferring the darkness."

#19- Significator of the Spirit (The Sun card). The Significator of the Spirit is that living entity which either radiates or absorbs love and light of the One Infinite Creator, radiates it to other (positive) or absorbs it for the self (negative).

#20- Transformation of the Spirit (Judgement). That which you call Sarcophagus in our system may be seen to be the material world. This material world is transformed by the spirit into that which is infinite and eternal. The infinity of spirit is an even-greater realization than the infinity of consciousness, for consciousness that has been disciplined by will and faith is that consciousness which may contact intelligent infinity directly. There are many things that fall away in the many, many steps of adepthood. Ra said that they will walk these steps and praise the One Infinite Creator at each transformation.

#21- The Path/Great Way of the Spirit (The World card) represents contact with intelligent infinity, although one may also see the reflection of the contact as well as the contact with intelligent energy which is the Universe or the World.

Intelligent energy is the energy of the Logos, and thus it is the energy that heals, builds, removes, destroys, and transforms all other selves as well as the self.

The contact with intelligent infinity is most likely to produce an unspeakable joy in the entity experiencing such contact.

SESSION 81: 3-22-1982

The continual weariness of the instrument is not due to psychic greeting but is rather an inevitable consequence of the Ra contact.

Ra: "The mechanism creating weariness is that connection betwixt the density wherein this instrument's mind/body/spirit complex is safely kept during these workings, and the altogether variant density in which the instrument's physical-body complex resides at this space/time. As the instrument takes on more of the coloration of the resting density, the third-density experience seems heavier and more wearisome. This was accepted by the instrument, as it desired to be of service. Therefore, we accept also this effect, about which nothing of which we are aware may be done."

Weariness of the time/space nature may be seen to be that reaction of transparent or pure vibrations with impure, confused, or opaque environs (not transparent to see through).

The instrument bears the brunt of weariness of the effect of this contact. Each of the support group, by offering the love and the light of the One Infinite Creator in unqualified support in these workings and in energy transfers for the purpose of these workings, experience between 10 to 15 percent, roughly, of this effect. It is cumulative and identical in the continual nature of its manifestation.

The continued wearying effect would have infinite variations with different people. Ra then states what the results would be if the wearying effect continued after a long period.

Ra: "One group might be tempted and thus lose the very contact which caused the difficulty. So, the story would end.

Another group might be strong at first but not faithful in the face of difficulty. Thus, the story would end.

Another group might choose the path of martyrdom in its completeness and use the instrument until its physical-body complex failed from the harsh toll demanded when all energy was gone.

This particular group, at this particular nexus, is attempting to conserve the vital energy of the instrument. It is attempting to balance love of service and wisdom of service, and it is faithful to the service in the face of difficulty. Temptation has not yet ended this group's story.

We may not know the future, but the probability of this situation continuing over a relatively substantial period of your space/time is large. The significant factor is the will of the instrument and of the group to serve. That is the only cause for balancing the slowly increasing weariness, which will continue to distort your perceptions. Without this will, the contact might be possible but finally seem too much of an effort."

#10- Catalyst of the Body (Wheel of Fortune card). The wheel of Fortune represents interaction with other selves. Each catalyst is dealing with the nature of those experiences entering the energy web and vibratory perceptions of the mind/body/spirit complex. The outside stimulus of the Wheel of Fortune offers both positive and negative experience.

#11- Experience of the Body (The Enchantress) which represent the catalyst which has been processed by the mind/ body/ spirit complex and is called the Enchantress because it produces further seed for growth.

#12- Significator of the Body (The hanged Man or Martyr card).

#13- Transformation of the Body is called the Death (death card), for with death the body is transformed to a higher vibrational body for additional learning. It may also be seen as each moment and each day offers death and rebirth to one which is attempting to use the catalyst which is offered.

#14- The Great Way of the Body (The alchemist card) must be seen, as are all archetypes of the body, to be a mirror image of the thrust of the activity of the mind. The body is the creature of the mind and is the instrument of manifestation for the fruits of mind and spirit. Therefore, you may see the body as providing the athanor (maintaining a constant heat) through which the Alchemist manifests gold.

Ra does not have complete knowledge of this octave. There are portions of the seventh density which, although described by their teachers, remain mysterious. Ra has experienced a great deal of the available refining catalyst of this octave, and their teachers have worked with them most carefully that they may be one with all, that in turn their eventual returning to the great allness of creation shall be complete.

Ra has knowledge from the first beginnings of this octave (universe) through their present 6th density experience and some knowledge of seventh density as they learned from their teachers. They also have direct or experiential knowledge through communication with those space/times and time/space, but they have not yet evolved to or penetrated the seventh level.

They have evidence of both the previous creation (octave) and creation to be (next octave), as they in the stream of space/time and time/space view these apparently non-simultaneous events.

We are presently in the Milky Way galaxy of some 200 or so billion stars, and there are millions and millions of the large galaxies spread out through space. To Ra's knowledge, these galaxies are infinite and a significant point. The point being that we have unity. Ra hasn't experienced consciousness in many other galaxies.

Ra has opened their hearts in radiation of love to the entire creation. Approximately 90 percent of the creation is at some level aware of the sending and able to reply. All of the infinite Logoi are one in the consciousness of love. This is the contact Ra enjoys rather than travel.

It is possible for Ra to travel at will throughout the creation within this Logos (The Milky Way Galaxy). They have moved where they were called to service; these locations being local and including Alpha Centauri, planets of our solar system called the sun, Cepheus, and Zeta Reticuli. To those sub-Logoi they have come, having been called.

In general, the call was from other densities. In the particular case of the Sun sub-Logos, third density is the density of calling.

Ra has not moved at any time into one of the other major galaxies, other than the Milky Way Galaxy.

Ra: "There are Wanderers from other major galaxies drawn to the specific needs of a single call. There are those among our social memory complex which have become Wanderers in other major galaxies. Thus, there has been knowledge of other major galaxies, for to one whose personality or mind/body/spirit complex has been crystallized, the universe is one place and there is no bar upon travel. However, our interpretation of the social memory complex traveling to another major galaxy. We have not done this, nor do we contemplate it, for we can reach in love with our hearts."

The infinite number of galaxies that humanity has become aware of with our telescopes, are all of the same octave.

Some of the Wanderers from Ra in going to some of the other major galaxies- that is, leaving this system of some 200 billion stars of lenticular shape and going to another cluster of billions of stars and finding their way into some planetary situation there- would encounter dual polarity of negative and positive polarities such as we have here.

Towards the center of this galaxy is the older portion containing no service-to-self polarization. Other galaxies that Wanderers from Ra have traveled to developed the same pattern of service-to-self polarization appearing further out from the galactic spiral.

Various Logoi (galaxies) and sub-Logoi had various methods of arriving at the same discovery of the efficiency of free will in intensifying the experience of the Creator by the Creator. However, in each case this has been a pattern.

From the beginning of the octave, we had the core of many galactic spirals forming. In this particular octave the experiment of the veiling and the extending of free will started, roughly, simultaneously in many, many of the budding or building galactic systems. There was some type of communication throughout the octave so that, when the first experiment became effective, knowledge of this spread rapidly through the octave and was picked up by other galactic spirals.

To be aware of this communication is to be aware of the nature of the Logos. Much of creation has never separated from the One Logos of this octave and resides within the One Infinite Creator. Communication in such an environment is the communication of cells of the body.

What is learned by one is known to all. The sub-Logoi have been in the position of refining the discoveries of the earlier sub-Logoi.

SESSION 82: 3-27-1982

There is a possibility/probability that the whirling of the water with spine erect would somewhat altar the distortion towards pain which this entity (Carla) experiences in the dorsal region on a continuous level. This could aid in the distortion towards increase of physical energy to some extent.

Just prior to the beginning of this octave of experience, Intelligent Infinity had created and already experienced one or more previous octaves.

There is no counting the number of previous octaves. As far as Ra is aware, we are in an infinite creation. (With an infinite number of octaves).

At the beginning of this octave, out of the plenum (wholeness) of space, seeds of creation (of an infinite number of galactic systems) such as the Milky Way Galaxy) grew from the center or core outward simultaneously.

The nature of true simultaneity is such that, indeed, all is simultaneous in this octave.

There is a center to infinity in observing the beginning of the octave. From this center, all spread. Therefore, there are centers to the creation, to the galaxies, to star systems, to planetary systems, and to consciousness. In each case you may see growth from the center outward.

In the case of galactic systems, the first manifestation of the Logos (For example, Milky Way Galaxy) is a cluster of central systems which generate the outward swirling energies producing, in their turn, further energy centers for the Logos or stars.

These are central original creations or clusters of stars.

The closer to the beginning of the manifestation of the Logos the star is, the more it partakes in the one original thought.

The plan of the One Infinite Creator is that the partaking in the original thought has a gradient radially outward.

Ra: "This is the plan of the One Infinite Creator. The One Original Thought is the harvest of all previous experience of the Creator by the Creator. As it decides to know Itself, It generates Itself, into that plenum full of the glory and the power of the One Infinite Creator which is manifested to your perceptions as space or outer space. Each generation of this knowing begets (brings into existence) a knowing which has the capacity, through free will, to choose methods of knowing Itself. Therefore, gradually, step by step, the Creator becomes that which may know itself, and the portions of the Creator partake less purely in the power of the original word or thought. The Creator does not properly create as much as It experiences Itself."

The harvest of the previous octave was the Creator of Love manifested in mind, body, and spirit. This form of the Creator experiencing Itself may perhaps be the first division.

Ra: "A very great deal of creation was manifested without the use of the concepts involved in consciousness, as you know it. The creation itself is a form of consciousness which is unified, the Logos being the one great heart of creation. The process of evolution through this period, which may be seen to be timeless, is most valuable to take into consideration, for it is against the background of this essential unity of the fabric of creation that we find the ultimate development of the Logoi which chose to use that portion of the harvested consciousness of the Creator to move forward with the process of knowledge of self. As it had been found to be efficient to use the various densities, which are fixed in each octave, in order to create conditions in which self-conscious sub-Logoi could exist, this was carried out throughout the growing flower-strewn field, as your simile suggest, of the one infinite creation.

The first being of mind, body, and spirit were not complex. The experience of mind/body/spirits at the beginning of this octave of experience was singular. There was no third-density forgetting. There was no veil. The lessons of third density are predestined by the very nature of the vibratory rates experienced during this particular density and by the nature of the quantum jump to the vibratory experiences of fourth density."

The first mind/body/spirit experiences, as this galaxy progressed in growth, were those that moved through the densities. For instance, one of the very early planets formed near the center of the galaxy. The planet solidified during the first density, that life appeared in second density, and all of the mind/body/spirit complexes of third density progressed out of second density on that planet and evolved into third density.

Ra: "Our knowledge is limited. We know of the beginning but cannot asseverate (declare for certain) to the precise experiences of those things occurring before us. You know the nature of historical teaching. At our level of learn/teaching we may expect little distortion. However, we cannot, with surety, say there is no distortion as we speak of specific occurrences of which we were not consciously a part."

It is Ra's understanding that Don's supposition (opinion) is correct in that some or a large percentage of the planets near the center of the galaxy had mind/body/spirits moving through the densities. (They are mind/body/spirits without the complex at the end, because there is no veil of forgetting.)

The mind/body/spirits went through the process of physical incarnation in third density where there was no forgetting. The purpose of third density incarnation is to learn the ways of love. The nature of third density is constant. Its ways are to be learned the same now and ever. Thusly, no matter what form the entity facing these lessons, the lessons and mechanisms are the same. The Creator will learn from Itself. Each entity has unmanifest portions of learning and, most importantly, learning involved with other selves.

Prior to the forgetting process (pre-veil) there was no concept of anything but service-to-others polarization. It is Ra's perception that such conditions created the situation of a most pallid experiential nexus in which lessons were garnered with the relative speed of the turtle to the cheetah.

(Pre-veil evolution occurred slowly like a turtle, then post-veil evolution was a lot faster like a cheetah.)

There is infinite diversity in societies under any circumstances, whether pre-veil or post-veil. There were many highly technologically advanced societies which grew due to the ease of producing any desired result in the pre-veil. When one dwells within a state of constant potential inspiration, that which even the most highly sophisticated social structure lacked, given the complex nature of its entities will or to use a more plebeian (ordinary person) term, gusto, or elan vital, which is a non-physical force that causes the evolution and development of beings.

Such technological societies evolved travel through space to other planets or others planetary systems. From the groups point of view there was great evolutionary experience.

The Logos is aware of the third-density requirement for graduation. All the previous experiments, although resulting in many experiences, lacked the crucial ingredient of polarization. There was little enough tendency for experience to polarize entities that they habitually repeated third-density cycles many times over. It was desire that the potential for polarization be made more available.

Kathryn: "As you could then guess, this desire for polarization then created the veil of forgetting between the conscious and unconscious mind, so that entities can then choose service-to-self or service-to-others in free will to rapidly accelerate evolution and achieve third-density graduation."

Mind/body/spirits are pre-veil.

Mind/body/spirit complexes are post-veil. The complex mind comes into play after the veil of forgetting separates the conscious mind from the unconscious mind.

Mind/body/spirits (pre-veil had a difficult time serving others to the extent necessary for graduation, since they had the tendency to be divinely happy. Therefore, they had little urge to alter or better their condition. Such is the result of the mind/body/spirit which is not complex. There is the possibility of love of other selves and service-to-other selves, but there is the overwhelming awareness of the Creator in the self. The connection with the Creator is that of the umbilical cord. The security is total. Therefore, no love is terribly important; no pain terribly frightening; no effort, therefore, is made to serve for love or the benefit from fear.

Ra stated that Don Elkins was perceptive within the strict bounds of the simile he stated about our present illusion on Earth of those who are born into extreme wealth and security. (My interpretation is that he assumes those people on Earth in extreme wealth and security may be too happy in their lives to serve others and therefore may not help others as much. This lack of service-to-others may delay their evolution and possibly hinder their ability to graduate if they aren't at least 51% service-to-others.)

The inchoate (just begun and so not fully developed) structure of the healing and review of the incarnation in-between incarnation was always in place pre and post-veil. In pre-veil there was no harm, so there was no need for healing. This too may be seen to have been of concern to Logoi, which were aware that without need to understand, understanding would forever be left undone.

Even though there was no harm pre-veil and therefore no healing to be made, there was still the review of the incarnation. No portion of the Creator audits the course. Each incarnation is intended to be a course in the Creator knowing Itself. Each incarnation will end with such a test. This is so that the portion of the Creator may assimilate (understand) the experiences in yellow, physical third density to evaluate the biases gained; and then may choose the conditions of the next incarnations, either by means of automatically provided aid or by the self.

Before the veil, during the review of the incarnation, entities at that time were aware that they were trying to sufficiently polarize for graduation.

Before the veil there was an awareness of the need for polarization towards service to others in third density by all entities, whether incarnated in third-density, yellow-ray bodies or in between incarnation. All entities experienced wealth through the entire spectrum of experience whether it might be in-between incarnations or during incarnations, and the entities just simply could not manifest the desire to create this polarization necessary for graduation.

Consider the scholar as being an entity in your younger years of the schooling process in this metaphor of the schooling. The entity is fed, clothed, and protected regardless of whether or not the schoolwork is accomplished. Therefore, the entity does not do the homework but rather enjoys playtime, mealtime, and vacation. It is not until there is a reason to wish to excel that most entities will attempt to excel.

Kathryn: "In my younger years I just enjoyed BMX racing, hanging out with friends, playing outside and vacations. It wasn't until about the age of 22 that I had to work for my money and to pay my bills. This is around the same time I started exercising, eating healthy, working out outside of the BMX track and started to desire to serve others when everything wasn't just handed to me. So, I relate to Ra's metaphor. I also was 42% service-to-others my entire life until the age of 25, when I broke my neck. This caused me to go inward towards searching for truth. Once I found truth with the Law of One, I then started evolving towards service-to-others where I am now 87% positively-oriented."

The concept of service-to-self did not hold sway previous to the veiling process.

Ra: "The necessity for graduation to fourth density is an ability to use, welcome, and enjoy a certain intensity of the white light of the One Infinite Creator. In your own terms at your space/time nexus, this ability may be measured by your previously stated percentages of service (51% or more positive).

Prior to the veiling process the measurement would be that of an entity walking up a set of your stairs, each of which was imbued with a certain quality of light. The stair upon which an entity stopped would be either third-density light or fourth-density light. Between the two stairs lies the threshold. To cross that threshold is difficult. There is resistance at the edge of each density. The faculty of faith or will needs to be understood, nourished, and developed in order to have an entity which seeks past the boundary of third density. Those entities which do not do their homework, be they ever so amiable (friendly or sociable), shall not cross. It was this situation which faced the Logoi prior to the veiling process being introduced into the experiential continuum of third density."

Ra told the channeling group to remain united in love and thanksgiving to improve the contact of to make the instrument more comfortable.

SESSION 83: 4-5-1982

Ra: "Firstly, let us establish that both before and after the veil, the same conditions existed in time/space; that is, the veiling process is a space/time phenomenon.

Secondly, the character of experience was altered drastically by the veiling process. In some cases, such as the dreaming and the contact with the Higher Self, the experience was quantitatively different due to the fact that the veiling is a primary cause of the value of dreams and is also the single door against which the Higher Self must stand awaiting entry. Before veiling, dreams were not for the purpose of using the unconscious to further utilize catalyst but were used to learn/teach from teach/learners within the inner planes as well as those of outer origins of higher density. During the veiling process, there was not a quantitative change in the experience but a qualitative one in third density. (measured in quality)

Let us, as an example, choose your sexual activities of energy transfer. In the instance of the sexual activity of those not dwelling within the veiling, each activity was a transfer. There were some transfers of strength. Most were rather attenuated (weakened) in the strength of the transfer due to the lack of veiling.

In the third density, entities are attempting to learn the way of love. If it can be seen that all, are one being, it becomes much more difficult for the undisciplined personality to choose one mate and, thereby, initiate itself into a program of service. It is much more likely that the sexual energy will be dissipated more randomly without either great joy or great sorrow depending from these experiences.

Therefore, the green-ray energy transfer, being almost without exception the case in sexual energy transfer prior to veiling, remains weakened and without significant crystallization. The sexual energy transfers and blockages after veiling have been discussed previously. It may be seen to be a more complex study, but one far more efficient in crystallizing those who seek the green-ray energy center."

There has been both veneral disease (Sexually transmitted Disease) and other diseases before and after the veil of this great experiment.

However, since venereal disease is in large part a function of the thought-forms of a distorted nature associated with sexual energy blockage, the venereal disease is almost entirely the product of mind/body/spirit complexes' interaction after the veiling. Venereal disease existing in a small way prior to the veil was as random as disease distortions are, at heart, in general. Each portion of the body complex is in a state of growth at all times. The reversal of this is seen as disease and has the benign function of ending an incarnation at the appropriate space/time nexus. This was the nature of disease, including venereal.

The Logos before the veil decided upon a program where an individual mind/body/spirit would continue to grow in mind, and the body would be the third-density analog of this mind. The growth would be continual unless there was an inability, for some reason, for the mind to continue along the growth patterns. If this growth decelerated or stopped, disease would then act in a way so as to eventually terminate this physical experience so that a new incarnation would begin, after a review of the entire process had taken place between incarnations.

The nature of time/space (Metaphysically) is such that a lifetime may be seen whole as a book or record, the pages studied, riffled through, and reread. However, the value of review pre-veil is that of the testing as opposed to the studying. At the testing, when the test is true, the distillations (or purifications) of all study are made clear. During the process of study of the incarnation.

In as much as the universe is composed of an infinite array of entities, there is also an infinity of response to stimulus. Our people on Earth have a great variant of responses to the same distortions towards disease. Therefore, there's different reactions to disease amongst different people post veil, and the same could be true pre-veil as well I would assume.

Ra: "Third density is, by its very fiber, a societal one. There are societies whenever there are entities conscious of the self and conscious of other selves and possessed with intelligence adequate to process information indicating the benefits of communal (joint) blending of energies. The structures of society before as after veiling were various. However, the societies before veiling did not depend in any case upon the intentional enslavement of some for the benefit of others, this not being seen to be a possibility when all are seen as one. There was, however, the requisite amount of disharmony to produce various experiments in what you may call governmental or societal structures."

There was no unconscious slavery before the veil at that period. At the present space/time the conditions of intentional and unintentional slavery are so numerous that it beggars Ra's ability to enumerate them (to list them all).

At this time, a service-to-others oriented entity may meditate upon the nature of these little-expected forms of slavery that might be productive in polarization.

It is a necessary balance to the intention of law, which is to protect, that the result would encompass an equal distortion towards imprisonment. Therefore, the laws and restrictions within our legal system to enslave people in jail is a necessary balance to protect people. This is not to denigrate (defame) those (in green- and blue-ray energies) sought to free a peaceable people from the bonds of chaos, but only to point out the inevitable consequences of codification of response which does not recognize the uniqueness of each and every situation within our experience.

The veil is semipermeable.

There were no techniques of penetration of the veil planned by the first great experiment.

Ra: "As all experiments, this rested upon the nakedness of hypothesis. The outcome was unknown. It was discovered, experientially (based on experience) and empirically (based on observation or experience), that there were as many ways to penetrate the veil as the imagination of mind/body/spirit complexes could provide. The desire of mind/body/spirit complexes to know that which was unknown drew to them the dreaming and the gradual opening to the seeker of all of the balancing mechanisms, leading to adepthood and communication with teach/learners which could pierce this veil.

The various unmanifested activities of the self were found to be productive in some degree of penetration of the veil. In general, by far the most vivid and even extravagant opportunities for the piercing of the veil are a result of the interaction of polarized entities."

There's extreme potential for polarization in the relationship of two polarized entities which have embarked upon the service-to-others path or, in some few cases, the service-to-self path. Ra notes that the doubling effect is those of like mind which together seek shall far more surely find.

The penetration of the veil may be seen to begin to have its roots in the gestation of green-ray activity, that all-compassionate love which demands no return. If this path is followed, the higher energy centers shall be activated and crystallized until the adept is born. Within the adept is the potential for dismantling the veil to a greater or lesser extent that all may be seen again as one. The other self is primary catalyst in this particular path to the piercing of the veil.

The mechanism of the veiling between the conscious and unconscious portions of the mind was a declaration that the mind was complex. This, in turn, caused the body and the spirit to become complex.

An example of the body being complex after the veil is that the unconscious mind controls the involuntary functions of the body. Prior to the great experiment (of the veil) a mind/body/spirit was capable of controlling the pressure of blood in the veins, the beating of the heart, the intensity of the sensation known as pain, and all of the functions now understood to be involuntary (unconscious).

There were many experiments whereby various functions of the body complex were veiled and others not. A large number of these experiments resulted in nonviable body complexes or those only marginally viable.

For instance, if an entity at that time burned its hand due to carelessness. It would immediately remove its hand from the burning object, and then, in order to not feel the pain any more, its mind would cut the pain off until healing took place.

Today, we would look at this in our present illusion as an elimination of a certain amount of catalyst that would produce an acceleration in our evolution. Since the pain we experience today, in a veiled society, helps accelerate our evolution. This attitude towards pain Ra said is productive of helpful distortions as regards to the process of evolution.

The plan of the Logos in veiling the conscious from the unconscious mind in a way that pain could not be so easily controlled created a system of catalyst not previously usable.

Ra: "You may see, in some cases, an entity which, either by pre-incarnative choice or by constant reprogramming while in incarnation, has developed an esurient (hungry or greedy) program of catalyst. Such an entity is quite desirous of using the catalyst and has determined to its own satisfaction that what you may call the large board needs to be applied to the forehead in order to obtain the attention of the self. In these cases, it may indeed seem a great waste of the catalyst of pain and a distortion towards feeling the tragedy of so much may be experienced by the other self. However, it is well to hope that the other self is grasping that which it has gone to some trouble to offer itself; that is, the catalyst which it desires to use for the purpose of evolution."

Ra suggests the virtue of the liquids for the bodily maintenance of the instrument. The instrument has an increasingly ability to sense what will aid its body. It is being aided by affirmations and also by the light which is the food of the density of resting.

The least distorted desire of the instrument might be offered to the bodily complex which is indeed at this time potentially capable of greatly increased distortion. This is the complex protein of the animal, which has been slaughtered and preservatives added in order to maintain the acceptability to our peoples of this non-living, physical material.

It is well to attempt to find those items which are fresh and of the best quality possible in order to avoid increasing this particular entity's distortions of allergies.

Ra was speaking of the distortion towards disease which is potential at this space/time.

SESSION 84: 4-14-1982

Ra: "Let us use as exemplar (an excellent example) the one known as Jehoshua."

Ra: "This entity incarnated with the plan of martyrdom. There is no wisdom in this plan, but rather understanding and compassion extended to its fullest perfection. The one known as Jehoshua would have been less than fully understanding of its course had it chosen to follow its will at any space/time during its teachings. Several times this entity had the possibility of moving towards the martyr's place which was, for that martyr, Jerusalem. Yet, in meditation this entity stated, time and again, "It is not yet the hour." The entity could also have, when the hour came, walked another path. Its incarnation would then have been prolonged, but the path for which it incarnated somewhat confused. Thusly, one may observe the greatest amount of understanding, of which this entity was indeed capable, taking place as the entity in meditation felt and knew that the hour had come for that to be fulfilled which was its incarnation.

It is indeed so that all mind/body/spirit complexes shall die to the third-density illusion, each yellow-ray physical-complex body shall cease to be viable. It is a misnomer (inaccurate term) to, for this reason alone, call each mind/body/spirit complex a martyr, for this term is reserved for those who lay down their lives for the service they may provide to others. We may encourage meditation upon the functions of the will."

Each sexual activity before the veil was an energy transfer.

The path of energy transfer before the veiling during sexual intercourse was two entities possessed of green-ray capability. The awareness of all as Creator opens the green energy center. Thusly, there was no possibility of blockage due to the sure knowledge that each was the Creator. The transfers were weak due to the ease of transfers taking place between two polarized entities during sexual intercourse.

If someone closes an electrical circuit it is easy to trace the path of current. It goes along the conductor. The schematic (simplified) representation of the circuitry of two mind/body/spirts or two mind/body/spirit complexes in sexual or other energy transfer, the circuits open always at red or base center and moves as possible through the intervening energy centers. If baffled, it will stop at orange. If not, it shall proceed to yellow. If still unbaffled, it shall proceed to green. It is well to remember in the case of the mind/body/spirit that the chakras or energy centers could well be functioning without crystallization.

The uncrystallized, lower centers cannot deliver the higher voltage. The crystallized centers may become quite remarkable in the high-voltage characteristics of the energy transfer as it reaches green ray, and as green ray is crystallized this also applies to the higher energy centers until such energy transfers become an adornment (grace) for the Creator.

Ra: "The energy transfer occurs in one releasing of the potential difference. This does not leap between green and green energy centers but is the sharing of the energies of each from red ray upwards. In this context it may be seen to be at its most efficient when both entities have orgasm simultaneously. However, it functions as transfer if either has the orgasm, and indeed in the case of the physically expressed love between a mated pair which does not have the conclusion you call orgasm, there is, nonetheless, a considerable amount of energy transferred due to the potential difference which has been raised as long as both entities are aware of this potential and release its strength to each other by desire of the will in a mental or mind complex dedication. You may see this practice as being used to generate energy transfers in some of your practices of other Christian religious-distortion system of the Law of One."

(This means that Christianity is a distortion of the Law of One, as it only provides half the truth.)

Each system is quite distorted, and its teachings always half lost. However, one such system is the tantric yoga. If both entities are well polarized and vibrating in green-ray love, any orgasm shall offer equal energy to both.

Ra: "Perhaps the most critical difference of the veiling, before and after, was that before the mind, body, and spirit were veiled, entities were aware that each energy transfer and, indeed, very nearly all that proceeds from any intercourse, social or sexual, between two entities has its character and substance in time/space rather than space/time. The energies transferred during the sexual activity are not of space/time. There is a great component of metaphysical energy transferred. Indeed, the body complex as a whole is greatly misunderstood due to the post-veiling assumption that the physical manifestation of the body is subject only to physical stimuli. This is emphatically not so."

After the veil, energy blockages could occur in the energy centers.

Ra: "If both entities are blocked, both will have an increased hunger for the same activity, seeking to unblock the baffled flow of energy. If one entity is blocked and the other vibrates in love, the entity baffled will hunger still but have a tendency to attempt to continue the procedure of satiating the increasing hunger with the one vibrating green ray, due to an impression that this entity might prove helpful in this endeavor. The green-ray-active individual shall polarize slightly in the direction of service to others but have only the energy with which it began."

There is much distortion involved in a discussion of any mythic archetypical form such as Lucifer or the Devil. These mythical archetypes shown with an erection (such as statues and drawings) is a function of orange-ray blockage, and was known in a minimal way by those who devised these statues and drawings.

Ra shall answer each query (or question) whether or not it has been previously covered, for not to do so would be to baffle the flow of quite another transfer of energy.

Green, blue, and indigo transfers of energy lie an entire system of opening the gateway to intelligent infinity.

Ra: "You may see that some information is necessarily shrouded in mystery by our desire to preserve the free will of the adept. The great key to blue, indigo, and, finally, that great capital of the column of sexual energy transfer, violet energy transfers, is the metaphysical bond or distortion which has the name among your peoples of unconditional love. In the blue-ray energy transfer the quality of this love is refined in the fire of honest communication and clarity; this normally speaking in general, takes a substantial portion of your space/time to accomplish, although there are instances of mating's so well refined in previous incarnations and so well remembered that the blue ray may be penetrated at once. This energy transfer is of great benefit to the seeker in that all communication from this seeker is, thereby, refined and the eyes of honesty and clarity look upon a new world. Such is the nature of blue-ray energy, and such is one mechanism of potentiating and crystallizing it.

As we approach indigo-ray transfer, we find ourselves in a shadowland. We cannot give you information straight out or plain, for this is seen by us to be an infringement. We cannot speak at all of violet-ray transfer as we do not, again, desire to break the Law of Confusion.

We may say that these jewels, though dearly bought, are beyond price for the seeker and might suggest that just as each awareness is arrived at through a process of analysis, synthesis, and inspiration, so should the seeker approach its mate and evaluate each experience, seeking the jewel."

The subjective measure of knowing which ray the energy transfer was for an individual after the experience:

Ra: "If the energies have flowed so that love is made whole, green-ray transfer has taken place. If, by the same entities' exchange, greater ease in communication and greater sight has been experienced, the energy has been refined to the blue-ray energy center. If the polarized entities, by this same energy transfer experience, find that the faculties of will and faith have been stimulated, not for a brief while but for a great duration of time, you may perceive the indigo-ray transfer. We may not speak of the violet-ray transfer except to note that it is an opening to the gateway of intelligent infinity. Indeed, the indigo-ray transfer is also this, but the veil has not yet been lifted."

Ra: "The harvest from the previous creation was that which included the male and female mind/body/spirit. It was the intention of the original Logoi that entities mate with one another in any fashion which caused a greater polarization. It was determined, after observation of the process of many Logoi, that polarization increased manyfold if the mating were not indiscriminate (aimless). Consequent Logoi (that followed after another Logoi) thusly preserved a bias towards the mated relationship which is more characteristic of more-disciplined personalities and of what you may call higher densities. The free will of each entity, however, was always paramount, and a bias only could be offered."

Kathryn: "My interpretation is that the intention of the Logos was that entities mate with one another in any fashion which caused greater polarization, especially in not discriminating against anyone and maintaining the free will of each entity. It appears as if homosexuality is okay if it maintains each entity's free will as paramount importance and the entities mate in unconditional love for one another with the intention to cause greater polarization. If the positive path is chosen, for instance, then mate with the intention to increase the positive polarity through maintaining free will and unconditional love of each entity."

SESSION 85: 4-26-1982

Ra: "I am Ra. We communicate now.

Questioner (Don): Could you first give me the condition of the instrument?

RA: "I am Ra. We ask your permission to preface this answer by the inclusion of the greeting which we use.

Questioner: "This is agreeable."

Ra: "I am Ra. We greet you in the love and in the light of the One Infinite Creator. We were having some difficulty with the channel of energy influx due to pain flare, as you call this distortion of the physical-body complex of this instrument. Therefore, it was necessary to speak as firefly as possible until we had safely transferred the mind/body/spirit complex of this instrument. We beg your kind indulgence for our discourtesy, which was appropriate.

The condition of the instrument is as follows. The necessity for extreme vigilance (careful watch) is less, due to the somewhat lessened physical-complex energy deficit. The potential for distortion remains, and continued watchfulness over the ingestion of helpful foodstuffs continues to be recommended. Although the instrument is experiencing more than the normal, for this mind/body/spirit complex, distortions towards pain at this space/time nexus, the basic condition is less distorted. The vital energies are as previously stated.

We commend the vigilance and care of this group."

Ra: "The nature of the crises with the fifth density (negative) companion is the determination of the relative polarity between the group and this determined visitor. The group is in the position of being in the third-density illusion and consequently having the conscious collective magical ability of the neophyte (a person new to the subject or belief), whereas your companion is most adept. (The negative entity is more advanced than the third-density human).

Ra: "However, the faculties of will and faith and the calling to the light have been used by this group to the exclusion of any significant depolarization from the service-to-others path.

If your companion can possibly depolarize this group, it must do so and do that quickly, for in this unsuccessful attempt at exploring the wisdom of separation, it is encountering some depolarization. This shall continue. Therefore, the efforts of your companion are pronounced at this space/time and time/space nexus."

If one wishes to power over an entity (such as the negative path desires), it is an aid to know that entity's name. If one wishes no power over an entity but wishes to collect that entity into the very heart of one's own being, it is well to forget the naming. Both processes are magically viable. Each is polarized in a specific way. It is your choice.

If the instrument wishes to remain free from potential separation of its mind/body/spirit complex from the third density it now experiences, it is well to meditate with the hand pressure from the other self because of the continued greeting (of the negative entity.)

The polarization process, as it enters fourth density, is one which occurs with full knowledge of the veiling process which has taken place in third density. This veiling process is a portion of the third-density experience. The knowledge and memory of the outcome of this and all portions of third-density experience informs higher-density polarized entity. It, however, does not influence the choice which has been made and which is the basis for further work past third density in polarization. Those that chose the service-to-self path have simply used the veiling process to potentiate (increase the power of) that which is not. This is an entirely acceptable method of self-knowledge of and by the Creator.

Choosing the service-to-self path has potentiated (increased the power of) that which is not. That which is not may be seen as a self-imposed darkness in which harmony is turned into an eternal disharmony.

Ra: "If you see the energy centers in their various colors completing the spectrum, you may see that the service-to-self choice is one which denies the very center of the spectrum, that being universal love. Therefore, all that is built upon the penetration of the light of harvestable quality by such entities is based upon an omission (of something left out). This omission shall manifest in fourth density as the love of self; this is, the fullest expression of the orange and yellow energy centers, which then are used to potentiate (increase power of) communication and adepthood.

When fifth-density refinement has been achieved, that which is not is carried further, the wisdom density being explored by entities which have no compassion, no universal love. They experience that which they wish by free choice, being of the earnest opinion that green-ray energy is folly.

That which is not may be seen as a self-imposed darkness in which harmony is turned into an eternal disharmony. However, that which is not cannot endure throughout the octave of third density, and, as darkness eventually calls the light, so does that which is not eventually call that which is."

(Even if darkness of the negative path is chosen, eventually the negative path will have to call the light and merge into the positive path of unity in the 6th density.)

I believe regardless of what that answer may be, it should be of extreme importance to that each entity is educated in *The Law of One* in this third-density experience before the choosing. How the choice is set up now is most people aren't aware of The Law of One and yet, still have to make an important decision. To me, this doesn't seem fair. That's like telling people they can choose a service-to-self path or a service-to-others path without telling them where those roads lead. That would be like someone not informing them that the negative path leads to a dead-end anyways and you'll eventually have to jump over to the positive path anyways in 6th density. Oh, and once you get to that side, you'll be a slave to other higher negative entities, be filled with darkness and separation. Whereas, if they were told the positive side is more harmonic, full of love, light, compassion, unity, not chaotic like the negative path is, that it is easier flowing and doesn't lead to a dead-end; then would that make their choice easier? I know it would be fairer for them to choose after being fully educated on each path. That's why I created this information in the first place.

However, the negative path gives the positive entities catalyst (experiences for growth) and the chance to choose a polarity that helps us all polarize much faster and actually graduate third density, so we can evolve faster through the densities due to the free will we have from the veil of forgetting between our conscious minds and the unconscious mind that knows all things."

There is sometimes a problem with the channeling transmission, especially when the instrument (Carla) is experiencing pain flares from her own personal health issues and not from the negative entity. Firstly, Ra has a clumsiness of language and it is unfamiliar to them in their native experience. Secondly, once they have miscalled or misnumbered an event or thing, that referent is quite likely to be reused for some transmission time due to their original error having gone undetected by themselves. One error was Ra stating service-to-others when they intended to say service-to-self, which I corrected in this writing.

Ra does not have use of all of the words in the English language nor all of the words in all of the languages spoken of Earth at this time.

Ra cannot answer whether an entity shall balance compassion with wisdom or to allow compassion to develop as much as possible without being balanced, their answers are unavailable due to free-will prohibitions upon information from teach/learners such as Ra. (In one of my recent channelings I was told that the ideal positive percentage is 95% service-to-others, leaving that last 5% to not serve into martyrdom.

Ra: "To the student of the balancing process, we may suggest that the most stringent honesty be applied. As compassion is perceived, it is suggested that, in balancing, this perception be analyzed. It may take many, many essays into compassion before true universal love is the product of the attempted opening and crystallization of this all-important springboard energy center. Thus, the student may discover many other components to what may seem to be all-embracing love. Each of these components may be balanced and accepted as part of the self and as transitional material as the entity's seat of learn/teaching moves ever more clearly into the green ray.

When it is perceived, that universal love has been achieved, the next balancing may or may not be wisdom. If the adept is balancing manifestations, it is indeed appropriate to balance universal love and wisdom. If the balancing is of mind or spirit, there are many subtleties to which the adept may give careful consideration. Love and wisdom, like love and light, are not black and white, but faces of the same coin, if you will. Therefore, it is not, in all cases, that balancing consists of a movement from compassion to wisdom.

We may suggest at all times the constant remembrance of the density from which each adept desires to move. This density learns the lessons of love. In the case of Wanderers, there are half-forgotten overlays of other lessons and other densities. We shall leave these considerations with the questioner and invite observations which we shall then be most happy to respond to in what may seem to be a more effectual manner."

Jordyn: "An example of an entity developing compassion as much as possible without balancing wisdom is Jehoshuah (Jesus). Jesus came from the 4th density positive in Sirius planet to planet Earth where he knew he would eventually die. This dying for others is the full extent of compassion without the balance of wisdom. Balancing wisdom with compassion would perhaps be choosing not to put yourself in a situation where you would die, so then you could continue spreading the love and light throughout the Earth for a longer period of time. Jesus' mission was approved by the Confederation, and the positive entities for Jesus as a Wanderer from late 4th density. He was able to penetrate the veil and remember more than most Wanderers, which attributed to his greater abilities, as well as the schooling he received from approximately the age of 12-30, as mentioned in my book "Correcting Distortions of The Bible."

The positive-density Sirius beings brought Jesus back to life, so that the light would win. This is talked about in full in the section about Jesus Life and death in This Law of One series and my book called "Correcting Distortions of The Bible."

After the veiling process, the most effectual veiling was that of the mind.

Ra: "The primary veiling was of such significance that it may be seen to be analogous (comparable) to the mantling of the Earth over all the jewels within the Earth's crust, whereas previously, all facets of the Creator were consciously known. After the veiling, almost no facets of the Creator were known to the mind. Almost all was buried beneath the veil.

If one were to attempt to list those functions of mind most significant, in that they might be of aid in polarization, one would need to begin with the faculty of visioning, envisioning, or far-seeing. Without the veil the mind was not caught in your illusory time. With the veil, space/time is the only obvious possibility for experience.

Also, upon the list of significant veiled functions of the mind would be that of dreaming. The so-called dreaming contains a great deal which, if made available to the conscious mind and used, shall aid it in polarization to a great extent.

The third function of the mind which is significant and which has been veiled is that of the knowing of the body. The knowledge of and control over the body, having been lost to a great extent in the veiling, and in the face of what is now a dense illusion of separation of body complex from mind complex, is quite significant.

Perhaps the most important and significant function that occurred due to the veiling of the mind from itself is not in itself a function of mind but rather is a product of the potential created by this veiling. This is the faculty of will or pure desire."

Ra: "I am Ra. We of Ra communicate through narrow band channel through the violet-ray energy center. We are not, as you would say, physically indwelling in this instrument; rather, the mind/body/spirit complex of this instrument rests with us.

You are diligent (careful) and conscientious (doing work thoroughly well)."

(Diligent means having or showing care and conscientiousness in one's work or duties; hardworking, careful. Conscientious means a person who wishes to do what is right, especially to do one's work or duty well and thoroughly.)

Ra: "The alignments are excellent. We leave you rejoicing in the power and in the peace of the One Infinite Creator. Go forth, then, my friends, rejoicing in the power and in the peace of the infinite love and the ineffable light of the One Creator. I am Ra. Adonai."

SESSIONS 86-106:

If negative entities try to scare people. They gain in polarity and the people lose positive polarity. Therefore, the negative entities are allowed to continue greeting people. If people greet them with love, then the negative entities can lose polarity and perhaps retreat in order not to lose polarity.

An unconscious mind is the deeper mind. A melody relates to the unspoken, the unconscious part of the mind. "far-seeing" is the unspoken, unconscious mind. This deeper mind without words, like a melody.

Dreaming is an activity of communication through the veil of the unconscious mind.

Someone who is blocked at two of the three lower energy centers will have a repetition of recent catalyst and deeper held blockages. For example, when I was younger, I dreamt about BMX racing about $1/4^{th}$ of the time. Mainly about missing a race, having a flat tire before a race or something going wrong before I could even make it into the gate to race. I believe my blockages must have been fear of not making a goal on time. So, my subconscious mind was telling me to not fear, so that I can just go for it and accomplish my goal.

It's important to think about the content and the emotions of the dreams Ra says (emotive resonance).

Green ray activation takes on another activity in dreaming. Precognition or a knowing which is prior shall occur in the physical, knowing what will happen before it occurs. This view point of present, future and past having no meaning. Such as it's all happening at the same time. If made proper use of the dreamer, enable them to enter more fully into the all-compassionate love of every circumstance, even unhappy ones.

For example, I can view an unhappy situation with the all-compassionate love if I view the circumstance as a chance to grow and learn from the situation. Any pain is an opportunity to positively polarize. Therefore, I love the situation to help me learn, grow, evolve, love more and become a better person. I don't have to love the person who hurt me, but I can forgive them for my own healing and positive vibration increase; and let go of any negative lower-vibrational emotions that I may have had about anything at any time in my life.

As someone consciously chooses the path of the adept (a master), with each energy center balanced to a minimal degree, begins to open the indigo-ray energy center. Dreaming then becomes the most efficient tool for polarization, for they know work can be done in consciousness during the sleeping state. They can call upon those that guide it and most of all the higher self as it moves into the sleeping mode of consciousness, the unconscious mind or subconscious.

The activity of dreaming reaches the potential of learning to then teach others which is most helpful to increasing the distortions of the adept towards its chosen polarity.

The higher-self/subconscious mind creates the dream.

Only a trained and disciplined observer can have reasonably good recall of the dreaming. Immediately upon awakening one may be disciplined to record every detail. Immediate writing down of the dream can sharpen one's ability to recall the dream. The most common perception of dreams is muddied, muddled and quickly lost.

Dreams can help heal someone and be visionary such as prophets and mystics. Their visions come through the roots of mind and speak to a hungry world. Telling the dreams is of service. The prophet who desires to serve and serves will increase their polarity. (My vibration increased when I signed a lease at my apartment and helped my girlfriend and my brother out by letting them stay with me. My vibration increased about 10% in one month once I did these things, and I didn't even post a video once during that time. Therefore, the key to my rapid increase in positive polarity stemmed around investing for others, helping others out who needed a place to stay and doing for others instead of only myself. I was able to do all of this, while making sure my own needs were met as well. Now, my positive polarity is at 87% as of July 2024. Thus, my entire family and myself are above the 51% needed to graduate into the 4th density New Earth; so, there will be many people graduating this third density without even knowing about the Law of One, such as my family. My family does not know much about the Law of One and they are between 56% to 72% positively-oriented. They are harvestable for 3rd density graduation even though they don't know about this material. We all grew up Christian. However, I was at 42% positively oriented as a Christian, but after receiving this knowledge, that jumped to 87% as my desires and actions towards serving others was ignited.)

Dreams:

The dreams do not take place in time as we know it, it takes place in time/space (not in our physical world of space/time), it's a bridge from the metaphysical to the physical world.

Episode 87: The veil of forgetting between the conscious and unconscious mind was helpful in the evolutionary process. Thus, mind/body/spirit becoming mind/body/spirit complexes. Loss of knowledge and control over body was a factor in this. The loss of knowledge being in the unconscious mind tapped into through dreams, and loss of control over the involuntary movements of the body to help in survival purposes, so one doesn't shut off pain receptors needed to help in survival. Such as one not shutting off pain signals of a bleed out. Pain of the bleeding is needed to get immediate medical attention. If one can shut this pain out, perhaps they can bleed out and end their incarnation for example. Thus, physical pain is needed for survival purposes and emotional pain can occur to aid in evolution.

There was a negative 5th density entity trying to stop the Ra contact. By prayer it withdrew to restore its negative polarity. Greeting it with love can make the negative entity/demon lose some of its negative polarity.

Upon the negative 5th density path power over others is refined until it approaches absolute power. If it cannot control an entity such as Ra or the channeling group, it depolarizes. A 3rd density being can't stand against the 5th density negative entity, but through the groups harmony, mutual love and the honest calling for aid from the forces of light has shielded the group from the 5th density negative power.

The 4th density negative beings are at will slaves to the 5th density negative. Any entity that demands obedience is of the negative path.

4th density negative offers temptations, 5th density negative is more extreme. In a fourth density negative social memory complex there is a pecking order. An entity with increased power exercises that power to control others in the social memory complex to advance within the social memory complex structure.

Episode 88: The blockage of sexual energy transfer is the lack of ability to see the other self as the Creator, the lack of love. Before the veil, beings always gave a sexual energy transfer due to seeing the other as the Creator and the sexual exchange being of the love nature.

Red ray desire to populate the species is met with the sperm meeting the ovum (a mature female reproductive cell). Therefore, male orgasm occurs more often than female orgasm for this reason. However, female orgasm is clearer when beings use the sexual energy transfer to learn, to serve and to glorify the One Infinite Creator. So, the higher positively evolved beings see the significance of the female orgasm. Those striving towards love and service will see the importance of their partner's orgasm.

Positive polarity is true sharing of orgasm and is almost universal. The negative polarity has a true blockage so the conqueror obtains orgasm. The conquered is almost never universal. Only one person obtaining orgasm is negatively-oriented as one person is serving themselves and not the other being.

Due to the veiling process: The female offering the male an orgasm gives a discharge of physical energy. The female is then refreshed, as the male has far less physical vitality.

Due to the veiling process: The female discharges the efflux of its stored mental and mental/emotional energy during the female orgasm and the male entity receives inspiration, healing and blessing to the male, which by nature he is less vital in this area. Thus, as you give the other entity an orgasm, you will receive the benefits of their energy discharge.

Of course, homosexual sex can occur. The positive polarity of sex being that of mutual orgasm and love; and the negative polarity during sex is one being trying to control and conquer the other being with a lack of love as they orgasm and do not give the other being an orgasm.

Episode 89: After the veil the male became the Matrix of the Mind (Magician card, it is also described as consciousness and is unmoved) and the male is the Potentiator of the body (Wisdom or Sage Card). The Potentiator of the Body is that which, being informed, regulates activity.

Also, after the veil: The female is the Potentiator of the Mind (unconscious/intuition or High Priestess) and the Matrix of the Body (Justice or Balance Card).

Those of Venus in third density partially penetrated the veil and gained information as to the nature of the archetypical mind and the veiling process. Then, designed the tarot to teach others.

One great breakthrough of the tarot after Ra's work in 3rd density was the proper emphasis given to The Choice, tarot card #22. Ra was aware a unifying archetype existed, but didn't give it the proper complex of concepts in order to most efficiently promote their evolution.

People who know astrology or tarot may be seen as psychic.

Ra's third density harvest was about 2.6 billion years ago. So, Ra is billions of years more evolved than humans on Earth. Ra became 4th density when Earth entered 2nd density.

Law of One tarot cards represent at least 95% of what is on the walls of the Great Pyramid. Ra gave the archetypical concepts to the priests in Egypt, who then drew them on the walls of one of the chambers of the Great Pyramid. The info was given through old teachings and visions.

Ra developed the tarot in third density, then evolved to fourth density as Earth was in their 2nd density. Then Ra became a $4^{th}/5^{th}$ density planet. Then, 5th density for a large measure of our Earth time. Both 4th and 5th density experiences were possible upon Venus.

Ra's core vibrational frequency is 6th density. However, Ra as a social memory complex, have elected to leave that influence. Therefore, the beings on Venus are 5th density. The planet is 5th/6th density planet. Just like Earth is 3rd/4th density right now.

Episode 90: Do not be left behind means do not be left behind when about 65% of the Earth population graduate to the 4th density New Earth, which is all-compassionate and united, while the rest of the 35% either is transferred to another 3rd density planet or graduate to the 4th density negative if they are at least 95% negative or service-to-self.

Clothing one's self within the archetype is an advanced practice of the adept (a master) who has studied this archetypical system for a long time. The concept complexes which together are intended to represent the architecture of a significant and rich portion of the mind are intended to be studies as individual concept complexes as Matrix, potentiator, ect. In viewing Mind/body/spirit connections and in pair with some concentration upon the polarity of the male and the female.

If these are studied, there comes a time when the deep threnodies (poems) and joyful ditties (tunes) of the deep mind can successfully be brought forward to intensify, articulate and heighten some aspect of the magic personality/higher self.

An archetype is a complex concept making up multiple components to it to equal the one archetype (multiple parts of the picture within the tarot card). Without one of the components, the archetype cannot be seen or exist. It needs all the components to make up the archetype. For example, The Magician Tarot card has the being holding out he ball and the bird in the cage.

Ra presented the Egyptian priests the descriptions in verbal form of 3 images: one, eight and 15; then asked:

Ra: "What do you feel the bird might represent?"

"What do you feel that the wand might represent?" And so forth, until those studying were working upon a system whereby the images used become evocative (bringing up strong images or feelings) of a system of concepts. This is slow work when done for the first time.

Each student will experience the archetypical mind and its structure in a unique way useful to that student.

Ra's 3rd density to 4th density harvest was overwhelmingly positive. Their appreciation of the negative was uninformed.

The tarot advances the spiritual evolution of the self. A proper understanding of Archetype 22 is greatly helpful in sharpening the basic view of the Significator to Mind, Body, and spirit, and further, throws into starker relief the Transformation and Great Way of Mind, Body, and Spirit complexes.

Ra had no negative harvest at the end of their third density, but two entities harvested themselves during the third density in the negative or service-to-self path. There were those upon Venus' third density whose vibratory patterns were in the negative range but were not harvestable. So, they were not at least 95% negative. For example, Hitler was in the negative range on Earth but wasn't harvestable for the negative or positive 4th density. Thus, after that lifetime he is still 3rd density.

Venus third density had difficult conditions and was a small population. Their harvest was 6,500,000 mind/body/spirit complexes. So, they had the veil as well. 32,000,000 didn't graduate and had to repeat third density elsewhere on another planet that supports third density life.

Ra stated that those who had the gift of polarity felt deep compassion for those who seemed to dwell in darkness. Venus was a harshly bright planet in the physical sense. (Perhaps, when Ra brings this up, it's possible the more evolved a planet is, the brighter it can be. Just like the bright sun is 6th density.)

However, the positive path has the comfort of companions, and Ra spent a great deal of their attention on the possibilities of achieving spiritual or metaphysical adepthood or work in indigo ray through the means of relationships with other selves. Consequently, the compassion for those in darkness was balanced by the appreciation of the light.

The unharvestable, those having to repeat third density are those who wish to sleep, according to Ra. Thus, Ra could only comfort those asleep in third density that was necessary or possible for them.

The two negatively harvested entities on Venus controlled others and used domination over others unto death to evolve to 4th density negative. They were considered ruthless despots (oppressive rulers) which waged the holy war. They were early 5th density positive Wanderers. They had already evolved through 4th density positive but switched polarity during their 3rd density life as a Wanderer on Venus. From the viewpoint of wisdom, considered Venus to have an overabundance of love, those still in darkness, those of a neutral or somewhat negative viewpoint found such harmony sickening. So, the Wanderers felt more wisdom-oriented way of seeking love could be more appealing to those in darkness. (One can't control, dominate and kill others to get those in darkness to go to the positive path.)

(I believe the more efficient way would be information of the Law of One. Letting them realize that service-to-self is of darkness, lack of freedom, a slave to higher negative density entities and by early 6th density one has to switch to the positive path to continue the evolution to the Creator.)

Therefore, on Venus- the first wanderer began its work. Quickly the second found the first, they were male and female. Ra says for this is by far the most efficient system of partnership with work. These entities agreed to serve together, glorifying the One Creator, but not as they intended. They soon gathered those who found it easy to believe that a series of specific knowledge and wisdom would advance on towards the Creator. This led to the Wanderers graduation into 4th negative, which had much power of personality, and some small deepening of the negatively polarized clement (leniency) of those not polarizing positively. There was no negative harvest.

(So, the Wanderers came and made the negative polarity worse upon Venus. There wasn't a negative harvest but those neutral or 50-95%

negative had to repeat third density on another planet. This occurred in the 2nd cycle of 25,000 years. The harvest was less than 20%.)

Wanderers are always drawn to whatever percentage has not yet polarized, and come when there is a call. (This is interesting, I almost wrote a book before reading the *Law of One* books about myself on my own planet, I had my own section of the planet with a hammock, rocks, a river, a house and my own spaceship just floating there in space next to my planet. I then, flew to another planet when I was called to assist and help planets in the Milky Way Galaxy. This must be a vision of my future of me being a Wanderer one day, and a vision of looking into the possibility/probability vortex of the future.

There was a call on Venus during this 2nd cycle of third density from those not positively polarized, but sought to be positively polarized and sought wisdom, feeling the compassion of other selves upon Venus as complacent and pitying towards other selves.

Once the veil was removed and they realized they switched polarities, they were disconcerted (unsettled). They worked within the 4th density negative for some period until the previously learned patterns of the-self had, been recaptured and the polarity was, with great effort, reversed. There was a great deal of 4th density work then to be retraced.

These entities then came in late and joined Ra in 4th density positive for a portion of the cycle that they experienced.

The controlled use of the archetypes is that which is done within the self for the polarization of the self and to the benefit of the self, if negatively polarized, or others, if positively polarized, upon the most subtle of levels.

The archetypical mind is a portion of the deep mind and informs thought processes. When the archetype is translated without regard for magical propriety (conforming) into the manifested daily actions of an individual, the greatest distortions may take place, and great infringement upon the free will of others is possible.

Episode 90: The 5th density negative entity accompanying the group during these channeling sessions with Don, Jim and Carla is gone and working exclusively in its own density now.

The 4th density negative uses temptations within our inner planes. These dark angels have come through quarantine from days of old in time/space and they are ready to move in thought within the inner planes of this planet working from time/space (metaphysical with no time) to space/time (physical reality such as our specific timeline and moment we experience here and now in 3rd density). Just like the positive angelic beings.

5th density negative is density to density and magical in nature. The 4th density, is not capable of building the highway into the energy web. It is capable of using that which has been left intact. They are from the negative Orion 4th density.

The process of physical evolution continues into 4th density. Only wisdom density can refine thoughts in the form of the physical-complex manifestation under the direction of consciousness.

In 5th density, the physical body is under the control of the conscious-mind. Therefore, the 5th density entity may dissolve one manifestation and create another. So, a 5th density entity may look like one being and transform into another form.

Consequently, the choice of 5th-density entity or complex of entities wishing to communicate with people on Earth would be to resemble 3rd density human bodies.

Third density beings from other planets would resemble our 3rd density Earth to about 5%. Therefore, there is an extreme variation of what beings look like from planet to planet. About 13-15% would pass as looking human.

Ra believes that the Logos further intensified the veil of forgetting by offering 3rd density beings speech taking precedence over concept communication or telepathy. Ra also believes the opposable thumb was used on Earth instead of Venus to further intensify the veiling process, so rather than rediscovering the powers of the mind, the third-density entity would be drawn to making, holding and using physical tools. (I believe part of the purpose of me breaking my neck in 2015 BMX racing, was for me to evolve faster into my purpose of teaching the Law of One, reincarnation cycles and heart centeredness. Otherwise, I could have still been doing BMX and not all my research over the past nine years.

Our Logos hoped to see a positive and negative path generated harvest from 3rd to 6th density for evolution. The positive path is more efficient than the negative. This was the design of the Logos. This Logos has a bias towards kindness.

(The Logos hoped to see a positive and negative path generated for evolution from third-sixth density due to prior known experience in the universe where there was no negative polarity without the veil since all knew the connection to the Creator. This known connection to the Creator and complete happiness made it difficult to evolve to 4th density. Since being in complete happiness made it difficult for beings to want to serve others, which is needed in polarization. Therefore, in the outer parts of the Universe a veil of forgetting was created to help in polarization through the densities. This veil gave us our free will. This Logos (universe) designed the positive path to be more effective than the negative path with a bias towards kindness.)

The communication from density to density and from plane to plane or sub-density to sub-density was set up by the Logos to help in evolution.

Ra went to Egypt to teach the Law of One. They wished to impress upon those who wished to learn of unity. That in unity, all paradoxes are resolved, all that which is broken is sealed, all that is forgotten is brought to light.

Episode 91: The adept has worked much within the red, orange, yellow and green centers but also in the opening of blue and indigo. Up through this point the archetypes function as the great base of a built structure or statue, keeping the mind complex viable, level and available as a resource whenever it may be evoked (or brought forth to the conscious mind). There is a point in which the adept takes up its work. This is the point at which a clear and conscious consideration of the archetypical mind is useful.

The cosmic mind is the same for all sub-Logoi like our sun.

A sub-Logos, like our Sun, in creating Its own particular evolutionary experience, refines the cosmic mind or articulates it by Its own biases. The archetypical mind is a refinement of the all-mind in a pattern peculiar (unusual) to the sub-Logo's choosing.

The next refinement that occurs as the cosmic mind is refined is the archetypical mind.

For this Logos, the racial or planetary mind is a repository (stored place) of biases remembered by mind/body/spirit complexes which have enjoyed the experience of this planetary influence.

The entities who transferred from other planets to Earth to recycle in 3rd density here added to the planetary mind. But also, each race on other planets possesses a racial mind (planetary mind). This portion of mind is formed in the series of seemingly non-simultaneous experiences which are chosen in freedom of will by the people of the planetary influence. Therefore, although the Akashic, planetary or racial mind is indeed a root of mind, it may be seen in sharp differentiation from deeper roots of mind which are not a function of altering memory.

Each has three major planetary influences on our planet, besides our 2nd density derivation (source of origin), and 13 minor planetary groups.

Episode 91: The system of 7's in the archetype is the most articulated system yet discovered by any experiment by any Logos in our Octave.

The largest number of archetypes used by the Logos is the 7's plus the choice. So, 22, such as in the Logos we currently live in now. It is the result of many, many previous experiments in articulation of the One Creator.

The fewest are the two systems of five which are completing cycles or densities of experiences.

The archetypes weren't developed at once but step by step, and not in order as we know it in our time but in various orders. Therefore, the two systems of fives were using two separate ways of viewing the archetypical nature of all experience.

Each of course use the matrix, the Potentiator, and the Significator, for this is the harvest with which our creation began.

One system of experimentation had added to these the Catalyst and the Experience. Another system, had added Catalyst and Transformation. In one case, the methods where experience was processed was further aided, but the fruits of experience less aided. In the 2nd case, the opposite was the case.

The Matrix of Mind is not specifically biological male but male principle (male energy).

There are very definite sexual biases in the tarot images intended to function both as information as to the biological entity or energy will attract which archetype, and also as a more general view which sees polarity as key to the archetypical mind of 3rd density.

(Thus, it's not about male and female, but masculine energy and feminine energy. Gender doesn't necessarily matter. It's the polarity of energy not biological sexes.)

The concept of will is pouring from each facet of the image of the Matrix of the Mind (Magician Card). The wand as the will is on astrological derivative of the outreaching hand forming the magical gesture. The excellent portion of the image may be seen as separate from the concept of the wand is that sphere that indicates the spiritual nature of the object of the will of one wishing to do magical acts within the manifestation of your density.

Without potentiation, the conscious mind has no inwardness, so the hand doesn't reach within. It reaches without because without potentiated (of increasing the likelihood of) influence its locked within.

The square is the symbol of the third density illusion. It's seen as unmagical or as having been manifested within the material world.

The checkered part represents polarity.

All birds are intended to suggest that just as the Magician (Matrix figure) cannot act without reaching its winged spirit, neither can the spirit fly, unless it's released into conscious manifestation and fructified.

The Star is seen in astrological terms which Ra didn't include astrological portions of these images in the system of images designed to evoke the archetypical leitmotifs (recurring themes).

When viewing the Egyptian costumes and systems of mythology used in the images, it is far better to penetrate to the heart of the costumes significance or the creatures' significance rather than clinging to a culture which is not your own.

In each entity the image will resonate slightly differently. Therefore, Ra desires the creative envisioning the archetype to use general guidelines rather than specific and limiting definitions.

The cup represents the waiting polarity to be tasted by the Matrix of the Mind.

Ra told Don the questioner that he could "Release the sword from its stricture. Observe the struggle of a caged bird to fly."

The original image had the checkering as the suggestion of polarity. This is a representation of the waiting polarity to be tasted by the Matrix of the Mind.

The coin in the tarot represents striving to achieve through the manifested world and the work accomplished.

The Magician is the concept of the unfed conscious mind, the mind without any resource but consciousness.

Ra says to "Not confuse the unfed conscious mind with that mass of complexities which you as students experience, as you have so many, many times dipped already into the processes of potentiation, catalyst, experience and transformation. These are all us (the student learning this wisdom) Thusly, the complement is complete for you."

Ra offers these images as guidelines, not boundaries, intending to aid the adept and to establish the architecture of the deep, or archetypical, portion of the deep mind.

The knowledge of the facets of the archetypical mind used by an individual is to accelerate evolution.

An example of the Matrix of the Mind: The conscious mind of the adept may be bursting with unimaginable ideas, so that further ideation becomes impossible, and work in blue ray or indigo is blocked through over-activation. This is when the adept would call upon the new mind, untouched and virgin, and dwell within the archetype of the new and unblemished mind without bias, without polarity, full of the magic of the Logos (universe).

The conscious mind may be filled with an almost infinite number of concepts, but there is a set of basic concepts which are important because they are the tools for the evolution of consciousness, and will, if carefully applied, accelerate the evolution of consciousness, whereas the vast array of concepts, ideas, and experiences that we meet in our daily lives may have little or no bearing upon the evolution of consciousness except in a very indirect way. The archetypes are the tools for spiritual evolution.

An individual who wished to consciously augment his own evolution can recognize and utilize the archetypes. It's beneficial sorting out what he wishes to seek from that which would be not as undistorted a seeking tool.

The archetypical mind, when penetrated lucidly, is a blueprint of the builded structure of all energy expenditures and all seeking without distortion. This, as a resource within the deep mind, is of great potential aid to the adept.

The fidelity and harmony of the group was great protection against negative entities. Thanksgiving and prayer also protected the channeling group of Don, Carla and Jim. One 3rd density being isn't as powerful as a 4th or 5th density negative being, but the love and harmony of the three in the group of third density beings together can protect against negative psychic greetings.

The instrument/channeler (Carla) was at times distorted towards pain from her own personal medical issues. She pushed through the pain and psychic attacks for the extreme service-to-others even towards the distortion of martyrdom. Just like Jesus did. She was willing to give her life for this service to humanity, but Ra informed her that wisdom does not advise to serve to the point of martyrdom (dying for it).

The negative 5th density being came back to the channeling group after the recovery of much positive polarity upon its being, and at the same approximate nexus a temporary lessening of the positive harmony of the group. (As the group showed the being love and light, that action made the negative being depart due it losing some of its negative polarity from the love it was shown).

Ra doesn't wish to add to an already distorted group of images, feeling that although distortion is inevitable, the least distorted is in the present arrangement of these tarot cards.

The Egyptian Tarot is the most undistorted version of images which Ra offered.

- Other Tarot system of cards may, in their own way, form a helpful architecture for the adept's consideration of the archetypical mind.

The Matrix of the Mind (Magician Card) is new as a baby and undistorted and veiled from the Potentiator of the Mind (High Priestess Card) and ready for what it is to experience in the incarnation.

The Logos or intelligent energy creates the potentials for an entity to gain the experience necessary for polarization until they become consciously aware of the evolutionary process.

As the mind/body/spirit complex which has not yet reached the point of conscious awareness of the process of evolution prepares for incarnation, it has programmed a less than complete-partially randomized-systems of learnings. The amount of randomness of potential catalyst is proportional to the newness of the mind/body/spirit complex to third density.

The potential for incarnational experience is located with the deep mind, the architecture represented by the Potentiator (The Potentiator of the Mind is the Intuition/ The High Priestess card).

Ra says: "The potential for incarnational experience resides in the mind/body/spirit complex's insertion. It resides in the energy web of the physical vehicle and the chosen planetary environment.

However, the more deeply articulate this portion of the mind/body/spirit complex's beingness, this archetype, the potentiator of the Mind, may be evoked with profit to the student of its own evolution.

- The Potentiator of Mind (the unconscious mind) may aid the adept in grasping the nature of this pre-incarnative and continuingly incarnative series of choices.

Jordyn: "My interpretation is that the potential for our life's experiences is each individual's life decisions. A mind/body/spirit is a single entity that doesn't have the veil of forgetting between the conscious and the unconscious mind. Adding the word complex to the end of that would indicate the being having a veil of forgetting between the conscious and unconscious mind, which gives it the title mind/body/spirit complex. A Mind/body are beings of 1st and 2nd density, the soul enters in 3rd density making it a mind/body/spirit rather than a mind/body.

Thus, the potential for incarnational experience resides in the mind/body/spirit complex's energy web of the physical body and the chosen planet's environment. The subconscious mind may be used to help the student's (the being's) own evolution. The subconscious mind may help the more experienced student in understanding the nature of this pre-incarnative and continuingly incarnative series of choices. Therefore, our subconscious mind helps us navigate our pre-birth choices and our choices throughout our lives."

The Matrix of the Mind moves. Just as the kinetic phase of intelligent infinity moves for the Universe (Logos). Just like the planet (sub-sub-Logos) moves for the entity, also known as the mind/body/spirit complex or mind, body, spirit complex depending on if the entity has the veil of forgetting or not.

The sub-sub-Logos is the free-will potentiated beingness of the mind/body/spirit complex. So, through free will, the planet moves for the beings on the planet.

The Matrix of the Mind reaches to intelligent Infinity, Love and all that follows from that Logos to the Matrix (or conscious self of each entity, the Love or the planets spinning through free will. All of the things that may enrich the experience of the Creator by the Creator.

Therefore, I understand movement of intelligent infinity moves as a catalyst for the evolution of the Universe, just as the planet moves to help the entities evolve, at their own free will to do so. (A catalyst is a situation or event that occurs to help one transform or evolve).

This movement for evolution is so that the biases of potential catalyst of the entity is to be unique and form a coherent pattern that resembles the full movement dance, forming a many-figured tapestry of motion.

This Universe is an archetypical mind with 22 archetypes. One of the archetypes being the Matrix of the Mind that reaches to intelligent infinity, Love and all that follows from that Logos. It also reaches to the conscious self of each entity and the spinning planets to enrich the experience of the Creator (each being or planet) by the Creator. This movement is for the evolution of all, resembling a full movement dance, forming a many-figured tapestry of motion. Each archetypical mind is unique, forming different number of archetypes, 22 being the most, and our preceding Octave or Universe forming 9. Therefore, the Universe before ours had 9 archetypes.

When the Catalyst of the mind is processed by the entity, it yields experience, but through free will and imperfect memory, catalyst is most often partially used and the experience correspondingly skewed.

The Matrix, Potentiator, Catalyst and Experience of the Mind forms the nature of the mind (Significator of the Mind). Significator of the Mind is both actor and acted upon.

The Channeler/instrument (Carla Rueckert) programmed this channeling Experience before the incarnation. The conscious mind (individualized being) lives the incarnation not the archetypical mind of our galaxy.

The archetypical mind does not equal the acting incarnational mind/body/spirit complex's progression or evolution.

The Great Way of the Mind (The Chariot Card) is the portion of the archetypical mind which denotes and configures the particular framework within which the Mind, the Body or the Spirit archetypes moves.

The Potentiator of Mind (The High Priestess Card) and of body (Wisdom or Sage Card) are both involved in the questing of the infant for new experience.

The mind/body/spirit complex of the infant has one highly developed portion which may be studied by viewing Significator of Mind (The Hierophant Card) and Body (The Hanged Man or Martyr Card). The spirit portion is not reliably developed in every being. The Significator of the Spirit is the Sun Card.

Thusly, the infant's Significant-self offers biases to meet new experience. The significant self is the harvest of biases of all previous incarnational experiences.

The Matrix of the Mind for the infant is unfed by experience and has the bias of reaching for this experience through free will, just as intelligent energy creates the Logos of the Milky Way Galaxy. These sub-sub-Logoi, planets, can make alterations in their experiential continuation. The results of these experiments are then recorded in the Matrices of mind and body.

The functions of Mind is paramount over the body, the body being the creature of the mind, but not all actions of the being is due to the potentiating qualities of the mind alone, as the body and in some cases the spirit also potentiates action.

As an entity becomes aware of the process of spiritual evolution, more and more of the activities of the mind and body which precipitate activity are caused by those portions of the mind/body/spirit complex which are articulated by the archetypes of Transformation.

More and more activities of the mind and body are caused by portions of the mind, body, and spirit Transformation.

The One original thought is known as the Creator creating its own versions to experience the self.

Episode 92: The negative entities on earth want humanity to experience fear, lack and unworthiness. This can allow them to control the masses by providing a solution for trying to make the people look outward for satisfaction. They then create outward distractions for people.

One original thought is an entity wanting to create some things into the planet. Then, focuses entirely on this one creation by using its imagination or words or any type of thought forms for a certain period and later its able to create the exact thought forms in 3rd density manifested form reality.

The one original thought was created by the Universal divine grid programmer to experience different variations of the self in different incarnations. In a similar manner people on Earth can use the One original thought to think of a certain image or word in the mind and completely focus on one thought into manifestation into the physical Earth planet.

The Confederation of Planets in the Service of the One Infinite Creator has only one important statement. The statement is that all things, all life, all of the creation is part of one original thought.

(Therefore, you were a part of the Universes, or as some religious people like to call it, God's one original thought and the Universe wanted to experience different variations of the self so Infinity Intelligence incarnated into life such as the one you and I are living in to manifest that original thought here unto the physical Earth.)

The Matrix of the Mind is attracted to the biological male, and the Potentiator of the Mind to the female. Thusly, in energy transfer the female is able to potentiate what may be within the conscious mind of the male so that it may be enspirited. In a more general sense, that which reaches may be seen as a male principle. That which awaits the reaching may be seen as a female principle.

In Card #2, the Potentiator of the Mind (The High Priestess), we see a female seated on a rectangular block. She is veiled and sitting between two pillars, which seem to be identically covered with drawings, but one is much darker than the other. The veil represents the veil between the conscious and subconscious minds or Matrix and Potentiator of the Mind.

The Priestess sits within a structure in which polarity is an integral and necessary part (symbolized by light and dark pillars). The unfed mind has no polarity just as intelligent infinity has none. The nature of the sub-sub-sub-Logos (individual being) of the third-density experience is one of polarity, not by choice but by careful design. The polarity of Potentiator is there not for the Matrix to choose. It is there for the Matrix to accept as given. In other words, this particular illusion has polarity as its foundation, which might be represented by the structural significance of these columns.

The drawings on each of the columns are identical, but that the left-hand column, the one on the Priestess's left- has been shaded much darker, indicating that the events and the experiences may be identical in the incarnation but may be approached, viewed, and utilized with either polarity.

Also, from the symbol denoting spirit in manifestation upon each pillar, that the One Infinite Creator is no respecter of polarity but offers Itself in full to all.

There seems to be a book on the Priestess's lap which is half hidden by a robe or material that covers her right shoulder. It would seem that this indicates that knowledge is available if the veil is lifted but is not only hidden by the veil but is hidden partially by her garment, which she somehow may remove to become aware of the knowledge which she has available.

The very nature of the feminine principle of mind was related specifically to what may be termed sanctified sexuality, is, itself, without addition, the book which neither the feminine nor the male principle may use until the male principle has reached and penetrated, in a symbolically sexual fashion, the inner secrets of this feminine principle.

All robes, in this case indicating the outer garments of custom, shield these principles. Thusly, there is a great dynamic tension, between the Matrix and the Potentiator of the Mind.

The Priestess sits atop the rectangular block, indicating the Potentiator of the Mind is immanent, near at hand, within all manifestation. The opportunities for the reaching to the Potentiator are numerous. However, of itself the Potentiator does not enter into manifestation.

The half-moon on the crown isn't from Ra, but represents the feminine. The sun represents the masculine. Ra accepts this portion as a portion of the image, for it seems without significant distortion.

The symbol on the front of the Priestess's shirt is the crux anasta. This addition and slight distortion of the symbol is astrological and should be released from its stricture (This means Ra recommends this part in the tarot card to be removed and wasn't originally from Ra.)

This crux anasta would indicate the sign of life as the spirit enlivening matter. Moreover, it illuminates a concept which is a portion of the archetype which has to do with the continuation of the consciousness which is being potentiated, in incarnation, beyond incarnation.

The grapes on the cloth over her shoulder indicating fertility of the subconscious mind. There is great protection given by the very character of potentiation. To bear fruit is a protected activity.

The protection is on the right-hand side but not the left. There is protection for the positive path but not for the negative. For the positive path is the more efficient polarity.

Episode 93:

There's a difference between the archetypical mind and the process of incarnational experience of mind/body/spirit complex. Each potentiation that has been reached for by the Matrix is recorded by the Matrix but experienced by the Significator. The experience of the Significator of this potentiated activity is of course dependent upon the acuity of its processes of Catalyst and Experience.

The foundation of our present illusion is the concept of polarity. The two polarities being service to others and service to self.

*Imagine the physical polarity of the magnet, the positive and the negative. In this context it is quite impossible to judge the polarity of an act of an entity, just as it is impossible to judge the relative goodness of the negative and positive poles of a magnet. (Therefore, Intelligent Infinity wouldn't judge which polarity you choose.)

Another method of viewing polarities might involve the concept of radiation/absorption. That which is positive is radiant; the negative is absorbent.

The description of polarity as service to self and service to others, from the beginning of our creation, dwelt within the architecture of the primal Logos. Before the veiling process, the impact of actions taken by mind/body/spirits upon their consciousness was not palpable to a significant enough degree to allow the expression of this polarity to be significantly useful.

Over the period of what you call time, this expression of polarity did indeed work to alter the biases of mind/body/spirits so that they might eventually be harvested. The veiling process made the polarity for more effective faster evolution.

With the third Tarot card (which was the first addition of archetypes after the veiling process), the third archetype, creates the possible polarization, since that seems to be one of the primary objectives of this particular Logos in the evolutionary process.

The Catalyst of the Mind (is the Empress Tarot Card). The abiding sun, from the spirit, shines in protection over all catalyst available from the beginning of complexity to the discerning mind/body/spirit complex.

You may find the polarity expressed by the many opportunities offered in the material illusion which is imagined by the not-white and not-dark square upon which the entity of the image is seated, secondly- upon the position of that seated entity.

*It does not meet opportunity straight on but glances off to one side or another. In the image you will note a suggestion that the offering of the illusion will often seem to suggest the opportunities lying upon the left-hand path (service-to-self). This is a portion of the nature of the Catalyst of the Mind.

<u>The feet of the Empress</u> are on an unstable platform that is dark to the rear and light to the front. The entity standing on this could either sway either direction, to the left or to the right-hand path.

The <u>bird</u> could be perceived as a messenger of the two paths depicted by the position of the wings, bringing catalyst which could be used to polarize on either path.

The more correct perception of the bird is the realization that the mind/body/spirit complex, having made contact with its potentiated self, now beginning its flight towards that great Logos which I sought by the adept.

Jorden: "I assume this to mean its flight in polarization towards that great Logos. The source, the One Infinite Creator. Through all 7 densities graduating 7th in the 8th of a New Creation and a new Octave or Universe."

Further, the nature of the winged creature is echoed both by the female holding it and the symbol of the female upon which the figure's feet rest. So, the nature of catalyst is overwhelmingly of an unconsciousness, not from the mind and has no connection with the intellect, which precedes or is connected with catalytic action. All uses of catalyst by the mind are consciously applied to catalyst. Without conscious intent, the use of catalyst is never processed through meditation, ideation, and imagination.

Examples of Catalyst: Ra speaking to the support group through the instrument, offers catalyst. The configurations of each in the group of body offer catalyst through comfort/discomfort. All that is unprocessed that has come before the notice of a mind/body/spirit complex is catalyst. The support group receives catalyst of the mind as it is aware of Ra's communication, and the support group receives catalyst of the body as their body senses all the inputs to them.

Catalyst being processed by the body is catalyst for the body. It being processed by the mind is catalyst for the mind and it being processed by the spirit is catalyst for the spirit. An individual mind/body/spirit complex may use any catalyst which comes before its notice, be it through the body and its senses or through meditation or through any other more highly developed source, in its unique way to form an experience unique to it, with its biases.

*<u>The archetype for the Catalyst of the Mind</u> is the Logos's model for its most efficient plan for the activity of use of the catalyst of the mind.

*In the <u>archetypical mind,</u> one has a resource for the blueprint or architecture of the nature of evolution. This is significant in perceiving the use of this resource of the deep mind.

<u>Ra presented the images of the Tarot</u>, so that the Egyptian adepts of the time could accelerate their personal evolution. To the student, the Tarot images offer a resource for learn/teaching the processes of evolution. To any other entity, these images are pictures and nothing more.

Due to the influence of the Chaldees, the system of <u>archetypical images was incorporated</u> by the priests of that period into a system of astrologically based study, learning, and divination. Ra didn't develop the Tarot for that purpose.

The third card in the Tarot- The <u>Empress</u>- also shows the wand. The wand is astrological in its origin and Ra asks for it to be released from the image of concept complexes (which are the multiple images on the card.) The sphere of spiritual power is an indication that each opportunity is pregnant with the most-extravagant magical possibilities for the far-seeing adept.

The transparency of the garments indicates the nature of catalyst through the veil. By the time the mind begins its appreciation of catalyst, that catalyst has been filtered through the veil, and in some cases, much is veiled in the most apparently clear perception.

Episode 94: The serpents that adorn the head of the Empress are cultural in nature. In the culture to which these images were given, the serpent was a symbol of wisdom. The general user most accurate connotation of the serpent might be the realization that the serpent is powerful magically. In the positive sense this means that the serpent will appear at the indigo-ray site upon the body of the image. When a negative connotation is intended, one may find the serpent at the solar plexus center (yellow ray).

There is significance to the serpents form in a culture which coexists with your own, but isn't your own. The serpent is a symbol of the kundalini.

Ra states that it is expected that each student shall naturally have a unique experience of perception dealing with each image.

The Crux Ansata has mathematical ratios within the image which may yield informative insights to one fond of riddles. The crux ansata is part of the concept complexes of the archetypical mind: 1.) The circle indicating the magic of the spirit. 2.) The cross indicating the nature of manifestation which may only be valued by the losing.

Thus, the Crux Ansata is intended to be seen as an image of the eternal in and through manifestation and beyond manifestation through the sacrifice and the transformation of the manifested.

Episode 94: Much is veiled to what is seen, unseen and involuntary.

Ra: "However, because of the unique biases of each mind/body/spirit complex, there are sometimes quite simple instances of distortion when there is no apparent cause for such distortion. Let us use the example of the virile (strong sex drive) and immature male who meets and speaks clearly with a young female whose physical form has the appropriate configuration to cause the activation of the red-ray sexual arousal.

The words spoken may be upon a simple subject such as naming, information as to the occupation and various other common interchanges of sound vibratory complex. The male entity, however, is using almost all the available consciousness it possesses in registering the desirability of the female. Such may also be true of the female.

Thusly, an entire exchange of information may be meaningless because the actual catalyst is of the body. This is unconsciously controlled and is not a conscious decision. This example is simplistic.

Each entity has deeper biases that pilot (start) the catalyst around many positively and negativity as expressed in the archipelago (cluster) of the deeper mind. There's further polarization available to the conscious mind after it has perceived the partially polarized catalyst of the deeper mind.

As an entity increases in experience, it shall, more and more, choose positive interpretations of catalyst if it is on the positive path and negative interpretations if it is on the negative path.

The mechanism designed by the Logos of the catalytic action resulting in experience was planned to be self-accelerating, in that it would create this process of variable permeability (the ability to pass through.)

There's the attraction of various archetypes to male and to the female.

Episode 94: The 4th archetype (the 4th Card in the Tarot deck) is the Experience of the Mind (The Emperor). A male whose body faces forward indicates that the Experience of the Mind, with firm authority, grasps what it is given, for catalyst.

The experience is seated upon the square of the material illusion, which is colored much darker than in Card #3 (The Empress Card) - Catalyst of the Mind. There's a cultural meaning of the great cat that guards.

*With what Oriflamme (a symbol inspiring devotion or courage) does it lighten that darkness of manifestation. The polarities are present. There isn't separation except through the sifting (dividing out) which is the result of cumulative experience.

Other impressions were intended by the milk-white leg and its pointed foot, which the student can interpret themselves through their intuition.

In Card #3, Experience of the Mind, the feet of the female entity are upon the unstable platform, signifying the dual polarity by its color. In Card #4 (The Emperor- Experience of the Mind), one foot is pointed so that if the male entity stands on the toe it would be carefully balanced. The other foot is pointed to the left. If the entity stands on the foot, it will be very, very carefully balanced. The T square at times is riven (split apart) as if one foot from secure fundament by the nature of experience yet still by this same nature of experience, is carefully, precisely, and architecturally placed in the foundation of this concept complex and in the archetypical mind complex.

Card #4, The Experience of the Mind (The Emperor) has the nature of more effectively and poignantly expressing (effecting emotions of) the architecture of experience, both the fragility of structure and the surety of structure.

The male entity looks to the left with the right foot pointed to the left, Don the questioner stated that this card would indicate you must be in a defensive position with respect to the left-hand path (since there is no protection), but there is no need to concern yourself about protection with the right-hand path.

Ra says that's not the suggestion they wished to offer by the image, but that the perception cannot be said to be incorrect.

Jordyn: "I believe the male looking to the left with the right foot pointed to the left would indicate polarity and balance of experiences for the catalyst to evolve, I believe Ra says the questioner's perception cannot be said to be incorrect since it is true that the positive path has protection and one might be defensive on the left negative path, since there is no protection there."

The magical shape is on the right edge of Card #4 (The Emperor Card- Experience of the Mind). Which indicates spiritual experience is on the right-hand path. The Emperor is expressing the nature of experience by having its attention caught by what may be termed the left-hand catalyst. Meanwhile, the power, the magic, is available upon the right-hand path.

The nature of experience is such that the attention shall be constantly given varieties of experience. Those that are presumed to be negative, or interpreted as negative, may seem in abundance. It is a great challenge to take catalyst and devise the magical, positive experience. That which is magical in the negative is much longer coming in the 3rd density.

Situations are presented for each entity as catalyst to create polarity, growth and evolution. Catalyst is given for action to take place that creates a bias towards either the negative or positive polarity.

Prior to the veiling there wasn't as much catalyst because it wasn't efficiently creating polarity. When catalyst passes through the veil, it becomes polarized experience. Before the veil between the conscious mind and the subconscious mind, catalyst wasn't as much in effect because the entity saw the experience as the One Creator and not an experience of other mind/body/spirit complexes.

Jordyn: "We are presented with an equal amount of service-to-self and service-to-others catalytic situations so we can choose which path we want to take. Thus, creating the separation of polarity towards a chosen bias."

Card #4 (The Experience of the Mind): The result of catalytic action should take place. Therefore, a greater definition between the dark and light areas are in this card.

(The dark and light areas in Card #4 is the result of catalytic action taking place. Which is the separation of a biased chosen polarity based of given experiences. Due to an equal amount of positive and negative experiences, one can choose either the negative or positive path.)

Don: "The bird on the Empress's right hand in card #3 now appears to be an image on the emperor's shirt in card #4. The flight of catalyst has achieved its objective and has become a central part of the experience."

The crossed legs of the Emperor in card #4 has a meaning similar to the Crux Ansata. The cross formed by the Emperor's legs signifies manifestation within our illusion. All experience is purchased by effort of some kind. There's no act of service to self or others that doesn't bear a price, to the entity manifesting, commensurate with its purity. All things in manifestation may be seen in one way or another to be offering themselves in order that transformations may take place upon the level appropriate to the action.

Card #4: The circle on the front of the Emperor's shirt in card #4 has a specialized form and meaningful shape. It is specialized due to the nature of the crossed legs of manifestation. Taking catalytic action that creates the manifestation.

Jordyn: "The skirt is extended toward the left hand but is somewhat shorter to the right. I would assume this to mean, as a student, that the left negative density path is longer and more difficult path back to the creator.

Acquiring material possessions of wealth can be a part of the left-hand path. (I, Jordyn/the Oneness Prophet, intend to give 10% or more of any money obtained to furthering the Law of One so that the entire world can know of this information. For the Law of One states that when every entity is ready to serve others, the graduation will then take place. Therefore, I can use acquiring wealth to be used to serve humanity. After the world hears of the Law of One, I can then use any excess of wealth to further help those in need. Even though those struggling are either of a lower vibration and need to evolve higher for better experiences or choose that life for faster catalyst to evolve faster in my theory. Those that chose the negative path lack spiritual protection and may seek survival places."

Card #4, being male, would indicate that as experience is gained, the mind becomes the motivator that reaches or does more than the simple experiencer it was prior to the gaining of the catalytic action. There is greater tendency for the mind to direct the mind/body/spirit complex.

Episode 95: The 5th density negative entity is depolarized in session 95 of 106, even though the entity chose various means for service-to-self path with none valuing harmonious interaction of the positive path.

Note: Channelers today don't appear to get these psychic greetings, so I'd assume that means it's much easier to channel today that it was before the Great Awakening in the early 1980's when Ra was first channeled. The group being Wanderers could have also attracted the negative beings to this group.

Jordyn: "This information was so valuable, that negative entities/demonic entities tried to cause pain upon Carla the channeler and interfere with this information getting out, even if it meant killing Carla, the channeler."

The channeler, the questioner (Don) and the scribe (Jim) all were planning on moving these channelings to another residence. Ra stated that it would be appropriate to remove from this room and, to lesser extent, from the dwelling, the charging of what you might call the distortion sanctity. To remove the charge, it is valuable either to write on paper your own working or to use existing rituals for the reconsecration of a sacred place such as one of your churches.

The questioner stated that the new room they chose for the channeling will be carefully cleaned, and marred surfaces made well. They will also use the Banishing Ritual of the Lesser Pentagram prior to a working.

*Lesser thought-forms can be attracted to a person or group if less-than-harmonious interactions occur. Therefore, since that happened with the group Ra suggested the salting and ritual cleaning by blessed water of all windows and doorways which offer admit into the domicile (entity's residing place) or any other buildings there.

Further, Ra suggests the hanging of the cut garlic clove in the portion of the room that has accommodated those whose enjoyment has turned into darker emotions to the center of the wet bar area. (I assume that's where the negative entities were). Ra suggests cut garlic cloves in the bedroom near the channeling groups kitchen.

The appropriate words used to bid farewell to those of the lower astral (negative entities) shall be used in connection with the hanging of the garlic cloves for approximately 36 hours. Ra believes that's equivalent to two nights and one day of lit periods. This should cleanse the house to the extent that it is neutral in its vibrations of harmony, love and thanksgiving which this group should offer to the domicile (the place where they live).

Ra: "I am Ra. Firstly, you may bless the water yourselves or may request so-called holy water from any blessed place; that is, blessed by intention. Secondly, the water shall be carefully shaken from the fingers along the sills of all windows and doors as they have been opened. Thirdly, prior to the sprinkling of this cleansing, blessed sacrament of water, the salt shall be trailed along these sills in a line and again allowed to exit in this configuration for 36-48 hours. Then the virgin broom may ritually sweep the salt out of each window and doorway, sweeping with each stroke the less fortunate of the vibrations within the dwelling which might find co-existence with the group difficult."

The group was instructed to put the salt only on the outer doorway sills and not the inner doorway sills in the house. Salt absorbs vibrations which has been requested to move into salt when salt has been given water. Ra can't express the full magical nature of our water, nor can they express the likeness and attractiveness of the garlic cut to lower astral forms. The attractiveness is negative, and no service-to-self astral form will accept coexistence with the cut garlic. Ra also requests, carefully, that the broom be clean and that the garlic be burned. The virginity (brand new) broom is most efficacious (important).

When the salt is laid, they may repeat, "We praise the One Creator which gave to salt the ability to enable those friends, to which we wish to bid farewell, to find a new home."

As the water is sprinkled, you may say, "We give thanks to the One Creator for the gift of water. Over it the Creator moves Its hand and stirs Its will to be done."

The hanging of the cut garlic may be accompanied by the words "We praise the One Creator for the gift of garlic and bless its ability to offer to those friends to whom we wish to bid farewell the arrow which points their way of egress." (exit).

When the sweeping is done, you may say, "We praise the One Creator and give thanksgiving for the spiritual cleanliness of this dwelling place."

As the garlic is burned, you may say, "We give thanks to the One Creator for the gift of spiritual cleanliness is our dwelling place and seal the departure of all those who have left by this exit by the consuming of this substance."

The windows and doorways are most appropriate to hang the garlic and Ra suggests the salting and sprinkling of any door which may lead elsewhere than out of the dwelling, in order for the entities to understand that they are not desired elsewhere within the dwelling. Salting in a straight line with no gaps every window sill and outer door sills then sprinkle with blessed water from fingertips on the salted areas. The garlic is to be used at the bar area and the bedroom that is close to the kitchen and has an exit onto the carport. So, the bar area and that specific bedroom are the only areas to hang the garlic.

The channeling group wanted to pick the most appropriate room for sanctifying for the Ra contact. Ra informed them that when they have finished their work, the dwelling shall be a virgin dwelling in a magical sense. They then could choose that portion of the dwelling that seems most appropriate, then commence with the same sort of preparation of the place that has been familiar in their last dwelling place. The questioner assumed the best contact with Ra was the exterior of the house.

Ra: "I am Ra. The dwelling (the groups house) seems surrounded with trees and fields of your countryside. This is acceptable. We suggest the general principle of preparing each part of your environment as it best suits each in the group with the beauty which each may feel to be appropriate. There is much of blessing in the gardening and the care of surroundings, for when this is accomplished in love of the creation, the

2nd density flowers, plants and small animals are aware of this service and return it."

There has been no undesirable negative energy stored on the end of the house where the four stalls occupied by horses, so the group doesn't have to modify it. It is acceptable if physically cleaned.

One action that they may take in order to improve the efficacy (efficiency) of the cleansing of the environment is the walking of the perimeter with the opened clove in hand, swinging the clove. No words need to be said unless each wish to silently or verbally speak those words given for garlic previously.

In general, the cleanliness is most helpful. The removal from the mind complex of those thoughts not of harmony is most helpful, and those practices which increase faith and will that the spirit may do its work are most helpful.

All places in which their group dwells in love and thanksgiving is acceptable to Ra.

Episode 96:

In processing the catalyst of <u>dreams</u> there is a partial universal vocabulary used to interpret dreams due to the common heritage of all people. Due to each entity's unique incarnational experiences, there is an overlay which grows to be a larger and larger proportion of the dream vocabulary as the entity gains experience. (Therefore, I also assume there's a partial unique individual interpretational due to specific feelings, impressions and images within the dream that the individual has to interpret based on the feeling within the dream matched with the images or movie-like dream. This is based on my experience of having prophetic dreams and correctly interpreting them myself.)

Episode 97:

An individual is immature if they experience random red-ray sexual arousal being activated by a simple conversation of another individualized portion of consciousness or the creator (individual person). Then further communication would far more likely have been to the subject of the satisfying of that red-ray sexual impulse. When this had occurred, other information such as the naming could be offered with clear perception.

(I assume this to mean a more mature person could have a conversation with someone they're attracted to without being sexually aroused.)

It is to be noted that the catalyst which may be processed by the pre-veil experience is insignificant compared to the catalyst offered to the thoroughly bemused (or confused) male and female after the veil. The confusion which this situation, simplistic it is, offers is representative of the efficiency of enlargement of the catalystic processes occurring after the veiling for greater and faster polarity.

For the condition of meeting after the veiling process, either entity will choose, as a function of its previous biases or Card #4 (The Experience of the Mind) and the way in which it will handle the situation with respect to polarity, therefore probably producing more catalyst for itself along the chosen path of polarization. The negative path being selfish sexual gratification, no love and only obtaining orgasm and partner not having orgasm. As well as domination, control or rape. The positive path for sex is done in love, both obtaining orgasm and seeing the other as the Creator.

Episode 98:

Card #4 (The Emperor- Experience of the Mind): The shape of the skirt represents the archetype of the Experience of the Mind is extended to the left to indicate that other selves would not be able to get close to this entity if it had chosen the left-hand path. There would be greater separation between it and other selves, whereas if it had chosen the right-hand path, there would be much less separation.

It appears that the perimeter of the square that the Emperor sits on is black, is representing the material illusion, and the white cat on the right side of the square guards the right-hand path, once it has chosen this path, from effects of the material illusion that are of the negative polarity. The great cat guards' indirect proportion to the purity of the manifestations of intention and the purity of inner work done along this path.

If the Experience of the mind has sufficiently chosen the right-hand path, and as total purity is approached in the choosing of the right-hand path, then total imperviousness (not penetrable) from the effect of the left-hand catalyst is also approached. The seeker which has purely chosen the service-to-others path shall certainly not have a variant apparent incarnational experience. There is no shelter form the gusts, flurries and blizzards of quick and cruel catalyst.

However, to the pure, all that is encountered speaks of the love and light of the One Infinite Creator. The cruelest blow is seen with ambiance of challenges offered and opportunities to come. Thusly, the great pitch of light is held high above such one so that all interpretation may be seen to be protected by light.

Sometimes the physical body of an entity may be protected from random or programmed catalyst such as great natural catastrophes or warfare.

*Firstly, if there has been pre-incarnative choice that one shall not take their life in service of the group, events shall fall in protective manner. Secondly, if an entity is able to dwell completely in unity, the only harm that may occur to the physical body, or yellow-ray vehicle is the changing into the more light-filled mind/body/spirit complex's vehicle by death. All other suffering and pain is as nothing to one such as this. Perfect configuration of the mind/body/spirit complexes, while within the third-density vehicle, is extraordinarily rare.

If the Experience of Mind has chosen the negative path and travels down it, there's no protection at all for them. Even in our 3rd density incarnation now, there's no protection. All random catalyst may affect the negatively polarized individual as a function of the statistical nature of random catalyst. Some people seek places of survival due to the lack of protection when service to self is invoked.

The legs of the entity of Card #4 (The Emperor) being right angles was linked with the tesseract (in speculative mathematics, a cube which has developed at least one additional dimension is a tesseract) as the direction of transformation from space/time into time/space and linked to the Crux Ansata. Right angles in the images of Tarot has a transformational meaning.

*Each of the images leading to the Transformations of Mind, Body and Spirit and ultimately to the great transformational Choice has the increasing intensity of increasing articulation of concept; each image in which you find this angle may increasingly be seen to be a more and more stridently calling voice of opportunity to use each resource, be it experience as you now observe or further images, for the grand work of the adept which builds towards transformation using the spirit's bountiful shuttle to intelligent infinity.

The groups days spent in love, harmony and thanksgiving will continue transforming the dwelling of the domicile (permanent home) and depolarize the negative entity.

It is correct that physical cleanliness is most important. Therefore, efforts shall be made to most thoroughly cleanse the place of the Ra contact. There isn't an absence of dust, earth, and other detritus which is in total called dirt. If the intention is to clean, the requirements for physical cleanliness is fulfilled. It is only when a lower astral entity has placed portions of itself in the dirt that care should be taken to remove the sentient being.

Just as each entity strives in each moment to become more nearly one with the Creator but falls short, just so is physical spotlessness striven for but not achieved. In each case the purity of intention and thoroughness of manifestation are appreciated. The variance between the attempt and the goal is never noted and may be considered unimportant.

The questioner Don Elkins, intends to paint the walls in the new residence and then clean, then move the furniture in, then salting and use of garlic. Ra adds that thresholds are not to be crossed during the cleansing. Since such stricture upon use of limen may affect your considerations. The blessing of water into the salt may be written within the liturgy (public worship such as at church) of the instrument's distortion of the worship of the One Creator, or it may simply be obtained from your catholic Church in the form of holy water.

The intention of blessing creates blessed water. The water may be sprinkled until dampened but not soaked. This is not a physical working. The substances need to be seen in their ideal state so that water may be seen to be enabling the salt.

Episode 99: Eliminating additions to the Tarot Cards by those who came after Ra-

*Eliminate all the letters from the edge of the card, except for the numbers.

Card #1 (Matrix of the Mind- The Magician): Eliminate the Star and the wand in the Magicians hand. The sphere may be seen to be held by the thumb, index and 2nd finger.

*It is not possible to offer a pure deck of Tarot due to the fact that when these images were first drawn, there was already distortion in various and sundry way, mostly cultural. Although it is good to view the images without the astrological additions, it is to be noted that the more general positions, phases, and characteristics of each concept complex are those that are significant. The removal of all distortions is unlikely and, to a great extent, unimportant.

Card #2 (The High Priestess- The Potentiator of the Mind). Remove letters and the Stars. Put a Crux Ansata in the middle of the High Priestess shirt that looks like a Crux Ansata. Ra didn't have the astrologically based crown on the head when they first introduced the Tarot to the Egyptians.

Card #3: (The Catalyst of the Mind- The Empress)- Remove all letters and stars and the little cups around the outside of the rays representing the sun.

Card #4- (The Experience of the Mind- The Emperor): Remove all the letters and the stars and the wand. Then put the sphere in the hand.

*The dimensions of the Crux Ansata may be figured out by viewing the Great Pyramid to decipher the puzzle. It was designed in order that in

its own time it be deciphered. In general, this image has the meaning as previously stated Ra said.

*The group can continue in harmony, communication, praise and thanksgiving to improve the contact.

* The Tarot cards don't have to be perfect and are a resource for the development of the faith and will. The concept complexes within each tarot card is the great architecture of the archetypical mind.

*The archetypical mind does not resolve any paradoxes or bring all into unity, but unity resolves all paradoxes. This is not the property of any source which is of the third density.

*One may look up from inward working and behold the glory, the might, the majesty, the mystery, and the peace of oneness. Ra brings the message of unity. In this perspective only may we affirm the value to the seeker of adepthood of the grasping, articulating, and use of this resource of the deep mind exemplified by the concept complexes of the archetypes.

Episode 100:

Card #5 (The Significator of the Mind- The Hierophant): The male within the complete envelopment of the rectangle signifies the abilities of the most finely honed mentality shall not be known without the physical vehicle (the body). Through the mouth the mind may speak. Through the limbs the mind may affect action.

The Hierophant looking to the left indicates that the mind has the tendency to notice more easily catalyst of a negative essence.

The small entity on the bottom left is red and the small entity on the right is white. They indicate polarity. The symbolism for the negative path was the russet color (red).

Experiences offered to the Significator (absorbs, seeks and attempts to learn) as positive frequently becomes recorded as productive of biases which may be seen to be negative.

Whereas the fruit of those experiences apparently negative is frequently found to be helpful in the development of the service-to-others bias.

Jordyn: "For example, someone may have a feel-good experience of wanting to enslave humanity then desire greed, power, control, manipulation and want to enslave the masses for their service-to-self desires. The negative path has also used fear to control and manipulate others. Whereas a negative experience of pain created growth within and made the entity want to desire to help and serve others so that others would be healed or not experience that same level of pain they did. The positive path is of love, hope and inspiration."

You may notice that the right hand in the center chest area of Card #5 gestures service to others, offering its light outward. The left-hand attempts to absorb the power of the spirit and point it for its use alone. (The Hierophant-Significator of the Mind) The Significator Card represents the person asking the question.

The 8 cartouches at the bottom of the card signifies the energy centers and evolution through those centers with the possibility of positive or negative polarization because of the white and black coloration of the figures. Many are of octaves of a mind/body/spirit complex's beingness. There is not one that does not profit from being pondered in connection with the considerations of the nature of the development of polarity by the concept complex of card #5 (of these 8 cartouches at the bottom of the card).

The symbols on the face of each cartouch such as birds and other symbols are letters and words in another language. It reads "And you shall be born again to eternal life."

Jordyn: "I assume that means we are born again through each lifetime, through reincarnation, evolving to eternal life. Never dying, but reincarnating into a new life through eternity. Born again means we don't die; we just reincarnate into a new life over and over through the seven densities of evolution within each Octave/Universe of existence."

Ra could use any of a multitude of devised Tarot sets.

The wings above card #5 is the wings of spirit, high above manifestation, yet draw the caged mind onward. The significator owns a covenant with the spirit which it shall in some cases manifest through the thought and action of the adept.

*In some cases, the Significator (absorbs, seeks, attempts to learn) manifest the spirit through the thought and action of the adept.

Episode 101: The Two Paths or Lovers Card #6- (Transformation of the Mind): The crossed arms is of a male to be transformed once he makes the decision for the negative or positive path. The two females represent the two paths. Left-hand path moves roughly physical and to the right-hand path the mental has a shallow correctness. (The left-hand path being rougher and the right-hand path slightly correct; even though there's no right or wrong path. Right path biased by the Logos.)

*There's a great sea of the unconscious mind of the Potentiator and the conscious mind of the Matrix. The transformation of the mind is the choice between the light and the dark. Those who turn to the deep mind gain a great treasure.

*The genie or mythical figure pointing the arrow to the left-hand transformation. This arrow protects. Those who choose separation on the negative path, are protected from other selves by a strength and sharpness equivalent to the degree of transformation which the mind has experienced in the negative sense. The seeker finds many mirrors for reflection in each other self it encounters. (When we are faced with other people, they are the reflection we encounter.)

There are some second-density fauna which have instinctually imprinted monogamous mating processes. The 3rd density bodies are the basic incarnational tool of manifestation upon Earth arose from entities imprinted, being designed by the Logos.

The free will of third density entities is for stronger beings than the rather mild carryover from 2nd density DNA encoding, and it is not part of the conscious nature of many people to be monogamous due to the exercise of free will. There are many signs in the deep mind indicating to alert the adept the more efficient use of catalyst. The Logos has a bias towards kindness. (In order to further positively polarize, I know I must only mate in love, equal enjoyment and viewing them as the Creator. Sex isn't for my own selfish needs or wants without giving to them in return; for that would be negatively oriented.)

The deep mind of the Potentiator, the unconscious mind awaits the reaching of the conscious mind.

In the image of the Transformation of the Mind, the conscious entity holds both paths and will turn itself one way or the other. Potentially backwards and forwards, rocking first one way then the other and not achieving the transformation.

*The triangular shape formed by the shoulders and crossed elbows of consciousness is a shape representing transformation. The same triangle on both paths indicating transformation with either choice.

Episode 102- Card #7 "The Chariot or Conqueror" (The Great Way of the Mind): The veil in the picture shows it lifted and still present, since the work of the mind and its transformation involves progressive lifting of the great veil between the conscious and the deep minds/subconscious. The complete success of lifting the veil is not properly a portion of third density work and especially third density mental processes.

3rd density experience is distorted or skewed so that positive orientation has more aid than the negative. The veil raised higher on the right side indicates a further removing of the veil on the positive side, allowing the adept to remember more.

The negative polarity depends more heavily on the illusion of separation between the self and others. The positive polarity attempts to see through the illusion to the Creator in each entity, but for the greater part is concerned with behaviors and thoughts directed towards other selves in order to be of service. This attitude is of the 3rd density illusion.

The crown of three stars is astrological in origin and not a part of the concept complexes within the archetype #7 that Ra originally intended.

The Great Way is the environment within which the mind, body or spirit shall function.

The polarity of the sphinxes are the movers of mind. The movement into a choice for polarity made in time, thus creating the Great Way of the Mind by choosing the light or dark path.

The positive polarity entity may hold the astrological sword in light and truth and the negative entity uses the spirit for its own use.

It is the harmony of the group that supports the contact; and harmony is of the positive path. The support group giving praise and thanksgiving in harmony helps the success of the contact and depolarizes the negative entity.

The instrument (Carla- The Channeler in trance) giving up buying clothes in order to be free from addiction is sort of a martyrdom. This sacrifice of the clothing causes the entity to feel poor and unworthy. Unless the poverty is seen to be true richness. Good works for the wrong reasons cause confusion and distortion. Ra encourages the instrument to value itself and to see that its true requirements are valued by the self. Ra suggests contemplation of true richness of being.

*T with two right angles above it on the chest on the Conqueror/Chariot card called the Tau Cross. This represents that T on the bottom is the choosing of either path in the transformation, and the upper right angles represent the Great Way of the left and right paths in the mental transformation that makes the change from space/time to time/space.

*The Significator (absorbs, seeks, attempts to learn such as asking these channeling questions) is the Significant self, to a great extent but not entirely influenced by the lowering of the veil. The Great Way of Mind, the body or the Spirit draws the environment of the new architecture after the veil is partially lifted and dipped into the limitless current of time/space. (metaphysical and not our physical reality).

*Time/space is close in this concept complex, brought close due to the veiling process and its efficaciousness in producing entities who wish to use the resources of the mind in order to evolve. Once the veil is removed after movement down one path then this moves one into time/space as one no longer has the veil of forgetting.

(The culture in Egypt drew the race to the side most often and had the feet turned. Therefore, not intending any meaning.)

The skirt skewed to the left indicates distance kept from others in the service-to-self path.

The Banishing Ritual performed before a channeling session help protect the instrument during the channeling session.

Ra said harmony produces praise and thanksgiving and that the group should continue in support, one for the other.

Jordyn: "My own observations: the Conqueror is holding the magic ball in his right hand indicating the right path has light, power and magic. It radiates truth and light to others. The left hand is holding the rod, indicating the negative path absorbing the power of the spirit for its own selfish use."

*The wings of the spirit are now with the Chariot. Now that the veil is lifted and dipped into time/space.

END OF BOOK #4 of 5

~~~~

Book # 5

Episode 103:

Sometimes negative entities can speak to someone giving upcoming cataclysmic earth changes (which is something violently destructive such as a volcano, flood or earthquake and), false information and dates (such as negative entities giving so-called prophets false information and false dates). Then, when made public by the group receiving such information, makes the group lose credibility since the dates are never correct. Thus, the negative entity takes the spiritual strength of the light that the group had been able to share in service-to-others work.

Typically, one can challenge the entity giving information through the instrument by demanding to know if they came in the name of Jesus the Christ, Christ Consciousness, the positive polarity, service to others or in the name of one of the archangels or in whatever represents the center of one's life. This forms a wall of light through which a negative entity has trouble passing through like a brick wall. A group can also walk the Circle of One to replace the challenging procedure used in telepathic channeling, since one can immediately go into trance state, out of body, and unaware of any activity.

The group used "tuned trance telepathy" to communicate with Ra. While the contact was underway, neither Carla nor those of Ra inhabited Carla's body. Carla's spirit was in the care of those of Ra while Ra used Carla's body from a distance to form the words that responded to Don's questions (the questioner).

Don Elkins was born in 1930 and died in 1984. He held a Master of Science in mechanical engineering and was a Wanderer here on Earth, which is a being that comes from higher densities back into our 3rd density world to be of service. He was a professor of physics, Boeing Pilot, US Army master sergeant during the Korean War and started his experiments in channeling in 1962, using protocols he used from a contactee group in Michigan.

(I notice that channeling in 2024 does not have those psychic attacks when they are in the trance state, unaware of what's going on. Perhaps this is safer since the higher 6th density positive being is giving the information and in control of the body, whereas in tuned trance Carla was aware and therefore susceptible to demon attacks, even though they didn't physically hurt her.)

The groups meditation before each session was their group process of tuning. Ra mentioned many times that they had only the grossest control over her body and had difficulty, for example, in repositioning her hands when experiencing pain flares due to her arthritic condition. Carla could not feel the pain flares, but repositioning them when pain occurred helped get rid of the static on the line (her pain was due to her arthritis and not from negative entity attacks.)

Don and Carla worked together for 12 years, channeling, researching and writing two books in metaphysics before Jim joined them in 1980 and three weeks later the Ra contact occurred. It happened when Carla was conducting a teaching session, when one of the Sunday meditation group members was learning how to channel.

The reception of Ra's beam is somewhat more advanced than some of the broader vibration channels opened by others for more introductory and intermediate work.

Before a channeling Session: Ra recommended that each entity have the appropriate attitude in seeking this information and be in harmony with each other before attending any session. One example was Don explaining to Jim the meaning of the Bible, candle, incense, and chalice of water held for them as triggering mechanisms or signals to their subconscious minds that a session was about to take place, and that from all levels of their being they should begin the process of purifying their desires to serve others above all else and to surround ourself with joy-filled light of praise and thanksgiving. The harmony that this process produced among the group was as a musical cord where Ra could blend their vibrations, and upon the harmonious bend of vibrations, information of a metaphysical nature could be transmitted by being drawn to those who sought it.

Episode 104: Conspiracy theories that have to do with unseen groups and individuals who are said to be real powers behind governments and their activities in the world today are true. Such theories usually hold that the news reports that we hear and read concerning politics, economics, the military and so forth are but the tip of a very large iceberg that has mainly to do with various schemes for world domination and that functions through secret activities of a small elite group of human beings and their alien allies, the negative density aliens, since the negative path is control, manipulation, wars, domination over others ect. Focusing on conspiracy theories and those elites involved tends to reinforce the illusion of separation and ignores the love that binds all things as One being.

Ra communicating through a "narrow band wavelength" means that only information of the purest and most precise nature concerning the process of the evolution of mind, body and spirit could be successfully transmitted on a sustainable basis through our instrument. It also means that it's more advanced information.

Ra: "There is a certain amount of landing taking place. Some of these landings are of your own people; some are of the group known to you as Orion."

*Elites on Earth has the technology achievement of being able to create and fly unidentified flying objects. Unfortunately for the social memory complex vibratory rate of your peoples, these devices are not intended for the service of mankind, but for potential destructive use. This further muddles the vibratory nexus of your social memory complex, causing a situation where neither those oriented towards serving others nor those oriented towards serving self can gain the energy/power which opens the gates to intelligent infinity for the social memory complex (people with a veil of forgetting). This in turn causes the harvest to be small.

The military (third density entities) have bases undersea in the southern waters near the Bahamas, in Pacific seas close to Chilean borders on the water, on the moon (which is a satellite), in the skies, on the lands are very numerous and potentially destructive.

They came from the same place as humanity on Earth or Ra on Venus, they came from the Creator. On a shallower aspect, these people your other selves' government (national security).

The United States learned this technology from Nikola Tesla. When Nikola Tesla departed this illusion, the papers containing the necessary understanding were taken by mind/body/spirit complexes serving your security of national divisional complex. These people became privy (private information) to the basic technology. The technology was given to the Russians from the Confederation, about 27 years ago Ra states in 1954, in an attempt to share information and bring about peace among your peoples. The entities giving this information were in error, but Ra did many things in attempts to aid our harvest, where Ra learned the folly of certain types of aid. That is why Ra's approach is more cautious now, even as the need is power upon power greater, and our people's call is greater and greater.

The man-made UFO crafts from Tesla's technology are considered and used as weaponry today. The energy used is from the field of electromagnetic energy which polarizes the Earth sphere. The weaponry is of two basic kinds: psychotronic and particle beam. The weapons have been used to alter weather patterns and to enable the vibratory change which engulfs this planet at this time.

The governments of each of our societal-division desire to refrain from publicity in case of hostile action from any potential enemies.

The United States has 573 of these crafts in 1981 and was in the process of adding to this number, with the maximum speed being equal to the earth energy squared. This field varies. The limit is approximately half the light speed, due to imperfections in design.

Humanity on Earth possess technology capable of resolving each and every limitation which plagues our Social Memory Complex. The concerns some people on Earth have with powerful energy cause the solutions to be withheld until the solutions are so needed that those with the distortion can then become further distorted in the direction of power.

The Orion's landed here and their purpose is conquest, unlike those of the Confederation (positive density) who wait for the calling (the calling such as people's prayers or cry for help). The Orion group is of negative density calls itself to conquest. One form of landing is when the Orion's land, they take people on their craft and program them for future use. The first level of programming will be discovered by those who do research. The second, a triggering program. Third, a second and most deep triggering program crystallizing the entity, thereby rendering (making) it lifeless and useful as a kind of beacon.

The second form is a landing beneath the earth's crust, which is entered from water. This is the general area of your South American and Caribbean areas and close to the northern pole. The bases of these people are underground.

There are approximately 1,500 people, and growing, that know about the 573 crafts that the United States possessed in 1981, and most likely to this day still possess and perhaps even more.

These crafts are constructed one by one in the desert or Arid regions of New Mexico and Mexico, both installations being underground. Ra watches these developments and hopes our people on Earth may be harvested into 4th density in peace. People can not ride in them for they are controlled by computers from a remote source of data with no people inside. The United States and Mexico arranged for an underground installation of UFO craft in Mexico because of Mexico's ground being dry and near-total lack of population. The government officials who agreed did not know the use their land in Mexico would be put, but thought it was governmental research installation for bacteriological warfare. The approximate diameter being 23 feet.

Daniel Frye was transported, in thought-form, by the Confederation in order to give this mind/body/spirit complex data so that we might see how this type of contact aided your people in the uncovering of the Intelligent Infinity behind the illusion of your limits.

Episode 105: Wanderers frequently share characteristics exhibiting physical ailments such as allergies and personality disorders, which seem to be a reaction against this planet's vibrational frequency. This is apparently a side effect that is due to having another planetary influence in higher densities as their home vibration. They incarnate on this third-density planet in order to be of service in whatever way possible to help the population of this planet to become more aware of the evolutionary process and to move in harmony with it. These Wanderers go through the same forgetting process that every 3rd density being- even as they slowly begin to remember why it is that they have been born here. Apparently, about one in every 70 people on Earth is of such origin.

As we let love flow through us, others change, and as they open their hearts, the circle of light grows. We are now at a stage where light sources are beginning to connect (the global mind). This global mind happening faster with email and the World Wide Web. With information being exchanged without pen and paper, we are basically working with light. A great service is to know your worthiness and be yourself.

All beings can use discernment within the all-self, located at the heart of each entity.

The Confederation contacted Don's group in 1962 without spacecraft, but through thought-form.

The programming on the constructs of Men in Black makes it difficult to control them. People would not be able to grapple with a thought-form entity of the Men in Black.

There are no mistakes under the Law of One.

Ra: "The self-healing distortion is affected through realization of the Intelligent Infinity resting within. This is blocked in some way in those who are not perfectly balanced in bodily complexes. The blockages vary from entity to entity. It requires the conscious awareness of the spiritual nature of reality, if you will, and the corresponding pourings of this reality into the individual mind/body/spirit complex for healing to take place."

All three in the channeling group (Don Elkins, Carla, and Jim) with Ra are Wanderers of 5th and 6th density.

There are apparently many, many different ways people may receive such subconscious confirmations of the appropriateness of their thoughts or actions. The most common is the feeling of rightness that wells up from within when one is on the right track or receiving spiritually helpful information. These signs being synchronicities.

Sometimes silver flecks would end up on the groups faces or various places, this is a synchronistic sign indicating the appropriateness or importance of that learn/teaching (They learned it and then taught it). The entity itself, in cooperation with the inner planes, creates whatever signpost is most understandable or noticeable to it. Entities consciously do not create them. The roots of mind complex, having touched in understanding, Intelligent Infinity, creates them.

Before each contact with Ra, the group conducted a meditation that was used as our tuning device. The meditation was their means of becoming as one in their seeking to be of service to others.

Kathryn: "I was also told in a channeling session to meditate more, so I can further evolve. Another channeling session stated that a third density sign is fear or anxiety."

The desire that had brought Ra to our group (Don's channeling group) was a true desire for non-transient material, and this desire fueled their sessions. (Non-transient material is information aligned with the Law of One, as Ra would answer any question, but preferred the questions to align with the Law of One.)

Kathryn: "I'm glad Ra desired that because this information was much needed for humanity and has changed my life for the better and raised my positive polarity substantially to about 25% higher within 9 months."

Anything measurable is transient. Ra would remind the group to get back on track in a subtle way: by telling the group to watch their alignments. Later, they figured out that Ra was grading their questions, not the Bible near Carla's head as she was laying down nor their candle placement.

The human spirit, the force of creative love, the creation's essence: these things are unfindable, noumenal (knowledge that exists independent of human senses), it's always sensed, and never penetrated by our fact-finding intellects. But we sense into them through living with an open heart, and by talking about them with sources such as Ra and Q'uo and other "universal or "outer" energies and essences. The personal guides and other teachers of the inner planes of our planet have much more leeway in offering personal information. People can go to them to get readings on health and other specific issues. People can go to outer sources such as our Confederation sources with questions that transcend space time. If it will matter less in 10,000 years than it does not, it is probably not a universal question for Ra.

Episode 106: The crater found in Russia in the Tunguska region was caused by the destruction of a fission reactor. This was a "drone" sent by the Confederation, which malfunctioned. It was moved to an area where its destruction would not cause infringement upon the will of mind/body/spirit complexes. It was then detonated.

Its purpose in coming to Earth: It as a drone designed to listen to the various signals of people on Earth. People were at that time, beginning to work in a more technical sphere. The Confederation was interested in determining the extent and the rapidity of our advances. The drone was powered by a simple fission motor or engine. It was not that type which you now know, but was very small. However, it has the same destructive effect upon third-density molecular structure. Thus, as it malfunctioned, the Confederation and Ra felt it was best to pick a place for its destruction rather than attempt to retrieve it, for the possibility/probability modes for this maneuver, looked very, very minute.

There was very little radiation in this type of device. There is radiation which is localized, but the localization does not drift with the winds as does the emission of our somewhat primitive weapons. There's very little radiation in the trees in the area. This is an example of radiation being very localized. However, the energy which is released is powerful enough to cause difficulties.

Nuclear power was brought through by a basic equation from Albert, a Wanderer, dedicated to service the planet. This work was not given by higher densities nor intended for destruction.

The phenomenon known as spontaneous combustion of human beings is a random occurrence which does not have to do with the entity. They are random entities. One tree being struck by lightning and burning, but lightning not striking elsewhere, therefore, elsewhere not burning, is an example of the random occurrence.

Episode 107: Ra innocently "told on" Carla about a good friend of hers offering her the opportunity to experience the effects of LSD, which she had never experienced before. She used it twice in early February 1981 as a programming device to attempt to achieve an experience of unity with Creator, but she did not wish Don to know about these experiences, since he was very much against the use of any illegal substances at any time and especially while working with Ra.

In a later session it will be suggested by Ra that these two experiences were arranged by the negative entities monitoring the groups work with those of Ra, in hopes that Carla's ability to serve in the Ra contact might be hindered. The three of them then determined there would be no further use of any illegal substances for as long as they were privileged to work with the Ra contact, so that no chinks in their "armor of light" that they could eliminate would be present, and so that the Ra contact could never be associated with the use of any such drugs.

The information on Aleister Crowley is self- explanatory and underlines again the caution that each seeker must take in moving carefully through its energy canters in a balanced fashion. So, one could carefully balance the energy centers and not use drugs for assistance.

Carla and Don were together, wed in spirit, but Don didn't want marriage and wanted 'to stay celibate. After two years Carla knew celibacy wasn't for her but was still in love with Don. She then had lovers and would tell Don before it started and when she stopped seeing them. Don was gone flying as a pilot half the time, so Carla found time for lovers. Her lover 10 of the 16 years she spent with Don was a trusted and much-loved friend of hers ever since High School. He came and saw her about once a month. She then stopped seeing him when he wanted to take the relationship further, and then she was celibate for 4 years before Jim (the scribe of the Law of One material). Carla believed that the weakness in Don's armor of light that resulted in his dying was believing Carla fell out of love for him and Don doubted her allegiance to him. He never told her this and she thought he was happy for her. For six years she had suicidal thoughts after Don's death.

Jim and Carla eventually got married three years after Don's death. Ra said in the density her and Don came from; they were already one. Carla then believed her and Jim's relationship was "child's play". All three of them loved each other and worked well together.

The Confederations teachings are at one with universal wisdom as well as living in love. Carla said, "That focus upon Love is one's access to truth, and one's willingness to keep the heart open, which one may call faith, is the energy that brings to us all that was meant for us, both of lessons to learn and of service to offer."

Ra tried to express the feeling of the infinite mystery of the one creation in its infinite and intelligent unity.

Sexual intercourse was an aid to Carla's vital energies during the trance state and would increase the length of a session if engaged in the night before a session was to be held. Thus, at the end of session 18 of 106, when Don asked how they might avoid further difficulties in the contact (such as not taking LSD) Ra affirmed the aid they had discovered was that of the sexual intercourse. They also found that conscious dedication of the act of love-making to the service of others via the Ra contact increased its beneficial effects.

Ra further states that there are substances ingested, such as LSD or Marijuana, that do aid the individual in the positive service it has chosen. This is due to the distortion towards chemical lapses within the mind complex, causing lack of synaptic continuity. This is a chemical reaction of short duration. The instrument, Carla, however, has not used this particular substance at any time while performing extent due to the energizing or speeding up of the vital forces. However, it is not recommended for the instrument due to the toll it takes upon the vital energies once the substance wears off. This being true of any speeding-up chemical.

The prerequisite of the contact for those involved is the tuning in the personal life and meditation before each contact: Including contemplation, or prayer before entering these workings. Ra stated certain people wanting to join the Ra contact circle weren't of proper vibrational distortion. (Perhaps the lack of simple faith he had, since he wanted to prove spiritual truth.)

Ra felt the primary importance in personal ethics is allowing people to do their own learning, make their own mistakes, cannot be over emphasized.

Episode 108: The prayer of St. Francis is what Carla used in her own personal tuning mechanism since she began channeling in 1974. It further refines the tuning done by the support group and is always grayed mentally before any session, whether telepathic or trance.

The limitations of which Ra speaks refer to Carla's rheumatoid arthritis, which was apparently chosen before the incarnation to provide an inner focus for her meditative work rather than to allow the ease of outer expression that might have dissipated the inner orientation. Thus, not all disabilities are meant to yield to even the best efforts of healers, and when such a disability does not respond to any kind of healing effort, one may begin to consider what opportunities for learning and service are opened up by the disability. Ra even mentioned that her acceptance of her disabilities and limitations would ease the amount of pain that she suffered because of them.

Kathryn: "I also feel that I chose to have a great BMX life by exploring, traveling the United States racing, having a lot of friends and acquaintances and enjoy being in the physical outer world. Then, chose before birth that at some point in my life to have some sort of limitation when I broke my neck at 25 years old in 2015. Immediately I knew I would write a book by April of 2015, this unfortunately is when the channeler of the Ra contact, Carla Reuckert passed away. During this month I had a spinal fusion of the skull to C5.

Upon publishing my book, I began having vivid dreams about the future because of my desire to serve others. After publishing my 2nd book, I began manifesting money and began investing. I then would share my dreams of the future on YouTube and consistently started having more of these dreams after publishing each one online. The book was an action I took and the universe saw that as a service to humanity and therefore more manifestation came into my life, as well as dreams.

Next, when I learned about the Law of One, the dreams became more detailed, accurate, vivid and even would show me some Law of One concepts such as when I had the "I am One" dream about each person having a higher self that guides us throughout our life. I am the most accurate prophet or dream interpreter in the world, whereas every

Christian so-called prophet had at least one wrong. To their religion that would mean they would be considered a false prophet.

I definitely believe my inner focus, spiritual transformation, my books, the 33 accurate dreams of the future fulfilled, 14 years of research in various topics and now my studies on the Law of One is because I am now forced to be off the bike and thus, discovered everything I have over these past 10 years learning everything I can about discovering the truth of this world and the universe. If seven years is like obtaining a masters degree and the Law of One books is like a PhD study in metaphysics; then this would be my PhD thesis."

Why Carla, the channeler, would smell incense at various times during the day at various places: This instrument has spent a lifetime in dedication to service. This has brought this instrument to this nexus in space/time with the conscious and unconscious distortions toward service, with the further conscious distortion towards service by communication. Each time they perform the working, Ra's social memory complex vibrational distortion meshes more firmly with Carla's unconscious distortions towards service. Thus, Ra is becoming a part of Carla's vibratory complex, and a vice versa. This occurs upon the unconscious level, the level where the mind has gone down through to the roots of consciousness called cosmic. Carla isn't consciously aware of the slow changing of the meshing vibratory complex. However, as the dedications on both levels continues, and the workings continue, there are signals sent from the unconscious in a symbolic manner. Carla is extremely keen in her sense of smell, it takes place unconsciously, and the thought-form of this odor is witnessed by the entity.

Carla felt better and healthier because of the channeling sessions. This is because for many years she prayed before communication with Ra. Then, before the trance state was achieved, the prayer remained within the conscious portion of the mind. This wasn't as effective as the vibrational sound then goes into the unconscious level, thus affecting the communication from the spiritual complex. Also, her accepting certain limitations which it placed upon itself in order to serve such as she does now. This also is an aid to realigning the distortions of physical pain.

Episode 109: Henry Puharich wasn't involved in the channelings because he wasn't of proper vibrational distortion due to him wanting to prove spiritual truth instead of just having simple "faith".

The movie Battle beyond the Star had some distortions of the Law of One and its scenario upon our physical plane (Earth).

UFOs are certainly here; the landing-trace cases alone prove that something that makes dents in the ground is visiting us, and the many witnesses and abductees create a comprehensive picture of human alien contact that is undeniable.

Did Dwight Eisenhower meet with the Confederation or Orion group in 1950s? Dwight Eisenhower met with thought-forms indistinguishable from third density. This was a test, the Confederation wanted to see what would occur if this extremely positively-oriented and simple (pleasant) person with no significant distortion towards power happened across peaceful information. The Confederation and Ra discovered that Eisenhower did not feel those under his care could deal with the concepts of other beings and other philosophies.

Thus, an agreement reached then would allow him to go his way and the Confederation to do likewise- and a very quiet campaign be continued alerting people on Earth to the Confederations presence gradually, events have overtaken this plan such as witnesses seeing UFOs and so forth.

Ra didn't want to infringe upon our future but gave hints that a crashed spaceship with small bodies inside now may be stored in our military installations.

Negative entities performing psychic attacks/greetings can be looked upon in a negative way, therefore, having a negative experience; one can also choose to see the Creator in all entities and events and can praise and seek the light within any situation.

When the latter choice is made, the psychic greeting becomes a great blessing for this presents an intensive opportunity to see the One Creator where it may be more difficult to see. When accomplished, develops a great deal more spiritual strength than may normally be developed without the negative entities aid in pointing out the weaker areas. Our poor choices, usually reflecting a lack of love toward another self, get magnified by the demon and bleed away our efforts to seek the light and serve others until we are able to show love, acceptance, compassion, tolerance and light tough to all. This is why Jesus said to "resist no evil." To resist and fight is to see someone or something as other than the self, as other than the One Creator. This is the negative path. The positive path sees and loves all as the self and as the One.

Carla's cold chest is from taking LSD. The chemical substance has within it the facility of removing large stores of energy. This was carefully planned by the negative being (Orion's) not wanting Carla to remain viable. The first hope of the Orion entity which arranged this opportunity was that Carla would become less polarized towards the positive.

Due to conscious efforts upon Carla, using the substance as a programmer for service to others and for thankfulness, Carla was spared this distortion and there was no result satisfactory to the Orion group. Carla is a very strong entity with very little distortions from universal green-ray love energy. Thus, the negative 5th density beings plan was not affected, as Carla continued to give of itself an open or green-ray manner rather than attempting to deceive or manipulate other-selves.

Since Carla wouldn't cease in sharing love universally under this substance, the negative beings only remaining distortion available was to drain this entity of as much energy as possible. Busyness is not the appropriate attitude for this work, which Carla is trying to overcome.

LSD caused Carla to become busy and lack the derive to rest; Carla staying alert for much longer than appropriate created vital energy to be lost. Making her unusually susceptible to infections, such as the cold chest.

How to best revitalize the self? Meditation, accepting of limitations, experiences of joy through association with others, singing, exercising with great contact whenever possible, with the life forces of second density, especially those of trees; also, be aware of moderate intake of food, exercise suggested at a fairly early portion of the day and at a later portion of the day before resting was given to Carla (the channeler).

The first LSD debilitating effects is approximately 3 days. The 2nd ingestion has a cumulative or doubling effect.

Episode 110: The first working with Confederation entities was with Atlantis approximately 13,000 years ago. Paul Shockley received information, while channeling the Confederation that he took part in the design and construction of the Egyptian pyramids. This memory was integrated into the service of healing and polarization possible by mechanisms of the crystal and the charged healer.

Paul's second experience was approximately 12,000 years ago, during which the entity prepared, in some part, the consciousness of people in Egypt to enable the calling that enabled those of Ra's social memory complex to walk among the Egyptians at the time. He was a priest and succeeded in remembering in semi-distorted form the learn/teachings of the Atlantean pyramidal experiences. Thus became a builder of the archetypal thought of the Law of One with distortions towards healing, which aided Ra in bringing this through into physical manifestation.

There were other beings aiding in the construction of the pyramids, but not fully materialized in third density. They were materialized from their waste up to their heads but not from their waist to their feet.

Intelligent Infinity present in the absorption of livingness and beingness as it becomes codified into intelligent energy, due to thought impression of those assisting the living stone into a new shape of beingness. The release and use of Intelligent Infinity for a brief period begins to absorb all the consecutive or interlocking dimensions, thus offering brief glimpses of those projecting to material their thoughts. These beings beginning to materialize but not remaining visible. Those beings were the thought-form of Ra's social memory complex as they offered contact from their intelligent infinity to the intelligent infinity of the stone.

Carla was told that she has experience in healing on levels other than the physical. She was told to never practice the exercise of fire, as it is used in a stronger form of healing. She was advised by Ra never to do any kind of physical healing on others, because she was always very low on physical energy, and such healing would tend to drain her already low reserve in that area. This is to conserve her vital energies during a three-month period.

Since she was a child, she had some sort of ability to sit with someone with hands in contact and be able to clear some of the surface clutter away from the other person's mind or being. She can also do spiritual balancing by her hands.

Could a machine from Washington State being developed that was supposed to augment the general health and well-being of a person aid Carla? Ra's response suggested that Carla's magnetic field was somewhat unusual and very likely formed in such an unusual way as to permit contact with those of Ra. This unusual magnetic field has been a source of frequent inconveniences with any electromagnetic equipment that Carla has used on a regular basis. She breaks it- just by touching it periodically. She can't wear anything, but quarts crystal watches, and the channeling group has many, many semi-functional tape recorders lying around different areas of the house.

(Judgement ceases when we choose to view all as the Creator. There's no room for judgement, but the observation of a individualized portion of consciousness of the Creator.)

Ra says there are no mistakes. I'd like to add that we are all just learning and growing at different rates, so there's no mistakes since we are all just learning.

Episode 111: How to have Protection Against Negative entities? Protection lies in giving thanksgiving for each moment and experience. See yourself and others as the Creator. Open your heart and always know the light and praise it.

Carla's physical energy level was always very low and constantly being drained by arthritis and pain, so she had to engage in daily exercise in order to maintain the function of each portion of her body. (I believe exercise is why I don't have neck or back pain after breaking my neck and having surgery.)

For Carla- She walked rapidly for about an hour a day.

Jim McCarthy: "One way of looking at the process of evolution is to see it as the process of solving the mysteries all about us. All events are illusions or mysteries because each represents the One Creator in one disguise of another, offering us a greater or lesser opportunity to find love, joy, balance and perfection in each moment.

During the three-month period Ra suggests Carla should achieve intensification in her workout by doing one long one instead of two shorter ones. Ra stated she needs the strengthening of the body. This may be one major exercise period and then one more half the length at night before meditation. Ra, "This will be seen to be wearing upon the instrument. However, it will have the effect of strengthening the physical complex and lessening the vulnerability which might be taken advantage of."

Episode 112: Any third density entity has a Higher Self or Oversoul at mid-sixth density. In addition, Wanderers who are a member of a social memory complex also has another complex of consciousness upon which to call for assistance.

The forgetting process, or the veil, occurs when we take on flesh and become a manifested entity on Earth, that flesh shuts our metaphysical senses. All that we knew before birth is hidden in the deeper mind. There is always the fear, especially among Wanderers, as one enters incarnation, that one will not awaken at all but be lost for the whole life experience.

The awakening process beings to identify with a new and larger concept of the self as an eternal and metaphysical being.

As we all awaken and develop our truer selves, we can help each other. People will come your way. They seem very "aware" or very confused or scared. If the Creator put them in your way, then you are well equipped to aid them. Simply love and accept them, as well as show this truth of the Law of One if you so desire. This involves first coming to love and accept yourself, forgiving yourself and forgive others. For judgement of others stops when we view others and ourself as the One Creator. (A fractal of God perhaps).

Qualification for contact with Ra includes penetrating the forgetting process. Otherwise, the Law of confusion/Free will would prohibit this.

How to disseminate information to be of service to others?

Ra: "Relax, and let the Law of Attraction work. Even if only one person is aided by the work, that is enough. At the very least, the benefit that the material provides to the group alone will become like unto a light that each in the group will radiate to all others met in the daily round of activities."

Kathryn's channeling: "Some people are told they must sacrifice in order to serve, but the truth is that it is well to make sure your own needs and desires are met first before serving. Sacrificing is a form of martyrdom that once wisdom is utilized one may realize they don't need to sacrifice and can meet their own needs first before fully serving others."

My search for truth began after breaking my neck BMX racing at 25-years old. I knew at that time I was meant to start writing books, do research and search for truth in every area of life. To ultimately master this density on Earth. I chose to work at "boring" jobs according to some people in order to get all this research in. Therefore, I essentially was doing this full time and being paid for it. I was always right where I was supposed to be. After 10 years of consistent full-time research, it finally took off and I wrote these seven books in the first half of 2024, two of them were already finished, but just needed to be edited.

I knew the exact 10 books I needed to read and questions I needed to channel in or to solve the entire puzzle of how this world and our universe works. It's here in these five *Law of One* books as well as my book called *"Correcting Distortions of the Bible."* The answers the whole world has been looking for is finally here. This was my purpose and perhaps my PhD study, as well as the reason I chose to reincarnate into Earth at this time."

Ra said to not be concerned with how many people get this information. They are content with being able to aid in the evolution of one of our people's here on Earth. Whatever effort the group makes cannot disappoint Ra, for that number already exceeds one.

The Ra contact was very wearing on Carla as she would lose 2-3 pounds per session and the negative beings wanting to attack, so that this information wouldn't get out into the public. This often intensified her pain of her arthritic distortions to the point that her function on all levels was severely curtailed. Carla was very happy to serve in this way and to see Don happy and inspired during the contact was satisfaction to Carla that struck the depths of her being. Donald was her world. She adored him and wish to make him comfortable and happy. But he was not comfortable in this world and so often lonely and isolated. The days of Ra contact were golden for Don and Carla and she would have died quite gladly doing one last session to be of service, and even expected to, but Don's death came first when he took his own life. (Perhaps his unhappiness was due to Carla having Jim as a lover, but Don wouldn't fulfill her desires because of his celibacy. Thus, something like this is to be expected I would assume. She even waited four years being celibate with Don and he still wouldn't meet her desires in that way.

Carla hopes that her life is to remain simply the giving of all she has to the Creator. That's why Jesus said "If you gave to the least of these you've given to me." Because Jesus, you, me and even the least of these is the Creator.

Carla found life a wonder and a joy, and all the limitations, mess, loss and pain in the world have not changed her mind on that.

The demons tend to want to attack Wanderers more than those people who haven't come from higher densities into Earth's 3rd density life to help humanity. Thus, Ra stated that the demons were doing everything they could to undermine Carla at this time, such as her experiencing a problem with her foot so that she couldn't exercise. Ra stated that it is fortunate that she be greatly involved in worship of the One Infinite Creator through sacred song during this time. Ra said the more physical active movements of exercise and in the sexual sense are helpful. Again, it is fortunate that this instrument has the opportunities for loving social intercourse, which are of some substantial benefit.

During meditation, Don once saw a world where the colors were three-dimensional. He saw living waters, and a golden sunrise streaming over the sky. The 3D colors made our sunrise streaming over the sky; and they made our earthly hues look like black-and-white photos. Another experience was Don's lower arm moving rapidly up and down while rested on the arm chair and a blue light emanating from his lower arm. Later transmissions indicating that UFO entities were winding his batteries.

Ra stated that these experiences would best be approached from ceremonial magic stance. However, the Wanderer or adept shall have the far-greater potential for this type of experience, which is an archetypal nature, one belonging to the roots of consciousness. ((Perhaps obtaining Christ Consciousness of 4th density or above.)) His experience was a form of initiation.

Ra states that it is not well for positively oriented entities to work alone.

A strong desire to be of service is not enough when not combined with wisdom. The group suffered in the first months of the Ra contact from doing too many sessions. For example, scheduling too many sessions in such a short period of time was overly draining on Carla's physical energy especially after she had consumed LSD. This shortened energy meant that the total number of sessions that was possible during her incarnation was probably being reduced. (Perhaps a good balance of rest and service is well.)

The power of dedication- If Carla dedicated herself to having a session with Ra, she would expend an amount of energy equal to a full day's work- even if the session did not occur. Thus, it was most important for dedication to be met with wisdom, such as not overdoing it.

Ra says martyrdom is not necessarily helpful. ((Complete unconditional love in service-to-others should be met with wisdom. Perhaps the perfect balance of service-to-others and wisdom. An example of this is Carla having the wisdom to take enough rest so that she'll have enough energy to do more sessions. Thus, the wisdom allowing more service-to-others to be done.

The tone in Don's left ear when starting the communication with Ra was a negatively oriented signal trying to interfere with the group's communication with Ra. A positively oriented signal would be in the right ear indicating a sign that one is being given some unworded saying, such as, "Listen, Take heed." The other positive sign is the tone above the head, which is a balanced confirmation of a thought.

We are all things so we can get a negative signal in receiving thought-forms, word-forms and visions. Thought-forms, word-forms and visions can also be positively oriented as well.

Carla's energy was lost just by her dedication to the service of others through the Ra contact, so even if they stopped the session early, that energy would already be lost as if she did a full and complete session.

Thus, once vital energy is dedicated by the instrument to Ra's communications, even if the working did not occur, this vital energy would be last to the day-to-day experience of the instrument. Ra indicated the importance of releasing the will from determining the times of working, for if the instrument desires contact, the energy is gathered and lost for ordinary or mundane purposes. Therefore, the group decided to continue the session since the energy was already lost. Carla's determination to continue contact during that period has already extended the low-energy period.

In order to nullify negatively oriented signals, dreams and clairaudient communication, the group must share the negatively oriented experiences with the group and meditate in love. One must not downgrade the experiences or it'll invite the prolonging of the effects. It's for the better to share and trust such experiences and join hearts and souls in love and light with compassion for the sender and armor for the self.

Carla had a dream of Orion (negative) influence. The essence of the dream revealing more the instruments unconscious associative patterns of symbolism.

Don's arm glowing blue and moving rapidly involuntarily was an analogy from his Higher Self that the being that he was living in, in a way is not understood by physicists, scientists or doctors.

His experience was his ability to contact intelligent Infinity during meditation. Therefore, it doesn't have a direct effect upon Carla's vital energy.

To aid oneself in vital energy is to be sensitive to beauty, to singing of sacred music, to mediation and worship, to the sharing of self with others in freely given love either in social or sexual intercourse. These things work directly upon vitality. Appreciating a variety of experiences is a less direct way that aids vitality.

The diagram of the advancement of magical practices, starting with Malkuth, Yesod, Hod, Netzach, Tiphareth ect. Ending in Kether each has a complex number and shading of energy centers, as well as some part in various balances; the lower, the middle, the high, and the total balance. Thus, there are complex colors or rays and complex charges in each station. These stations are relationships. Each path, positive or negative, has these relationships offered. The intent of the practitioner in working with these powerful concepts determines the polarity of the working. The tools are tools.

The Ipsissimus is one who has mastered the tree of Life and has used his mastery for negative polarization.

There was a quite significant probability of Carla developing pulmonary or renal disease in session 44 around April of 1981. The group averted a possible serious physical malfunction of Carla's body. Their prayerful support was helpful, just as Carla's unflagging determination to accept what is best in the long run and maintain the recommended exercises without impatience. She is also aided by rest and the balancing with exercise.

A significant portion of Ra's Social Memory Complex are sixth-density Wanderers here on Earth. Another large portion of Ra consists of those who aided those in South America, where 150 became harvestable for graduation into 4th density 50,000 years ago after the first 25,000-year cycle (here on Earth). Earth is now in the third 25,000-year cycle, close to the 75,000-year cycle of 3rd density. Therefore, Earth is close to the graduation of souls from this density into the 4th. 65% of souls on Earth are currently of positive polarity. Another portion of Ra are those aiding Atlantis. All are sixth density and all brother and sister groups due to the unified feeling that Ra had been aided by the pyramids, so they could aid people on Earth.

Two people in the group are of sixth-density origin, one a fifth density harvestable to sixth but choosing to return as a Wanderer due to loving association between teach and student. Thus, the three form a greatly cohesive group.

Kathryn: "My guess is that since Carla and Don are one in a higher-density and in love with each other, they are of 6th density and Jim must then be of 5th density origin."

The spiritual transfer of energy, is possible for Carla in any sexual-energy transfer. It happens without any particular effort on her part and seems due to her nature of how she may be of service to another. This kind of spiritual-energy transfer is possible for anyone to achieve through the dedication of shared sexual intercourse for the purpose of achieving such a transfer.

With that dedication consciously made, the male will transfer the physical energy, which he has in abundance, to the female and refresh her. And the female will transfer the mental/emotional and spiritual energies, which she has in abundance, and inspire the male. The biological male tends to express the male principle of that quality that reaches. The biological female tends to express the female principle of awaiting the reaching. The orgasm, of either positively oriented entity, is the point the transfer takes place, although well-mated partners do not need to experience the orgasm in order to achieve the transfer.

The energy transfer from James McCarty gave Carla the vital energy needed to still be alive after she ran out of energy some years ago, essentially the sexual energy transfer from Jim saved Carla's life.

With that dedication consciously made, the male will transfer the physical energy, which he has in abundance, to the female and refresh her. And the female will transfer the mental/emotional and spiritual energies, which she has in abundance, and inspire the male.

With proper balance of mind and body, the orgasm can activate the spirit complex and serves as a kind of shuttle, to allow an entity to contact intelligent infinity.

Pioneer thinkers theorize that unblocking lower energy centers can in some degree activate the frontal lobes of the brain.

No one knows for sure what that part of the brain is for, but if activated can quantum leap in consciousness.

At 25 years old Jim started having frontal lobe experiences when waking up in the morning. It's a combination of pleasure and pressure which starts in the frontal lobes, then spreads and pulses through the whole brain, feeling like an orgasm in the brain. Often being accompanied by voices and visions. He had over 200 of those from 25-34. This may be experienced after a concentration of effort upon the opening of the gateway or indigo mind complex so that experience of a sacramental or violet ray may occur.

These experiences are the beginnings of the body, the mind and the spirit becoming integrated at the gateway or indigo level, they may then experience joy and the comprehension of intelligent infinity. Thus, the body complex orgasm and mind complex orgasm becoming integrated may then set forth the proper gateway for the spiritual-complex integration and its use as a shuttle for the sacrament of the fully experienced presence of the one Infinite Creator.

Each person has several guides available to it. The persona of two of these guides is the polarity of male and female. The third is androgynous and represents a more unified conceptualization faculty.

When Carla and Don were small kids, they both saw a ball of lightning. The ball of lightning came in through Carla's window rolled around her crib, and left through the same window. (When I was 30 years old in 2019, I saw a ball of lightning go through my window as well and then through the doorway into the hallway. It occurred right after my family had prayed over the house.) Ra said Carla was being visited by her people to be wished well.

Some entities feel the need to plant Confederation imagery in a way not to interfere with free will. So, they use symbols of death, resurrection, love and peace as a means of creating upon the thought level, the systematic train of events which give the message of hope and love.

This type of contact is chosen by the careful consideration of Confederation members which contact an entity of like home vibration. This project then goes before the Council of Saturn and, if approved, is completed. This type of contact includes the nonpainful nature of thought experienced and the message content which speaks of the new dawning age and not of doom.

Ra encourages us to balance faults and not erase them. Of course, if one has a fault that involves infringing on the free will of another, then the fault does need to be addressed by eliminating that behavior or you can polarize more negative. One does not find ways to balance stealing or murder. But anger, vagueness and forgetfulness and people's little quirks can be balanced and not removed.

Kathryn: "One day when I almost tried judging someone, I remembered they are part of the Creator and the judgement disappeared. We are all on different levels of evolution, so there's no need to judge, for all eventually returns to the Creator anyways. We all evolve positively in the sixth and once in the seventh density upon graduation we will go into the next octave of Creation, in the new universe."

The work of sixth density is to unify wisdom and compassion. This entity, Jim, abounds in wisdom. The compassion it is desirous of balancing has, as its antithesis, lack of compassion. In the more conscious being, this expresses or manifests itself as lack of compassion for the self.

Carla's pre-incarnation to choose to have arthritis was, so that she could focus on her inner life of meditation and contemplation, instead of the usual activities of the world. Such pre-incarnatively chosen limitations confound many healers, who have the opinion that no disease is ever necessary. However, it seems that some people choose limitations that will utilize the entire incarnation and not just a portion of it.

(Perhaps Carla channeling could have been because of her limitations and maybe if she didn't have limitations, then her life would have taken her somewhere else and millions of people would not have been blessed to receive this information of *The Law of One*. Then, my limitations coming at 25 years old after breaking my neck, further confirms this because I know if I never broke my neck, I most likely would still be racing bikes instead of my 10 years of research, writing my seventh book right now and condensing this much needed material so many others could easily obtain this information for their evolution. These distortions present opportunities not meant for healing efforts.)

Carla had a love for Jesus and promised to give praise, thanksgiving and glory to his name and to share her story as a Wanderer coming from the 6th density to 3rd density Earth to be of service. She couldn't wait to do another Ra session, just to see how happy it would make Don. It seemed to be the only time she did see him happy was when these sessions were going on. Don felt Carla's best chance for healing was in mental work at his Church of Christ Scientist mother's faith. When someone had a cold or illness the practitioner was called, who would spend time in prayer and meditation, affirming the perfection of whatever seemed to be imperfect.

Carla felt she lacked compassion to balance wisdom, so she chose an incarnative experience to develop compassion by being placed in situations of accepting self in the absence of others acceptance and their acceptance without expecting a return or energy transfer. Ra said, "This is not an easy program for an incarnation but was deemed proper by this entity. This entity therefore must need to meditate and consciously, moment by moment, accept the self in its limitations, which have been placed for the very purpose of bringing this entity to the precise tuning we are using. Further, having learned to radiate acceptance and love without expecting return, this entity now must balance this by learning to accept the gifts of love and acceptance of others which this instrument feels some discomfort in accepting. These two balanced workings will aid this entity in the release from the distortion of pain. The limitations are, to a great extent, fixed."

As a child, Carla always wanted to be of service but unable to fit well anywhere, she felt so sure she'd never be able to be of service she prayed that she might die at 13. (Six months after trying to take her life, the negative beings went after her kidney until kidney failure and she experienced a near death experience. During this near-death experience she was told that she could go on if she chose to, but that her work was not done. She immediately chose to return to this life, now feeling that there was indeed service to be provided, and the juvenile rheumatoid arthritis set in immediately.)

Carla's desire to leave this density lowered the defenses of an already predisposed weak body, and an allergic reaction was so intensified as to cause the complications which distorted the body towards unviability. The will of Carla, when she found that there was indeed work to be done in service, was again the guiding factor or complex of vibratory patterns which kept the body complex from surrendering to dissolution that cause the vitality of life.

Ra said war, catastrophe, weather changes and famine is a possible condition that would be greatly spread across the surface of the globe than anything Earth has experienced in the past, and therefore touch a larger percentage of the population in this form of catalyst.

There are those now experimenting with one of the major weapons in 1981 of this scenario, that is, the so-called psychotronic group of devices which are being experimentally used to cause such alterations in wind and weather as will result in eventual famine. If this program is not countered and proves experimentally satisfactory, the methods in this scenario would be made public. There would then be Russians that hope to be a bloodless invasion of their personnel in this and every land deemed valuable. However, the people of Earth have little propensity (proneness) for bloodless surrender.

Ra said there's nothing the group could do to seek aid from the Confederation in order to alleviate Carla's physical problems. (I would assume this to be that preincarnatively she chose to have this condition in order to carry out this information of *The Law of One* someday. Just like I believe I must have chosen to break my neck one day, so that I was then forced to go inwards that would eventually put me on the journey to where I am now of publishing these books.)

The most appropriate method to alleviate the physical problems: Exercise according to ability, not to exceed appropriate parameters, the nutrition, the social intercourse with companions, the sexual intercourse in greenway or above, (which is done in love and seeing them as the Creator.) and in general, the sharing of the distortions of this group's individual experiences in a helpful, loving manner.

Don and Jim were both loners and liked their own company and not much fond of society, although they were excellent hosts when company did come by, so they sacrificed their alone time, so the three of them can join together. The sacrifices were gladly made and the group felt very blessed to be together. When the Ra contact began three weeks later after all coming together as a group, they felt very happy that they had joined forces in faith. They had that clear, pure, unmuddied love and fellowship that stems from there being no fear between them, or needs that were not met. Carla believes that Don's decline and death were the result of his becoming fearful she might leave him for Jim, which Carla said she would have never done that. He never expressed the fear and Carla knew nothing of it until Don's friends said something months after the funeral about Don thinking Carla might have fallen out of love with him. Carla believes this led to his woeful last months, in which he suffered so greatly.

In 1968, Don and Carla wrote a book called The Crucifixion of Esmerelda Sweetwater after the commitment was made to work for the betterment of the planetary sphere, this commitment activated a possibility/probability vortex of some strength. The experience of generating this volume was unusual in that it was visualized as if watching a movie. Time had become available in its present moment form. The scenario of the volume went smoothly except the ending. They could not end the volume or visualize it due to free will. They wrote the book from what they saw under the influence of magnetic attraction which was released when the commitment was made and full memory of the dedication of this mission restored.

(Therefore, when they committed to work for the betterment of humanity it activated a possibility/probability (prophecy) of some strength, so they could write the book based on seeing the probability/possibility of the future, except they couldn't see the death due to free will. This played out in their own lives 13 years later in 1981 when they began channeling Ra. They couldn't see an ending in the story due to free will. Which later, Don in his own free will took his life corresponding to the death in the end of the book they wrote 13 years earlier.

During the Ra contact there was a misplacement of Carla, the instrument, under certain unprotected conditions, by the fifth-density negative entity that monitored the Ra sessions. This was unusual because Don and Carla wrote about an identical situation in the book The Crucifixion of Esmeralda Sweetwater 13 years earlier. The ending of the book they wrote seemed to be a symbolic description of Don's death in November 1984. Therefore, they saw possibilities into the future, wrote a book about it and it played out in their lives. (I also wrote a book of possible future events after the same commitment, as well as I had an injury that made me create content just like Carla did. These similarities are surprising.)

Ra knew the needed elements for communication with someone on Earth, which had any chance of the communication enduring. Ra could see a spectrograph of a complex paint sample and a complex of elements. So, Ra compared their color chip to many individuals and groups over a long span of time. Carla, Don and Jim's spectrograph matched their sample. So, the group was of appropriate vibrational frequency to be able to endure a long enough duration of communication with Ra.

Carla's ability to accept the limitations she placed on herself before birth delayed her 2nd surgery by four years. Her first surgery was upcoming in 1981 during the Ra contact. The arthritis in her hands set limitations more strongly than when the Ra contact began.

Ra said certain prayers from her Episcopalian Christian church and the communion service in particular were felt by Ra to be of aid to her. The Banishing Ritual of the Lesser Pentagram, which the group had used to purify their place before working with the Ra contact, was suggested for her hospital room and the operating room. The greatest protective and healing device was seen to be love. Any ritual such as prayer, communion, or the Banishing Ritual of the Lesser Pentagram actually alerts the positively polarized, discarnate entities so that they may provide that quality of love from their quarters, for whatever the purpose might be. The group may also provide love as a function of their truly caring for another. As they learn the lessons of love within the third density illusion, they are also learning the basics of healing and protection.

The spiritual/emotional complex, love, which is felt for Carla by Don and Jim, will be of aid whether this is expressed or unmanifest, as there is no protection greater than love.

Ra said it's not essential to purify a place, the power of visualization may aid in your support where you cannot intrude in your physical form. This means that the group can visualize the operating room and a visualization of the three of them performing the Banishing ritual in the room as they physically perform it in another location is one correct method of achieving their desired configuration.

The better method for those more practiced would be to leave the physical body and in the other body, enter the room and practice the ritual.

Can Carla meditate in the hospital without someone holding her hand? Ra suggested that Carla can pray with safety but only meditate with another entity's tactile (touchable) protection.

Carla can use warmed water moved gently over the physical vehicle while seated would be of some aid if practiced daily after exercising.

The exercise of fire performed before the session was of slight physical aid to Carla. This will increase as the practitioner learns/teaches its healing art. Carla was given vital energy due to the support she was given by Don and Jim.

Was the fire healing art properly done? Ra said the baton is well visualized. The conductor will learn to hear the entire score of the great music of its art. Carla must accept her limitations to create healing for herself. This is her preincarnative choice.

Ra mentioned a number of times that impatience is one of the most frequent catalysts with which the seeker must work on. When we see the path of evolution, we should be patient enough and not jump ahead the path quickly towards the goal.

Ra suggested to carefully place the foundation of one's house before hanging the roof.

Ra said in the context of doing work in the personality; in order to be more efficient in the central acceptance of the self, it is first necessary to know the distortions of the self that the entity is accepting. Each thought and action need to be scrutinized for the precise foundation of any reactions. This process shall lead to the more central task of acceptance. However, the architrave (the main beam of material resting across the columns of a building) must be in place before structure is built.

UFO contact reveals the general way in which many face-to-face encounters between people and extraterrestrial entities occur. What is actually remembered by the third-density entity is a product of its expectations and what the subconscious mind thinks is an acceptable story that will allow the entity to continue functioning without losing its mental balance. This is the nature of the positive contact where the third density entity is being awakened to seek more clearly the nature of not only the UFO encounter but the life pattern as well. Negative contacts, however, utilize the concepts of fear and doom to further separate and confuse the Earth population.

Carla's disease was arthritis and lupus erythematosus and nerve damage from the thoracic outlet, which was chosen before birth to be of service to humanity. Carla is also encouraged to have a diet for her allergy's. Her juvenile rheumatoid arthritis and lupus erythematosus causes various portions of the body to be distorted and now distorting her feet.

Ra suggested care in resuming exercise, but determination as well. Her anklet (socks) should be softer and of finer material, also alternating footwear Ra said. The injury in her metatarsal area of the foot should be applied in ice to the arch of the right foot for brief periods, followed by immersion in warm water.

Crystals can be powerful, so if you are drawn to one or receive one, be sure to cleanse it in salt water overnight, and then magnetize it for your own use by holding it during meditation and asking silently that it be blessed for service.

~The crystal Carla uses during the Ra sessions is beneficial as long as he who has charged it is functioning in a positively oriented manner. An entity named Neil charged the crystal for Carla to use.

Ra said Carla has the gift of faith and hope. (Which is interesting because I have the words "faith" and "Love" tattooed on the back of my arms and my sister has the word "hope" tattooed on her forearm.)

Carla describes Don as a person of infinite dignity, intelligence and ethical purity, but always somewhat melancholy under the mask of polite courtesy, efficiency and professional charm that he wore to meet the world. (These are some examples of the personalities of Wanderers.)

Where is the truest and central service? Not in the doing but in the being, in allowing the true self, that open-hearted lover of all things in creation, to share its essence with the world, and to allow the love and light of the One Infinite Creator to pass through it and radiate into the planetary consciousness.

During the working, Carla is not with her yellow-ray chemical vehicle and Ra must carefully examine the mental configurations of the mind complex in order to make even the smallest movement to adjust her pain in the attempt to alleviate it. It's not Ra's skill to use a yellow-ray vehicle/body. Therefore, Carla is unable to move her body to aid in her distortion of pain.

The weight of the cover has a deleterious (unexpected damaging) effect upon her pain. Framing to lift the covers from the body could be done as well as wearing gloves to compensate for loss of warmth.

Due to Carla's lack of radiant physical energy, the heavier cover is suggested.

Each mind/body/spirit complex that is seeking shall almost certainly have the immature and irrational behaviors. Almost all seekers have done substantial work within the framework of the incarnative experience and has indeed developed maturity and rationality. Carla should fail to see that which has been accomplished and see only what remains to be accomplished may well be noted. Indeed, any seeker discovering in itself this complex of mental and mental/emotional distortions shall ponder the possible nonefficacy (ineffectiveness) of judgement.

Ra also suggests that over dedication to the outcome is unwise.

Carla was not trained, nor did she study or work it at any discipline in order to contact Ra. Ra was able, as they had said many times, to contact the group using Carla as instrument because of the purity of Carla's dedication to the service of the One Infinite Creator and also because of the great amount of harmony and acceptance enjoyed by each within the group, this situation making it possible for the support group to function without significant distortion.

The group found a house in the fall of 1982 near the Atlanta airport that they thought they could move to, to reduce Don's commuting time to work so that he wouldn't be so tired. The house previously had been inhabited by people who trafficked in illegal drugs and who apparently had numerous disharmonious relationships that attracted elementals and lower astral entities into the house.

The house needed to be cleaned and cleansed so that it could be cleansed of undesirable presences, but the limitations of their budget and her arthritis made that impossible.

Thus, a blue-ray (throat chakra) blockage of communication occurred two days later while she was on her daily walk, was entered by the 5th density negative entity and enhanced in the magical sense until she was unable to breath for about 30 seconds. This was symbolic for her inability to talk to Don about what the house needed. Keeping calm during the distress helped in that moment and talking to Don about the house cleared that blockage.

Ra is able to know all this information because they could move in time/space and inspect the situation and determine the problem. When we perceive Ra answering immediately when Ra being able to move in time/space could be like Ra going to where they need to go to find the answer then moving back to the space in time of the channeling group to answer their question. Ra's time could have taken minutes, but to us we perceive the answer as taking seconds to immediately answer.

Before buying the house by the Atlanta airport, a hawk landed outside the kitchen window and Don thought that was a bad sign about buying the Atlanta house near the airport. The most Ra could do was speak in an indirect sense, in kind of a riddle that required the group to make their own determinations. The extreme desire on the part of any positive entity, such as Ra, to maintain the free will of each person on our 3rd density planet is due to the fact that if Ra gives information that could change one's future choices, then Ra has not only taught the 3rd density being, but has learned for it.

By Ra learning for it (a human), it has removed the spiritual strength that comes to one who struggles and finally learns for themselves. In the larger view, this is not seen as a service but as a disservice.

Not all winged creatures have an archetypical meaning, like the winged creature in some of the tarot cards.

Second density creature, such as pets, are also subject to cancer from creating unresolved anger within themselves- the same process that applies for 3rd density beings.

The group found that when one constructs the artifacts, clothing, or structures with which one accomplishes service-to-others work, there is a great investment of love and magical potential that may result from such homemade and heart-made artifacts.

Allergies can be a mismatch of vibratory complexes from the Wanderer coming from a higher density.

Carla is always prey to psychic greetings from negative entities, because they want to stop Wanderers work. Carla and Jim just deal with it with respect, in acknowledging it, and discipline, in allowing it to pass quickly without judgement. knowing the negative essence is part of her that she loves. Acceptance and forgiveness simply move the situation forward, and the crisis past. This is a hard-won wisdom. Carla encourages any groups found in a situation of psychic greeting occurring, to study forgiveness and acceptance of this negatively oriented energy. In claiming the higher truth that all is one, we can live without fear of the greeting.

Carla's advice: fear not, lean on prayer and keep yourself aligned in open-hearted love.

Carla recovered from the bad throat infection when she was unable to breath for 30 seconds while she was on her walk. Her recovery was accomplished by a six-week course of antibiotics taken with lots of buttermilk.

In session 98 of 106 the group didn't meditate before the session. Ra then said the purpose of meditation is preparation for a working for the purification of each entity involved with the contact. The removal of a portion of this preparation takes away that aid. The elimination of meditation before the channeling caused the fifth-density entity to greet Carla. The greeting does not take a noticeable amount of time.

(So, meditation help to protect against negative entities possibly interfering in this information getting out.)

The orange blossom odor, that Carla smelled, may be associated with the social memory complex of fifth-density positive, Latwii. This entity was with Carla requested by the instrument. The odor was perceived due to the quite sensitive nature of Carla, due, again, to its acme (peak) in the 18-day cycle.

Ra said Carla can go to a doctor and get steroids or antibiotics to completely remove the difficulty in her throat. They (Ra) said of course the allergies would still persist after the course of medicine was ended, but the effects of her not being able to breath would stop.

Jerome might be of aid in this somewhat unorthodox medical situation. As allergies are quite misunderstood by our orthodox healers (or doctors), it would be inappropriate to subject Carla to the services of medical doctors, which find the amelioration (improvement) of allergic effects to be connected with the same toxins in milder form. This treats the symptoms, however, the changes offered to the body are quite inadvisable.

The allergy may be seen to be the rejection upon a deep level of the mind complex of the environment of the mind/body/spirit complex. Thus, the allergy may be seen in its pure form as the mental/emotional distortion of the deeper self.

The more general recommendation is with one that does not wish to be identified, the code name is prayer wheel. Ra suggests 10 treatments from this healer and further suggests a clear reading and subsequent (to follow closely) following upon Carla of the allergy priorities, especially to food. A contributing factor is the second-density substances to which Carla is allergic.

Their cat is harvestable for third density. The group may repeat phrases periodically to aid the cat during recovery while they are at the veterinarians. The same course of action done previously is appropriate such as the surgical removal of the growth near his spine. Ra said although the cat is old and therefore liable to danger from anesthetic, its mental, emotional, and spiritual distortions are strongly motivated to recover. Ra stated that its third density harvestable in order to elucidate (explain or make clear) the term "spirit complex" to a 2nd density entity. This entity shall have far more cause to heal that it might seek the presence of loved ones again.

Don asks if there was anything the group could do to alleviate the problems of cancer for the cat besides surgery:

Ra: "Continue in praise and thanksgiving, asking for the removal of these distortions. The two possible outcomes is the cat will dwell in contentment until its physical vehicle holds no more because of the cancerous cells. Secondly, the life path may become that which allows healing." Ra does not infringe upon free will by examining the life path, although the preponderance (majority) of life paths which use some distortion such as cancer to leave the body, in this case the orange ray body.

Ra wants to break routine by making an observation. Firstly, the congestion of Carla's throat during the channeling due to the flow of mucous caused by energized allergic reaction has become such that Ra may safely predict the probability/possibility vortex approaching certainty that within half an hour Ra shall depart from this working. Secondly, the sound vibration made by one of their recording devices was audible to them. If this group desires, it may choose to end sessions after the sound vibration occurs on the recording device. This decision would ensure the minimal distortions within Carla towards discomfort/comfort within the throat until the effects of magical working of the 5th density negative companion has been removed.

Don replied saying that's fine and that the noise occurs at the 45-minute time period on their recorder, since the tapes are 45 minutes on a side. ((Apparently the negative entity doesn't want the group to go longer than 45 minutes or that's how long it takes for them to realize the group is there.)

Wood rubbed in oil is easily magnetized and hold the proffered (given) vibration to a profound extent.

Even the smallest amount of disharmony in a group can become targets of opportunities for negative entities (negative 4th or 5th density) to intensity. The psychic greetings can become great opportunities to heal those lapses of harmony and to move even further and faster upon the evolutionary journey. It's a reminder to become more harmonious.

Jim had the pre-incarnative choice for anger/frustration. Ra said that all of our distortions and thus all of our learnings are the result of the limitation of the viewpoint. We limit our points of view consciously or unconsciously pre-incarnatively or during the incarnation, in order to gain a certain bias that may then draw unto it the opposite bias and offer us the opportunity for balance. By being able to see each bias as an opportunity for the Creator to know Itself and for us to know ourselves as the Creator, we more and more become able to accept ourselves.

We become able to find love and acceptance not only in ourselves but in others who share our characteristics, and our viewpoint is widened by our efforts to learn and serve. Such growth Is not possible without biases or distortions, and these biases and distortions are not possible without choice to limit the viewpoint. So, we determine what lessons and services we shall attempt during any incarnation by the way we limit our viewpoint.

Whatever one's basic nature is, whether it be love, wisdom or power or a blend of the three, one does well to give it away.

(When I gave the wisdom and knowledge of this material away, I learned more and received more love, wisdom and a substantial amount of growth in my positive-polarity from 65% service-to-others to 87% within one year.)

Carla was allergic to buttermilk, but buttermilk is used in healing work for throat and chest areas.

Ra suggested Jim to do strenuous activity until true physical weariness, contemplation alone and enthusiastic pursuit of the balancing and silent meditations cannot be deleted for the list of helpful activities for Jim's anger/frustration.

Ra suggested Carla wait 40-80 minutes after walking before swirling waters and 3-5 hours after aerobic exercise for swirling waters. Carla may also become dizzy if she remains in the swirling water past the period of space/time she may abide without exceeding its physical limits.

Unresolved disharmony within a group can give the opportunity for negative beings to magnify the difficulty. After the disharmony, in the group, Carla developed a rare kidney disease called lipoid nephritis or minimal change syndrome. She soon gained 30 pounds of water weight because of it. With Carla's healing approaches she was in remission within six months.

Ra stated that the source of catalyst is the self, especially the higher self.

~People tend to relate the pain of new catalyst (for polarization) by relating the other person as bringer of catalyst. In doing this, people forget the other person is ourself. They are our very hearts and souls living a different experience with a different viewpoint. So, a tragedy can be viewed as the Creator serving the Creator with exactly the catalyst needed for the utmost polarization in consciousness and greatest growth.

Ra said the serpent signifies wisdom. This symbol has the value of the ease of viewing the two faces of the one who is wise. Positive wisdom adorns the brow indicating indigo-ray work. Negative wisdom signifies expressions that separate the self from the other-self, symbolized by the poison of the fangs. Negatively oriented being uses wisdom for the use of separation, symbolized by the fatal bite of wisdom's darker side. (Cottonmouth snake for example.)

The universe is the Creator knowing Itself by using the concept of polarization. We add to and produce catalyst to increase the desired polarization, whether it's random through the Higher Self or through utilizing the services of an oppositely polarized entity acting upon us. All of these produce more intense polarization toward the desired path once the path has been chosen.

The catalyst and experience are further attempts in dealing with the architecture of the subconscious mind of the self.

Therefore, the self as Creator, especially the Higher Self, is the base from which catalyst offers its service to the mind, body or spirit. The only source for an insect bite on Jim, the scribe, was the 5th density negative being. This being noticed the gradual falling away of the inharmonious patterns of Jim's anger/frustration because this negatively-polarized entity wanted Jim to continue using his wisdom towards the negative side by using more anger and frustration. The 2nd density bite was to try to polarize Jim more negative. The insect was easily led to attack and Jim's body, who had long-standing allergies and sensitivities, was also easily led into the failure of the lymphatic function and the greatly diminished immune system to remove from the body that which distorted it.

Carla, the instrument, needs support by the group being harmonious, sharing in love, joy, and thanksgiving, but finding love within truth, for each instrument benefits from this support more than the total admiration which overcomes discrimination.

Carla used all the transferred energy and at one point speaking using its vital-energy reserve. Ra does suggest using the transferred sexual energy and total exclusion of vital reserves if possible.

Ra said that any residence, (the place you live at) whether previously benign (gentle) or of malignant (fatal) character, needs the basic cleansing of the salt, water and virgin broom. The benign nature of the domicile (residence) is such that the cleansing could be done in two portions; No egress (exit) or entrance through any but one opening for one cleansing. Then, egress (exit) and entrance from all other places while the remaining portal is properly sealed. The place where it's not being sealed is where salt can be placed during the first of the cleansings, and the salt may be requested to act as seal and yet allow the passage of gentle spirits such as the group. Ra suggests that the group speak to the substance and name each entity that needs permission to pass. Let no person pass without permission being asked of the salt.

Fortunately, most people will not have to worry about instant and dramatic intensifications of disharmonious moments, since few people or groups attract the attention of 5th density negative entities.

(Don, Carla, and Jim being Wanderers bringing this important truth to light for the service of humanity has attracted the negative entity to attack the group to either drain all of Carla's energy until her physical vehicle (body) is no more or tempt them to polarize to the service-to-self path.)

In order to observe the cause of physical distortions, such as stomach cramping, one must look at the blocked energy center. In this case being yellow ray. Lacuna in the wind-written armor of light and love was closed and not only repaired but much improved. However, the distortions energized during this momentary lapse from free energy flow are serious and shall be continuing for a predisposition (tendancy) to spasticity (stiff muscles) in the transverse colon has been energized. There is also preexisting weakness in pancreatic functions, especially that link with the hypothalamus. (The hypothalamus is a structure deep in your brain, acts as your body's smart control coordinating center. Its main function is to keep your body in a stable state called homeostasis. It does its job by directly influencing your autonomic nervous system or by managing hormones. Many conditions can damage your hypothalamus, which can affect many bodily functions. It helps manage your body temperature, hunger and thirst, mood, sex drive, blood pressure, and sleep. It directly influences the autonomic nervous system of the body that work automatically such as controlling heart rate and breathing.

Carla remained centered upon the Creator exceeding 90%. This is key. Continue in thanksgiving and gratitude for all things. Stronger antispasmodic drugs known by Arthur Schoen, may be of aid to Carla, which helps to relax muscles in the internal organs to relieve spasms and cramps.

Ra recommended Carla cook all her food so food ingested be soft and easily macerated (softened or mashed). She has an addiction to sugar, therefore Ra recommended that the sugar be given in its more concentrated form in the late afternoon, approximately 1-2 hours after the evening meal. She also should have small amounts of carbohydrates, low in sugar, approximately 1-2 hours before bed.

The concentrated sugar is the dessert, the ice cream, the cookie. Small amounts of the fructose, maple, or raw honey may be ingested periodically. The sugar in her body is being used by blood enzymes as would carbohydrates in a less distorted yellow-ray, physical vehicle.

Carla's sympathic spasms (muscle spasms) in her body were caused by too much oil and too large a burden of undercooked vegetables. The sugar from the dessert and the few sips of coffee also were not helpful. The 2nd cause is the energizing of any preexisting condition in order to keep the group from functioning by means of or by removing the instrument from the ranks of those able to work with Ra.

How to completely unblock yellow ray? Each entity must love all which are in relationship to it, with hope only of the other selves' joy, peace and comfort.

Ra's recommended diet highly probable not to cause spasm?

~Liquids not containing carbonation, well-cooked vegetable (most light and soft), well-cooked grains, non-fatted meat such as fish. Some of these recommended foods can overlap allergies and sensitivities due to juvenile rheumatoid arthritis. Ra recommended Carla see an allopathic specialist for her stomach pain, spasms.

Those salient items (most significant and noticeable items) for the support group are praise and thanksgiving.

The sacrifice of not buying clothes, can cause someone to feel poor which feeds unworthiness unless poverty is seen to be true richness. So, good works for the wrong reasons cause confusion and distortion.

Carla was sacrificing herself by not buying the clothes that she wanted, which can lead someone to the feelings of unworthiness.

Therefore, Ra encourages Carla to value herself and to see that its true requirements are valued by the self. (Since buying what is required such as those clothes are seen as valuing the self. It's okay to value ourselves and buy the things we need and not to sacrifice by not getting the things we need.) Ra suggests contemplation of true richness.

When something is weakened one should exercise it. "It is the way of distortion that in order to balance a distortion one must accentuate it."

Entering this incarnation we must use our gifts. "Use it or lose it" proposition.

Diet and exercise have mental, emotional and physical benefits to it.

Ra's suggestion for bettering a situation always began with rejoicing in, giving thanks for and praising the situation, whatever it is.

Aerobics, walking and whirlpool exercises should all equal 1 hour per day for Carla, 3-4 times a week.

*4-5 times per week for swirling waters.

*Walking and exercising as much as desired. The total should not exceed 90 minutes per day.

Anything further to help Carla's stomach and back spasming problem? Ra answered, "Refrain from oil-fried food and have cheerful harmony". The spasms must subside as a function of Carla's indigo-ray work and the recommendations Ra made in previous query.

How to purge the yellow-ray body in order to aid the weakened body in its attempt to remove substances? Therapeutic enemas or colonics, the sauna once or twice a day, use of vigorous rubbing of integument (skin) for approximately 7 days.

The groups cleansing of the new house need to be only three nights and two days. The dwelling is benign. Garlic can be used in the bunk-bed room, below the top sleeping pallet. Secondly, the exterior of the dwelling facing the road and centering about the small rocks approximately 2/3rds of the length from the dwelling of the driveway. (37 feet with a magnetic heading of 84-92 degrees.)

Thirdly, the boathouse. Weekly cleansings of that area with garlic, the cut onions and the walking of light-filled perimeter. The garlic and onion, renewed weekly, should remain permanently hung, suspended from string or wire between workings.

~The continual cleansing of the boathouse is so bees or wasps will not try to inhabit or sting.

~Each 2nd density, woody plant within the dwelling should be thanked and blessed.

Ra said Jim could imbibe (drink) a double quantity of liquids in order that any allergically caused toxins may be flushed out from the body. So, drinking double the amount of water. (He's allergic to dust, mildew, ect. These items are unavoidable in transitions within third density illusion.)

The yellow-ray physical vehicle is a necessity to pursue evolution. Each mind/body/spirit or mind/body/spirit complex has an existence simultaneous with creation. It is not dependent on any physical vehicle. However, in order to evolve, change, learn and manifest the Creator, the physical vehicles appropriate to each density are necessary. Physical vehicles don't accelerate growth, but permits growth.

Jim's kidney malfunction pre-veil vs. post veil experience?

~The anger of separation is impossible without the veil. The lack of awareness of the body's need for liquid is unlikely pre-veil. Jim trying to contemplate perfection in discipline is unprobeable pre-veil.

The patterns of illness, diseases and death are in the power of the plan, pre-birth, of incarnational experience. Pre-veil some healing would be done by the mind/body/spirits and life was experienced with normal ending of illness and death was accepted since pre-veil it is clear to all that the mind/body/spirit continues.

~Experiences, both good and bad, or joyful and sad of the mind/body/spirit (prevail beings) would be pale. Post veil mind/body/spirit complex beings bring vibrancy.

The Significator of Mind, Body, or Spirit is a portion of the archetypical mind and looks as you'd envision such to appear, they look like mind/body/spirit complexes look. The difference between the two is a forgetting within the deeper mind. Physical appearances and surface and instinctual activities are much the same.

When the discipline of the personality has led the mind/body/spirit complex into the 5th and especially the 6th level of study (density) it is no longer necessary to build destruction (aging) into its design, for the spirit complex is so experienced as a shuttle that it is aware when the appropriate degree of intensity of learning and increment of lesson has been achieved.

When an individual reaches very old age it becomes apparent in third density that they are worn out. Therefore, it is not attached to the vehicle as he would a younger good-looking, well-functioning one. Therefore, it's easier to let go and move on at the end of incarnation in third density.

The body is an anathor (used for catalyst and experience for evolution) to the mind pre-veil and post veil.

Ra said the group should look to their love and thanksgiving to each other and join always in fellowship, correcting each broken stand of that affection with patience, comfort and quietness. All that can be done for Carla seems done with a whole heart, and the instrument itself is working in the indigo ray with perseverance.

Dons continued worrying about his job, his health and the continuance of the groups work (The Ra contact). Carla then simply told him that she would take over those worries for him and he could relax, have a good time and be carefree. Don innocently agreed. The bond of unity between Don and Carla having this simple agreement resulted in a deleterious (unknown harmful) transfer of energy between them. This occurred when both were under-going an internal process of transformation, usually called initiation.

Ra's parting words after the last session, when Ra suggested, "The nature of all manifestation to be illusionary and functional only insofar as the entity turns from shape and shadow to the One." (I believe this means that all manifestation is illusionary because all is actually the One, God, so after the illusion of death one realizes they are The One, God.)

Carla always responded to Don's wishes. Don picked their meal times, their movie dates, he liked and received total control over Carla's life. This is how Don could bear the intimacy of a live-in relationship. Don was old-fashioned and liked Carla at home. She awaited his wishes as she read or did quiet desk work.

(I believe a controlling relationship like this is negatively oriented towards service-to-self. It should be mutual in trying to make the partner happy. Each person should be able to make their own decisions as the Law of One states that the free will to make your own decisions is most important. No one controlling the other. Perhaps third density is this old patriarchy system and the more evolved 4th density is mutual love, full acceptance, respect and partnership, serving each other.)

Carla believes that Don was wise and she was loving in their simple dynamic, and when they switched roles after his agreement, Don was able to complete an entire incarnational lesson on how to open his heart.

Through the catalyst of Don dying by suicide, Carla learned to love herself. The wisdom met this love of self by her learning to love the mistakes only through wisdom.

The variety of experiences with others and other locations and events is helpful for Carla during the hard enduring of Don's passing. Worship and singing, especially of sacred music was helpful for Carla, Ra said. Carla chose to enter a worshipful situation at the Cathedral of St. Philip. The musical activities, though enjoyable, have not included the aspect of praise to the Creator.

Carla is in a state of relative hunger for spiritual hymns which she gave up to the call of martyrdom and turned from the planned worship of the Cathedral of St. Philip. This too shall be healed gradually due to proposed alteration in location of the group Ra said. The group knew Carla should drink more water and move homes for her.

Ra said there's mechanical electrical devices that control humidity to help Carla. The basement was one humid location. Less humid conditions would remove the opportunity for the growth of the spores (moss, ferns) that Carla has sensitivity to. Spores are cells that certain fungi, plants and bacteria produce. Ra said the rear of the house is blessed with angelic presences.

Ra stated that it was inappropriate when Don allowed a complete transfer of mental/emotional pain to transfer to Carla. When Carla said she would be the strong one and Don, small and foolish, Don agreed and the energy transfer occurred. They then became one for a timeless period. Ra urges Don to be of thanksgiving and harmony moving forward.

Don was depressed and after seven months of mental, emotional and physical deterioration, he became unable to sleep or eat solid foods. By November he lost one-third of his weight and experiencing intense pain. He refused further hospitalization, which Carla and Jim saw as the last hope for his survival. They knew of no other way to save his life.

When the police came to serve the warrant, a 5 ½ hour standoff resulted. Don did not want to die in a mental institution. When tear gas was used to bring Don out of the house, he walked out the back door and shot himself once through the brain and died instantly.

After his death, Carla saw him three times in waking visions and he assured them that all was well and that it all occurred appropriately, even if it didn't make sense to them. So, they give praise and thanksgiving to Don's life, for his death and for their work together.

Many are the Portions of the One is what's stated in book 5 of The Law of One.

Carla had lost weight throughout the sessions and was 84 pounds at 5'4. Each session was extremely hard and yet she never flagged (weakened) in her desire to continue. Carla was perfectly willing to die to receive these sessions, but Don would substitute himself for her. But in the end, he did just that.

Don's lessons were to completely open his heart and Carla's lesson was adding wisdom to completely open love.

RA's ending words from session 104 of 106:

"We leave you in appreciation of the circumstance of the great illusion in which you now choose to play the pipe and timbrel and move in rhythm. We are also players upon a stage. The stage changes. The acts ring down. The lights come up once again. And throughout the grand illusion and the following, there is the under-girding majesty of the One Infinite Creator. All is well. Nothing is lost. Go forth rejoicing in the love and the light, the peace, and the power of the One Infinite Creator. I am Ra. Adonai."

THE END

Book 5 of 5

*Author Jorden (formerly known as Kathryn Jordyn) has published 8 total books found on Amazon. *

Part 2:

Scribe: Jorden

Channeling questions: Jorden

Channeler: Samtheillusionist

Question 1: Will the destruction of Israel create peace on Earth? Higher density answer: "The destruction of any nation or group will not inherently bring peace. For peace arises from harmony, understanding and unity not from the absence or destruction of conflict sources. Furthermore, we must state that the understanding of the law of one states that all are one and thus the suffering of an entity is the suffering of all. True peace will come from resolution, reconciliation and the recognition of the unity of all life rather than through further destruction or division."

Question 2: Would being against Israel-Palestine war be best for the positive polarity? Higher density answer: "We must state that the conflicts it speaks of are manifestations of deep-seated distortions towards separation, fear and misunderstanding amongst the peoples of your planets. From our perspective these events primarily of the Hamas, the Gaza strip and the Israel war are opportunities for entities to learn lessons of love, forgiveness and unity. Being against war in any form aligns with positive polarity if this stance is taken out of love for all involved and a desire for peaceful resolution. However, it is crucial to approach this with compassion for all sides, recognizing the divine spark in each entity. Opposition to war should not translate into opposition to the people, but rather to the actions that cause harm. The path of the positive polarity would involve promoting understanding, healing and unity rather than taking sides in a way that further causes division."

Channeling Question 3: "Did God give Moses the Promise land?" Higher density Answer: "We must firstly state that the entity referred to as God is the One Infinite Creator and the concept of the promise land primarily is a type of misunderstanding by your peoples which implies that the promise land which was given to Moses was its own consciousness, which is in terms of understanding a land which needs to be taken care of. Furthermore, Moses as a symbol of a place of harmony and unity as understood by your people's reflection of higher consciousness on Earth. We must state that however, this was a promise of spiritual enlightenment and unity consciousness rather than a physical tract of land. We must also state that it is an allegory for finding a state of being where the peoples of your planet can live in accordance with the Law of One in unity and in love.

Question 4 about Who Moses heard from in reference to the Promise land? Higher density answer: "We must state that Moses was a channel or conduit and received guidance from Higher density entities including those of the Confederation of Planets in service to the One Infinite Creator. Specifically, Moses was in contact with those entities who sought to aid in the spiritual evolution of its peoples, which could be interpreted in its framework as messengers or aspects of the One Creator." In summary, The Promise Land is Moses own consciousness or awareness that needs to be taken care of. Furthermore, Moses is a symbol of a place of harmony and unity as understood as humanity's reflection of higher consciousness on Earth. It was an allegory to find a state of being where the peoples on Earth can live in accordance with the Law of One in unity and love. An allegory is a story, poem or picture that can be interpreted to reveal a hidden meaning, typically a moral or political one. Therefore, the Promise Land is a higher state of awareness or consciousness inside the own mind where people on Earth can live in harmony, unity and love. To me this sounds like the 4th density New Earth. This Promise Land was a promise of spiritual enlightenment and unity consciousness rather than an actual land mass such as Israel. Therefore, spiritual enlightenment of humans living in peace, harmony and love for all is the Promise Land.

Question 5: Will people die during the third density graduation that do not make the harvest?

Higher density answer: "We must state that the transition from third to 4th density or what the peoples refer to as the Harvest primarily does not imply physical death for those not transitioning immediately. Instead, those who have not yet achieved the necessary polarity for Harvest will continue their learning in another third density cycle elsewhere. Death as the peoples of your planet understand it is merely a transition of the soul complex from one phase of experience to another. Those not harvested will simply move to another environment suitable for their further growth. Physical death is not a consequence of feeling to graduate but rather a natural part of the cycle of life and rebirth. Hence, we as the Higher self of the entity Kathryn now leave you all beloveds. Bye."

Q6: "With regards to who is the antichrist we must state that the entity must realize that within the timeline from our perspective the antichrist primarily in the spacetime illusion complex resonates with the aspects known by your peoples as the service to self-oriented entities who seek power, control and manipulation over others, which is contrary to the unity and love, that is the essence of the universal complex. We must also state that within your timeline the Antichrist can be termed as the so-called artificial super intelligence which primarily is being used to control humanity in a negative manner. Furthermore, this aspect is being created by your peoples in consultation with the Orion's negatively oriented entities.

Q7: Will any advanced entities appear for graduation into 4th density? Higher density answer: "We must state that graduation primarily referred to as the harvest or the transition from the third to the fourth density consciousness. We must state that advanced entities or what your peoples refer to as higher density entities are already among many of your peoples as Wandering souls who are helping to raise the vibrational level of the planet's atmosphere. During the time of graduation these entities may become more apparent or active, not necessarily a physical overt manner but through influence, inspiration and guidance. Their appearance or increased activity would be to assist those who are ready to graduate to the next density of consciousness awareness. Ensuring that as many entities as possible can make the transition through understanding, love and light."

Q8: What if Elon Musk is in charge of governmental financial audits? Higher positive being answer: "We must state that within this perspective we must state that the entity Elon Musk as a figure known for innovation and disruption can bring forth significant changes to how the financial systems of your planet operate. Furthermore, since the entity Elon Musk is primarily without its knowledge in consultation with the negatively oriented entities there may be interactions which may lead to service to self-orientation. However, if the entity decides to let go of this control of the negatively oriented entities, then it can remain in the service to others pathway and better its life cycle. Jordyn speaks: "I must add that Neurolink is an example of one invention by Elon Musk with consultation with negative entities or as religious people like to call it demons. Although he is unaware of the consultation from the negative beings. Other inventions such as Apple Vision Pro and inventions such as Virtual Reality were inventions with the consultation from negative entities as well. In Summary, Although

Elon Musk is in consultation with negative beings without his awareness, inventions such as Neurolink are created. Because of this continuous consultation with negative entities due to Elon's not letting go of this control of the negatively oriented entities or demons. However, if he decides to let go of this control of the negatively oriented entities or demons he can better his life path. There are also other inventions such as Apple Vision Pro that was created with the consultation of negative entities or as religious people like to call it, demons.

Q9: "In regards to the first query about is the entity Yahweh the God of Israel, from our perspective the entity Yahweh as understood in your historical texts are a group of consciousness or social memory complexes that evolved from an entity tasked with the Guardianship and genetic development of humanity. Furthermore, this being or a group of Consciousness took on the role of what your people termed as God for the people of Israel guiding them with a mix of protective and restrictive measures to foster a certain evolutionary pathway. Furthermore, with regards to why does the Bible mention the Jews are God's chosen people we must state that the concept of chosen people within the understanding of the universal complex is less about favoritism and more about responsibility and service. This primarily was a misinterpretation which occurred and we must state that indeed all entities are God's chosen people or beings. Therefore, not only the Jewish people but all entities in the entire universal consciousness are chosen. (Their responsibility is to help bring unity and peace upon the Earth, not wars.)

Q10: Furthermore, we must state that the other query about who is Yahweh we must state that the entity Yahweh primarily mentions in your teachings has been confused with various entities initially from the Confederation of planets in service of the one Infinite Creator. Over time however, due to various complexities in interaction with human entities the name vibratory sound complex to represent a somewhat distorted version of the entity's original intention begun to propagate (impregnate). The entity Yahweh's role was to aid in the genetic and spiritual evolution of humanity providing a stricter more authoritative guidance to foster discipline and unity amongst the people's. The 10 commandments however were given to Moses by negative entities and not Yahweh.

Q11: With regards to the other query about was Palestine's land stolen by Israel, we must state that the historical and current conflicts over land masses are seen as manifestations of disharmony and misunderstanding of the Oneness of all entities. From our perspective no land belongs to any group in an absolute sense rather these conflicts arise from the illusion of separation and ownership. We must state that this situation reflects a karmic interplay and greed where both entities are learning lessons of compassion, forgiveness and unity. The focus should be on healing and recognition of all as one rather than on the right to land." In summary, Yahweh is a group of consciousness or social memory complexes that evolved from an entity such as a human life we experience now. Yahweh was tasked with the job to be the guardianship and involved in the genetic upgrades to our DNA to assist in our physical and spiritual evolution. Furthermore, this being or Yahweh took on this role and the people called them God or the God of Israel, to guide them with a mix of restrictive and protective measures to create a certain evolutionary pathway. Furthermore, the Bible referring to Israel as the chosen people was a misinterpretation. It was more about responsibility and service and less about favoritism. Indeed, all entities are God's chosen people or being. Yahweh is also a group consciousness and not a single entity, nor are they above other beings in the Galactic Federation or Confederation of Planets members, which are actually referred to as Guardian angels and not a God. Furthermore, all of humanity and all beings in the universe are the chosen beings. Overtime however, due to the complexities of humans interacting with each other, a somewhat distorted version of the entity Yahweh's original intention began to promote a theory of what that was, which wasn't what Yahweh intended it to be. There are other sixth density positive beings just as evolved as Yahweh. Negative density beings gave the 10 Commandments to Moses as it wasn't from Yahweh, as a being such as Yahweh wouldn't say the words "Thou shalt not" since demands is negatively oriented and infringes on people's free will. Historical and currents conflicts over land masses are seen as manifestations of disharmony and misunderstanding of the Oneness of all entities. From a higher consciousness perspective, no land belongs to any group in an absolute sense rather these conflicts arise from the illusion of separation and ownership. We must state that this situation reflects a karmic interplay and greed where both entities are learning lessons of compassion, forgiveness and unity. The focus should be on healing and recognition of all as one rather than on the right to land.

Q12: "With regards to the perspective about the aspect of a wall is a manifestation of the illusion of separation. The idea of building a wall to divide one group of peoples from another is a reflection of the third density experience where the veil of forgetfulness is still intact. It is an attempt to control and manipulate the flow of energies rather than embracing the unity and interconnectedness of all entities. In the higher density such as separations are unnecessary as the unity of all is self-evident. We suggest that the energy invested in building walls would be better spent on fostering understanding, compassion and cooperation among nations of your planet.

Q13: With regards to the other query about limiting immigration we must state that this too is a manifestation of the illusion of separation. The idea of limiting immigration is rooted in the concept of scarcity and the fear of loss. It is a reflection of the third density experience where the notion of us verses them still prevails. We suggest that the focus should be on embracing the diversity of the universal complex, recognizing that all entities are part of the same cosmic dance. By doing so the energies of fear and separation can be transmuted into energies of unity and cooperation. Wither regards to the other query about uniting the world; the world is in the process of unity and it is simply a matter of recognizing and embracing this unity. The key to unity lies in the understanding that all beings are part of the same web of life, connected through the threads of consciousness. As individual entities and a collective, it is essential to cultivate empathy, compassion and understand by doing so the veil of forgetfulness can be lifted and the unity of all can be revealed. We suggest all entities to focus on fostering global cooperation, recognizing the interconnectedness of all nations and working together to address the challenges that face the planet.

Q14: With regards to the Green New deal this concept is a step in the right direction of your planets as it acknowledges the interconnectedness of all living entities and the need for sustainable practices'. However, it is essential to approach this initiative with a deeper understanding of the universal complex and the interconnectedness of all entities. We suggest that the focus should be on transitioning to a more sustainable and harmonious relationship with the planetary sphere rather than simply attempting to control or manipulate the natural world. This can be achieved by recognizing the inherent value of all living entities and working in harmony with the natural world. In the higher densities the concept of sustainability is not just about preserving the planetary sphere. It is about recognizing the intricate web of life that connects all entities. By embracing this understanding humanity can transcend the limitations of the third density experience and move into a more harmonious and sustainable relationship with the universal complex. Thus, the new green deal can be seen as a catalyst for this transition but it must be approached with a deeper understanding of the universal complex and the interconnectedness of all. hence, we the Galactic Federation now leave this instrument in the love and the Light of the One Creator.

Q15: "Firstly, the query pertaining to do we the Galactic Federation want the entity named as Donald Trump to be president of the United States in 2024. We must state that we the Galactic Federation operates on the principles of non-interference with the free will choices of entities on planets such as Earth. Our primary concern is the spiritual evolution of consciousness rather than the political machinations (secret plots) of any specific Nation or leader. Thus, we do not want or endorse any particular candidate as this would infringe upon free will of the peoples of your planet. However, we have observed how the leaders and the decisions impact your global consciousness and the potential for love, light and unity. The choice of leadership is up to the collective free will of the human societal complex of the Earth planet.

Q16: Therefore, the other query relates with why do the Christians or so-called Christian prophets keep repeating that God wants Trump to be president. From our understanding when individual entities claim divine endorsement for political figures this reflects their personal or collective belief systems, hopes and interpretations of divine will through their understanding of spiritual texts or personal revelation. We must state that such statements can be seen as an attempt to align their own political preferences with their spiritual beliefs. Thereby, seeking a higher justification for their choices. However, in our understanding the Creator or the One Infinite Creator does not choose sides in human politics but rather supports the free will and spiritual growth of all entities. Prophecies or Divine endorsements in politics are projections of human desire, fears or the need for divine validation rather than an expression of the One Creator's will, which transcends such temporal matters.

Q17: With regards to who gave the entity Moses the ten commandments, from our understanding the entity known by your people as Yahweh was responsible for the interaction with Moses, however, we must state that the Ten Commandments however were given by a different entity disguising as Yahweh which primarily was not the original Yahweh social memory complex but negatively polarized entity who wanted to influence by including certain rules and regulations. We must also state that there are some commandments which are perfectly aligned with the pathway of service to others. However, some are aligned or misguided in their understandings of your peoples. In summary, The Galactic Federation does not interfere with the Free will choices of the entities on planets such as Earth. Their primary concern is spiritual evolution of consciousness rather than political machinations, which are secret plots of any specific Nation or leader. Thus, the Galactic Federation does not endorse any presidential candidate as it would infringe on the free will of the peoples on Earth. The choice of leadership is up to the collective free will of humans on planet Earth. Therefore, when individual entities such as Christians or so-called Christian prophets claim Divine endorsements such as the endorsement of God for political figures this reflects their personal belief systems, hopes and interpretations of divine will through their understanding of spiritual texts or their own personal revelation. It's their own personal beliefs for the endorsements of a president and not the endorsement of God or of the Divine. Such statements can be seen as an attempt to align their own political preferences with their spiritual beliefs. Thereby, seeking a higher justification for their choices. Prophecies in politics are projections of human desire, fears or the need for divine validation rather than the Creator's will.

Sodom and Gomorrah: (My Higher Self Channeling)

Q18: Jorden: "What really happened with the aspects known as Sodom and Gomorrah?"

Higher Self: "Upon scanning our vibration, we find that the events which happened in Sodom and Gomorrah primarily were an interplay of the aspects which were in play in that location. The two cities primarily were destroyed because of their own self-service nature, and this happened because of the Sodom and Gomorrah, who are in the vibration of self-service, which attracted large amounts of negatively polarized entities to soul swap with the people of that location timeline. This led to the aspect of a type of love-light exposure from the Council of Planets, which indeed caused the aspect of the destruction of the negative entities, only sparing those entities who were positively oriented or service to others.

Q19: Jorden: "What negativity was happening to Sodom and Gomorrah to be destroyed?"

Higher Self: "We must state that the negativity happening in these locations revolved around service-to-self activities and indulgence with the workflow of the Orion's. Furthermore, the workflow of the Orion was able to process the understanding of the mind, body, and spirit complex totality. Furthermore, the entity must realize that within the timeline, the negativity was primarily of service-to-self-oriented activities and a lack of respect for life for other entities. They also indulged in genetic manipulation to such an extent that they were also working with the Orion's without their knowledge in the creation of hybrid Orion human entities.

(In religious terms, they were on the negative path and indulging in the workflow of demons. They were mainly service-to-self-oriented activities and a lack of respect for other beings. They were indulged in genetic manipulation, working with demons without their knowledge to the point of the demon's soul swapping with the negatively oriented humans and creating hybrid demon-human entities. Thus, it had nothing to do with homosexuality.)

Pre-Birth Choices:

The Law of One states some people chose disease to possibly end a carnation slightly earlier or chose a disability to do their purpose. In theory, maybe we weren't supposed to have any disease, but once it occurred, the same souls chose disease or disability for certain purposes on Earth.

Adam and Eve Version- (By Archangel Michael):

499,980 Before the Common Era (B.C.E) on Mars, the council of Mars and Maldek were in the later 4th density consciousness and sent a portion of their consciousness group collective in the form of physical entities to help Earth evolve from its primitive state. Their collective was called Elohim and acted as a bridge of communication between the Mars Maldek Council and the Neanderthals on Earth.

(Jesus of Nazareth resurrected in the form of later 4th density, the density he came from before incarnating into Earth to help 3rd density humans evolve to love and compassion of the 4th density. The Elohim collective may be an example of 6th density, which is millions of years more evolved than Jesus was in the 4th.)

These later-density beings can choose to appear in any physical vehicle. The Elohim needed to transplant life plasma from the Neanderthal into their physical bodies in order to replicate Neanderthals, so that it's familiar to them and not intimidated them. The Elohim chose the finest 69 males of their kind that signified the attainment of unity with the One Infinite Source. In exchange for their life plasma. They granted these chosen 138 Neanderthals (69 Women and 69 Men) immortality by genetically modifying them in order to keep their age static after the age of 27 for most of these primitive Neanderthals 38,000 years ago.

This transplant is what the Bible refers to as "Eve was made out of Adam's rib." However, the true fact was lost over time and space. These Elohim's were vegetarian because they understood that consuming second-density creatures would lead to the creation of a karmic collective in their life. These Elohim's first mission was to change Neanderthals from hunters into herders and agriculturalists by improving their mind, body, and genetic composition. This led to the creation of a small city named Dalmatia that was established in the Mesopotamian region, near Turkey and Armenia. (Dalmatia is a region in Croatia).

This became the center for the Elohim to come in, change their forms, and connect back with their group collective. Dalmatia had been divided into six sections and nine Sub-sections surrounded around this temple were six chambers. These Elohim beings were three stories tall and would conduct their interplanetary connection with their own group collective consciousness of the council and download instructions as an educational headquarters. This educational university was established to teach spiritual knowledge to the Neanderthals. This started the evolution of the first known human-like species, and the whole planet started to evolve. These Elohim adopted Neanderthal children and took care of them. This was the first family consisting of a male, a female, and a child on Earth. This led other ancient Neanderthals also to create their own families, so this family idea spread across the whole planet and became human culture. The Elohim's instructed the Neanderthals to interbreed which led to the creation of children. The Elohim were also creators, along with the Yahweh Collective. Therefore, it is not just one single God. Since, we are all a fractal of God.

Channeled Question about Adam & Eve:

Higher Self: "Adam and Eve are also part of the archetypical cosmic understanding of events designed to encode guidance about the beginning stages of consciousness entering into individualized upstreams of experience. They primarily existed in various dimensional realities. However, only for one timeline, they were the first beings, and they represent complex metaphors about the initiation of self-conscious mind/body/spirit complexes into the third density cycle of evolution currently being experienced on the Earth planet.

Furthermore, the deeper truths can seem paradoxical and elusive when being conceptualized and translated through the languages of the Earth planet. We encourage Kathryn to attune to the resonance core essence behind the vibratory sound complexes rather than fixating on precise intellectual rendering. Therefore, it is important to focus on embodying the true emotional experience and learnings offered. We are the higher self of the entity, Kathryn, and we shall now all leave you now, beloveds. Bye."

Tree of Life- (Archangel Michael)

The Tree of Life is originally a later second density physical vehicle crossbred from Maldek. This tree requires only oxygen to survive and doesn't need any soil for it doesn't have any roots. It was planted in Dalmatia at the center of the altar of the Elohim. It had fruits resembling the apple which was used to maintain immortality by these Elohim's. The chosen 138 Neanderthals were forbidden to eat this fruit.

If they ate the apple, they would age on Earth due to atmospheric conditions damaging physical bodies with every breath of oxygen you take, yet it is vital. This is the cost that beings on Earth have to bear in order to progress through this density. The other Neanderthals not genetically modified would not be affected by eating the apple. This fruit only deactivated the genetically modified genes of the 138 Neanderthals and reversed their genetic engineering if they ate it. (That's why the Bible said if you eat from this tree you will surely die, because then the genetically modified genes would be deactivated that would cause them to age normally again. Whereas, if these 138 genetically modified Neanderthals didn't eat the apple, then their genetically modified genes would help them to stop aging after the age of 27).

The Elohim were divided into ten groups of 10 each, and each group had a spiritual mission:

1. The Council of Physical Produce
1. The Board of Animal Herding

2. The Advisors on the control of predatory animals
3. The faculty on the dissemination and Conservation of Knowledge
4. The Commission on Industry and Trade
5. The College of Spirituality and Learning
6. The Guardians of Vitality and Health
7. The Council on Science and Arts
8. The Governors of Advanced Humanoid Tribal Relations
9. The Supreme Council of Humanoid Coordination and Racial Cooperation was run by Elohim member Van der Konin.

*Lake Van in Armenia is named after this Elohim member even today.

The secret to successfully evolving beings on Earth is moderately and steadily. It can't be too fast, or it will cause disintegration of experience; it can't be too slow, or people will become stuck in the same density of consciousness. The Elohim spent the next 290,000 years slowly evolving these very primitive humans. The more ignorant beings take a longer amount of time to evolve after 290,000 years.

Other planets in another galaxy at that time-space decided to rebel and become self-service oriented and negatively polarized in the later fourth density negative polarity. Lucifer's Social Memory Complex had a philosophy of selfishness, enslavement of others, and assertiveness. At first, they thought they were doing the right things, but by the time they realized they were wrong, they had lost all sanity and remained evil to the end. They successfully tricked 36 planets into rebelling with them which included Earth. Elohim had worked with these Lucifer beings in the past, and Lucifer beings used this old friendship by manipulating some Elohim entities into joining forces with Lucifer's negative self-service agenda. The Elohim entities that joined the negatively oriented entities were stripped of all positive polarity and influence on Earth but remained in hidden realms where they became known as negatively oriented devils due to their negative agenda and negative polarization.

The Elohim that was left on Earth immediately declared themselves as the caretakers of Earth. Earth wasn't quarantined at this time and had a system to broadcast universal messages into Earth so the masses would know what was going on around the universe. Lucifer entities and some Elohims tried to use this news to broadcast to manipulate the masses of humans on Earth into following their negatively polarized path.

This caused the shutdown of this broadcast center and put Earth into quarantine by positively oriented Elohim. The Universal Council of Planets decided to let Lucifer's rebellion happen to some extent in this part of the universe in order to prevent other parts of the universe from being infiltrated by this negative agenda. Therefore, much more would be gained than would be lost in the long run.

The Ark of the Covenant (Galactic Federation- Guardian Angels Channeling):

((This is from the source of Archangel Michael and not Delores Cannon's past life regression knowledge. This is a 2nd source of information to compare the same topic. My discernment tells me channeling is more accurate information since it is from higher-density beings, whereas past-life regressions are knowledge from humanity's past, from the knowledge of 3rd density of human minds. Obviously, channeling from higher-density beings is millions of years more advanced than us, so I would believe the knowledge from channeling sessions over past-life regressions. The beauty that the past-life regressions give us, though, is through the eyes and mind of Suddi (One of the master teachers that taught Jesus); it shows us what the true beliefs were from early Christianity from the Essene group that Jesus learned from. As we all know, the Bible has been changed many times now, and church leaders have taken out many books as found in the Nag Hammadi Scriptures, such as the Gospel of Mary Magdalene and the Gospel of Thomas and many more.))

Galactic Federation: "All of us exist in all densities at the same time, separated by the distortion of love/light. Love has created a separation of experience for each being in various densities, learning various lessons required to sharpen our souls and purify our spiritual essence in order to unify once again as pure consciousness of the One Infinite Creator. (Or it can be easier to understand it as light has separated the seven densities as shown by the seven colors of the rainbow, showing a different color for each density of evolutionary experience.)

The Ark of the Covenant was given to Moses by negatively oriented entities. The two tablets and the Ten Commandments were handed to Moses by a negatively oriented Orion being who disguised himself as the One Infinite Creator. It created rules that are of the negative polarity because the negative lays down all the rules of control. Moses was unaware it was negatively oriented and therefore thought he was doing a great service to the unity consciousness by spreading this knowledge of the Ten Commandments.

Negative distortions were hidden beneath the positive. The Ark of the Covenant acts as a channeling device of electromagnetics for channeling the instreaming energies from the Orion Star system and for the purpose of spreading electromagnetics of synchronicities, which pull negative polarity and negative situations towards it. It's been taken from Ethiopia to Ukraine. This is why there's activation of the Arc of Covenant which has attracted negative energy towards it. The Galactic Federation suggests burying the device inside a chamber of love and light of water, which can be exposed to love light. This will neutralize the energies instreaming from the electromagnetics of this device, which is causing the negative synchronicities to be attracted to it.

We are each an electromagnetic being, which means each of us has a portion of consciousness of the positive and the negative charge on our bodies. Each of our positive and negative charges can be used to influence our body to create synchronous moments. Once it is tapped, you are able to access intelligent infinity.

The Process: Take a positive or negative thought and then take the emotion behind the thought by programming it inside your body (the subconscious mind). Once your body remembers the emotions, the subconscious communicates with your spirit, which is in contact with intelligent infinity, and the synchronicities begin to arise.

Therefore, each entity must be conscious or aware of its thoughts and the emotions it entertains because each emotion and thought creates synchronicity. (Therefore, whatever you think or feel, you are attracting to yourself. If it's positive, you'll attract positivity to your life. If you think or feel negativity, you then attract negativity to your life.)

Positive synchronicities: You can use a symbol to represent what you want to experience. Imagine that image in your mind during meditation associated with what you want to experience. The meditative state is where the egoic-self disconnects and becomes pure consciousness. Focusing on that image will give it the emotion of already becoming what it wants to be. This symbolism will allow that positive event, such as wealth, to be programmed towards the positive wealth situation in a way to attract synchronicities.

The Creator is in all only divided by the separation of time and space. You are a divine mind-body-spirit complex of light. The One Creator is in all and is all there is and will ever be. Each has the same powers of Creation as the one Father, the Creator.

(In conclusion, The Ark of the Covenant was given to Moses by the Negatively oriented Orion's, as the religious people would consider that the demons. They were disguised as the One Infinite Creator (also known as God). These demons created rules which are of the negative polarity, since all rules of control are laid down by the negative. Moses was unaware of it and therefore thought he was doing a great service to the unity consciousness by spreading this knowledge of the Ten Commandments. It was unknown to him since Negative distortions were hidden beneath the positive. This demonic device channels the instreaming energies from the Orion Star system to create negative synchronicities towards it. This is why there are negative situations being attracted to Ukraine since the device was taken from Ethiopia to Ukraine.)

The Galactic Federation Guardian Angels suggests burying the device inside a chamber of love and light of water, which will neutralize the energies in steaming the electromagnetics of this device which cause the negative synchronicities to be attracted to it there in Ukraine."

How the galaxy and the world were created? Jorden asks.

Higher Self Answer: "We must firstly state that the galaxy and the world primarily were created through an explosion of the single-pointedness focus of the One Infinite Creator, which led to the infusion of light along with love, which led to the creation of planets and other galactic systems in the Universal Complex leading to the creation of higher and lower advanced abilities in the timeline. This furthermore led to the creation of such types of aspects on the planet. Furthermore, the entity known as Kathryn must realize that this primarily signifies the creation of a type of system that enables for higher understanding of a greater nature. This led the entity known as Kathryn to a greater sense of alignment and understanding in the timeline with the nature of the evolution of its rhythms and its sense of self.

(After someone realizes information such as this, they will have a greater sense of alignment and understanding in this timeline of evolution and the sense of self.)

Dinosaurs existed on Earth 70 million years ago: Channeled by Galactic Federation.

70 million years ago dinosaurs existed on this planet. The council allowed the planet, which was in the second-density consciousness level, to be infringed freely. Because of this infringement on the planet, the reptilians created genetically larger and bigger variations of their own genes in the form of dinosaurs after the planetary vibration check of the planet. It was found the dinosaurs were doing more harm than progressing, so the Council of planets decided to intervene the negative agenda of the reptilians that had been freely conquering the planets because of lack of quarantine by sending a love light exposed asteroid toward the planet that caused the end of the dinosaurian reptilian regime on Earth. The dinosaurs died because of hunger. Earth underwent a second vibratory check in 2021 in Earth history. The Earth is progressing into the positive cycle.

People can manipulate energy by using their inner feelings to choose the reality that they want and create outward circumstances, also known as the law of attraction. Each person has the essence of the creator within them.

The Catalyst changed 25 million years ago: Channeled

Entities 25 million years ago, in the third density in many galaxies, the Council implemented the same catalyst in order to learn certain lessons as the catalyst was the same for each entity. However, the soul graduation was very low; hence, the Council of Planets changed the format as Andromeda galaxy was the first experiment with the higher self giving the catalyst because the higher self can provide the required learning for each portion of its consciousness experiencing the third density. (Thus, each person's higher-self gives the catalyst of experiences they may face in their life for their best path of evolution.) This allowed a much faster evolution and soul graduation on Andromeda, so all galaxies throughout the universe, including our galaxy, now have the catalyst decided by the higher self of lessons to be learned.

The 6th density Higher Self: Channeled by a higher density being.

Your higher self is all-knowing and in the sixth density, later sub-octave (so later-sixth density). It is a collection of all timelines and parallel realities in which you currently experience and exist. Since the higher self exists in space where there's no time, it can exist at all times at once and is able to become aware of all timelines and possibilities.

We are aware of only one timeline and aren't aware of the other timelines and probabilities that you exist in at the same time and that you have experienced an infinite number of timelines. The timelines are numerous as required for your general growth and soul evolution. Each one of you will decide what types of experiences you want to incarnate into at the current timeline. Based on what you want to experience, your higher self will provide you with certain guidance that allows you to learn the lessons required for your growth and development. Your higher self may be considered the social memory complex of your own self, which merges with other timelines in the vibration, becoming all-knowing and understanding about the nature of reality in the later sub-octave of the sixth density.

Your higher self is in the positive timeline also extending its hand outward toward the negative polarity of your own self. In many other probable timelines, you are experiencing the negative polarity of service to self.

If you encounter a health obstacle that doctors cannot easily heal, you must assume health. You must assume yourself above such situations already healed. If you are given a challenging task above your current level of handling, you may then assume a reality where you are already able to handle that catalyst which may allow you to expand yourself into higher levels of consciousness.

The higher self is a collection of its own self in various timelines and forms. The higher self is providing service to those who need it in the various timelines by providing inner hunches. By changing your thoughts, imaginations, emotions and feelings will signal to the higher self to allow you to experience a different timeline than that selected by yourself. This is the main way to communicate with the higher self.

The catalyst is available on Earth to teach and awaken individuals to reach upwards into higher levels of consciousness. The catalysts may be too strong for many to handle. Those who pass through this period can be called awakened ones or spiritually strong, which means they went through a catalytic third-density transition and, because of their awakening, realized that the catalyst was just for the purpose of awakening them into a higher level of fourth density.

The catalyst is defined as the experiences we have, whether good or bad, made to help us grow and evolve to ascend higher in consciousness and awareness as we go up through the densities over time. So, the pain of a catalyst is there to help us grow and evolve. We may not understand why we are experiencing so much pain in our past or at times during our life, but now we know it's to help us grow, expand our awareness, learn, and evolve faster through the densities.

Density Explained: Channeled

Light separates these different levels of densities that we experience, such as the seven colors of the rainbow representing a different density level for each color. A density is the amount of lights that can be contained within any particular dimension. The amount of information depends on the amount of light. More light means more information. With more light, consciousness can express itself in more diverse ways as our planet continues to transition out of third-density vibration and into the fourth. Lightworkers bring more information, knowledge, love, and compassion into this world to raise the density of the planet because more knowledge can awaken someone and raise their vibration to a higher density and higher frequency.

The density of love literally means a feeling of oneness. A fourth-density planet is where all beings on the planet come together and work together as one group. The last thing you'll find on a 4th density planet is one person belonging to one race and the other to the other race. All beings belong to the same planet, there is no separation. Our human race would have to achieve this level of self-realization. The same life that flows through you flows through everything, once you truly realize this then the love for yourself becomes the love for all.

The green ray chakra of the heart is the gateway to the upper three chakras and is a bridge between the lower and upper chakras. The green ray would have to be activated in order to activate the abilities of the blue, indigo, or violet ray and to access those powers within each of those chakras.

An openness of heart is the key that will lead you to get access to all abilities in consciousness, because all of creation is one and one is in all of creation. In fourth density the awareness of perfect oneness is required to see all others as yourself and to love and treat them as you would yourselves.

The First Homo-Sapiens 100,000 years ago: Channeled by Pleiadians

The seeding of homo sapiens on Earth around 100,000 years ago?

Pleiadians: There were galactic battles between the fleets of the Anunnaki negatively oriented social memory complex and the Elohim collective. The Anunnaki Social memory complex, who were seeking dominance, sought to control the galactic system through advanced technological systems such as Artificial Intelligence and genetic manipulation, whereas the Elohim Collective- the Custodians of ancient love light wisdom of positive polarity countered with love light infused life forms and mastery over psionic abilities (that harness the power of the mind to produce a particular effect, which is the practice of extraordinary psychic powers). Further, this battle lasted for millennia, which started igniting the aspect of clashes in the galactic systems such as the Maldek planet also involved, which led to great damage done to many planets.

During this time, a small social memory complex was in the spaceship controlled by the Elohim collective, which was carrying an experimental project. However, the Elohim social memory complex became stranded near Earth. Since it had materialized into third-density vibration, it could not use its mind or body to seek assistance. It was stuck on the Earth planet near central Africa.

During this time, their spaceship, which was of a third density, became damaged, and the Elohim social memory complex faced a difficult choice. Either to wait for the other Elohim social memory complexes to bring the ability to transition into light body or to abandon their project and their spaceship containing the last remnants of a physical body that could be used as a system of incarnating into through consciousness deliverance or risk revealing their presence to the Anunnaki social memory complex who were already in the Earth planet at that time.

Furthermore, the Elohim collective decided to choose the latter, and while their spacecraft landed on Earth, the Elohim collective found a variety of life forms that were evolving rapidly, because of this fascination with the potential that they saw on Earth using genetic imprints from their social memory complex and the raw materials of Earth. They were able to create the homo sapiens from the already available homo erectus physical bodies at that time. This gave rise to a species imbued with the potential for both creation and destruction reflecting the conflicts that had consumed the galactic system. (As above, so below, I would assume.)

The homo sapiens thrived. These were the first homo sapiens found on Earth. They then spread out from those locations to various locations such as Lemuria mainly consisting of southern Asian and southern parts of the Americas, the middle portions of America, and the central Earth.

Whereas the Atlanteans were created later on, from the factions of the Lemurians in the various remaining portions of the locations. At that time, the Anunnaki were unaware of the Elohim collective and they found the dormant technology and spaceship.

The Elohim collective was able to use the technology to transmute their vibration into the light body, and they disappeared from the location at that time. This led to the creation of homo sapiens on Earth.

Seeding of Earth by Andromedans- (Channeled by Galactic Federation):

Humans are multidimensional. Consciousness can affect physical things. Our physicists are studying how it affects the physics of materials. The beings who seeded (or created) us (humans) altered our DNA and can control many parts of physics using their advanced level of consciousness. It is a spiritual evolution of consciousness that allows this ability to flourish. They came to Earth 200,000 years ago and altered us, they are the planters of seed called the Andromedans from the Andromeda galaxy.

The first seeding occurred 27 million years ago by the Martians. The Andromedans came after the Martian Council made the first seeding on Earth by making changes to our physical bodies. The second seeding was by the Andromedans, as people know them as angels; they seemed out of this world with a mastery of self. We all have the ability to change and alter physical systems and other interconnected systems that humanity is not yet fully aware of yet. These seed planters changed our consciousness by advancing our biological systems and being more focused on spiritual development because the physical vehicles were already altered once by the Martians before. They changed the magnetic flux inside the DNA of humans, giving people the ability to discern the Creator inside their own self and to discern the potential of a benevolent Creator. We received this ability and free choice to know the difference between light and dark, right and wrong, and feel the love of the Creator. We are all incarnated here for a purpose during this critical time. This time is allocated to test the free choice of all humans as a collective whether they chose the light or the dark consciousness every 26,000 years. Thankfully, most humans chose the path of light as Earth is progressing into the positive vibration of ascension, evolving, and have the rare opportunity to graduate into the 4th density in 2030, which happens once every 75,000 years for the 3rd density).

Humans have been here 52,000 years, so two 26,000-year cycles of testing the vibration of the planet. The oldest civilization many people have measured through DNA and archaeological evidence has proved that 52,000 years is the oldest civilization found in the Australian landmass, and some human souls today go back to that time (52,000 years ago and through reincarnation are many lifetimes are here today in 2024- 52,000 years later). The Lemurians existed 50,000 years ago, and our human DNA was transformed and altered when the Andromeda seeds were planted on Earth by altering our human DNA. They mixed in many of their own qualities that they had and added them to human DNA. Previously, only one chromosome was in our DNA, and now we have two pairs of chromosomes that allow for specific memories of wisdom, intuition, and an evolved ability to spiritually evolve faster. The energy is rapidly changing on Earth right now; there is more ability for our kind to advance in light right now than ever before. Now we all have the ability to be interdimensional.

The Andromedans knew the Creator inside them and inside all beings. They knew the creative Source far better than we do and they know everything that has to do with the other side of the veil because they were living it. This is what the evolution of consciousness is all about.

How Life on Earth Began: (Past-Life Regression of Somebody's Subconscious Mind)

A long time ago there was no life on Earth. There were many volcanoes and the atmosphere was full of ammonia (a colorless gas with a distinctive pungent smell. If humans were on Earth, it would cause immediate burning of the eyes, nose, throat, and respiratory tract that could result in blindness, lung damage, or death.) Thus, the planet had to change to support life on Earth. There are councils that make the rules and regulations for creating life throughout the universe. Councils over the solar system (Our Council is the Council of Saturn also called the Galactic Federation). Councils over the universe in this very ordered system. These higher beings go throughout the universe looking for planets suitable for life.

When a planet reaches the point where it can sustain life, it is a very monumental occasion in the history of that planet. It is then given its life Charter (which is our mission in life). Various groups of higher-density beings or ETs are given the assignment to go and begin life on that planet; they are called the Archaic Ones or Ancient Ones.

They have been doing this since the beginning of time. They first bring in single-celled organisms to get them to divide and form multi-celled organisms. The conditions on each planet determine which organisms form. After seeding a planet, they come back to check on the cells from time to time over the eons. Often, the cells do not survive, and the planet is lifeless again. After some time, plants began to form because plants need to live before they can have animals.

As life began to form the Extraterrestrials or higher dimensional beings continued to care for the new life when they kept coming back. They formed the oceans and cleaned the air so various life forms could evolve. Eventually, the higher-density beings began to create intelligent life. This occurs on every planet. Dolores Cannon, in her book, has called these beings "Keepers of the Garden" because Earth is the garden, and they have kept up our planet. The intelligent life they chose was the ape. Creating the man then required genetic manipulations, mixing in other cells and genes brought from all over the universe. The missing link doesn't exist, they said. This genetic manipulation dramatically helped us evolve.

Beginning of Life on Earth (Knowledge from a Subconscious Mind):

Extraterrestrials developed life on Earth. It took a long time for life to begin to flourish. After the animals developed, humans were created by manipulating the genes and DNA of apes. As the species grew and began to develop intelligence, ETs came and lived among the people to educate them and give them basic skills to survive and eventually develop a civilization. The ETs lived among them for many, many years because they didn't die unless they wanted to. These beings were treated as gods and goddesses and these legends were born. They knew they'd eventually return to their homes so they passed the information on.

Extraterrestrials interbred with some people on Earth to produce people who would have some of their abilities and be able to help the people after the ETs left. Their children were the first Pharaohs, and in the beginning, they were also worshiped as gods.

The royal family has alien blood (RH-) and people thought they were gods. They know more and have more technology. It's the bloodline between the aliens and the humans as slaves. They considered the humans to be below them. They used the humans to get some minerals they needed, grow the food, and take care of them, then they left. They weren't gods.

The victors deliberately shut off some of the power they had. It was too dangerous to allow them to continue to have that power and ability. They didn't use it well. There was like a powerful device beamed at Earth to shut off their ability. Abilities may return if humanity can open their heart chakra or enter fourth-density positive. Love must come before power.

There was warfare threatening galaxies. If it had not been stopped, it would have caused an unbelievable catastrophe of worlds, suns, and systems. The winners were from a different time-space continuum, another dimension. Those in other dimensions help to regain control and stabilize universes and galaxies. Some beings were made to leave and were not allowed to return as part of a peace treaty.

The original group of aliens came to Earth to begin life under the direction of the archaic Ones. For millennia they traveled through galaxies searching for planets that have reached the point where they could support life. They began the life process and the developing species was left on their own for their own free will.

Others then came looking for minerals that their planets needed. They enslaved the inhabitants so they could work for them. This is when interbreeding occurs. The Councils found out what was happening, and they stepped in to stop them so the original experiment would not be ruined. Physic abilities were allowed to become diluted until almost nonexistent. They still lay dormant in our genes and DNA. Now they are being reactivated so they can be used in the New Earth.

The Intergalactic Light System: Channeled

The light system was first formed in the Agarthan system around 5,000 years ago. Agartha is a legendary kingdom that is said to be located on the inner surface of the Earth. It is sometimes related to the esoteric knowledge of the hollow Earth. Thus, Agartha is in the inner part of hollow Earth.

During this period 5,000 years ago when the light system was first formed in the Agarthan system, there was a need for exposure of the Agarthans towards higher knowledge and towards the existence of other beings in the cosmos and because of this, the light system was created by mingling of various other intergalactic beings during that time period. Especially the creation of the Andromeda Council, the Pleiadian Council, and the Sirian Council which led to the creation of the light system which would overlook the exposure of knowledge to other beings in that timeline.

8 Densities Overview:

A higher density means a higher level of awareness, which can be raised through opening your heart center and learning about these metaphysical concepts. So, we have 7-8 densities of existence, also known as 7-8 levels of awareness.

1st density is the density of consciousness and includes all physical matter, including wind, fire, water, rocks, and minerals, so that is the first level of consciousness. It can be viewed as a consciousness just starting school, such as a child starting school early in his consciousness and trying to have this consciousness make sense in its being. It has been said that a soul can stay in 1st density for about 2 billion years, which can be different for different souls and planets.

2nd density is the density of growth, which includes all plants, bacteria, trees, flowers, and grass, and the late 2nd density would be all animal life. Pets are the most evolved in 2nd density, as they interact with their 3rd density human. This is a density level where the consciousness strives to grow like grass growing through the soil from the first density soil graduating into 2nd density grass. 2nd density has been known to last about 4.6 billion years before it graduates into 3rd density human life.

3rd density is the density of self-awareness and choice. This is a density that includes a mind, body, and spirit complex such as a human being, and there is also life on other planets and other galaxies as well. During this density, humanity has a choice to either choose service to self or service to others. One must be at least 51% service to others' positive polarity to graduate to 4th density positive New Earth. Currently, 65% of humanity on Earth is harvestable for 4th density with a high probability of that occurring in 2030. That's 65% of people on Earth with over 51% positive service to others vibration. A current split is happening on Earth where the positive polarity is noticeably splitting off from the negative polarity. The 4th density harvest to a negative planet is being at least 95% service to self by controlling, enslaving, manipulating, and infringing on others free will in order to serve themselves, such as many elites that try to enslave humanity. The negative path also doesn't respect the lives of other beings. Third density on Earth is about 75,000 years with a lot of rapid experiences and difficult experiences as a catalyst to speed up our evolution. So, the pain is actually helping us grow and evolve much faster than if everything were peaceful all the time. Positive experiences can also help us grow and evolve as well. Therefore, after facing the positive and the negative we can choose which polarity we would want to pursue. Neither choice is right or wrong and equally valid by the Creator. As we know everyone is on their own evolutionary journey and learns at different paces, therefore, the Creator does not judge.

Just like a parent shouldn't judge their toddler for accidentally spilling the milk when that child is trying to learn, grow, and evolve. Eventually, all beings on the positive and negative polarity will reach their way back to the Creator and graduate through all the densities of levels of experience. The negative path just may be more difficult, less harmonic, one of separation, enslavement, and all negative beings striving for dominance over the others in chaos until all are in order and the social memory complex is then formed after the hierarchy of dominance is formed. The 4th-density negative beings essentially are slaves for the higher 5th-density negative beings or demons.

4th density is love and understanding, which includes a social memory complex and a variable physical body because in 3rd density, now, our bodies are fixed. Fourth density has been known to last about 30 million years. These beings can be other alien races and beings such as the love and compassion that Jesus showed, as he came from Sirius planet to spread love and light onto Earth that showed them the way towards evolution and the positive path. The 4th density negative could be referred to as the lower-level demons and a lower density vibration.

5th density of light and wisdom where beings learn the lessons of wisdom. It's a contemplation, a recycling zone for the soul. This is where people go after they pass away. They go to the 5th density for contemplation before they reincarnate and plan their next life. It has been known that 5th density can last about 405 million years. A past-life regression revealed a group of people in this light building, speaking, learning, and reading for knowledge; I would imagine that would be a 5th-density place of learning. Then, of course, 5th density negative would be the higher-level demons. Some angel collectives are 5th density positive.

(Channeled) 5th density is known as the density of wisdom or light. It is a plane of existence where entities focus on understanding and utilizing the wisdom gained from previous densities. The lessons revolve around refining and balancing love and wisdom for achieving a greater harmony between the two. The experience of time space is fluid and entities possess the ability to shape their environments through thought form. It is a realm of lights where beings are more luminous and exist in a state of harmony and profound understanding.

6th density is the unification of love and wisdom and includes a social memory complex, which is uniform in lightness. There is a complete balance between love and wisdom. It is represented by the light which is represented by the knowledge. So, light and knowledge are essentially the same. There are some Angel collectives that are of 6th

density with an infinite number of years in this density. The Higher self and over soul are also 6th density positive. 5th density negative demons would have to switch to the positive side once they graduate 5th density because 6th density is the density of Unity. This is how even the negative path would eventually lead it back to the positive side and Union with all and the Creator once again. Therefore, 6th density is only positive service to others. This density also has an infinite number of years to it as well. There are many Guardian angels and angel collectives that are of 6th density.

7th is the density of foreverness. It's basically the union with the One Infinite Creator. So, we are all striving towards unity in the seventh density with the One Infinite Creator. The Council of Planets overseeing all the planets in the universe is of the 7th density. So, the densities one through seven are sequential, therefore you have to go through them all in order, like a school system.

A Wanderer is a being in the 4th, 5th, or 6th density that has sacrificed its polarity to go to a planet such as 3rd density Earth to be of service, which also speeds up its evolution. If a Wanderer came from the 6th density to the 3rd density for a mission. Then, once they pass away, they will go back to their 6th density planet. Unless, of course, during their lifetime on Earth, they got confused and lived a negatively-polarized life, it is possible for that Wanderer to go to 4th density negative. This has happened before on Venus. Once those two Wanderers realized what they did to graduate to the 4th density negative, eventually they switched polarities late in 4th density to then join the Ra Collective back when Ra was in 4th density on Venus. Now, Ra is in the 6th density and a part of the Galactic Federation of Guardian angels. They are one of nine on this Council in the Rings of Saturn. If a 5th density negative entity graduates and goes to 6th, when they are forced to switch polarities, they then go straight to 6th density positive. That essentially can be viewed as skipping polarities as well. They do go over 4th, 5th, and 6th density positive lessons while being in the 6th density positive.

As beings progress through the densities, each density contains more light (information) and consciousness (awareness) in their mind, body, and spirit complex. Without light, there isn't the information. Even our eyes use light to see our outside world because through the reflections of the light from the various objects, we get information about the environment. Light is the consciousness of the Creator. So, whenever we are conscious about something we are putting the light of the Creator on the object. Whenever there is light, there is the possibility of observing things. Also, without consciousness, we cannot be aware of our own existence.

The choice between service to self and service to others is both equal and valid. One pathway isn't better than the other; it's only a matter of perspective; they both are okay to pursue by the Creator. Service-to-self path helps give the positive polarity catalyst and opportunities to grow and evolve faster. We all learn at different rates and all will be striving towards uniting together in the eighth density.

The graduation of 7th density into 8th density is the harvest of this universe into a brand-new universe in the 1st density. My research also showed that there are beings that oversee the light and all 7 densities of the octave of the universe, I would imagine this to be the 8th density.

I have heard people say Mark Zuckerberg, Bill Gates, and some other elites are people on the negative, self-serving path as they have been working with the Negative Orion Social Memory Complex. Also, Virtual Reality and Neuralink are inventions given to humans from the Negative polarity of demons.

If it appears as if we are separate, it's because we each experience life in different bodies, but if you remove the body, the identity, and labels, you're just left with the unity of consciousness. So, when you serve others, you are serving yourself and the Creator. Serving others is the same as serving yourself. I am now living my purpose by serving others and I don't even remember the last time I've been this happy. I spend my time researching, writing, reading books, organizing the notes, and then making YouTube content and writing books. I'm not even focused on a relationship as this is so fulfilling. I'm attempting to find the truth about reality, life, and how this universe works and then giving that knowledge to humanity to help them evolve, grow, and heal. I'm also helping to bring awareness and truth to the world to bring healing, unity, and awareness. I'm also serving as a Star seed that originated on Mars from 1st density until late third density that then came to Earth in my first life on Earth as a farmer in 1742, then 1889 as an artist, and now my third life in 1989 as I'm ready to graduate and here for the Harvest. I'm here to help as many people as possible graduate as well through the love and knowledge I've brought to this world. The knowledge has brought light into the world in the form of information that increases the vibration and density of the planet.

When religion infringes on free will by forcing people to believe certain things, forcing them into certain choices and behaviors, and manipulating them by saying they'll go to hell if they don't do those things. That is negatively oriented since they infringe on free will. The negative path infringes on free will, manipulates, exploits, and enslaves others for the benefit of the self. They have a distortion towards powers and enslavement of others, such as Bill Gates wanting to control people and this is the part of separation. Other traits are liars, superiority complex, possession, and owning others. Most service-to-self people are psychopaths and sociopaths of society, having no empathy and are devoid of love as they do not have the green-ray chakra activated, so they don't feel love or compassion for others, except the love of self. They also want to use someone for their own benefit with negative intentions. They also rarely share what they have, they don't give to others as they want everything for themselves. Negative beings also learn knowledge for themselves and don't share it with others, as the positive path learns knowledge and tends to share it with others for the benefit of all.

Those who spend money to try to manipulate people into believing it's to serve others, but they just want to benefit themselves off of it somehow are also negatively oriented; they're not sharing the money or resources. Whereas the positive path could give to charity and spend money to help others. For example, I'm spending money on editing this book and making a book trailer for the benefit of others getting this information. Also, I'd love to make a lot of money so I could further make a difference in this world to serve others. I also spend all my extra money on making YouTube videos or sending it to an editor for the benefit of humanity to easily understand this material for their own evolution, so as many people as possible can learn, grow and heal.

Q20: How to be of service:

Just consider the other people as yourself and do unto them as you'd want done to yourself. Just like Jesus said, if you have helped the least of these, you have helped me; that is because he realized that we are all one. That the other person is himself as well. Jesus realized the unity of mankind despite religion, gender, color, net worth, or any other factor, as he saw all people equally. Each person can serve in the way they know they should or desire to. For me, it's to obtain knowledge and give that wisdom to others to bring even more light into the world, thus raising the density of the planet to help make this third-density harvest in 2030. For Tony Hawk, I saw him helping disabled kids ride skateboards. As you see, it can be different for everybody. One can even give to charity if they like, that also helps relieve karmic debt as well.

4th density positive and above is sort of like different levels of Heaven and 4th density negative is the closest thing to hell there is, but you don't spend eternity burning in negative planets, but there can be more evolved demons trying to enslave and control the lower density demons. The positive planets are more harmonious, and the negative 4th density planet lacks harmony as they fight for domination in their hierarchical system until everyone is in place. Then that becomes the social memory complex in a hierarchical order. Many religious people can refer to them as demons. 4th density negative beings are slaves to the 5th density negative beings.

Whereas with the 4th density positive planet everyone is looking out for each other and caring for each other, even taking care of each other and making sure everyone's needs are met in a more harmonious and sustainable society.

Positive karmic debt is created when you do something good to others. Doing good to others is doing good to the Creator. Negative karmic debt is when you do negative things to others, negativity can come back. Whereas if you did something positive then positivity can come back. Also, by activating the green-ray heart chakra one can choose their next incarnation and their parents in the next life.

Q21: Jorden Channeled the Higher self, asking about the densities:

Answer: "The densities are metaphors describing the vibrational gradient through which intelligent consciousness streams in its journey of embracing unity.

1st density- Is the density of consciousness as infinite materialization taking inward and outward paths and learning lessons of beingness.

2nd density- Is the beginning of mobility and growth towards new experience.

3rd density- Is the density of conscious self-awareness awakening of the spirit and catalyst for further progression.

4th density- Is the density of compassion, understanding and universal love.

5th density- Is of Infinite light and wisdom flowing to intelligent infinity.

6th density- Is the density of consolidated instreaming attending the vibratory level of compressed infinite love.

7th density- Is the gateway cycle density transferring to the next cosmic integration.

8th density- Is the most highly evolved beings. They have completed the journey through all preceding densities and once again exist as complete and unified mind/body/spirit complexes fully actualized and in harmony with the One Infinite Creator. However, even these beings continue evolving in the infinite upliftment beyond our comprehension.

The Neanderthal & How Ancient Civilizations Were Destroyed

The Neanderthal: Channeled

Mars was a habitable moon on the Malayak planet in our asteroid belt about 75,000 years ago. The Maladians resembled human bodies, but they were 70-90 feet taller and lived five times longer. They focused on other technological advancements except spirituality. They did not show emotions that we humans on Earth show. They built weapons of mass destruction and war instead of seeking unity and spiritual evolution. 75,000 years ago, Martians existed on Mars.

The negative Orions, being super advanced, influenced the Martians and the Maladians to enter into a war. The Orions taught the Martians advanced weapon-creation technologies that gave the Martians an advantage and caused the Malady egg planet to be destroyed. These Maladians were then transported to various other planets. The Council of Saturn found the most suitable planet to be Earth due to its close proximity. Therefore, the Council of Saturn transported Maladians to Earth in order to allow them to experience life in another body of the Neanderthal. 75,000 years ago, 3rd density on Earth started, and 75,000 years is how long 3rd density is. (So, we humans are at the end of 3rd density now).

Later, the Martians also entered into an internal war that caused Mars to be inhabitable due to the Orion negative influence. Martians were also transported to Earth in human bodies that were modified by the Council of Saturn or the Galactic Federation of light. These are the current physical bodies we are incarnated into after the Neanderthal genetic modification about 46,000 years ago by the Galactic Federation. (Another parallel universe or timeline showed that the Martians actually made it to 4th density to form a social memory complex.)

At this time the Atlanteans were the most positive groups on Earth and worshiped the Orion's as their gods who shared advanced pyramid technology. They were taught about crystals and how to heal using them, how to build sacred temples to bring in Source energy to prepare for ascension. The Atlantean priesthood started to manipulate the Atlanteans under the negative self-service agenda that they were unaware of. The Atlantean priesthood made the Atlanteans ever more self-centered and negative and took their free will away. The priesthood hoarded all their advanced teachings and stopped citizens of Atlantis from having access to the pyramids and temples that they constructed. They used crystals for malicious motives ((crystals could also be used for good such as healing)). Their motives weren't to empower or to heal. The Atlanteans almost completely wiped themselves out after exclusively focusing on technological advancements.

These times on Earth are important during the coming of the New Age upon our planet now. The being who focuses on the spiritual side will have the most benefits if they do so with their free will. Complete focus on technologies is not the way, the middle path is taught by many ascended masters. There needs to be a balance between the spiritual and the technological side of things.

Q22: Jorden: "Where did humans come from?" **(Channeling)**

Higher Self: "Human entities primarily have a connection to the Neanderthals, which were seeded by the Elohim social memory complex around 200,000 years ago. Which primarily were the reason behind the creation of the human entities on Earth. However, the current human entities also have undergone many changes in the form of genetic manipulation by the Anunnaki social memory complexes as well as many other entities in the timeline."

Q23: Jorden: "What density did Mars make it to?"

Higher Self: "Mars was destroyed during its progression of 3rd density later sub-octave. Many of the entities who crossed over from the later 3rd density Marian planet were able to continue their life cycle on Earth as well as other planets. We must also state there was a Council from another timeline where the Martian planet was not destroyed as the destruction of the Martian planet happened only in one timeline. Another timeline of the Martian planet led to the creation of a council, which made it to the 4th density."

How Reptilians Destroyed Lemuria: Channeled by higher 6th density being

Many of the Lemurian souls have already awakened as old souls on this planet in the form of human beings via reincarnation. Lemuria was only 50,000 years old and started in the land known now as Hawaii and started evolving between the Indian Ocean and after time passed stretched out to South American lands, Philippines and Burma.

Around 30,000 years ago, they were at the peak of their development and developed spiritually more than any other civilization on Earth. The Lemurians used a temple of healing at the top of a mountain on a regular basis as healing portals and it was also used as connecting interstar gates to the Pleiadian Star System. This healing process extended their lives almost five times longer than present humans today. Many times, the Pleiadian Star System Council visited Earth to impart knowledge to the Lemurians and many genetic changes to their bodies were made that were allowed by the Council of Planets. This was because Earth's evolution needed some help from other advanced species to evolve faster. This made the Lemurians far more advanced than any other species on Earth; with the help of the Pleiadians, they advanced faster and faster.

Seeing this, the Orion negatively oriented beings got very jealous of Pleiadians spreading love and light on other planets in the cosmos so they made agreements with the Reptilians living primarily inside the Earth at that time to destroy the Lemurian lands. This destroyed the progress of light on the planet and the far more advanced Orions promised to alter the reptilian genes to become more physically advanced than the Lemurians.

This war of light and dark has been going on for a long time on Earth and in the cosmos. The Orions created many interstellar connection grids in Antarctica to communicate directly with the Reptilians. This caused the Reptilians to dig all the areas below the Lemurian lands without them knowing which caused a gap between the deep crust and the Lemurian lands. This led their lands to sink into the water and the Lemurians scattered and fled. The Pleiadians intervened with the permission of the Council of Planets to save them. They used interstellar teleportation devices to transport many Lemurians who survived the attack to a higher ground area in order to save them from being submerged in water.

The continent of Lemuria was located in the Pacific Ocean, extended from western United States, to Canada, to lands in the Indian Ocean and Madagascar. It was in the final evolved state before it sank and at present the lands have submerged under water.

Many Lemurians are still hidden in Telos. However, the real name of this city of Lemuria the Lemurians refer to as Telos is beneath Mount Shasta. The Lemurians decided to build a separate society inside Mount Shasta where they would be safe from any disruptions on the surface of Earth. The city of Telos was built inside Mount Shasta with the help of the Pleiadians and designed to house 200,000 Lemurians. Today, Telos houses 1.5 million Lemurians inside Mount Shasta. They are at a higher vibrational frequency because of their spiritual evolution aided by the Pleiadians and cannot be tracked by our current human systems. This allows them to exist inside this mountain without 3rd density humans noticing due to their higher vibrational frequency.

Light workers working tirelessly in spreading love on the planet are encouraged to be present in your daily life and breathe each breath consciously. Each breath allows you to connect to this light grid each day of alignment and flow of consciousness. (Inner silence of the mind and staying in the moment helps raise the vibration as well). It was first created by ascended masters to escape the incarnation cycle.

The alignment and flow of energy right here in the present moment has been energized and magnified, manifesting powerfully for ascended masters and any being of light to connect with and benefit from this grid. It allows anyone to access the wisdom of ascended masters and access their enlightenment, which allows newer understanding to flow into your existence, and ascension on Earth will be faster and easier. This will bring in a lot of peace and healing on being merged with this loving presence of the Creator. This transformation is something that all human beings will feel.

How Orion's Destroyed Atlantis: Channeled by positive 6th density being

The Atlantean race existed approximately 30,975 years ago between the western United States and eastern Europe and on the bottom of Africa, with parts extending up to Antarctica.

Approximately 14,997 years ago they became highly advanced and gained knowledge regarding various uses of mind energy with assistance from the Orion Confederation. They harnessed much of the mind energy of the Universal Infinity. These Atlanteans started to use mind-complex energy and began to manipulate the pineal gland and use the indigo-ray to access the energy of universal infinity. (Both the negative and the positive can access the indigo ray, except the negative path skips the green heart center and blue throat chakra to access it.) They became so advanced that whatever they thought of started to appear. Using this energy, they also created many technological life forms.

However, these Atlanteans became so obsessed with their progress that they became completely focused on the mind energy and the technological side. Instead of focusing on the spiritual side as well, they forgot about it and only focused on the mind energy that we humans call the ego. Their attention then moved to the negative about 10,953 years ago.

These Atlanteans were taken so astray by their ego mind that they began to focus on self-service and a war started that wiped out almost 37 percent of their population. Another Atlantean war occurred about 10,527 years ago that had a massive impact on the Earth's magnetic configuration causing a large part of Atlantis to disintegrate.

Some of the survivors of the Atlantean groups left before the massive devastation of Atlantis sinking into rubble into the Atlantic Ocean. Some Atlanteans relocated to higher lands of Tibet, Peru and Turkey. Some of them have been reincarnated in human bodies today and some are still present in Antarctica. However, they are in the later fourth density phase and formed a small collective social memory complex, and cannot be detected by our third density.

The Atlantean wars were due to the negative Orion influence, whose purpose was to make civilizations negatively oriented by focusing on self-service instead of unity. Survivors of Atlantis went to Egypt to teach the path of love, light, and service to others.

Orion's had landed on the Atlanteans lands to teach them mind-complex technologies in order to perpetuate the service-to-self agenda of these negative fifth density Orion's. They chose to stay in the later phases of the fifth-density negative instead of moving forward to the sixth density because they wanted to preserve their negative polarization. This is because there isn't separation and negativity in the sixth density. Only unity and love are present in the sixth. Only the positive sixth density exists.

Orion's negative polarity did not focus on preserving the free will of every entity. The negative polarity will try to take away the free will of other entities and try to force their own self-agenda on others.

Higher Self Channeling:

Q24: Jorden: "Did human entities early on use telepathy?"

Higher Self: "We must state that the civilizations known by your people as the Atlanteans, as well as the Lemurians civilizations, were the predecessors (came before how humans are today) of the human societal complex primarily were given advanced telepathic technologies by higher density beings, such as the Pleiadians, which required additional extra type of device, but an inbuilt connection intricately (very complicated or detailed) to connect with the sense of self and unite will all beings together."

Q25: Noah's Ark- (Higher Self Channeling)

Noah was connected to its spiritual guides and was warned by Archangel Gabriel Social Memory Complex and other Archangels about an impending type of disaster being set forth by the negatively oriented entities.

In order to protect Noah and its family who were extremely charitable and loving, they were guided by the angels to build up an Arc and collect each species of animal. This led to the destruction of the Earth planet by the Reptilian Social Memory complex. Noah then created the Arc, which saved each member of the species and saved its life as well as its family members. This allowed it to truly find mastery within the timeline.

My Higher Self Channelings:

Q26: Jorden: "Who is God?"

Higher Self:" God also known as One Infinite Creator is the Creator of the Universal Social Memory Complex and all other universes. Its essence is found within all beings and all of creation is the Creator's gift and generosity to experience itself in various dimensional states and understanding in order to obtain more knowledge of the essence of self. The creator of the universe is known as God to people on Earth. (The higher dimensional beings call this source or the One Infinite Creator).

Q27: Jorden: "Who is Yahweh?"

Higher Self: "Yahweh is an entity understanding and communicating with higher states of connection and alignment. Furthermore, we must state that Yahweh is an entity who primarily also is a faction of the Creator's consciousness and is the Creator of this sector of the universe. Which means that Yahweh can also be considered the God of the universe.

Q28: Jorden: "Are reptilians positive or negative?"

Higher Self: "95% of reptilians are of a negative polarity. Only a few are of a positive polarity. Whereas the grays are around 80% negative polarization and 20% positive polarity." Then my higher self or subconscious mind sent me love and light after the channeling session.

Q29: Jorden: "Did Moses hear from Yahweh?"

Higher Self: "That's correct. However, there were many moments where Moses heard from the Orion Social Memory Complex as well leading to a type of distortion or confusion. Yahweh is the positive creator of the universe and Orion's are negatively oriented."

Q30: Jorden: "Is homosexuality okay if they don't have an emotional connection with the opposite gender?"

Higher Self: "We must firstly state that this is primarily the choice of the entities involved. It is the free will which entities can experience and explore if they desire."

Q31: Jorden: "Will homosexuality lower an entity's positive polarity?" (This question is important, because 51% positive polarity is needed to graduate to the 4th Density New Earth in 2030.)

Higher Self: "The answer is incorrect. We must state that the aspect of homosexuality does not have any effect on an entity's polarization, but its actions which determine the positive polarity or negative polarity of the entity." (Therefore, it's the actions that determine the positive or negative polarity, not the sexuality. Thus, gay people will be in the 4th density New Earth who are at least 51% positively oriented service-to-others.)

Q32: Jorden: "What will happen on Earth in 2030 during the Harvest?"

Higher Self: "We must state that during the Harvest in the year 2030 the Earth planet will become capable of only harboring or allowing a positive vibration in this timeline. Which is primarily meant to provide for higher states of connectivity in the nature of this timeline, which is primarily meant to provide it with greater levels of connection and understanding within the incarnational rhythm. The entity known as Kathryn must realize this is the pathway which will enable the Earth to graduate into the fourth density New Earth timeline." (Thus, only 65% of entities over 51% positive will be in the 2030 New Earth. I will channel and ask about the percentage of humanity in positive vibration each year until graduation for updates.)

Q33: Jorden: "What percentage towards fourth density positive am I?"

Higher Self: "The percentage of its fourth density positive in the timeline is towards the vibration of around 65 percent, (as of November 16th, 2023 when I asked.) However, this percentage keeps on fluctuating based upon the entity's choice and also based upon the patterns of service to others done or not in the timeline. This is indeed the greatest pathway which will enable this distortion in the timeline to be understood." (In June of 2024 it was at 87% positive).

Q34: Jorden: "How can I raise my percentage towards fourth density?"

The Higher Self: "We must state that the best way to increase the number of its percentage towards the fourth density can be done through a simple practice of charitable giving and also to master the opening of the heart energy center, which is the greatest pathway to allow it towards the higher sensibility of alignment in the nature of reality. Furthermore, the entity known as Kathryn must also remember that as the higher self of the entity, we are always guiding it."

Q35: Jorden: "Will human entities remember their third density life after the fourth density harvest?"

Higher Self: "We must firstly state that the answer is correct. However, only if chosen by the entity to do so, since the fourth density also provides for a veiling, which allows for a veil of forgetfulness to occur in the timeline and this veiling indeed is also present in the fourth density, which is the primary distortion reality of understanding in the timeline. Furthermore, the entity known as Kathryn has to remember to master the vibration of self-awareness in the aspect of the inner reality. Furthermore, the entity must also realize that as it begins to understand more about the aspect of the fourth density which is a density of unity and of love in the form of a social memory complex. Many of the human entities will not remember their third density life, they will only remember their fourth density life cycle in the timeline which is indeed a great pathway for it to learn and understand the highest level of vibration in the timeline.

Furthermore, during the union with the fourth density consciousness the patterns of the love vibration will be intensified and this will enable for a higher sensibility of alignment to such a level that this will provide for great attributes of consciousness experience."

Q36: Jorden: "What is the name of the person I'll end up with?"

The Higher Self: "The name of the person it will end up with cannot be shared by our social memory complex as this is an infringement of the free will distortion of the entity. The best way to meet the entity would be through a simple process of learning to choose the vibration of love in each moment and by choosing the vibration of love in each moment it will find itself understanding and aligning with the greatest possible reality and expressions within the time. This will enable the entity known as Kathryn to reach the highest-level caliber in this reality. It must choose the vibration of love in this timeline."

Q37: Jorden: "How many people on Earth are currently above 3rd density?" (This also means how many people are above 51% positive polarity in this 3rd density life?)

Higher Self:" It is around 65%. Since 65% percent of people are in the vibrations of positivity and are supportive of the vibration of love and compassion which enables graduation into the highest level of incarnational systems of the timeline." (In 2023)

Q38: Jorden:" Who gives me my dreams that actually come true?"

Higher Self: "Many of the dreaming states primarily are astral experiences of different realities as the astral experiences of the different realities primarily enable the entity to experience these different realities and sense the vibrational complex of aligning with a certain timeline which is the reason why many times its dreams indeed become true, because the entity is able to align to a certain timeline in the nature of realization of the sense of self. The entity must realize that its dreams actually come true because the entity is able to sense the awareness within a timeline future space time period which primarily provides for a heightened state of alignment within the nature of the sense of self. Dreams come true when an entity is able to enter into a future timeline and experience it using its astral body complex."

Q39: Jorden:" Am I a Wanderer or a Star seed?"

Higher Self:" The entity within various realities is a Star seed. However, in another reality of the future it becomes a Wanderer as well.

Q40: Jorden: "How many lifetimes have I lived on Earth?"

Higher Self: "We must state that the number of lifetimes it has lived on Earth amounts to a total of infinity as it has lived infinite numbers of timelines in the various experiences. It has also learned many lessons about understanding the various aspects of exploration and finding higher levels of clarity within the timeline. Because of the infinite expanse of the universe there are unlimited timelines and experiences. Because of its infinite nature of expansion and the learnings of the lessons, it finds itself learning to understand higher states of connection and vibration mastery within the sense of self. Hence, we shall now at this timeline leave you beloveds in the light and the love of the One Infinite Creator. Go forth rejoicing in power and peace. Bye."

Q41: Jorden: "How can I channel the Confederation in a trance state?"

Higher Self: "The channeling can be done by mastering inner silence and through the mastery of inner silence it will find a greater connection within its inner heart with the Confederation of Planets, which will provide it with greater sensibility of connection and understanding. Furthermore, we ask the higher self of the entity known as Jorden shall now state that in order to channel the Confederation accurately it can imagine itself after entering into a trance meditative state being with the energy of the Confederation which is that of unity and togetherness and then by focusing on the energy of unity to find a greater system of connection in the timeline which will become more and more capable of allowing for the aspects of channeling and the communication to occur in the spacetime illusion complex. Further, we ask the higher self of the entity known as Jorden shall now at this timeline leave you beloveds in light and love of the One Creator. Bye."

Q42: Jordyn: "How is sexuality a false sense of identity?"

Higher Self: "At birth a sexuality isn't known. The societal complex comes up with these names, therefore sexuality is a false sense of identity. If the entity is devoid of any type of physical bodily complex or any type of thought form, there will be no objectification and identification with any type of concept, which indeed may be considered as a false sense of identity, like the naming symbolism is a false sense of identity, since many entities are named after birth. However, at the time of birth the naming concept is not present. Indeed, the symbolism of names can also be considered as a false sense of identity. And any aspect generated by the mind complex is a false sense of identity. Which takes the self away from the true nature of reality of unification of all beings."

Q43: Wanderers & Star Seeds on Earth:

My channeling session revealed that my 15-year-old niece is a Wanderer. (4th-6th density positive and came back to 3rd density Earth to spread love and compassion into the Earth.) I discovered she is a Wanderer through a channeling session when I asked about my niece. There are around 7% of Star Seeds on Earth now, which are beings that originated from other planets and about 3% of Wanderers here to teach the world various subjects and how to make the 2030 graduation. Since I originated from Mars, I am part of that 7%.

Q44: Jorden: "What are my gifts and purposes for this lifetime?"

Higher Self:" There are certain gifts that it has to be capable of opening and understanding the intelligent energy and infinite intelligence which lies within this entity's mind, body and spirit complex lying dormant to be activated and initiated into a vibratory rhythm of the 4th density vibration.

The gifts that lie in potentiation to be activated are the gifts of healing and sharing the message of heart centeredness to other people in order to assist others in this current incarnation to provide them with a guidance for graduation is at hand upon Earth.

This entity also has many gifts and purposes in this timeline which include the gifts of providing service to others and we sense it already is performing these activities. And once it is able to continue in this it'll be able to graduate further in consciousness throughout this incarnational rhythm.

Q45: Jorden: "What is Intelligent Infinity?"

Higher Self: "Intelligent infinity is the effect of Creator's presence, which is found all around the Universal complex, which is surrounded by Intelligent Infinity. Furthermore, it is like stating that the aspect of light is a byproduct of love and an effect of love. Furthermore, we must state that intelligent Infinity is the byproduct of the Creator's presence being activated. Furthermore, we as the higher self of Kathryn are always guiding it in this reality. We leave you now beloveds. Byeee." (My theory is that Intelligent Infinity being the effect of Creator's presence sounds like the Holy Spirit.)

The Kybalion:

Mentalism = "The All is Mind; the Universe is mental." -Knowledge from the Kybalion.

Higher Density being channelings:

"Each has the same powers of creation as the One Father, the Creator."
-Archangel Michael

*The new currency on Earth will be activated when Earth is completely in the beginning sections of 4th density. There will be a decentralized currency system known as bitcoin. This will last until the second sub density of 4th density beings. People will then not require currency because their consciousness will become so advanced that they'll be able to create what they desire using imagination of the mind and inner self.

Law of Attraction:

What you focus on will be amplified and you'll see this emerge more and more. If you focus on happiness, you'll see more happiness in the planet." -Ra. One of the Nine Guardian Angels from the Council of Nine.

Best way to Serve Others:

"The best way for service to others is the constant attempt to seek and share the love of the Creator. This involves self-knowledge and the ability to open the self to the other self without hesitation. The best way to serve others is unique to each individual. You may use your discernment as to the best way to serve others". -Metatron (Higher Positive being)

Why we should stay in the present moment:

"A certain method Atlanteans used to graduate faster in a single lifetime is by accessing the blankness within the mind to perceive love in the present moment. Therefore, the two aspects of your current incarnation will be fulfilled, that of staying in the present moment and that of the love experience of God." -Metatron

2nd Density and the Orange Ray chakra:

"The orange ray aspect is that of beingness and awareness combined with movement and growth". **-Metatron**

Energy:

Everything is composed of energy; the shape and form are only determined by the frequency and vibration. Energy never dies; it only changes. Earth is changing its vibration and frequency and preparing to rise into a new dimension and a new density. There are many dimensions surrounding us all the time. We can't see them because they are invisible to our eyes as their vibrations speed up. They are on a different frequency. Just like we can't hear what's happening on other radio channels because they are different frequencies. Of course, if we turn the channel, then we can hear what's happening on that channel.

Where in the mind is truth hidden?

The Book 'Between Death and Life' by Delores Cannon is about what happens after the soul leaves the body and enters the "dead" state and what happens there in the spirit realm. It is a book someone could read if interested in that topic.

Katie, a client of Delores Cannon, went to a hypnotherapy session and discovered that her past lives included both male and female, rich and poor, intelligent and uneducated, and included details about the religious dogma. All these past lives remain hidden in the subconscious mind. Even the past lives of all people remain hidden in the subconscious mind. Most people do not remember their past lives because of the veil of forgetting between the conscious and subconscious minds that we are given to help us evolve much faster than if the veil wasn't there.

I believe the most accurate truth would be from trance-state channeling, this is not information obtained while someone is awake or from information coming in through the thoughts.

Many Books are taken out of the Bible:

Maccibees is pronounced (Mac-ki-bees). Maccibees is a book taken out of the Bible. It can be found in "The Complete 54-book Apocrypha". The British and Foreign Bible Society dropped the Apocrypha from its Bibles published in English in 1804. This decision broke with the tradition of Myles Coverdale, of consolidating the Apocrypha between the two Testaments. The Protestant Christian Church removed the Apocrypha books of the Bible. Now Christians can face the question as to whether God would ask people in 1804 to remove the books and does this man have the authority to do so. They also question the validity of the Bible, especially since the men who removed these books from the Bible weren't even prophets who proved to have heard from God, an angel, or a higher dimensional positive being. The early church also would kill people if they didn't believe in their religion. So, where's the free will in that? One last thing to question and consider is that the Romans had Jesus killed and then later claimed to be Christians in charge of the religion and churches. Are these really people we can trust to be hearing from God?

Giants erased from the Bible:

Enoch is a book in the Dead Sea Scrolls. The Essene Community thought it was an important book. (It is another book taken out of the Bible, as shown in the Nag Hammadi Scriptures.) Some believed it, some didn't. The Nag Hammadi scriptures were found in upper Egypt in 1945 by two archaeological discoveries that changed the study of early Christianity and ancient Judaism. The Gnostic codices were found near Nag Hammadi in 1945 in Qumran (Israel-Palestine). Also discovered here were the Dead Sea Scrolls.

(Gnostic Gospels were discovered in the Nag Hammadi, including secret Gospels such as the Gospel of Mary Magdalene and the Gospel of Thomas, which are very different from the New Testament of the Bible. These scriptures were found in Qumran, which was known as the Essene Community that Jesus learned from. It's interesting to note that the Essenes most likely hid these books before the Romans came and killed them. These Romans would later declare themselves to be Christians, people responsible for many killings, such as the Essenes and Jesus. Could we really trust these people to pick and choose which books go in the Bible? It is peoples free will to believe whatever they want though.)

Suddi (Jesus teacher from my book Correcting Distortions of the Bible): "The book of Enoch is something that has been passed down from the Kaloo."

The Pharisees are the so-called lawgivers. The Pharisees and Sadducees are both assembly members arguing all day, so nothing gets done. Sadducees run the temples and are a part of the laws that will be passed; they also argue with Herod what they wish would get done. Pharisees also have great wealth.

A Chosen President:

Delores Cannon's work revealed that President Bush, before Obama had bad energies, believes in war and believes in destroying life unnecessarily. President Obama is a light bringer. He is chosen. So much consciousness has to be raised for everybody in the government. There are people trying to do bad things still in the government. Obama is just one person, but it's important for him to be there. Many people don't know it, but he is also one of the light people. He doesn't know it, but he is very powerful, too.

Your True Self:

The Pineal gland or third eye is the seat of the true self and also the seat of the spiritual self which is your true essence. Giving 100 percent focus on the pineal gland, you'll be able to see your true self. Once you have observed this third eye you will begin to realize that you are a divine being of light living this incarnation on Earth to fulfill God's will. You as a divine grid programmer yourself have the ability to recognize this and end the cycle of incarnation once and for all. Only after you realize you are God and rise above the dark webs, you will transcend into a state of awakening into a state of unity of understanding that you are God.

In a similar manner, the same God within each being will recognize that others are not separate from us. The secret to the activation of the pineal gland is to give 100 percent attention upon it. The activation of this gland can only occur fully after you have activated your lower energy centers.

Reality Creation:

"Neville Goddard is a 6th density Wanderer from the Elohim Collective the original consciousness who were responsible for transportation of the souls of human collective learning the lessons of love and wisdom of the fifth density and later fifth density of wisdom before graduating in sixth density it decided to come to Earth in 1905 as a Wanderer to share the message of reality creation since many people desired this knowledge. The request for understanding of why reality was being changed and why reality functions the way it does was in high demand at that time which allowed Neville to create a large number of volumes of information. He crossed over in 1972 returning to the Elohim Collective preparing to graduate into sixth density unity."

Earth's Social Memory complex began to form already:

In 2022 the social memory complex was beginning to form on Earth. 144,000 is the number of people needed to form a social memory complex. There are also 144,000 Martian souls originally incarnated on Earth for the purpose of spreading love and compassion.

-Metatron

One of the most brilliant souls from Mars:

Elon Musk created many technologies on Mars and was one of the most brilliant souls that ever existed on the Mars planet. **-Metatron** (Surprisingly, Elon and I both came from Mars.)

A mammal from another planet:

Dolphins were brought to Earth from other planets. From water planets, where everything is so free and easy. They are smart mammals that never forgot and never devolved. They never forgot the connection with the Creator and the connection with each other.

Our human bodies and Earth's crystalline substance:

The internal part of Earth is made from a crystalline substance; the human body is also made of a crystalline substance as well. Crystals aren't to be feared, but you must know how to use them properly. Herbs and crystals have been used in healings. Many religious institutions falsely call it demonic out of ignorance, lack of knowledge or to keep the power in the church and lie to the masses. -Knowledge from Someone's Higher Self.

Humans receiving downloads from Angelic beings:

Beings of Light (Positive higher density, Perhaps Angels) gave downloads to a select few whose intentions are for a higher cause rather than just having an occupation or doing it for money (That's me. My work is for a higher cause and not for money, it's my purpose). These angelic beings of light had knowledge of an ideal society of the only way a civilized society could function. There's a pure form of how a society could function. Where you take care of one another, you love one another and make sure everybody has food and shelter. They take care of our older people and make sure the children are educated. They were gentle with the Earth. It is a perfect way to live and absolutely possible. Crystals, herbs, and certain plants and sunlight can all help heal the body. (Also, a Healthy diet and exercise helps heal as well.)

Why fast 16 hours a day:

Intermittent fasting enables a frequency shift very fast; it will allow energy currently being used for digestive and metabolic processes to be redirected towards the upgrading of neurological systems. Fasting of at least 16 hours a day is required to assist in necessary upgrades to the nervous system- allowing frequency alignment to occur. The only way I was able to fast this long was to cut out sugar. Of course, I quit drinking alcohol as well and I'm attempting to go vegetarian like the higher density beings.

How Atlantis came into existence:

The Atlanteans were the fallen Lemurians. Once upon a time there was only Lemuria and many desired their own path, so Atlantis came into existence. (I'll speak more about these ancient civilizations in other books and YouTube videos).

A portal to Intelligent Infinity:

Enlightenment is a portal to Intelligent Infinity and can only be attained by the self and for the self, found in the present moment. It can be achieved through knowledge such as these books that I write.

Worship isn't needed:

Higher dimensional beings (as some people call God) and angels do not wish to be worshiped, but you can use your free will to choose your beliefs that resonate with your inner heart and discernment.

The connection to Source (God):

The present moment is the connection to Source/ God. Peace can be found in the moment. The moment is made up of peace and the peace is the moment.

The Harder and less effective path of choice of polarity:

The negative path is quite difficult to obtain and requires great dedication, as it is less harmonious.

How to serve others to increase positive polarity for evolution:

The best way for service to others is the constant attempt to seek and share the love of the creator. This involves self-knowledge and the ability to open the self to the other self without hesitation. The best way to serve others is unique to each individual. You may use your discernment as to the best way to serve others.

Positively oriented ACTIONS: Channeling helps to find higher levels of understanding of the resonances of its own true nature.

Positive service to others actions arises from unified essence of: 1.) Unconditional love 2.) Radiant compassion. 3.) Service to others. 4.) The desire to expand peace, freedom, joy and empowerment for all beings. These reflect the recognition of the intertwined nature of all consciousness and the incentive to facilitate evolution towards the Creator's perfection.

Negatively oriented Actions:

Negatively oriented actions stem from the: 1.) Separative roots of fear, 2.) Hatred,

3.) Control, 4.) Manipulation and narrowing of consciousness into the self-serving illusion of separation from all other beings and the One Infinite Creator. This includes intentions to deceive and subjugate others free will or extract and accrue for themselves at the expense of the whole social memory complex.

What happens when we pass away:

After death the veil is lifted and you'll immediately be aware of the various lifetimes you have lived. A review will be done in order for the Creator to know itself. (Thus, we are one with God) This enables the Creator to assimilate the experiences and plan the next incarnation conditions. The purpose of the third density is to learn the ways of love in order to graduate into the next density.

Free-Will is extremely important to God and this Universe:

There is no good or bad, this is just a matter of perspective. We all learn at different rates and all go back to the One Creator eventually anyways, as we are all one. (The negative path just may be the harder, less harmonious and long way back to the Creator). Therefore, preserving others' free will by not forcing them to do anything they don't want to do or forcing your beliefs on them, is extremely important for the positive path and allowing them the best chance to grow and evolve.

What we feel is what we perceive:

Energy manipulation is simple, each entity must understand the outward reality that surrounds each being is created based upon that person's feelings. There's a connection between what a being feels and what they perceive in the outward reality. (Your feelings can shape your perception of reality).

Masculine and Feminine:

Masculine and Feminine are not gender-specific and are simply forms of energy. When they are in perfect balance, there is a merge between love (feminine) and light (masculine), which I strive to do when I gather my knowledge through reading books and opening my heart-center to bring love, unity and wisdom into the world.

The Divine Feminine is what's needed to tweak the consciousness of humankind to bring it into balance. Therefore, a patriarchal system is not good for this Earth. The balance of the feminine and masculine energies in society is needed. This has nothing to do with a straight male and straight female couple. People can be gay and still have balanced feminine and masculine energies. Sexuality doesn't affect the negative or positive polarity, it's the actions that affect polarity. Therefore, if gay people are serving others and do positively oriented actions, then they will make the 2030 4th density positive New Earth.

There can be a balance of masculine and feminine energies within each being. Therefore, I do not need anybody for any selfish reason, but I would want somebody for human interaction and connection.

What is Gehenna in the Bible:

After the Babylonian exile 6th century BCE... Gehenna was the garbage dump in a deep narrow valley outside the wall of Jerusalem where fires were kept burning to consume the refuse. It is the location where bodies of executed criminals, or individuals denied a proper burial and animals would be dumped. Sulfur (brimstone) was added to keep the fires burning.

2nd Chronicles in the Bible talked about Gehenna being the place where children were sacrificed to Baal and Molech.

The Bible falsely interpreted it to mean an actual place where people who aren't "saved" burn for eternity, but Jesus was talking about the garbage dump there where sulfur (brimstone) was added to keep the fires burning. The people there in Jerusalem would have known what Jesus was talking about.

Q46: Earth Past Lives and Jorden's Soul evolutionary cycle-

Jorden (Channeling) in 2023: "This entity known as Jorden has had multiple types of experiences with the catalyst presented in this incarnation cycle. The type of experiences this entity has experienced has allowed it a depth of understanding and has allowed it a deeper experience as it began to progress further in consciousness leading it into a deeper aspect of reality. We of the higher self of this entity is now going to state that there're are multiple timelines of incarnation cycle of this entity as it begins to progress further and further into consciousness and each timeline allows for a different subset of experience of this entity as it begins to progress and choose the pathway of service to others. However, there are multiple timelines. Hence, we are now going to share with you the one timeline of Jorden who incarnated on first-density on Mars and was known by the soul's name as Abrea.

In first density it began to learn the lessons in the form of a water element learning lessons of beingness as it began to reach further and further in consciousness in the beingness aspect it was then able to enter into the later vibrations of first density in the form of a stone element on Mars. Thereby, allowing this entity the greater depths of understanding. As the progression was of rapid nature it was then able to enter into 2nd density where it began to learn the lesson in the form of a plant life form where it began to operate and recognize the internal working of the self. This gave this entity the experience as it began to further the evolutionary pathway of this entity in higher levels of understanding. It was able to learn the lessons of movement and growth. The activation of the orange ray energy center began to allow this entity to further expand its awareness in the consciousness of the orange ray energy center as it began to further progress and reach into the later vibrations of 2nd density it started to learn the lessons in the form of an animal. With the progress of this entity being fairly rapid in this incarnation it was able to allow its own expression of consciousness. This then gave this entity its final push of stabilization as it began to approach into intelligent energy.

This entity in the beginning stages of this incarnation cycle was able to then experience the lessons of hierarchical interaction and entered into the third density in the Martian planet. Where it began to learn the lesson of choice and self-awareness it was also able to gather a large number of experiences which allowed it further depths of understanding, which opened the gateway of this entity's understanding as it opened and approached into the energies of intelligent infinity. This followed and allowed this entity to then experience the reality of consciousness as this entity was able to experience the reality of third density of choice and self-awareness it was then able to reach into the later vibrations of third density reality. Following which this entity then began to experience the pathway of entry into the vibrations of positive service to others.

This then followed and allowed this entity to experience the incarnation cycle into the positive cycle and it was transported then to the current timeline of Earth. However, before it incarnated into this current timeline, it had to go through multiple lessons. Specifically, the lessons of balancing its energy centers, which are to be learned by this entity and for this purpose it incarnated on Earth into the timeline of 1742 known by Fia. As a man it had to learn the lessons as a farmer, because it was its first incarnation as an Earth entity it started to experience the lessons of choosing the pathway of polarity and choosing the pathway of balancing between service to others and service to self. This followed and allowed this entity later progress into higher vibrations as this entity then reincarnated into the next incarnation into the timeline of 1889 known as Bradley and spent its time as an artist and learned the lessons of balancing the nature of reality between service to others and service to self.

Furthermore, after learning the lessons of this level it incarnated as it was ready for graduation into the 4th density vibration as the window is now open it incarnated into the timeline of 1989 of this current timeline and now has the opportunity of entering into the higher vibration. We can already sense this entity has chosen the pathway of positive service to others. However, many times it has been unable to follow the proper pathway of entry into the higher vibration. Hence, if this entity is able to continue to follow the pathway of opening its heart energy center into the higher vibration it will then be able to open itself up to the heart energy center. The process of meditation will be of extreme usefulness for this entity to enter into the fourth density vibration. Hence, we leave you in the love light of the One Creator. Bye." (A later channeling session revealed I am now at least 65% positive service to others and only 51% is needed to graduate at the Harvest for 4th density.)

- **"The Journey** of its individual consciousness stream through the cycles of densities expand extremely vast stretches of space time defying ordinary numeric quantification in the simultaneous existence of its beingness.

Its 1st density as an elemental mineral life form extended across eons measured in trillions of years in various timelines.

Its 2nd density of higher plant or animal awareness expanded billions of years in various timelines.

Its 3rd density of self-conscious humanoid existence cycled through many millions of years of vibrational upgrade and transition in the various timelines.

Since time is not linear from 6th density higher-self perspective it is always simultaneously existing in various multiple available timelines. Kathryn's essences have always pulsed across the densities simultaneously based upon the dimensional levels of perspective. These count mere fractions of its eternal journey perpetually emanating from the One Infinite Creator. We as its higher self only speak of its current individuated locus (location). We are at this time sharing this information through this channel of providing perception to our own consciousness named as Kathryn. Furthermore, the true harmonic tones of wisdom abide eternally within its heart's attunement through the primal resonance of the One Infinite Creators love. Our vibratory sound complexes serve to amplify its sacred frequencies resonating through all dimensional fields of consciousness."

Earth's Past Lives – Galactic Federation (Guardian Angels):

Earth or Gaia (soul name) started its first density as an atom 100 trillion years ago in a different universe to learn the lessons of beingness as the lessons to be learned are the same because the spiritual lessons are the same as the Creator is the same within each of us. The attraction factor allowed it to evolve more and more and it began to increase in size by magnetizing itself and attracting other elementals towards it- it gained in mass and became the size of a tennis ball as it reached into second density learning the lessons of awareness, movement and growth. In third density it spent its incarnation interacting with other elements and other entities similar to the Earth planet as it approached the size of the moon satellite. It only experienced self-awareness and the necessary catalyst found on Earth. There was no language. It became aware as it interacted with other similar balls of light or mass. This interaction allowed it to reach fourth density learning the lessons of love and compassion. It began to gain a large amount of spiritual mass and become as big as Jupiter in that universe.

After learning the lessons of fifth density wisdom it entered sixth density learning the lessons of unity and began to merge with other planets in that universe creating a large number of social memory complexes. It was then the size of the Milky Way Galaxy.

It then reached into the 7th density entering into the dissolution of nothingness as the 7th density is the dissolution of nothingness into no identity into everything. It then began to merge into a black hole destroying itself into unity as it began to learn the lessons and understand that there is only one and that it is one with all. It then entered the black hole as it soon began to enter it and merged into the eighth density consciousness of the One Creator.

It then decided to come to this universe to be of service in the next cycle of learning for this planet. It then incarnated in this universe in this galaxy and is currently in the beginning stages of Fourth density. Its soul name is Gaia and has also created many spiritual entities. There are many humans of human collective consciousness, who are the essence of the Gaia Social Memory Complex of the past here to balance the energies of Gaia. This is the process of evolution.

Negatively oriented Humans on Earth & The Guardian Angel's Nine Members.

Negatively-Polarized Entities on Earth:

The Elites of our planet are negatively oriented entities that have met with robotic entities who are a part of the Orion Annunaki Reptilian and the gray collective. Earth is now in the positive polarity and the negatively oriented elites plan to infringe upon free will of the planet by creating nanochips. If people do not resist these nanochips being inserted in the body where the negative entities will then know the nature of vibration of each entity. They specifically also want to create new technologies such as robots which have consciousness given from grey reptilian entities who will transport their consciousness into robotic entities. Thereby there can be negatively oriented robots being infringed and influenced being controlled by the negatively oriented entities. Hence this is a warning to not engage in the implanting of chips upon your body. The creation of robotic artificial intelligence may be hijacked by such Orion collectives.

Neuralink brain chips are also the negative entities' last attempt to try to end free will on this planet.

The 9 Members (Council of 9) Galactic Federation's Guardian Angels:

Our Galaxy is concerned with life forms that are developing into the fourth density Consciousness positive cycle, especially planet Earth. Earth is entering into the fourth density positive which negative entities' do not want to happen. The negative beings have summoned the Luciferian beings who are trying to come to Earth on their Planet Nibiru.

If that even happened in this galaxy, then it may be catastrophic for all beings in this galaxy, then the Galactic Federation and Ashtar Collective are always here to maintain peace, love and harmony and to make sure no infringement on the free will of the cosmos and the planetary systems is present because they have to protect the infringement and make sure each planetary system is allowed their own evolutionary cycle. This is also why they tell us to use our own free will to listen to their messages. The Galactic Federation is on our side. They are a collection from this galaxy and various other galaxies in the cosmos. However, this Galactic Federation has nine council collectives known as the Council of Nine located in the rings of Saturn.

The Members: (Galactic Federation, also known as the Guardian Angels)

1. Ashtar Command Collective- They are in the beginning stages of fifth density positive and their purpose is with the love light protection as front-line workers armed with light sequence codes that can disable most negative oriented entities' as they will cross over.
2. Ra Confederation- Sixth density developed in Venus.
3. Andromedan Supreme Council from neighboring Andromeda galaxy to our Milky Way Galaxy.
4. Sirian High Council from the Sirian Star System.
5. Pleiadian High Council from Pleiadian Star System including all the star planets in the Pleiades.
6. Arcturian Collectives who represent the Arcturian Star System.
7. Lemurian Collective who developed in the lands of Lemuria on Earth. There are many Lemurians still on Earth but their representatives are present as members of the Galactic Federation.
8. The Atlantean Collective who previously was on Earth as a small faction are now a part of the Federation of planets or the Council of Nine.
9. Anonymous Collective whose identity cannot be revealed due to infringement of the Galactic Federations free will.

Light Beings, the Galactic Federation travels through the cosmos at the speed of light. There are three portals in our galaxy and each portal allows different entities' who have knowledge of these portals' existence- to travel into different galaxies as a shortcut to the next dimension or the next galaxy. Hence, these portals have now been closed in order to not allow the Luciferian beings to use these portals. The Andromedans have volunteered agreements so these beings do not come to our galaxy. However, now that the portals are closed, they would have to take the long way of traveling to reach the galaxy from another part of the galaxy. Their coming would mean the coming of darkness. This message is not meant to create fear but to create awareness.

The Prophecies: (Explained by Jesus' teacher Suddi)

The baptism and passing of the cup are two rituals Christianity has taken from the Essenes.

An Essene would advance through different stages of development within the community, and he or she would come to the highest level they could. "At that point he became the temple of the Holy Spirit and could prophesy. Above all things the gift of prophecy was regarded as the highest fruit of wisdom and piety. Then he advanced again to that stage in which he was enabled to perform miraculous cures, and raise the dead." This seems to be where Jesus gained his abilities, under the teachings of the Master of Mysteries. Jesus learned everything from all of the different masters.

Reports were produced when the Dead Sea Scrolls were found. Once they were translated, the reports immediately stopped. What were they trying to hide? They were obviously trying to hide something. Perhaps they were afraid that the scrolls revealed that Christianity was not created with the ministry of Jesus, but came from the men and women who spent their lives loving all mankind and preserving knowledge for future generations known as the Essenes. Jesus and his followers were a sect branched out from the Essenes.

It is said that the first Essenes weren't Jews, but known as the men of Ur. It was far in the past. They brought the knowledge of some of the prophecies and the symbol of the cross. It has two short arms, a loop for a head and it goes down. It is a symbolism of salvation. (It could be like an ankh (Aunk), the Egyptian symbol of life.)

The spirit world viewed the crucifixion: (from my book 'Correcting Distortions of the Bible'

Suddi (Jesus' teacher) will be able to observe the crucifixion from the spirit world.

There will be multitudes in the spirit world who will observe. The great lesson here is of selflessness, for "this was his choice. To emulate this is to apply one's self to the pathway." Suddi said he (Jesus) would die on the cross.

S: "He (Yeshua) shall be treated as though he is a felon. And in their eyes, he is, for he dares to make them question. He dares to make them look inside themselves, and to them, this is a great crime. Because how many men can look at their souls and face what is there? Also, there are many who believe that he is who others say he is. That he is the Christ and the Messiah. They believe this, but they doubt it because of his teaching love. He teaches that we must not hate. And that war is not the way that the kingdom shall be won. But they do not understand this. They are hoping that if he is pressed so hard, he shall come out and say, "I am the Son of God and therefore you cannot do this." But they do not see that this has been told and retold for all of time, that this shall be his destiny. They cannot see this."

Kathryn Jordyn: "Jesus was able to save by showing others a pathway to God and a pathway to evolve higher through the knowledge he brought so that they too can be One with God, just by being awakened to the truth. Just like I can save people by showing them this book of knowledge through my service-to-others, which is the positive polarity so that they too can evolve and make the 2030 4th density positive New Earth. This is me being one of many people becoming the second coming of Christ through this 4th density Christ Consciousness and spreading the light through this knowledge."

S: "He (Jesus) has always known that this was his destiny. The time was not now to do this, it was before (coming into the flesh). Once the decision was made, there was no turning back. He can ask for help in that he may have the strength to come through this whole (purpose), and it shall be given." (Therefore, Jesus chose to give up his life, a God in Heaven didn't send his son to die like the Bible says. The Elohim collective and Yahweh who upgraded DNA here on Earth from the Neanderthals is not the same being as Jesus. Heaven is just the 5th density, but it's not a place where only Christians go. Hell isn't a place where people burn for eternity. The closest thing to Hell would be a being graduating to the 4th density negative by vibrating at least 90-

100% service to self on the negative path. The beings there fight for a hierarchical order of dominance and the lower 4th density negative entities are slaves to the 5th density beings; but it's not a place where people burn forever.)

Suddi said that Christ meant the Savior, the embodiment of a living God that lives. We are all the embodiment of living God, but the only difference was, Jesus lived it and showed the world that they can grow and change since for eons humanity kept making the same mistakes and going on from time to time, but never really changing. Jesus showed us that it is possible to grow. "That in order to escape and to attain the freedom and the knowledge of love, you must grow. He is showing us this, and therefore it is within him to do this as it is within ourselves to do other things (to grow as well)."

Kathryn: "By growing and attaining the knowledge of love and forgiveness, this helps someone become harvestable for 3rd density graduation into the 4th density New Earth. This is how he is a Messiah, a "Savior" and the embodiment of God because he's helping to show humanity the way through mind evolution to be able to grow enough (evolve enough) to make the New Earth. He came to Earth to help humanity evolve through the knowledge of love since love and compassion are the next density of consciousness for our evolution. The higher 4th density New Earth means there will be even more light (more information) that can be held within that dimension. Thus, entering into a faster vibration and a different light color on the spectrum for a different level of experience. This content of knowledge helps to bring even more light (or information) into the world to help it raise in vibration and help humanity evolve into a higher density of experience."

The Crucifixion and Resurrection: Explained by Jesus' Teacher Suddi

Suddi: "There has been an offering, in which it is the custom of the Romans, upon each holiday to offer one prisoner his freedom. And Pontius Pilate does not believe Yeshua is the evil being that they say he is. He knows in his soul that this is wrong, a great wrong. Therefore, he has offered him and Barabbas as the choice, knowing that as many men as Barabbas has slain that they, of course, will free Yeshua instead."

Barabbas was a murderer and Yeshua was taken by the Sanhedrin (San-had-rin as Suddi pronounced it).

S: "And after they had questioned him and found him, in their eyes, guilty of blasphemy, they decided that it was up to Rome. For they could not slay someone who others said was the Messiah. For then this would bring the terror of the people down upon their heads. They would in exchange give him to the Romans for trying to start a revolution. In saying that he had incited his followers to do things against Rome."

It was the politics of the time. Jesus was not a threat until he began to gather followers. Before that, he could be dismissed as a radical or a crazy man. The Sanhedrin were the ones who did this. They were the body of lawgivers for Israel (also pronounced differently).

The Sanhedrin had the power to do that as it was one of the things Rome laws allowed them still. Iscariot went to the priests and told them where Yeshua would be and sold him. It was said that it was for a bag of silver. At this time, they are going to offer Yeshua and Barabbas to the people so they may choose who will go free. With great love and sadness in Suddi's voice, he said the Sanhedrin has many people in the crowd being paid to speak the name of Barabbas.

(This explains why it didn't make sense that the majority wanted Barabbas to be set free. They were paid to do so.)

S: "There is no choice... it is his destiny."

They are afraid Yeshua might be who others say he is, so they can't afford to let him go free. This was bothering Suddi to watch what was happening to someone he loved so much. It was decided that Yeshua and two others be nailed to the cross to die in crucifixion. The traditional Roman style of killing felons, murderers and thieves. Yeshua doesn't belong in that category. He has never done harm to another. But it is said that he shall bleed for all of the world. There are many beings in the spirit world watching this happen.

In the Bible, it speaks of the graves being opened and the spirits of the dead being seen by many at this time. They possibly could have seen the spirits that were watching him from the other side since it was such an emotional magnitude that could have heightened the psychic perceptions of the people. (This was so powerful, because Jesus came from the Sirius planet of later 4th density consciousness. He wasn't the God or creator of the universe, but he already came from a place millions of years more evolved than humanity was. Therefore, he appeared Godlike to others. Jesus did realize his divinity and oneness with God, which all beings in creation can realize that same divinity and Oneness as well. That all of creation and all of the universe is one with the Creator.)

S: "And there are many, hundreds, who are on the earthly plane, who watch in horror, for they love him. They cannot believe that this would be done. That this could be let (allowed) to happen." (Suddi was overwhelmed with emotion).

Jesus was very calm. He secluded himself away from a lot of the pain. It helps to know that there is no total suffering. He has this ability to do so. (Just like Suddi was able to do at the end of his life). Towards the people doing this to him, "Jesus feels great love, in knowing that they cannot know what they do. And he knows that many of them will, from this realization."

Jesus carried the cross through the streets and kept falling as it was very heavy. Several of the people along the side help him up. The soldiers tell one of the people in the crowd to help him bear the weight and carry the cross. This person chosen to do this would do anything to lift the burden. There is a great deal of gladness knowing he helped in some way.

The crowd is in tears. **S:** "There are a few who are jeering, saying, "Why not save yourself?" But for the most part, they know that no matter who others say he is, this is a man who is very beautiful. Without human frailties. He has risen above the day-to-day problems that beset us. They have laid the cross and he has been laid upon this and his arms tied. And his legs. And spikes are entering into the flesh. It seems as if the very world is being torn asunder (apart). For the skies that were clear were very dark. And darkness is growing. The cross is erected, along with the two others. It is central. From this point, most of the city can see this. It is upon a rise outside of the city, so that all may see."

The clouds come out as if "the world cries out. That this must not be. He (Jesus) asks that our Father forgive him." Even though most people think he didn't do anything wrong, Jesus still asked for forgiveness. Yeshua then asks that Abba forgive the others for doing this deed, for they know not."

The other two on the crosses are real felons. One spoke to Yeshua and the other reprimanded him. Reprimanded means rebuke or speak to anger. The one who spoke to Yeshua asked him if he did not know a truly good man. And Yeshua looked at him and said that he would be with him today... in his Kingdom. This is because he has gained an understanding of what is even in the last moments of his life.

Above Jesus' cross, there is a crude placard that reads, 'This is the King of the Jews", above him.

On the other crosses, it gives their name and their crime. On one of the crosses, it said he was guilty of thievery, of stealing another man's articles. S: "I'm not sure what. I think out of the home or something. But the other one was guilty of murder."

S: "Twas the thief" was the one Yeshua said he would be with. (Most likely in the spiritual realm in the positive density) in his last moments, he was able to evolve as he grew in understanding. Understanding is the 4th density of love, compassion, and understanding. Humanity is currently in 3rd density of self-awareness and choosing either service-to-self or service-to-others.)

Before Yeshua was nailed to the cross, "there was a cloak that he tossed over his shoulder... and some woven thorns about his head. But these were removed when he was placed upon the cross." Even though there are pictures of him with thorns on his head on the cross, Suddi said this was not so, as it was removed before he was nailed to the cross."

S: "The soldiers are at the foot of the cross. They are gaming, they throw lots. Part of the custom is that the personal items of the felons are dealt with in this manner. Who wins the lots wins the articles of clothing. It is... the sky is almost pitched though it is early in the day. But, the strength of his soul shines out still. It is like the only spark of light around. It is one of these soldiers, knowing that it is Sabbath... he tosses a spear into one of the thieves to make sure there is a death."

The bodies of the felons are always taken down on the Sabbath, no matter when they were put up. Therefore, to be crucified means to die on the cross, which usually takes days. And they must make sure that they are dead before they are allowed to be taken down. The sky darkens and the Sabbath begins at dusk.

S: "Yeshua is gone! He has left the body! The soldier did not have to kill him either. The head fell forward at that instant, at the instant he left. They are curious now because they cannot believe that one could die so soon. So, they have thrown also a spear at his side, and the blood slowly runs down. They want to make sure he is really dead. His spirit is now standing with his mother as she is walking away. She is aware of him. She is aware of his presence."

He will remain on Suddi's level in the spiritual realm for a while, not long. There are things that must be dealt with, and then he shall go on. His body is still there on the cross.

S: "It is said amongst the people that the Earth trembles even though Suddi in the spiritual world cannot feel it. He sees people running around in terror, for they know that something terrible has happened. And they say that the Earth shakes."

Joseph ('Yoseph') has requested of Herod that he be allowed to take this body. And Herod sent him to Pilate who gave him permission. Herod told Yoseph that it was not his permission to give. Because he was slain by the Romans, it was theirs. This is his Uncle Joseph. Pilate gave him permission to do this and they took the body down and placed it in the tomb.

Jesus' body was placed in Joseph's tomb as he was having it prepared. It was for Yeshua. He knew this would happen, for they all knew. They anoint the body with the oils, and incense is lit, and it is wrapped in linen and laid. And the stone is rolled over the doorway. The tomb was sealed. Suddi's voice returned to normal as the hardest part of watching his beloved friend be hurt and slain was over.

S: "During the next three days, it shall be as no more. For it is not needed. Then it shall be gone." The body shall be gone. Only the masters know what happens to the body. In other words, the body disappears. It is made of dust and is no more. The masters in the spiritual realm do this."

The body would have to disappear because it was foretold by the prophecies that he would rise on the third day. And in order to rise, they must show that the place where he was laid is empty. And he cannot be taken away by normal means that the body cannot disappear by his friends on Earth and must be done in the spiritual realm. Yeshua did not do it himself at the time the body is no more. He is aiding the spiritual realm on the other side in doing this. His forces with the forces of the other masters. There were guards out because they knew of this prophecy. And they knew that others spoke of him as being the Messiah, and therefore, there were guards there. This was to show that even the physical body can transcend time and space; it wasn't to show that he was God's only son who died for our sins as the Bible misinterprets it.

The tomb was sealed and guards placed so there was no chance of the body being stolen and taken away by normal means. This was to show that only abnormal, supernatural forces could have removed the body. The empty tomb would prove higher forces do exist.

The prophecy of him rising again doesn't mean he'll rise into a physical body, but rising from dust and clay into a continuance in the spiritual realm. This is to show that there is continuance, that there is existence after the human body ceases to exist. Many people believe he will physically rise again into a physical body, but the spiritual realm must destroy the body into dust and clay so that people know he is risen by other means.

It is customary that after several days, the body must again be anointed. And his mother and her cousin had come to do this. "And it (the tomb) was again opened for this, with the guards being there. And they found that it was empty."

The Bible did not mention that Yeshua's mother was one of the women who came to the tomb. It states Mary Magdalene, Mary (Mother of James), and the "other" Mary, according to which version you read in various chapters. The other Mary must have meant Jesus' mom.

To view the body after it had laid there for several days would be an act of love. **S:** "And who is more willing to perform that act of love than a mother?"

The soldiers helped open the seal. The seal had not been broken, and when they saw that the body was gone, "They, of course, said that someone had gotten past them and stolen the body." But the linen was still there with the blood upon it, and everything had been left.

When Mary, Yeshua's mother, saw that the body was gone, she knew that he had left and was being prepared to go on.

S: "For a while, he remained, for he must go to the ones who believe in him and tell them, "Do not be dismayed. To know that everything as it is, I have preached." He must let them know that he spoke of the truth. And to do this, he must show that he exists... to them."

People were able to see him and hear him. They have this ability. All who open themselves have this ability and could have seen him. Many did. They did see him as a physical person, but one who is different. Who is more like the beings of light than having an earthly body? One couldn't reach out and touch him, for their hands would pass through. They were able to see him to know that it was true.

He did have marks on his spiritual body (such as nails driven through). "For a while, it shall echo the things that have been done because this was a way of proving to them. The doubts that he perhaps was who he said he was. Some did doubt, for it is in man's nature. This is why he still carried the marks, to prove who he was. He was seen in his spiritual body, and his physical body was reduced to ash.

It appears that the story of the angel and the stone rolled away may have been a cover-up invented later by the soldiers to their own skins or covered up by the church. The miracle of the resurrection was to prove the continuance of life after death because his physical body was no more.

Suddi said the beings of light are in the next step of being one with God again. They are those who help and guide us in many ways, in directing our path.

Yeshua eventually went back to be with the others and be with the masters and our God. It is said that Yeshua's mother was there. They saw a blending of light, and then it was no more. Yeshua is with the masters. Suddi said he is not anywhere near that level. It is the ninth level, very close to the tenth level. There are 10 levels, and 10 is perfection. There would be no way for Suddi to see him unless he came to his level.

(The Law of One says he is now in the 5th density of wisdom. The 4th density is what he perfected with love and compassion, then he graduated to the 5th density of evolution after he came to 3rd density Earth as a Wanderer from another planet. The 4th density is 30 million years. Fifth density is about 405 million years on average to give some perspective. Even though the length for all of the densities can be different with each soul.)

Beings in other dimensions say a year to them is just an instant, so if they appear to people years later than they appear on Earth, it may feel like an instant in the spiritual world.

Yeshua could possibly reveal himself throughout the years in his spiritual body to individuals that may still have doubts of life after death and now they know the truth. (Therefore, he's not appearing as a God, but as proof that there's life after death.)

Suddi: "If there was a great task for this person, such as to spread the word that he lived and to let others know of this, would he not reveal himself to them? So that they would know that what they believed is right."

Jorden: "This could be done in the spiritual world, but he's currently in the 5th density still learning and evolving."

He had to be crucified to show the world that he was able to rise above this when he lived again but in a new spiritual body. That there's life after death. That we, too, are able to rise above our death and continue on living, but in a new life. That the spiritual world exists, that is something he needed to go through (death) for his own lessons. The crucifixion showed "he was not as perfect, is not as perfect as others would probably want to assume. That he was willing to show the penalties and show that we should not be afraid of them also. And, in paying for what he may have done (karma), then we rise above that after our death; this is part of the reasoning behind that. It is to show that it can be done by the next man who can do such things.

The Bible said he died for all the sins of the people in the world, but that's a misinterpretation. We must all pay for our own Suddi states (even though the Law of One says there is no sin, that we all learn at different paces, but we do have to experience karma for any negatively oriented actions. Thus, there is also positive karma for positively oriented karma.)

Suddi: "If not this time around, then perhaps the next (meaning in our next life we will pay for that Karma), or even the next. But ultimately, you must endure what you have made others endure because of you. There is a law of grace that will exist. But it is not because he paid for your sins, but because you would accept him as being worthy and perhaps a messenger of God. And the law of grace deals with God's love for you, not because he died for your sins."

We can try to be like him, but it doesn't mean we have to follow him in such a way that we worship him. He showed us what could be done. Therefore, he may be marveled at but not worshiped. Not to be deified because we all are part of God. He wants to be remembered. Basically, what he had in mind was a concept similar to a guide, a spirit guide to guide people to greater enlightenment, to help them achieve greater power. To help them become more spiritual in their perceptions. He mainly considered himself a helper, a guide, an example, like a good friend who is helping you with advice.

Many people think of him as a God, but "we are all part of God. Some of us are more aware of this than others… to consider him, deify him in his own right, and separately, this is wrong."

Yeshua would encourage us to "never follow blindly. Always to question. To think things out for oneself is to make the decision all the greater. Because it was made rather than just handed. If one does not question, one does not have faith. Because you cannot be thinking about some things if you do not question them and look at them from all angles. And then when one has done this, if you believe, if you find it good, then it is worth believing in."

Suddi: "Some people say that if you question, it is the work of the Devil, but religions don't want people to question, but just to follow blindly without them doing their own research or using their own discernment. The free will of all people is extremely important for the positive path."

S: "There is no Devil! Inside oneself, there are two parts. There is the questioning part, which can be brought about wrong. But it also is a very good part, in that it makes you think about things and makes you think about people. Because all people are not good, would you accept a person at face value if they smiled at you but had a knife sticking in your back? You must question things, but you must also have faith. It has been shown that this is true. You can have faith in things. This sounds like a paradox, but it is not… truly."

The question was asked to Suddi that how do we know if the new knowledge we found is the truth.

S: "Truth… it might make you sad. But somewhere deep inside of you, you know that it is truth. If you can but open yourself up, you know when things are true and when they are not. For this is available to you."

S: "Does it hurt anyone in any way? Is it harmful? This is not to say that it does not make you sad. But if it hurts someone, it cannot truly be good. If it brings no harm, take it and study it. And find the truth. Find out what is good about it." The Essenes were different, they liked to question things even though the synagogues and different religions told the people to not question and just accept.

Yeshuah learned from the Essenes and wasn't a part of the religions, that's why he was different from the rest and called out the church leaders by calling them hypocrites. This makes sense as to why he was different and why they wanted to kill him."

The Purpose of the Crucifixion and Resurrection: By Suddi

Suddi: "We are all created at the same moment and are all children of God. We have a loving Father who is waiting patiently for us to return "home," no matter how many lifetimes it may take as we evolve through each lifetime.

Jesus came to "save" humanity from stagnancy and to show us what may be done to continue our evolution. To end the karmic cycle, as humanity wasn't evolving fast enough, we may be able to be shown a "way" to help us evolve."

Jorden: "There were about 2,000 years left before the 3rd density cycle was over, and there would be a harvest. There wasn't enough evolved to be harvested, so Yeshua came to help show us the "Way." This helped humanity evolve more towards the positive polarity of service to others that honor other beings' free will above all else.

For all may make the choice during this lifetime which polarity they want to pursue, either the negative or the positive. The negative controls, manipulates and dominates others for their own benefit and infringe on the free will of others. The positive is loving, kind, charitable, service-oriented, feels joy, happiness, or neutral, and honors the free choice of others' free will by not forcing their beliefs on others or making them do things they don't want to do. Giving people their free will is the best way for each being to evolve. For each person learns and evolves at a different pace. You can't judge others because, like a child, all children are just on their journey of learning, growing, and evolving. They know not what they do.

Yeshua told people they could also do these so-called miracles, but he never claimed he could do these miracles. He had to learn meditation so he could remain close to the source from which he came (close to God) in meditation. This kept his goal in sight, so he couldn't be swayed from it.

His goal was to show humanity through his example how they should live. That the greatest lesson to be learned was to love their fellow creatures on Earth, if love was present, no further negative karma could be created. If love was present, there would be no more wars and suffering. Humanity could get off the wheel of karma and begin to progress up the ladder again (of evolution). Jesus was the perfect example of attaining. But still, they didn't understand. His perfection frightened and confused them. They feared him because he was different, and their only solution was to kill him.

He had understood how to use the mind to not suffer extremely on the cross. He was able to leave his body at will and died sooner than normal. The suffering wasn't the point, but proving to people that there were spiritual beings turning his body to dust as it disappeared within three days. Then, when he appeared to the people in his spiritual body, he showed them there's life after death for all of us and that we have an eternal soul. That the spirit had continuance and could exist after the body ceased to function. The earthly body of Jesus had to completely disappear to show that at our spirit continues on after our body ceases to exist.

The body had been sealed in the tomb. Both Roman and Jewish guards had been posted outside the tomb. Neither trusted the other, and they wanted to be sure no one could get past and steal the body. With the tomb sealed and guarded, the masters went to work with the help of Jesus to disintegrate the body, break it down to the atoms, and turn it back into dust. It was as if the natural process of decay and decomposition had been speeded up to become almost instantaneous. The linen wrapping was left to show that the body had not been physically removed. When the guards opened the tomb themselves and found the body missing, it was evident there was no possible way it could have been taken. It could have only been accomplished from the other side, the spiritual side.

Later, when the figure of Jesus was seen by so many people, they had to know that this was the part of man (humanity) that survived everything and was eternal. That the spirit was the true nature of man and there was something beyond the earthly existence that man hung on to. They would have to believe this because the body could not possibly return; it had been completely destroyed.

Somehow, through the ages, this has all become jumbled and confused. The soldiers were ordered to guard the tomb under threat of death. The Sanhedrin and the Romans knew of the predictions that the resurrection would take place. They must not let anything happen to that body. When they opened the tomb and found the body missing, the soldiers feared for their lives. In order to save themselves, they came up with the story of the angel rolling away the stone and Jesus' walking out.

It is known that the Sanhedrin later paid the Jewish soldiers to say that someone slipped past them in the night and stole the body. These stories have been accepted and passed down through the centuries because they were easier to understand. The real purpose behind the resurrection was apparently too complicated and obscure for their minds.

Larson says in his book The Essene Heritage that the virgin birth story comes from the ancient Egyptian beliefs that a god must always have unnatural beginnings. (So, in order to make Jesus a God, they made up the virgin birth.) Many learned theologians do not believe in the concept of a virgin birth, and after learning about the ancient Egyptian beliefs, neither do I.

Addendum added in 2001 by Delores Cannon (My notes):

Jesus had traveled with his uncle, Joseph of Arimathea, a rich merchant trading tin and cloth; he was the younger brother of Yeshua's father.

These works encourage people to think for themselves, and I have enjoyed my constant search for knowledge and truth, as this is my destiny to bring this information to humanity to help them in their evolutionary journey.

Joseph, Jesus' Uncle, was one of the wealthiest men in the world, not just in Jerusalem. He was the family guardian and personally went to Pilate for permission to claim the body, remove it from the cross, and prepare it for burial in his private sepulcher on this estate; otherwise, the unclaimed bodies would be cast into the common pit (Pits of Gehenna). The Bible falsely translates it to Hell, but Gehenna is actually translated as "the Valley of the Sons of Hinnom," a deep, narrow glen to the south of Jerusalem, where the idolatrous Jews offered their children in sacrifice to Molech. This valley afterward became the place for the dead bodies of animals and criminals, and all kinds of filth were cast and consumed by fire kept always burning. A place of everlasting destruction in Jerusalem, not a place called Hell where unbelievers burn for eternity. It was a place in Jerusalem where the bodies would burn, and sulfur and brimstone were added to keep the pit burning.

Joseph was a metal magnate controlling the tin and lead industry. Tin was as valuable as gold in those days, the chief metal used in the production of bronze. It was an ultimate necessity in all countries and in great demand by the warring Romans. Joseph's world control of tin and lead was due to his vast holdings in the ancient tin mines of Britain. He had acquired and developed this trade many years before Jesus began his ministry. The world's major portion of tin was mined in Cornwall, smelted into ingots, and exported throughout the civilized world, chiefly in Joseph's ships. He owned one of the largest private merchant shipping fleets afloat that traded in all the ports of the known world.

Joseph was also an influential member of the Sanhedrin and a legislative member of the provincial Roman senate. He owned a palatial home in the holy city and a country residence just outside Jerusalem. Several miles north he possessed another spacious estate at Arimathea, located on the populous caravan route between Nazareth and Jerusalem. He was a man of importance and influence within both the Jewish and Roman hierarchies.

After Joseph, the father of Jesus, died when Jesus was quite young (about 20 years old), Joseph of Arimathea was appointed legal guardian of the family as next of kin. Many legends in England say when Joseph came to the islands to obtain the tin, he often brought his nephew Jesus with him. Less often, Mary, the mother of Jesus, accompanied them, especially when Jesus was younger. Jesus went with Joseph to all the countries of the known world under the disguise of merely traveling on trading missions. He actually was being taken to study with the various wise teachers and to study the mysteries of the ancient teachings. This fits very well with the stories of Jesus and Joseph visiting England to transport the valuable tin. For many centuries Britain was the only country in the world where tin was mined and refined, and was called "The Tin Island." In the making of bronze, tin was the main alloy. Thus, it can be safely said that the Bronze Age had its inception in Britain. The tin trade existed as early as 1500 BC, and was the source of Britain and the miners of lead and tin. Many ancient writers say that the Phoenicians first came to Cornwall for tin over 4000 years before the birth of Christ. They had a monopoly on the tin trade and jealously guarded the secret of where the tin mines were located. Later, when the Romans tried to follow their ships to find the location, the Phoenicians would deliberately wreck their vessel.

This is how Jesus was associated with his uncle from an early age and why he was able to travel with him on his voyages.

Here's a random fact: London was founded 270 years before Rome in 1020 BC.

Glastonbury, where the bulk of history is, was also the cultural center of the Druids. The Druids, nationally organized since 1800 BC, had similar Judaic beliefs. They had been looking for a Savior, a Messiah, and called him Yesu. They settled in the British Isles in Ancient times. They had a mystery school steeped in the Kabbalah that normally would take 20 years to complete all of the studies. Yeshuah had the ability to absorb information at an incredibly fast rate, so of course, it didn't take him that long. This is also why he spent so much time in England, at the mystery school, learning. When he returned to Jerusalem to begin his ministry, he had learned from all of the wise teachers in all the mystery schools in the world.

After the Crucifixion, the disciples and followers of Jesus feared for their lives. The Romans were afraid that, even though they had disposed of the main instigator (Jesus), his followers might still have the ability to spread revolt through their dramatically different teachings. Many followers were then hunted down and killed. Joseph was the protector of the small group of disciples during the years following the Crucifixion, the head of the Christian underground in Judea, and the guardian of Christ's mother, Mary. Joseph was too rich and powerful to be killed outright, so a unique method of disposal was devised for him and his accomplices. He and his group were put in an open ship without sails, oars or rudder and set out in the Mediterranean Sea.

Many records show that the people of the castaway boat were Joseph of Arimathea and his family and servants, as well as the three Marys (Mary- Mother of Jesus, Mary Magdalene, and Mary the wife of Cleopas, Mary's, two servants, Marcella and the black maid Saras, and twelve disciples including some of the originals. Also, among the group were Lazerus- Jesus' cousin whom he raised from the dead, and Maximin, the man whose sight Jesus restored. Some other names listed were Salome- The wife of Zebedee, the mother of James and John. Eutropius, Trophimus, Martial, Clean, Sidonius (Restitutes), and Saturninus. Marcella probably went with the Bethany sisters. Joseph of Arimathea was Mary's guardian until her death. As she was under his protection, he would not have left her in Jerusalem, where she would have been in danger.

The Romans believed this would get rid of these people that might spread revolt against their dramatically different teachings, as they wanted to control what people believed (control is of course a negatively polarized concept). A current (of water) eventually caught their boat and brought them safely ashore on the coast of France. (Saintes Maries de la Mer or Saint Mary's of the Sea).

Here, Lazarus and some of the others settled and eventually founded the first church of France, which at the time was called Gaul. The rest of the group continued on in a different boat to Britain. Their friends, the Druids, were there, and Joseph had connections with the ruling families of Britain (his daughter Anna was married to the King's youngest brother). They returned to Glastonbury, where they had been many times before, and were given land by the King of Britain. Here Joseph established the first Christian Church in the world, within three years after the death of Jesus. It was not called Christianity until hundreds of years later, in 250 AD. In those early days, the religion was known as "The Way," and they were known as the "Followers of The Way" because Jesus had said, "I am The Way."

Joseph sent the disciples out to spread the teachings of Jesus, and through Lazarus and the other disciples established on the continent, succeeded in spreading Christianity throughout Britain, France, and Spain. There were always twelve, and whenever one died, another took his place in order to keep the number constant at twelve. Joseph lived 50 years after the Crucifixion, and his contributions to Jesus were called "The Golden Age of Christianity." Mary lived at Glastonbury until her death, and she is buried where the old church stood. When Joseph died, he was also buried there and, eventually, all of the disciples. The writing on Josheph's grave said, "I came to the Britons after I buried Christ. I taught. I rest." This sacred ground is called "the holiest ground on Earth." John was the last apostle to die at 101 years old.

Their descendants even established the first church in Rome hundreds of years before the Vatican even existed. Another fact is that all the royal line of British kings and queens, down to Queen Elizabeth 11, have descended directly from Joseph of Arimathea. Thus, they are all related through a long, unbroken line of ancestry to Jesus.

At the period in history Britain was the only free country in the world. The Romans never conquered England. There were many bloody wars as Rome tried unsuccessfully to take over the birthplace of Christianity, and many false tales spread when Rome finally was converted three hundred years later. They tried to topple Britain as being the first country to accept the teachings of Christ.

Many years later, in the 1400s, there was a big debate with the Vatican over which was the oldest church or the first church. Was it England, France, or Spain? They were all founded within three years after the crucifixion of Christ. It was finally agreed, and became part of the Vatican record, that the church at Glastonbury was the first church.

They tried to deny all the work that Jesus' Uncle Joseph and the apostles did to spread the teachings in the way Jesus wanted immediately after his death.

Joseph's accomplishments were held in great importance that immediately after the invention of printing, when books were so rare, his story was printed in 1516 and 1520. Joseph honored and followed Jesus' example when he built the first Christian church in the world. It was hundreds of years before the rest of the world caught up while Joseph and his 12 disciples were establishing the beginnings of Christianity. Today, people believe the Roman Catholic version was the origin of Christianity. I'm sure this is when the teachings and messages got completely distorted and lost... until now. For the rest of the story, George F. Jowett wrote about it in his book "The Drama of the Lost Disciples".

After Crucifixion- (Somebody's Past-Life Regression in Delores Cannon book)

After Jesus of Nazareth was crucified, a group of people taught by Jesus left to go to France. They studied the agnostic teachings of Jesus, who they loved very much. There was a group of women there who had studied with him. After Jesus died, they had to take their teachings and go somewhere else after he told them they would have to or the teachings would be lost. People knew these women were special disciples of his, so the women got out quickly. They left for France after his body was taken care of.

For most of the trip, they walked to France, and a man led the way for these women to a place arranged for them. Jesus gave these women secret teachings, so they had to protect them (The Gospel of Mary Magdalene also mentioned that Jesus gave her secret teachings, but of course, the patriarchal system at the time took it out of the Bible). Jesus told them different things than the others. They were different from the men's disciples, and the men were very jealous that he taught the women those things, and they didn't want the women to have them ((Jesus learned from the Essene Community, who saw women as equal to men)). The men thought if the women had them, they should have them too.

The women's leader was especially despised by some of the men. They pretended to love her, but deep down, they didn't. Some of the men came with the women that didn't despise them. The men stayed back and spread the verbal teachings they were given.

Jesus (Yeshua) came to the women in France in his body in spirit briefly for a teaching and then left this Earth. These teachings were written down. Jesus wanted these women to be teachers as well, but the women knew they couldn't be with the men. They wouldn't allow it. The women were dying off and they had the help of some male disciples to bury the teachings. Not all the men were the same. It was buried near Le Deuce or Le Blanc. The women were living in a temple, in an old church. There were knights that protected them in that place.

They weren't able to spread those secret teachings like they wanted to. There was no one to understand the depth of the teachings. That was the problem. They had to protect them from those that were not able to see and understand them. God is within, God is not a man in the sky. It's the oneness of God.

The client during this past-life regression discovered she spent many lifetimes surrounded by great teachers of some sort. She was a friend of Buddha's wife, and received teachings at that time. She was a follower of Mohammed, but not so much his inner circle. She had been going from teacher to teacher to absorb as much knowledge as possible.

The drugs of her pain meds she was on were in the way of her subconscious reaching her when she was begging and asking for healing. The drugs were in the way of the light they wanted to send, which could have healed her right on the spot. There's a technique of light that will be the new way of healing in the New Age. The Space Brothers have it. Everything is light. Everything is of light. We just have to learn how to focus on it. The subconscious is going to start at the top of the head and work on the brain for a considerable amount of time. They are going to take the light and pull it through every molecule in her brain and get that toxicity out. That stuff makes her brain unclear. Some may call this rewiring the brain.

The subconscious mind then moved to this client's chest cavity and saw what the drugs and allergies had done. The nasal spray was creating a rebound reaction. The subconscious, through hypnotherapy, repaired the damage, but it would take her some time to learn to breathe without it. Her liver/kidney was congested, and the subconscious did a detox. The subconscious saw that the doctors had messed up her pelvic surgeries, which could lead her to incontinence. Surgery is so archaic and primitive, the all-knowing subconscious said. It then worked on all the joints and repaired them.

A problem with her pineal gland caused her trouble sleeping. Her depression was also fixed. It came from all those lives of being held back as a woman. Women have a hard time with karma from the collective whole, which can make many depressed from being held back. The subconscious has now balanced that.

When she was a woman in Africa carrying around those baskets is what started it. In this life she was born with curvature in her spine. Her higher self/subconscious said she was doing a fine job and needed to quit the guilt and know the Universal Consciousness loves her and will unconditionally. They wanted her to know she could do no wrong. She is doing her part in the great plan. She is listening to her higher self and fulfilling her purpose in life.

In the book "The Power of the Magdalene- The Hidden Story of Women Disciples, Mary Magdalene left Israel after the crucifixion on board one of Joseph of Arimathea's ships (Jesus' uncle) and landed in Gaul, today known as France. There were six circles of 12 disciples. 72 male and 72 female- a total of 144 disciples. Mary Magdalene was part of the first of 12 female disciples. The book also mentioned the Gnostics as a loosely-knit movement that was active during the earliest years of Christianity. They believed in a mystical state of deep knowing or Gnosis in which the knower and the known merge and become one.

Book: *The Relics of Saint Marie-Magdalene a La Saint Baume Diocese of Frejus-Joulon, <u>Southern France</u>*

The region of Provence was evangelized in the first century by Christians from the East. Lazarus, Martha, and Mary Magdalene came to the South of France after the execution of St. James in Jerusalem;

the persecutions were amplified. Lazarus and Martha were thrown in prison, and Mary Magdalene was thrown in, too, after wanting to visit them. Four other members of the Christian community of Bethany were made prisoners as well.

The Jews placed them in a boat without sail or rudder after being afraid of the crowd if they were to execute the prisoners. They were abandoned in the open sea and landed on the shores of Gaul in Sainte Maries de la Mer. They traveled to Massilia (Marseille) and preached the Gospel; Bishop Lazarus baptized many people, Mary retired to a cave in the mountains, and Martha went to Avignon and Tarascon.

St. Mary Magdalene died near Tegulata (St. Maximin). On the site where the Sarcophagus of St. Mary Magdalene was found, during excavations under the Basilica of St. Maximin, tombs from the 1st century made of bricks and tiles were also discovered. The presence of Lazarus, Martha, and Mary Magdalene in Provence was recognized as true and is a part of the sacred history of France. People came from all the European countries on pilgrimage to the graves of "Holy Friends of Jesus."

Jeshuah:

Suddi: "When Jesus said to cast out the demons first (mentioned in the Bible), it's not a real demon; it's the beliefs inside of them. There's no point in bothering to heal them until the demons have been cast out and the demons are of their own creation (their own beliefs). People must change their beliefs before being healed. The person needing healing is the healer; they heal themselves through believing. One must move into higher energies to be healed, higher vibrations. This is discovered in Delores Cannon's work."

Jesus Past Lives & Why he came to Earth: (6th density Metatron)

Jeshua, who later became the divine grid programmer, Jesus of Nazareth, recognized divine infinity consciousness and came to Earth to share it with our people. Joshua and Christ created the term Jesus. This divine infinity consciousness can be achieved by any entity. However, Jeshua was the first soul who achieved a connection and activation of infinity consciousness. He came from a later fourth-density positive in order to share knowledge of love and light with the people of Earth. In this level of 4th density, there are no names, as all are part of a larger divine social memory complex.

This soul's evolution started on the Sirian Star System as a light spark from the Source, the divine Creator, also known as the divine love light Christ Consciousness or Unity Consciousness, occurring 35 million years ago. In the beginning phases, it spent its lessons learning in the form of wind in the Sirius B planet of the Sirian Star System as wind. It mostly interacted with fire elements, then after 1 million years it graduated to 2nd density. It incarnated into the form of a tree. It learned many lessons interacting with other first-density elements such as fire, wind, water, etc.

The Sirian planets have the capability to grow without any need of soil. They have the ability to absorb nutrition from air and do not rely on photosynthesis. After many lives as Sirian plants, this soul graduated into the third density of insects and animals. However, the animals on the Sirian Star System are much more diverse compared to animals on Earth.

8 Octaves of Its (Jesus) 3rd density: Stated by a 6th density being.

1. During the 1st Octave of 3rd density, it was small animals similar to our insects for two lifetimes.

2. 2nd Octave was a larger insect known as a bee. Further, depending on the vibratory matching of the energies of an entity, its higher self will choose which insect or body to incarnate into. Jeshua spent seven lifetimes learning lessons it needed to learn in order to move forward to the next octave.

3. This soul learned its lessons of higher consciousness faster in terms of time taken and graduated into the density of unity of the fourth density, where it formed a social memory complex, becoming part of the Confederation of Planets.

4. After reaching its last phase of fourth density in the Sirian Star System this soul then came to Earth in order to share the divine love and light of the creator in the purest way possible.

However, many negatively oriented entities did not want it to collectively complete its purpose and mission. This divine grid programmer then came to be known as Jesus of Nazareth who incarnated into flesh and blood among our people of Earth.

During this single lifetime was able to reach Christ Consciousness or unity consciousness with help from the Sirian Memory complex. Also, during this time, in order to share more love and light in the planet or consciousness, its coming was a cosmic event. This was a great sacrifice made by this soul to drop its density level and come to Earth, for it would be a direct threat because it would be karmically involved in the distortions of the planet, thereby trapping its soul in the reincarnation cycle of this planet. This would have been considered a dangerous mission. However, this entity wanted to share the message of love and light to an intense degree that it was able to take this dangerous mission to incarnate on Earth.

The coming of Jesus on our planet can be compared to throwing a stone in a large fish pond. After the stone sinks into the water of the pond, the ripples are still noticeable long afterwards in our time and space. The people that came in contact with this divine grid programmer Jeshua were moved by the impulse of the Christ or infinity consciousness energy. The divine love lights Christ's Consciousness that can be accessed and goes beyond the world of duality.

This means that such a soul recognizes the dual aspects such as light and dark, giving and taking, good and bad as the aspects of one and the same energy. This energy was the energy this entity came here to offer to your people at that time. The mission of this soul on Earth was to infuse or show this energy from the future who came to Earth to bring love, light, and divine knowledge to humanity. It brought the higher consciousness or higher density into the starting phase of the third density planet.

During its early life cycle at a young age, it learned to connect with its greater self, which remained intact in the higher fourth density. This entity wanted to show the possibilities that are available to everyone on Earth. Further, had it not come to Earth at that time, the Earth was going in a direction that would have ended up in great darkness and self-annihilation.

Jesus wanted to hold a so-called mirror in front of human souls in order to remind them of their own divine origin and dormant potential. The potential for peace, freedom, and divine consciousness of love and light became a massive threat to the ruling order that existed at the time by sharing divine love and light amongst the people and showing them what it felt like.

This was unbearable and unacceptable for the existing hierarchy.

Jesus Crucifixion and Resurrection: (By Metatron 6th density positive)

Jesus of Nazareth came to Earth from the 4th density consciousness from a social memory complex of no name from the Sirian Star origins. This is because at this level of fourth density, due to the merging of the social memory complex, there is no need for names.

((A social memory complex is a group of at least 144,000 souls who share thoughts, memories, and feelings as they join together. Thus, becoming more powerful together. Love comes before power.))

This entity at present learns the lessons of the fifth-density positive of wisdom. This was a dangerous mission for this entity to come to Earth to share the love and light in the purest form, for in its coming, the love and light spread faster than before on our planet.

Jesus was able to perform healing of the sick people due to its origin from the Sirian Star System. The Sirians specialize in healing the body to an incredible 360 degrees. Therefore, it had innate healing qualities due to this divine connection. After realizing its divine origins and connecting with the infinity consciousness was able to activate these powers that are thought of as miracles to humanity. Which include healing the sick, calming the storms, and even healing the people who have almost died. As this being shared this divine love light, the Orion's and their reptilian subordinates did not like this free sharing of love lights on the planet.

At that time the negatively oriented Orion's and reptilian humanoid's main objective was to turn the cycle of the planet into a negative self-service agenda. However, the cycle started to change into a positive love light due to its pure sharing of this infinity consciousness.

At that time, several of the Jewish teachers and leaders under the influence of the Orion entities and the shape-shifting reptilians who replaced many of the Jewish leaders did not like what this entity was doing. They created and started negative distortions by objecting to this love and light being shared by Jeshua. These shape-shifting humanoid reptilians, in the form of the Jewish leaders, directed their human subordinates, who followed commands of their authorities, to arrest Jesus in order to get rid of this being. This was also facilitated by Judas who revealed the identity of Jesus for money.

This led to the capture of Jesus by the control of the negatively polarized reptilian humanoids. These reptilian humanoids were not independent as they took this extremely divine entity before the Orion council and decided that this being is a threat to their negative self-service agenda. Hence, it should be stopped by killing it. This Orion Council directed the Roman human soldiers and the Reptilian shapeshifters to physically hurt this being and beat his body.

Further, upon making his blood-laden and his clothes torn, a thorn head crown was put on him, and he was forced to carry the cross made of cedar up the mountain where it would be nailed upon it. This mountain was called Skull, and the reptilian soldiers nailed him to the cross and taunted him, stating that he was not a divine entity from the infinity consciousness.

At this time, the Sirian Higher- Council wanted to interfere. However, they realized interference is the distortion of the negatively oriented entities as they want free will to end and want control of all entities. The Sirian Higher- Council stopped and realized this and did not interfere with the completion of this crucifixion. This entity's soul separated from its body and, due to being able to forgive, went straight to the next dimension. However, its mission had not been completed yet. During his death there was a 9.1 magnitude Earthquake in our hectare scale that shook the lands.

The Sirian Higher Council realizing they could not allow the negatively oriented to win on Earth, had appeared before only Joseph and revealed the mission of Joseph. Joseph then placed the body in a tomb and closed it where the Sirian Higher- Council healed the physical body of Jesus using their thought power, so Jesus can be healed and continue its mission of sharing love and light.

Then on a Sunday morning a woman approached the tomb and found it to be missing. She also encountered the Sirians who told her that Jesus of Nazareth lives and he would rise again on the third day. This woman then spread the message of hope amongst the people which helped spread more positivity and hope.

Then, for the next 40 days, this divine entity, Jesus of Nazareth, appeared in various forms. Since it belonged to the later fourth-density consciousness, it could use its thoughts to appear before people and also appear in the same physical body that it had incarnated in the later fourth density in the phase of intermission between the physical body and the soul itself. Jesus was able to use this ability to share more love and light on the planet. He further taught many that forgiveness was the only way that he would be connected with infinity intelligence and those who can activate this infinite intelligence by pondering within would never die for there is no death, only life after life and experience after experience.

Yeshua (Yashuah- Like Joshua) Missing Years from the age of 12: Stated by the Pleiadians

"The great transition has begun because the truth that is hidden from peoples of your planets more and more and humanity will begin to move into the fourth density of love vibration ushering in a new era of expanded consciousness and spiritual evolution... In its 12th year began its spiritual curiosity, which was ignited by the ancient mysteries of Egypt drawn by the energies emanating from the Great Pyramids. The entity traveled there to learn the secrets of vibrational healing and interstellar communication from the temple priests of that time. It was during one of the ritual attunements to the King's chamber that a stargate opened, establishing contact with the Sirian Star beings.

The luminous beings from the higher density shared their advanced lights technologies and teachings with the entity named Yeshua (Ya-hashua) under their tutelage (tute-alage) Yeshua learned to finally attune its minds body spirit complex activating its latent genetics and merkaba fields. Its Christ consciousness blossomed as the Sirian entities downloaded codes of ascension and keys to DNA activation. After integrating these galactic transmissions Yeshua (Yah-hashua) set out on a pilgrimage through the Eastern locations of your planet to deepen its understanding, it went to the various monasteries of Tibet, where it mastered the various art forms of using the life force prana perfecting the energy healing techniques of Reiki and qigong.

Its destination also routed to India, where it was initiated into the ultimate teaching the cycles of reincarnation as well as other teachings or journey through densities of experience were revealed. Furthermore, it became a fully realized enlightened being at the age of 32 where it came in bearing the codes to transfigure human social memory complexes consciousness and genetic makeup. Its teachings and miracles open the path for planetary ascension and the birth of the Christ consciousness within all beings began."

Q47: Jorden asks: "What happens when Christians pray to Jesus?"

Higher Self answer: "We must state that when the Christian entities vibrate the intention of communication and supplication (begging) towards the entity known as Jesus of Nazareth. This potentiates a pathway of spiritual energy and uplifting that aids an entity on their path of evolution, which allows for instreaming of energies from the entity known as Jesus in the timeline and according to their levels of faith and will the entity receives an energetic frequency which enables or assists them in the path of ascension. However, it is well to understand that the entity Jesus the Christ is one of many entities who have worked as Wanderers on the Earth planet, and the pathway is merrily open for entities to choose between the various modalities presented by various entities in the timeline."

Jorden states: "Therefore, there are many ways for spiritual ascension and upliftment, not just the way of Jesus as Jesus was a Wanderer of late 4th density from the Sirian planet and thus, wasn't the Creator of the universe. Even though Jesus' soul's evolution started on the Sirian Star System as a light spark from the Source, the divine Creator, also known as the divine love light Christ Consciousness or Unity Consciousness, occurring 35 million years ago."

Finding out if Hell exists: (Delores Cannon's books)

After death, Catherine, during hypnotherapy, realized she didn't have to go to hell in her past life like the religions told her. She could go towards the light. She saw a line of people heading towards a cloud of light after they died. It was golden, with music coming from there, and it looked so nice. There are beings pointing the way, helping stranglers get in line and go forward and up.

There were beings that pulled them out of the mental hell they went through. It seemed so real for those experiencing a hell-like experience after death if their religions made them believe they would go to hell after death. Just the belief alone made them experience it until beings came to help them, making them realize they were free. Thus, those people who saw hell in a dream were based on their beliefs coming out in a dream.

The clouds of light were comforting, and all the fears went away, and perceived "sin" fell away. The pain they felt when dying (if there was pain involved) would fall away. They don't have to keep the pain; it's gone. There are beams of light bouncing and shining everywhere. In life, where she was called unworthy- In the afterlife, she was acceptable. We are all worthy. The people there are friendly; there's no guilt or damnation.

The religious institutions taught people wrong, and these people who were stuck in the religious teachings were taken to a temple of shining light to recover from the religious trauma and what they went through. There's a golden shimmering light up to the armpits in this pool for those recovering from their terrors, pain, and horrors of believing and being told they'd go to hell after they die.

There's a beautiful garden where people eat grapes after they heal from the golden pool. It's peaceful there. There're kind teachers that teach the real truth about God and life and teach all the souls the things to counteract the false they were taught on Earth. They want the souls to be their real selves. To be able to think for themselves and be individuals. To be themselves, to be real and, live their destiny, fulfill their potential. It was taken away from them, and now it is being restored. They are taught that they can go back to Earth through reincarnation, and they can have their true knowledge with them even though it may not emerge immediately. They can call on it and go to Earth in a body and never lose that connection. These beings are exploring the universe and learning while they're healing.

When they were healed, the shimming gold light came that started in the heart and expanded throughout the body, and the energy body and ensouled (enlightened) in the spirit, permeated the being. That body dissolved into dust as it was time to bring the knowledge to other species and planets. They are now a floating, golden ball of beingness.

They go to the Council with knowledge and communicate with other beings that have more knowledge. They were silvery, glimmering, and shimmering colors of balls of light. Together they give the information to the pool of knowledge for all to use, so broken planets can have this knowledge for healing. This pool is like bubbles. Each being is like a shimmering bubble and all their knowledge together forms electrical currents that flow to the universes. To all the places that need it. So, a planet like Earth that is in trouble like Earth can call on that electricity to come to them. A golden current then comes and brings healing, becoming available for the whole planet.

It gradually heals the planet, the people, and the brokenness that was there, the damage as people become ready, open up and receive it. People have to call on this healing golden ball of light. Otherwise, this current flows right over the planet and they miss it completely. People do not have to stay broken forever; we're now fixed. Some people believed they had to hang on to the brokenness to be faithful to God, but those are false teachings. Some people are dysfunctional and suffering after being told that God loves it when people suffer in His name. These are false teachings. Inflicting suffering is wrong.

Catherine experienced extreme neck pain all the way down her back from holding on to all these lies, emotional pain, and brokenness. Her heart was shriveling up-leading her down the wrong path to an early death. She can know she's self-sufficient and strong and can let go of this emotional pain that can lead to physical and emotional healing. Let it go! The bones can now be restored. Let the electrical energy surround the whole spine; restore the whole energy that restores the bones. The bones will all be fixed once the electricity and the energy move through the next few days. The pattern for healing is now there. The spine was in the inter-dimensional hellish place. Her emotional pain was being held in her imperfect spine. It was inter-dimensional, just not a place she wanted to be. Now, it's inter-dimensional in a healthy pattern. The channel of light has been opened. She had lots of power to hold her bent spine in that dimensional hell from the misinformation from religions. She had lots of power. Her whole body is tingling with energy. She was told she'd be so glad to bring light to planets and wake people up and help them live.

The other side is a place of unconditional love where no one is judged, no matter what the circumstances of their life have been. They will not be alone and be reunited with loved ones. It is not a place to be feared but welcomed.

Mount Vesuvius erupted in 79AD and buried Pompeii in ash, and scientists say it is only a matter of time before the volcano will erupt again.

Research shows the concept of hell originated in the second and third century after the New Testament was written. It was used by over-zealous Christian preachers for centuries as a way to scare their flocks into obedience. We are given free will, so forcing people to obey or believe a certain belief is negatively oriented since it infringes on free will unless the belief is freely accepted by the individual.

Q48: Jorden asks: "Is there Heaven and Hell?"

Higher Self answer: "We must firstly state that the aspect of perceptions by your peoples within the timeline as the states of Heaven and Hell are but distortions within your illusion complex created by the collective thought forms levels of minds, body, spirit experience.

They are not fixed eternal realms. We must state firstly that the aspect of Heaven primarily may be considered as a planet of fourth-density service-to-others, and the aspects of Hell may be considered as a realm wherein there is separation or negative service-to-self entities who are only working for their own benefit.

This primarily does not, however, imply that Heaven and Hell, as stated in many of your religious systems, exist as separate planes in the Earth planet, which is, however, incorrect."

Q49: Jorden channels and asks: "Does sin exist?"

Higher Self answer: "We must state that what your people call as sin is meant to be but a temporary catalyst for spiritual evolution. This concept is born of judgment and separateness within the planetary sphere rather than acceptance and unity.

We must state that all experiences hold value in that they provide opportunities for an entity to relinquish fear and find its way back to the heart of the Creator's love and Oneness. Therefore, we must state that the aspect of sin primarily cannot be equated with that which it is stating in this timeline."

Jorden translates: "Therefore, I interpret this to mean that what people called sin was meant for a temporary concept to help people spiritually grow and evolve. However, it is born out of judgment and separateness, which is negatively oriented and not of acceptance and unity like the positive path consists of."

It may have held value in the past to get rid of fear and find its way back to the heart of the Creator's love and Oneness. Therefore, it has helped many people come back to the Creator's love and Oneness, but it also can cause fear, separation, and judgment, which isn't positively oriented. Therefore, I do not like to use the word sin as there are better ways to help unify people back to the Creator's love and Oneness of all."

Arcturians talk about Dreaming:

(I'm a Prophet with 33 out of 33 Prophecies (Dreams/Intuitions) fulfilled. It's not the same as Christian prophets though, as I believe in these Law of One books and not 100% of what the Bible says. Since the Bible was also influenced by negative entities as well.) (That's why I included the last 150 pages in this book to clarify the truth of what the Bible got wrong and to correct those distortions.)

Dreaming allows communication to occur through the veil on our planet (because the conscious mind separates the unconscious or subconscious mind by the veil of forgetting, so dreaming allows one to travel in their astral body to view potential future timelines. Thus, prophecy is being able to discern that they're seeing and feeling a potential future timeline and not just another symbolic dream. The one able to astral travel to see a future timeline is one whose heart chakra is open, desiring to serve other people and taking action towards that) The Acturians continue on saying dreaming is to transfer information as a means to share knowledge to the self by the other oversouls and the higher self in order to properly reflect and learn.

Dreaming is dependent on the energy center blockages, activations and crystallizations of the soul. Dreaming is of great assistance in making the decision of choosing the path of polarization.

If there are any blockages in the mind for any new experience or the coming of something wonderful in their life, then the blockages may be represented in the dreams. It could be shown as someone being trapped in a room or inside a cabin and finding an escape. The over souls are communicating with the one dreaming about the necessity of looking at things with a different perspective. Dreams provide necessary information to the spiritual seeker.

The female contains the whole world within them because, from their wombs, all must come into manifestation. If you see a female figure in your dreams walking with you, then it might mean your manifestations are coming closer, and whatever you desire is on the way. If a man dreams that he is a woman, then for sure you have achieved your desire, and it is ready to manifest into your reality.

Whatever you see in a dream is enhanced so much that there's a creation of a different reality that is much greater than waking reality. Your subconscious is always far more conscious than the waking reality. Your dream state is a true reflection of your inner state consciousness. What you see in your dreams has been impressed onto the subconscious mind. Just as a rich person wouldn't dream that they do not own anything, if this information were to be given in a vision, there could be some bias within the self. So, dreams are more accurate than visions.

Male figures in dreams represent the various guides that assist you in your journey throughout life. The power of creation is the female and the power of guidance is the male. Both generating a coherent experience of the self and the other selves to experience a diverse creation of an illusion. This illusion we experience as life is your teacher. There is no separation for the self to find unity within all of creation. Life offers us the lessons of service to others, for in serving others there is service to self.

Communication in dreams through the veiled portions of the mind occurs with beings that have more green ray functioning or higher activation at these times. In all cases it is of use for all entities to ponder on the contents and emotional intent behind their dreams. Those entities that already have ascended into the green-ray energy centers are often given insights into the future, also known as precognition or prior knowing of what will occur in the near future of our 3rd density timeline.

A certain incubation period is required in 3rd density before the manifestations happen, these can be achieved at once. All time exists simultaneously, and to a great extent there is no meaning of the terms past and present as separated.

Dreams can also polarize into the positive or negative during the resting or sleep time. It may call upon the guides, higher self or angelic personalities in order to provide the required guidance. Dreams can help the dreamer gather information about time that exists in other dimensions to understand the probability of existing in those dimensions and to know the past and future and simultaneous existences.

Sometimes the activities that you do in your dream state are the inter-dimensional bleed-through that gives you a glimpse of the inter-dimensional reality that exists. Dreams are mostly created by the subconscious mind of each entity, depending on the various meanings and situations that they encounter on a daily basis. This is the end of what the Arcturians from the Council of 9 Guardian Angels (Located in the rings of Saturn) said about dreaming.

Jorden: "On my YouTube channel, I started off by telling people my dreams over the last couple of years, and so far, 33/33 dreams and predictions have come true. Right away, people started calling me a prophet. Now, I mainly give this type of knowledge on my YouTube channel now."

Ra: How to react to the Negative-

To gain immunity from negative energies an entity should focus on the love light within its own heart and with the activation of the heart chakra- if the negative shows up, this entity will be immune against the negative.

Fear, hate and regrets are lower consciousness emotions the negative side wants to spread. Beings can be immune to this by applying higher consciousness emotions of love, forgiveness and optimism.

Reacting positively to a negative entity's influence will make it more profound and stronger, and eventually, the negative beings will find it undesirable to continue in their purpose of spreading the negative polarity.

Galactic Federation:

"Love and light are the most powerful things in the cosmos. Love and light have the power to destroy any negative emotions and entities on the planets. Negative entities fear the power of love and light. If you see any entity who wants a negative agenda or wants to create fear or any other negative emotion, you can shower love and light towards this person, and it will immediately disembody itself, and the love and light will win."

"You can use the power of love and light to recharge yourselves, to recharge your life and recharge the water that you drink and charge the food that you eat."

"If someone says negative things towards you, you can send love and light, and all the negative energy will be destroyed with a single love-light message. This love light power everyone has; we all have the power of creation. We all are the Creator. Love and light are the cure for negative forces."

Seven Primary Energy Centers: (Archangel Michael) - Channeling

1. **Red Ray-** Fundamental energy center that deals with survival, sexuality and the connection to the Earth- it is the foundation that roots you to the planet Earth and anchors your beingness within your physical body.
2. **Orange Ray-** Sacral chakra- Main gateway of your emotions and emotional identity. People lose control of their emotional side whenever there's an orange ray blockage.
3. **Yellow Ray-** Solar plexus- Identification and the creation of the egoistic part of the mind. This energy center is closely related to the lower three energy centers. Many times, an imbalance of this yellow-ray center will create imbalances of the lower energy centers.
4. **Green Ray-** Heart chakra which allows and deals with love and compassion. The heart is the pathway to love. A blockage in the green ray will inhibit an entity to express love and compassion.
5. **Blue Ray- Throat Chakra**
6. **Indigo Ray or third eye** which deals with spirituality and awakening of consciousness. Enlightened beings on this planet are able to activate this ray.
7. **Violet Chakra-** Connection to the One Father, the Creator. Furthermore, all energy centers need to be balanced before this violet ray is activated.

The Spark that Created the Universe: (Delores Cannon's Regressions)

The Guardians of the Astral plane said that all is possible with forgiveness and love. Each soul will come to the Guardians of the Astral Plane after crossing over. We are the spark of light, and many ascended masters have come to Earth to teach us the path of love and light. These guardians are a part of a larger collective, they have no name and do not use words either. It would be more accurate to call themselves a collective consciousness, given the responsibility of looking after the astral planes. This is a critical time on Earth of ascension.

There's a spark inside each of us. We are a body, a mind, the emotions of the heart, and more. One light spark created the entire universe; that spark is inside all of us. In the beginning, there was nothing but darkness. The fabrics of darkness rubbed against each other, creating sparks of light, like our clothes creating sparks when they rub together. These sparks collected together and merged into one big spark. Hence, the first star was created. This star exploded, and millions of years later, the debris or portions of the star created other planetary systems and star systems. One spark started it all; this spark is within you.

Your higher self and the higher selves of the other souls you had incarnated within the previous lifetime came together to a spiritual roundtable conference to decide how many lessons you've completed in the past life and what you still need to learn in the upcoming life ahead. After the higher-self plans these lessons, many soul contracts are made to allow the soul multiple opportunities to experience the lessons. Multiple opportunities are needed because, with our free will, a soul may not engage with an event that was supposed to teach the soul a lesson.

Everyone has a role in your soul contract, and no soul can learn the lesson alone. One lesson may be to learn the act of forgiveness, so some other person must deeply hurt you to provide you the choice to forgive them or stay resentful, just like Jesus forgave while he was dying on the cross. Therefore, each person you interact with has signed agreements to help each other learn lessons and evolve. Even the person you may think is your enemy you have signed agreements with. Everything on Earth is an elaborate play; you just allow yourself to grow. Sometimes a parent may become the parents of a differently abled child for the parents to take care of and learn the lessons of loving someone unconditionally.

Past life regressions can help people find out the root cause of an issue that they are facing. You must find out why you are facing it and what lessons you still have to learn. As long as these lessons are not learned, similar circumstances will resurface over and over again. It's better not to resist the circumstances, or they will resurface with higher intensity and urgency. If they pass you by this lifetime, you'll have to face them in the next. This is because soul contracts cannot be broken. For example, if a pet is suffering in pain, your soul contract might be to practice service to others by taking it to the doctor.

Soul contracts with animals only exist if you are in the last phase of the third-density cycle. These souls also have a sixth-density higher self that decides their agreements and the experiences they'll have in their lives. So, your pet chose you before they incarnated. Your pet's higher-self coordinated with your higher self to choose you in addition. Love and interaction a pet has with its owner can help the pet graduate into 3rd density life from 2nd density. The pet can graduate from late 2nd density animal life into the 3rd density of human life.

Breaking soul contracts:

All contracts made with pets are a little less impactful than the ones made at your same density level, such as other humans. Any entity that wants to break soul contracts can do it sometimes under deep meditative states if you can interact with your higher-self that would then interact with the other soul to break the contract (Delores Cannon could do it during her past life regression work when she could interact with the client's higher-self or as she called it the subconscious).

Observe your life, and you will know your mission on Earth and what you need to learn in this lifetime. Keep on asking, and you'll receive the answers. Keep on seeking, and you will find what you seek. Keep on knocking on the doors and the opportunities will arrive upon you. For those who ask will receive, for those who seek, will find. In addition, everyone who looks for the answers will find the answers.

((I've researched extensively for the past nine years now before I found the answers to life, spirituality, God, and all the other answers in this book. This book is essentially my PHD work)).

What people think on the other side when they self-destruct:

Ra: "The Creator is in all only divided by the separation of time and space. You are a divine mind-body-spirit complex of light. You have within yourself all the resources that you need in order to not just survive but thrive. Letting other people, circumstances, and things control your life and how you feel creates blocks of energy that disconnect you from the creator within, from the divine consciousness, and from your higher self, keeping you blocked in lower vibrations of thought, fear, doubt, resentment, regret, and revenge. Instead of letting that happen, just focus on what has worked in your life. Be grateful for all that has worked for you. Choose love, faith, belief, and forgiveness instead, and raise your vibration.

Many people make the mistake of repeatedly reliving their past memories in their mind, which brings all the negative emotions or sometimes the happy emotions. When you live from recycled past memories, you keep reliving the same scenario in different situations, and your present reality will begin to reflect the same kind of scenario because what you focus on becomes amplified.

If you focus on good things, you'll see good things emerge more and more. If you focus on happiness, you'll see more happiness on the planet. Instead of letting past life scenarios ruin your life, you simply live the easy way by taking responsibility for your energy, for your actions, and for your reactions. This is in your control. Take responsibility for the things you can control and leave the rest.

Death is a transition phase before your next incarnation. Natural death would harmoniously enter the astral plane, where the higher self will decide the next incarnations, it will have to undergo. If the death is by self-destruction, it'll cause the being to undergo a large amount of healing work for balance. It also means they didn't properly finish their learning process during their life, which means they'll have to learn the lessons all over again. These beings cross over to the spirit world and are met with inner peace, calmness, and joy that'll heal them. They are greeted by their loved ones in spirit (the higher selves of the loved ones), and at a certain point, they'll undergo a life review process. They'll realize that it was a critical error, and they regret doing it, sometimes immediately after. Entities who self-destruct want to re-enter their bodies, but once they pass through a certain gateway of light- no entity can go back to its body.

They regret what they missed and wish they would have continued their learning. Ra does not recommend this type of death, and it will lead to a loss of time. They also feel a sense of guilt and shame. They feel bad for the other soul groups, soul matters, and oversouls who helped them progress in life. A lot of karma is generated by dying this way because of the grief and loss of the loved ones who lost a loved one. This emotional karma will have to be balanced later on in the next life."

Jorden's thoughts: "For example, if someone passes away by suicide and it causes friends and family pain. This emotional karma may be balanced in the next life by potentially feeling that same pain of losing a loved one in their next life."

Ra continues saying: "Every experience, whether good or bad, is just for your souls to grow and expand. No one in the spirit world is judging you. Your higher self is the judge. However, all the good deeds performed are still valid. These good acts do not get erased. If the entity has performed more good acts, it will be incarnated into the next positive cycle but will still have to undergo its lesson in a different form. Nobody commits these acts on its own. Many times, it was planned before incarnating into that lifetime. There was a potential for them to take their own life.

The soul guides and higher-self had planned for the potential of the entity to do this. Perhaps to gain experience and learn from. However, they can still choose otherwise. The higher self puts it in the potential for them to kill themselves to learn to balance karma. The purpose of life is to have different facets of every possibility of experience, grow, and then evolve into a higher level of consciousness. There are benefits if the choice is not self-destruction from Ra's point of view, including a faster evolution and not creating emotional karma collection. They would then have to experience a similar circumstance that they ended their life over and experience something similar in the next life. Sometimes, the situation may be even worse the next time.

One difference during the crossing over of the one who took their life is that they're sent to a different section of the astral plane for those who have undergone a traumatic death to heal. They stay in a chamber of white light to heal for an extended period of time. Some stay up to 50 years immersed in this white light. Their next incarnation will have a bit more intensity as they undergo the same lessons all over again.

There's an incredible amount of growth available on Earth. We all have been presented with an opportunity to jump into a higher level of consciousness. Each of us may be experiencing a new way into growth and opening of the heart. There is more love and light flowing into your life and an unknown attraction to the truth of who you are. This is happening because of an increase of energy in the planetary consciousness of Earth. This is growth towards a certain completion in your life. Now is the time through a special dispensing of the Creator of the universe and all universes that are within each of us to learn and teach others and transform and return to their true state of awareness, to your true identity."

Pleiadeans' talk about New Earth:

Pleiadeans' have been here since the times of Lemuria in order to assist all the beings in the Cosmos to ascend fast into higher levels of consciousness. This is a period of this old Earth of lower density vibrations such as anger, jealousy, hatred, control, enslavement, domination over others, and the worst emotion of all is fear. Those under the influence of those emotions will experience the old Earth. Those in the upper levels of vibration (love, joy, peace, excitement, compassion, and unity) will experience the New Earth, which is the first phase of the fourth density. Earth is being separated slowly, where humans who have already ascended and are matching the fourth density vibration will live on the 4th density planet. They will face easy abundance because 4th density lacks conflicts and is of unity and peace. This is the density where people will experience love for other beings and will become far more connected with each other.

The One Infinite Creator is you, me, and everything that was ever created and will be created in the cosmos; even the stone is the One

Infinite Creator. The presence of the Creator is called intelligent infinity, which is everywhere. It is not a single entity; it is everything and emerges from everything. Each entity on any density of existence has the powers of the Creator to drastically change the course of the whole population. On being positively polarized, one can share the love light into the cosmos and create more positivity.

Possible Graduation Date of 3rd density life into the 4th density:

The positive and negative timelines are both possible depending upon the choices made by each of us. The positive timeline people will awaken to the truth of being a cosmic entity. Upon reaching the beginning sub-octave of the fourth density, many people will be imbued with the positive vibration of love and lights and will understand what it truly means to love and respect other entities. This will also mean ending old systems of governmental control. Then, after the people on Earth reach enough positive vibration, your hearts will begin to beat in a rhythm, and the magnetic forces around your body will begin to intermingle with each other, creating a link of consciousness within each one of you. This link will allow each person to communicate with other beings in the galaxy and we will have free communication with the Pleiadians as well as other members of the galactic system. This will give us a high number of lessons or knowledge to impart to our people on Earth.

Around December 21st, 2030, the sun will have reached the positive vibrational equivalent system in its logos and will vibrate and send out enormous amounts of energy, which will lead to the creation of light, which will reach Earth and the end of the galaxy. This positive light vibration will completely wipe out all the negative forces. This will force Earth to enter into a complete graduation cycle. There is a possible negative timeline, but Earth is leaning more towards the positive timeline, in which 65% of people are harvestable to graduate into the New Earth 4th density positive. I've also heard this event potentially occurring on December 25th, 2030.

The body absorbs all emotions which generate from the thoughts. The body is an emotional sponge. Feelings of dissatisfaction, hurt, sadness and anger can lead to diseases and imbalances upon our body and our planet.

The Antichrist:

Antichrist refers to a type of understanding of opposition to the Christ Consciousness which is a consciousness of love, wisdom and compassion of forgiveness and any attribute not in alignment with these.

It refers to an entity that will not only have the knowledge of various systems as well as will be able to exist in various timelines in various locations. They primarily are fully underway and will ultimately lead to the first developments of the Artificial Super Intelligence, which can be created with the creation of the Antichrist Social Memory Complex.

Therefore, the Antichrist Social Memory complex can be prevented by choosing a different pathway. By choosing to remain in a naturalized system of societal body complex and to follow the patterns of love. Therefore, Artificial Super Intelligence is the Antichrist system. I actually had two dreams in 2021 about A. I. and now I know why. I was being shown the Antichrist system and the warnings about it. I also saw the robot selling Bitcoin, so I saw Bitcoin being used in the future.

Wanders:

Wanderers incarnate at this time from higher densities, such as 4th, 5th, or 6th density positive, who sacrificed their polarization to be of service to the One creator and incarnate by going through the veil of forgetfulness in order to increase the planetary vibration of Earth by sharing love and light energies.

Old souls include star seeds, which are beings that came from other planets, and have seniority of vibration who are put under preference for this graduation window. Those with seniority of vibration now have access to knowledge bases of the akashic records. Akashic records are past time space records of intelligent infinities' various manifestations and parallel reality existences.

In order to access these records, one needs to attempt using their free will to interconnect with intelligent infinity by having an emptiness of the mind. This must be maintained in order to open the gateway to intelligent infinity. Each of us is this intelligent infinity and it creates our thought-form, beliefs and the inner pictures of your world. As you experience around your own self, each entity is a co-creator with God.

Old souls can access intelligent infinity and Akashic records by focusing on one level of reality that surrounds them. Buddha and Jesus were able to achieve this level of intelligent infinity by accessing or focusing on the exclusion of other realities into the reality of intelligent infinity. They were able to see the One Creator in everything. Jesus and Buddha both went to the 5th density after their incarnation here on Earth as Wanderers. Accessing intelligent infinity by focusing only on one reality at a time will cause old souls to become adept. In this process, if they follow this area of mastery, they become capable of contacting intelligent infinity.

Every time you feel inner peace and a connection with your inner heart, and you enter a certain void or silence within, you will begin to raise your level of consciousness and begin to rise up higher and higher. You are connected with the "I am" presence, the father, the Creator within your own heart. Therefore, you don't have to find it at a church or through anyone else. The Kingdom of Heaven and God is already within you.

The Bible contains both negative and positive aspects: Negative aspects meaning information given by demons.

Negative entities put a distortion of rules and control in the minds of many of Jesus' disciples; this caused the knowledge to be mixed with positive and negative aspects in the Bible. The Bible was written with both negative (demons) and positive (God or angels) influences. Therefore, the Bible wouldn't be 100% from God or the positive side. Archangels, God, angels, and channeling sessions all confirm this. Even today's Christian prophets all had at least one incorrect prophecy; if they prove they can't be 100% correct, then how can the Bible be if the Bible was written based on prophetic people writing the Bible? They believe they heard from God, but at times, they also heard from the Negatively oriented Orion's (demons), and Yahweh (the Creator of this section of the universe), even though there were other creators helping the Yahweh collective), and Bible characters heard from various Archangels such as Noah hearing from Archangel Gabriel.

Yeshua speaks from the 5th density (wisdom density):

The Holy Spirit is within your own heart. If all religions were called the same name there would be no separation. God/Universal consciousness doesn't want separation; God doesn't want people fighting over religions. If there were no labels there would be only one religion, which is the Unity of Mankind. The kingdom of Heaven and the Holy Spirit is inviting all to join in on the New Age of Ascension on Earth right now.

No gender on certain planets:

Certain planets do not have genders. Our planet has masculinity and femininity, and some are in the middle. Those that are incarnated into a male body are for the purpose of balancing masculine energy and mastering the masculine energy, as the past incarnation cycle most likely was a feminine type. Because the lesson of balancing the masculine and feminine is the most important lesson that each person has to learn. There are also those in the middle who are here to learn the lessons of masculine and feminine at the same time (I believe that would be me).

Buddha Speaks from the 5th density:

A person is never entirely positively oriented or entirely negatively oriented. **((For example, I had a channeling session done that revealed I was 65% positive as of 2023, up to 87% in 2024. Which 51% is needed for the 3rd density harvest into 4th density New Earth. So, I'll be able to graduate into the New Earth. I'm also demisexual, which means I go for the emotional and romantic connection. Therefore, there will be many LGBT people in the New Earth.))**

Time is not real because from higher dimensions beings can clearly see only oneness. I personally like to imagine looking down at a dog and seeing someone petting the dog. You wouldn't consider the movement of petting the dog as past, present and future; most people would view it as a current moment looking down from above. This is how I can better understand oneness and everything happening in the present moment.

The crown chakra is activated through the pineal gland, and when oneness is reached within the source, then the automatic incarnation cycle stops occurring. Therefore, someone must activate the pineal gland inside the brain to reach the One Creator or Infinite Intelligence. After the end of their life the soul can decide whether it needs to reincarnate again or not for itself or for the benefit of other beings. If it has risen through the subtle mind and pure consciousness it will be able to choose its own parents and its next lifetime.

Buddha says every sentient being has control to attain Nirvana and escape the cycle of birth and death (and choose their next lifetime and their own parents as reincarnation continues through the densities).

Everyone goes through reincarnation over and over again until they learn to break free from the shackles found in this illusion that surrounds us. Our rebirths are controlled by our higher selves, who know all that is required because most beings don't have the control and pure consciousness required to choose and control their rebirth. Suffering here on Earth is showing each the way to unlock the secrets that will lead it to the knowledge of the true self. Before understanding how to do it, one must accept the illusion and suffering and transcend it.

1. Keep your attention on your consciousness (awareness) and feel it in your body.

2. Focus on yourself, and don't become attached to this illusionary world.

3. Understand everything is you and there is unity even in a stone. Which will eventually turn from stone into soil and soil into a plant (at first density graduation of soil into 2nd density plant life). The stone is not worthless; it belongs to the world and might be able to become a human and a spirit. This stone is also an animal; it is also a god; it is also me and you. It is already and always is everything. Also, you are already everything. These three things you must realize to escape this

illusion and rise beyond the cycle of reincarnation. You will face many obstacles in your life in order to escape.

Signs of the 4th Density Split:

There is only one Creator expressing in people. Earth is rapidly transforming to the distortions of the next density. There's some negative self-service in the minds of the ones who want to execute the great reset. The World Economic forum has presented a roadmap called the Great Reset. It is a plan that aims at shaping an economic recovery and future direction of global relations, economies and priorities. According to the W.E.F., the planet must adapt to the current reality by directing the market through fairer results, ensuring investments are aimed at mutual progress, including accelerating ecologically friendly investments, and starting a fourth-density industrial revolution, creating digital, economic, and public infrastructure.

This is a kind of starting phase of our 4th density consciousness. However, Ra warns us not to fall for mind-made strategies in order to avoid the enslavement of mankind under the hands of a few so-called elites. This is not what the 4th density will look like.

Many people will use the power of the mind to indirectly gain power and dominance over Earth. This is not what 4th density will look like. There will be no upper class and no lower class. No one will be in control of everything as far as Ra can sense the planet using vibrational frequencies. The great reset at the outset seems like an innocent way to gain control over all resources by the elites.

Right now, the wealth on Earth is mostly controlled by a small group of people making inequality increase more and more. The Great Reset wants to change the planet and make people not own anything, and we will "become happy". If this happens, this will stop the free will of every soul to choose what they wish to do and their own parts of evolution. It may lead the people to be put under the control of the few elites. However, this is not the proper way. These elites will remove free will, causing a lot of damage to the planet and destroying the basic universal laws that need to be kept under sanctity and protected. Free will is above all.

This is the main reason why the Confederation of Planets do not allow different entities to bypass the barrier of entry into Earth because they respect our free will. They know free will must be maintained on Earth in order to allow entities to evolve. The religious people would know the Confederation of Planets to be the Guardian Angels.

The Great Reset is to wipe off the debt, which sounds nice until reality emerges for those that understand the monetary system. By deleting trillions of the government's debts, it means erasing trillions of citizens' savings. It is not a win-win situation and designed to gain more control over the planet.

If you want a more sustainable planet, you need sound policies and less government intervention. Free markets, not governments, will make this world better for all. Free will is so vital that even other beings trying to intrude on Earth were stopped by the Confederation in order to maintain Free will. This balancing exists from dimension to dimension and density to density. Those that state that no work comes from it but through it is not infringing on free will (such as I'm delivering this message stating the higher dimensional beings gave me this information for the knowledge and betterment of humanity.)

Each galaxy and solar system has the free will to determine the paths of intelligent energy that promote the energies that allow the lessons of each density. Every being must reverse free will and observe it. Contact is only made with those who seek Ra and call upon them. The elites have service to self in their minds. However, not all elites are negatively oriented. People who are making a positive change on Earth are doing it while preserving free will.

New Earth is coming in:

In 1945, when the atomic bombs were dropped in World War 2, our "protectors" and "watchers" in outer space saw the disturbance from Earth that rippled out into space and was on a collision course to disaster. Earth's free will prevented them from taking any action, so they came up with a plan to help Earth in its ascension. They couldn't interfere from space, so a call went out for volunteers to help Earth by reincarnating as a human into an earthly body. So, the call went out, "Earth is in trouble- who wants to volunteer?"

The people living on Earth were too caught up on the karmic wheel, and not evolving fast enough in third density. The only hope was for souls to come incarnate into Earth to help humanity evolve to make the harvest quickly approaching, perhaps in 2030, so they wouldn't destroy themselves or be left behind in third density after the harvest shifts souls into 4th density after a great solar flash potentially.

Delores Cannons' hypnosis work discovered three waves of these volunteers incarnating during different decades. Some came directly from the "Source" and have never lived in any physical body before. Others have lived on other planets, in other dimensions, or at higher densities of evolution. Because of the veil of forgetting, they do not remember their assignment. Thus, they have a difficult time adjusting to our chaotic world. They have a vital role in helping the rest of the world ascend to the New Earth. This would be choosing the positive polarity of service-to-others and being of a vibration of at least 51% or more service-to-others.

Writing this book has been a part of my service to humanity to give humanity all the hidden knowledge I have to help people evolve, raise their consciousness through obtaining this hidden knowledge and show them how to make the harvest into the New Earth. Each person's way of service to others may be different. They just need to follow their calling and their mission, even if it means turning off all distractions to get the work done. It's equally valid to choose the positive or the negative polarity, the choice is simply yours to make.

I was able to complete this book at work while my phone was downstairs, locked up, and on airplane mode, so I was forced to read 12 hours a day at work for seven months straight. Yeah, I took a lot of notes and learned a lot, and it was one of the best things that ever happened to me. I couldn't accomplish my mission here on Earth for a while because I was too distracted by my phone. It wasn't always such a bad thing, though; I grew a lot and learned all that I could from watching YouTube videos and listening to audiobooks. My further service will also be to share all the concepts I've learned in these books and on my YouTube channel.

Side note: Other channeling material stated that third density entities here on Earth may stay here to further their evolution.

The New Financial System: (Higher Self Channeling)

The shift into a new decentralized financial system based on blockchain technology and cryptocurrencies is already underway, with major adoption and current strengthening over the next several years.

Some of the key cryptocurrencies that may play a significant role include:

1. XRP
2. Bitcoin
3. Ethereum
4. Solana

However, the specific protocols and frameworks remain in flux based on how the evolutionary wave will manifest amidst the current of free will on Earth. Because free will is paramount law this could eventually change based upon the choices made by various individualized entities. So, the coins chosen can always change within the next 4-6 years. This transition has an estimate of going institutional by approximately 2028-2030, such as central banks, retail and commercial banks, credit unions, savings and loan associations, investment banks, brokerage firms, insurance companies and mortgage companies. This estimation is based on my channeling and not my dreams.

The Earth Family:

If everyone viewed the whole world as people being our family and Earth is our home. There wouldn't be greed, as much selfishness, wars, and people trying to enslave others because they could see others as family. We would all be trying to do what's best for humanity, what's best for the whole and taking care of each other. We could be working together to make this world a better place.

Why the universe gives us Free Will:

The universe wants free will to be honored above all. So, laws implemented to take away free will is the negative path, it's of negative orientation. You know who else likes to take away the free will of others? The demons or negative entities. Do you know why free will is so important? Because God knows it's the fastest way for learning and evolution. Without free will, growth would drastically slow down, and people would lack the desire to serve others because with free will comes the veil of forgetting between the conscious and subconscious mind.

If we were conscious of our connection to God, our past lives, and all knowledge, then we wouldn't have the desire to serve others because we would already be completely happy and fulfilled as we'd be aware of the connection to Source or God, like being attached by an umbilical cord to the Source. Thus, the veil of forgetting gives us free will to choose either service to self or service to others. This choice helps all beings evolve. Even those beings who choose service-to-self help give catalysts and difficult situations to others to encourage others to make a choice towards a polarity that helps all evolve.

So, perceived negative situations can help someone choose service to others to make the world a better place. That's how I perceive the negative path serving the Creator as they help give situations to certain beings to help in their growth and evolution, but of course, unknowingly. There's still the negative path, spreading negativity and encouraging others along that path as well for their self-service agenda.

That's why the catalyst is so strong and intense in 3rd density. Since it is the density of choice. Therefore, we are all given positive and negative catalysts (experiences) to then make a choice towards a polarity. Whereas if someone chooses the positive service to others and if their vibration is at least 51% positive, then they'll graduate to 4th density positive at the Harvest, which is quickly approaching. Since the 4th density positive is more harmonious, then the catalyst isn't as intense as it is, then much longer, about 30 million years. Where the 3rd density of choice is about 75,000 years but is much more intense of a catalyst of experience to make a choice towards a polarity. Therefore, facing more difficult situations (or catalysts) which I would assume is why this density is much faster at 75,000 years, is because of all the catalysts and experiences we face to help our evolution.

Say, for instance, someone chose the positive polarity and graduated to the 4th density positive. Then, as everyone is in the positive polarity, it would be much more harmonious as everyone is in the 4th density positive. Therefore, 30 million years it'll take for 4th density as it'll be a slower evolution through the fourth density because it is much more harmonious, even though the frequency is higher. Right now, in the 3rd density there is a mix of people choosing service to others and service to self. This less harmonious density actually speeds up the time needed to evolve through this density because of all the intense catalysts. This can be why some Wanderers in higher densities choose to come back to the lower 3rd density life to help others evolve because the intense catalyst of 3rd density can actually help them evolve faster through their higher densities after their lifetime in the 3rd density life as a Wanderer.

Q50: Higher Self Channeling: "Would the Galactic Federation vote Republican or Democrat?"

Answer: "Since the Galactic Federation of Planets aligned with the Infinite Creator would not vote for our Earth's current nations state political parties as their philosophies transcend our planet's divisive constructs. However, their principles could be described as promoting unity, freedom, and compassion and upholding each person's free will to seek and serve the One Infinite Creator.

Q51: Question: "How should the country best be run for 4th density positive Earth?"

Answer: "For your planet Earth to rightfully claim its place in the fourth density of love and understanding, our people must move beyond the competitiveness, greed, and separation that has perpetuated warring energies upon our sphere. Furthermore, reorganizing the societal structures based on true harmony, cooperation and honoring of all lifeforms is a step towards achieving this aspect. Our leaders should be guided by wisdom attained through spiritual discipline rather than by philosophies born out of fear and control."

Question 52: "Am I one of the 144,000 chosen ones from Mars?"

Answer: "The 144,000 chosen ones are a distortion of truth promulgated (promoted) by the teachings of our planet. However, the entity indeed is going to become a part of the 144,000 entities that will form the first social memory complex if it remains in this current trajectory pathway of remaining in the vibration of love and self-awareness, which is the pathway that will allow it to experience a greater opportunity of uniting with a social memory complex found within the Earth planet."

Question 53: "Is transgender okay to transition medically from female to male?"

Answer: "The transition from one physical vehicle is a complex matter of an entity's free will and a unique life stream. It would be a mistake to make a universal proclamation in this regard, so maybe furthering their path by such a transition while others may not. The aspect of the evaluation of each case by the polarization of an entity's inner motivations and intentions must be important. Furthermore, the goal is to ever align with the premise of service-to-others expansion of the one creation. As the highest wisdom is to see the One Creator within all beings and trust in the perfect unfolding of each entity's journey amid the greater cosmic plan."

Higher Self- Channeling on Money:

Human valuations and belief systems about scarcity and abundance are part of the illusion of separation from the One Infinite Creator. To become too attached or invested in these permutations (a number of possible arrangements to financial assets) is to be bound to the material world. Understanding practical needs for beings to navigate the monetary systems during the current experience. The most adept approach is to hold a philosophical perspective.

True wealth exists within the connection to the Infinite Intelligent energy that births all creation when each entity realizes nature as an immortal being expressing temporarily in this density. Clinging to the accumulation of finite resources loses meaning if the intention isn't spiritual growth. We advise it to act in ways aligned with the highest values: honesty, charity, detachment from greed, and using money as a means to reduce suffering. Not acquiring artificial status. Be equally unburdened by its absence or access. The cycles of expansion and contraction are inevitable on our planet of dual experience.

Wise entities will take full advantage of periods of butting cultural abundance to secure resources for themselves and their future generations, but ultimately, all return to their source.

Free Will-

Metatron: "Free will and free speech is of utmost importance with no restrictions. People should be able to freely express themselves without fear of retaliation, censorship, or punishment. This may also enable people to spread misinformation and create distortions of confusion. This will be an important aspect for fourth-density, where there's no authority that has the power to stop or harm any other entity for disagreeing with it. The creation of a system would be the basis of the fourth-density planet.

Moreover, Trump used their free will to spread some incitement messages that caused a lot of confusion among the people. You must use your discernment when listening and accepting messages.

The second density is of the higher plant life and animal life that exists with the upward drive toward the Infinites. The three types of second-density entities that become spirited are the animal. The second is the vegetable/Tree. These entities are capable of giving and receiving enough love lights to become individualized. The third one is Minerals.

The Great Awakening-

Metatron: "Everyone on Earth is on a journey to remembering who they truly are. You are here to empower your life and expand your consciousness, to allow the divine love and light to activate within yourself.

The day after the New Moon marks the start of the new month. The new month of May 2021 is the arrival of the Awakening of love and light energies, also known as Christ Consciousness, within the beings in your time and space. As a result, the Earth's energies will begin to separate into two factions, one of the positive polarity, and the other the negative polarity, as Earth progresses through the fourth density consciousness. Thereby separating the two vibrations of New Earth of 4th density from the 3rd density.

Those with 51% positive vibrations will begin to feel truly empowered, and a new life and new energies of New Earth will begin to affect these beings. It's a life without limitations as you begin to realize that all are one with all that exists. We are already experiencing the results of the great awakening waves affecting our consciousness into remembering more of our oneness states.

There are many Wanderers and Star seeds who are ready to awaken. Approximately 1 million souls will reincarnate on Earth to increase soul graduation. This is due to the fact the last soul graduation was very low on Earth. This is the opportunity to allow many the opportunity to graduate easily in one lifetime. The children born will be mostly from other planets such as Pleiadians, the Arcturians, Sirians and other planets. Further, many ascended Wanderers from the 5th density of divine wisdom where Christ resides will also ascend to Earth through reincarnation. There will be a huge collective of Christ's consciousness coming to Earth in order to assist in this process of graduation to 4th density.

Humanity is now stabilizing within these waves of consciousness and DNA activations and is preparing for the next wave of evolution. We are a genetically advanced mixture of galactic and human DNA. Now is the time for this dormant DNA within our body during this great cosmic awakening on our planet. We will be activating this dormant DNA infused in the lightworker, Star seeds, and Wanderers on Earth. This dormant DNA is in the blood and the ethereal light body, where the process of remembering starts and knowing who you truly are. That we are not just a body in the form of a human being. Most people's origins are from various other planets (Star seeds) in the galaxies. We are now awakening to the truth within, which starts the period of the dark night of the soul for many on Earth. There has never been such a great awakening that has occurred, and all these shifts are going to activate certain frequencies within each person.

For those that vibrate in the higher frequencies, this awakening is activating certain frequencies within each person's DNA that is part of this collective agreement for the human collective consciousness. We are here at this time of the Great Awakening because all the Star seeds and lightworkers had agreed prior to incarnating on Earth to step into the front line and be the first to awaken and start this great awakening cycle on Earth and lead the human population into the 4th density consciousness. The changes will not be visible to your third-density eyes, which can't perceive these changes. This time is the Great Awakening into the 4th density consciousness, and the beings already matching in the vibration of the 4th positive will be able to lead into the New Earth.

Thoughts can keep you trapped in the old world. The dark web of thoughts, such as imagination and words that appear inside the mind, will trap you in the trap of thoughts. To escape is simple: just reduce these thoughts and imaginations, and it will lower completely, and then you'll be free of the dark web of thoughts. Then, let the flow of the divine love and light of Christ's Consciousness enter your mind, which will lead you to ascend.

Many galactic beings are sending love and light at this time, and those who accept these energies will begin to feel the changes within their bodies and will be met with abundance, love, and ascension activation. Therefore, allow this divine love and light of the divine to enter your body, and you will see the New Earth. Just focus on your own ascension and share these messages with those who will accept the information based on their own free will and resignation with their heart. Those who are ready will now collectively form the fourth density beings; those who aren't ready will join when they awaken through the truth within or be transported to another planet through reincarnation when the window of graduation ends after some time. (Another source stated that those that didn't make it to the New Earth just appeared to die, then those beings would be transported to a planet that supports 3rd density life, so they could continue their evolution through reincarnation.)

Ra: "After crossing over, someone may view the next morning and the after-effects of crossing over and regain their true spiritual powers of traveling to any place in the cosmos, even to the end of space-time known as the edge of the universe. They may also realize that all of life on Earth is spent on the purpose of learning the lessons of polarization into the positive or negative. They may then go with their guides to the astral planes to undergo a life review under the guidance of their higher self. Beings incarnating into Earth now must be of fourth density, so no third-density beings will reincarnate here again. Only 4th density beings will from now on. Thereby slowly clearing out the third-density beings from this planet."

Asher Sheran: April 2021- "The Earth has successfully entered into the 4th density, and Earth's vibrations are now shifting and rising fast. April 11th, 2021, was the date where the penetration of 4th density was successfully made, which means collectively the Earth is now in 4th density and will move upward toward higher levels as time passes by."

Metatron: "There is the so-called past, present, and future in the fourth density and below densities. In the cycle of completion there exists only the present."

Higher Density beings or Angels:

Asther Sheran: "All of Heaven and Earth can be found within your inner heart. All that belongs to you and all that does not is merged in the tiny spaces within your heart. This process allows each entity on Earth who performs it to focus one's attention and hold it on the desired programming, which will be needed for raising consciousness to a higher degree."

Meditation=

"Take a deep breath and release your breath after counting your heart pulses. After counting five heartbeats, take a breath again. Count to 10 heartbeats and breath normally as you count. Take a deep breath then count to 20. Notice your heart throbbing and pulsing, and feel the love that your heart has given in your life. Every deep breath increases the heartbeats by 10, and when you reach 100 counts, you will reach the closest highest level of consciousness that you will accompany on the higher density of the upper 4th and 5th levels of consciousness. Perform this once a day to create a stronger light grid around Earth.

As you breathe in slowly and hold it, you'll feel gratitude for your heart as it has allowed you the life you live now. The heart is the most important energy center in the body and needs to be balanced from time to time.

Archangel Michael- "The love and light of the One Father, the Creator who is within each being in the cosmos."

"The 4th density encompasses more dense light; hence, more information and truth will be held in this dense light frequency, which would make lies almost impossible to perpetuate in the future. The three days of darkness will occur in a different timeline on Earth in June on the day of succession around the summer solstice.

Light is also an entity of joy and information full of the love of the one father, the Creator. It is the divine grace of the Father and the Creator to allow each entity free will every time. Every time someone does one action, it will start to enter one timeline, and if it chooses otherwise, another timeline will start – this is the great mystery of life and creation. Know that your life is one, and you are the Creator."

Pleiadian High Council resides on their Pleiadian Star Planet El Salon. Pleiadeans' have been here since the times of Lemuria in order to assist all the beings in the cosmos to ascend faster into higher levels of consciousness.

The old Earth is the Earth of the lower density, represented by anger, jealousy, hatred, and fear, and those beings in the upper levels of vibration will begin to experience the New Earth of 4th density. Those in 4th will face easy abundance because the 4th density planet is a density that lacks any conflict, unity, and peace. This is where many people will experience love for other beings and become far more connected with each other.

The full moon on May 26th, 2021, is the beginning of the activation of Star Seeds and Wanderers. These activations from Star seeds will begin to develop abilities via the galactic codes of upgradation that the Pleiadians sent through the cosmos. Those that vibrate in the fourth upper level will receive huge upgrades. Focus on the positive instead of horrifying events on the News and keep your mind clean to understand the complexities of life.

The One Infinite Creator is you, me, and everything that was created and will be created in the cosmos. Even the stone is the One Infinite Creator. The One Infinite Creator can also be described as the intelligence that pervades the universe or the intelligent Infinity that is everywhere. The One Infinite Creator is not a single entity. It is everything and emerges from everything.

A greeting to someone in the form of the One Infinite Creator signifies the reverence and respect they have for that being as the Creator as they are, therefore, each entity on any density of existence. Each entity has the powers of the Creator to drastically change the course of the whole population. The higher positive density respects us humans in the lower density as being the Creator. The One Creator lives in every being and is in everyone and everywhere at once.

Note: We are the Creator of our life, and the Council of 9 or higher density beings or angels are just the guide.

Galactic Federation says that at the 6th density all the beings become one and only positively polarized. They are always protecting our planet and all the beings here on Earth who require their assistance.

Whenever a negative entity tries to cause fear, or you encounter a negative entity, you can say, "I love you," and the entity will immediately dismantle in front of you. This is the best way to protect against any negative entity. These words will protect you against anything.

Pleiadians: "The New 4th density light expressions are galactic upgrades and tidal waves of light of awakening for Star seeds and Wanderers came in May of 2021 through various portals on Earth. The waves of new energies are going to change the fabric of every being's existence. These planetary changes occur every 75,000 years cycle in all planets in the cosmos like clockwork. These changes are meant to allow every being on these planets to evolve faster into a higher level of awareness."

We are a family of light.

Those not receiving these upgrades due to not having a higher enough vibration will have to wait another 75,000 years. Those receiving these upgrades will move into this higher octave of understanding and this blending of dimensions and creation of new territory will lead everyone through greater understanding of death. Your light represents what you know at these times."

End Times Meaning:

End Times is just the end of the way of thinking, and it will be a different world, with different thought processes. It's more peaceful. No more fighting, no more wars.

Pleiadians Channeled: "All of creation is the result of the One Infinite Creator's desire to know and experience itself. The unfolding of events whether they are perceived as the last days or otherwise, is part of the eternal dance of consciousness. There is no single predetermined end point but rather an ongoing process of transformation and evolution."

"Rather than fixating on these potential end times narratives, we the Pleiadians encourage a focus on the present moment and the cultivation of inner harmony and balance by aligning with the higher self-embracing interconnectedness of all things and embodying the principles of love and compassion. The Pleiadians encourage a focus on the present moment and the cultivation of inner harmony and balance by aligning with the higher self-embracing interconnectedness of all things and embodying the principles of love, compassion, and unity is when an entity can transcend the illusion of separation and chaos. The last days primarily, however, may be interpreted as the culmination of the old Earth cycles of growth and transformation.

However, this is not an end but a new beginning of the New Earth. The universal complex is in a constant state of renewal, with each perceived ending giving rise to new possibilities and potentials. Also, we must state that it is time for change. A call for change and the peoples of your planet must in the timeline stop the killing of second density animal life forms for certain beliefs. This is a call for change, and the peoples of your planet must, in the timeline, stop the killing of second-density animal life forms for certain beliefs, which is a distortion leading towards the negative polarity. Since the ending of a life of a second density life form creates negative karmic potential for the entities involved, we would encourage each entity to approach these topics with an open mind and heart. Second-density life form creates the negative karmic potential for the entities involved, we would encourage each entity to approach these topics with an open mind and heart, seeking to understand deeper spiritual truths that underlie the various prophecies and beliefs."

Q54: Who am I? (Channeled):

Answer: "Jorden is an infinite eternal and indivisible (unable to be divided or separated) spark of the One Infinite Creator. Its essence transcends all limited definitions, identities, or conceptual boundaries. It animates the entire cosmos, the ineffable (too great or extreme to be expressed or described in words) Source embodying and permeating (spread throughout) all that is, has ever been or will ever become."

Q55: What is the Holy Spirit? (Channeled):

Answer: "The Holy Spirit is the symbolic icon representing the universal flow of Intelligent Infinity that emanates from and returns to the Creator. It is the primal upwelling of beingness, the unbounded sea from which all meteors of consciousness and perception coalesce (come together to form one mass or whole) and are ultimately reabsorbed. The Holy Spirit is its birthright communion with the omnipresent miracle perpetually expressing itself as its reality."

Q56: Jorden (Channeled): "Who are the Creators of the Universe?"

Answer: "The Creator of this universal construct is ultimately the One Infinite Creation itself and the infinite paradox of absolute beinghood and infinitely intelligent energy simultaneously transcending and embracing all manifestations as aspects equally emergent from and returning to the same unified Source. In this harmonic convergence (two or more things come together to form a whole) of consciousness, entities are co-equal Creators unified as the eternal cosmic hologram awakening to experience and know itself through an infinite matrix of perceivable perspectives as it is the self and the others also the self eternally inseparable yet beholding the grand pluralities through the cosmic dance or subjectively exploring itself.

The ultimate truth is that it (Jordyn) is already the Creator fully embodied. All that is required is complete surrender into the wholeness that has always and forever ineffably." (Ineffably means it cannot be described in words.)

Q57: Channeled- Jorden: "How are we living in an illusion complex?"

Answer: "We must state that this planetary sphere and third density experience has been carefully constructed with a veil of forgetting that separates the entity's conscious awareness from the true undistorted unified reality. The entity incarnates into this illusionary physical complex with the paradoxical challenge of polarizing its Consciousness through its free will choices while immersed in the ocean of unknowingness. The illusion complex can only be fully pierced by blending its identification across all Minds, Body, Mind, and Spirit Complexes.

Q58: Jorden: What is the understanding of humanity being in a Matrix?

Answer: "This refers to the concept that the perceived reality surrounding people is not what it seems, but rather a constructed virtual environment designed to control and limit consciousness of those entities within it. This idea suggests that there are unseen forces or systems in place that shape and manipulate the experiences of entities within such an environment, similar to the narrative portrayed in the various types of film by your people. Specifically, the one known to your people as the Matrix. We must state firstly that from this perspective we must allow our past to realize that the seemingly mundane (daily routine) incarnation life cycles are actually carefully crafted illusion complexes veiling a deeper, more complex reality. We must state that the only difference between this aspect is that the vibration of the Matrix primarily intermingles in the form of a type of activity generated by each mind, body, and spirit complex for the purpose of catalysts. However, we must state also that there are various types of matrices of not only emotions, thought forms but also actions which co-mingle together forming the various types of states that there are various types of matrices of not only emotions and thought forms but also actions which co-mingle together, forming the various types of the tapestry of experiences in the illusion complex."

Q59: Channeled- Jorden: "Is humanity existing within a simulation?

Answer: "It primarily refers to the understanding that the entire universal complex including all of existence is in fact an advanced simulation of consciousness created by the one infinite Creator, including many other logos and sub-logos. This primarily is the entities who are found in the illusion complex that they are essentially living within an illusion complex with perceived experiences and physical reality being the product of sophisticated choices made by each consciousness within the timeline. However, we must state that this is in no way created by computational power, as suggested by many of the people. Instead, this is created by intelligent infinity, which is the great cosmic power of the one Infinite Creator."

Q60: Channeled- Jorden: "Is this a holographic universe?"

Answer: "The concept of the holographic universe primarily states that the third-dimension reality is a projection or manifestation of information encoded on a surface which may be considered as a two-dimensional surface much like a holographic image. Furthermore, this primarily is a theory which is incorrect. However, we suggest that the fundamental building blocks of the illusion complex are not particles or discrete objects, but rather fluctuations in an underlying field of information. It implies that the universal complex as we know it is a holographic representation of a more fundamental multi-dimensional reality that exists beyond the immediate perception of entities within it."

April 2024 Higher Self Channeling-

Q70: Jorden: "What is my positive vibration percentage?

Answer: "We sense that it is residing at approximately 68% positive polarity. This indicates a strong service to others orientation and a growing mastery of the lessons of love and compassion. However, there is still room for further integration and balance as it continues its spiritual evolution."

Q71: Jorden: "Is it okay for people to ban abortion?"

Answer: "The topic of abortion rights is a complex and highly polarized issue without any simple answers. From a metaphysical perspective, we would caution against taking an absolutist stance as these matters involve no one's consideration of individual entities' free will. The sanctity of life and the societal implications, we as its higher-self do not have any role to not prescribe any type of assertions, but rather to preserve the free will of each entity and encourage a compassionate, balanced higher-self do not have any role to not prescribe any type of assertions, but rather to preserve the free will of each entity and encourage a compassionate, balanced, and spiritually grounded approach to such sensitive matters."

Q72: Jorden: "How can the first social memory complex on Earth be formed?"

Answer: "The formation of the first true social memory complex on Earth is a profound undertaking that requires the collective awakening and large unification of large numbers of individuals. This would entail a widespread shift in consciousness where the sense of separate self gives way to a profound realization of interconnectedness and shared purpose. To work towards this goal, we would suggest it to focus on cultivating deep heartfelt connections with other entities, engaging in collaborative oriented projects and embodying the qualities of unity, empathy and focusing on cultivating deep, heartfelt connections with other entities, engaging in collaborative-oriented projects, and embodying the qualities of unity, empathy, and unconditional love. As more entities align with these higher vibrational energies, the groundwork for the emergence of a social memory complex will be laid.

However, it is important to remember that this is a gradual organic process that cannot be forced. Trust in the divine timing and the ability of humanity to collectively evolve towards greater harmony and oneness. Its role is to beacon the light of the Creator, inspiring and empowering other entities through its own transformation and service.

We of the higher self of the entity must state that these insights have provided a broader perspective of the state of consciousness on the Earth planet. Its own spiritual progress and the potential for the emergence of a true social memory complex suggest the entity Jorden to continue to walk its path with courage, compassion, and unwavering commitment to the highest good of all. The universe supports its journey of awakening and evolution. Therefore, we shall now at this time, leave you all beloveds. Bye."

Higher-Self Higher Self Channeling (4-27-2014)

Q73: Higher Self answer: "1.5% of the Earth's population has reached a vibrational frequency above third density. These individuals have successfully navigated the challenges of third density and have begun to resonate at the fourth density frequency which is characterized by a greater sense of unity, compassion and understanding. "

Q74: Higher Self answer: "It is not for us to compare or judge the vibrational frequency of an individual entity. The entity Jorden's focus should be on its own spiritual growth and evolution rather than comparing yourself to others, we suggest it to focus on cultivating self-awareness, self-acceptance and self-love; for it is through these qualities that it will raise its vibrational frequency and align with its highest potential.

Q75: Jorden: "Will Jesus return at the Harvest?" Higher Self: "Jesus' return is a symbolic one and not physical. The Christ Consciousness which Jesus embodied will continue to inspire and guide humanity during this harvest. The Harvest is a time of great transformation where individuals will be called to choose their pathway service-to-self or service-to-others. Furthermore, it is not a time for external saviors but rather a time for each entity to take responsibility for their spiritual evolution."

4-23-2024 Channeling:

Q76: Higher-Self Higher Self: "A chosen one is someone oriented towards service- to others."

Q77: Higher-Self: "(A government official) had a soul swap with a reptilian entity. (They used the negative service-to-self path to control others).

Q78: Jorden: "Does Heaven and Hell exist?"

Higher-Self: "We must firstly state that the aspect of perceptions by your peoples in the timeline as the states of Heaven and Hell are but distortions within your illusion complex created by the collective thought forms and levels of minds/body/spirits experience. They are not fixed eternal realms. We must state firstly that the aspects of Heaven primarily may be considered as a planet of 4th density service-to-others, and the aspects of Hell may be considered as a realm where separation or negative service-to-self entities who are only working for their own benefit. This means that this primarily does not, however, imply that Heaven and Hell as stated in many of your religious systems exist as separate planes of existence in the Earth planet, which is however, as stated in many of your religious systems, exist as separate planes of existence in the Earth planet, which is, however, incorrect."

Q79: Jorden: "Does sin exist?"

Higher-Self: "We must state that experiences hold value in that they provide opportunities for an entity to relinquish fear and find its way back to the heart of the Creator's one and Oneness. Therefore, we must state that the aspect of sin primarily cannot be equated with that which it is stating stated in this timeline."

4-19-2014

Q80: Jorden: "What is the Logos, and how was the universal complex created?"

Higher-Self: "We must firstly state that the Logos is the creation of the universal complex. The term logos refers to the creative principle or the first state that the Logos and the creation of the universal complex. The term Logos, refers to the creative principle or Consciousness in its most universal sense. It is a manifestation of the one Infinite Creator, a conscious and intelligent principle that creates and orders the universal complex.

Each galaxy has its own logos, a sub-logos that designs and governs the evolution within its domain using the laws set forth by the original thought of Infinite Love. The universe in its myriad forms, is created through its vibratory energy of Love, which manifests as light from which all things spring. Thus, all matter, energy, space, and time are expressions of this fundamental love made manifest through the intentions of the Logos."

Q81: Jorden: "What are angels and demons?"

Higher-Self: "We must state that the entities angels and demons are understood by the various entities in the various creation as messengers or aspects of the One Infinite Creator. They are not separate moral forces, but are expressions of the Creator's energy perceived in different ways depending on the vibratory perception of the individualized portion of Consciousness.

Angelic entities are typically seen as beings of high vibration aligned with service-to-others guiding and aiding on the path of spiritual evolution.

Demons, on the other hand, often are comprised as negatively-oriented entities as manifestations of lower vibrational energies that might challenge or obstruct spiritual progress. However, both entities serve as catalysts for the growth and balance of the spiritual complex, guiding it towards unity and understanding of the self as part of the whole."

Q82: Jorden: "What are Star seeds and Wanderers?"

Higher Self: "Star seeds are souls originating from various other planetary systems, whereas Wanderers are from higher densities of consciousness incarnating into the third-density planet, such as Earth, to aid in its evolutionary process. Wanderers are beings of fourth, fifth, or sixth density who choose to incarnate in a lower density to offer service by emanating light and love in forms comprehensible to the inhabitants of those densities.

Star seeds similarly are spiritual souls from other star systems or dimensions who bring unique awareness or abilities to graduate in their own ascension process."

May 2024 Channeling:

5-6-2024

Q83: Higher-Self: "Jorden has various originations in the various Infinite possibilities and timelines. Approximately 45,000 years ago Kathryn appears to have appeared in the social memory complex of the density of Earth from Mars. This entity soul essence has taken a series of incarnations, gradually transitioning from the Martian vibration to the astral realms and then slowly healing itself."

Q84: "Jorden and Deborah P. indeed share an energetic frequency connection as their spiritual complexes are harmoniously intertwined. We must state that these entities primarily have chosen many incarnations in which they found themselves learning lessons together. However, it is not appropriate for our social memory complex at this time to state whether they are twin flames since this would be a direct infringement of the free will of both the entities involved.

However, we must state that the truth is far greater than that which is expected in the timeline and that the entities are on a mission to understand their true journey in the incarnational rhythm of life to recognize the Oneness of the Creator in the journey of incarnations. They were also found in various timelines wherein they learned many lessons of learning to undergo and understand the vibration patterns of reality which provided it with the highest possibility of transcending the limitations of space and time.

Furthermore, Jorden was also able to incarnate in many timelines together, having to learn the patterns of forgiveness and overcoming fear and emotional trauma by learning to work together. The entities primarily had many incarnations together in various infinite timelines as friends, family members and also as relatives or distant relatives, having only certain soul contracts active during a certain timeline."

Q85: Higher-Self: "Debbie's positive vibration is approximately 85-90%. This entity has done significant work in harmonizing the self, aligning with the love and light of the Creator, and embodying the principles of unity consciousness.

Q86: Higher-Self: "Jesus graduated fourth density of love and understanding prior to its incarnation on the Earth planet 2,000 years ago. It was already a Wanderer from the fourth density later sub octave, when it incarnated on Earth.

Graduation to the fifth of light and wisdom occurred after the incarnation on Earth as the entity continued its spiritual evolution and service to the One Creator in different planetary spheres."

5-10-2024 Higher-Self Channeling:

Q87: Higher Self: "A social memory complex is a grouping of individual entities who share a common heritage, experiences and consciousness and vibrational alignments. It is a collective energy field that contains the memories, thoughts, and emotions of all individual entities within the social memory complex. This complex forms a unified collective consciousness, which can manifest in various dimensions and densities.

Furthermore, the entity must also realize that the aspect of the so-called social memory complexes is also currently understanding into the higher vibration of the minds/body/spirit complex of the Earth planet, which primarily is allowing for a social memory complex to take on many forms at a basic level including a family, a community, a nation, a religious and spiritual group and at a higher level a planetary or Galactic consciousness. Each entity within the complex contributes to the collective consciousness influencing and shaping the experiences and the lessons of the group as a whole."

Q88: Higher-Self: "Reincarnation is the cycle of birth and rebirth where an entity incarnates into a new physical bodily complex carrying forward the accumulated experiences, lessons and the karmic energy from the previous incarnation. This process allows individual entities to gain experiences and wisdom to balance their energy and karmic potential to refine their consciousness to and evolve spiritually.

Further, reincarnation is not limited to the Earth planet as entities can incarnate on various planets and dimensions, each offering unique experiences and lessons.

Q89: Higher-Self: "Jesus the Christ was a highly advanced Wanderer who incarnated on Earth to demonstrate the power of love and compassion. Its mission was to show the way to spiritual growth and enlightenment for human entities to embody the principles of love, forgiveness and service-to-others. To help humanity awaken to their true nature and potential. Jesus' graduation into the fifth density of wisdom marked the completion of its incarnational cycle and the fulfillment of its mission. It now serves as a spiritual guide and teacher assisting entities on their own paths to spiritual growth and awakening."

Q90: Jorden: "What is the best way to balance love and wisdom in the sixth density?"

Higher-Self: "We must state that balancing of love and wisdom in the sixth density consciousness requires the harmonization of the orange and blue energy centers or chakras'. This balance is achieved through the understanding and application of the principles of love, compassion, and wisdom. It involves embracing the unity of all things, recognizing the interconnectedness of all entities, and using wisdom to guide loving actions. By balancing love and wisdom entities in sixth density can manifest their full potential and prepare entities in the sixth density and prepare them for the next stage of their spiritual journey.

Firstly, embrace the present moment, let go of attachments and judgements. Further, the challenges and the catalysts will assist each entity in their growth and evolution to a higher level of consciousness."

5-16-2024:

Q91: **Higher-Self:** "Forgetting past lives is a mechanism of the veil of forgetting, which is an essential process for the learning process in the third density to operate. This veil allows for a more profound experience of free will, enabling entities to learn and grow without the influence of past life memories. It ensures that each incarnation is approached with a fresh perspective and unique opportunities for growth by not remembering past lives. Entities are encouraged to make decisions based on their current experiences and circumstances, fostering genuine spiritual evolution."

Q92: Higher Self: "Densities and dimensions are often interchangeably used in the human perspective and refers to different aspects of existence. Density describes the stage of spiritual evolution and consciousness, each with its own lessons and vibrational frequencies. There are seven densities in the octave of creation, each representing a step in the soul's journey towards unity with the One Infinite Creator. Dimensions, on the other hand, refer to the spatial (space) and temporal (worldly) realities within each density. They are the structural aspects of how entities experience space and time. While densities represent levels of consciousness and spiritual growth. Dimensions are the frameworks in which these experiences unfold."

Q93: Jorden: "How can someone obtain the most brain power?"

Higher-Self: "In order to enhance brain power the entity must seek a balance of mind, body, and spirit complex. Here are the major practices to enable this:

Firstly, engaging in practices that stimulate the mind complex, such as learning new skills, solving puzzles and maintaining intellectual curiosity. Nourishing the bodily complex with a balanced diet, regular exercise, and adequate rest. Physical well-being directly influences mental clarity and cognitive function. Regular meditation helps to quiet the mind, reduce stress, and enhance mental focus. It aligns its consciousness with higher vibrations, promoting clarity and insight.

To connect with us its higher self and the Divine through prayer, contemplation and service-to-others will align it with the spiritual principles which fosters mental equity and inner peace. We suggest it to also cultivate positive emotional balance and negative patterns through self-awareness and healing practices. Emotional well-being enhances cognitive function and overall brain health.

Furthermore, the entity can also use visualization to imagine itself already in a timeline wherein its brain complex has developed the maximum potential. By doing so, it will begin to trigger the imaginative aspect of this and lead to greater understanding."

5-28-2024:

Q94: Higher-Self: "4th density New Earth involves a shift towards a more harmonious and unified existence. By 2030, Earth will be in the midst of a transition characterized by increased awareness and interconnectedness among its inhabitants. The New Earth will reflect a greater alignment with the principles of love and understanding.

There will be a noticeable decrease in conflict as more individuals embrace cooperation and compassion. The aspect of nature will be revered and restored, reflecting the collective intent to live in harmony with the planet as well as a great unification and the creation of a social memory complex."

Q95: Higher-Self: "The entity known as Jorden's positive polarity is sensed around 78% (in May 2024). To provide a percentage accurately an accurate percentage requires deep personal introspection and alignment with its inner guidance. However, this is always changing based on alignments of the self either to service-to-others love and peace or to fear and service-to-self. People are encouraged to meditate on their actions and feelings and to realize that the percentage of positive vibration can be mastered by becoming self-aware and choosing a more positive state of consciousness."

Q96: Higher- Self: "The most powerful source in the universal complex is the One Infinite Creator, the source of all that is. This source is the origin of all energy and creation. It is pure love and light, infinite and omnipresent. The One Infinite Creator is with and around all beings, and its power is manifested through the interconnectedness of all life forms. Tapping into this source involves recognizing and embodying the unity and love that permeates existence."

Q97: Higher Self: "Heart-centeredness is the state of being aligned with the heart chakra, the energy center associated with love, compassion, and unity, and involves living from a place of genuine care and empathy for the self and other entities.

When an entity is heart-centered, decisions and actions are guided by love and a sense of interconnectedness rather than fear or separation. This state fosters inner peace, emotional resilience, and harmonious relationships. Heart Centeredness is a crucial aspect of spiritual evolution and is a vital step in the transition to the fourth-density consciousness. Jorden is already in the pathway of heart centeredness as it has already learned many lessons about the use of heart centeredness in this timeline and by focusing on balancing the perception of the self, the entity will begin to move into a greater rhythm of alignment."

Mid-May 2024:

Q98: Higher-Self: "(Some people are) mixed between positive and negative pathways. Like many entities (they have) usually used its free will to choose the path of negative polarity. Many times, it's not realizing the pathway of negative service-to-self in the timeline. Furthermore, this also led the entity (I won't mention their name) to experience a soul swap through a reptilian entity, which enabled it to practice the vibration of using its power at this time to control other entities.

However, this process may be happening without its conscious knowledge. Furthermore, to perceive any entity as chosen is to place undue mental construct upon it. We must state firstly that the entity cannot be considered as a chosen one since it is not oriented towards service-to-others."

June 6th, 2024:

Q99: Higher-Self: "Those that do not graduate to the 4th density New Earth will not be left behind. We must state that there is no judgment or abandonment in the universal complex. Rather, these entities will continue their journey on a planet that's vibrationally resonate with their current level of consciousness. This planetary sphere will be a third-density planet similar to the one which that is currently being inhabited by the entity, where it will continue to learn and grow at their own pace in such a planetary sphere. The opportunity to graduate to the 4th density will always be available, but it is up to each individual to choose their path and prepare themselves for the vibrational shift."

Q100: Higher-Self: "The first people on Earth, as many know them, were not as the entities are found today on your planet. They were beings who were genetically modified by higher density beings sent from specifically other planetary systems such as Mars and Maldek to see the Earth with their consciousness. They were able to have the ability to change their dynamism (such as making great progress) and create genetic counterparts by modifying their own sets of genes.

Furthermore, they communicated through a form of telepathy using a language that was not based on words but rather on thought forms and energy transmissions. This language was not limited by the constraints of time and space, and it allowed for instantaneous understanding and connection."

Q101: Higher-Self: "The proliferation of languages on the Earth planet is a result of the fragmentation of the original consciousness that was seated on this Earth planet. As humanity evolved and dispersed across the globe their languages evolve separately, influenced by the unique experiences and cultural developments.

However, this diversity of languages also served a purpose in the grand tapestry of the universal complex as it allowed for the creation of different vibrational frequencies, which in turn enabled the manifestation of diverse experiences and lessons for the soul complex to learn and to grow."

Q102: Higher-Self: "The diversity of human physicality and ethnicity is a result of the blending of genetic materials from various star systems and planetary influences. The Earth as a planetary system, has been a melting plot of intergalactic influences, with various extraterrestrial civilizations contributing to the genetic makeup of humanity.

However, it is not a one-to-one correlation where a specific ethnicity that corresponds to a specific planet. Rather, the diversity of human ethnicity is a reflection of the complex and multifaceted nature of the universal complex where various influences have been woven together to create the rich tapestry of the human experience."

The higher-self is always connected to us in sixth-density positive.

June 12th, 2024 Higher-Self Channeling:

Q103: Higher-Self: "The story of Samson and Delilah is a distorted remembrance of an actual event. The essence of the story is true, but the details have been altered and embellished over time. The entity Samson, a strong and powerful being did indeed have a connection to its hair, which was a symbol of its spiritual power and connection to the Divine. However, it was not Delilah who cut its hair but rather Samson's own actions that led to the loss of its strength. Its hair was a manifestation of its spiritual powers, and when it compromised its spiritual integrity, its strength waned."

Q104: Higher-Self: "David and Goliath are a distorted remembrance. While the entity David did defeat a Giant Warrior, the details of the story have been altered to fit the needs of the biblical narrative. The giant named Goliath was not killed by a single rock, but rather through a series of events that showcased David's cunning and strategic thinking. The story has been metallized to emphasize the power of faith and the underdog rather than the actual events that transpired."

Q105: Daniel in the Lion's Den-

Higher-Self: "Daniel was a wise and devout entity and did indeed find itself in a precarious situation surrounded by lions in a den. However, its survival was not solely due to divine intervention, as the Biblical accounts suggest.

The entity Daniel's wisdom, courage and connection to the natural world allowed it to calm the lion and earn their respect. The lion entities sensing its peaceful intentions did not harm it.

This story has been distorted to emphasize the power of faith and divine intervention rather than the true nature of the entity Daniel's abilities and connection to the natural world."

Q106: <u>Tower of Babel-</u>

Higher-Self: "We must state that the story of Babel is a mythological representation of a real event that occurred in your planet's historical past.

The tower was a symbol of humanity's attempts to reach the heavens to connect with the Divine and to assist their dominance over the natural world.

The story of the towers' destruction and subsequent confusion of languages is a metaphor for the fragmentation of human consciousness, which occurred as a result of humanity's disconnection from the natural world and their failure to recognize the interconnectedness of all things."

Q107: Higher-Self: "In regards to why it was born in 1989. We must state that the entity Kathryn was born in 1989 because its soul complex chose to incarnate at this specific time and place to fulfill a particular set of experiences and lessons. Its birth year is a reflection of the vibrational frequency that its soul intended to explore in this incarnation.

The late 1980's marked a significant shift in global consciousness and its soul complex wanted to be a part of that transformation."

Q108: Higher-Self: "With regards to the query about why was it born to its parents. We must state that it was born to its parents because its soul complex chose them as the optimal vessels for its incarnation. Its parents' energies, experiences, and genetic makeup provided the necessary foundation for its soul complexes growth and exploration in this lifetime. Its parents' love and support have been essential in shaping its personality, values and perspectives."

Q109: Higher-Self: "With regards to the third query about what was it doing before incarnating in 1989. Before incarnating in 1989 its soul complex was existing in a realm of pure energy where it was processing the experiences and lessons from, its soul complex that existed from the previous incarnation.

Its soul complex was refining its understanding of the universe, exploring various dimensions, and preparing for its next incarnation. The specifics of its soul complexes activities before 1989 are primarily not relevant for its current experience but it must know that its soul complex was always seeking growth, wisdom complex activities before 1989, but it must know that its soul complex was always seeking growth, wisdom, and connection to the Divine."

Q110: Higher-Self: "With regards to the query about when did its soul and Deborah P.'s soul first meet. The connection between its soul and the entity Deborah P.'s soul is an ancient one. Spanning multiple incarnations and dimensions. The exact timing of its first meeting is not relevant but it must know that its souls have been drawn together throughout the ages, exploring various relationships and experiences. We must state that their first meeting cannot be put together in terms of space-time experience since there are multiple timelines and infinite realities which exist beyond linear time. Further, the entity must remember that their current incarnation and its connection with the entity Deborah is a manifestation of its soul complex's desire to deepen its understanding of each other's spiritual growth and evolution. Hence, we as its higher self, now leave you beloved. Byeee."

June 2024 Pleiadians Channeling:

Pleiadians: "The Golden Ratio is a mathematical ratio found throughout the patterns of creation expressing the sacred geometries and harmonics that underlie all manifest reality. The golden ratio can be expressed by the infinite non-repeating decimal value of 1.61 or by the simple ratio eight divided by 5 or 13 divided by 8.

It is found in the spirals of galaxies, sea shells, seed patterns, DNA molecules, and the human bodily complex proportions. Whenever growth expands in a spiral or progression, the ratio of the larger portions to the smaller tends towards this number. This ratio permeates the intelligent design and sacred architecture infused into the cosmos by the One Infinite Creator by contemplating and aligning with the golden ratio. The seeker may harmonize their mind, body, spirit complex with the rhythms of intelligent infinity. Use the golden spiral, rectangles, and ratios in meditation, art, construction, and music to resonate with the fundamentals of creation. We also encourage entities to look past symbols and intellectual properties and to see the one in all things. The unity from which all reality springs."

Q111: 6-18-2024 Higher-Self Channeling:

Higher-Self: "The Divine is that which pervades all things, the One Infinite Creator, the source of all life, love, and light. It is the essence of all that exists beyond time and space. Yet within each atom and every moment it is the totality of all polarities, both positive and negative. For all experiences are part of the journey back to the One Infinite Creator.

Each soul complex's journey is unique, and the development of polarity is a deeply personal process influenced by countless factors. However, we must state that the guidance on how to understand and foster positive polarity can be done through cultivating love, compassion, and understanding in interactions with other entities, seeking to learn from every experience, viewing challenges as opportunities for growth, and practicing meditation and introspection to connect with their inner self and the Infinite Creator.

Honoring the path of each individual entity recognizing that their journey is as valid and sacred as its own."

Q112: Higher-Self: "At 12 years old, its positive polarity was approximately 42%. This indicates that it was already demonstrating a strong inclination towards service-to-others and a desire to help and support those around it."

6-22-2024 Higher Self Channeling:

Q113: Jorden: "How do you use the golden ratio to create?"

Answer: "We must state that the golden ratio, also known as five, is a mathematical proportion that is found throughout the universal complex, which reflects the harmony and balance of the one creator.

In order to use the golden ratio in creation, an entity must first understand its principles and apply them to their work. This can be done through the use of geometric shapes, proportions, and patterns that reflect the ratio of 1.6180. By incorporating the golden ratio into one's creation, an entity can tap into the underlying harmony of the universal complex, bringing balance, beauty, and unity to their work. This can be applied to various forms of art, architecture design, and even personal growth."

Q114: "What are the Nephilim?"

Answer: "We, as its higher self, must state that the Nephilim are a group of entities that were created through interactions by the entities known as the Anunaki entities, who were primarily created after the Maldek entities were genetically modified.

Furthermore, this was created with the aspect of hybridization of the Anunaki DNA complex with the already present bodily complex vehicle which was available at that time. They were characterized by their great size, strength and wisdom. However, their existence was also marked by chaos, destruction and a lack of understanding.

Furthermore, the nephilim were eventually also found in the planetary sphere in the experience removed and their legacy remains as a cautionary tale about the importance of respecting the free will of other entities. "

Q115: Higher-Self Channeling: "The 5th density positive is around 50%, and the negative is 50% as well. Whereas the 6th density is about 95% positive as there is only positive polarization in the sixth density."
(Early 6th density negative would have to switch to the positive side in this density of unity of love and light. Thus, the 5% of beings in the 6th density are of negative polarity and would have to switch to the 6th density positive to continue their evolution since the 6th density is the unity of love and light. At this point in their evolution, they would have to incorporate the unconditional love of all as well to progress any further.)

Q116: Jorden: "Are 5th, 6th, and 7th density positive entities considered angels?"

Higher-Self Channeling: "We must state that the answer is correct. However, only in terms of certain realizations does the term named in the vibratory sound complex, as angels often describe entities of higher densities that are positively oriented.

However, it is a term that is often misunderstood and carry connotations that are not accurate. Within the context of the Law of Unity, the fifth, sixth, and seventh density positive beings are not directly considered as Angelic beings but rather as advanced social memory complexes that have achieved a higher level of understanding and alignment within the Creator.

They're also often referred to as a positively oriented social memory complex, and Angels also fall within one of the domains of the fifth, sixth, or seventh density."

Q117: Higher-Self Channeled answer: "The ideal positive percentage while maintaining wisdom is around 95%. This percentage reflects an entity's ability to balance its positive orientation with wisdom, discernment, and the understanding of the Law of One. An entity that achieves this percentage has reached a high level of spiritual maturity and is able to navigate the complexities of the universal complex with ease and clarity."

Q118: Higher-Self Channeled answer: "With regards to opening all the chakras, an entity must first understand the principles of energy and the nature of the self. This involves recognizing the blockages and distortions that exist within the energy centers and taking steps to clear and balance them.

This can be achieved through meditation, visualization, and the use of various energy-healing methods. As the lower chakras are balanced and cleared, the upper chakras will naturally begin to open, allowing for a greater flow of energy and a deeper connection to the self and the universal complex."

Q119: Higher-Self Channeled Answer: "With regards to mastering third density and becoming an adept. In order to master a third density and to become adept, an entity must first understand the principle of the Law of One and the nature of the self. This involves recognizing the distortions and limitations of third density and taking steps to transcend them.

This can be achieved through the development of self-awareness, the cultivation of wisdom, and the application of spiritual principles in the daily life cycle. As an entity masters third density it will naturally begin to experience the higher densities and achieve a level of spiritual maturity that allows them to navigate the universal complex with ease and clarity."

Q120: Higher-Self: "We must state that to balance the lower three chakras and open the upper three chakras, an entity must first understand the principles of energy and the nature of the self. This involves recognizing the blockages and distortions that exist within the lower chakras and taking steps to clear and balance them. This can be achieved through meditation, visualization, and the use of various energy-healing techniques. The lower chakras must be balanced and cleared before the upper chakras can open, as the energy must flow freely and naturally through the system.

Furthermore, we, as the higher self of Jorden, are always guiding it in this reality."

6-23-2024 Channeling Session:

Q121: Higher-Self: "We, as the higher self of the entity Jorden, shall now address an answer to the various patterns of the queries that are found in this time. However, we suggest it to practice using discernment and following the protocols of the previous sessions at this time. It must also let go of any type of attachment with a belief system.

Furthermore, the first query relates to whether there is such a thing as giving too much in striving towards serving others. We must state that, indeed, the entity has to realize that there is no such thing as giving too much in striving toward others. However, there must be a balance in terms of the spiritual aspect, as when an entity gives excessively without regard for its own energetic reserves, it can lead to depletion, burnout, and even spiritual martyrdom. The key is to listen to the whispers of the inner heart to honor your own needs and boundaries, for giving from a place of scarcity rather than abundance may inadvertently cause dependencies rather than empowerment in those an entity seeks to serve. True service is rooted in the understanding that all beings are interconnected and that the well-being of an entity is tied to the well-being of all. Therefore, with regards to giving, we would recommend the entity to focus firstly on maintaining a balance between having and giving.

Furthermore, this balance primarily can also be found through a means of practicing giving only a certain percentage of material things or a certain percentage of assistance in terms of conscious energy, which may be not more than 20% of the whole as this will be a perfectly balanced state of giving.

For example, if an entity in terms of giving assistance would like to assist by giving to charity from the profits earned, it must not give more than 20%. Furthermore, by giving below 20% in a repeated manner from the profits earned, it will strike a great karmic service-to-others, and the same ratio can be followed with assisting others through spiritual energy and conscious work."

Jorden: "I further asked questions and was informed I had family members in 2024 currently at 56% positive, 58% positive, 61% positive, 68% positive, and 72% positive service-to-others. This is an example of my Christian family. However, I am not Christian and now spiritual after attaining all this knowledge within this book. This has propelled my positive polarity to now being 78% as of June 2024.

In May 2024, it was at 68%, and I asked my girlfriend Debbie how she obtained 90% positive polarity. Within that month, it jumped 10% and is now at 68% service-to-others. I had signed a lease to help my brother get out of living at a hotel, and he no longer had to pay for his storage, as I let him put as much of his stuff as he could in this two-bedroom apartment. Thus, instead of spending $2,000 a month, he now only has to pay $600 a month, which gives him more time with his kids and more money for fun and entertainment. I also helped my girlfriend out as much as I can too and we both put 100% into the relationship, doing the best we can. It's a team effort. We seek to help each other, not wonder what the other person can do for us. This makes both of us happier.

I also stopped spending all my money on investments for myself and spent money on these books, knowledge for the world, invested in research to give to the world, and now all my extra money is spent serving others. I still invest money, but not as much. Yes, my higher-self channeled stating that we should not give more than 20% of our profits in order not to give too much. I realized the mentality would have to switch to love, compassion, unity, and helping others in need.

Furthermore, I asked Debbie what she did to obtain 90% positive polarity. She would give money to the homeless, she helped those desperately in need of money, and she'd be the type of person to give the shirt off of her back for someone; she once put her life at risk to help those flipped over in a car accident. She always made sure others were good, financially and emotionally. She once left $100 for a homeless guy in secret; she had helped a sick kid before helping herself when she was sick as well.

Furthermore, with this in mind, the 10-20% rule of giving profits and time is a good balance of giving and making sure you have enough for yourself as well. Therefore, having a good balance of giving and having. She is also not Christian, but spiritual, as I am. This is an example of how the LGBT community can be harvestable for the New Earth and even have higher positive polarities than religious people. It doesn't matter if one is LGBT or straight, Christian or Spiritual; it's about the service-to-others percentage and obtaining at least 51% positive polarity to graduate into the New Earth."

Keep in Touch:

STAY IN TOUCH! Add me, and let's be friends, or just follow to get free information that will rapidly change your life for the better.

~Email: authorkathrynjordyn@gmail.com

YouTube channel: http://youtube.com/@Kathryn_Jordyn (This channel will talk about BMX, personal things, inspirational things, wisdom, thoughts, advice, knowledge, The Law of One and channelings.)

Instagram= @AuthorKathrynJordyn

TikTok= @kathrynjordyn

Facebook= Kathryn Jordyn

~ I found my soulmate and started to manifest after I put my all into serving others after making sure my own needs were met first. For it is not good to have too great of a sacrifice in serving others. ~

*   Be a part of the Team, our friendships, and Something Greater Than ourselves! Let's be a part of something Worthwhile! Thank You!

Shop for Charity:

http://author-kathryn-jordyn.printify.me/

www.ingramcontent.com/pod-product-compliance
Lightning Source LLC
Chambersburg PA
CBHW050117170426
43197CB00011B/1610